Encyclopedia of the Commemorative Coins of the United States

History, Art, Investment & Collection of America's Memorial Coinage

ENCYCLOPEDIA
OF THE
COMMEMORATIVE
COINS OF THE
UNITED STATES

History, Art, Investment & Collection
of America's Memorial Coinage

EDITED AND COMPILED BY

Anthony J. Swiatek

KWS
PUBLISHERS
CHICAGO • LONDON

Published 2012 by KWS Publishers

KWS Publishers
1516 North State Parkway
Chicago, Illinois 60610
USA

or

11 Tower House
Candover Street
London W1W 7DQ
UK

www.kwspub.com

British Library and Library of Congress
Cataloguing in Publication Data are available.

ISBN 978–0–9817736–7–4

Book design and production by Studio 31
www.studio 31.com

Printed in China

DEDICATION

This work is dedicated to my lovely wife, Gloria Rubio Swiatek, for her inspiration, time, and remarkable input, and to Gregory N. Mirsky, consummate computer professional and numismatist, for his work, time, effort, and top-notch suggestions, especially with the modern commemoratives.

Special thanks must be given to Gregory's son and daughter, Kevin and Nicole Mirsky, for their computer graphic talents. I also want to thank Bill Corsa, Daniel Kirkpatrick, and James Wasserman for their efforts throughout the creation of this book. Thanks also to Brad Reed, Armen Vartian, William T. Gibbs, Beth Deisher, and my adopted "numismatic mother," Margo Russell, for their assistance in making this opus a reality—and a dream come true.

It is also dedicated to those individuals who inspired me along the numismatic trail and have passed, such as Lester Merkin, one of the most honest dealers of his time and my adopted "numismatic father," as well as to Abe Kosoff, Sol Kaplan, Norman Stack, Richard Picker, John Jay Pittman, et al.

Likewise to those individuals who have been a major inspiration during my travels along my numismatic path. These individuals are key contributors to my success and deserve honorable mention: Mary Ellen Withrow, past Treasurer of the United States, Mark Salzberg, David Hall, Steve Ivy, Jim Halpern, Dave Camire, Rick Montgomery, Miles Standish, David T. Alexander, Brenda Bishop, Gary and Mary Beedon, Edward C. Rochette, and James Taylor. Others include Q. David Bowers, Bob Brueggeman, Robert B. Lecce, Rich Schemmer, Harvey Stack, Scott A. Travers, and Fred Weinberg.

It is also dedicated to the American Numismatic Association, the Society for United States Commemorative Coins, and to all coin clubs that promote the series and our coin collecting hobby.

TABLE OF CONTENTS

INTRODUCTION

Welcome to the numismatic world of United States commemorative coinage. I think of these coins as special remembrance preservers. Many collectors, as well as dealers in the hobby and industry, refer to them as "commems." To me, though, they are special in a much broader sense of the word—not just because they are different, but because in many ways they are really better. If you stop for just a minute to think about our regular U.S. coins, and compare them to our commems, you'll soon see what I mean.

Regular U.S. coinage until recent years has lacked variety. Commemoratives, by contrast, offer enormous diversity. Since 1982, we've had more than 100 different designs in all (not counting the 1999–2010 Fifty State Quarters and the 2010 territorial coinage), and we could get many additional issues in the years to come. Commemorative coins represent the work of some of the finest artists this nation has ever produced.

Commems also possess tremendous historical appeal. They have been issued to honor a broad cross-section of the people, places, and events that have shaped the nation's history.

On top of everything else, U.S. commems have great diversity, too, from a market standpoint. In other words, they come in a wide variety of rarity levels and prices. Some of them are common and extremely inexpensive, others are rare and costly, and most of them are somewhere in between. Thus, they can be pursued and enjoyed by just about any collector or investor, regardless of his or her level of personal income or expertise.

Before going further, perhaps I should pause and define just what I mean by commemorative coinage. A commemorative is a coin that is produced primarily to honor a historically significant person (living or dead), place, or event. Often, a commemorative is issued to mark an anniversary: the centennial, perhaps, of a person's birth or death, the sesquicentennial of a place's founding, or the 300th anniversary of a great event. (More on what defines a commemorative a little later.)

Commems have been produced since the time of Alexander the Great (356–323 BC), the illustrious Macedonian Greek conqueror who was said to be the very first person to have his likeness placed on a coin. My research indicates that Tissaphernes (died 396 BC), a Persian satrap (governor) of Lydia, was the first historical figure with his portrait or likeness on a surviving coin. On the ancient coinage of Egypt, Arsinoë II, wife, of Ptolemy II Philadelphus (308–246 BC), was the first woman to be accorded the honor of a portrait.

A National Photo Album

Commemorative coins generally serve as reminders of a heritage—and U.S. commemoratives focus attention on vignettes from America's past. They might be viewed as snapshots from a national photo album, but captured on metal, instead of on film.

Some of the people portrayed in America's "album" are famous historical figures whose presence on these coins is predictable. People such as George Washington, Thomas Jefferson, Abraham Lincoln, Ulysses S. Grant, and Robert E. Lee. Others, however, are totally unexpected. I suspect that most Americans would be utterly amazed to learn that this country has issued special coins honoring such little-known individuals as Alabama's governor in 1921, Thomas E. Kilby. What is most incredible is the fact that he was the first living person to be depicted on this nation's coinage. Others to be honored were Admiral Gaspard de Coligny of France; William the Silent of the Netherlands; Dr. John McLoughlin of Fort Vancouver, Washington; William Wyatt Bibb, first governor of Alabama; and John Pell, Lord of Pelham Manor in 17th-century New Rochelle, New York.

As it happens, each of the coins depicting these particular individuals is primarily a tribute not to the person, but rather to a place or an event with which they were identified. Admiral de Coligny and William the Silent, for instance, both appear on the same U.S. half dollar: a commemorative issued in 1924 to mark the tercentenary, or 300th anniversary, of the settlement of New Netherland (present-day New York) by the French Huguenots and the Dutch Walloons. Each was chosen because of his close relationship with one of the two groups.

McLoughlin is depicted on a 1925 half dollar marking the centennial of Fort Vancouver, a settlement he founded along the Columbia River in Washington State. Today, it is the site of the city of Vancouver. Both Bibb and Kilby are portrayed on a 1921 half dollar issued to commemorate the centennial of Alabama's statehood. Pell turns up on a 1938 half dollar marking the sesquicentennial (or 250th anniversary) of New Rochelle's founding.

Browsing through our album, we also find the portraits of other historical figures whose names are more familiar: Christopher Columbus; Spain's Queen Isabella, the first woman and foreign monarch to be depicted on U.S. coinage; England's Sir Walter Raleigh; and such native-born Americans as Virginia Dare, Daniel Boone, P.T. Barnum, Stephen Foster, Booker T. Washington, George Washington Carver, "Stonewall" Jackson, Robert E. Lee, Jackie Robinson, the Wright Brothers, and Benjamin Franklin. No, you won't find that a genuine U.S. Mint made a William Jefferson Clinton 50 State Quarters commemorative coin: those are novelty coins over-struck on genuine coinage outside the government facilities!

By interesting coincidence, the U.S. Mint issued its first commemorative coin at a time when the Mint itself was exactly 100 years old. The subject of that first commem, in 1892, was an earlier event, though, and one with far greater implications: the coin was issued to commemorate the 400th anniversary of Columbus's landing in the New World.

Actually, the coin—the Columbian half dollar—wasn't conceived entirely as a historical tribute. It also was intended as a money-making device: to help raise funds for the World's Columbian Exposition, a world's fair that took place in Chicago. In this respect, the Columbian set an important precedent, for every subsequent U.S. commem also has been issued—to some extent, at least—with the goal of raising revenue for some particular agency or cause.

The portrait of Columbus on the first U.S. commem was an artist's conception. Since no authentic portraits of Columbus were available, the Mint's Chief Sculptor/Engraver, Charles E. Barber, had no choice but to use his imagination. But, while the portrait may not have been a true one, it represents a landmark in the history of U.S. coinage—for, up until that time, no U.S. coin had depicted a real-life person. Most people would guess that Abraham Lincoln was the first actual person to appear on U.S. coinage: he is seen on the 1-cent piece. (We produce the cent and not the penny.) But Columbus was the first, not Lincoln. In 1909 Lincoln became the first president to appear on U.S. coinage meant for circulation and commerce. George Washington was portrayed on the 1900 Lafayette dollar, but this was a commemorative issue that sold for double face value when offered to the public by the Lafayette Memorial Commission. The Lafayettes were special collector coins, not issued at face value by banks.

One of the great beauties of U.S. commemorative coins is the fact that we can collect them in so many different ways.

Traditionally, regular-issue coins have been saved in two principal ways: in comprehensive date-and-mint sets, including one example from every different Mint for every year of issue; and in type sets, containing just one specimen of any particular coin.

With commems, we have a great deal more flexibility.

If our budgets are big, we can save them by date and mint. A complete set from 1892 to 1954 would contain 144 different pieces, and can cost about $100,000 in Mint State 65 (MS-65) condition (see Topic 3, "About Coin Grading"). In circulated condition, this set can sell in the $17,000 to $23,000 range, depending on the actual condition of each coin.

If we're not wealthy, but decently well off, we can put together a type set of every different commem. This would consist of 50 different coins from 1892 to 1954 and would cost perhaps $62,000 in MS-65 condition. In circulated condition, the set would cost in the $8,000 to $11,500 range, based on the state of each piece. Thus values will naturally vary, depending on the strength of the coins making up the set in question.

These are not the only options open to us, though. We also can assemble topical sets, if we wish, bringing together commems that share a common theme or are similar in design. One approach, for instance, would be to put together our own "who's zoo": a collection of all the commems on which there is a portrait of an animal or a bird. There are more than two dozen of these, and their animal-kingdom subjects range all the way from a fatted calf (on the New Rochelle half dollar) to a hippocampus (on a 1915 quarter eagle, or $2.50 gold piece, issued to commemorate the Panama–Pacific Exposition). In case you're ever asked, a hippocampus is a mythological creature with the head and forequarters of a horse and the tail of a fish.

Another approach would be to save commems with architectural portraits—designs that feature buildings or bridges. Some examples are the 1935–36

California–Pacific Exposition (San Diego issues) half dollar, which shows the observation tower and the State of California Building at the exposition; the 1936 San Francisco–Oakland Bay Bridge; and the 1996 Smithsonian Institution 150th Anniversary, which shows the "Castle," the original Smithsonian building on the Mall in Washington, D.C. An excellent way to get started collecting commemorative coins is to acquire those coins that are related to your other interests. Civil War buffs, for example, could acquire Ulysses S. Grant memorial half dollars or gold dollars, the Stone Mountain Monument coin, the Battle of Gettysburg half dollar, or the Battle of Antietam half.

The Golden Age

The golden age of U.S. commems—more correctly, the gold and silver age—was the two-decade period of the 1920's and 1930's. About three-fourths of all commemorative coins were issued during that time. Gradually, however, objections began to arise, and some of these objections appear to have been justified.

Critics complained, for instance, that some of the commems were issued for occasions of questionable importance, and that Congress was approving them only because of their sponsors' political clout. There was also criticism because some of the coins were issued for extended lengths of time. In one case, the same commem—the Oregon Trail half dollar—was issued on and off for nearly 15 years. Because of this, collectors who wanted complete sets were forced to buy duplicate pieces year after year. President Franklin D. Roosevelt actually vetoed a commemorative bill in 1938—one that had been passed at the last moment before Congressional adjournment in 1937. This bill called for an authorization of 100,000 half dollars to commemorate Coronado's exploration of the southwest in 1540.

Production of commems was suspended during World War II. After the war, they really never got rolling again—and finally, in 1954, the program ground to a total halt. For nearly three decades thereafter, the series was dormant. Worse than that, it was dead. The U.S. Treasury took the position that issuing commemoratives would be counterproductive. As one treasury official put it, such coins would "violate the principle for which our coinage system was established, introduce confusion in the system, and encourage counterfeiting."

Thankfully, that attitude has changed. It is sad to realize, though, that during those "dark ages" we lost the opportunity to issue special coins for many events of truly great significance to the nation: medicine's triumph over polio, the Civil War centennial, the civil rights achievements of the 1960's, and the first moon landing, to name just a few.

The series was revived with the issuance of the George Washington half dollar in 1982. The renaissance was reinforced by the three Los Angeles Olympics coins. Except for 1985, U.S. commemorative coinage has been continually produced.

Circulated examples, in the Very Fine or Extremely Fine (VF-EF) grades, of the commonest pre-1955 commem—the 1892 and 1893 Columbian half dollar, with a total combined mintage of 2.5 million—can be purchased for little more than the value of the silver they contain. At the opposite extreme, the Panama–Pacific $50 gold piece—with just 483 Round and 645 Octagonal examples—are valued in MS-65 condition at $120,000 and $133,000 respectively.

Compared to regular-issue coins of comparable mintage and quality, commems can be excellent buys at current market values. As with any coins, however, the buyer must be careful that the coins he or she is acquiring are accurately graded. And I can't stress enough that there isn't any substitute for knowledge: invest time in learning all you can before investing a dime in any coin. I recommend that you never buy a coin valued at $125 or more unless it has been encapsulated by a major grading service, such as the Numismatic Guaranty Corporation (NGC) or the Professional Coin Grading Service (PCGS). Why? Such coins usually bring the most money when sold at a coin convention or auction, and these grading services are recognized and accepted within the numismatic industry.

By now, I think, you should see what I mean when I say that commemoratives are "special." They have great diversity, attractive designs, unusual historical appeal, low mintages, and relatively modest price tags compared to other U.S. coinage. If you're looking for a specialty in coins, try the uncommon commem. You, too, will find that, as specialties go, this one is really super-special.

The Commemorative Nature of Regular Coins

In coin collecting circles, the word "commemorative" has a particular meaning. We generally refer to just those coins produced in limited numbers for a limited time to mark a specific event. In fact, we could say that commemoratives are the coins produced by the U.S. Mint that were *not* intended to be used as money.

However, that definition is a fuzzy one. For one thing, all commemorative coins are *legal tender*. That means they can be used as money for their face value, if you so choose. There are some instances in our commemorative past where a special issue was minted, but did not sell as well as expected, and the unsold coins were simply dumped into circulation. This accounts for the high number of some issues showing significant wear.

The early commems were generally sold to the public at near face value. A 90 percent silver commemorative half dollar could be acquired for as little as $1. What a bargain that seems at today's prices! Today's commemoratives, however, have a much higher spread between purchase cost and face value: a copper-nickel clad half dollar may cost upwards of $10 or a silver dollar be priced at $37.

There is, however, one big exception. If our definition is broad enough, many coins produced for circulation may qualify as "commemoratives." Doing so may not endow them with any special financial worth, but pursuing these coins can make for an interesting—and inexpensive—collection.

First, let us review a little U.S. coinage history. When the Founding Fathers first contemplated the nation's coinage, many believed we should follow the custom of the time and portray the current head of state. Most European nations followed this practice, and many continue it today. George Washington and others objected, however. It was their intention to throw off the old ways. "No King George" was their cry, and our first lawmakers eventually agreed. It was decreed that the nation's coins bear designs "emblematic of liberty." Now, Liberty is a complex social issue, a deeply philosophical one, and doesn't lend itself well to visual portrayal. A design "emblematic of agriculture" could show corn or wheat or plowing, but what does Liberty look like?

Early American coinage artists looked to Europe for help. There, many artists used the technique of *allegory* visually to represent abstract social concepts. Allegorical representation reaches back to the dawn of civilization, but it has also served us moderns quite nicely. In 1792, in the fledgling United States of America, Liberty acquired the face of a woman. Through the years, Liberty's features changed with the prevailing fashions, and with the engraver's abilities. Sometimes, other symbols of Liberty were used: a national shield, perhaps, or a proud Native American. But never was a design representative of a single individual.

In 1892, the half dollar created for the World's Columbian Exposition in Chicago broke the mold. A portrait, albeit a fantasy, of Christopher Columbus was placed on legal tender coinage of the United States. This was quickly followed in 1893 with Queen Isabel of Spain's portrait on the commemorative quarter dollar for the same event.

But the nation's "real" coinage, the circulation coinage, remained allegorical or symbolic. In 1900, the following designs were used to portray Liberty: 1 cent—young woman wearing a Native American-styled headdress; 5 cents—a somewhat stern-faced woman wearing a tiara with the word "LIBERTY" stamped on it, in case you miss the point; dime, quarter dollar, and half dollar—Charles E. Barber's classically-styled youth wearing a laurel wreath in the Greek style; silver dollar—George T. Morgan's now-popular woman wearing a tiara and a headdress of various vegetable matter; gold $2.50, gold $5, gold $10, and gold $20—a woman wearing a larger coronet.

Now, with the door having been cracked open in 1892 with the Columbian, followed by commemorative coin portraits of Isabel, of Washington and Lafayette in 1900, of Thomas Jefferson and William McKinley in 1903, and of Lewis and Clark in 1904, a major shift in circulating coinage began in 1909.

The year 1909 was the 100th anniversary of Abraham Lincoln's birth. His profile portrait was placed on the 1-cent's obverse, replacing the former Indian head design. The Lincoln head cent, with minor engraving changes, has survived longer than any other U.S. coin design—more than a century! In fact, in 2009 the Treasury Department and the U.S. Mint produced (as authorized by Public Law 109-145, the Presidential $1 Coin Act of 2005) and issued new reverse designs of the 1-cent coin to commemorate the centenary event. The reverses featured Lincoln's birth and early childhood in Kentucky (1809–16), his formative years in Indiana (1816–30), his professional life in Illinois (1830–61), and finally his presidency in Washington (1861–65). Like the 50 State Quarters program, the new reverses were released approximately every three months during 2009. Additionally, the Secretary of the Treasury had the authority to mint and issue numismatically-oriented 1-cent coins in 2009 with the exact metallic content as contained in the 1909 1-cent coin (95% copper, 5% tin and zinc). This will bring the total number of varieties for collectors to procure to eight coins for just one year and one denomination. In 2010, in accordance with Public Law 109-145, the Treasury Department and the U.S. Mint again modified the reverse design of the 1-cent coin. The 2010 reverse features a union shield inscribed "E Pluribus Unum", with a scroll draped across and the text "One Cent".

Don't forget, the 1-cent piece you have in your pocket change today is commemorative too. In 1959, Lincoln's 150th "birthday," the wheat design on the reverse was replaced with a depiction of the Lincoln Memorial. Therefore, it can be argued, the least expensive "commemorative" coin in the United States is the Lincoln cent. The cost? 1 cent each.

In 1932, Liberty was again bumped from a denomination. The 200th anniversary of George Washington's birth seemed a fitting time to honor him with a coin design of his own. His portrait was placed on the quarter of 1932, and that was that, as no quarters were made in 1933. But in 1934 nearly 32 million commemorative portraits of Washington were released into circulation, and the floodgates were opened wide. Allegorical designs quickly fell out of favor, at least with the Washington officials who decide such things. For the 50 State Quarters program, Washington's portrait was slightly reduced to accommodate the addition of the statutory inscriptions and denomination. These appeared on the eagle reverse, which will not be used until 2009.

In 1938 (for no apparent reason) the splendid Native American portrait/bison 5-cent design was replaced by a hollow-cheeked Thomas Jefferson, with a picture of his house on the back. In 1946, a year after his death, Franklin Roosevelt's portrait forced the "Mercury" design off of the dime, ironically replacing a Winged Liberty head representing "freedom of thought" with yet another "commemorative" portrait. (The 10-cent denomination was chosen in part because of Roosevelt's involvement with the March of Dimes polio organization.)

In 1948 Benjamin Franklin ascended to the half dollar, but for no apparent commemorative reason. In 1964 he was bumped in favor of John F. Kennedy who, like Roosevelt, attained coinage status by dying in office.

A "real" commemorative was produced in 1921. Following World War I, it was decided to issue a silver dollar commemorating the concept of Peace. Treasury officials misunderstood the directive, however, and dusted off the dormant Morgan Liberty design. Tens of millions were struck before Anthony de Francisci's beautiful (albeit allegorical) Liberty design could be implemented. (The word "Peace" appears on the rock on which the eagle stands on the reverse.)

Dwight D. Eisenhower got the nod when a new dollar design was begun in 1971, and the reverse does show an eagle (representing the Apollo spacecraft *Eagle*) landing on the moon. But these designs are not generally considered to be commemorative.

The 1976 Bicentennial of the Declaration of Independence was the biggest birthday party this nation has seen. In 1975 and 1976, the usual year-of-issue dates on the quarter, half, and dollar coins were replaced with the dual date 1776–1976. Also, a widely publicized design contest had yielded three special reverse designs specifically commemorating the Bicentennial. The three coins were sold at various prices for various sets, including 40 percent silver versions. They were also struck in the hundreds of millions and placed into circulation. They can still be easily found among pocket change.

The Bicentennial coins are not generally cataloged as part of the "commemorative" coins of the United States. Nor are the others just mentioned here, except for the 50 State Quarters. Why? I believe for a coin to be labeled a genuine commemorative, and not just commemorative in nature, the coin must be referred to as a commemorative coin in the official Act of Congress that approves the issue. If the Act's wording indicates only that we are "commemorating" an event, such as the ending of World War I and the arrival of peace, and does not cite the coin as a "commemorative coin," I would simply label the particular coin commemorative in nature. Nevertheless, we enjoy this coinage, since it adds much to the joy of collecting.

Some even consider the 1848 gold $2.50 quarter eagle with a "CAL" counter-stamp to be the first U.S. commemorative coin. The "CAL" was punched into the reverse, just above the eagle's head, while the coin still rested in the obverse die. This was done to commemorate the fact that the gold came from California (this was during the Gold Rush). The number of pieces so marked was limited, and the marking was done for a particular reason—but it entailed no real design change, and to call this coin a commem is admittedly a stretch.

How to Use This Book

The listing is in chronological order. A chronological listing allows the reader to follow the evolution of coin designs, to trace the comings and goings of key designers, to witness the disintegration of the coin boom after the excesses of the 1930's, and then the long gap and rapid acceleration of the modern commemoratives. Many other sources organize commemoratives alphabetically, but this can cause readers difficulties, since there is no widely accepted, standardized naming system. (An Alphabetical List, with name variants, is provided, however, to help in locating a particular coin if its date is unknown.) Be aware that some commemorative coins are referred to by several names. One notable example of this is the 1936 "Arkansas–Robinson", also known as the "Robinson–Arkansas" or just the "Robinson" or the "Arkansas". Another example is the 1918 "Illinois Centennial Half Dollar", sometimes called the "Lincoln" because of Abraham Lincoln's portrait on the coin.

Each coin type is shown, with its date of issue, reason for issue, the numbers struck and sold, and a market value in several levels of preservation. The issuing authority is listed for commemoratives through 1954. Modern commemoratives are issued by the U.S. Treasury and the U.S. Mint. Collectors should please be aware that the coin market can and does change very quickly. Certain coins are "hot" for a time and can fall out of favor as promotion ebbs.

How can we determine a coin's grade and associated value? These are based on a number of factors:

1) What does the surface of the coin in question reveal? Bag marks? How many are present? Where are they located? How severe are they?

2) Do you observe surface hairlines possibly caused by numismatic abuse? If present, where would they rate on a scale starting from miniscule to heavy?

3) Are these hairlines caused by improper cleaning or surface doctoring, such as whizzing (wire- or plastic bristle-brushing)? This will drastically lower a coin's value and it will not be encapsulated in a major grading service's holder.

4) Does the coin in question possess a weak strike, while most of the issue is known for a strong strike? Is the strike just average?

5) Does the coin in question possess attractive flashy bright luster, or beautiful colored toning, or is its luster dull or just average for the grade?

6) How alluring or eye-appealing is the coin in question? All of these factors combine to give a coin its grade. And remember: coin grading is an art and not a science. (More detail is given in Topic 3, "About Coin Grading," and Topic 4, "What is Eye Appeal?")

When the evaluation is complete, we can end up with a low-end coin, or solid-for-the-grade coin, or an upper-level encapsulated coin. (Simply associate this with a school grade of B-, B, and B+.) A low-end coin (B-) should not bring as much money as an upper-end coin (B+). If it is a common issue, a low-end coin could bring 20% to 30% below market value. A solid-for-the-grade coin should be worth approximately "red book" money or more. The upper-end or premium quality (PQ) coin (B+) usually will bring more than market value. There is always the possibility that an encapsulated coin rated MS-64 or higher is or was under-graded. In such cases, the knowledgeable will pay much more than the retail value listed for the grade on the encapsulation or slabbed grading label. A dealer or collector who sees an encapsulated or slabbed MS-65 coin as having the potential to be upgraded to an MS-67 will pay much more the item. But at an auction an MS-65 coin that is average for its grade will bring only the current value for an MS-65 coin. The secret is in spotting an under-graded coin.

Individuals wanting to have the best or finest graded set possible for a particular grade are sometimes prepared to pay eye-opening prices for their registry set(s). These individuals have the funds, and money appears to be no object. My attempt in this book is to present retail values that are solid for the grade. The Topic sections below go into more detail about the evaluation and pricing of commemorative coins, the market for them, the various types of collector, and the approval process for a new commemorative.

I have attempted to provide a realistic assessment of the commemorative coin market. However, any statements regarding current or future value of any coin or other collectible item in this book must be considered the sole opinion of the author, and in any case is not a promise or guarantee of future value. Readers are advised to seek independent and individualized advice before purchasing or selling any coin for purposes of financial gain. Readers can also contact Anthony J. Swiatek at P.O. Box 684, Saratoga Springs, N.Y. 12866, e-mail: uscoinguru@aol.com; Telephone: 1-518-587-9451

Whatever your primary objective may be, have fun as you journey the numismatic trail.

1. Pricing Commemorative Coins

Classic Commemorative Pricing

The pricing of classic commemorative coinage (coins issued intermittently from 1892 to 1954) differs from the pricing of the modern commemorative coinage (coins issued since 1982) in several ways. The factors to take into account when attributing value to classic commemoratives are:

- Mintage
- Collector distribution or issue dispersion in relation to possible undiscovered hoards of the issue
- Promotion potential by dealers
- Allure and attraction of the specific coin

Modern Commemorative Pricing

Pricing of modern commemorative coinage differs from the pricing of the classic coinage in several ways. For one thing, classic coins had a fixed issue price. With the modern coinage, the U.S. Mint often has a pre-issue discount: this is given in the "Pre-Issue Price" column of the mintage tables listed for each coin. Also, the old axiom of a lower mintage being better does not always translate into a higher price. The factors to take into account with attributing value to modern commemorative are:

- Base metal content
- Mintage
- Collector distribution or issue dispersion
- Scarcity and collector demand
- Promotion potential by dealers

The base metal content can by itself be a significant factor in a coin's price increase or decrease if the commodities market has a sharp upturn or downturn. The next factor that comes into play is the mintage figure: what people are willing to pay for is "scarcity." By the law of supply and demand, great demand—or the perception of potential demand—is responsible for higher prices. The dispersion of an issue can also play a factor in a coin's price. If a coin is fully dispersed into the collecting public and there are no known hoards of it, the price can rise because there is not a steady supply for the coin market. On the other hand, the price will eventually stabilize and sometimes lag behind other similar issues if no dealer can accumulate enough stock to promote the coin. At times, issues can and will be promoted by dealers. Prices generally tend to rise during a promotion and then to settle down after the promotion has run its course.

In this book, prices are quoted for MS-69/PF-69 (Mint State-69 / Proof-69) examples that are not certified unless otherwise noted. All pricing is offered as a guide only, since demand, promotions, and collector sentiment can change without warning. For more accurate and up-to-date pricing the author suggests that the reader check various sources, such as numismatic auction sites (http://teletrade.com; http://coins.ha.com; http://www.goldbergcoins.com) and hobby trade papers, such as CoinWorld (http://www.coinworld.com) and Numismatic News (http://www.numismaticnews.net).

A Note about Population Numbers

Populations from grading services can be volatile and depend on several factors including, but not limited to: promotions by coin dealers, hoard discoveries, and general collector sentiment. Those familiar with the population reports of coin grading services already know that bulk submissions to these services by coin dealers hoping to promote an issue have occurred in the past and will occur in the future—and have been responsible for sharp increases in graded coin populations from time to time.

In the classic coins listings, the Numismatic Guaranty Corporation (NGC) is the only grading service that attributes coins with a Proof-like (PL) status: for clarity, these coins have been segregated from the normal population figures. See the section "Pricing Proof-like Commemorative Coinage" in Topic 2, "Commemorative Proof-like Coinage," to learn how to determine if your coin measures up to Proof-like standards.

I have made every attempt to represent accurately the population figures at the time of the updating of this third edition. The reader should note that NGC often denotes proof coinage as PF (proof), PFCA (proof cameo), and PFUC (proof ultra cameo), while the Professional Coin Grading Service (PCGS) will denote proof coinage as PF (proof) or PFDC (proof deep cameo). To simplify the listings, I have combined all the proof categories together in the population reports.

MODERN POPULATION NUMBERS

For more up-to-date population numbers for any individual modern issue, I suggest that collectors check the websites of the leading grading agencies (fee required), the Professional Coin Grading Service (http://www.pcgs.com) and the Numismatic Guaranty Corporation (http://www.ngccoin.com).

Collector sentiment is also a factor in coin grading population numbers. When news of a 1982 George Washington half dollar obtaining an MS-69 from PCGS hit the general collector community there was a marked increase in submissions by collectors also hoping for the same lofty grade. The George Washington half dollar had a reputation, because of its somewhat "rough" handling during the coining and packaging process by the U.S. Mint. It was generally regarded as a coin that would not achieve high Sheldon scale values when professionally graded. However, this particular coin did not receive the same abuse a coin made for circulation purposes would receive via counting, bagging, transport, handling, etc. Once a coin broke the MS-69 barrier, the population figures inflated because of the sheer number of hopeful submissions. This phenomenon occurred yet again when one George Washington half dollar attained a PF-70 grade. A previously infrequently submitted coin saw a marked increase in population figures, as other collectors and dealers tried to attain the same lofty PF-70 grade.

Be aware that there are many in the numismatic arena who criticize the documentable grade inflation among populations given by the certification services. When the initial revisions for the third edition of this book were being compiled in 2005 many of the modern commemorative coins had either zero or single-digit populations for MS-70/PF-70. Now, some five years later in 2010, some issues show MS-70/PF-70 populations in triple digits. Why? Were grading criteria for modern commemoratives too strict or have the standards been loosened to satisfy demand? The debate continues. Just be aware that the graded census landscape has changed drastically and will probably continue to do so for some years to come.

Also be aware that population ("pop") or census figures for most modern issues will be lower than expected in grades PF-68 and MS-68 and below. Why? Modern coinage is produced with such tender loving care that the lowest grade created for the most part by the Mints will NGC and PCGS grade PF-69 or MS-69. This is why the reader will notice that the population charts in the modern section will generally feature only the 69 and 70 grades. Only those coins with significant lower populations will have the lower grades illustrated for comparison.

Usually, when collectors or dealers improperly handle a coin when removing it from its Mint-packaged capsule, they can create some numismatic abuse. If this occurs, the coin's grade will now be lowered to a PF-68 or MS-68, or less, by the grading services. On rare occasions, the Mints will ship coins where a letter or two of a word or peripheral inscription has been abraded or flawed by frictional action. Such coinage will rate no higher than MS-68. Their lower population figures do not indicate rarity for the grade, especially when the rarer higher ratings such as MS-69 or PF-69 have a much higher census. If you are told you are buying a rare MS-68 or PF-68 coin, be cautious: it is all spin!

When modern commemorative coins are sold by the Mints, they are generally placed in a plastic capsule for protection, and the accompanying literature notes that they are "encapsulated." This word does *not* mean that a professional encapsulation service has been involved.

2. Commemorative Proof-like Coinage: An Enigma

There is an aspect of the coin collecting hobby that is neglected and remains virtually undetected: it has no notoriety or infamous rarities. This is the world of early or classic silver commemorative 1892–1954 proof-likes.

Statistics are easily obtained by year of issue, Mint marks, mintage figures, and populations, but pricing remains an enigma. Coin dealers, collectors, buyers, and sellers for the most part had no idea of how much a proof-like commemorative should sell for. There is no pricing available in *CoinValues*, *Numismedia*, or even *Coin Dealers Newsletter*. Auction results are the only current sources that offer us some assistance.

To date, the Numismatic Guaranty Corporation (NGC) has graded and encased more than 210,000 silver commemoratives. The Professional Coin Grading Service (PCGS) has graded about 330,000, but has never labeled any as proof-like, even if the coins are proof-like. ANACS does recognize the condition and labels them accordingly.

There are 144 issues in the early silver commemorative series, but only 33 have received the proof-like or the PL designation on the grading label insert by NGC.

The total number of graded coins that comprise these 33 issues amount to about 47,000. Of these, a mere 1,400 are labeled proof-like. Eight issues account for 1,192 coins or 85% of all proof-likes.

Year	Issue	Population
1892	Columbian	361
1893	Columbian	187
1936	New Rochelle	174
1937-S	Boone	125
1892	Isabella	97
1947-S	B.T.W.	96
1936	Rhode Island	85
1937	Roanoke	67

Conversely, there are 20 encapsulated PL issues that account for 69 coins.

One Coin		Two Coins		Three Coins	
1935-S	Boone	1936	Cincinnati	1937-D	Boone
1936-S	Boone	1936-S	Rhode Island		
1918	Illinois (Lincoln)	1948	B.T.W.		

One Coin		Two Coins		Three Coins	
1920	Maine	1951	Washington–Carver		
1949-S	B.T.W.	1952-S	Washington–Carver		
1951-D	B.T.W.				
1953-D	Washington–Carver				
Five coins		Six Coins		Eight coins	
1954-D	Washington–Carver	1937	Boone	1938-S	Boone
		1935-S	San Diego	1937-S	Texas
				1949	B.T.W.
				1952-D	Washington–Carver

Of the proof-like coins, only three issues, a total of six coins, have been granted NGC's deep mirror proof-like (DPL or DMPL) designation. The 1892 Columbian has two pieces graded MS-63 and MS-65, and the 1893 Columbian has three: one each in MS-63, MS-64, and MS-66. The 1951-S Booker T. Washington (B.T.W.) was granted by NGC an MS-67 DPL ¶ (star) designation, exemplifying exceptional eye appeal.

There are only nine coins with such a marking, including the B.T.W. This coin sold at the January 2007 FUN Auction in Orlando, by Heritage, for $11,557, possibly the highest price paid for a proof-like commemorative.

Others, with star, are: the Isabella; 1892 Columbian with two; 1892 Columbian and Roanoke with one each; and the New Rochelle with three. Of the 210,000 NGC-graded silver commemoratives, there are about 900 coins with the star designation.

There are 31 commemorative issues that contain three coins each. We refer to them as PDS Sets, containing pieces struck at the Philadelphia, Denver, and San Francisco Mints. Examples are the Boone, Texas, and Cincinnati issues. However, the only available proof-like set is the Boone production. The Philadelphia coin has six, the Denver has three, and the San Francisco has 125 available proof-likes. As there are no pricing figures for proof-likes, only a seller and a buyer will establish the value and act accordingly.

These coins are produced from polished pristine coin dies. After fewer than a hundred strikings the dies lose their polished surface and produce frosty looking coins instead of mirror-like surfaces. Therefore these coins are not as abundant, as one can observe. I know of collectors who will pay many times over bid for the proof-like issue. The coins resemble near brilliant proofs. There is excellent future potential in all proof-like grades. In today's market, how does one ascertain the value of these coins? Look up the cost of a regular issue and add a premium? Good idea, but how does that work if the coin is a 1936-S Rhode Island with a population of two, in MS-62 PL and MS-63 PL, or a 1920 Maine MS-64 PL, with a listing of one coin. In a Heritage auction on May 12, 2007, a 1951-S Booker T. Washington MS-66 PL sold for $1,380. The Coin Dealer

Newsletter value was $140, so the sale price was ten times more than the going price. In past auctions, a 1938 New Rochelle graded MS-67 PL by NGC sold for $2,587 in July 2003, $2,415 in June 2005, $4,168 in September 2005, and $3,450 in January 2006; an MS-66 DMPL¶ sold for $9,775 in December 2009. Some pricing guidance is needed.

PRICING PROOF-LIKE COMMEMORATIVE COINAGE

Value has to be based on several factors. One is the depth of the proof-like or PL surface on each side of the coin. A semi-proof-like surface on one side of the coin and a full PL surface or even deep mirror proof-like (DPL or DMPL) on the other side eliminates the issue from a true PL designation. One side only does not make the PL designation. In order to be labeled PL, the coin must reflect 10-point print (about one-eighth of an inch high, such as that often found on a standard business card) in the coin's fields as you hold the coin at a minimum of a strict two inches (50.8 millimeters)—not 1.8 or 1.9 inches—to four inches (101.6 millimeters) from the printing. If the reflective printing in the coin's field begins to blur or looks out of focus before your two-inch marker is reached, then this side of the coin cannot be labeled proof-like: it is semi-proof-like. Don't cheat or delude yourself. One proof-like side does not make the whole coin worthy of a PL rating.

Should you have a coin labeled PL and it does not meet this standard—sell the encapsulation. B.T.W.s, Boones and the New Rochelles, for example, just might fall into this category. If you can't make the positive determination, have the coin sent in for encapsulation. The closer you are to the four-inch marker while still being able to read the print clearly, the stronger the depth of the PL surface.

One dealer informed me about cracking out an MS-65 PL Booker T. Washington because the belief was it would upgrade. This did happen, but the PL designation was taken away. Suggestion: do not crack out the coin, but send it in for a re-grade and note that the PL designation must remain. Contact the customer service department prior to submitting the coin about your concern to have the PL appellation remain on the label. If this cannot be guaranteed, do not submit, and sell that coin at your selected venue.

The next factor is the grade of the coin. For the most part, I do not get too excited about the 1892–93 Columbian issues or the 1893 Isabella quarters or B.T.W. and Carver half dollars rated between AU-55 and MS-62. Usually they look too scruffy. When rated MS-63, the coin's eye appeal and total makeup must be taken into consideration. I would prefer a piece that grades MS-63+, rather than a low-end coin for the grade. Collectors should pass on a PL issue that displays unattractive toning or has too many hairline imperfections. Needless to say, the attained value is directly related to the coin in question and the buyer.

For a piece to be labeled DMPL it must without question have a minimum of four to six inches of clear field reflectivity of 10-point print on both sides of the coin. Sorry, but 3.9 inches or less will not qualify. One B.T.W. MS-67+ DMPL sold for over $11,000 at Heritage's auction on January 6, 2007. It was an amazing coin—and, no, I did not procure this fantastic piece at that level.

What is an Ultra Deep Mirror Coin?

I do not believe any classic U.S. commemorative coin issued between 1892 and 1954 will ever receive this rare grade. Morgan dollars that have a mirrored surface on both sides and that have 12 inches of clear reflectivity of 10-point print are the only coins worthy of this rare designation.

Let us take a look at the proof-like values of the PL 1892 (population 363) and 1893 (population 188) Columbian half dollars:

Grade	Value	Populations 1892–1893	DMPL Populations 1892–1893
MS-63	$80–$110	(14;6)	(0;0)
MS-62	$175–$220	(44;37)	(0;0)
MS-63	$225–$375	(95;49)	(1;1)
MS-64	$425–$525	(125,67)	(1;1)
MS-65	$750–$1,265	(57;22)	(2;0)
MS-66	$1,350–$1,700	(16,1)	(0;1)
MS-67	?	(1;1)	(0;0)

A 1893 Columbian MS-66 DMPL sold for $6,325.

Now let us examine the Booker T. Washington price ranges:

Grade	Price
MS-63	$180–$250
MS-64	$500–$625
MS-65	$500–$1,300
MS-66	$800–$1,500

And the Booker T. Washington proof-like census and populations:

Year	Population	MS-63	MS-64	MS-65	MS-66	MS-67
1946-S	12	1	7	3	1	0
1947-S	97	4	23	48	17	5
1948-P	2	0	0	2	0	0
1948-S	26	0	12	11	1	2
1949-P	8	0	2	6	0	0
1949-S	1	0	0	1		0
1950-S	45	0	8	24	13	0
1951-D	1	0	0	1		0
1951-S	29	0	2	14	12	1

Proof-like Carver–Washingtons (C.W.s)

The few proof-like C.W. pieces that have sold, and that I am aware of, are the 1954-D MS-63 PL ($1,035) and the 1952-D PL rated MS-64 ($1,100). I do not get too excited about the MS-63 PL C.W.s that I have seen because they look too scruffy or bag-marked, or lack eye appeal. The coin's design doesn't help, and the reflective fields do little for me—though this doesn't seem to matter to the registry set collectors or dealers who must have the coin, and will pay record prices to procure one.

The proof-like Carver–Washington census and populations:

Year	Population	MS-63	MS-64	MS-65	MS-66
1951-P	2	2	0	0	0
1952-D	8	1	5	2	0
1952-S	2	0	1	1	0
1953-D	1	0	1	0	0
1954-D	5	3	0	2	0

These are the only issues that have received the PL designation from NGC. Expect lofty prices when they enter the marketplace.

In various auctions in 2009, the 1938 New Rochelle PL half dollar graded MS-65 sold in the $600 to $800 range; rated MS-66, it sold for between $950 and $1,725; and with the MS-67 label, it sold for $3,450. Also in 2009, the 1937 Roanoke PL issue rated MS-64 (population: 20) brought between $400 and $500. Graded MS-65 PL (population: 34), the coin sold at the $1,000 level. In MS-66 PL condition (population: 9), the value attained was between $1,100 and $1,300. Granted the lofty level of MS-67 PL (population: 2) the coin brought only $2,000. Why? Was it because the PL surface was not deep enough?

The four most available PL coins are the 1892 Columbian (363), the 1893 Columbian (188), the 1938 New Rochelle (177), and the 1937-S Boone half dollar (127). Let us look at the Boone's population figures:

Date	Population	MS-63	MS-64	MS-65	MS-66	MS-67
1935-S	1	1	0	0	0	0
1936-S	1	0	1	0	0	0
1937-P	6	0	2	3	1	0
1937-D	3	0	3	0	0	0
1937-S	127	3	53	44	24	3
1938-S	8	3	4	1	0	0

Proof-like 1937-S Boone price ranges:

Grade	Price
MS-64	$325–$400
MS-65	$725–$1,100
MS-66	$1,200–$1,400
MS-67	$2,100–$2,500

Please be aware that *if* another less populated issue were to make its appearance, depending on the depth of reflective surface, grade, and the coin buyer, a record price could be paid, especially in the higher grade. This Boone is an excellent coin to possess when it has strong reflective fields. Should an offering be listed as semi-proof-like, or somewhat PL or mildly PL or possesses PL tendencies, it should be worth what the regular issue is worth based on similar eye appeal and makeup.

Let us not forget the 1893 Isabella quarter (population: 99):

Grade	Value	Population
MS-61	$650–$700	5
MS-62	$675–$725	6
MS-63	$750–$1300	35
MS-64	$1,300–$1,700	34
MS-65	$2,000–$2500	8
MS-66	$3,500–$4,000+	6
MS-67	$8,500–$9,000+	1

This coin has excellent future potential in grades MS-64+ and higher. It is the only classic commemorative quarter dollar struck between 1892 and 1954. There wasn't a second until 1999, when the Delaware State Quarter entered the marketplace. Technically, or by strict interpretation of the rules, for a coin to be labeled an official commemorative coin, the term or words *commemorative coin(s)* must be part of the issuing Act. This was not the case for the 1932 George Washington quarter or the 1976 Bicentennial quarter.

Summation

The amount of clear reflectivity of 10-point print, when measured between a minimum of two to four inches, is certainly one of the main value factors when determining what to pay for a coin. Should an eye-appealing coin show reflectivity closer to four inches, rather than two inches, it will bring greater value than a piece that is moderately mirrored or just manages to make the PL designation. Beware of offerings described as having mild or proof-like tendencies. They are only semi-PL coins. Other factors are the coin's allure or drawing power, color, grade, issue, population, and the buyer. Let us not forget the buyer. Collectors should pass on those pieces that look very hazy or cloudy. It could well be that these coins were once a bit too heavily toned. They were then dipped in a tarnish-removing solution that was not strong enough to remove the toning completely. Such a coin might be made much brighter looking—but your natural surface is lost forever. Also pass on the dark and ugly-looking coins. Again, beware of those offerings described as mildly proof-like or possessing proof-like tendencies or semi-proof-like surfaces. They usually are worth no more than a similar issue of equal quality without such a description.

U.S. Commemorative PL Purchase Recommendations

Needless to say, I would want to own a U.S. commemorative coin exhibiting a strong to very strong PL surface on both sides of the coin. The PL commemoratives that I have examined over the last 35 years number more than 300 pieces. Those of the same issue varied in mirror or PL depth. As an example, two years ago, I examined a collector's collection containing 53 encapsulated B.T.W. PL issues. They graded from MS-64 through MS-66: this was a lesson in PL variance. The coins ranged from the questionable—how could this be called PL?—to the just-made-it PL pieces, of which there were many; to the few strong PLs. This is what the future owner of PL coinage should consider before acquisition. Know how to evaluate what you want to buy and/or have someone who knows the area well, and whom you trust, guide you. This is a section of U.S. commemorative coinage that possesses exceptional future potential.

Now Those PL Issues to Ponder

I highly recommend commemorative issues with strong PL surfaces on both sides of the coin. First is the 1893 Columbian PL striking in MS-63+ condition and loftier. It is rarer than the 1892 PL coin, but I also will take the 1892. The next impressive issue would be the 1938 New Rochelle PL coin. To date, 177 coins have been labeled PL—but it is the coin with those strong PL fields that should be sought. Pass on the borderline or questionable offering: some of these are out there in the marketplace. Also pass on the 1937 Roanoke PL half dollar, the B.T.W. PL half dollars, and the Boone 1937-S PLs. On the other hand, collectors should love the Isabella quarter with its 99 census figure.

I have seen some of the other issues with low populations. I was not impressed, as I would prefer more surface reflectivity on both sides of the coins. Possibly, buyers of these issues are mesmerized by the PL designation and must procure. A dealer may pay a hefty price for a coin, but only because he or she firmly believes that their client will not refuse it. Keep in mind that when a population or census figure is high for one issue and low for another, values should vary greatly—especially when we compare a population of 97 to 5 or 45 to 2. If they don't vary, it might be that the level of reflective depth for the offered coin is not very impressive. Those assembling registry sets, or possibly just the person who must have these proof-like issues, will pay big money for the PL label, regardless of the reflective surfaces. The degree of variance will be quite noticeable, when the set is being assembled or finalized.

Should you have any questions about proof-like issues, kindly contact with the author.

3. About Coin Grading

"Making the grade" is more than just an abstract concept when it comes to collectible coins. It is a stark reality that can translate into thousands of dollars of added value.

As you would expect, top quality coins—coins with little or no wear and few if any imperfections—command higher prices than those that show signs of extensive use or careless mishandling. With that in mind, we'll concern ourselves here only with coins in the upper echelon—those in or close to what is called "uncirculated" condition.

Dealers and collectors use a numerical scale to designate the condition—or "grade"—of a coin. This serves as a form of shorthand that simplifies transactions by giving both sides a reasonably accurate profile of the coin's level of preservation and other important attributes.

In determining this grade, evaluators consider several major factors. These include the extent of any *wear*, the presence or absence of *imperfections*, the *sharpness* of the features in the coin's design, the amount of *luster*, if any, and the degree of *eye appeal*. Some of these, such as wear and imperfections, are readily discernible, even measurable. Others, such as eye appeal, can be highly subjective: beauty, after all, is in the eye of the beholder.

Grading coins is an art. It is not an exact science. Several numismatic experts can render different grades for the same coin. The major professional coin grading services grade according to a consensus of numismatic opinions.

The grading scale ranges from 1 to 70, with "1" denoting a coin that is barely recognizable and "70" corresponding to a coin that is absolutely perfect. The numbers from 60 to 70 are reserved for uncirculated—or "Mint State" (abbreviated MS)—coins. The evaluation process has become so sophisticated that dealers and collectors now recognize 11 different Mint State grades (MS-60 to MS-70); each with subtle distinctions that set it apart from grades just a trifle higher or lower on the scale.

The difference in appearance between one grade and the next may seem slight, but the difference in value can be enormous. That is why it pays to learn as much as possible about the finer points of grading Mint State coins—or, alternatively, to buy such coins only from dealers who are highly knowledgeable and thoroughly reputable.

Here is a brief rundown on the generic key characteristics that identify each Mint State grade. Please note that each coin issue has its own nuances for grading that is tied to that particular coin's design, strike, and metallic composition. The Mint State categories are:

Mint State-60 (MS-60) The coin will probably have extensive marks or hairlines (fine lines visible when the coin is viewed at an angle). Hairlines, in fact, may cover its entire surface. It also can be weakly struck and have little or no luster or eye appeal. Nonetheless, it can be considered uncirculated—though barely—if there is no evidence of wear and the shortcomings are not the result of circulation.

Mint State-61 (MS-61) The coin can have the same kinds of deficiencies as an MS-60 example, but they will be somewhat less pronounced. Marks and hairlines, in particular, will be less extensive—and on larger coins such as silver dollars, entire areas may be free from such flaws.

Mint State-62 (MS-62) There can be light marks and hairlines across the entire coin, but if there are several sizable marks, the rest of the coin should be relatively free from such detractions. Sharpness of strike, luster and eye appeal are less significant factors in this grade, but typically will be weak and at best no better than average.

Mint State-63 (MS-63) For collectors who strongly favor higher-quality coins, this grade—known as "choice uncirculated"—is the lowest level they normally buy. An MS-63 coin can have numerous marks and hairlines, but these will be less noticeable than on lower-grade Mint State coins. There can be full detail in the strike, and the eye appeal can be positive. But there also can be significant detractions, such as spotting or unattractive toning.

Mint State-64 (MS-64) Imperfections become fewer and less obvious in this grade. There still can be readily detectable marks and hairlines, but they won't be severe and will be limited. Sharpness of strike will be full as a rule, but luster may be impaired and there can be moderate spotting. Overall, coins in this grade are attractive and tend to have better-than-average eye appeal.

Mint State-65 (MS-65) This is a watershed grade, separating lesser lights in the Mint State firmament from stars of higher magnitude—including the grading scale's superstars. It is a highly respectable grade in its own right, regarded by even the most discriminating collectors as fully acceptable for coins in a first-rate set. An MS-65 coin can have minor defects, but these will be overshadowed by its pleasing overall appearance. Marks and hairlines will be scattered and frequently hidden in details of the design. The coin will be well struck and its luster and eye appeal will generally be above average. This is the lowest rung on the grading ladder to qualify for the designation "gem uncirculated."

Mint State-66 (MS-66) There can be a few defects in a coin graded MS-66, but they will be minor and the coin's total impact will be overwhelmingly positive. Marks and hairlines will be minimal, the coin will be well struck, and the luster and eye appeal will be above average—sometimes well above.

Mint State-67 (MS-67) Any flaws will be slight. Marks or hairlines will be minimal and well-hidden, the strike will be very sharp, and the luster will be exceptional. The overall impression: this is an exceptional coin, well deserving its designation as "superb gem uncirculated."

Mint State-68 (MS-68) Coins in the three highest grades can be likened to supernovas. They dazzle the eye of the beholder with their virtually—or completely—flawless brilliance. An MS-68 coin will have only the slightest imperfections—tiny hairlines, for example, or very small breaks in otherwise spectacular luster. There may be minor unevenness in toning, but not to the point that it detracts from the totally positive impression.

Mint State-69 (MS-69) A coin that is graded MS-69 will be just a hair's breadth—or perhaps a hairline's breadth—from perfection. The coin may appear to be perfect, in fact, until it is examined in minute detail. Any imperfection can be, quite literally, microscopic—barely perceptible, very localized hairlines; the merest hint of softness in the strike; the slightest disruption in luster. Such a coin can only be described as superb.

Mint State-70 (MS-70) Perfection! To merit this supreme designation, a coin must be free from any flaw—however slight—detectable with a 5-power magnifying glass. There can't be marks or hairlines; details must be razor-sharp; the luster must be stunning and totally undisturbed; and the eye appeal must be truly magnificent.

The 1-to-70 numerical scale also is used in grading proof coins—specimen pieces minted on high-quality coin blanks that are struck several times with highly polished dies to give them a jewel-like appearance. These coins are much more likely to merit the highest grades—from Proof-68 (PF-68) to Proof-70 (PF-70)—because so much care is taken with their production and preservation. Those receiving lower grades, such as Proof-60 to Proof-62, are downgraded in almost all instances because of flaws resulting from mishandling or improper storage.

Modern proofs, including both regular and commemorative specimens, are far less elusive in lofty grades than business strikes (coins intended for use in circulation) or proofs from earlier periods—those from before 1950. Among classic commemorative coins, struck between 1892 and 1954, certain coins are given "super-high" grades in greater proportions than others. This tends to reflect greater care in their preparation and distribution.

Serious collectors generally steer clear of circulated coins. However, the highest grade reserved for such coins—About Uncirculated-58 (AU-58)—is often applied to coins much more attractive than lower-level coins in Mint condition. That is because these coins bear signs of circulation, disqualifying them from Mint State grades—and yet have positive attributes, such as sharp detail, nice luster or strong eye appeal, that would stamp them as MS-63, or even better, if there weren't any wear.

There are numerous coin grading services—companies that evaluate coins submitted for their review and certify them as being in designated grades. Two of these grading services enjoy far greater market acceptance than their competition: the Professional Coin Grading Service (PCGS) and the Numismatic Guaranty Corporation (NGC).

PCGS and NGC both have been in business since the 1980's, and both are well regarded for the accuracy and consistency of their experts' grading decisions. Most importantly, both stand behind these decisions and guarantee that coins reviewed by them and housed in their special holders are authentic and properly graded.

4. WHAT IS EYE APPEAL?

Eye appeal is a subjective factor when grading or appraising coinage. It is the amount or degree of luster emanating from the coin's surface. The amount of luster can vary from coin issue to coin issue, depending on the coin's design and the die surface used to strike the coin. If the die had a dull satiny surface, then that is the finish that will be imparted on the coin. If the die is polished to a greater degree than the normal production die, the coin will have a more brilliant surface. If the die is highly polished the coin will have a mirror-like finish.

Strike is also another component to eye appeal. A sharply-struck piece that clearly highlights the smallest details of the coin's design will grab the eye more than that its weakly-struck cousin.

Surface luster and strike are only part of total eye appeal. There is an aesthetic component to this quality as well, which is based on the coin issue and the collector population collecting that issue. For example, collectors of the Standing Liberty Quarter (1916–30) adore blast white brilliant uncirculated shining coins; collectors of Morgan silver dollars (1878–1921) also adore blast white brilliant uncirculated shining coins, but rainbow effect tarnished dollars also command high premiums because of the beauty of the iridescent patina. Commemorative collectors are similar to Standing Liberty Quarter collectors and tend to gravitate toward specimens that exhibit lustrous reflectivity coupled with sharp striking. Commemorative collectors by reflex avoid dull, dark, and unattractive coins; such coins should not be purchased except for the pride of ownership only. A tarnished commemorative should generally be avoided unless it elicits an almost unanimous excitement from everyone who sees it.

5. What is a Numismatic Collector?

There are several different categories of numismatic collector. From the many gradations I will try to categorize with broad strokes the most widely found.

- **accumulator** This collector will seek to procure as many example of a numismatic item as possible. These are the people who you hear about having anywhere from a mason jar filled with circulated U.S. and foreign coins up to, if not more than, 100,000 Lincoln wheat back (1909–58) cents in buckets.
- **hobbyist** This is the collector who collects for the joy of collecting. They tend to want a representative example of an issue for their collection and are not always preoccupied with the coin's grade or rarity.
- **academic** Serious collector who carefully researches particular coins and their history. These collectors fixate on higher grade specimens or rare die marriages as illustrated in *The Comprehensive Encyclopedia of Morgan and Peace Dollars* by Leroy C. Van Allen and A. George Mallis (revised edition 1991). We touch upon such esoteric numismatic information in the 1900 Lafayette entry. This information is limited because there is so little die variation in the commemorative series.
- **investor / speculator** This is the purely financially driven collector who seeks a return on his numismatic investment in the future and is not concerned with the aesthetic qualities of the coin.
- **unscrupulous** This is the worst breed in the hobby. They are most likely responsible for selling over-graded, cleaned, or altered surface coins to the neophyte collector. The worst of the worst have perpetrated some of the most hideous frauds, such as the counterfeit coinage coming from China complete in a PCGS or NGC holder, or, worse yet, boiler room salesmen who sell generic or over-graded coins at exorbitant prices. Unscrupulous collectors/dealers have been known to doctor coin surfaces by artificially toning coins, cleaning with wire brushes (known as "whizzing"), applying fillers such as epoxy to hide abrasions, cut, nicks, scratches, and overall wearing in order to deceive the collector and grading services.
- **dealer** Can be best described as a combination of all the above categories. Dealers are notoriously known for the collections of miscellaneous coins and odd lots they accumulate from past deals and estate buys. Most dealers started off in the trade as a hobbyist and morphed into a full- or part-time dealer for a number of reasons. As an academic, dealers often research coinage history or die variations to set their inventory apart from other dealers' offerings or to pique interest in an issue so they can promote their offerings. Of course dealers are also investors and speculators: otherwise they would not be in business very long. Hopefully your dealer is reputable and not among the "unscrupulous."

6. The Business of Buying Coins

After coins are dispersed by the U.S. Mint or its agents, where do the coins available on the secondary market come from? Coins sold by numismatic dealers generally come from the following sources:

- Estate sales
- Walk-in's to store-front coin dealer shops / pawn shops
- Private sales from collectors whom the dealer has in his social / hobby network
- Online sales, such as seen in classified ads on eBay.com, CraigsList.com, UPillar.com, etc.
- Shows / conventions
    Local coin shows usually held at a VFW hall, Elks lodge, etc., by local coin clubs
    Regional shows held at larger venues such as hotels
    National shows held at convention centers such the American Numismatic Association's World's Fair of Money and the Florida United Numismatics (FUN) show
- Auctions
    Online auctions on eBay.com, Teletrade.com, Heritage.com, etc.
    Regional auctions from auction and estate companies, etc.
    National cataloged auctions from renowned numismatic auction houses

Coins that are procured by coin dealers are then either sent to a grading service or, if the condition and value warrant, the coin may be sent to a conservation service before being submitted to a grading service. At times, a coin may come back with a lower than expected grade on the slab (grading service capsule). A dealer may choose to remove the coin from the slab, called "cracking out," and resubmitting the coin to another grading agency in hopes of a higher grade. "Cracking out" is also performed on newly acquired graded coins, generally in older holders, that the dealer feels could be upgraded to a higher rating. Over the years many grading insert labels have been thrown away by dealers and collectors, instead of being returned to the relevant grading agency so that the agency's reported populations could be adjusted. This is why in this book I state that the reader should adjust known populations by a certain percentage.

7. THE MARKET HIGH OF MAY 26, 1989

In early 1989 coins enjoyed an unprecedented bull market in which coin prices skyrocketed to dizzying heights only to plunge in June 1989 and languish for nearly a decade, defying any expected upswing usually found with financial waves.

Why did coin prices surge in late 1988 and early 1989? There were several factors:

- Wall Street money, and consequently uninformed investors, poured into the numismatic market when graded or slabbed coins were judged to be quantifiable commodities that could be tracked, traded, and speculated on by financial institutions. Coins were allowed to be included as investments in Individual Retirement Accounts (IRA) and Keogh accounts (full-fledged pension plans for self-employed people, named after U.S. Representative Eugene James Keogh of New York). Mutual funds also invested in rare coins as they sought new types of investments for the money that flooded in as millions of Americans took advantage of the 1981 Economic Recovery Tax Act, which allowed all taxpayers under the age of 70½ to contribute to an IRA.
- Known populations were low at the time for many issues (see the 1936 Elgin entry) and various sources for the populations were considered dubious at best. With the rise of grading services, the population data from these sources became the new numismatic standard. Some issues, once thought difficult to find, were soon realized to be quite common and available.
- Coin dealers successfully promoted many issues to Wall Street fund managers and generally uninformed investors.
- The marked increase of coin prices garnered media attention that inadvertently brought into the marketplace many collections that had been squirreled away by surviving relatives of deceased collectors, thus inflating known populations.

All these factors conspired to push the numismatic market into an overdrive much akin to that of the tulip mania in February 1637, the Florida real estate craze in 1926, or the stock market speculation of 1929.

8. The Approval Process of a Modern Commemorative Coin

1) The sponsoring group of a potential commemorative coin petitions Congress for a new commemorative coin issue.
2) If the petition is successful, Congress passes a law authorizing the production of a design for the sponsoring group and authorizing the U.S. Mint to produce the issue.
3) The U.S. Mint places the design in its schedule.
4) The U.S. Mint allots two weeks to create from four to as many as 15 designs.
5) The U.S. Mint engages the eight outside artists in the Artistic Infusion Program (AIP), established in 2003, to assist in the creation of the designs.
6) The U.S. Mint's internal committee selects four or five of the designs for approval.
7) The designs are sent to the sponsoring group for approval.
8) The designs approved by the sponsoring group are sent to the Citizens Coinage Advisory Committee (CCAC) for approval. The CCAC was established in 2003 by Congress under Public Law 108-15. The design is also sent to the U.S. Commission of Fine Arts (CFA), established in 1910, in Washington, D.C. The CFA makes the final decision regarding the design of the issue.
9) Upon approval of the designs by the CFA, the director for the U.S. Mint approves the design.
10) The approved design is sent to the Secretary of the Treasury for approval.
11) Modeling and tooling by the U.S. Mint begins.
12) Test striking and trial strikings are performed before production begins.

1892–1893 WORLD'S COLUMBIAN EXPOSITION

Reason for Issue:	To raise funds for the World's Columbian Exposition in Chicago and to commemorate the 400th anniversary of Christopher Columbus's landing in the New World.
Authorization:	Act of August 5, 1892, with a maximum of 5,000,000 pieces.
Issued by:	World's Columbian Exposition
Official Sale Price:	$1

Production Figures

Date	Business Strikes	Assay Coins	Proofs	Melted	Net Mintage
1892	950,000	?	103	0	950,000
1893	4,052,105	2,105	0	2,501,700	1,548,300

Current Market Values

Date	MS-60	MS-62	MS-63	MS-64	MS-65	MS-66	MS-67	MS-68
1892	$25	$38	$80	$130	$300	$750 to $1,250	$3,000 to $4,500	$14K+
1893	$25	$38	$75	$130	$440	$800 to $1,100	$3,000 to $6,000	$14K+

DESIGNS

Obverse by Charles E. Barber

Bust of Christopher Columbus, facing right. This is a fantasy portrait based on the work by Olin Levi Warner (1844–96), who copied from a Spanish medal. "UNITED STATES OF AMERICA" arcs above; "COLUMBIAN HALF DOLLAR" circles below. Incused on the left truncation of the collar is Barber's initial (B).

Reverse by George T. Morgan

Three-masted caravel (representing the flagship Santa Maria) sailing to the left, in a westerly direction, above two cartographic hemispheres, representing the opening of the New World to Europeans. The "14" and the "92" of the year of Columbus's first voyage are to the left and right of the hemispheres. "WORLD'S COLUMBIAN EXPOSITION CHICAGO" circles the design. The date 1892 is at the bottom. At the lower right edge of the center sail is Morgan's initial (M) in relief.

Origins of the Columbian

It was the initial hope of the Exposition Commission's manager to have 40 million half dollars struck to be used as admission tokens to the Exposition and souvenir keepsakes. However, only 5 million were authorized. Thus, the first United States commemorative half dollar was sold at double face value to help defray expenses. It was supposedly produced from melted-down obsolete silver coins (3-cent pieces, half dimes, etc.) as mandated by the authorizing legislation.

Struck in 1892, the was not included as part of the yearly Proof set which now boasted the new Liberty Head coinage, also designed by Charles E. Barber. The reason was that a Proof Columbian half dollar would have to cost more than $1, while the Barber half dollar would cost the collector only a few cents more than face value.

For publicity purposes, Wyckoff, Seamans and Benedict, makers of the Remington Standard Typewriter (the official writing device of the Exposition) offered to pay the Commission $10,000 for the first specimen of the half dollar. Harlow N. Higinbotham, President of the Exposition, was content merely to set aside the first regular strike. However, Commissioner Colonel James Ellsworth, one of history's most famous coin collectors, lobbied for a Proof 1892 Columbian half dollar to be produced. Without Higinbotham's permission, Ellsworth had arranged for this coin to be produced in Proof condition. On November 19, 1892, 103 pieces were struck by hand at the Philadelphia Mint.

All of the 1892 coinage—the first U.S. coins to depict a foreigner—was produced in November and December of 1892 and distributed. The Exposition was dedicated on October 21, 1892, but did not open until noon on May 1, 1893.

President Grover Cleveland officiated at the ceremony that opened the event to the public. After the Exposition closed its doors in 1894, some 3.6 million 1893-dated commemorative halves remained unsold, and the Treasury Department offered the coins to the public at face value. There were few takers, though: 2,501,700 were melted and the rest were dumped into circulation. In the 1890s, the average factory worker earned between $4.50 and $7.00 per week, and a half dollar represented quite an investment.

The Columbian Today

Both dates are readily available in grades EF-40 through AU-58. Strict MS-60 Columbians are not scarce, but they are not as abundant as many would believe. The real MS-60 or MS-60+ coin offers little that appeals to the eye. Surfaces can range from proof-like, to blazing and pristine luster, to dull, to dipped-out and gone-forever luster on baggy and hair-lined surfaces. There are too many "About Uncirculated" coins offered as BU-60 or MS-60. "BU" usually means "been used." Thus, caution should be exercised; there are few genuine bargains in numismatics.

Current MS-63 pieces can be located with little difficulty. If possible, collectors should concentrate on MS-63+ specimens, which offer better future value, as they are sought by those hoping to have them slabbed MS-64. Collectors should apply the same reasoning to MS-64+ specimens. However, there is little chance these coins would be slabbed MS-65 if a detracting deep bag mark, too many field hairline scratches, or hits in the primary focal areas (such as Columbus's portrait) are present. Collectors should be aware that these bargain-priced slabs do exist. Strictly graded MS-64 specimens are somewhat undervalued. More highly recommended are the MS-64+ coins, some of which were once bought and sold as MS-65. For those who cannot afford MS-65 prices, the MS-64+ can be an excellent purchase.

The 1892 Columbian specimens grading Proof-55 and higher will enhance any collection. Past sales have ranged from $800 to $75,000. After re-examining the alleged Proof 1893 first-struck specimen housed at the Chicago Historical Society, I've come to the conclusion that it is an exceptional presentation coin: it simply does not possess total Proof characteristics. I believe that no 1893 Proofs were produced. Even those few encapsulated pieces are in fact actually just amazing early deep mirror proof-like (DMPL) strikings.

Columbian surfaces will range from DMPL to semi-proof-like, to blazing brilliant, to bright satiny, and to dull luster. Because of die preparation, the business strike production 1893 issue will offer the buyer more of a DMPL surface, with stronger mirrored fields, than the proof-like specimen of 1892. Such coins

were either struck from new dies, which retained their initial finish, or were produced from dies re-polished by the Mint to obliterate existing clash marks. Die
polishing marks were created by this polishing into the die surface. These marks
will be seen as fine raised lines, superficially resembling scratches, but they do
not cut into the coin's surface in the way that scratches do.

As observed on the Morgan silver dollar, the obverse of this coin can display
as proof-like, combined with a satiny reverse or vice versa. Collectors need only
be aware of the fact that the existing die surface at striking time will create an
identical surface on the newly minted coin.

Variations in strike will run from full to strong to acceptable (for the issue)
to weak. Areas of importance are Columbus's eyebrow, his hair detail (situated
next to his forehead), his wide bottom hair curl (which normally displays little
detail, and is contiguous to his lower jaw), the *Santa Maria's* sail seams (especially the center sail) and her vertical ribs and horizontal planking.

There are 1892 Columbian halves with the digits "9" and "2" re-punched at
the Mint. The same holds true for the 1893 issue with its digit "3" re-punched
(at the top). At present, little additional premium, if any, is offered for such
pieces. This situation could quickly change, however, as a result of the emer-
gence of many new collectors and their interest in these details. These half dollars will also exhibit machine, or strike doubling (on the letters of a word or date
or Mint mark, if present), usually caused by the hammer die being loose. There
is no extra value for any such coinage—die doubling is another matter, however.

Originally, 5,002,105 pieces were struck for this issue. To date, only three
error coins with errors have been reported. Two are reverse Mint State lamina-
tion errors—which are questionable. They have an error in "1892" as well as a
before-and-after looking *Santa Maria*, as if it had been struck in the bow by a
torpedo. (One such coin sold for $8,800 in 1994.) The third error is a circulated
VF piece struck approximately 35% off center. It sold for $400 in 1984.

Detecting Counterfeits

To date, no counterfeits have surfaced. Coins lacking a reeded edge are doctored
pieces or have been worked on outside the Mint. The edge is usually rounded.

Is Your Columbian Circulated or Mint State?

Obverse

Columbus's eyebrow and cheekbone are the first locations to indicate a metal
loss: they present a grayish-white metal texture. A collector should not confuse
the lack of metal fill marks in these areas or on the coin's devices with small
nicks, cuts, or scratches: they can look similar. The latter are created during
striking when metal does not flow into the recesses of the die (the high points
on the coin). Also, a blank coin can be damaged before striking. Sometimes, the
damage cannot be eradicated by the minting process. Thus, there can be a coin
"born" MS-63 or lower in grade.

Reverse

The relief is well-protected by the rim. Were anyone to place this issue obverse-side down and gently do a "rub test" by pushing the coin forward four inches, then examining it, he would immediately notice a loss of metal on the obverse high points. However, were he to try a rub test on the ship's side, the results after five back-and-forth movements would show only on the coin's reverse rim. Metal loss will first be noticed on the upper point of the rear sail, then on the center and upper sails, followed by a trace of wear on the Eastern Hemisphere. The observer should not confuse striking weakness on the center sail's seams or the slight loss of light cameo frost with wear.

Since the obverse design's relief is higher than the reverse design's, the obverse can display slight friction or wear, making it AU or ("almost uncirculated" or "about uncirculated"). But the reverse of such a coin can be full Mint State MS-63 or better. It is important to remember that one grades a coin—and buys it—by its lowest grade. This rule should be applied to all coinage.

Related Material

There are no official Exposition Commission holders or mailing envelopes for this issue. However, the coin was distributed by various banks in small, purse-like, round or square burgundy or brown leather holders with velour interiors and the bank's gold imprint. Some of the rarest bank issues are the "Third National Bank Merchants" and "Manufacturers National Bank" (both from Pittsburgh) and the "Paterson National Bank" (Paterson, New Jersey). Similar holders are known with only "Columbian Exposition" encircling "1492—Chicago—1892" gold-stamped on the upper cover. Wells Fargo & Co. produced a lovely distributing holder for the issue ($300+). The distribution material can be quite rare and expensive. The leather pouch can be worth $75 to $500+, depending on its condition. If accompanied by a coin, its value must be determined by both the state of the half dollar and the condition of the holder. The rarity of an item will also be a factor. At times, a pouch contains a toned, proof-like coin that can be AU or UNC. The seller's primary objective is probably to encourage the potential buyer to believe that a proof is contained; justifying the higher asking price.

Leather holders

One should be vigilant. A rare presentation box was distributed by the McConway & Torley Co., an iron foundry in Pittsburgh; one of these sold for $1,380 at the American Numismatic Rarities auction in Baltimore in March 2005.

Special ribboned badges with the Columbian Exposition half dollars were produced for special days at the event. The first was Chicago Day (October 9, 1893) when badges were red-ribboned, followed by Manhattan Day (October 21, 1893), when they were blue. The last was Columbus Day (October 30, 1893), when gold ribbon was used. This set of three brought $2,070 also at the American Numismatic Rarities auction in Baltimore in March 2005. The accompanying coins graded VF-EF. It is likely that the buyer paid too much for the set. Individual badges have brought between $100 and $300—real value should be based on the coin, however.

Future Potential of the Columbian Half Dollar

I have yet to see a 1893 Columbian that I would classify as defnite Proof: too controversial. Only NGC uses the proof-like (PL) designation.

Date	Service	EF 40	AU 58	MS 60	MS 62	MS 63	MS 64	MS 65	MS 66	MS 67	MS 68	MS 69
1892	NGC	3	154	9	544	1079	1723	802	177	43	0	0
1892	PCGS	5	341	88	895	1610	965	685	226	12	0	0
1892	Combined	8	495	97	1439	2689	2688	1487	403	55	0	0

Date	Service	EF 40	AU 58	MS 60	MS 62	MS 63	MS 64	MS 65	MS 66	MS 67	MS 68	MS 69
1893	NGC	10	315	18	702	1196	1170	619	152	26	2	0
1893	PCGS	9	495	114	1067	1548	1438	490	165	9	0	0
1893	Combined	19	810	123	1769	2744	2608	1109	317	35	2	0

Date	Service	PF 40	PF 55	PF 60	PF 62	PF 63	PF 64	PF 65	PF 66	PF 67	PF 68	PF 69
1892	NGC	0	1	0	0	4	14	8	2	0	2	0
1892	PCGS	0	0	2	4	17	12	6	5	1	0	0
1892	Combined	0	1	2	4	21	26	14	7	1	1	0

Date	Service	PF 40	PF 55	PF 60	PF 62	PF 63	PF 64	PF 65	PF 66	PF 67	PF 68	PF 69
1893	NGC	0	0	0	0	1	0	0	0	0	0	0
1893	PCGS	0	0	0	0	0	1	0	0	0	0	0
1893	Combined	0	0	0	0	1	1	0	0	0	0	0

Date	Service	PL 40	PL 58	PL 60	PL 62	PL 63	PL 64	PL 65	PL 66	PL 67	PL 68	PL 69
1892	NGC	0	6	3	50	94	133	61	19	1	0	0
1893	NGC	0	4	1	38	52	73	24	1	1	0	0

Date	Ser-vice	DMPL 40	DMPL 58	DMPL 60	DMPL 62	DMPL 63	DMPL 64	DMPL 65	DMPL 66	DMPL 67	DMPL 68	DMPL 69
1892	NGC	0	0	0	0	1	0	2	0	0	0	0
1893	NGC	0	0	0	0	1	1	0	1	0	0	0

A DMPL 1893 Columbian, rated MS-66, sold for $6,235 at auction.

Aside from the Booker T. Washington and Carver–Washington issues, the 1892 and 1893 Columbians are the second most abundant commemorative half dollars in circulation. An average worn specimen is worth between $15 and $18. Dealers will pay between $18 and $20 for attractive AU pieces. An increase in silver bullion prices will trigger a rise in value for them. This is the kind of coin used in a decorative frame or sold in a holder and is advertised between $35 and $75. One can buy them for the fun of ownership, or as a "numismatic seed" for some youngster or future collector. Appealing AU coinage, acquired in the $18 to $25 range, can be offered to novices in various uncirculated grades. There is a respectable price spread between MS-60 and MS-63. Based on their availability, one should acquire them for the joy of ownership.

In 1992 radio, television and telemarketing campaigns heavily promoted the MS-63 rating. Some MS-63 and MS-64 slabbed—and raw—coins were sold for $4,000 per coin. Bid values in the open secondary market were $375 and $1,200, respectively. Those investments are lost forever; only divine Intervention would increase values to past levels. NGC and PCGS coin grading and encapsulation services figures can be reduced between 18% and 22% for MS-64 coins: one should buy them only for the joy of ownership.

During the last market high in May 1989, the 1893 issue was bid at almost $6,000, while the 1892 striking was bid at about $1,000 less in MS-65 condition. At current levels, the higher mintage 1893 Columbian (which is rarer—because it received more abuse or less angelic protection) is the most desirable and undervalued coin; it possesses more potential than the 1892 coin. I would reduce the census between 17% and 20% for each date. One should not consider the unattractive or questionable offering, or buy an unslabbed coin, if it can't be graded. Given its higher population, the MS-65-rated coin is not difficult to locate.

Columbians strictly graded MS-66 offer very good to excellent future potential, depending on the attractiveness and how strictly the coin was graded. I would lower the census between 11% and 13% for the 1892 issue and between 12% and 14% for the 1893 coin. Population figures are quite low for the loftier MS-67 category, which would be an excellent addition to one's collection.

Proof 1892 coinage is good to own in all categories. 1892 Columbian Proof census figures are not accurate. PF-63 and higher rated pieces were churned out and sent—and re-sent—to NGC or PCGS for a higher grade, making census figures questionable. Too many grading labels were discarded and coins resubmitted.

Business strike on the left and proof on the right. Note the depth
of the hairlines on the stronger-struck proof example.

To date, 73 1892 proofs have been encapsulated by NGC and PCGS. They
grade between PF-60 through PF-68. Some pieces showing wear have been
rated lower. The price depends on the coin's eye appeal, strength of grade, and
on the buyer and seller. Values can range from $1,500 to $20,000+. Expect to
pay about $3,800 for a PF-63 example; $4,500 to $5,500 for a PF-64; possibly
$6,500 to $7,500 for a PF-65; and $8,000 to $10,000 for a PF-66. PF-67 pieces
have been marketed for between $11,000 and $15,000, while a PF-68 striking
sold for $20,000. Two 1893 strikings were encapsulated by both services. They
range from PF-63 to PF-64. The reader must be the arbiter on this issue. They
should rate as non-proofs. One sold for approximately $2,300 at auction, which
probably says something about its proof status. I highly recommend the 1892
Columbian proof in grades PF-63 and higher. You may have one in your collection without knowing it. It has excellent long-term potential.

Is It or Isn't It a Proof Columbian?

Over the years, collectors, dealers and the inquisitive have crossed my path at
coin shows, or, having forwarded a coin, have asked the question: "Is my 1892–
1893 Columbian a proof?" They simply don't know and hope that, because they
possess a coin that looks like a proof, it is a proof. After all, it might display a
proof-like or deep mirrored surface on both sides. Sometimes they know it isn't
a proof, but still strive for confirmation that it is, because a proof coin is very
valuable.

Is it that difficult to tell the difference between a proof and a proof-like coin?
Not if one follows certain rules of observation. When examining a raw specimen
with seemingly proof-like surfaces, one should be certain the beaded border is
fully rounded and sharply struck on both sides. Should a section display any flatness on either side, it will only be an early-struck proof-like coin. Next, observe
the coin's striking details. Sharp definition should be observed on Columbus's
hair and the ship's rigging and planks. This uncommonly well-defined sharpness will not be present on the business strike or the collector issue. Do not use

Columbian proof-like coin. Note flattened denticles.

the coin's wire rim as—shall we say—proof that the coin in question is a proof coin. Wire rims, also referred to as a wire edge or a knife edge, are created when the coin's metal flows between the die and collar. The collar is a device placed around the lower die. Its function is to prevent metal spreading and to create the coin's grooved notches (reeding) or edge device, such as lettering. I've seen wire edges on 1892 and 1893 Columbian coinage with proof-like, frosted as well as satiny-finished surfaces. The same is true of the 1893 Isabella quarter.

To determine if your coin is proof-like, you should be able to read the reflected small print (10-point: approximately one-eighth of an inch high) on a standard business card held from two to approximately four inches away from the coin. How strong is the coin you are examining? At what distance does the print begin to blur on both sides? Is it 2.5 inches or 3.8 inches? (For more information, see the section "Pricing Proof-like Commemorative Coinage" in Topic 2, "Commemorative Proof-like Coinage.")

The author examining the sealed proofs in 1978.

The 1893 Proof Columbian is a controversial coin. It can possess deep mirror-like fields that are deeper than the 1892 coin, but that lack the characteristic total proof-striking requirements. In 1983, after examining for a second time the very first 1893 piece struck, I determined it to be a first-strike coin, and not a proof.

In 1978, I asked the Chicago Historical Society's Chief Curator, Joseph B. Zywicki, to petition the Society's Director, Dr. Harold K. Skramstad, Jr., to open the three linen envelopes that housed the 1892 anniversary-related

400th, 1492nd and 1892nd proof strikings that had been sealed since November 1892. We carefully opened the envelopes, each of which contained a small circular box, which in turn contained the grey-toned proof coins. They had last been admired nearly 86 years previously.

Those who can't afford Columbian proof commemorative half dollars should attempt to acquire the next best thing. That is a proof-like coin struck with highly polished or even proof dies—but given only one blow from the press. A collector should seek such a coin in MS-64 condition (or higher) because lesser grades show too many scratches and other surface negatives that are magnified by the proof-like fields. There is nothing wrong with owning lower-graded pieces.

There is great potential in attractive pieces of either date, graded MS-64+ or better. One should beware the buffed or polished raw coin offered as a proof or proof-like specimen.

Additional Related Material

The World's Columbian Exposition Admission Tickets

The large number of admission tickets sold prior to and during the 1893 World's Columbian Exposition in Chicago were of the inexpensive variety. However, some of the most beautiful admission tickets created for any exposition were those engraved and printed by the American Bank Note Company of New York City. Resembling fractional U.S. currency (5-, 10-, 25-, and 50-cent notes), they were printed on specially prepared paper, and had a mottled appearance. These "spots" can be detected by holding the item up to a light source. In fact, they can be felt by rubbing one's fingertips across them.

The tickets were elaborately engraved and printed—in order to discourage attempts at counterfeiting. They were sold on April 1, 1893 in Chicago, to companies and individuals at 50 cents each—one month before the Exposition opened on May 1, 1893—in order to fill advance orders. The original group of tickets offered four different portraits: an American Indian chief; Columbus; and presidents Washington and Lincoln. The portraits represented four eras of U.S. history. Approximately 1 million of each of the four sets of tickets were originally printed. Because more tickets were needed, nearly 500,000 extra were produced with the addition of the letter "A," which was positioned on the lower right of the portrait. These portrayed the American Indian and George Washington. Roughly 450,000 depict Columbus; 400,000 picture Lincoln, the rarest of the group. They have sold for $50 each, or more if they are in brand-new condition. If they have been improperly handled, they are worth only $15–$35.

Also printed—but not with the initial four—were tickets depicting Benjamin Franklin and Georg Friedrich Handel. Franklin was honored for his "electrical association" with the use of electricity at the Exposition. Bearing the word "Complimentary," these tickets were engraved and printed for the Exposition free of charge. Approximately 126,000 were produced: all feature the letter "A." I previously owned serial #125,905. Eventually, most of these tickets were given

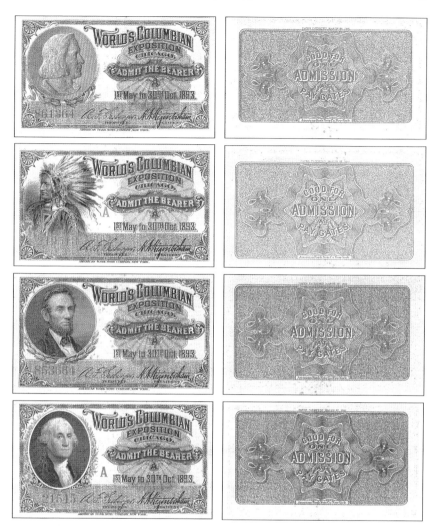

Original set of four admission tickets elaborately engraved and printed
by the American Banknote Company.

free of charge by various institutions to potential clients and friends. Their estimated value: $65–$85+ new; $30–$40 used.

Handel, whose ticket features the word "Music," was selected because of
a work that was viewed as being closely associated with most of the Exposition's subject matter: buildings, water, and music. Handel composed the *Water
Music* suite for George I of England; it which was performed in 1717 on a vessel
near the royal barge, while they cruised the River Thames. Roughly 100,000 of
Handel tickets were printed, all without the letter "A," making it the rarest of
these beautiful American Bank Note Company creations. Their estimated value
is $75–$100+.

The scarcer Franklin and Handel admission tickets.

Rare Chicago Day Child's Ticket—front

Rare Chicago Day Child's Ticket—back

Front of common Children's Special Ticket that is often
inserted in sets of tickets in place of the rarer
Chicago Day Child's Ticket.

Back of the common Children's Special Ticket.

Two months before the Exposition's closing, it was virtually impossible to obtain these little works of art. Instead of destroying those on hand, the Exposition's managers decided to recommence their sale, on October 26, 1893. When the Exposition closed six days later, it was determined that all unsold American Bank Note Company special day and general admission tickets would be sold to the Caxton Company of Chicago. Eleven different versions were packaged in Caxton's printed envelopes and were offered as a collectible. I estimate that between 2,500 and 3,000 sets of the 11 tickets were originally assembled: possibly 400 sets are extant. They have recently been offered for sale at between $250 and $500 each.

The rarest item within the group is the Chicago Day Child's Ticket, with the stub attached. The stub is a must on all special-day tickets. This 5½ x 2-inch peach-colored ticket shows the mythical Phoenix rising from the ashes of the Chicago Fire, which occurred on October 8–9, 1871. 50,000 of these were printed. It has sold for between $100 and $250+. Should you acquire the 11-piece package, make certain this ticket is present and has not been replaced by an unattractive light brown Children's Special Ticket (CST) measuring 3 × 1¼ inches, or those return passes (red or brown) that resemble door-prize tickets. These CSTs (series "A" for ages 7–11 [1,000,000] and series "V" for ages

Front of Chicago Day Ticket

Back of Chicago Day Ticket

7–17 [500,000]) have a combined 1,500,000 printing and can be obtained for between $3 and $7 each.

Finally, the Chicago Day Ticket, also depicting the Phoenix rising, announces the date of October 9, 1893. The reason, of course, was that most of the city was burned exactly 22 years earlier, and was thereafter rebuilt. This ticket used the series letters "A" through "H." Each involved a printing of 99,999, totaling almost 800,000 pieces. Some 700,000 Chicago Day Tickets were purchased, mostly by locals. The Manhattan Day Ticket, portraying the Statue of Liberty, was also created by the Western Bank Note Company of Chicago. Its date has no special significance. The primary objective was to attempt to increase attendance for this special day. The 500,000 pieces made for the New York affair did not sell as well as expected. Either can be obtained with some difficulty with the stub attached for between $20 and $30, as a result of limited demand. Should you be interested in these items, purchase them for the fun of collecting. The three admission tickets that are the most popular and have the best chance to increase in value are the Chicago Day Child's and the Handel and Franklin issues, followed by the very popular admission ticket depicting Columbus with a letter "A" added.

1893 Isabella Quarter Dollar

Reason for Issue:	To commemorate the World's Columbian Exposition and Isabel (anglicized to "Isabella"), Queen of Castile, who sponsored Columbus's voyage of discovery.
Authorization:	Act of March 3, 1893, with a maximum of 40,000 pieces.
Issued by:	Board of Lady Managers, World's Columbian Exposition
Official Sale Price:	$1

Production Figures

Date	Business Strikes	Assay Coins	Proofs	Melted	Net Mintage
1893	40,023	23	103	15,809	24,191

Current Market Values

Date	EF-40	AU	MS 60	MS 63	MS 64	MS 65	MS 66	MS 67	MS 68
1893	$450	$450	$550	$650	$850	$2,100 to $2,500	$4K to $5.5K	$7K to $8K	$40K

Designs by Charles E. Barber

Obverse

The crowned bust of Queen Isabel of Spain, facing left. "United States of America" circles the rim. In the right field parallel to the word "America" is the date 1893.

Reverse

A kneeling spinner facing left, holding a distaff (a staff used for holding the flax, tow, or wool in spinning) in her left hand and a spindle (emblematic of a woman's industry), in her right hand. Encircling the inner border, and inside the beaded border that is present on both sides of the coin, is the inscription: "BOARD OF LADY MANAGERS COLUMBIAN QUAR. DOL." This commemorative is the first American coin to portray a foreign sovereign and a royal crown, and was the only purely commemorative quarter dollar issue struck between 1893 and 1999.

Origins of the Isabella

Mrs. Potter Palmer, a wealthy Chicago matron, headed the World's Columbian Exposition's Board of Lady Managers, which was formed at the request of Susan B. Anthony. This was a group of women designated by officials of the Exposition to promote the interests of women at the event. At Mrs. Palmer's suggestion, the Appropriations Committee of the U.S. House of Representatives assigned $10,000 to the Board in the form of souvenir 25-cent pieces. This issue gives special recognition to women in government, as well as in social and industrial movements.

Records indicate that the Philadelphia Mint began production of the Isabella quarter dollar on June 13, 1893. As with the Proof Columbian 1892 issue, was it possible that the 400th, 1,492nd and the 1,892nd coins struck were selected and documented by the Mint, and then forwarded to the Board of Lady Managers in Chicago? To date there is no proof for this. I speculate that 100 proof pieces of this issue were struck, as were the Columbian 50-cent proofs; it could even be 50 or 75 pieces, but my research, as well as other investigations concerning this matter, has uncovered no conclusive evidence.

As a result of a lack of publicity, only small quantities of the Isabella were sold at the Women's Building on the Exposition grounds. Of the approximately 15,000 coins purchased by the public, most were vended via mail order to collectors and dealers during the celebration year. Scott Stamp & Coin Company procured several thousand of these commemorative quarters. Mrs. Palmer and her friends purchased 10,000 pieces at face value in 1893. These were apportioned through coin dealers and others for the next 34 years. Still, 15,809 coins were returned to the Mint's melting pot.

The Isabella Today

Based on present grading standards, most of the existing mintage for this issue is between the EF-AU to the low-end MS-63 category. "Low-end" refers to a borderline coin that just makes the grade. It will be worth less than current values. However, some dealers refer to it as a questionable grade: they believe that the coin, though labeled MS-63, is really MS-62+. When acquiring EF-AU specimens, make certain they are original, un-doctored and not heavily toned brown or black. One should not consider the polished or wire-brushed job, as they offer little to no future value. When acquiring an MS-63 Isabella, be certain the coin you are examining possesses decent eye-appeal and originality. One should reject those coins with deep cuts or scratches or those that are heavily marked, unless the price is a great bargain. Attractive quarters labeled MS-64, while not considered rare, offer good to very good potential. Alluring pieces graded MS-65 can be elusive and are certainly quite desirable and undervalued. I suggest passing on unattractive, heavily toned dark brown coins or dull-surfaced, artificially bright-looking slabbed MS-65 Isabellas. These coins will likely bring a disappointing price when the time comes for selling them.

Proof Isabella quarters graded PF-55 and higher make an excellent addition to one's collection. Prices will range from $750 to $75,000; the loftier rating brings the loftier price. Value must be based on the coin's makeup, such as its attractiveness, strictness of grading, etc. The same is true of the Columbian or any other issue. First, they will be double struck. (A proof-like specimen will have received only one blow from the coin press.) One should beware of the raw (un-encapsulated) offering accompanied by a letter declaring that the coin is a proof or a special striking, as it might just be the exact opposite. One should look for a coin that has been rated by a major grading service—this is for the buyer's protection. The double striking will bring out much sharper detail on both obverse and reverse designs. One should beware of the lightly polished or buffed coin which at times is offered as a proof. A safe acquisition is one purchased in a major grading-services holder.

As with the Columbian issues, most naturally toned specimens will possess colors of sea green and electric blue, as well as magenta and a combination of these colors. The combination is produced naturally over time, and an MS-64 or higher grade can bring double or more the value of an un-toned coin. This is one of the reasons why unscrupulous sellers artificially tone coins. One should beware of vivid peacock blue accompanied by deep purple and brilliant yellow-green. The coin's strike will seldom will be responsible for a grade and/or value drop. A partial wire edge will be observed on many specimens. Luster will range from deep mirror proof-like, to proof-like, to semi-proof-like, to brilliant frosty, to brilliant satiny, to dull satiny.

Detecting Counterfeits

No error coinage or counterfeits have surfaced to date.

Is Your Isabella Circulated or Mint State?

Obverse

A metal loss will first be observed as a dull grayish color on the crown's central oval jewel and the Queen's cheek. Beware of doctoring in the latter location: it can appear in the form of wire-brushing, light polishing, texturing, puttying or artificial toning. Wire-brushing is sometimes used in this primary focal location on uncirculated specimens to hide facial cuts, hairline scratches, slide marks, etc.

Reverse

The reverse design will display a metal loss on the strand of wool that seems to rest on the kneeling spinner's left thigh.

Related Material

To date, no official mailing holders or envelopes housing the original coin have been found. I have seen several Board of Lady Managers envelopes while examining the complete personal correspondence of Mrs. Palmer, which is housed in the Chicago Historical Society. Possibly, the coins were placed in smaller unmarked envelopes or simply wrapped in tissue paper and inserted in the larger printed mailer.

Future Potential of the Isabella Quarter Dollar

Population Figures

To date, only one of these special quarters has been graded MS-69. *Only NGC uses the proof-like (PL) designation.

Date	Service	EF 40	AU 58	MS 61	MS 62	MS 63	MS 64	MS 65	MS 66	MS 67	MS 68	MS 69
1893	NGC	2	220	181	456	682	966	425	145	49	8	1
1893	PCGS	5	361	192	772	1115	1143	395	161	32	4	0
1893	Combined	7	581	373	1228	1797	2109	820	306	81	12	1

Date	Service	PF 40	PF 58	PF 60	PF 62	PF 63	PF 64	PF 65	PF 66	PF 67	PF 68	PF 69
1893	NGC	0	0	1	5	7	12	7	3	0	0	0
1893	PCGS	0	2	0	1	0	0	1	0	0	0	0
1893	Combined	0	2	1	6	7	12	8	3	0	0	0

Date	Service	PL 40	PL 58	PL 60	PL 62	PL 63	PL 64	PL 65	PL 66	PL 67	PL 68	PL 69
1893	NGC	0	1	2	5	37	38	9	6	1	0	0

Isabellas graded EF-AU through MS-64 are fairly priced at current levels. The value should be based on the coin in question. You might want to focus on the eye-appealing MS-64+ specimen, which has good potential. The spread between the MS-64+ and the MS-65 coinage during the May 1989 high was $3,700. I would delete some 21% from the census, and I expect values to rise.

In MS-65 condition, the Isabella quarter is undervalued—depending on eye appeal. During the last market high, there was a $5,000 spread between grades MS-65 and MS-66; that spread exists no longer. I would lower the census by anywhere from 23% to 26%. There is excellent future potential for this popular issue. In the higher grades, the Isabella is a great coin to have in one's collection. A wonderful future awaits the only commemorative quarter dollar produced in the United States in 106 years—until the 1999 Delaware 50 State Quarters Program issue.

For those who can afford a genuine Isabella proof, I suggest buying the coin, if it is available. A limited number were slabbed. Its approximate values: PF-63: $3,400; PF-64: $5,300+; PF-65: $13,000.

Dealers keep lowering the bid on the coin, because they know that money and buyers are in short supply. The Isabella proof offers great potential, but for those who cannot afford these popular coins, the NGC proof-like (PL) encapsulations should be considered.

An Isabella's worth—which can be double or greater than the listed grade —depends on the coin's allure. Let us assume that four Isabella quarters graded MS-66 appear consecutively at auction. The variance between the prices realized can range from $2,900 to $4,900. The reason is that there is an "allure" factor that comes into play: how attractive is the coin? Does it possess beautiful genuine or natural color-toning on one or both sides? What percentage of this rainbow play of colors, or iridescent toning, covers the coin? How do surface negatives such as marks, hairline scratches, etc., affect the coin's grade because of their location, frequency and eye-appeal? Is the surface luster blazing or average? Is the proof-like surface deep or shallow? If encapsulated, is the MS-65 coin enclosed really an MS-66 coin by today's grading standards, or is it a questionable MS-64+ coin worth less than the current MS-65 value? The potential buyer(s) is another key. All of these factors come together to determine the worth of a coin. Also, please refer to the Topic 2, "Commemorative Proof-like Coinage," for the procedure that experts use to determine if a coin is proof-like (PL) or deep mirrored proof-like (DMPL) or ultra proof-like (UPL).

Apply these procedures to all the classic commemorative coinage (1892–1954) presented in this book, and, indeed, to all U.S. coinage. The modern mint productions will be the exception, since they are produced with tender loving care from creation to sale. MS-69 is a common grade, as is MS-70. The same is true for ratings in proof condition.

1900 Lafayette Memorial Dollar

Reason for Issue:	To commemorate the construction of a monument to General Lafayette in Paris as part of the U.S. government's participation in the Paris Exposition of 1900.
Authorization:	Act of March 3, 1899, with a maximum of 50,000 pieces.
Issued by:	Lafayette Memorial Commission
Official Sale Price:	$2

Production Figures

Date	Business Strikes	Assay Coins	Proofs	Melted	Net Mintage
1900	50,000	26	10?	14,000	36,000

Current Market Values

Date	EF 40	AU 50	MS 60	MS 63	MS 64	MS 65	MS 66
1900	$500	$570	$900	$1,850	$2,800	$6,000 to $10,000	$11,000 to $18,000

Designs by Charles E. Barber

Obverse

Conjoined heads of George Washington (based on Jean Antoine Houdon's bust of Washington) and Marie-Joseph Paul Yves Roch Gilbert du Motier, Marquis de Lafayette, possibly designed from a French medal of François-Auguste Caunois, which was made at the French Mint in 1824. (However, it does appear that Barber used Peter L. Krider's Yorktown Centennial Medal of 1881 to create his mock-up.) "UNITED STATES OF AMERICA" arcs above; "LAFAYETTE DOLLAR" below. This was the first time that George Washington appeared on a legal tender U.S. coin. Technically, he is the first president to appear on U.S. coinage, although this coin was commemorative in nature (selling for double face value), and was not intended for general circulation. The first person to appear on U.S. coinage was Christopher Columbus (1892), and the first woman to be pictured was Queen Isabella (1893). Both coins are commemorative issues. Abraham Lincoln, the 16th President, was the first person and the first president to be portrayed on circulating U.S. coinage, the Lincoln cent (1909–present).

Reverse

An equestrian statue of General Lafayette (who is also depicted on the obverse). He rides left and holds a sword pointed, hilt upwards. Symbolically, if a horse is depicted with two feet up, it died on the battlefield. If one foot is up, it was wounded on the battlefield, and died elsewhere. If all four feet are down, it died a natural death. Located at the base of the statue is the name "BARTLETT" which is believed to be the name of the designer of this issue. As noted, the coin was designed by Charles E. Barber. Paul Wayland Bartlett, whose early sketch was used by Barber, was the sculptor who designed the Lafayette statue in Paris. Situated below and on the base of the statue is a palm branch, and within a beaded border is the inscription, "ERECTED BY THE YOUTH OF THE UNITED STATES IN HONOR OF GEN LAFAYETTE PARIS 1900".

American youth did, in fact, raise $50,000 for the creation of the Lafayette statue in Paris.

Origins of the Lafayette Dollar

The Lafayette Memorial Commission at first requested that Congress authorize the production of 100,000 half dollars. The Memorial Commission later thought a silver dollar would make a better souvenir, and this was approved by Congress on March 3, 1899. The Lafayette dollar became a reality on December 14, 1899, the 100th anniversary of the death of George Washington. When the press operator Miss Gleary created the country's very first commemorative dollar, George Washington became the first president to be depicted on legal tender U.S. coinage. At the same time, Lafayette became the first person to be represented on both the obverse and reverse of a U.S. coin.

On this day, using an old coin press that was able to produce 80 coins per minute, the Philadelphia Mint struck 50,000 coins plus 26 assay pieces. The coin does not bear the actual production date of 1899. The Memorial Commission wanted the coins to bear the date 1900, but U.S. coinage laws did not permit the predating of coins. To please the Memorial Commission, the date 1900 was included within the coin's reverse border inscription. This date, however, does not indicate the minting date, but rather the year in which the Lafayette monument was erected, as well as the year of the Paris Exposition. The coins were then sold for $2 each by the Memorial Commission.

The Philadelphia *Public Ledger* reported:

> Present at this small Lafayette dollar ceremony were several Mint officials, members of the Lafayette Memorial Commission and a few members of the press. After Miss Gleary removed the first Lafayette dollar struck, she presented it to Mint Superintendent Henry Boyer. Mint Chief Engraver Charles E. Barber then inspected it. It was then shown to Robert J. Thompson, secretary of the Memorial Commission, and then given to Director of the Mint, George E. Roberts. It was placed in a coin or medal case and brought back to Washington, D.C., by Mr. Roberts, to be given to President William McKinley. The coin was then to be sent in an elaborate $1,000 presentation case, to be given to the president of the French Republic.

Secretary Thompson, who had traveled to France aboard the SS La Champagne, presented the gift to President Émile Loubet on February 22, 1900. It is not known whether any of the 12,000 pieces shipped to the Memorial Commission's headquarters in Paris accompanied Secretary Thompson on his voyage.

The Memorial Commission refused an offer of $5,000 for the first coin struck, the first to depict a president as well as the first to depict an American citizen. It had been previously decided that President McKinley would forward the first strike to President Loubet. It was the government's intention that the coin be used in a special ceremony, to be held on Washington's birthday. The event, however, did not occur on that date, but took place instead on March 3, 1900, in the Elysée Palace.

After the striking ceremony was over, the coin press began producing 4,800 Lafayette dollars per hour.

Four obverse and five reverse dies were used in six die combinations. Probably, several coin presses were used to strike the 50,000 coins (and not the one Merrick press) over the course of about 10½ hours. No die cracks have been seen on any of these coins. I have seen that first Lafayette dollar, housed in what appeared to be a heavily toned, casket-like presentation case. The darkened piece has a satiny type of surface. It is the Obverse 1, Reverse A variety. The coin is in the Musée du Louvre in Paris.

In 1925 George H. Clapp discovered a Lafayette dollar that differed from the piece described by Howland Wood in *The Commemorative Coinage of the United States* (Numismatic Notes and Monographs 16), published by the American Numismatic Society in 1922. After a discussion with Clapp, Wood examined several hundred Lafayette dollars over a period of years and discovered two more varieties. He concluded that there are three obverse and four reverse varieties. The following descriptions are based exactly on Wood's arrangement of the examined varieties and later discoveries first presented by Clapp in the *Coin Collectors Journal*, November 30, 1934.

Obverse 1	"AT" in "States" high; point of Lafayette's bust above top of "L"; small point on bust of Washington. Found with reverses A, B and C.
Obverse 2	"A" in "States" high; last "A" of "America" double-punched at left foot. Found with Reverse C.
Obverse 3	Last "S" in "States" low, "AT" re-punched; both "F's" are defective; "America" poorly spaced, "RI" close; pallet between "OF.A" is closer to "A" than to "F"; point of Lafayette's bust is beyond right top of "L". Found with Reverse D.

Obverse 1	Obverse 2
Left leg of "M" is raised slightly in relation to right leg of "A".	Left leg of "M" is on an even plane with the right leg of "A".

"I" in "United" points directly to denticle.	"I" in "United" points between the denticles.

Tip of Lafayette bust close to first "L" of "Dollar".	Tip of Lafayette bust away from first "L" of "Dollar".

Reverse A	Palm branch with 14 long leaves and long stem; point of lowest leaf above "1" of 1900; "B" below "Y" in "by". Found with Obverse 1.
Reverse B	Palm branch with 14 shorter leaves and long stem; point of lowest leaf over space between "1" and "9". With Obverse 1. Later die states are cracked through the legend.
Reverse C	Palm branch with 14 medium leaves and short stem bent down; point of lowest leaf above center of "9". Found with Obverse 2.
Reverse D	Palm branch with 15 thin leaves and short stem, bent up; point of lowest leaf above center of "9". Found with Obverse 3.

These make the following combinations:

Clapp–Wood 1	Obverse 1 Reverse A: Scarce.
Clapp–Wood 2	Obverse 1 Reverse B: Probably the most prevalent of all the varieties.
Clapp–Wood 3	Obverse 2 Reverse C: Rare.
Clapp–Wood 4	Obverse 3 Reverse D: Very Rare.
Swiatek 5	Obverse 1 Reverse C: Very Rare.

Numismatist John Merz has eloquently simplified these descriptions. He has also made a first-class study of the comparative scarcity or abundance of these varieties. He says:

> None of the prior reference information on Lafayette Dollar varieties has been numerically specific as to the relative scarcities (or populations) of the four different varieties. In all previous cases the attempt to differentiate the scarcities has been adjectival, rather than specific percentages, and in many cases, as it turns out, was inaccurate. The reason for this, I'm sure, is that all Lafayette Dollars are scarce and expensive, and it would have been financially prohibited for anyone to own 250 or 500 Lafayette Dollars to get a statistically valid comparison of scarcities.

This situation has changed dramatically in the last couple of years because of the development and widespread use of the Internet. My database for this paper is comprised of over 500 coins, and I actually possess very few of them. All of the others have been seen by me because of excellent photographs available on the Internet and contained in auction archives, in current auction catalogs, on eBay, and on dealer web sites. My records have been collected over a period of a year or so, and go back about 2½ years.

To facilitate easy identification of die varieties, I studied the coins in my collection to come up with some new "pick-up points," that is, the die markers that allow differentiation of one die from another. I am including close-up photos of the pick-up points, so that in many cases variety identification can be made, with a little practice, with the naked eye. Five-power magnification makes it really easy. Most, if not all, of the Internet photos can be magnified.

The most difficult problem is identifying the difference between Obverse 1 and Obverse 2. Identification of Obverse 3 is simple. All four of the reverses can be easily identified.

Obverse 1	Obverse 2
"At" in "States" is raised slightly relative to "T" and "E".	"A" in "States" is raised in relation to surrounding "T's"

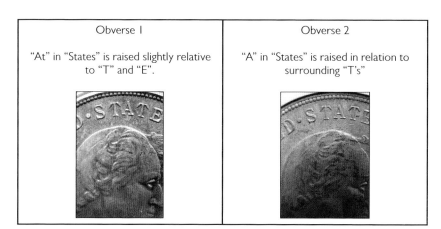

Reverse A	Reverse B
Tip of lowest leaf in palm branch is over "1" of 1900. 14 leaves. Confirm to see that the top of "B" is below top of "Y" in "by".	Tip of lowest leaf in palm branch is over the space between "1" and "9 "of 1900. 14 leaves.
Reverse C	Reverse D
Tip of lowest leaf of palm branch is over "9" in 1900. Lower leaves lie flat against the stem. 14 leaves.	Tip of lowest leaf of palm branch is over "9" of 1900. Lower leaves spread apart from stem. 15 leaves.

- Obverse 1 is paired with Reverse A and B.
- Obverse 2 is paired with Reverse C.
- Obverse 3 is paired with Reverse D.

The populations for the four collectible Lafayette varieties, based on my examinations of 501 coins (or photographs of coins), are as follows:

1A	10/501	2.0%
1B	265/501	52.9%
2C	196/501	39.1%
3D	30/501	6.0%

Clearly, variety 1A is the "stopper," appearing only infrequently, and comprising 2% of the Lafayette population.

Varieties 1B and 2C are common, together comprising more than 90% of the Lafayette population. Variety 3D, with 6% of the population, is interestingly scarce.

In examining photographs of Lafayette coins on the Internet, I have tried, as much as possible, to avoid counting a coin that I have seen before. I established some, but probably not all, of the multiple sales of the same coin. Double counting would tend to inflate the population figures for the common coins, but probably not to any great degree.

I would like to speculate on the manufacturing scene at the Philadelphia Mint on December 14, 1899, the day all 50,026 of the Lafayette dollars were struck. Bullowa, in his 1938 article, states that they were all struck on one press, which took more than ten hours of production time.

In a 2005 article in Coin World, I speculate that several presses were used. It would seem logical that one press would be fitted with a 1B die pair and another with a 2C die pair: these two presses then produced more than 90% of the Lafayette dollars, and the entire run could have been completed in five hours.

The Breen–Swiatek Encyclopedia of United States Silver and Gold Commemorative Coins 1892–1954 (1981) states that reverse B eventually showed a die crack across the legend. If that die broke, it would have been replaced by reverse

A for the short remainder of the production run, and this probable event is consistent with today's small population of 1A coins. A similar situation could have occurred with the 2C die pair on the second press, or possibly a third press could have been activated for the limited production of 3D coins that we see reflected in today's small population. It is impossible to know for sure, but it is interesting to guess.

It would enhance any commemorative collection to include the four-coin variety set of Lafayette dollars. A nice AU Lafayette dollar can be purchased for $450–$525. Also, at the moment, there is no premium attached to the scarce 1A and 3D varieties. Some vigilance will be needed on the part of collectors to obtain a 1A, but they will feel good about having done so.

Everyone reading this entry should begin looking carefully at the Lafayette dollar varieties. Frank Du Vall and I have done so in the past, and both of us have reported the discovery of a new variety. Since there have been no other reported sightings of these two new varieties, each of them should, at this time, be called non-collectible. It would be reassuring and encouraging if more examples were found, but it takes many eyes looking. Variety collecting is an avid pursuit among those who specialize, for example, in large cents and bust half-dollars. The Lafayette dollar provides a venue to do this in a commemorative series.

In total, 36,000 pieces of the Lafayette dollar were sold. Nearly 1,800 were sold in Paris, but 10,000 were returned to America. As sales came to a halt, 14 bags, each containing 1,000 Lafayettes, were returned to the Treasury Building in Washington, D.C. In 1945, while examining government records, Aubrey Bebee, of Omaha, became aware of the existence of this holding. When he inquired, he was informed that the commemorative dollars were melted into silver bullion. No one knows for sure whether the Treasury Department knew that the $14,000 lot was worth $140,000, or simply chose not to create problems for themselves—and melted the lot.

The Lafayette Dollar Today

Most of this popular issue is in EF-AU through MS-63 condition. Many of the circulated pieces encountered by collectors over the years have been whizzed, buffed (in areas displaying a loss of metal or detracting marks), or simply polished to dupe the uninformed. There is satisfaction in acquiring for the joy of collecting a circulated coin that displays natural, un-doctored surfaces that do not possess ugly cuts, digs or scratches, and are not toned black. Pieces showing no trace of actual wear and graded MS-60 or MS-61 are underrated and can be rather difficult to locate. This is because of abuse, as well as because the coin's rims offer little protection for the high points (the first areas that lose metal from friction). Lafayettes that are graded MS-62 and MS-63 are easier to obtain.

Attractive pieces that are graded strictly MS-64 are not as abundant as is widely believed. One would be surprised especially at the number of times those identical MS-64 Lafayette dollars were resubmitted to the same and different grading services by the original, the second or the third owner over the years, in hopes of attaining the upgrade—which never materialized. The reason is that bag marks, cuts, or scratches in the primary focal area are too deep or too long to permit a higher grade. Unfortunately, many identification labels were destroyed, and not returned for population deletion. This practice hinders a determination of the issue's true population. It doesn't matter how flashy or mark-free the coin might appear upon inspection. It's the long, fine hairline scratch or two, usually located on Washington's portrait or across the portraits, that will prevent the coin from grading higher—and thereby making it possibly worth between $4,000 and $6,000, or more. Collectors should beware of those coins that have had these areas lightly puttied in order to create a false, mint-frosty appearance that hides the surface negatives. Some pieces have eluded the close inspection of the grading services.

Should the obverse make the grade, too many reverse bag marks, a large and deep dig or fine hairlines on Lafayette's horse or in the field will prevent the coin from being graded MS-65. Strictly graded MS-65 coinage is elusive. The slabbing, resubmittal scenario has also affected this category. Specimens graded MS-66 and better are very difficult to locate.

I saw—then levitated several times, numismatically—a genuine double-struck brilliant proof along with the Panama–Pacific $50 Round and Octagonal coin struck in silver, without the S Mint mark, in a Philadelphia collection in 1976. I saw another in New York City in 1982 at the late Lester Merkin's office. The Lafayette proof was said to be one of a possible ten such pieces struck.

Luster for this issue will range from almost semi-proof-like, to very flashy brilliant frosty, to bright frosty, to dull frosty. Unfortunately, specimens displaying the first two desired surfaces are seen infrequently. Those that appear to have a mirrored surface are probably left-over coins from the group of 14,000 that were melted. Bright to dull frosty luster is the norm for them. In the attempt to create a more eye-appealing bright or better-than-new surface for the bright frosty and dull frosty luster conditions, pieces were over-dipped in a tarnish-removing solution or were carelessly cleaned in some other manner, forever damaging their original surfaces.

Strike rarely affects the value or grade of this issue. The sharpness of detail on the saddle blanket design and/or the engraving line separating Lafayette's boot from his leg (known as the full boot specimen) and/or the folds in the General's lower coat design will typically be lacking, appearing somewhat undefined or indistinct. All depends on the reverse variety. Neither grade nor value will be affected unless the coin possesses a major strike weakness on the devices. No error coinage has surfaced to date.

Detecting Counterfeits

A counterfeit specimen will often display surface roughness, graininess and roundness of lettering. Look for raised metal spikes, or tooling marks, above the words "States" and "the" of the inscription, and on the reverse, examine for this defect below the letter "L" in "Lafayette".

Is Your Lafayette Dollar Circulated or Mint State?

Obverse

The primary focal area is the bust of both figures. Wear will initially develop on Washington's cheekbone because of a difference in metal texture: it will look grayish-white. A lack of metal fill, the result of insufficient striking force, can resemble rub or friction and can create what look like small cuts—plus scar marks on the portraits. If uncertain, check with a knowledgeable person when buying such a coin. This is the part of the coin where unscrupulous individuals will wire-brush (whiz), buff, lightly polish or putty in an attempt to conceal metal loss, a deep cut, slide marks, a reed mark, or a grade-lowering bag mark.

Reverse

The primary focal area is the equestrian figure of Lafayette—which is also the target (but to a lesser degree) of doctoring. A metal loss will be noticed first on the horse's blinder, as the rim offers little high-point protection, then on the hindquarter. Bag marks, cuts, digs, reed marks, hairline scratches, and abrasions, which can easily cause a lowering of the obverse grade, can do the same to this reverse design. One should also beware of artificially-toned raw (unencapsulated) coins that attempt to hide surface marks and doctoring. Most specimens should display a genuine blue and/or sea green iridescent toning, or on rare occasions, a rainbow play of colors.

Related Material

The issue was placed in paper coin envelopes and mailed in a manila envelope imprinted: "Office of Commissioner-General for the United States to the Paris Exposition of 1900, Lafayette Memorial Commission, Chicago". The mailing envelope indicated the number of coins enclosed. It was also accompanied by an information letter from the Lafayette Memorial Commission, dated January 1, 1900, which described the coin and the reason for its issue. The letter also advised that 15,000 paid advance orders had already been received, and, as a result, orders would be limited to a maximum of 500 pieces, until the first 40,000 had been sold. The envelope, with its related items, is valued at $150–$500.

I have seen a toned or lightly polished Lafayette dollar counter-stamped with three digits. One was higher than the other two, as if the counter for one of the numbers jammed or moved only half way. Such a lack of craftsmanship suggests work done by an amateur. My research has never revealed such a coin, but dealer Billy Paul informed me that a friend in Paris had handled this type of coin, which was accompanied by a documented letter and housed in a box. I would especially want to have the letter, as anyone can counter-stamp any coin.

Lafayette mailing envelope—front.

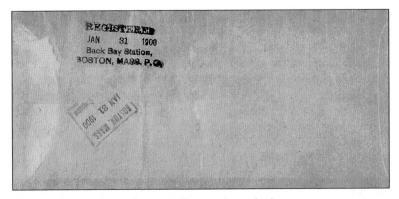

Lafayette mailing envelope—back.

Future Potential of the Lafayette Dollar

Population Figures

To date, none has been graded higher than MS-67.

Date	Service	EF 40	AU 58	MS 60	MS 62	MS 63	MS 64	MS 65	MS 66	MS 67	MS 68	MS 69
1900	NGC	1	101	21	381	494	755	191	62	8	0	0
1900	PCGS	13	234	61	433	679	941	246	75	5	0	0
1900	Combined	14	335	82	814	1173	1696	437	137	13	0	0

The 1900 Lafayette dollar, which was struck in 1899, is the only commemorative cartwheel to be produced before the 1983 Olympic dollar. On the surface, this issue appears to be somewhat undervalued in grades AU through MS-65. It is an extremely popular coin with collectors. There is now a great interest in the Lafayette varieties that sell for little or no premium—depending on the rarity of the variety. That's not to say a collector wouldn't pay more if he wishes to complete a five-piece variety set. The high spread between grades MS-63 and MS-64 was $5,000. It was $9,500 between the MS-64 and MS-65 rating, and $13,000 between the MS-65 and MS-66. It is hard to say in what manner history will repeat itself; our census was much lower when these prices were obtained. Populations are now probably between 24% and 28% lower in the MS-63 and MS-64 conditions, and between 22% and 26% lower in the MS-65 category. Four beautiful MS-64 Lafayette cartwheels were submitted 17 times each over the years—with no upgrade, because the grading labels were destroyed every time. (The coin's surface negatives kept these beautiful, original, lustrous pieces in the MS-64+ category forever.) The same is true of five different MS-65 specimens that made 26 journeys each in the hope of a higher grade. There were no scores. Unfortunately, those population figures can never be deleted and corrected.

One should pass on the dull, dark, unattractive and arguable offering—even if it declares itself an MS-66. Certainly, do not buy raw or unslabbed specimens if you do not know how to grade. One should beware the "bargains," as they are seldom what they might appear. Do not expect to receive a $3,000 coin for $300; rather, seek the advice of a recognized expert in the field when assistance is needed.

One MS-67 PCGS encapsulation sold for $66,700 at a January 1, 2004 Heritage auction. A coin's total makeup determines its value. For example: during the September 25, 2004 Heritage auction (Sale 384), five MS-64 Lafayette dollars were sold: Lot 3854 NGC $2,875; Lot 3855 PCGS $2,990; Lot 3857 PCGS $4,312.50; Lot 3858 PCGS $3,450; Lot 3859 NGC $2,300; and Lot 3860 PCGS $3,737. It is worth remembering that eye appeal, luster flash, upgrade potential, and the buyer are the primary factors that determine a coin's value.

1903 Louisiana Purchase

Reason for Issue:	To commemorate the Louisiana Purchase Exposition, held in St. Louis in 1904, and the 100th anniversary of the purchase of the Louisiana Territory.
Authorization:	Act of June 28, 1902, with a maximum of 250,000 pieces (125,000 for each variety).
Issued by:	Louisiana Purchase Exposition Company
Official Sale Price:	$3

Production Figures

Date	Business Strikes	Assay Coins	Proofs	Melted	Net Mintage
1903 Jefferson	125,000	129	100	107,625*	17,375*
1903 McKinley	125,000	129	100	107,625*	17,375*

* Estimate

Current Market Values

Date	AU-50	MS-60	MS-63	MS-64	MS-65	MS-66
1903 Jefferson	$575	$650	$875	$1,300	$1,800	$2,350
1903 McKinley	$570	$650	$725	$1,100	$1,875	$2,250

DESIGNS BY CHARLES E. BARBER, ASSISTED BY GEORGE T. MORGAN

Obverse

Type I: the bust of Thomas Jefferson, architect of the Louisiana Purchase from France for $15 million while he was the third president of the United States (1801–09). Seen facing left, his portrait was designed from a Mint Indian peace medal created by John Reich, Assistant Mint Engraver, who used a Jean-Antoine Houdon bust as a model.

Type II: the bust of William McKinley, the 25th president (1897–1901), who signed the bill that sanctioned the Louisiana Purchase Exposition. His "life" portrait was copied by Charles E. Barber from a presidential medal. On both coins, within a beaded border almost encircling the bust, is the inscription "United States of America".

Reverse

The same for both coins: the anniversary dates 1803–1903, separated from "ONE DOLLAR" by part of an olive branch. Around the coin's circumference, within a beaded border, is the inscription "LOUISIANA PURCHASE EXPOSITION ST. LOUIS".

Origins of the Louisiana Purchase Coins

Initially, this coin was to depict Jefferson only. However, after McKinley (who originally signed the Exposition into law on March 3, 1901) was assassinated at another Exposition six months after the signing, officials decided to make his likeness part of this issue.

The Louisiana Purchase Exposition Company's management requested that Congress use part of its $5 million appropriation to create commemorative gold dollars.

The Philadelphia Mint struck 75,080 gold dollars in December 1902, an apparent infraction of government procedure because these coins were dated 1903 but are supposed to bear the date of striking. (See the 1900 Lafayette Memorial Dollar entry.)

In January 1903, 175,178 additional pieces were struck, for a total production of 250,000, plus 258 assay coins. There were 125,000 of each type produced. Shortly thereafter, the Philadelphia Mint melted 250 specimens of the 258 assay pieces. To date, we do not know which design was the first to be produced. All coins bear the date 1903—the anniversary date.

Sold at $3 each, the coins were kept as souvenir gold pieces and memen-
toes, possibly because 16 years had passed since the United States had issued
its last gold dollar. To increase sales of the coins, the organizers offered different types of mountings, such as gold stickpins and brooches. Some specimens
were mounted in such jewelry with solder: such pieces are worth much less than
the conventional coins. Despite these gimmicks, sales were poor; approximately
35,000 coins were sold. Retail value fell to $2 within a year. The numismatist
B. Max Mehl acquired thousands of pieces from the promoter and fellow numismatist Farran Zerbe, which he sold over the next two decades. In 1914 the Mint
received some 215,000 coins, which were then melted. Today, the estimate is
that there are some 17,500 coins of each variety, a small portion of the total
production.

The Louisiana Purchase Coins Today

With some effort, either issue can be located in circulated EF-AU condition. A
collector's goal should be to find pieces that have not been polished, or display
repair work or file marks, and that have not been doctored in some way. You
should purchase such coins only if the price is right or if you simply want a low-
grade representative example. They weren't worth much in the past, are worth
much less today, and will be worth even less in the future in comparison to an
un-doctored coin.

The Louisiana Purchase issues are not scarce in grades MS-60 through
MS-64, but they have become very popular and are sought after by more collectors than ever before. The rarer issue is the McKinley design in the MS-65 and
MS-66 categories. In the MS-67 state, the Jefferson production is rarer. Future
value resides in coins rated eye-appealing MS-64+ and higher.

There were 100 Proof coins of each design struck for the "selected" few: government officials and insiders. They certainly were not produced for the average
numismatist. Technically, these Proofs are the first official gold commemorative
coins produced in the United States. These rarities were placed in the opening
of an imprinted card, covered by a wax paper window and signed by J.M. Landis,
Superintendent, and R.R. Freed, Coiner of the Philadelphia Mint. The coin
was secured with heavy string, which was embedded in a dark red Philadelphia
Mint wax seal at its end. Since then, some of the seals have been doctored, and
the proof coin substituted. Some wax seals have been pressed flat (destroying
their embossing) with string enclosed to appear officially sealed. The *proof-like*
replacement coin now hides behind its wax paper window. Collectors should
beware of any broken wax seal, as this may indicate a replacement proof-like
coin. When offered a raw specimen out of its holder, the collector should be
certain it is double struck, and should have the seller encapsulate it—by a major
service.

Luster will range from proof-like (not the norm), to semi-proof-like, to brilliant satiny, to dull satiny. Strike rarely affects the grade and value of this issue.
As a result of die wear, the Jefferson design at times will exhibit a slight flatness
in hair detail over the ear and flatness in denticle design. The latter flaw will

keep such coins from being categorized as MS-66. No error coinage is known. There are some trial strikings, struck on a heavy stock paper, in the Smithsonian national collection. The rare coin auctioneers Bowers and Merena auctioned a similar item, which obtained $5,500. Its owner had discarded the heavy stock paper impression of the coin, thinking it had no value; it was, however, spotted in time by Ray Merena and rescued to be auctioned—to the owner's delight.

Detecting Counterfeits

There are counterfeits of each issue. Examine coins for lack of strike sharpness, field depressions, and small raised lumps of metal in the field.

Is Your Louisiana Purchase Circulated or Mint State?

Obverse

Metal loss will be noticed first on the cheekbone. Flatness around the ear area can be the result of die wear. Examine these areas for crisscross scratches and a difference in metal texture.

Reverse

Wear will occur on the olive branch, to the right of the digit "3" of 1803, then on the anniversary dates and the denomination on this lower-relief motif.

Related Material

No official mailing holders housing the issue, with accompanying mailing envelopes, have surfaced to date. The Exposition's Souvenir Coin Department issued a self-addressed embossed 2-cent envelope known as postal stationery (U-86). Enclosed was an order form for the coins and coin jewelry. These are not often seen; one could be worth $100+, based on its condition. There does exist, though it is not often encountered, a rectangular off-white cardboard box, which housed either gold coin or gold mounting resting on cotton. Imprinted on the top cover is: "Louisiana Purchase Exposition, 1904 Souvenir Gold Dollar, Jefferson–$3.00–McKinley". This box is worth $150–$500, depending on its state of preservation. (See next page)

Population Figures

To date, no Jeffersons and only one Louisiana Purchase gold dollar have been slabbed MS-69. Neither issue has been granted MS-69 or PF-69 status.

Date	Service	AU 58	MS 60	MS 61	MS 62	MS 63	MS 64	MS 65	MS 66	MS 67	MS 68	MS 69
1903 Jefferson	NGC	80	4	47	176	258	571	466	402	83	1	0
1903 Jefferson	PCGS	87	18	47	217	543	928	690	519	71	0	0
1903 Jefferson	Combined	167	22	94	393	801	1499	1156	921	154	1	0

Souvenir coin jewelry and
original box.

Date	Service	AU 58	AU 60	MS 61	MS 62	MS 63	MS 64	MS 65	MS 66	MS 67	MS 68	MS 69
1903 McKinley	NGC	53	9	64	219	269	495	385	357	105	4	0
1903 McKinley	PCGS	113	34	66	307	546	845	538	434	75	1	0
1903 McKinley	Combined	166	43	130	526	815	1340	923	791	180	5	0

Date	Service	PF 58	PF 60	PF 61	PF 62	PF 63	PF 64	PF 65	PF 66	PF 67	PF 68	PF 69
1903 Jefferson	NGC	0	0	1	2	4	2	4	9	3	0	0
1903 Jefferson	PCGS	0	2	1	3	8	9	8	3	2	0	0
1903 Jefferson	Combined	0	2	2	5	12	11	12	12	5	0	0

Date	Service	PF 58	PF 60	PF 61	PF 62	PF 63	PF 64	PF 65	PF 66	PF 67	PF 68	PF 69
1903 McKinley	NGC	0	1	1	1	3	10	7	2	2	1	0
1903 McKinley	PCGS	0	2	1	0	7	12	12	6	1	0	0
1903 McKinley	Combined	0	3	2	1	10	22	19	8	3	1	0

Date	Service	PL 58	PL 60	PL 61	PL 62	PL 63	PL 64	PL 65	PL 66	PL 67	PL 68	PL 69
1903 Jefferson	NGC	1	0	0	3	6	3	0	1	0	0	0
1903 McKinley	NGC	0	0	0	4	4	0	1	1	0	0	0

Future Potential of the Louisiana Purchase Gold Dollars

In grades EF-AU through MS-62, both issues appear somewhat underrated.
Rated MS-63 and MS-64, they are undervalued—if strictly graded. There is
good potential for MS-64+ specimens of each design. The May 1989 market
high spread between MS-64+ and MS-65 coinage was about $1,600. I would

reduce the census by between 21% and 25%. One can expect both popular issues to move upward—if fully original and not puttied or artificially colored. In the MS-65 condition, the rarer McKinley Louisiana Purchase gold dollar possesses a bit more potential than does the Jefferson striking. If not attempting to collect the 11-piece gold set, collectors should choose the McKinley, though both popular coins will rise in value. The last high differential between the MS-65 and MS-66 was approximately $7,500. The MS-65 census, which was much lower, can now be reduced further by between 20% and 25%.

In MS-66 and especially MS-67 conditions, both designs offer very good to excellent potential—if fully original and strictly rated at present levels. For those who can afford the rarer Proof coinage, acquiring one is a good strategy. The price depends on:

- The attractiveness of the Mint State or Proof gold coin and location of copper spots.
- The possible surface-doctoring that has suddenly become more obvious.
- The desire of the buyer to own the coin.

PF-63 through PF-67 sell prices can range from $11,000 to $55,000. The coin's value is based on the total makeup of the specimen being offered. If purchasing an unslabbed coin in the original frame, collectors should be certain the enclosed Proof is not a replaced proof-like issue. There are several such frames that house proof-like coins instead of the actual proof. I know of one dealer who purchased an original frame, with proof coin enclosed, from a New York auction in the late 1980s. The coin was substituted with a proof-like piece, and the red-wax seal was carefully secured to the heavy string. An attempt was made to place the coin in this firm's next auction. When I visited the establishment, and examined the coin, it was returned to the consigner. I have since determined that the coin was later sold to an unsuspecting buyer for $18,000 at a major California show.

Original frame with proof coin.

One should also beware if offered a set in which the red wax seal that secures the heavy string lacks any design, and is completely smooth. I have seen several sets in which the proof coin was substituted with a proof-like business strike. The wax was melted, or put back together in some way, and the string was placed within the red mass of wax—which eventually hardened. An iron was used to make the wax look even and flat.

This issue is a great one to own, especially if the coin lacks surface copper stains in the primary focal areas and flaunts a cameo contrast.

1904-1905 Lewis and Clark Exposition

Reason for Issue:	To commemorate the 100th anniversary of the exploration of the Northwest (the Louisiana Territory and the Oregon country in North America) by Captain Meriwether Lewis and Captain William Clark and the Exposition that was held in their honor in Portland, Oregon.
Authorization:	Act of April 13, 1904, with a maximum of 250,000 coins.
Issued by:	Lewis and Clark Centennial and American Pacific Exposition and Oriental Fair Company
Official Sale Price:	$2 (some sold at $2.50 individually and for $1.67 each if six coins were purchased).

Production Figures

Date	Business Strikes	Assay Coins	Proofs	Melted	Net Mintage
1904	25,000	28	4?	15,003	9,997
1905	35,000	41	4?	25,000	10,000

Current Market Values

Date	AU-50	MS-60	MS-63	MS-64	MS-65	MS-66
1904	$925	$1,050	$1,700	$2,300	$4,500	$7,500
1905	$975	$1,400	$1,850	$3,100	$7,500	$13,000

Designs by Charles E. Barber

Obverse

A bust of Meriwether Lewis, facing left. Within the beaded border is the inscription "Lewis–Clark Exposition Portland Ore."; the date of striking (either 1904 or 1905) appears below the bust.

Reverse

A bust of William Clark, facing left. Within the beaded border are the inscriptions "United States of America" and "One Dollar". These inscriptions appear within a beaded border. It seems that the designer copied both portraits from Charles Willson Peale's oil painting of the two explorers.

Origins of the Lewis and Clark

In September 1904 the Philadelphia Mint struck 25,000 Lewis and Clark gold dollars, plus 28 coins for assay purposes, bearing the date of 1904. The next year, 35,000 gold dollars dated 1905, plus 41 assay pieces, were produced during the months of March and June. The Lewis and Clark dollars were the first gold designs to be produced in consecutive years, just as the Columbian Exposition coins were the first consecutive silver issues. The Lewis and Clarks were sold for $2 each, but not all were sold, and some had to be melted by the Mint: 25,000 specimens of the 1905 issue never left Philadelphia, since they were not needed. These coins were not popular, and they received little publicity.

The famous numismatist and promoter Farran Zerbe used D.M. Averill & Co. of Portland to handle some of the orders received. To encourage public acceptance of the coin, he had Averill state that the 1904 issue was almost sold out and had them raise the price to $2.50, while the newly released 1905 issue could be acquired for $2, or six pieces for $10. Most of the coins from both issues were sold to individuals who treated these little jewels very badly. A small number of both issues were offered mounted on silver spoons or housed in brooches and stickpins. Their value today has been compromised by such treatment.

The Lewis and Clark Today

Although not abundant, the Lewis and Clarks can be obtained in EF-AU condition. The collector's goal should be to acquire a specimen that has not been "rim repaired," polished, or doctored in some way. The coins in grades MS-65 and higher offer the best future value. The 1905 striking is twice as rare in MS-65 and MS-66.

The luster of each production will range from proof-like (not the norm), to semi-proof-like, to frosty satiny, to dull satiny. Strike rarely presents a problem for the issue, nor does the surface porosity observed on a small number of these gold coins. The only error coinage known is in the Smithsonian: it exhibits a partial brockage.

Detecting Counterfeits

There are counterfeits of this issue. One should examine the field for depressions and small raised pieces of metal, as well as for crude-looking, faded inscriptions and statutory lettering.

Both Sides

Look for the barest trace of metal loss on the cheek and temple areas of the portraits. As a result of die wear, a slight flatness of the strike can be observed on the hair definition, above and to the left of the portrait's ear.

Related Material

No official holders or mailing envelopes have been found to date. A Lewis and Clark Centennial admission ticket (obverse printing only) sold for $65 recently.

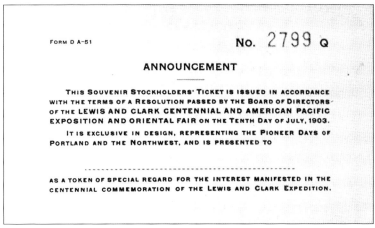

Lewis and Clark Centennial admission ticket.

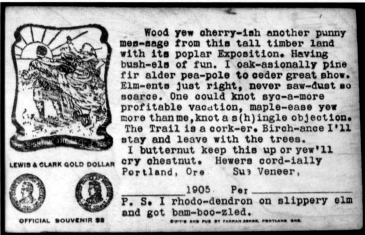

Souvenir wooden postcard.

The wooden postcards depicted above have recently sold from $75 to $150.

Future Potential of the Lewis and Clark Gold Dollars

Population Figures

Date	Service	AU 58	MS 60	MS 61	MS 62	MS 63	MS 64	MS 65	MS 66	MS 67	MS 68	MS 69
1904	NGC	39	9	52	146	183	407	193	116	25	1	0
1904	PCGS	97	17	46	243	344	629	279	122	15	1	1
1904	Combined	136	26	98	389	557	1036	472	238	40	2	0

Date	Service	AU 58	MS 60	MS 61	MS 62	MS 63	MS 64	MS 65	MS 66	MS 67	MS 68	MS 69
1905	NGC	55	5	79	205	214	413	127	54	4	0	0
1905	PCGS	107	38	83	266	455	670	230	66	3	0	0
1905	Combined	162	43	162	471	669	1083	357	120	7	0	0

Date	Service	PL 58	PL 60	PL 62	PL 63	PL 64	PL 65	PL 66	PL 67	PL 68	PL 69
1904	NGC	0	0	2	6	5	1	0	0	0	0

Date	Service	PF 58	PF 60	PF 62	PF 63	PF 64	PF 65	PF 66	PF 67	PF 68	PF 69
1904	NGC	0	0	0	1	1	0	0	0	0	0
1904	PCGS	0	0	0	1	1	0	0	0	0	0
1904	Combined	0	0	0	2	2	0	0	0	0	0

Most circulated offerings of the only two-headed U.S. coin have been abused in some way. One should pass on the damaged or once-soldered piece—they are worth much less than an un-doctored gold coin. That is, unless the price is very reasonable and/or the collector doesn't care. The coin is popular in all grades. At present, the Lewis and Clark gold dollars are undervalued, and their acquisition can be recommended in grades EF-AU and higher. The key to a wise purchase is to procure a nice looking, un-doctored, circulated piece that is free of deep cuts, digs or scratches. The same is true of pieces graded up to MS-62. MS-63+ offerings should still have most, if not all, of their original luster. When funds permit, consider the MS-63+ offering. There is an excellent future for both dates in the strict MS-64+ and higher grades—especially in the 1905 production.

During the May 1989 numismatic market high, the price spread between the 1904 and 1905 coins in grades MS-63 and MS-64, respectively, was $2,500 and $5,500; in MS-64 and MS-65, $14,000 and $22,000; in MS-65 and MS-66, $20,000 and $43,000. Although it appears that history will not repeat itself by duplicating these prices, pleasant surprises do occur during a hot market. Currently: delete 23% to 27% from the MS-63 census; delete 33% to 38% from the MS-64 count; delete 24% to 29% from the MS-65 figures; and delete 13% to 19% from the 1904 MS-66 population. In MS-64 condition, the 1904 coin is somewhat rarer; those labeled MS-65 are more difficult to locate. In the higher grades, the 1905 is almost twice as rare as the 1904 issue. Only seven 1905 pieces to date have been granted MS-67 status, but the 1904 was encapsulated forty times. It appears these may have had a limited amount of upgrade success in grades MS-63 through MS-66, or, quite simply, coin values brought these pieces out of collections and into slabs. Collectors ought to consider purchasing Lewis and Clark dollars before they move forward, figuratively, on their next lucrative journey.

Proof pieces were struck for this issue. To date, only two 1904 PF-63 (one cameo) and two PF-64 pieces have been encapsulated. One should pass on raw offerings. All the coins that I have examined were early-struck, proof-like pieces—some of which were accompanied by a letter of authenticity from a late, well-known numismatist.

You should consult true experts in the field and have you coin encapsulated by a major grading service.

1915 Panama-Pacific International Exposition

For photos, see individual denominations on the following pages

Reason for Issue:	To commemorate the Panama–Pacific International Exposition celebrating the completion of the Panama Canal. The Exposition was held in San Francisco.
Authorization:	Act of January16, 1915, with the following limits for each denomination: Half dollars - 200,000 Gold dollars - 25,000 Quarter eagles ($2.50) - 10,000 $50 Octagonal - 1,500 $50 Round - 1,500
Issued by:	Panama-Pacific International Exposition Coin and Medal Department
Official Sale Price:	Half dollars - $1, or six coins for $5 Gold dollars - $2 Quarter eagles - $4 $50 (both types) - $100 Set of all denominations - $100

Production Figures

Date	Business Strikes	Assay Coins	Proofs	Melted	Net Mint-age
1915-S 50¢	60,000	30	4?	32,866	27,134
1915-S $1	25,000	34	?	10,000	15,000
1915-S $2.50	10,000	17	?	3,251	6,749
1915-S $50 Round	1,500	10	?	1,017	483
1915-S $50 Octagonal	1,500	9	?	855	645

Current Market Values

Date	AU 58	MS 60	MS 63	MS 64	MS 65	MS 66	MS 67
1915-S 50¢	$400	$500	$725	$1,100	$2,000	$2,500	$7,000
1915-S $1	$525	$550	$650	$800	$1,400	$2,000	$7,000
1915-S $2.50	$1,525	$1,900	$3,700	$4,500	$6,100	$7,200	$10,500
1915-S $50 Round	$47,000	$53,000	$85,000	$98,000	$140,000	$190,000	$250,000
1915-S $50 Octagonal	$46,000	52,000	$81,000	$90,000	$133,000	$208,000	$225,000

HALF DOLLAR DESIGNS

Obverse by Charles E. Barber

Columbia facing left and scattering flowers. Behind her is a naked child holding a large cornucopia, symbolic of the many resources of the West. The Golden Gate and the rays of a setting sun are in the background; below the sun, separated by a wave motif, is the date. At the left of the numeral "1" of "1915" is the San Francisco Mint mark (S). Around most of the coin's border is the inscription "PANAMA–PACIFIC EXPOSITION".

Reverse by George T. Morgan

American eagle with raised wings, standing on the national shield. In the right field is an olive branch, representing peace; an oak branch, symbolizing stability, is in the left field. "UNITED STATES OF AMERICA" circles the rim above; "HALF DOLLAR" is split by the shield below. The Panama–Pacific half dollar is the first commemorative to bear the motto "IN GOD WE TRUST" (above the eagle). It was also the first issue for which the authorizing Act specified a place of production.

GOLD DOLLAR DESIGNS BY CHARLES KECK

Obverse

Head of a Panama Canal worker wearing a peaked cap, facing left. Some people think the worker resembles a baseball player. In the lower field is the date of issue. The worker faces directly into "UNITED STATES OF AMERICA" in two crowded lines. The sea god Poseidon and the famous explorer Balboa were also suggested as obverse design candidates.

Reverse

"ONE DOLLAR" in the center, almost encircled by two dolphins, which indicate the meeting of two oceans. Around the border encircling the coin is the inscrip-

tion "Panama–Pacific Exposition San Francisco". Located below the "DO" of "Dollar" is the Mint mark (S).

Gold $2.50 Designs

Obverse by Charles E. Barber

Columbia seated on a hippocampus, a mythical sea monster, which is plunging to the left: it represents the use of the new Canal. Facing right, Columbia holds in her hand a caduceus (the symbolic staff of a herald), which consists of a staff with two entwined snakes and two wings at the top. In the upper border is the inscription "Panama–Pacific Exposition"; in the lower border is the date. At the extreme right of the date is the Mint mark (S).

Reverse by George T. Morgan

American eagle with raised wings, facing left and standing on a classical standard. Inscribed within the standard is the motto "E Pluribus Unum" (for the first time on a commemorative coin); directly below is the denomination "2 1/2 –Dol"; "United States of America" arcs above. This design was copied from

the 1877 pattern half dollar design (item 1512 in J. Hewitt Judd's United States Pattern Coins).

Gold $50 Designs by Robert I. Aitken

This $50 gold piece was produced in an octagonal shape as well as in the usual round shape because California used these shapes for coins following the Gold Rush. When most people refer to this particular issue, they claim that the only difference between the two coins is their shape. This is not the case, however. The design image of the Octagonal issue has been reduced from 44mm to 36.5mm, making space for the addition of eight dolphins (symbolizing the uninterrupted water route made possible by the Canal) in the angles of the coin's obverse and reverse. This is the first commemorative to bear both of the mottoes "In God We Trust" and "E Pluribus Unum". The Round issue has the lowest mintage (483) of the entire commemorative series, followed by the Octagonal (645).

Obverse

Minerva, goddess of wisdom, skill, contemplation, spinning, weaving, agriculture, and horticulture, wearing a crested helmet and facing left.

At her left shoulder is part of a shield, bearing the date of issue in Roman numerals, "MCMXV" (1915). In the lower border is the coin's denomination, "Fifty Dollars". "United States of America" arcs above; "In God We Trust" is in the upper field above and to the left of Minerva's helmet.

Reverse

An owl, sacred symbol of Minerva and symbolic of wisdom, perched on a branch of western pine, with pine cones and needles. Between the milling and a double dot and dash border is the inscription "Panama–Pacific Exposition San Francisco"; the designer's initials (RA) are incused in small letters below the owl's right talon and above the letters "FR" in "Francisco", beyond the double dot and dash border. The motto "E Pluribus Unum" is in the right field; the San Francisco Mint mark (S) appears after the letter "M" in "Unum".

Origins of the Pan–Pac

More than $50 million dollars was spent to make the 1915 Panama–Pacific Exposition the greatest of all fairs. It celebrated the opening of the Panama Canal, by the S.S. *Ancon*, on August 15, 1914. The Exposition's doors opened February 20, 1915. By the time the event closed on December 4, 1915, it had attracted more than 19 million visitors.

S.S. Ancon in the west chamber of the Mira Flores Upper Locks, August 15, 1914.

This issue was the first commemorative half dollar to be struck at a branch Mint, in San Francisco (June 29, 1915). The dies were created at the expense of the event's organizers and 60,000 half dollars, plus 30 assay coins were produced. They were priced at $1 each, but not all of them sold, and 32,866 pieces had to be melted (September 7, 1916). The coin was issued by the Exposition's Official Coin and Medal Department and sold at the Exposition.

There are some extremely rare trial pieces of this issue, made at the Philadelphia Mint. These were struck without the S Mint mark. Two were created in gold, six in silver, and four in copper for Treasury Secretary William Gibbs McAdoo—a coin collector.

The San Francisco Mint struck 25,000 $1 gold coins, plus 34 assay pieces. The first ten pieces struck during the striking ceremony of June 10, 1915 were accompanied by a letter from Mr. Robert W. Woolley attesting to the coin's status. Since not all of the pieces offered for sale at $2 each were sold, 10,000 coins were returned to the Mint and melted. Thus, the net mintage stands at 15,000.

There are two extremely rare silver plain-edge trial pieces, as well as nine much sought after gold $1 specimens of different thicknesses. Seven of these proof pieces have reeded edges ($50,000) and two have the plain edge ($65,000–$75,000). The most sought after coin out of the gold trials—created for McAdoo—is the plain-edge fourth impression specimen. It was struck on a very thick planchet (weighing 55.6 grains), and is listed as E.1588 in David T. Alexander's *Coin World Comprehensive Catalog and Encyclopedia of United States Coins* (also item 1793-a in Judd, $50,000). This coin reminds me of the lesser French Piefort or specimen coin which is struck on a planchet twice the normal thickness. None of these proof pieces has a Mint mark, as all were struck at the Philadelphia Mint before the Mint mark was added. White metal bronzed obverse and reverse trial pieces were struck without the S Mint mark on thin planchets with plain edges.

Originally, Evelyn B. Longman, a New York City sculptor, was chosen to design the $2.50 quarter eagle. The obverse was to depict the head of an eagle, the reverse was to portray a cluster of fruit (symbolic of the state) and a dollar sign ($) instead of "Dol". Unfortunately Longman became ill and could not complete her work.

The San Francisco Mint struck 10,000 Pan–Pac quarter eagles, plus 17 assay coins in June 1915. Die trials were struck in copper and brass. Sales were sluggish, and 3,251 pieces were returned for melting.

During the months of June, July, and August 1915, the San Francisco Mint struck 1,500 Octagonal and 1,500 Round $50 pieces, plus 9 and 10 assay coins, respectively, with the aid of a special 14-ton hydraulic press. The press was shipped from the Philadelphia Mint, which used it to produce medals. On June 15, 1915, the first 29 out of 100 Octagonal pieces were struck by guests and officials of the Mint. These guests included T.W.H. Shanahan, Superintendent; Charles C. Moore, President of the Exposition; and Farran Zerbe, the well known numismatist and head of the Coin and Medal Department at the Exposition.

When Superintendent Shanahan was about to strike the first $50 Octagonal, he made the claim that this would be the first $50 coin issued under authority of law in this nation—but he was incorrect. August Humbert (appointed U.S. Assayer) produced $50 Octagonal pieces in 1851 and 1852, under the Act of September 30, 1850. (These are the very pieces, generally cataloged as "Pioneer gold," that inspired the Pan–Pac Octagonal design.) To date, this is the only U.S. coin not struck in the common round shape.

The Round version it is the lowest commemorative mintage (483) issue after melting. The production of this rarer coinage had to be halted after the 62nd striking because the dies broke. Production was postponed until additional dies were received from Philadelphia; the 63rd striking is thus #1 from the new dies.

The Octagonals were favored at the fair, because of their shape and the representation of dolphins in the border. They were sold individually at $100, in a purple velvet-lined leather case with a descriptive card and an imprinted inner top, which provided Exposition Coin Information in gold ink, at $100. They could also be acquired along with a boxed set containing the three minor coins, at $100. (Buyers had the choice of either $50 coin.) With gold valued at $20.67, these large and beautiful coins contained $49.99 worth of gold: their gold weight is 2.68 ounces or 1,290 grains or 83.59 grams. There are extremely rare hub trial pieces for each issue, as well as a set, or possibly two, of each design struck in silver as well as in copper without the S Mint mark.

The Pan–Pac $50 piece (Round or Octagonal) was offered in a set with a half dollar, gold dollar, quarter eagle, and the $50 piece for $100. Originally the $50 piece sold for $100 but was later discounted when included in a set.

Sales of Pan–Pacs were not limited to single coins, but could be purchased in several packages. A set of five could be obtained in a presentation box, or in an elaborate copper frame suitable for hanging like a picture. A few "double" sets are known; these are in copper frames, showing both sides of each denomination. (The selling price of these sets is unknown at this time. They may have been special presentation sets given to notable guests or dignitaries—research is still ongoing. No sales receipts or correspondence regarding these sets have been found by the author.) Sets of five coins in a presentation case or displayed in a copper frame were sold for $200. Four-piece coin sets were sold later in the year, giving purchasers the option of an Octagonal or Round $50 denomination for $100, the same price originally charged for a single $50 gold piece at the opening of the Exposition. For less affluent collectors a three-piece coin set, featuring the half dollar, gold dollar, and quarter eagle, was available for $7.

The Pan–Pac Half Dollar Today

The very popular half dollar, the first commemorative to portray Columbia, can be located with some effort in EF-AU condition. Most specimens will display some form of abuse, such as polishing, cleaning, or various degrees of whizzing—especially on Columbia's body and the reverse eagle's breast. This coin is somewhat undervalued in grades AU-58 through MS-65. At present the exceptions are the unattractive or average looking MS-64 pieces. Luster, strike, and marks cause many grade-value problems. I suggest looking for a specimen grading a minimum of MS-64+ and possessing fully original attractive surfaces. There is a definite future for strictly graded MS-65+ and loftier labeled specimens.

Luster will range from brilliant satiny (not the norm) to lifeless-dull. Beware of toned specimens, which could lack natural surface luster. Possibly they were placed in a tarnish-removing solution in order to brighten or improve a surface appearance that otherwise could not be improved. Instead, this re-toning has lowered forever the grade-value of the coin.

A faulty strike can affect this issue's value, keeping it out of the MS-65 category. Columbia must not possess too much flatness at the head, cap, arm, or body. The same applies to the reverse eagle's breast, neck, and claws. Another characteristic of the strike, but one that should not affect coin's grade, is termed a rim indentation. This is can be seen close to Columbia's Phrygian cap. Another wide indentation caused by the die and striking technique can be observed in both fields near the periphery. The primary focal areas, such as Columbia and the reverse eagle, are plagued by such numismatic villains as bag marks, reed marks, slide marks, hairline scratches, etc.

A matte proof has been reported. I do not believe the coin labeled a satin finish proof deserves the rating: it is a coin produced from new dies. No error coinage has been reported to date. Two varieties are available with re-punched S Mint marks below and to the right of its final placement. Currently, there appears little interest in this variety, but interest can change quickly. Coins with a squiggly mark at the right base of the second letter "I" of "Pacific", caused by die damage, are not too difficult to locate.

Detecting Counterfeits

The Pan–Pac counterfeit half dollar displays the following: a weak strike, fuzzy lettering, lack of detail on Columbia and the reverse eagle, an uncharacteristic flashy proof-like to frosty surface, lack of die polish lines in the date's field, and tool marks located at "FIC" of "PACIFIC".

IS YOUR PAN–PAC HALF DOLLAR CIRCULATED OR MINT STATE?

Obverse

A metal loss will first be observed on the shoulder of Columbia and on the area between her waist and dress fold, directly above her exposed foot.

Reverse

Wear will first occur on the left side of the eagle's breast and leg as you view the coin. Look for a difference in metal texture and crisscross scratches in this location—it is a prime target area for the coin doctors.

Related Material

Each of the smaller coins—the half dollar, gold dollar, and $2.50 quarter eagle—was distributed in an imprinted paper envelope (2 1/4 × 4 7/16 inches), describing the enclosed coin and listing its designer and ordering address. One envelope for the half dollar gives the price as "$1.00 each"; another "$1 each—6 for $5.00." The gold dollar versions indicate a price of "$2.00 each" or "$2.00—6 for $10.00." The envelope for the quarter eagle was marked "$4 each." The envelopes for the half dollar and gold dollar are worth in the range of $50–$125+; envelopes intended for the quarter eagle can bring $45–$125+, depending on condition.

PANAMA-PACIFIC INTERNATIONAL EXPOSITION

OFFICIAL SOUVENIR MEDAL

The medal delivered herewith is the Exposition's Official Souvenir Medal. Authorized by act of Congress, the designs selected by the Government Exhibit Board (for which the designer received $1,000), produced at the Government's minting demonstration at the Exposition and sold by the Exposition Department of Official Coins and Medals.

DESCRIPTION BY THE DESIGNER

ROBERT AITKEN, N. A., *Sculptor*

The obverse shows a winged Mercury, the Messenger of Heaven, the first of inventors, the furtherer of industry and of commerce, opening the locks of the Canal through which passes the Argo, symbol of navigation. Upon her canvas the setting sun is reflected as she sails for the west.

The quotation "On! Sail On!" from Joaquin Miller's poem to Columbus, is used as a suggestion of the uninterrupted voyage made possible by the Canal. There is also the inscription, "To commemorate the opening of the Panama Canal, M C M X V."

Upon the reverse is shown the central motive, The Earth, around which are entwined two female forms suggesting the two hemispheres, holding in their hands cornucopias typifying abundance. These are so arranged in the design as to become one, the idea being that the Canal brings together the wealth of the world.

Below these flying forms is shown the sea-gull, the bird of the Canal Zone. The inscription upon this side reads, "The Panama-Pacific International Exposition, San Francisco, California, M C M X V."

Half dollar envelope.

PANAMA-PACIFIC COMMEMORATIVE HALF DOLLAR

OFFICIAL SOUVENIR COIN OF THE PANAMA-PACIFIC INTERNATIONAL EXPOSITION

Authorized by Act of Congress
Issue limited to 200,000 pieces

Coined at the San Francisco Mint

PRICE $1 EACH - 6 FOR $5

Designs by Charles E. Barber

DESCRIPTION

OBVERSE: COLUMBIA SCATTERING FLOWERS; ATTENDANT WITH CORNUCOPIA, TO SIGNIFY THE BOUNDLESS RESOURCES OF THE WEST. BACKGROUND, GOLDEN GATE ILLUMINED BY THE RAYS OF THE SETTING SUN. INSCRIPTION: PANAMA-PACIFIC EXPOSITION - 1915.

REVERSE: SHIELD OF THE UNITED STATES SURMOUNTED BY AMERICAN EAGLE AND SUPPORTED ON THE ONE SIDE BY A BRANCH OF OAK, EMBLEM OF STRENGTH AND STABILITY, AND ON THE OTHER SIDE BY THE OLIVE BRANCH OF PEACE. INSCRIPTION: UNITED STATES OF AMERICA - HALF DOLLAR IN GOD WE TRUST.

Address Orders to
OFFICIAL COIN & MEDAL DEPARTMENT
SERVICE BUILDING, P. P. I. E.
SAN FRANCISCO.

Medal envelope.

PANAMA-PACIFIC
COMMEMORATIVE
GOLD DOLLAR

OFFICIAL SOUVENIR COIN
OF THE
PANAMA-PACIFIC
INTERNATIONAL EXPOSITION

Authorized by Act of Congress
Issue limited to 25,000 pieces

Coined at the San Francisco Mint
Sold for the Exposition at $2.00 each

Designs by Charles Keck

DESCRIPTION

OBVERSE: HEAD REPRESENTING LABOR
THROUGH WHOSE EFFORTS THE PANAMA
CANAL BECAME A REALITY.   UNITED
STATES OF AMERICA - 1915.

REVERSE: TWO DOLPHINS, INDICATING
THE MEETING OF THE TWO OCEANS- ONE
DOLLAR - PANAMA-PACIFIC EXPOSIT-
ION - SAN FRANCISCO.

Address Orders to
OFFICIAL COIN & MEDAL DEPARTMENT
SERVICE BUILDING, P. P. I. E.
SAN FRANCISCO.

PANAMA-PACIFIC
COMMEMORATIVE
QUARTER EAGLE ($2 1-2) GOLD

OFFICIAL SOUVENIR COIN
OF THE
PANAMA-PACIFIC
INTERNATIONAL EXPOSITION

Authorized by Act of Congress
Issue limited to 10,000 pieces

Coined at the San Francisco Mint
Sold by the Exposition at $4.00 each

Designs by Charles E. Barber

DESCRIPTION

OBVERSE: COLUMBIA SEATED ON THE
MYTHICAL SEA HORSE. COLUMBIA WITH
THE CADUCEUS, THE EMBLEM OF TRADE
AND COMMERCE, INVITING THE NATIONS
OF THE WORLD TO USE THE NEW WAY FROM
OCEAN TO OCEAN.   PANAMA-PACIFIC
EXPOSITION - 1915.

REVERSE: AMERICAN EAGLE ON A
STANDARD BEARING MOTTO E PLURIBUS
UNUM - UNITED STATES OF AMERICA
2½ DOL.

Address Orders to
OFFICIAL COIN & MEDAL DEPARTMENT
SERVICE BUILDING, P. P. I. E.
SAN FRANCISCO.

Gold dollar envelope.   Gold $2.50 envelope.

Future Potential of the Pan–Pac Half Dollar

Population Figures (NGC and PCGS combined)

Date	MS-63	MS-64	MS-65	MS-66	MS-67
1915-S	935	1403	756	364	115

To date, two Pan–Pacs have been encapsulated MS-68.

Date	Service	AU 58	MS 60	MS 61	MS 62	MS 63	MS 64	MS 65	MS 66	MS 67	MS 68	MS 69
1915-S	NGC	98	1	25	218	410	933	492	256	63	0	0
1915-S	PCGS	149	30	49	309	654	864	487	244	76	2	0
1915-S	Combined	247	31	74	527	1064	1797	979	500	139	2	0

Many circulated offerings of this very popular issue will exhibit some form of cleaning, polishing, or whizzing. Collectors should avoid these, unless the price is very right or your objective is only to acquire a representative example of the issue. At current levels, pieces grading MS-63 and higher are somewhat undervalued. Lesser ratings should be acquired only for the joy of collecting. Attractive halves categorized as MS-64+ offer good future potential. During the 1989 market high, the price spread between the MS-63 and MS-64 specimen was more than $1,100, while the MS-64 and MS-65 variance was $4,000.History will not repeat itself in such a robust fashion for these and loftier grades. I would reduce the census between 20% and 24% for the MS-63 and MS-64 categories. As prices rose the issue came out of collections to be encapsulated.

Strictly graded MS-65+ Pan–Pac halves are certainly undervalued at current prices, and it is a wonderful and very popular coin to possess. The May 1989 price spread between the MS-65 and MS-66 ratings was $7,500. The census can be reduced between 25% and 29% for these ratings. These coins have very good future potential for increasing in value. For the underrated MS-66 coins, I expect a bright tomorrow. Should you be able to afford this rarer level, or the MS-67 grade, I recommend purchase.

Beware of the so-called specimen Pan–Pac Half Dollar strikings. In my opinion, these, as well as the so-called satin finish proofs, are nothing more than pieces struck from a new die—giving them a slightly more satiny appearance. They do look beautiful, and I have seen a few pieces graded MS-65 and MS-66, but buyers should be careful what they pay.

The Pan–Pac Gold Dollar Today

The Pan–Pac gold dollar is one of the more available commemorative gold dollars in EF-AU condition. Specimens will display naturally worn as well as doctored surfaces. The coin can be obtained with little effort in grades MS-60 through low-end MS-66. It is undervalued in eye-appealing MS-66+ and better condition, and it is in these grades that values may increase.

Luster will range from blazing frosty to dull matte-like frosty. Strike rarely presents a grade-value problem for this coin. The primary focal area portrait is usually plagued by grade-lowering hairline scratches (such as on the worker's cap), slide marks, and bag marks. On the reverse, numismatic negatives usually show up on the smooth dolphins design. No error coinage is known. Examples can be observed with a re-punched S Mint mark located to the lower right, but these offer no added value at present.

Detecting Counterfeits

There are counterfeits for this coin. On one, small die scratches can be observed among the normal metal flow lines to the right of the first "A" in "America", directly under the worker's chin. The reverse displays file marks and die scratches between the "P" and "A" of "Pacific". Also there are several blobs of extra metal between the "A" and "N" of "Francisco" at the six o'clock position.

Another counterfeit Pan–Pac dollar displays a depression in the center of the "9" in the date 1915 and another depression about midway down on "DO" in "Dollar".

Is Your Pan–Pac Gold Dollar Circulated or Mint State?

Obverse

Metal loss will first appear on the peak and center section of the worker's cap, as well as on his cheekbone.

Reverse

Wear will first be observed on the letters "One Dollar" and on the heads of the two dolphins.

Future Potential of the Pan–Pac Gold Dollar

Population Figures

Date	Service	AU 58	MS 61	MS 62	MS 63	MS 64	MS 65	MS 66	MS 67	MS 68	MS 69
1915-S	NGC	140	93	376	447	1076	753	595	62	1	1
1915-S	PCGS	287	63	413	991	1633	1193	730	50	2	0
1915-S	Combined	427	156	789	1438	2709	1946	1325	112	3	0

During the 1989 market high, the spread between the MS-63 and MS-64 coins was more than $1,400; the MS-64 and MS-65 variance was a walloping $4,500. I do not believe these variations will recur. I would reduce population figures between 24% and 28%.

The population figures do appear high, but collectors should remember that this gold commemorative series is very popular.

In MS-66+ condition, this issue is under priced, with a good future for eye-appealing strikings. The May 1989 variance between the MS-65 and MS-66 ratings was an enormous $19,000. This is unlikely to happen again. I would reduce census between 24% and 28%.

Tomorrow can be bright for the fortunate owners of the lofty MS-66+ and higher graded encapsulations: if funds are available, I would advise buyers to take the plunge.

The Pan–Pac Gold $2.50 Today

This popular low mintage issue is not abundant in EF-AU grades. Specimens usually will show some form of abuse, and collectors should look for pieces that have worn naturally. These should be purchased only for the pure joy of collecting. Luster will range from bright satiny (not the norm), to dull grainy, to satiny. Strike will vary, but too soft a design definition on the headdress of Columbia and head and neck of the hippocampus, as well as the reverse eagle's head, neck, and claw, will affect the grade-value. On the obverse, the primary focal area is Columbia's body, plus the head and neck of the hippocampus; on the reverse, it is the eagle and the exposed field, opposite the word "United". A non-detracting characteristic of these coins are raised metal swirls caused by steel brushing the dies at the Mint. Hairline scratches caused by abuse cut into the coin's surface and lower the grade and value. No error coinage is known for this issue.

Detecting Counterfeits

Counterfeits exist, displaying a soft strike, field depressions and tooling marks within inscriptions and above the S Mint mark.

Is Your Pan Pac Gold $2.50 Circulated or Mint State?

Obverse

A metal loss will first be observed on the knee and breast of Columbia. Look for a difference in metal texture and crisscross scratches in these locations.

Reverse

Wear will first be seen on the leg, breast, and upper wing of the eagle, then on the base of the classical standard.

Future Potential of the Pan–Pac Gold $2.50

Population Figures

Date	Service	AU 58	MS 61	MS 62	MS 63	MS 64	MS 65	MS 66	MS 67	MS 68	MS 69
1915-S	NGC	35	24	96	137	435	502	594	125	0	0
1915-S	PCGS	58	17	142	324	665	537	403	21	0	0
1915-S	Combined	93	41	238	461	1100	1039	997	146	0	0

At present levels, all grades of this extremely popular coin are somewhat under-valued. There is upside potential—especially in pieces graded MS-66+ and higher. Population figures have now risen to unexpected levels. The May 1989 peak variance between the MS-63 and MS-64 levels was $2,400; the MS-64 to MS-65 difference was approximately $4,500. The census count for those grades can be reduced between 19% and 24%. It may not be easy for history to repeat itself in terms of valuations, but it certainly will make the attempt.

In strict MS-65 condition, the $2.50 commemorative gold strikings make a wonderful addition to one's collection, should funds be available. The last market high between this and the MS-66 rating was a gargantuan $16,000: a repeat performance is unlikely. From collector, dealer, and personal experience, I can report that the $2.50 coins were often submitted—and resubmitted—to grading services. Numerous resubmissions—after the crack outs—were made with the hopes of upgrades, which rarely occurred. Many grading labels were destroyed—

without concern for future population accuracy—in the rush to resubmit the coins. Dealers were cracking out coins on the bourse floor, or in convention lavatories, or in hotel rooms at 1 a.m. I would reduce the population count between 28% and 33%, and predict an average future potential for the Pan–Pac quarter eagle in this grade. But there are very good possibilities for coins in MS-67 condition, should one be lucky enough to have the available funds.

The Pan–Pac Gold $50 Today

Who wouldn't like to own this rare coin? The higher the grade, the rarer the coin. More specimens in the EF-AU state will exhibit some form of abuse, in the form of cleaning, various degrees of whizzing and light polishing, than will not. The future looks bright for the issue in any uncirculated grade: it is very undervalued in all categories. In grades MS-60 through MS-64, the Round is the rarer of the strikings. In the higher states, only 26 Rounds were rated MS-66, with four graded MS-67. Four Octagonals were granted the lofty grade of MS-67. Luster will range from blazing frosty to frosty. Strike presents no real problem for this issue. At times, the hair by Minerva's ear and the feather design on the owl's breast will display a slight weakness of strike, but not enough to lower the coin's grade or value. Value is definitely lowered, however, by surface negatives, caused by some form of abuse. The rare $50 strikings were originally acquired by those with money to spend: they were sold individually in a leather case for $100 each. Buyers who ordered the four-piece set, received the three-piece minor coinage ($7.50) at no extra charge.

No error coinage or counterfeits are known. Medallic copies, however, do exist. I know of one, which was triple gold plated and was sold to an ill-informed buyer for $24,000!

Is Your Pan–Pac Gold $50 Circulated or Mint State?

Obverse

A metal loss will first be noticed Minerva's cheek, as well as on her crested helmet in the center of the leaf design. Coins should be examined for portrait and left field doctoring.

Reverse

Look for wear and difference in metal texture on the owl's wing, directly across from the word "Pluribus" and on the upper part of the owl's breast.

Related Material

The $50 issue was offered as a complete set with the three smaller denominations and the choice of either $50 coin for $100; with both $50 coins for $200;

Counterfeit ribbon used along with bogus inserts for inclusion
in the counterfeit copper hammered frames.

and as a double complete set, which would show the obverse as well as the reverse, for $400. Also included at no extra charge was a glass-fronted copper hammered frame or a leather presentation case. Printed descriptions of each coin were part of the sets.

Individual $50 cases can bring between $400 and $800 at present. The five-piece case can sell in the $2,500–$5,000 range. The hammered frame made by Shreve & Co. housing the five-piece set can be worth $5,000 to $8,000. The double set holder, which once brought $18,000—empty—is now valued in the $8,000 to $12,000 range. Collectors should be aware that there are counterfeit frames, housing counterfeit descriptive coin inserts, as well as the upper representative ribbon. The type of gold print used is different from the genuine, as is the color and type of ribbon. Counterfeit frames have a faded purple color, and the inserts and printing show a low quality of workmanship. These false frames lack the counter-stamped maker's name. Replicas of the Pan–Pac $50 Round, dated 1915 and housed in a red leather case gold-stamped "Coca-Cola, etc., Convention 1915 USA" were produced in 1971. These sell for between $50 and $80, depending on condition.

A set of the three denominations was sold in a leather case lined with purple velvet at $7.50. The inner cover is imprinted with "Exposition Information" in gold ink. Leather cases lined with white velvet are said to be later replicas. The genuine item can today bring between $250 and $900, depending on condition. The leather cases also house the individual $50 gold pieces. (See next page.)

Future Potential of the Pan–Pac Gold $50

Population Figures

Date	Service	AU 58	MS 60	MS 61	MS 62	MS 63	MS 64	MS 65	MS 66	MS 67	MS 68
1915-S Round	NGC	18	1	23	46	81	150	52	17	4	0
1915-S Round	PCGS	23	5	22	69	111	75	10	1	0	0
1915-S Round	Combined	41	6	45	115	192	225	62	18	4	0

Panama–Pacific leather cases.

Date	Service	AU 58	MS 60	MS 61	MS 62	MS 63	MS 64	MS 65	MS 66	MS 67	MS 68
1915-S Octagonal	NGC	20	4	34	62	106	165	44	7	4	0
1915-S Octagonal	PCGS	36	11	29	98	144	113	18	1	0	0
1915-S Octagonal	Combined	56	15	63	160	250	278	62	8	4	0

Both the Round and Octagonal issues are well distributed and extremely popular, fully enjoyed and treasured by most who own them. I compare them to the rare fancy diamonds naturally colored pink, red, blue, or green. They are the truffles and Beluga caviar of commemorative coinage, and outstanding celebrities in our coin world.

In the EF-AU through MS-63 categories, the Round $50 Pan–Pac is rarer than the Octagonal. I would reduce their census count between 14% and 19%. Pieces rated higher are equally rare. The population count indicates otherwise, but I know of one MS-64 Round that was submitted ten times (in total), via three different dealers. Its collector-investor owner threw away seven of their insert grading labels—which can never officially be deleted from the census and population reports.

These strikings are now seriously sought after in all grades, and have become difficult to locate in grades MS-63 and higher. The census may appear somewhat high, but plenty of well-to-do collectors want these quintuple eagles—but certainly not the cleaned, doctored, whizzed or polished-examples, unless the price is right. Collectors should remember that dealers will ask for a certain dollar amount to sell—but their buying price will be a completely different matter. If you own one of these coins, you should consider its immediate sale now. Pieces rated MS-62 and lower could possess a steep downside especially if the surface is problematic within a slab or if the coin market becomes soft for six months to a year. Beware of the doctored pieces—even in slabs whose surfaces have been puttied, etc. Blessed are they who can afford to procure original-surfaced $50 Pan–Pac Round or Octagonal strikings: future potential is just tremendous, and history can easily repeat itself for this issue.

Reason for Issue:	To commemorate the completion of a memorial to President William McKinley in Niles, Ohio.
Authorization:	Act of February 23, 1916, with a maximum of 100,000 pieces.
Issued by:	National McKinley Birthplace Memorial Association
Official Sale Price:	$3

Production Figures

Date	Business Strikes	Assay Coins	Proofs	Melted	Net Mintage
1916	20,000	26	4-6?	10,023	9,977
1917	10,000	14	4-6?	0	10,000

Current Market Values

Year	AU 58	MS 60	MS 63	MS 64	MS 65	MS 66	MS 67
1916	$525	$600	$650	$900	$1,225	$2,300	$4,800
1917	$560	$700	$925	$1,300	$1,925	$3,200	$5,300

Designs

Obverse by Charles E. Barber

Head of McKinley, facing left. "United States of America" appears around the upper border; "McKinley Dollar" around the lower border.

Reverse by George T. Morgan

Facade of the McKinley Memorial Building, with inscriptions "McKinley Birthplace—Niles Ohio", located in the upper border and field respectively. The date is above the word "Memorial", which is in the lower border.

Origins of the McKinley

At first, it was proposed that a silver dollar be created for this commemorative coin. But this was recognized as inappropriate, since McKinley was elected primarily because of his support for the gold standard. The Philadelphia Mint struck 20,000 coins plus 26 for assay purposes during August and October 1916; in February of the following year, 10,014 pieces dated 1917 were minted. Die trials for the 1916 issue were struck in silver and nickel and bronze, as well as two separate obverse and reverse pieces struck in nickel with a reeded edge. The dies were then destroyed: this was a provision of the authorizing Act, which also designated the Mint responsible for the coin's production. I note this because no other Act had ever made such a specification, with the exception of the Panama–Pacific issue, for which San Francisco was the designated Mint.

Both coins were offered for sale at $3 each by the McKinley Birthplace Memorial Association. According to B. Max Mehl, the great Texas coin dealer, the Association in 1917 realized that collectors would not absorb any more coins at $3 each. Sales were slow, and eventually came to a standstill. Mehl acquired 10,000 coins from the Association and sold these extensively among collectors at $2.50 each. The Association decided to return 10,023 gold dollars to the Mint. It was believed these coins were all dated 1916, but today it appears that one-third to one-half of the returned coins were dated 1917.

The McKinley Today

The majority of specimens in circulated condition have been cleaned or numismatically abused in some manner. Original surface coins grading AU-55 or AU-58 will at times exhibit uncirculated reverses: the obverse relief is much higher, while the reverse's rim better protects its lower relief. The 1916 is not difficult to locate in grades MS-60 through MS-66. Collectors should focus on a specimen that is appealing and grades at least MS-64+. Lower grades should be acquired only for the joy of collecting. There is a real future for coins in MS-66+ and better condition. The 1917 McKinley is rarer in all grades, up to MS-67, and has excellent future potential when rated MS-66 and loftier.

Luster will range from proof-like, to semi-proof-like, to brilliant satiny, to dull satiny. Gold planchets used to create the issue will vary from yellow to orange in appearance. Vertical die polishing marks in the reverse field above the Memorial are characteristic for the 1917 issue. Strike rarely presents a problem for either date. On the obverse, McKinley's hair detail has a soft design and will lack the strike sharpness of the 1903 McKinley Louisiana Purchase dollar. In fact, although the coins show portraits of the same person, they seem to be commemorating two different men. McKinley's image acts as a magnet for bag marks, hairline scratches, etc. If these defects occur in the smooth fields the coin's value will be lowered.

Detecting Counterfeits

There are counterfeits of each date. Collectors should look for lack of detail in the obverse and reverse devices, as well as for field depressions and lack of lettering sharpness on the 1916 coin. The fake 1917 striking will display raised parallel striations between the rim and the letters "ERICA" of "America", field depressions below the letters "IO" of "Ohio", and a round depression on the steps of the Memorial building, directly below the statue.

Is Your McKinley Circulated or Mint State?

Obverse
Metal loss will occur on the cheek and temple of McKinley.

Reverse
Wear can first be observed on the flagpole base, and on the top section and steps of the Memorial building.

Related Material

Both issues were distributed in plain coin envelopes and rubber-stamped on the reverse in red ink with "The Niles Trust Company, Niles Ohio" within a circle. There was also a paper coin envelope imprinted with "The National McKinley Birthplace Memorial Association, Youngstown, Ohio" plus the notation that it contained a "Souvenir McKinley Gold Dollar". Both envelopes are rare. The coin was also sold in a large white coin envelope (2 ¼ × 2 ¼ inches), imprinted with a red berry and green holly Christmas wreath with "A Merry Christmas"

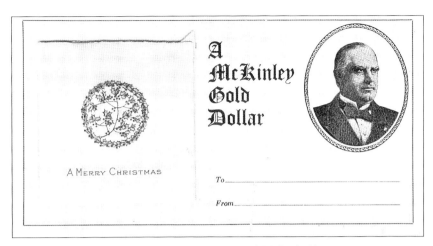

Souvenir Christmas McKinley gold dollar holder.

printed in red, glued to a printed white card (6 ¼ × 3 ¼ inches). The card features a portrait of McKinley and the words "A McKinley Gold Dollar"; "to" and "from" are situated below. This item makes an occasional appearance. I have seen but two of the coin envelopes, and would value each at $400. The Christmas item is worth $125 to $275.

Possibly the rarest item is a blue eight-sided box with a cream-colored white border on the upper outer cover. Within the upper inner cover is a satiny material with the inscription "McKinley Memorial Oct. 5, 1917". The lower cream-colored velour section has a slot for the dollar. This box may have housed special

Rare McKinley gold dollar box.

coinage, such as a proof. One crushed box sold for $775, another sold for $3,000. Another rare item is the 1917 leatherette holder with a picture of McKinley and the Memorial.

Future Potential of the McKinley Memorial Gold Dollar

Population Figures

One piece dated 1916 has been rated MS-68.

Date	Service	AU 58	MS 60	MS 61	MS 62	MS 63	MS 64	MS 65	MS 66	MS 67	MS 68	MS 69
1916	NGC	62	16	11	256	353	742	460	330	70	1	0
1916	PCGS	120	35	96	376	769	1338	946	576	63	0	0
1916	Combined	182	51	107	632	1122	2080	1406	906	133	1	0

Date	Service	AU 58	MS 60	MS 61	MS 62	MS 63	MS 64	MS 65	MS 66	MS 67	MS 68	MS 69
1917	NGC	56	7	42	218	473	785	575	358	53	0	0
1917	PCGS	85	5	48	158	221	395	269	200	55	0	0
1917	Combined	141	12	90	376	694	1180	844	558	108	0	0

Date	Service	PF 40	PF 58	PF 60	PF 62	PF 63	PF 64	PF 65	PF 66	PF 67	PF 68	PF 69
1916	NGC	0	0	0	0	0	0	0	0	0	0	0
1916	PCGS	0	0	0	0	1	2	0	0	0	0	0
1916	Combined	0	0	0	0	1	2	0	0	0	0	0

Date	Service	PL 40	PL 58	PL 60	PL 62	PL 63	PL 64	PL 65	PL 66	PL 67	PL 68	PL 69
1916	NGC	0	0	0	1	1	1	0	0	0	0	0
1917	NGC	0	0	0	1	1	5	2	0	0	0	0

There are no proofs for the 1917 coin, which is the rarer of the two dates. While census figures are not exactly low, the point to remember is that both strikings are popular collector items: many collectors want to complete the 11-piece gold commemorative set (1903–1926). Anyone buying only for the joy of ownership should concentrate on affordability. Attempt to locate an attractive, undoctored, original surfaced gold disk that does not display a large or deep scratch across the portrait or fine hairline scratches across the coin. Buyers interested in the coin's future value should seek, if funds permit, an attractive, fully original MS-64+ specimen, particularly the 1917 issue. The past high price spread between the MS-64 and MS-65 ratings for the 1916 and 1917 coins were $5,600 and $5,000 respectively, but that is unlikely to recur. I would lower the census by 29% to 33% for each coin.

In MS-65+ condition the 1917 issue is especially undervalued at present. Buyers should attempt to procure an attractive slabbed 1917 specimen, but don't reject the 1916 McKinley dollar. The May 1989 market high between grades MS-65 and MS-66 was a whopping $9,500 (1916) and $16,000 (1917). But, again, there is unlikely to be such a price spread again: fewer coins were encapsulated during this period, plus demand was high. I would reduce census between 23% and 29%. The 1917 issue offers better potential in this grade. In MS-66 condition, however, the 1917 issue is the rarer. McKinley gold dollars offer a bright tomorrow for their owners, especially in the loftier MS-67 rated coinage.

1918 Illinois Centennial (or Lincoln) Half Dollar

Reason for Issue:	To commemorate the 100th anniversary of the admission of Illinois into the Union.
Authorization:	Act of June 1, 1918, with a maximum of 100,000 pieces.
Issued by:	Illinois Centennial Commission
Official Sale Price:	$1

Production Figures

Date	Business Strikes	Assay Coins	Proofs	Melted	Net Mintage
1918	100,000	58	4–10?	0	100,000

Current Market Values

Year	AU 58	MS 60	MS 63	MS 64	MS 65	MS 66	MS 67
1918	$130	$155	$165	$180	$400	$600	$3,500

Designs

Obverse by George T. Morgan

Bust of Abraham Lincoln, facing right. The design was created from a photograph of Andrew O'Connor's statue at the Illinois State Capitol Building in Springfield; the statue shows a beardless Lincoln as President-elect, and was unveiled in 1918. Around most of the coin's border is the inscription "CENTENNIAL OF THE STATE OF ILLINOIS". "IN GOD WE TRUST" is in four lines in the left field behind Lincoln's head. "LIBERTY" appears in the lower right, just in front of the president's collar. The date is below. Neophyte and experienced collectors often mistakenly call this issue the "Lincoln" because of Lincoln's prominent bust on the obverse.

Reverse by John Ray Sinnock

American eagle with raised wings facing left, and standing partly on the shield of the United States and partly on a rock. The eagle holds in his beak a ribbon bearing the incused Illinois state motto "State Sovereignty — National Unity"; the motto "E Pluribus Unum" is in the right field above the rising sun with extending rays. Above the "HA" in "Half Dollar", in the lower border area, is an olive branch, symbol of peace. "United States of America" arcs above.

Origins of the Illinois

In August 1918, the Philadelphia Mint struck 100,000 coins plus 58 for assay purposes. None of these coins was returned to the Mint. Most of the issue was sold through the Springfield Chamber of Commerce, and other County Centennial outlets for $1. The famous numismatist B. Max Mehl acquired more than 3,000 pieces for between 55 cents and 60 cents each. He notes that a particular bank in Springfield housed 30,000 specimens, which were handled by that city's Chamber of Commerce. During the bank holiday of 1933, that particular bank also took a holiday and the remainder of these pieces were acquired by several dealers at less than $1 each. The market became flooded with them, but the coins were ultimately absorbed during the commemorative boom that began in 1935.

This issue was the first to commemorate an occasion, event, or undertaking that was confined to a single state.

The Illinois Today

This coin is not at all difficult to obtain in EF-AU condition. The majority of Lincolns are in the MS-60 through MS-64 grades. Collectors should focus on the latter classification, since there is little value spread at present. Attempt to acquire an original eye-appealing specimen: the coin's portrait and smooth obverse field should be almost free of detracting hairlines, scuff marks, and scratches. It is those surface negatives, such as a reed mark or large bag mark on the portrait or a few fine hairline field scratches, that downgrade many would-be MS-65 specimens. Luster can range from blazing proof-like brilliant to dull satiny. Strike rarely causes a coin to be downgraded. On the reverse the eagle can display a slight flattening of its breast feathers, because of die wear, but this seldom affects the coin's value. Collectors interested in future gains should look for coins strictly graded MS-66 and loftier, if funds are available. Two or three die trials, each struck in copper, nickel, and white metal, show incomplete design details: they were struck without a collar. To date no error coinage has been observed, and no counterfeits are known for the issue.

Is Your Illinois Circulated or Mint State?

Obverse

Metal loss will first appear on the cheekbone and hair above Lincoln's ear. Look for a difference in metal color and for crisscross scratches in this area, as well as surface doctoring.

Reverse

The lower relief eagle will indicate wear by a loss of surface metal on the breast. Should the area display some flatness because of die wear, examine the coin carefully for signs of a silver loss.

Related Material

Original holders for this issue are unheard of to date. The only official numismatic centennial item I have encountered is the wearable silvered nickel shield-shaped badge housing an Illinois, with an attached ribbon, and a top hanger with the date 1818 over "Illinois Centennial", and the date 1918 at bottom. Several versions of the ribbons exist. The most common is the white, blue and white striped ribbon with 21 stars. Next is the same design, but with the word "Official" imprinted in gold. Another design is reported to have a red and blue striped ribbon. Could it be that some individual simply substituted this ribbon for a damaged official version? The value of these items is based mostly on the condition of the enclosed coin, and could be anywhere between $250 and $2,500.

Future Potential of the Illinois Half Dollar

Population Figures

Date	Service	AU 58	MS 60	MS 62	MS 63	MS 64	MS 65	MS 66	MS 67	MS 68	MS 69
1918	NGC	34	1	153	552	1686	1073	276	74	4	0
1918	PCGS	79	18	392	1325	2144	1190	501	83	1	0
1918	Combined	113	19	545	1877	3830	2263	777	157	5	0

Date	Service	PL 58	PL 60	PL 62	PL 63	PL 64	PL 65	PL 66	PL 67	PL 68	PL 69
1918	NGC	0	0	0	0	1	0	0	0	0	0

This beautiful souvenir piece is not difficult to obtain in circulated condition. There is no significant price spread between the circulated and the MS-64 rating. However, this coin is a collector favorite. The real future potential begins in flashy MS-66 coinage. The past price difference between material rated MS-64 and MS-65 during the May 1989 market high was $2,000, but I do not see history repeating itself to this degree. I would reduce population figures by 30% to 35% for the MS-65 grade. There is average future potential for pieces grading MS-62 through MS-65.

As noted, the popular Lincoln coin is somewhat undervalued in MS-66 and MS-67 condition. The dollar difference between the MS-65 and MS-66 classifications has been $1,700. I estimate that the census can be reduced between 25% and 33%. This issue will almost certainly be pushed by sellers when the market next goes high.

Graded MS-66 and MS-67 this coin is underrated, and is a wonderful coin to have in one's collection. A bit of history: the first president to appear on U.S. coinage was George Washington –on the 1900 Lafayette commemorative dollar. Lincoln was the first president to appear on our business struck coinage, in 1909 on the 1-cent piece.

1920 Maine Centennial

Reason for Issue:	To commemorate the 100th anniversary of the admission of Maine into the Union.
Authorization:	Act of May 10, 1920, with a maximum of 100,000 pieces
Issued by:	State Treasury Department of Maine and the Maine Centennial Commission.
Official Sale Price:	$1

Production Figures

Date	Business Strikes	Assay Coins	Proofs	Melted	Net Mintage
1920	50,000	28	4?	0	50,000

Current Market Values

Year	AU 50	MS 60	MS 63	MS 64	MS 65	MS 66	MS 67
1920	$145	$175	$175	$300	$500	$700	$4,300

Designs by Anthony de Francisci

The Maine was designed by Anthony de Francisci based on specifications furnished to him by the State of Maine. He also created the Peace silver dollar design (1921–35).

Obverse

Arms of the State of Maine, composed of a sunken relief pine tree and moose in a lying position, on a shield supported by two male figures representing Commerce (the anchor) and Agriculture (the scythe). Above the shield is the word "DIRIGO" ("I direct") on a scroll; above that is a star with five short rays. Below the shield is another scroll bearing the word "MAINE" situated between two rosettes. "UNITED STATES OF AMERICA" arcs above; "HALF DOLLAR" below.

Reverse

Wreath of pine needles and cones. Within appears the inscription "MAINE CENTENNIAL 1820–1920"; "LIBERTY" connects the tips of the wreath at the top. "E PLURIBUS UNUM" is squeezed between the wreath and the rim above; "IN GOD WE TRUST" is similarly placed at the bottom.

Origins of the Maine

Originally it was the idea of Maine's delegate to the House of Representatives, John A. Peters, to have this issue placed into circulation. Its primary objective would be free advertisement for the Centennial event. The concept, however, garnered little support. The design was severely criticized by the judges at the U.S. Commission of Fine Arts.

During the late summer of 1920, the Philadelphia Mint struck 50,000 Maine half dollars, plus 28 assay coins. These coins were sold at $1 each from the Office of the State Treasurer. Although delivery was not made until after the Centennial celebration at Portland was over, more than 30,000 pieces sold immediately and the remainder of the issue was offered for sale until all pieces were sold.

The Maine Today

This coin is abundant in EF-AU condition. It was used as a pocket piece by the locals, and many specimens will show some form of abuse. It is not a difficult coin to acquire in grades MS-60 through MS-65. Future value increase will be in specimens that are very attractive, possess a strong strike, and grade at least MS-64+. Luster will range from proof-like, to semi-proof-like (not the norm), to brilliant satiny, to satiny, to dull satiny. A proof-like coin is the result of a coin struck from a new die that was highly polished. Dies are also re-polished after a die clash, which occurs when the obverse and reverse dies have come together with no planchet (coin blank) in between them during the minting process, resulting in damage to the coin dies. The subsequent re-polishing is a die repair technique that can result in proof-like or semi-mirrored coins being created right after the coin dies are put back into production. Proof-like coins are not proof coins. They are attractive simply because of the way they look. With every blow from the press, the partial mirrored surface quickly changes to a more brilliant lustrous condition.

Strikings produced from the original die state will offer the beholder a bright to dull satiny appearance. Strike seldom affects the grade or value of the issue. Coins produced after heavy die polishing will lack sharpness, especially on the faces of the obverse male figures. The primary focal area is the obverse shield, which is usually plagued by numismatic negatives such as bag marks or slide marks. The critical locations for the reverse design are the wreath and the area above the word "MAINE". One large detracting mark in this area can downgrade an MS-65 to an MS-64. The same applies to the shield on the obverse.

To date no error coinage has entered the marketplace, nor has any counterfeit coinage. Several examples were artificially surfaced and offered as matte proofs. Collectors should seek the advice of the truly knowledgeable before making any acquisition.

Is Your Maine Circulated or Mint State?

Obverse
Metal loss will first be noticed on the hand of each male holding the shield, and the center of the countersunk pine tree will appear worn. This is the result of die design and striking—not wear. If luster has been disturbed, metal loss is a certainty. Fine crisscross scratches in the shield will indicate metal loss and not handling marks.

Reverse
Examine for wear on the wreath's ribbon at the six o'clock position and the top section of the pine wreath extending from the four to almost the nine o'clock position. Raised lines appearing in the left field and above the word "MAINE" are the result of die polishing. They do not lower the coin's grade. However, scratches, whether hairline or heavier, cut into the surface metal and do lower a coin's value.

Related Material
To date, I have encountered no original distribution holder or printed material.

Future Potential of the Maine Half Dollar

Population Figures
To date, one of these 1920 commemorative half dollars have been graded MS-68, with none rated higher.

Date	Service	AU 58	MS 60	MS 62	MS 63	MS 64	MS 65	MS 66	MS 67	MS 68	MS 69
1920	NGC	25	1	92	317	1086	843	243	33	1	0
1920	PCGS	41	14	160	659	1224	890	316	18	0	0
1920	Combined	66	15	252	976	2310	1733	659	51	1	0

Date	Service	PL 58	PL 60	PL 62	PL 63	PL 64	PL 65	PL 66	PL 67	PL 68	PL 69
1920	NGC	0	0	0	0	1	0	0	0	0	0

The Maine is available in circulated condition, since many coins were used as pocket pieces. There is no large price spread between MS-60 and MS-64 coinage. The coins are valued fairly in grades EF-AU through MS-65. Collectors should acquire eye-appealing coinage in these grades only for the joy of ownership. The May 1989 market high valuation for an MS-65 specimen was $2,525, but that value is unlikely to repeat barring massive bullion revaluation or hyper-inflation.

Eye-appealing MS-65+ specimens are somewhat undervalued at current levels. The market-high values between grades MS-65 and MS-66 was $4,200, but collectors should not count on a similar performance in the future, despite what future promoters will want you to believe. The census can be reduced between 19% and 22%.

Thirty years ago the owners of a nearly full original bag of this issue said that the coins would be sold only on an individual basis. I bought 10 pieces, before this statement was made. The population count over the last two years has risen in the MS-65 and MS-66 categories. Were coins from this original bag that were sold individually and slabbed over the years responsible? If not, then the population figures will rise in the future. At present I think this coin has good potential; it is a popular issue, and is currently undervalued in the MS-66. I would reduce the census between 20% and 25%. The Maine is a rare coin in MS-67 condition—I wish I owned one of the 51 encapsulated pieces to date.

1920-1921 PILGRIM TERCENTENARY

Reason for Issue:	To commemorate the 300th anniversary of the landing of the Pilgrims at what became Plymouth, Massachusetts.
Authorization:	Act of May 12, 1920, with a maximum of 300,000 pieces.
Issued by:	Pilgrim Tercentenary Commission
Official Sale Price:	$1

Production Figures

Date	Business Strikes	Assay Coins	Proofs	Melted	Net Mintage
1920	200,000	112	4?	48,000	152,000
1921	100,000	53	4?	80,000	20,000

Current Market Values

Date	AU 58	MS 60	MS 63	MS 64	MS 65	MS 66	MS 67
1920	$90	$115	$125	$145	$330	$600	$3,900
1921	$175	$200	$220	$240	$465	$850	$4,500

DESIGNS BY CYRUS E. DALLIN

Obverse

Half-length portrait of Governor William Bradford (indicative of the Pilgrim of his time), wearing a conical hat and carrying a Bible under his left arm. Below his elbow appears the incused initial "D" for Dallin: not for the Denver Mint.

Separated by two decorative stars are the inscriptions "UNITED STATES OF AMER-
ICA" and "PILGRIM HALF DOLLAR". The words are separated by dots. Behind the
Governor's head is the motto "IN GOD WE TRUST". On the 1921 issue, the date
is in the left field opposite Bradford's upper chest. The words "HOLY BIBLE" on
the book's front cover were removed from Dallin's original design; Dallin's full
initials (CED) met the same fate.

Reverse

Side view of the Mayflower sailing to the left, as well as the Pilgrim Tercentenary dates 1620–1920. This reverse met with some technical criticism from
historians. Ships of the day were equipped with a square water sail that hung
under the bowsprit (a spar extending forward from the stem of the ship, to which
the stays of the foremast are fastened), or the large spar (support rigging) which
projected forward from the bow or ship's nose. The Mayflower on the half dollar
is depicted with a flying jib, a triangular sail set on a stay extending from the
head of the foremast to the bowsprit, or the jibboom (a spar that extends the
bowsprit). This type of sail was not actually in use when the Mayflower sailed.
"PILGRIM TERCENTENARY CELEBRATION" and the tercentenary dates circle the
outer border.

Origins of the Pilgrim

This issue was produced by the Philadelphia Mint in October 1920. Its original
mintage of 200,000 pieces was placed in the hands of the Pilgrim Tercentenary
Commission for distribution in November through the National Shawmut Bank
of Boston; coins could also be ordered at any Boston or Plymouth Bank. They
were offered at $1 each.

   The sale of the 1920 souvenirs must have been very successful, since no one
at that time thought of returning any coins to the Mint. However, when sales
slackened, the Pilgrim Tercentenary Commission believed they could do just as
well with another issue. During the following July, the Philadelphia Mint struck
an additional 100,000 half dollars (plus 53 pieces for assay purposes), to the
exact design as the 1920 issue, but with the date 1921 added in relief in the left
field on the obverse. There are thus three dates on the coin: the tercentenary
years and the year of striking.

   In the end, sales turned out to be poor. The Tercentenary Commission
returned 48,000 pieces dated 1920 and 80,000 dated 1921 to the Mint for melting. This leaves us with a low mintage figure of 20,000 half dollars dated 1921,
and 152,000 dated 1920.

The Pilgrim Today

The 1920 Pilgrim is abundant in circulated EF-AU condition. It can be found in
any state from naturally worn to unnaturally abused. The 1921 striking is not as
abundant, and usually shows some form of cleaning or doctoring. It is certainly
the better buy of the two, since the value spread is little.

In grades MS-60 through MS-64, there is little value spread currently in the easily obtainable 1920 issue. Collectors should seek out a somewhat undervalued eye-appealing MS-64+ specimen, unless the purchase is simply for the joy of collecting and grade is of no concern. The 1920 coin will increase in value at MS-66 levels. But the real value for this issue lies in the 1921 striking, the coin that introduced me to the world of U.S. commemorative coinage. It is underrated in all grades MS-66 and higher. Luster will range from proof-like, to semi-proof-like, to blazing satiny, to dull satiny. I have seen only a few first-strike examples of the 1921 coin with proof-like obverses and blazing satiny reverses. Otherwise, both dates will display reverses in the satiny range. The 1921 Pilgrim is more likely to exhibit the "luster look" than the 1920 issue.

Strike can be responsible for lowering the grade-value of this issue, especially if the border inscription lettering—"States" or "Half" on the obverse, or, on the reverse, parts of the word "Tercentenary", the anniversary dates, or ship's mast—appear too flat or weak. One authentication bureau believes Type 1 (non-upset) coin blanks were fed directly into the coin press to help prevent weakness of strike on the inscriptions. If this is what happened, the blanks or planchets did not fit into the press. Numismatic abuse, in the form of bag marks, slide marks, reed marks, etc., usually appear on the primary focal locations, such as Bradford's portrait (and then the surrounding fields) and the reverse Mayflower. One ugly, large bag mark in the obverse field or a slide mark across the Governor's likeness on a blazing, eye-appealing specimen can drop the coin's value dramatically. These focal locations are often whizzed (wire-brushed), polished, or doctored in some fashion.

While studying this issue, I discovered several 1921 half dollars that showed evidence of die-clashing, and called it the Pilgrim 1921 Type 2. My discovery concerns a lump in front of Bradford's nose, several tiny bumps behind his head above the hat brim, a raised area below the "RU" in "Trust", and the conical hat that doesn't quite fit Bradford's head.

Through the use of film positives we can prove that the lumps were the result of clashed dies and the ill-fitting hat the result of die polishing, probably an attempt at eliminating the clash marks. Clash marks occur when a blank fails to feed into the press. The dies hit each other without the blank between to absorb the blow. As a result, the outline of the design details from each die is transferred to the other die.

The faces of dies are normally slightly convex so that they impart a slight concavity to the field of the coins they strike. And because the dies are convex the centers of the dies hit first and hit hardest, with the result that the design nearest the center is more subject to the die clash transfer.

The film positives were used as overlays to show that the lump in front of Bradford's nose corresponds to the area below the sail of the foremast, the tiny bumps behind the head match spaces between the waves below the center of the ship, and the raised area below "RU" corresponds to the curved lower edge of the sail at the Mayflower's stern. The reverse has no clash marks, indicating that

Die clash mark diagnostics.

possibly the reverse die had been changed after the clash and probably because of it.

There are 1920 Pilgrims that exhibit obverse die clash marks and/or display the clash marked letters "US" (inverted) from the word "Trust". This too can be seen on many of the 1921 specimens, indicating the reverse die used to make the 1920 coin was used for the 1921 coin. Using ten power magnification, the Governor's index finger and collar can also be observed beneath the letters "ER" of "Tercentenary" and under the sail design, to the left of the rear mast, respectively. Be aware pieces exist on both issues displaying die break (raised metal).

There are possibly 100 such 1921 pieces, but the premiums asked for the offered grade have thus far been negligible, though that could change. There is die doubling on the inscription "1620 Pilgrim" and the letters "NARY" of "Tercentenary" on the 1920 reverse.

Detecting Counterfeits

On December 8, 1987 the 1920 die trials struck in pure silver (3 pieces), brass (2 pieces), and lead (2 pieces) were sold via Christie's of London for $44,000 (Lot #295). Ironically, a pawn shop was selling fakes at exactly the same time. I informed the new owners (who had forwarded some pieces) that their coins were fakes, and presented them with documentation for Christies for their refund. The dies were created by a non-professional, as were other recent die trials that have surfaced. Were they the real thing, these items would have been bought for way over their $2,500–$3,500 asking price by several dealers, including myself.

Counterfeit coins obverse. Note that Governor Bradford eyes are depicted closed—
as if he were asleep. Compare with the genuine issue.

Counterfeit reverse on the right. Compare with the genuine reverse on the left.

Is Your Pilgrim Circulated or Mint State?

Obverse

A metal loss will first occur on Bradford's cheekbone, then in the hair area covering his ear. These are prime targets for coin doctors, so collectors should examine the portrait very carefully.

Reverse

Examine the crow's nest, center mast, and stern of the *Mayflower* for a metal loss or difference in metal texture.

Examples of the rare distribution boxes.

Related Material

The 1920 coin was sold by the banks in a plain coin envelope or just over the counter. The issue was also distributed in a gold-colored coin box with an emerald green slit-pouch. The top cover is imprinted in black: "People's Savings Bank, Worcester, Mass", with a coat of arms. The coin was also distributed by the Second National Bank of Boston in a long green rectangular box. The two styles of coin boxes sold for $1,610 and $2,530 respectively, with MS-64 and MS-65 coins enclosed, at the March 8, 2005 American Numismatic Rarities auction in Baltimore.

The 1920 coin was also sold in a white coin box. The box had a light tan velour interior with a circular coin slot, and included a small printed insert with information about the coin, the striking, and the designer. The top cover is imprinted in orange-brown ink: "Society of Colonial Wars, in the State of Rhode Island and Providence Plantations, by its Governor, Henry Dexter Sharpe, Esq." Other boxes may exist. Buyers should beware of a gold-colored box with a sailing ship on the box top cover. It is not in any way connected to the original issue.

Genuine boxes are very rare and valuable today, and original specimens may be valued in the lofty $500 to $700 range. There is also a plaster model reverse of the coin, which once hung on the wall of the old Mayflower Coffee Shop in the Statler Hilton in New York City. It was purchased for $700 by Stanley Apfelbaum, owner of First Coin Investors (FCI), as a gift for the coin expert and writer Walter Breen.

Future Potential of the Pilgrim Half Dollar

Population Figures

Date	Service	AU 58	MS 60	MS 62	MS 63	MS 64	MS 65	MS 66	MS 67	MS 68	MS 69
1920	NGC	112	4	215	633	2020	996	183	23	0	0
1920	PCGS	43	24	462	1429	1914	929	320	34	0	0
1920	Combined	155	28	677	2062	3934	1925	5-3	57	0	0

Date	Service	AU 58	MS 60	MS 62	MS 63	MS 64	MS 65	MS 66	MS 67	MS 68	MS 69
1921	NGC	14	1	38	177	826	697	153	26	0	0
1921	PCGS	17	2	141	474	981	677	257	22	0	0
1921	Combined	31	3	179	651	1807	1374	410	48	0	0

In circulated condition, the 1920 Pilgrim is not difficult to locate. There is little price spread between grades EF-AU and MS-64. Collectors should look for coins graded at least MS-64+. The past dollar variation between MS-64 and MS-65 coinage during the May 1989 peak was a huge $1800; this will be difficult to repeat. The census can be deleted by 25% to 29%. There are decent possibilities for pieces grading MS-64+; for lesser grades the prospects are only average.

In strict MS-65 condition, the 1920 coin is somewhat undervalued at current levels. The price spread between the MS-65 and MS-66 ratings during the last high was an enormous $4,000; history may repeat itself to a degree, but not to this extent. I would reduce population figures between 20% and 27%. A 1920 Pilgrim, strictly graded MS-66 and MS-67, would be a significant addition to one's collection, offering excellent future potential.

The 1921 Pilgrim, which introduced me to U.S. commemorative coinage, is somewhat undervalued in EF-AU condition, as well as in the MS-60 through MS-67 ratings. Its future potential ranges from average in grades EF-AU through MS-64.

In May 1989, the dollar variation between MS-64 and MS-65 coinage was a big $2,100; history will repeat, but not to this extent. I would lower the census by between 26% and 33%, and see good possibilities for the MS-64+ coin.

In strict MS-65 condition, the 1921 coin is somewhat undervalued at current levels. The 1989 spread between MS-65 and MS-66 was a massive $4,300; again, the current spread will increase, but not this much. I would lower the population count by 20% to 25%.

Die-clashed 1921 Pilgrims displaying the blob in front of Bradford's nose are seldom seen in MS-65 or better condition. This coin is a future sleeper; examples have sold for up to 20% more than the regular issue.

A 1921 coin grading MS-66 is a fantastic way to enhance one's collection and is definitely undervalued at present. As noted, both the 1920 and the 1921 coins are rare in the loftier MS-67 rating, and both are highly recommended.

1921 ALABAMA CENTENNIAL

Reason for Issue:	To commemorate the 100th anniversary of the admission of Alabama into the Union.
Authorization:	Act of May 10th, 1920, with a maximum of 100,000 pieces for both types.
Issued by:	Alabama Centennial Commission
Official Sale Price:	$1

Production Figures

Date	Business Strikes	Assay Coins	Proofs	Melted	Net Mintage
1921 2X2	6,006	6	4?	0	6,000
1921 Plain	64,038	38	4?	5,000	59,000

Current Market Values

Year	AU-58	MS-60	MS-63	MS-64	MS-65	MS-66	MS-67
1921 2X2	$310	$325	$535	$66-	$1,475	$3,100	$20,000
1921 Plain	$215	$230	$440	$470	$1,300	$2,600	$18,000

DESIGNS BY LAURA GARDIN FRASER

Obverse

Portraits of William Wyatt Bibb, Alabama's first governor, and Thomas E. Kilby, the governor in 1920. Beneath their busts in small letters are their names, the date 1921 and the words "HALF DOLLAR". "UNITED STATES OF AMERICA" arcs above; "IN GOD WE TRUST" appears in smaller letters between that and the portraits. In the field at the lower right are 10 five-pointed stars, set up in three rows. In the lower left field, also arranged in three rows, are 12 five-pointed stars. These 22 stars denote that Alabama was the 22nd state granted admission into the Union.

Until the issuance of the Alabama Centennial half dollars in 1921, no living person had ever been portrayed on coinage of the United States. The representation of Governor Kilby was not opposed at the time, since it was not in violation of the congressional Act of May 16, 1866, forbidding the portrayal of any living person on U.S. currency. Numismatists today argue both sides—some say that "currency" should refer to any legal tender, including coins; others that the term refers to paper money only.

The "2X2" incused in the center of the right field of the low mintage variety additionally stresses that Alabama was the 22nd state. Commonly referred to as the "two by two" the "X" does not represent the word "times" or "by"; it represents the red X-shaped cross of St. Andrew, patron saint of Scotland, who was martyred on such a cross. The St. Andrew's cross is also emblematic on the British Union flag, the flag of the Confederate States of America, and the state flag of Alabama.

Reverse

The seal of Alabama: an eagle with raised wings, facing left, set on the shield of the United States, holding arrows in its talons and a scroll in its beak bearing the state motto, incused in small letters, "HERE WE REST". "STATE OF ALABAMA" arcs above; "1819 CENTENNIAL 1919" below; at the three o'clock position are the designer's initials (LGF).

The half dollars that received Congressional authorization in 1920 to commemorate the centennial of 1919 were not minted until 1921. Under the coinage laws at that time, a coin must bear the date of the year in which is was minted, so the Alabama Centennial has both the date of striking (obverse) and the anniversary dates (reverse).

Origins of the Alabama

Initially, this issue was designated a quarter dollar, but an amendment of April 21, 1920, changed the denomination to a half dollar. Mrs. Marie Bankhead Owen, Chairwoman of the Alabama Centennial Commission—appointed by Governor Kilby—informed Kilby that the Centennial Commission judges rejected all the Alabama coinage designs that had been submitted. The subsequent selection was an obverse depicting the State Capitol, and a reverse portraying James Monroe and Woodrow Wilson, presidents during Alabama's admission and centennial.

On June 19, 1921 Mrs. Owen submitted new sketches. The obverse depicted the state seal of Alabama, the reverse depicted Bibb and Kilby. These designs were forwarded by the U.S. Mint Director Raymond T. Baker to Charles Moore, Chairman of the U.S. Commission of Fine Arts, and then to the sculptor member of the Commission, James Earle Fraser. Fraser commissioned his wife, Laura Gardin Fraser, to create the models. She informed the Commission of Fine Arts that the Centennial Commission should be made aware of the special 2✶4 marking used on 5,000 of the Missouri Centennial coins, which were sold at a premium. Representative Lilius Rainey received this information and forwarded it to Mrs. Owen—who was already aware. The completed models were approved—with the reverse designated the obverse—and submitted to the Mint on September 22, 1921.

According to official records, the Philadelphia Mint struck 6,006 coins in October 1921 with the St. Andrew's Cross dividing the figure 2X2 at the back of Governor Kilby's head. In December 1921 an additional 10,008 pieces—presumed to be the 2X2—plus 54,030 extra specimens of the Plain variety were produced (after the 2X2 was removed from the hub). These figures conflict with currently accepted mintage figures. The figures in the table at the beginning of this entry are considered to be the widely accepted mintage figures by numerous experts in the numismatic field.

According to John H. Morris, Jr.:

> The Alabama halves were sold on October 26, 1921. President Harding, being a Mason, was invited to come to Birmingham to lay the cornerstone at the new Masonic Temple on October 26th, 1921. The Alabama halves were sold on that day. It was a holiday here and all the public schools were closed. I went down to the park to hear President Harding speak. After his speech, he walked two blocks to the Masonic Temple to lay the Corner Stone. I was at both places.
>
> I started collecting coins in 1915, so naturally I had to buy the Alabama half. As I had collected two of each commemorative coin issued up to this date, I had to buy two of these coins. Both coins were the Plain variety, not 2X2. These Alabama halves were sold by several banks here and on the main street corners, downtown. They were sold from stalls about four feet square with a shelf on three sides, about three feet from the sidewalk. During the late 1930s when the

commemoratives were very popular, I ran an ad in our local newspaper offering to buy the Alabama halves for $1.50 each. I would go to your house to pick them up. I bought thirty-two at this price and none were the 2X2 type. A friend of mine who worked at a bank here saw my ad and called, telling me the bank had a roll of the Alabama halves in a $10 wrapper. They had to get $20 for them, since they paid $1 each for the roll of 20. I bought the Alabama halves and they were all Plain, not 2X2. Having bought two the first day and 52 about 16 years later—and none with 2X2—they could not have been sold in Birmingham.

Since the Plain issue was offered first, according to eyewitnesses who attended the celebration in Birmingham, on October 26, 1921, it would appear Mint records were incorrect and the Plain variety was struck first. However, according to Mrs. Owen, "the first 5,000 of these coins received showed a St. Andrew's cross between two figure '2's,' with the cross being emblematic of the state flag." (The idea of this special mark was previously conveyed to her by Representative Rainey.)

It appears that the Alabama Centennial Commission wanted no more than 5,000 2X2 specimens and that no additional pieces would be produced by the Mint, for whatever reason. Thus, all that was offered for sale on October 26 were the 1,000 "Plains" delivered along with the 2X2's.

The Alabama Today

The Alabama Plain issue is not at all difficult to locate in EF-AU condition. Most pieces will exhibit natural wear; some will display forms of numismatic abuse, such as a degree of whizzing, polishing, cleaning, etc. Should you be interested in collecting 2X2 EF-AU or AU specimens, they are available at present, but not in great numbers. People needed money to live during the Depression— and these issues were spent. Many were also kept as pocket pieces, especially the Plain issue. Buyers should attempt to acquire a specimen with eye appeal and with only slight wear on its natural surface. The 2X2 coin is preferable.

Both Alabamas can be located with some effort in grades MS-60 through MS-63. Their values are currently underrated, and the coins can be acquired for the pure joy of collecting. Pieces grading strict MS-64 are somewhat undervalued. Grading strictness and eye appeal are the key considerations if you wish to buy an example that will increase in value. A collector may be offered a most eye-appealing Alabama Plain issue, something that is not often encountered in MS-64 and higher condition. These beautiful coins possess semi-proof-like fields and frosted devices varying in depth. They will also have what appears to be a scratch or cut in the field behind Kilby's head. This should not make you afraid to purchase the coin. In the early stages of striking, the dies clashed; the fields were then polished at the Philadelphia Mint, creating a blazing new semi-proof-like surface. However, a small clash mark was left behind in the above-mentioned field. Higher graded specimens (MS-64+) can be a most rewarding

Note die clash behind Kilby's head.

find. About Uncirculated (AU) coins are more of a challenge to find, but you will appreciate their beauty, even in this grade, if they are un-doctored.

Alabamas grading MS-64 had better be fully original, bright or attractively toned, and have but a few marks, spread irregularly, in the primary focal areas. Coins grading MS-65 should have no detracting marks in these areas. The primary focal locations especially prone to attack by numismatic negatives such as slide marks, cuts, bag marks, and scratches, are Kilby's cheek, forehead, and lower jaw. Then, to a lesser degree, Bibb's cheek and forehead. The central part of the reverse eagle can also take a good hit, lowering both the specimen's grade and value. Those who can afford MS-65 examples should be aware that the Plain is somewhat rarer than the 2X2. In MS-66 they are equally rare. Both possess a good future and are definitely undervalued if strictly graded. In the lofty MS-67 grade the Plain, again, is slightly rarer.

Fully struck examples are seldom seen. Locating specimens with a strongly defined eagle's front and back claw holding the arrows will be almost impossible—especially on the Plain issue. By strongly defined or struck, I mean that some definition on the legs of the eagle, along with slightly defined claws and arrow shafts, should all be visible. Continuous die wear in this area, during the 2X2 strikings, caused these details to vanish forever. When the same dies were used to strike the Alabama Plain issue (without the 2X2), the condition was not remedied. It will only be those very early-struck 2X2 coins that possess the stronger strikes. Thus the coin's reverse generally possesses the poor strike—and this can be grade and value lowering. On occasion, a planchet split may be seen on the coin's edge, arising from a flaw in the design and manufacture of the dies. This split can lower a coin's value.

The original Mint State specimens for both coins will display a luster ranging from a bright satiny (which is usually not the norm), to medium, to a dull satiny (usually the norm). Should a coin be toned, collectors should be certain that its original luster is visible beneath this veil, for the toning might be hiding a surface that possesses no luster because it was improperly cleaned and has toned with time or is a toned AU coin. Toning represents permanent destruction: someone believed they could change the minted finish, which accompanies most of the issue, from satiny to blazing. This doesn't work.

Detecting Counterfeits

To date, no examples of error coinage or any counterfeits have made their presence known.

IS YOUR ALABAMA CIRCULATED OR MINT STATE?

Obverse

Wear will first be observed on Governor Kilby's forehead and earlobe. The slight flatness on his upper ear directly above the lobe was caused by the strike. Look for a loss of metal, and an unnatural shine where metal has been worn away. Such friction will cause a difference in the texture of the metal. I like to use no more than ten power to look at the high points of wear. However, be certain you know what you are looking at: you could possibly interpret a flat strike as wear.

Reverse

When grading this issue, first examine this side of the coin. Wear will be most evident on the top of the eagle's wing diagonally below the letters "ERE" of the word "HERE" in the scroll and in the upper breast area of the eagle.

Related Material

No original distributing holders or mailers have surfaced to date.

Future Potential of the 1921 Alabama Half Dollar

Population Figures

Date	Service	AU 58	MS 60	MS 62	MS 63	MS 64	MS 65	MS 66	MS 67	MS 68	MS 69
1921	NGC	32	10	87	273	709	355	81	3	0	0
1921	PCGS	79	14	154	438	809	430	73	2	0	0
1921	Combined	111	24	241	711	1518	785	154	5	0	0

Date	Service	AU 58	MS 60	MS 62	MS 63	MS 64	MS 65	MS 66	MS 67	MS 68	MS 69
1921 2X2	NGC	62	21	120	324	791	376	81	6	0	0
1921 2X2	PCGS	53	9	189	447	742	421	75	5	0	0
1921 2X2	Combined	115	30	309	771	1518	797	156	11	0	0

Circulated coinage should be acquired only for the joy of ownership. While the 2X2 is several times more difficult to locate than the available Plain specimen, it is fully priced and offers little chance of future advancement. The current price spreads between the MS-60 and MS-63 grades are somewhat undervalued. However, the real growth for this issue lies in coins properly graded strict MS-65+ and loftier: these are "sleepers," or future winners.

I would estimate that at least 29% of the MS-64 population figures can be safely deleted, because of crack outs and resubmissions. Grading labels were thrown away—in many cases—without concern for the importance of population accuracy: the hope of receiving a higher grade was all that mattered. During the last bull market, there was a $3,500 spread between MS-63 and MS-64 encapsulated coinage. How many times would you resubmit your coin, if you though it had a chance of making the next highest grade? I know of several individuals who sent in the same five Alabama Plains a total of 43 times. (One coin was granted higher status.) Strictly graded, eye-appealing MS-64 coinage for this issue is at present undervalued, and I highly recommend such coins to collectors.

Pieces rated MS-65 offer very good future potential; the 2X2 is slightly rarer in this grade. I would cut the given population figures for each issue by more than 26% because of resubmission and the thoughtless disposal of grading insert labels. I would stay away from dull or dark coinage, or material that causes one to exclaim, "How in the world can this unattractive coin be slabbed MS-65 or higher?"

In MS-66 condition, both issues are equally rare. However, with census figures as low as presented, either coin should be a thrill to own, and both have tremendous future potential. Very few pieces have been granted the lofty MS-67 rating: one of these would be a wonderful coin to own, should you have $25,300 to spend. That is what Lot 4141 in the Heritage Sale 366 sold for on February 26, 2005.

In August 2011 an MS-65 2X2 variety rated MS-65 sold for $28,750 in a Stacks/Bowers auction. Why? The issue rarely comes iridescently toned. Were it graded MS-67 I could justify the price. No Alabama issues have been graded higher than MS-67 to date.

Buyers should beware of anyone offering you, for many thousands of dollars, an unencapsulated or raw coin housed in a Lucite holder and described as grade MS-67. Chances are the piece can grade anywhere from circulated to MS-64 and be worth less than $1000. Trust only a coin slabbed by a major grading service, such as NGC or PCGS.

Reason for Issue:	To commemorate the 100th anniversary of the admission of Missouri into the Union.
Authorization:	Act of March 4, 1921, with a maximum of 250,000 pieces.
Issued by:	Missouri Centennial Committee
Official Sale Price:	$1

Production Figures

Date	Business Strikes	Assay Coins	Proofs	Melted	Net Mintage
1921 2★4	5,000	0	4?	0	5,000
1921 No 2★4	45,000	28	4?	29,600	15,400

Current Market Values

Date	AU-58	MS-60	MS-62	MS-63	MS-64	MS-65	MS-66
1921 No 2★4	$350	$550	$550	$800	$1,100	$2,800	$8,900+
1921 2★4	$550	$700	$700	$950	$1,200	$3,000	$9,800+

DESIGNS BY ROBERT I. AITKEN

Obverse

The bust of a frontiersman intended to represent Daniel Boone wearing a coon-skin cap and deerskin jacket, facing left. The centennial dates are in the coin's lower field. "UNITED STATES OF AMERICA" arcs above; "HALF DOLLAR" below. In the field of the low mintage variety above the "21" of "1821" is the incused 2★4, which indicates that Missouri was the 24th state to enter the Union.

Reverse

The standing figure of Daniel Boone or a frontiersman wearing a powder horn and holding a rifle with his right hand, while extending his left hand. Standing beside him is a Native American, wearing a war bonnet, holding a pipe and a shield. The 24 five-pointed stars signify again that Missouri was the 24th state to be admitted into the Union. Situated around the upper border is the inscription "MISSOURI CENTENNIAL"; the word "SEDALIA", the site of the Exposition and State Fair that took place August 8–20, 1921, is incused in the lower border. Robert Aitken, who designed the Panama–Pacific $50 gold piece as well as the 1935–1936 San Diego issue, has his initials (RA) incused in the lower right field near the rifle stock. "IN GOD WE TRUST", "LIBERTY", and "E PLURIBUS UNUM" were omitted from this issue, possibly because of the lack of space in the coin's field after the design was accepted.

Origins of the Missouri

The Philadelphia Mint struck a total of 50,028 Missouri 50-cent pieces in July 1921. Five thousand of the 2★4 variety were struck first. To save the expense of making new dies, the 2★4 was simply polished off the first working die and 45,000 pieces plus 28 assay coins without the special symbolic mark were produced. They were first distributed at $1 each, by the Sedalia Trust Company. Several pieces were shown at the August American Numismatic Association Convention in Boston that year.

The incused symbol was the idea of James T. Montgomery, Chairman of the Executive Committee of the Centennial Commission. His primary objective was to have 5,000 pieces struck, and then have the special mark removed. It was intended that these coins would produce enough profit to cover the model and die cost of $1,750.

```
                                    COPY
                            Medallic Art Company
                            137 East 29th St.
                            New York City
                                          Bill No.62126

        Sold to    Mr. James T. Montgomery, Chm.
                   Missouri Centennial Exp.
                   Sedalia, Mo.


        Hubs for the Missouri Centennial Half-Dollar        $250.00

        Expressage and packing                                1.63

                                                            251.63


        Date Shipped   6/29/21   to   U. S. Mint   via   Am Ry. Exp.
```

Invoice for Missouri Centennial hubs by the Medallic Art Company.

This issue was very popular with collectors, but sales eventually started to decline and not all of the larger mintage issue was sold: 29,600 "Plain" (No 2✶4) Missouri coins were returned to the Mint and melted, leaving the present net mintage figure for this issue of only 15,400 No 2✶4 coins. The Missouri was the second issue to depict the same person on both the obverse and the reverse. General Lafayette was the first example, on the 1900 Lafayette dollar.

The Missouri Today

Circulated examples of either coin in EF-AU condition will display some form of abuse, such as whizzing or polishing. Smart collectors attempt to locate coins whose surfaces may be worn, but that display no nasty scratches, digs, etc., and are un-doctored. The 2✶4 variety is the rarer issue in EF-AU through MS-65 condition. The incused symbol is responsible for the higher price tag. Any potential for future gains begin with eye-appealing MS-63+ coinage of either variety. The Missouri is a very popular collector coin, and in grade MS-64 is a wonderful, and rare, part of any collection. The 2✶4 variety was subjected to much numismatic abuse. Most of the No 2✶4 issue was also sold to non-collectors and heavily abused, making these coins almost equally rare in MS-65 condition. Luster will range from flashy, to brilliant (not the norm), to satiny, to dull satiny. The coin's original granular and irregular surface affects the luster.

Only a small percentage of the entire issue can be classified as sharply struck; the remainder are at best satisfactory. The vertical leather strap extending upwards from the powder horn will show definition approximately halfway up the left shoulder. Because of the shallow design definition and die wear, only the earliest strikes from the new dies will display the full leather strap. This will not affect the grade of most coins, nor does the slight flat area, caused by die wear. The flat area can appear grainy from the original planchet or coin blank surface.

Being struck first, the incused variety displays more definition. Detracting features, such as slide marks, small scratches, and cuts on the primary focal area (the face of the frontiersman) quickly eliminate many of these coins from the MS-64 and MS-65 grades. These same negatives will do likewise to the reverse primary focal location, the smooth-looking back of the frontiersman. Attempt to acquire strictly graded and appealing MS-64+ and higher material. Some pieces may exhibit a small planchet split on the edge, resulting from a flaw in the design and manufacture of the dies. This split can lower a coin's worth. To date no error coinage has entered the marketplace, except for a proof 2✶4—which is not an error. However, there is one slabbed PCGS PF-66 Missouri 2✶4 matte proof example.

Counterfeits of the No 2✶4 variety do exist. I have seen a few examples, which have proof-like to semi-proof-like surfaces, weakness of strike, and raised metal.

IS YOUR MISSOURI CIRCULATED OR MINT STATE?

Obverse
Wear will first be observed on the cheek of the frontiersman, as well as on his shoulder and on the hair behind his ear. Examine the cheek area for doctoring, in the form of whizzing, surface texturing, and light buffing. The rest of the coin can glow in the dark from originality: collectors beware.

Reverse
A metal loss will make its appearance on the left shoulder and upper arm of the frontiersman.

Related Material
No original mailing holders or official coin envelopes have surfaced to date. The 14 carat gold badge worn by chairman Montgomery sold for $4,000 in August 2003 at the Baltimore American Numismatic Association Convention. It is a very rare and desirable piece of commemorative history.

Extremely rare 14 carat gold badge worn by James T. Montgomery.

Future Potential of the Missouri Half Dollars

Population Figures

Date	Service	AU 58	MS 60	MS 62	MS 63	MS 64	MS 65	MS 66	MS 67	MS 68	MS 69
1921 2★4	NGC	30	0	93	299	835	243	50	0	0	0
1921 2★4	PCGS	63	9	170	410	775	275	24	0	0	0
1921 2★4	Combined	93	9	263	709	1610	518	74	0	0	0

Date	Service	AU 58	MS 60	MS 62	MS 63	MS 64	MS 65	MS 66	MS 67	MS 68	MS 69
1921	NGC	47	5	135	335	991	300	33	2	0	0
1921	PCGS	131	16	205	498	788	241	30	0	0	0
1921	Combined	178	21	340	833	1779	541	63	2	0	0

That excessively rare matte proof was submitted to NGC (PF-65), as well as PCGS (PF-66). The NGC grading label was finally returned, for census deletion. There is actually only one encapsulated proof coin.

Many of the circulated offerings will display some form of cleaning, whizzing, or polishing: collectors should pass on these pieces, unless the price is very right or all you want is a representative example of the Missouri issue. Flashy, un-doctored AU-55 and AU-58 pieces are more desirable. In grades EF-AU through MS-62, both coins are somewhat undervalued, and should be purchased only for the joy of ownership. The same applies to the borderline or unattractive MS-63 specimen. Very good to excellent future potential begins with pieces rated strict MS-65+. Alluring MS-64+ examples of each striking are worth much more than current levels. Average-looking pieces appear somewhat fully priced at present; these are coins that might look MS-65, but possess some detriment. They usually sell fast when offered at coin shows, unless the asking price is unjustly high.

Sometimes a seller believes he or she possesses more of a coin than they really do. I know of examples of both strikings that have been submitted more than 29 times each, in hopes of an upgrade. The labels were cast away. The past high spread between MS-64 and MS-65 No 2★4 and 2★4 rating was $10,000 and $12,000 respectively. I would reduce both population figures between 26% and 29%.

Any strictly graded MS-65 Missouri is a quite undervalued and wonderful commemorative to have as part of your collection, should you be able to afford it. The May 1989 price high between grades MS-65 and MS-66 was approximately $9,500 for each striking. The census can be reduced between 31% and 29% for each coin. There is very good future potential for these coins. In the loftier underrated MS-66 category, the issue is difficult to locate strictly graded. If you can afford the rating, buy it: there are tremendous possibilities for its owner.

1922 Grant Memorial

Reason for Issue:	The centenary of the birth of General Ulysses S. Grant, 18th President of the United States.
Authorization:	Act of February 2, 1922, with a maximum of 250,000 half dollars and 10,000 gold dollars.
Issued by:	U.S. Grant Centenary Memorial Commission
Official Sale Price:	1922 Half Dollar: $1 (later $1.50) 1922 No Star Half Dollar: $1 (later $0.75) 1922 Star $1: $3.50 1922 No Star $1: $3

Production Figures

Date	Business Strikes	Assay Coins	Proofs	Melted	Net Mintage
1922 ★ 50¢	5,006	6	4?	750	4,250
1922 50¢	95,055	55	4?	27,650	67,350
1922 ★ $1	5,016	16	4?	0	5,000
1922 $1	5,000	0	4?	0	5,000

Current Market Values

Date	AU-58	MS-61	MS-62	MS-63	MS-64	MS-65	MS-66	MS-67	MS-68
1922 ★ 50¢	$950	$1,175	$1,250	1,600	$2,800	$6,000	$9,000	$17,000	$35,000
1922 50¢	$100	$120	$145	$150	$200	$655	$1,100	$3,700	$8,000
1922 ★ $1	$1,370	$1,425	$1,475	$1,575	$1,600	$2,200	$2,500	$4,000	$12,000+
1922 $1	$1,370	$1,400	$1,450	$1,575	$1,600	$2,200	$2,600	$3,600	$12,000+

DESIGNS BY LAURA GARDIN FRASER

Obverse

Both gold and silver issues: the bust of General Ulysses S. Grant, in uniform, facing right; the image was adapted from a photo by Matthew Brady. Grant's name is in the left and right fields, divided by his portrait. Below the bust are the anniversary dates; "UNITED STATES OF AMERICA" arcs above; "HALF DOLLAR" or "ONE DOLLAR" below. A small letter "G," representing the artist's maiden name, was placed between the dates by the Mint, as was previously done in other locations with the Columbian and the Pilgrim issues. In the right field above the "N" of "GRANT" on the Star variety is the incused five-pointed star. The only difference in design between the issues is the word "HALF" and "ONE" indicating the denomination.

The President was born Hiram Ulysses Grant. In 1838, the congressman who appointed Grant to the U.S. Military Academy at West Point, New York, thought Ulysses was his first name and that his mother's family name (Simpson) was his middle name. Grant never corrected the error, because he knew he would be jested about his actual initials, "H.U.G."

Reverse

Both gold and silver issues: a fenced clapboard house symbolic of the house where Grant lived as a boy in Georgetown, Ohio. (He was born in Point Pleasant, Ohio, where he apparently lived until he was 11 months old—his autobiography says two years old.) Maple trees are shown in the coin's field, with "E PLURIBUS UNUM" to the left and "IN GOD WE TRUST" above. Laura Gardin Fraser (who also created the Alabama, Fort Vancouver, and Oregon Trail obverse) makes no reference to a Grant memorial in her design: the design itself tells the story. Her maiden initial (G) was used by the Mint, probably because her husband James Earle Fraser's initial (F) was placed on the Indian Head ("Buffalo") 5-cent piece, which was also being produced in 1922.

Origins of the Grant

The coins were struck at the Philadelphia Mint during March 1922. The first 5,000 gold coins (plus 16 for assay purposes) were struck with the "Star." After the star was removed, 5,000 gold dollars were struck (these are referred to as "No Star" dollars). With the gold production completed, 5,006 silver half dollars were produced with the Star. Then with the star removed 95,055 No Star half dollars were coined. Eight obverse and six reverse dies were used to make the silver issue. The U.S. Grant Centenary Memorial Commission suggested that a single star be placed on the gold dollar coin to earn extra funds. They were amazed to see a star was also added to 5,000 silver half dollars.

There is an obverse hub trial for the Grant Star half dollar issue, as well as die trial pieces struck in silver, copper, nickel, and brass. A reverse die trial was struck in silver, nickel, and white metal, and there were hub trials of the Grant Star gold dollar: obverse and reverse die trial pieces struck in copper and white metal. There is also a piece struck on a broad bronze planchet with an uneven impression; it is 23.20mm in diameter.

Does the incused star have any significance? Had Grant been a one-star general, the device might have been appropriate. However, Grant's rank in the Union Army requires three additional stars. In actuality, the star bears no significance, unlike the incused 2X2 on the Alabama variety and the 264 on the Missouri variety.

All coins were offered for sale in April 1922, with the silver half dollars selling at $1 each, and the No Star gold dollars selling at $3 each. The Star variety sold for $3.50. No gold coins were returned to the Mint. When silver sales, previously excellent, finally came to a standstill, the Memorial Commission decided to offer approximately 29,000 specimens of the No Star variety at 75 cents each in lots of 10 or more coins. About 800 unsold Star specimens were offered for sale at $1.25 each.

There were few buyers, thus 27,650 No Star specimens were returned, along with 750 Stars, to the Mint and melted. This leaves us with a present day mintage of 67,350 No Stars ("Grant Plains") and only 4,250 Star specimens.

The Grant Half Dollar Today

The Grant No Star half dollar is quite available in EF-AU condition. I suggest that collectors look for naturally worn, un-doctored pieces without detracting surface cuts. Most of these coins are in the MS-60 through MS-64 state. Surface attractiveness should be your key when deciding what to buy. The real future potential begins at the MS-65+ level; any lesser grade should be acquired only for the pure joy of collecting. Eye-appealing MS-66 and loftier rated specimens are not that easy to find.

Luster will range from blazing frosty (not the norm), to dull frosty, displaying a powdery look. Strike rarely presents a problem for this issue. The detail in Grant's hair, beginning from the temple area and going inward above the ear about 60 percent toward the back of the head will be faint. This was caused by the wearing of the obverse dies in that area as the coins were being struck, and because little detail was present to begin with. The faintness of hair detail is accepted as characteristic for the issue. (The same is not true for the small gold dollars: all hair details are visible in these coins.)

The rarer Grant Star issue, a very popular collector coin, can be obtained in EF-AU condition. Unfortunately, most pieces will display some form of surface doctoring, done in order to hide surface wear, bag marks, slide marks, etc. Grades MS-60 through MS-64 are scarce, and the coin is rare in the loftier classifications: this is the result of much numismatic abuse. Luster will range from semi-proof-like, to blazing lustrous (both not the norm), to dull satiny. One seldom sees blazing lustrous pieces. Strike will pose no problem for the issue. Early specimens with no die clash marks will show fine hair detail in the center of Grant's head, while coinage with the clash mark will not. Approximately 50 pieces were created before the dies clashed. Coins were produced from perfect, clashed, and lapped dies. The raised lines that can be observed in the obverse field are die polishing marks. If the lines cut into the surface, they become detracting scratches and lower the coin's value. To date, no error coinage has entered the marketplace.

Detecting Counterfeits

In 1935, when the Grant Star issue was selling for $65 and the Grant No Star for $3.50, a dentist decided to purchase a quantity of the less expensive issue and personally incuse his own star. Since we cannot appreciate his effort in attempting to make more Grant Star specimens—the highest priced of all U.S. commemorative issues in 1935—available to collectors and investors, we must be able to distinguish between the dentist's "addition" and the Philadelphia Mint's "edition."

The following distinguishing characteristics will help you determine whether the star is genuine:

An obvious clash mark will be present around Grant's chin and in the area of his necktie, and by the letter "G" of "GRANT", just to the right of his tie. Virtually all of the genuine issue will display these characteristics.

Those much rarer specimens produced before the dies clashed will not show these clash marks, but they will reveal a small raised pimple or lump of metal within the star just below the nine o'clock position. The lump can also be seen on the clashed die variety.

The star should be located above the letter "N" and not the letter "A" of "GRANT", as it is on some altered pieces. This coin is genuine.

Note the "little island" inside the star.

Fake star punched over letter "A" instead of over letter "N"

The "Dental Star" altered surface coin.

Because the star was added to this coin, it is correctly labelled as an "altered surface coin." While the coin is a genuine No Star issue, the star punched in by the dentist has created a counterfeit known in the trade as a "Dental Star" altered surface coin.

Is Your Grant Half Dollar Circulated or Mint State?

Obverse

Wear first occurs on Grant's cheekbone. The coin's rim does little to protect this area, which is virtually equal in height to the rim. The slightest abuse will cause friction, and collectors should look for a difference in metal texture in this location. The portrait is the primary focal area: marks and negatives are detrimental to value and grade here, and this is the prime target for whizzing and other forms of doctoring.

Reverse

The issue's rim does an excellent job of protecting the first area to display wear. This is the central section of leaves located directly above the second and third tree trunks from the left. If Grants do display wear, it will occur on the obverse.

Related Material

To date, no original mailing holders accompanied by stamped envelopes, or any other associated material, have surfaced.

Future Potential of the Grant Half Dollar

Population Figures

Date	Service	AU 58	MS 60	MS 62	MS 63	MS 64	MS 65	MS 66	MS 67	MS 68	MS 69
1922 No Star	NGC	67	2	207	638	1463	675	211	27	1	0
1922 No Star	PCGS	126	25	324	1005	1367	700	237	35	0	0
1922 No Star	Combined	193	27	531	1643	2830	1375	448	62	1	0

Date	Service	AU 58	MS 60	MS 62	MS 63	MS 64	MS 65	MS 66	MS 67	MS 68	MS 69
1922 Star	NGC	19	0	105	233	575	214	45	6	0	0
1922 Star	PCGS	48	15	127	341	446	149	31	4	0	0
1922 Star	Combined	67	15	232	574	1021	363	76	10	0	0

In circulated condition, the Grant No Star is available. Pieces exhibiting a small dot between the "22" of the date "1922" bring no premiums at present. The rarer Star issue is usually encountered whizzed or cleaned. These coins are worth less than the un-doctored coin's bid level. The higher mintage No Star is fairly priced in grades MS-60 through MS-64. During the May 1989 market high, there was an approximate $1,500 difference between the MS-64 and MS-65 grades. The higher grade coins will probably be promoted during the next upturn. I would reduce the MS-65 population figure between 20% to 25%. Any future potential begins with attractive flashy MS-64+ No Star pieces; certainly worth 25% to 50% over bid levels.

A strictly graded MS-65 Grant No Star is moderately undervalued, though reject dark, dull, and debatable coins. The past price spread between this category and MS-66 was $3,500. I would lower population figures by 15% to 22%. There is excellent future potential in the rarer MS-66 and MS-67 grades. Were a buyer to believe an auction offering can upgrade from an MS-67 to an MS-68, he or she will pay much more for the coin. Simply remember to pass if such a Grant No Star should cross your path claiming these lofty values, but doesn't look striking indeed.

Silver Grant Stars grading MS-60 through MS-62 are currently fairly priced. Good future potential really begins with those pieces grading MS-63 and higher. Collectors should prefer an attractive original un-dipped MS-63+ or MS-64 coin. The non-clash-mark variety can bring more money, but not always: all is dependent on the coin. I would lower the census between 26% and 30%. The 1989 price spread between MS-64 and MS-65 was a whopping $14,000, because so few had been encapsulated at the higher level.

This is a great coin to possess in MS-65 condition. Make sure you can see original surfaces if the coin you are examining is lightly toned. I would lower the census between 16% and 20%. There is excellent future potential for this, the rarest silver commemorative struck since 1892, in grades MS-64 and higher. In MS-66 condition we are talking about a rare item. I would reduce its population by 32%. What a great coin to have in one's collection. The very rare MS-67 and MS-68 ratings would be great coins to have in one's collection.

The Grant Gold Dollar Today

Specimens of either issue in the EF-AU state are not abundant. Based on their history, Grant gold dollars grading from MS-60 through MS-63 (either variety) should be considered only for the pure joy of collecting. The No Star is equally as rare in grades up to MS-64. Future value definitely lies in those strictly grading MS-65+ and better, with the No Star being more difficult to acquire. The present value spread does not reflect this situation because of the demand for either coin. This is the reason why most price guides list close to equal value for both issues in grades MS-64 and higher. No error coinage has yet entered the market scene.

Detecting Counterfeits

Die struck counterfeits do exist. The telltale signs to look for are file marks between "UNITED" and the rim, and die scratches above and between the "OF" and the first "A" in "OF AMERICA", on the reverse. Also, a number of spikes will angle into the field from the "P" of "PLURIBUS" halfway up to the "I" of "IN". Also look for depressions on the reverse fence. Cast fakes display a blurry or dull powdery appearance.

Related Material

To date, no original mailing holders accompanied by stamped envelopes, or any other associated material, have surfaced.

Future Potential of the Grant Gold Dollar

Population Figures

Date	Service	AU 58	MS 60	MS 62	MS 63	MS 64	MS 65	MS 66	MS 67	MS 68	MS 69
1922 No Star	NGC	23	2	84	117	288	257	262	100	4	0
1922 No Star	PCGS	49	8	123	296	541	441	392	120	0	0
1922 No Star	Combined	72	10	207	413	829	698	654	220	4	0

Date	Service	AU 58	MS 60	MS 62	MS 63	MS 64	MS 65	MS 66	MS 67	MS 68	MS 69
1922 Star	NGC	7	1	44	97	313	309	319	103	4	0
1922 Star	PCGS	25	7	48	218	573	503	585	224	1	0
1922 Star	Combined	32	8	92	315	896	812	904	327	5	0

When examining the entire commemorative production from 1892 through 1954, the most expensive coins available in about uncirculated (AU-58) condition (except for the $50 issue) are the Grant gold dollars ($1,425), followed by the $2.50 Pan–Pac ($1,375). There are silver issues such as the Hawaiian ($1,650) and Spanish Trail ($1,150) found in circulated condition that are worth more than all and most lightly worn gold issues respectively within the 11-piece gold commemorative set (2 Louisiana Purchase, 2 Louis & Clark, 2 Panama–Pacific, 2 McKinley Memorial, 2 Grant, 1 Sesquicentennial). During the 1989 market high, the price spread between MS-64 and MS-65 Grant gold dollars was approximately $3,300. I would lower population figures between 23% and 27%.

Grant No Stars grading MS-65 are undervalued at present levels; eye-appealing pieces offer very good future potential. Collectors should consider this variety as preferable to the Star. The difference in value between this and the MS-66 striking was approximately $6,100 during the 1989 high, but populations were much lower at that time.

There is a very good future for the No Star issue in the MS-66 category. Both Grants would have cost you $32,000+ in 1989. I warned against their purchase then because I was aware of too many small high-grade raw hoard pieces that would eventually increase populations and drastically lower values. I wouldn't mind owning one of the lofty MS-67 Grant No Stars—a wonderful coin, as is the MS-68. Collectors should just be certain to examine carefully Grant's portrait on these high-grade pieces.

1923 Monroe Doctrine Centennial

Reason for Issue:	The 100th anniversary of the announcing of the Monroe Doctrine.
Authorization:	Act of January 24, 1923, with a maximum of 300,000 pieces.
Issued by:	Los Angeles Clearing House representing backers of the First Annual American Historical Revue and Motion Picture Industry
Official Sale Price:	$1

Production Figures

Date	Business Strikes	Assay Coins	Proofs	Melted	Net Mintage
1923-S	274,000	77	4?	0	274,000

Current Market Values

Date	AU-58	MS-60	MS-63	MS-64	MS-65	MS-66	MS-67
1923-S	$62	$75	$125	$240	$1,400	$5,000	$13,000+

Designs by Chester Beach

Obverse

The accolated busts of James Monroe, fifth president, and John Quincy Adams, sixth president. Their names are seen directly below, separated by two links. "United States of America" arcs above; "Half Dollar" below. "In God We Trust" is in the left field, just below Monroe's chin. The date is to the right of Adams, with the Mint mark (S) directly below the date.

Reverse

A representation of the Western Hemisphere, depicted as two female figures: North America, holding a horn of plenty, is presenting South America with what appears to be a twig. Ocean currents are represented by faint lines in the field. The centennial dates are flanked by a scroll and quill pen, symbolic of the Monroe Doctrine manuscripts. "MONROE DOCTRINE CENTENNIAL" arcs above; at the four o'clock position is the artist's circular monogram (CB). In the lower border are the words "LOS ANGELES", the location of the centennial celebration. The design was copied from Ralph Beck's 1901 Pan-American Exposition medal, which he created in 1899 and copyrighted. (See the Related Material section for a photo of the badge.) Beck's claim of plagiarism on July 23, 1923 was rejected by the sculptor James Earle Fraser and the Mint. No lawsuit was initiated, since Beck's design had been used in different contexts during and after the Exposition (held in Buffalo, New York), by steamship and other major companies in the import and export trade.

Origins of the Monroe

The motion picture industry had had its share of bad press before 1923. To help clean up its image, a public film show, The American Historical Revue and Motion Picture Industry Exposition, was organized, and was sponsored by the film industry. The idea by some unknown individuals to have a commemorative coin struck as a revenue and publicity tie-in was set in motion. Political help was required, and to their aid came not a movie star, but Republican Representative Walter F. Lineberger of California. He introduced a bill that attempted to interpret how Monroe's declaration supposedly prevented Britain, France, and Russia from striving to acquire California from Mexico and that proposed to commemorate this event with a coin. (In point of fact, the U.S. at the time probably lacked the power as a nation to enforce the Doctrine.) Despite some opposition, the bill became law. The Los Angeles Clearing House, an association of local banks, received 274,000 commemorative halves of the 300,000-coin authorization from the San Francisco Mint. The coins were produced during the months of May and June 1923, along with 77 coins for assay purposes. Trial pieces exist in copper of both the obverse and reverse without the S Mint mark. Approximately 27,000 coins were sold at double face value through the banks and mail, for the most part, and at the Exposition. When sales came to a dead stop about four months later, the balance on hand was released into circulation.

The Monroe Today

This issue is quite abundant in EF-AU condition. Collectors should attempt to locate an attractive natural specimen: these are readily available up to MS-64 condition. The future lies in the MS-64+ eye-appealing coinage, and definitely in the higher grades if funds are available. Alluring virtual MS-65+ pieces with exceptional eye appeal and luster flash or blast can bring double the MS-65 value. This is the main reason why population figures for the grade are high—

the same coins are cracked out and submitted many times over in the hopes of an upgrade. You can bet that many of the grading insert labels were thrown away.

Luster will range from blazing frosty, to dull frosty. Because of the low relief reverse design, the reverse surface brightness may not be equal in flash to the obverse; strike can also affect grade and value. At times, the reverse design can be too soft or flat, lacking the face and head definition of the obverse. A coin lacking definition will grade no higher than MS-64. Detracting marks, such as fine hairline scratches, digs, cuts, etc., definitely have an effect, especially on this coin's smooth obverse surface. The primary focal areas are the portraits, especially Adams's face, and the reverse continents and fields. Beware of the whizzed or wire-brushed example with a bright aluminum lustrous look: they are worth EF-AU money, and no more.

Detecting Counterfeits

No error coinage or counterfeit pieces have surfaced to date.

Is Your Monroe Circulated or Mint State?

Obverse

A metal loss will first occur on the cheek of John Quincy Adams. His portrait is usually a target for the whizzing specialists in their attempt to hide wear or surface negatives.

Reverse

A loss of surface luster, then metal loss, will first be noticed on the arm of Miss North America.

Related Material

The issue was distributed in a small imprinted white envelope (which could be easily duplicated today), as well as in unprinted white envelopes. For the collector, the coin itself should be of first importance, as the envelopes carry little or no premium value. (See next page.)

Future Potential of the Monroe Half Dollar

Population Figures

Date	Service	AU 58	MS 60	MS 62	MS 63	MS 64	MS 65	MS 66	MS 67	MS 68	MS 69
1923 S	NGC	67	10	336	878	1523	352	53	7	1	0
1923 S	PCGS	140	28	451	1067	1452	363	54	4	0	0
1923 S	Combined	207	38	787	1945	2975	775	107	11	1	0

Badge medal - front.　　　　　Badge medal - reverse.

This is one of the most common commemoratives in circulated condition. In grades EF-AU through MS-64, it is fairly priced at present. The coin is not very popular, and collectors should buy only for the joy of ownership. Future potential lies in the flashy, underrated MS-64+ Monroe. The past high between this grade and the MS-65 category was a tremendous $7,000. I would lower population figures by 35% and 42%

In strict MS-65 condition, the coin is a very undervalued, as long as it is not one of those dull, dark, and questionable offerings. The May 1989 high between grades MS-65 and MS-66 was $4,500. The census can be lowered between 21% and 24%, and these grades have excellent future potential. The same applies to the very rare and undervalued MS-66 Monroe, which would be a great coin to possess, funds permitting. Likewise for the loftier grades such as MS-67: Lot number 1454, rated PCGS MS-67, sold for $29,900 at Heritage's sale 1128, July 31, 2009.

Reason for Issue:	To commemorate the 300th anniversary of the settling of New Netherland in 1624 by Walloon, French, and Belgian Huguenots, under the Dutch West India Company.
Authorization:	Act of February 26, 1923, with a maximum of 300,000 pieces.
Issued by:	Huguenot–Walloon New Netherland Commission
Official Sale Price:	$1 ($1.50 plus 2 cents postage in 1929)

Production Figures

Date	Business Strikes	Assay Coins	Proofs	Melted	Net Mintage
1924	142,000	80	4?	0	142,000

Current Market Values

Date	AU-58	MS-60	MS-63	MS-64	MS-65	MS-66	MS-67
1924	$120	$135	$165	$235	$390	$675	$2300

DESIGNS BY GEORGE T. MORGAN
(APPROVAL AND MODIFICATIONS BY JAMES EARLE FRASER)

Obverse

The accolated busts of two Protestant leaders of the Reformation, which occurred during the 16th century. Admiral Gaspard de Coligny of France and

William the Silent of the Netherlands, whose names appear below their respective busts, are seen facing right and wearing hats of their period. The Admiral has the letter "M" incused on his shoulder, which represents the surname of the designer, George T. Morgan. "HUGUENOT HALF DOLLAR" arcs around the lower border; "UNITED STATES OF AMERICA" arcs above; "IN GOD WE TRUST" is in four lines in the right field, in front of William the Silent's nose.

Reverse

The ship *Nieuw Nederlandt*, sailing to the left. Above the ship is the inscription "HUGUENOT–WALLOON TERCENTENARY" below the vessel, around the bottom border, is the inscription "FOUNDING OF NEW NETHERLAND". The anniversary date 1624 is in the left field, 1924 in the right.

Origins of the Huguenot–Walloon

This particular half dollar was supposed to commemorate an event, but instead it portrays two Protestant leaders of the Reformation who had really nothing to do with the actual founding of New Netherland, since both men died several decades before the Dutch West India Company (formed in 1621) and its colony became a reality. Their relationship with the 1624 founding was strictly spiritual in nature.

This coin also has the distinction of being promoted by the Federal Council of Churches of Christ in America through the Huguenot–Walloon New Netherland Commission. The American Numismatic Association President Moritz Wormser acted as its adviser of sales promotion, but several groups became disturbed and looked upon the issue as a carrying religious misinformation and being un-American.

The term Huguenot refers to the French Protestants who studied the teachings of John Calvin; the term Walloon to French Protestants who lived in southern Belgium.

During February to April 1924, the Philadelphia Mint struck 142,080 Huguenot–Walloon Tercentenary half dollars. Brass obverse and reverse die trials specimens are known to exist. These coins were later distributed through the Fifth National Bank of New York, which paid the Treasury 50 cents for each piece and offered them for sale at $1 per coin, as well as through other sources. According to Reverend John Bear Stoudt, the New Netherland Commission's director, 44,000 coins were sold by April 1, 1924. Of the total mintage, 87,080 coins were sold to the public, leaving a total of 55,000 unsold half dollars. They were returned to the Mint to be melted, but for some reason they were placed into circulation. Could it be that because this commemorative 50-cent piece was the only U.S. half dollar struck in 1924, someone in the Treasury Department said, "Let the collectors enjoy the coin at face value"? Bless him if he did.

The Huguenot–Walloon Today

The issue is not at all difficult to find in EF-AU condition. Simply beware of those new-looking pieces with portraits that have been doctored to hide metal loss. The bulk of the production is in MS-60 through MS-65 condition. Collectors should zero in on at least an eye-appealing, higher graded original coin, unless all that is needed is a representative example. Bag marks and other surface negatives keep many glamorous-looking coins from attaining higher grades. The primary focal areas are the obverse portraits and reverse ship. Luster will range from brilliant frosty to dull frosty. The reverse will display a die polishing mark in the upper field at the eleven o'clock position. A number of specimens will show what appears to be some type of damage, or scratches, on Coligny's cheek. This is actually a clash mark resembling the letter "V," with an additional vertical bar to the right. Strike will rarely affect the issue's value or grade. Slight die doubling can sometimes be observed on the letters "HUG" of "HUGUENOT" on the reverse.

Detecting Counterfeits

No error coinage or counterfeits are known to exist.

IS YOUR HUGUENOT–WALLOON CIRCULATED OR MINT STATE?

Obverse

A loss of metal will first be observed on the cheekbone, eyebrow, and mustache of Admiral Coligny. Collectors should look for doctoring in the form of whizzing, light buffing, etc., on this image.

Reverse

The coin's rim does an excellent job of protecting the shallower relief of the *Nieuw Nederlandt*. When wear makes itself known, it will begin on the center of the main mast, crow's nest, and rear supporting sail pole.

Related Material

No official distribution holders with accompanying mailing envelopes have surfaced to date. I have seen only a brochure depicting a sketch of a memorial stone and photo of the first coin struck being presented to President Calvin Coolidge. The brochure has sold for between $100 and $200, depending on condition.

Future Potential of the Huguenot–Walloon Half Dollar

Population Figures

Date	Service	AU 58	MS 60	MS 62	MS 63	MS 64	MS 65	MS 66	MS 67	MS 68	MS 69
1924	NGC	15	1	71	273	1335	998	294	41	0	0
1924	PCGS	54	11	188	800	1452	911	315	44	0	0
1924	Combined	69	12	259	1073	2787	1909	609	85	0	0

There is little price spread between coins grading EF-AU and MS-64. Coins graded from MS-60 through MS-64 are fairly valued, and should be acquired only for the joy of collecting. There is average future potential in attractive pieces rated MS-64+. During the market high of May 1989, there was a $2,600 spread between grades MS-64 and MS-65. I would reduce population figures between 22% and 24%. At current levels, MS-65 eye-appealing Huguenots are somewhat undervalued. The past value spread between this grade and MS-66 was $5,200. I would lower the census between 22% and 25%, and I expect these coins to be promoted during the next market upturn.

I have been questioned at coin conventions and on the phone as to the reasons why five of the same coins which have the same grade and are encapsulated by the two major grading services might bring an extreme variation of realized auction prices. There are a variety of reasons why a coin with a price guide value of $2100 might realize between $1800 and $4800. The full numismatic makeup of each coin translates into the value realized. The amount of outstanding, average or ugly eye-appeal, the flash displayed, how vibrant is the iridescent colors (if present)... How exceptional is the strike for the issue, the state of the market, as well as the number of bidders desiring the item. Even equally graded, which pieces can be classified as a low-end (B-), on grade (B), or hight-end (B+), and which might be candidates for an upgrade if resubmitted. Or perhaps, "What was the buyer thinking?"

At the August 2011 Chicago ANA Stacks/Bowers auction a buyer paid $34,500 for a PCGS MS-66+ Huguenot Walloon commemorative half dollar!! An MS-67 example brought $29,000!! The MS-66 market value range was $460–$750. MS-67 pieces have sold in a value range of $1400 to $2100. Why so much for the MS-66+ or M-S67 examples? The buyer believes the issue never comes with color. Thus, the prices paid.

To me, such is a "value anomaly." Several individuals wondered what the eventual owner(s) would receive when the coins are sold. Who knows? In my opinion, I'd have a hard time paying these prices or these pieces for my personal collection or for a client.

In MS-66 and MS-67 condition, Huguenots are definitely undervalued, and have excellent future potential for those who can afford these lofty grades.

1925 California Diamond Jubilee

Reason for Issue:	To commemorate the 75th anniversary of the admission of California into the Union.
Authorization:	Act of February 24, 1925, with a maximum of 300,000 pieces.
Issued by:	San Francisco Citizens' Committee
Official Sale Price:	$1

Production Figures

Date	Business Strikes	Assay Coins	Proofs	Melted	Net Mintage
1925-S	150,000	200	4?	63,606	86,394

Current Market Values

Date	AU-58	MS-60	MS-63	MS-64	MS-65	MS-66	MS-67	MS-68
1925-S	$180	$220	$295	$495	$925	$1,250	$2,000	$10,000

Designs by Joseph Mora

Obverse

A prospector kneeling to the left, working with a gold miner's pan in his quest for gold. This portrayal symbolizes the Gold Rush spirit, as well as the tremendous growth of California that took place after the discovery of gold. Above the prospector, who appears to be looking at "In God We Trust" in the left field, is the word "LIBERTY". Below are the words "CALIFORNIA DIAMOND JUBILEE" and the date of issue, 1925.

Reverse

A grizzly bear facing left, a symbol of California's independence from Mexico. Above the bear is "E PLURIBUS UNUM"; below is "UNITED STATES OF AMERICA". The Mint mark (S) appears at the six o'clock position, below the "D" in "HALF DOLLAR".

Origins of the California

One of my favorite numismatic works of art was created by Jo (Joseph Jacinto) Mora. This local sculptor was selected by the San Francisco Citizens' Committee, which was in charge of the 75th anniversary celebrations, held in September 1925. Mora's initial sketches were proudly forwarded by the Committee Chairman Angelo J. Rossi to U.S. Mint Director Robert J. Grant on May 4, 1925, and were eventually received by the sculptor member of the U.S. Commission of Fine Arts, James Earle Fraser. Unfortunately, Fraser was not impressed, labeling the drawings "inexperienced and amateurish."

He did suggest some improvements, but truly believed the work should be done by a competent medalist, such as Chester Beach or Robert Aitken, who had designed other commemorative coinage.

The Citizens' Committee was not swayed by the criticism, and ignored the recommended changes. The proposed medalist, Aitken, was rejected because of his fee. The design was accepted by Committee members, though one member, Louis Ayres, suggested "IN GOD WE TRUST" be placed in another position, "where it does not seem as if the 49ers were frying it in oil." The location remained unchanged, however.

Rossi was eager for a coin to commemorate the California Jubilee, and California Representative John Raker also wanted to help achieve this objective. Nevertheless, the Bureau of the Mint was directly opposed to additional keepsake production, and influenced the thinking of Representative Albert H. Vestal of the House Coinage Committee. On January 9, 1925 Senators Dale and Green introduced a bill calling for the creation of a Vermont gold dollar and 50-cent piece. By January 24, it was decided to eliminate the larger denomination. On February 16, Raker offered to amend their bill further, by authorizing the California souvenir coin. This bill was further amended by Representative Albert Johnson of Washington State, attempting to authorize production of the Fort Vancouver coinage. Authorization was signed by President Coolidge, whose boyhood home was in Plymouth Notch, Vermont. This is the first time a commemorative coin authorizing Act covered more than one issue.

Between August 12 and August 26, 1925, 150,200 pieces of the California Diamond Jubilee issue were produced at the San Francisco Mint. Obverse and reverse lead die trials were struck on an oversized lead octagonal planchet without the S Mint mark; a trial piece was also struck in silver with a reeded edge. They were offered for sale at $1 each by the San Francisco Clearing House Association and the Los Angeles Clearing House Association. The first coin struck was presented to the museum located in Golden Gate Park. Also, 494 coins were donated to children born on the Diamond Jubilee date (September 9, 1925).

Unfortunately, 63,606 pieces were returned to the Mint and destroyed. Rossi had requested that the San Francisco Mint produce 100 special presentation pieces, and he got his wish. One pair of dies had its fields polished to what we might label a bright, chrome-like reflectivity for the special striking, which took place on August 12, 1925. (These were not brilliant or satin finish proofs, just business strike presentation coins.)

The California Today

A large percentage of this issue is between the EF-AU and MS-65 categories. Today's circulated specimens were used as pocket pieces, or were lightly polished or cleaned to look bright and shiny. Another circumstance that removed many coins from the Mint State category is the issue's high relief. The bear's shoulder and the miner's upper shirt sleeve folds—the high points—are virtually as high as the protective rim. Even slight abuse will cause a rub or metal loss. Such coins can be lightly whizzed in these locations to dupe the unknowledgeable.

Most MS-60 through low-end MS-63 specimens that I have observed are less than beautiful, downgraded by bag marks, field abrasions, slide marks, reed marks, over dipping, etc. Collectors should pay close attention to the miner's back and shoulder, as well as the bear's shoulder or the near front leg and central portion of his body: these are the issue's primary focal areas. These negatives in combination or individually darken the future of affected coins. However, to the collector with limited funds or to the young numismatist, the thrill of ownership can register an MS-68 on the enjoyment meter; such pleasure is too precious to bear a price tag.

Coins grading MS-64, which can appear to grade MS-65 or better to the non-professional, can be located with some effort. Yet those grading MS-64+ are somewhat elusive. For the most part these would have been graded MS-65 in the past, but have been downgraded because of numismatic negatives that were once acceptable but no longer are.

Strictly graded MS-66 and MS-67 coins are undervalued.

Luster for the issue will range from proof-like, to a deep semi-mirrored surface, to chrome-like, to flashy, to dull satiny. Upon examination of the surface, one may detect a greater degree of mirroring on the 49er's side. The reverse design occupies more of the field, and there is thus less area to polish; this in turn offers a look of less intensity or a diminished luster.

Approximately the first 75 strikings will display various degrees of frosting (or cameo effect) on the devices. The effect was created by a surface roughness on the incused parts of the design which scatters or spreads the natural reflectivity of the metal. The die was not sandblasted to create this effect, as many have noted. After the 75 strikings, a flattening or smoothing or wearing down of these incused areas occurred, because of the cold metal flowing horizontally, to some extent, against the die surfaces. These areas now became polished, and the surfaces exhibit little field–device contrast. Overall, this creates a chrome-like, no-contrast silver coin.

A second pair of dies was used to strike additional coins, but was not prepared in the same manner, resulting in some satin finish specimens. The Mint mark of these coins is punched at a slightly different angle.

As far as strike is concerned, a small number of the chrome-like specimens will display excessive flatness on the bear's snout. This will influence the grade, as well as the value of such a coin. Weakness in the word "LIBERTY" and in the bear's near front leg can also affect a Jubilee's worth, depending on its degree of flatness and eye appeal. The same also applies to a weakness on the word "JUBILEE" and the date and reverse words on the "HALF DOLLAR". As noted, only a very small percentage of this issue is influenced by the weak strike.

Detecting Counterfeits

To date, no error coinage or counterfeit coinage has entered the marketplace.

IS YOUR CALIFORNIA CIRCULATED OR MINT STATE?

Obverse

A metal loss, indicated by a grayish-white metal texture, can first be observed on the 49er's upper shirt sleeve folds. This primary focal location is a target for the coin doctors.

Reverse

Because of the slightly higher reverse design, the slightest abuse will first cause a loss of high-point metal or wear on the bear's shoulder. Drop imaginary lines down from the letters "LU" of "PLURIBUS". Then draw a line about three times the width of the bear's ear. Where they intersect is the location collectors should inspect. This is also a primary focal location for doctoring.

Related Material

To date, I have come across no distribution holders. On occasion, a tricolored ribbon that was worn by members of the Coin Distribution Committee will surface. The ribbons are usually unaccompanied by the Jubilee half dollar, which was placed into a holder and initially attached to the ribbon. A ribbon's value is based on the accompanying coin. Without the coin, the ribbon alone should be worth $75 to $125. Two other vertical tricolor ribbons, one displaying the colors red, yellow, and green and the other green, red, and orange—with the gold stamping "Official Souvenir"—were accompanied by a copper medal. This depicted a prospector with pan, a city, and a bear at a cliff's edge. These ribbons sell for between $50 and $125, depending on condition.

A number of local businesses, such as pharmacies and department stores, attempted to help sales by offering the coin in cardboard holders. The cutout or slot for the coin was in the upper left corner. Usually the uncirculated coin is now replaced with an AU piece; value is dependent on the grade of the enclosed coin. Originally each coin was accompanied by a thin red and golden yellow informative flyer. An identical business address sticker (similar to a large mailing address label as received in the mail via some charitable institution) was placed on both the flyer and the coin holder ($250–$500).

Future Potential of the California Half Dollar

Population Figures

Date	Service	AU 58	MS 60	MS 62	MS 63	MS 64	MS 65	MS 66	MS 67	MS 68	MS 69
1925-S	NGC	99	99	180	560	1428	893	428	150	14	0
1925-S	PCGS	218	38	454	1106	1470	737	297	84	5	0
1925-S	Combined	317	137	634	1666	2898	1630	725	254	19	0

This popular issue exhibits a small price spread between the EF-AU and MS-63 ratings. These grades, as well as MS-63 coins, should be bought only for the joy of collecting. When possible, collectors should zero in on MS-64 coinage. During the past market high, the price spread between MS-64 and MS-65 coinage was almost $2,000. I would deduct approximately 17% from the census figures. A strictly graded MS-65 specimen is slightly undervalued at today levels. What drives prices down in an illiquid marketplace are the large numbers of unattractive and sometimes questionable MS-65 offerings. These are usually offered to novices or bargain hunters. These coins have very good potential, but only when the miner and bear have a stunning look.

During the high of late May 1989, there was almost a $3,000 spread between the MS-65 and MS-66 categories. I would lower population figures here by 18%. Pieces grading MS-66 are undervalued in today's coin world, and are recommended. If iridescent toning is present, that rainbow-like play of colors should look alive, and not as if the colors are trapped within a smoky surface. I would lower census figures for the grade between 20% and 25%. California Jubilees grading MS-67 and MS-68 offer excellent potential: they are highly recommended.

The first piece that had been slabbed MS-68 was an NGC rainbow-toned coin; it brought $8,337.50 at the Heritage July 2002 New York Signature Sale. The population has risen considerably since then.

Another MS-68 PCGS encapsulation brought $17,250 at the Heritage 2009 August Los Angeles coin auction (lot 1426). Again, price will vary depending on the coin offered for sale.

Beware of the satin finish proof offering—even if it is accompanied by a letter of authentication: in my judgment, they do not exist. I think such coins were produced from an obverse–reverse die combination that had just been placed into production. Extra striking pressure was employed (two blows were not applied). This, and the new die surface–planchet encounter, results in a coin with a different look. If such a coin was additionally fortunate enough to receive angelic protection against bag marks, etc., it will certainly appear captivating even to the astute. This allows it to be labeled what it never was meant to be. Collectors should consult the real experts, if uncertain.

1925 Fort Vancouver Centennial

Reason for Issue:	To commemorate the 100th anniversary of the founding of Fort Vancouver by the Hudson's Bay Company.
Authorization:	Act of February 24, 1925, with a maximum of 300,000 pieces.
Issued by:	Fort Vancouver Centennial Corporation
Official Sale Price:	$1

Production Figures

Date	Business Strikes	Assay Coins	Proofs	Melted	Net Mintage
1925	50,000	28	4?	35,034	14,966

Current Market Values

Date	AU-58	MS-60	MS-63	MS-64	MS-65	MS-66	MS-67	MS-68
1925	$300	$355	$410	$500	$1,050	$1,400	$4,000	$14,000

Designs by Laura Gardin Fraser

Designs based on original rough sketch by John T. Urquhart and plaster models by the sculptor Sydney Bell.

Obverse

The bust of Dr. John McLoughlin, the Hudson's Bay Company employee central to the founding of Fort Vancouver in what is now Washington State, facing left with his name beneath in curved letters. "UNITED STATES OF AMERICA" arcs above; "HALF DOLLAR" below. Split by the portrait are the anniversary dates 1825 and 1925, and "IN GOD / WE TRUST".

Reverse

A standing trapper in a buckskin suit holding a musket, facing right. In the background is Fort Vancouver with its defensive enclosure; in the distance is Mount Hood. The outer inscriptions read "VANCOUVER WASHINGTON FOUNDED 1825 BY HUDSON" and "FORT VANCOUVER CENTENNIAL". Below the stockade posts at the extreme right are the designer's initials (LGF). The Mint mark was unintentionally omitted, but all coins were struck at the San Francisco Mint.

Origins of the Fort Vancouver

John McLoughlin (1784–1857) was able to convince the native tribes in the area that he and his company intended no harm. If they wronged a white man, they were punished—and vice versa. The evil practice of "trading firewater to the Indians" was forbidden. In fact, McLoughlin was so just in his dealings that he was acknowledged by these Native Americans as their "Big Chief." The San Francisco Mint struck 50,000 Vancouvers, plus 28 assay coins on August 1, 1925. On the same day, 1,378 pounds of these coins were shipped by air aboard a 12-cylinder engine DeHavilland to Vancouver by Lt. Oakley G. Kelly, flight commander of the Vancouver Pearson Field Barracks. The coin was distributed by the Fort Vancouver Centennial Corporation at $1 each in August and September 1925. The Centennial Corporation's president, Herbert Campbell, presented Lt. Kelly (one of two pilots who made the first transcontinental non-stop flight in 1923) with the first coin from the delivered shipment. Likewise receiving coins at the small ceremony were Mayor N.E. Allen, Councilman O.W. Stone, and Donald Sterling, managing editor of the *Oregon Sunday Journal* in Portland, who accompanied Lt. Kelly on the 1,100-mile round trip.

Did a lack of sales destroy a dream and cause a suicide? Sales prior to and during the week-long Centennial celebration, which began on Monday, August 17, 1925, were not as brisk as expected. Five days later, Charles A. Watts, Secretary of the Fort Vancouver Centennial Corporation, committed suicide.

Why? Campbell, the editor and general manager of the *Evening Vancouver Columbian* in addition to his role with the Centennial Corporation, noted that "Mr. Watts was the real force behind the coin program. He was the Centennial. He loved the coin and the event. It could never be a failure. All corporation members simply lent their names and did what they were told to do. He was the real person in charge, who had plans for a big follow-up campaign on coin selling and other means of producing revenue. He was most respected."

Unfortunately, fate dealt him a cruel blow. On August 24, during a Centennial Corporation meeting, Campbell informed all present that "the late Charley Watts had told us that Mrs. Laura Gardin Fraser, creator of the Vancouver coin design, was previously paid $1,200 for her services. Funds were derived from the stock subscriptions and not from the revenues. He also told us the night before his death that we were over the top, with enough funds in sight to pay all bills."

Sadly, this was not the case. Fraser had yet to be paid. In fact, she sought help in obtaining payment—even in souvenir coins at face value from the Centennial Corporation and through her Washington connections. (What a deal: by early 1929, the coin was offered at $10 each.) She was paid almost a year later by check.

Concerning the Centennial Corporation's accounts payable, including Fraser's, it was discovered by Lloyd DuBois, Watts's administrator, that the unpaid bills amounted to $6,000, with no funds to pay them.

One might ask why the Centennial Corporation did not sell the coins on hand and pay all involved? The answer to this question is that the Corporation did not own any coins.

The Vancouver National Bank advanced the money for the commemorative half dollars and took them as collateral, advancing what coins were needed during the selling campaign. In total, 14,966 pieces were sold. By late October, sales came to a standstill.

According to George Palmer, cashier of the bank and secretary-treasurer of the Centennial Corporation, the coin dealer B. Max Mehl made an offer to buy all 35,034 unsold coins held by the bank, at face value, in lieu of their return to the Mint for melting. The offer was rejected, since many people previously paid $1 for their souvenir. Thus, 35,034 specimens were returned for reincarnation into some other coinage.

It has recently been discovered that while on a visit to the Pacific Coast in August 1926, Governor Charles Sale of the Hudson's Bay Company purchased 1,000 of these coins. They were shipped to the Provincial Archives Building in Winnipeg, Manitoba, in 1974. These coins were stolen between August 1 and September 1, 1982, by a caretaker. A civil law suit was filed by the Province of Manitoba, in connection with the theft and sale of 568 Vancouver commemorative half dollars. More than 400 coins, each with a minimum numismatic value of at least $800, were allegedly spent at face value over a short period of time by the person who stole them. According to the Canadian dealer who handled the remainder of these coins, most would not grade MS-65 by today's standards. He personally sold 522 pieces to third parties in the United States and Canada and held about 46 pieces, before the problems with the government materialized. For the record, he did check with the FBI and the Royal Canadian Mounted Police, who reported at the time that there existed no record of these coins being stolen.

The theft was not discovered by the Archives until January 28, 1983, when inventory was taken. Supposedly needing money to buy a used car, the thief took the remaining 568 to a bank. There they were exchanged by a Winnipeg bank teller at face value, or $284 in Canadian paper funds. The teller then received permission from her supervisor to purchase the lot from the bank at face value. The pieces were counted via a counting machine. In turn, she sold them to a Canadian dealer for $37,500. The dealer presented a written statement of information to the police department, particularizing the transaction. Clearance was received after several weeks. Nevertheless, the Province of Manitoba filed suit against all involved, even though all proper procedures were followed. In the end, the dealer's 46 pieces were returned to him and settlements were made. Manitoba made no effort to reclaim those pieces sold in the United States.

The Fort Vancouver Today

Specimens in the EF-AU category for the most part will display some form of numismatic abuse. Depending on one's current financial situation, I would suggest locating a coin that shows most of its original surface and possesses slight wear. That is unless you require a representative example only. Specimens grading MS-60 through MS-65 are not that difficult to locate at present. Since value spread between MS-63 and MS-64 is not that great, consider a flashy eye-appealing MS-64+ or a higher graded specimen, if possible.

During the 1989 market high, the price variation in grades MS-63 and MS-64 was $400; between the MS-64 and MS-65 ratings it was a whopping $3,300. That now seems too great. Between the MS-65 and MS-66 categories, it was a lesser $2,800: this figure may come back at the next upturn. I would lower census figures by 20% to 26% for the MS-64 and MS-65 grades and by 17% to 24% for the MS-66 class. This is an excellent issue to have in one's collection, especially rated MS-66 and higher. Depending on the coin's eye appeal and possible upgrade, examples have brought between $4,000 and $7,800.

Luster will range from an almost semi-proof-like satiny, blazing satiny, to satiny, to dull satiny. Strike weakness, especially on the reverse trapper's hands, face, right thigh, and chest, will be seen on a small percentage of this issue, and may cause a grade-value lowering.

The primary focal areas are the obverse portrait (then surrounding fields) and the reverse trapper, then Mount Hood. Numismatic negatives, such as abrasions, nicks, cuts, hairlines, slide marks, and bag marks, plague McLoughlin and his clean fields. The reverse trapper should not appear to have been shot by some weapon, nor be flatly struck, though do not be overly concerned if the leather powder horn strap is not fully visible. Only the earlier strikings will display good definition in the strap. Do, however, expect to see a series of raised die chip marks; their irregular pattern extends from the peak of Mount Hood, to the letter "C" in "CENTENNIAL".

Detecting Counterfeits

Counterfeits were made for this issue, and can be recognized from numerous surface depressions. One certain indication is one nose's length in front of

McLoughlin's nose, just above the tip of this area. Another is directly below and to the right of the "O" in "GOD", as well as above the "1" of the date 1825.

Tooling marks below the "CEN" of the word "CENTENNIAL" make their presence known on the reverse. A circular depression can be seen close to the foot of Mount Hood. Making a straight line, starting at the one o'clock position of the "O" in the word "FORT", go right to see the marks. Also semicircular striations will be seen starting at the base of the right stockade section and continuing upward over the buildings within.

IS YOUR FORT VANCOUVER CIRCULATED OR MINT STATE?

Obverse

Look for signs of wear on the hair covering McLoughlin's temple area and on the hair that covers the top of his ear, as well as on his cheekbone. This portrait is the prime location for the coin doctors.

Reverse

Any loss of metal will be noted on the actual right knee of the pioneer (to the left as you view the coin). Beware of light buffing, polishing, or whizzing in this location.

Related Material

To date no special distribution material has surfaced.

Future Potential of the Fort Vancouver Half Dollar

Population Figures

Date	Service	AU 58	MS 60	MS 62	MS 63	MS 64	MS 65	MS 66	MS 67	MS 68	MS 69
1925-S	NGC	15	0	82	260	789	575	261	49	1	0
1925-S	PCGS	66	10	198	690	941	673	280	45	1	0
1925-S	Combined	81	10	280	950	1730	1248	541	94	2	0

Most circulated offerings of this issue are usually seen whizzed, polished, or abused. Collectors should look for an un-doctored and attractive piece. The coin is at present fairly priced in all Mint State grades up to MS-64. Populations have risen to levels that make it somewhat overvalued at MS-65. The real future is now in the MS-66 and MS-67 categories. At the January 2011 Tampa FUN Heritage auction (Lot #5704) an MS-68 PCGS encapsulation housing an iridescent Vancouver brought $14,950.

1925 Lexington–Concord Sesquicentennial

Reason for Issue:	To commemorate the 150th anniversary of the battle of Lexington and Concord, Massachusetts.
Authorization:	Act of January 14, 1925, with a maximum of 300,000 pieces.
Issued by:	United States Lexington–Concord Sesquicentennial Commission
Official Sale Price:	$1

Production Figures

Date	Business Strikes	Assay Coins	Proofs	Melted	Net Mintage
1925	162,000	99	4?	86	161,914

Current Market Values

Date	AU-58	MS-60	MS-63	MS-64	MS-65	MS-66	MS-67
1925	$88	$98	$115	$185	$650	$1,375	$6,000

Designs by Chester Beach

Obverse

The statue of the famous Minute Man in Concord, Massachusetts, seen holding a musket. In the lower right field is a plow with the Minute Man's coat hanging from the handles. The image was adapted from Daniel Chester French's statue. The inscriptions "United States of America" and "Patriot Half Dollar" separated by two decorative stars are seen in the outer field. In the lower left field are the words "Concord Minute-Man"; in the upper right field is "In God We Trust".

Reverse

The Old Belfry in Lexington, Massachusetts; this housed the bell that sounded the call to arms. Originally built on its present site in 1762, the Old Belfry was moved to Battle Green in 1768. It was destroyed in 1909 and a replica was constructed in 1910. Beneath are the words "Old Belfry, Lexington", with two triangles at the sides. Around the outer border are the inscription "Lexington–Concord Sesquicentennial" and anniversary dates 1775–1925.

Origins of the Lexington

The Philadelphia Mint produced 162,000 coins of this design during the months of May and June 1925. Only 86 were returned to the Mint to be melted. Celebrations occurred between April 18 and 20, during which 38,000+ and 20,000+ specimens were sold in Lexington and Concord respectively.

The Lexington Today

The issue is abundant in EF-AU condition, since many pieces were treated as souvenirs. There is no major value spread between the circulated coins and specimens grading up to MS-64. The Lexington is not that easy to obtain in strict MS-66 condition. No sign of wear should be present on the thigh of the Minute Man, or on the left corner section of the Old Belfry to the left of the door. I have seen pieces showing some metal loss graded MS-65. Collectors should be alert.

The primary focal areas are the Minute Man and the belfry. However, a dig or reed mark in the surrounding fields can easily cause a value downgrade, as can a long hairline scratch or scratches. Luster will range from semi-proof-like, to brilliant frosty, to dull frosty. Strike rarely causes a loss in grade or value. Because of slight die wear, the Minute Man can display soft design definition from the waist up.

Detecting Counterfeits

No error coinage or counterfeit pieces are known.

Is Your Lexington Circulated or Mint State?

Obverse

Metal loss will first be visible on the thigh of the Minute Man, adjacent to his rifle. Collectors should examine the high points for some form of doctoring.

Reverse

Examine the lower corner of the belfry, directly above the "R" in "Belfry" and parallel to the left door frame for metal loss, visible in a dull grayish white appearance. The coin's rim is virtually equal in height to the higher area of its design, and at the slightest abuse wear becomes noticeable. You should ascertain whether or not beneath the "luster loss" is actual metal loss.

Related Material

The Lexington was distributed in a small wooden box with a sliding top. The box bears a blue ink stamping of the Minute Man statue plus the anniversary dates. The Old Belfry is illustrated on the bottom section of the most common coin holder. Often a coin possessing some degree of wear, hidden by dark toning, accompanies the pine box. The asking price is usually twice as much as such an item is worth. The value should be based on the grade and eye appeal of the coin, as well as the condition of the holder. Exceptions must be made if the commemorative holder for the issue is rare. Unofficial copies of the Lexington box exist, manufactured from a different type of wood. Also, one of the anniversary dates, 1775 or 1925, will be lightly stamped on, but not into, the top cover. The secret is to know the features of pine. Several banks distributed the issue in their own imprinted boxes (as the Second National Bank of Boston), as well as in flamboyant mailing envelopes: these are not often seen.

The wooden boxes may be valued at $20 to $100 without the coin, depending on condition.

Future Potential of the Lexington Half Dollar

Population Figures

To date, one Lexington specimen has been graded MS-68.

Date	Service	AU 58	MS 60	MS 62	MS 63	MS 64	MS 65	MS 66	MS 67	MS 68	MS 69
1925	NGC	99	0	163	590	1778	865	208	14	0	0
1925	PCGS	87	27	305	1052	1758	938	278	8	1	0
1925	Combined	216	27	468	1642	3536	1808	586	22	1	0

This coin is not difficult to locate in circulated condition. Try to buy an undoctored, attractive coin with original surfaces. There is only a small price difference between grades EF-AU and MS-64. Avoid dull or dark coins and borderline MS-64 or low-end pieces for the grade, should a future profit be part of your objective.

The price variation between MS-64 and MS-65, during the May 1989 high was $1,900. Some very flashy coins with half-inch hairline scratches in the field should not be graded MS-65, though many of this type were constantly resubmitted. I would lower population figures between 27% and 31%.

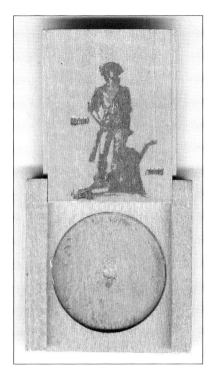 

Wooden box—front.   Wooden box—back.

Strictly graded, eye-appealing MS-66 Lexingtons are undervalued at cur-rent levels. At present, the abundance of unattractive and questionable coins in the marketplace is driving the issue's value downward, and the nicer pieces into hiding. The dollar difference between the MS-65 and MS-66 rating was a whopping $4,500 during the market high. I would reduce the census by 22% to 25%. This is a popular coin and can be elusive in MS-66+ condition; I would lower the census between 15% and 23%. There is a wonderful future for this undervalued coin. To date 22 Lexingtons have been granted MS-67 status. I would re-examine one of them for grade lowering because of surface negatives in the reverse field. A single coin has been rated MS-68. This PCGS coin sold in Heratige's 2005 Long Beach auction for $69,000! Should another Lexington be granted this lofty grade, review the section on coin pricing nd those factors involved in giving the said coin its worth.

1925 Norse American Medals

Production Figures

Date	Business Strikes	Assay Coins	Proofs	Melted	Net Mintage
1925 Thick	33,750	Unknown	0	0	33,750
1925 Thin	6,000	Unknown	0	0	6,000
1925 Gold	0	Unknown	100	53	47
1925 2 5/8 Inch Copper/Bronze	Approximately 75 struck known	Unknown	0	0	Approximately 75 struck known

Current Market Values

Date	AU-58	MS-62	MS-63	MS-64	MS-65	MS-66	MS-67
1925 Thick	$115	$160	$345	$425	$480	$850	$3,000
1925 Thin	$130	$225	$350	$575	$575	$3,150	$5,000
1925 Gold	$7,000	$10,000	$15,000	$20,000	$25,000	$30,000	$40,000
1925 2 5/8 Inch Copper/Bronze					$3,000		

How did the Medals Become a Reality?

An individual very proud of his Norse descent wanted to contribute to U.S. recognition of its Norse heritage, as well as having an important Norse American centennial remembered—preserved "in metal" and in "paper time capsules." The individual's name was O. J. (Ole Juulson) Kvale (1869–1929), a Congressman from Minneapolis and a member of the Coins, Weights and Measures Committee.

On February 3, 1925, accompanied by his son, Congressman Kvale visited his friends in the Treasury Department in order to present the first draft of his bill, which was to be introduced the following day, authorizing the Secretary of the Treasury to prepare and issue silver medals commemorating the Norse American Centennial. During the discussion it was immediately pointed out that objections would be raised over the production of a round medal because of its size, between that of the quarter and the half dollar. Acting Mint Director Ms. M. M. O'Reilly, present at the meeting, indicated that the only alternative would be to strike a round medal that was larger, thicker, and heavier than a silver dollar.

At this point the Congressman's son suggested the medal be made octagonal or hexagonal. Both Ms. O'Reilly and Under-Secretary of the Treasury Garrad Winston immediately loved the idea.

During the day the Congressman also spoke to legal representatives in the House Legislative Drafting Service and the legal counsel in the Treasury to be certain the bill would contain no "imperfections" that would cause later troubles. Shortly thereafter he was informed that the Treasury Department would assure him—from the beginning—of all the possible cooperation to help him make his goal a reality.

All silver used to strike these medals was to be advanced by the government from its supply at the Mint, thus relieving the Norse American Centennial Commission from the necessity of purchasing silver in the open market. Its cost would represent only production (up to a maximum of 40,000 medals) and die-making. But why wasn't a commemorative coin struck instead of a medal? Looking back to 1925, we note that Congress authorized six commemorative issues:

The Lexington–Concord Sesquicentennial half dollar	January 14
The Fort Vancouver Centennial half dollar	February 24
The California Diamond Jubilee half dollar	February 24
The Vermont–Bennington half dollar	February 24
The Sesquicentennial of American Independence half dollar and $2.50 gold issues	March 3

Kvale and the others were aware of the agitation concerning the Huguenot–Walloon Tercentenary half dollar of 1924. It was labeled a vehicle for religious propaganda, un-American, and unsuitable for U.S. coinage: Kvale knew that striking a special coin was impossible because of the current attitudes of Congress and the Treasury Department. There could be no commemorative coin honoring the arrival of the first shipload of Norse immigrants, so a medal and not a coin was produced.

Why were the Norse Medals Struck?

On March 2, 1925, one day before the Sesquicentennial coin was approved, Congress authorized the production of a maximum 40,000 octagonal medals by the Philadelphia Mint for the Norse American Centennial celebrations. These were to be minted to preserve remembrance of the arrival in New York (Orleans County), on October 9, 1825, of the first group of Norse immigrants to America, on board the sloop *Restaurationen*. Festivities were to take place at the Minnesota State Fair Grounds between June 6 and June 9, 1925.

Who Created This Issue?

In search for a well-known designer, Kvale had hoped his friend Senator Henrik Shipstead would be able to contact Gutzon Borglum, creator of the Stone Mountain half dollar, and request his services for a nominal fee—or even gratis. The famous sculptor, who was to leave the Stone Mountain project to carve the gigantic heads of presidents Washington, Jefferson, Theodore Roosevelt, and Lincoln on Mount Rushmore, South Dakota, was just too busy.

Since time was of the essence, James Earle Fraser, husband of the famous designer Laura Gardin Fraser, sculptor and member of the U.S. Commission of Fine Arts, was asked to do the honors. The Frasers later prepared the designs for the Oregon Trail half dollars: these are considered among the finest in the commemorative series.

On the reverse the medals are signed "Opus [work of] Fraser" Examining the die and designing costs incurred by the Centennial, I am of the strong opinion that Mr. Fraser was paid $1,500 for his efforts. Collectors should bear in mind that Fraser's wife was paid $1,200 for the creation of the Fort Vancouver half dollar issue of 1925. My research indicates that this was the kind of fee charged by a top designer when creating a coin design.

The *Minneapolis Journal* on March 29, 1925 presented a sketch of the Norse medal. Some objected that Americans might get the impression that the Norsemen in 1825 still dressed like Vikings. Others felt the date AD 1000 or Vinland 1000 should be located below the Viking pictured on the obverse, thus indicating the proper time period. However, these objections had no effect on the planned design.

Orders for the Norse issue—which was as yet to be struck by the Mint—started to arrive at the Centennial Commission's Medal Department, 11 Washington Ave. S., Minneapolis, in late April. Silver Thick specimens were offered first, at $1.25 each. Rules stated that no customer was permitted to purchase more than one. However, buyers could order for all "500" people in their family, if they wanted to, via an individual order for each medal. It was also made known that this could be the only method of acquisition, for none were to be offered at the celebrations or delivered in person at the time of purchase. This procedure allowed an exact record to be kept of what was sold, and to have postal receipts for each sale.

As an added incentive to purchase the medal, it was made known that they would become more valuable as time passed because the Norse American was the first medal authorized by the Congress of the United States. Actually, this is not true—as the Centennial Commission was later to discover.

Are there Round Die Trial Pieces for This Issue?

A letter sent by Ms. O'Reilly to Charles Moore, chairman of the U.S. Commission of Fine Arts, dated April 14, 1925, was accompanied by one "round" obverse and one "round" reverse or uniface trial strikings of the Norse, issue struck in copper.

The strikings were received and approved on the following day (April 15); the only suggestions from the Commission of Fine Arts was that the article "the" be removed from the reverse inscription before the word "Congress". It originally read "AUTHORIZED BY THE CONGRESS OF THE UNITED STATES OF AMERICA". Such a phrase would never be used in writing or speaking, and it was changed.

There is no record in the National Archives of the corrected die trial piece or round copper uniface specimen, but this piece was officially made. It measures 3.6cm x 3.6cm with a .2cm thickness or almost 1½ inches wide with a 1/16-inch thickness. Thus we may conclude that there are one round obverse die trial piece—since the medal's obverse was approved—and two round reverse trial pieces, with and without the article "the" as mentioned above, struck in copper.

Copper trial pieces.

The Issue's Symbolism and its Interpretation

Observing this medal's obverse, we can see a full-length figure of a Norwegian Viking chieftain who has left his ship and has just come ashore on the American continent. He is depicted in his full fighting regalia, which consist of a horned helmet, breastplate, *svard* or dagger, sword (in right hand), and battle shield (in left hand).

Actually, the protective head covering was not worn in battle. Recent studies reveal that the horned helmet was only ceremonial in nature and used more than 3,000 years ago during the Bronze Age. Most likely, it was worn by one who was thought to possess supernatural powers for healing and invoking spirits—a kind of medicine man.

The Vikings, who are also called Norsemen, were seafaring warriors who raided and colonized wide areas of Europe from the 9th to the 11th centuries. Their disruptive influence was to have a profound effect on European history. These pagan Danish, Swedish, and Norwegian warriors undertook such raids because of many factors, ranging from overpopulation at home to the relative helplessness of their victims abroad—especially the Irish monks, who recorded the acts of the Vikings.

One might now question the reasoning behind the portrayal of the Viking on this issue. Would not a figure of Leif Ericson, the 11th-century Norse explorer who is said to be the first European to set foot on the American continent at a place called Vinland (and "without a horned helmet") be a more appropriate choice?

This was not how Kvale saw things: he was interested in pure romanticization. He saw a Viking ship and its chieftain in full fighting gear. Located in the upper field is the inscription "NORSE AMERICAN CENTENNIAL" with the dates 1825–1925 separated by the figure.

In 1824 the "pioneer pathfinder" Kleng Peerson presented glowing accounts of the possibilities to be realized in America, based on his trip there. Inspired by Peerson's enthusiasm for the country, Norse-immigrant traders and farmers arrived in New York the following year on the *Restaurationen*; they were the first of many to journey westward over the years.

This issue's reverse does not portray the *Restaurationen*, but a Viking ship with full crew at sea, Above in the Congressional inscription. In the lower field is the date AD 1000, indicating the approximate date Leif Ericson landed at Vinland. "OPUS FRASER" is near the eight o'clock position.

What are the Mintage Figures for the Norse Issues?

It appears that the Philadelphia Mint struck this issue in the early part of May 1925. Records indicate that 39,850 silver pieces in total were struck—like ordinary business strikings—then counted, bagged, and shipped to the Fourth Street National Bank of Philadelphia for the Centennial Commission. (Included in this figure were the gold medals.)

The totals were:

- 33,750 pieces struck on a thick octagonal silver planchet; 3.0cm × 2.9cm (diameter) with a 0.2cm thickness or a 1 ¼-inch medal with a 1/16-inch thickness; production dates: May 29; June 1–6; and June 8–13, 1925.
- 6,000 pieces struck on a thin octagonal silver planchet; 3.0cm × 2.9cm (diameter) with an approximate 1.6cm thickness or a 1¼-inch medal with a 1/20-inch thickness; production dates: May 21, 2,000 pieces; May 22, 3,000 pieces; and May 23, 1,000 pieces.
- 100 matte proof pieces struck twice on a .900 fine octagonal gold planchet. 2.45cm × 2.4cm (diameter) with an approximate 0.2cm thickness or just short of 1 inch wide with a 1/16-inch thickness. Production dates: June 3–4, 1925.
- 75 pieces were struck approximately seven months later on a copper-bronze planchet; 6.95cm × 6.7cm (diameter) with a .45cm thickness or a 2 5/8-inch wide medal with almost a ¼-inch thickness; production dates: after November 27, 1925.

Note: A copper version of the gold medal, most likely a trial piece, was graded MS-63 Brown (i.e, with a brown patina) by NGC.

In early October 1925, it was learned that the Norse medals were not the first to be authorized by Congress, as claimed by the Centennial publicity committee. Kvale was informed by Mint Director Robert J. Grant that a medal issued for the American Centennial, which took place in Philadelphia in 1876, was the first. Kvale was now to discover further that this medal was also produced in different sizes.

The larger size intrigued Kvale. Immediately he informed the Secretary of the Centennial Commission, Mr. J. A. Holvik, that he believed 50 three-inch bronze medals should also be struck, for it would show the detail more clearly—especially in display cases in museums and other institutions. In fact, Kvale said he would purchase all the medals—at cost—in the event they were not sold

Large-size Norse bronze medal.

after July 1, 1926. Holvik was against this idea and would vote accordingly. But since all other members of the Cenntennial Commission board were in favor of the new medal, Holvik changed his mind. According to his papers, he hoped this was the last phase of the medal situation. On November 27, 1925 the board authorized Kvale to make the "bronze" a reality.

Seventy-five copper-bronze medals and not 50 were struck, most likely in December by the Philadelphia Mint. (Some numismatists believe that only 60 were produced.) However, for reasons known only to Kvale, possibly all of the medals were silver triple plated outside the Mint by a private firm in Washington. Could it be that silver looks more prestigious than bronze? Thirty pieces were presented or mailed to official guests from Norway, who attended the later celebrations, as well as to President Coolidge. This was probably the reason as to why 75 medals were struck. Should silver dip (a liquid that removes tarnish from silver) be used several times and rubbed against that plated metal, expect it to vanish in part from the surface, exposing a little bronze.

The Centennial received the following medals from the Mint at cost:

- Silver Thick at $0.45 each
- Silver Thin at $0.30 each
- Gold at $10.14 each

The Thick was sold for $1.25 or almost three times cost. No information is available as yet on the Thin's selling price, but I would estimate $1.75. The reason why a thin blank was struck also remains elusive. Max E. Brasile of Jackson, Michigan, remembers purchasing the gold specimen from the Centennial for about $20 back in 1925.

First strikings of the silver and gold medals were retained by the Centennial Commission. Kvale was presented Gold Medal #2, or the second piece struck, in appreciation of his services; George L. Croker, W. J. Clark, and J. Carmichael were presented with Gold Medals #3 through #5, respectively, in appreciation of courtesies extended the Centennial.

As of July 31, 1925, 7,697 Norse Thicks were sold, leaving 26,053 pieces in stock, as well as 53 gold specimens, plus the entire 6,000 Norse Thins—which were not offered for sale until November or December. They were reportedly sold out to non-collectors (*The Numismatist*, June 1933).

By October 14, 1925 Holvik expressed his lack of understanding as to why few "Norsemen" purchased the medal. He believed it was possibly the delay in obtaining the medals from the Mint: when the medals finally did arrive, the initial interest might have been lost. Or was it that the price was too high?

According to a letter published in the June 1933 issue of *The Numismatist* (page 397), all unsold medals were called in by the Centennial Committee. The result, according to Treasurer Lars O. Haugh, was the return of 2,000 Thick pieces from a Chicago bank as well as a few Thins—all of which were then in his possession. Possibly these 2,000 Thick pieces were returned to the Mint and melted, leaving us with a total mintage of 31,750 eventually sold. Additional research will confirm this. Since the Centennial Corporation owed the U.S. Treasury money, the 53 gold matte proof specimens were returned and melted. That leaves us with a mintage of 47 pieces.

By December 1936 the Thin was selling for $5, whereas the Thick could be purchased for $3. The gold and silver plated medals were rarely offered for sale.

As previously mentioned these medals were struck like coins and treated in the same manner. They will exhibit bag marks, nicks, scratches, varying degrees of striking qualities—especially near the inner rims—differ slightly in measurement, and exhibit little to heavy wear. The medals—mostly the Thick—were kept as pocket and dresser drawer pieces, improperly handled, and even worn (on a neck chain) by visitors to the celebration and thereafter. The coin dealer Selby Ungar showed me several pieces that would grade numismatically from About Good to Very Fine from his stock. The variations near the inner rim were evident.

Can the Norse issue be considered a coin? Congress authorized them as medals. Thus they are not legal tender at a face value that can be acceptable in the discharge of debts. However, these specimens have been collected along with U.S. commemorative coins since 1925 and have shown good appreciation, considering they have seldom been in the limelight.

The very rare matte proof gold specimens have sold for between $2,500 (cleaned) and $40,000+. An ANACS PF-66 piece sold for $20,062.50 at a Heritage auction. The price range depends on the condition or quality of the piece. Scratches, cuts, digs, and doctoring lower the value. I have seen a coin that was polished lightly to remove a fine scratch, then acid-dipped to simulate the once original surface. I suggest that collectors purchase from the truly knowledgeable.

The large silver triple-plated 3-inch (or 2 5/8-inch) medal that was so well distributed has sold for between $500 and $3,500. As with every coin or medal or associated packaging, etc., value is based on condition.

Collectors should procure NGC or PCGS graded specimens. The rarer Thin specimen can at present be purchased for between $80 and $3,150, depending on quality and encapsulated grade. Do not buy the raw or un-encapsulated piece if you are spending more than $100.

Thanks to the dealer David F. Schmidt of Tacoma, Washington, we know that 6,000 Norse Thins were struck between May 21 and May 23, 1925. What we don't know is the reason for the halt in production.

My hypothesis is that the Centennial Commission was displeased with the thin planchet striking and thus requested a thicker planchet. Or could it be just that 6,000 pieces were purposely ordered to create a rarer item with a view to future interest and increased sales?

We can then equate this medal to the Alabama 2X2, Grant Star and Missouri 2✯4 low-mintage commemorative issues that were produced along with larger mintages bearing the same design to help increase sales. Kvale knew about these earlier issues. Whatever the case, 33,750 Thicks were produced between May 29 and June 13, 1925.

The gold medal production of 100 numbered pieces took place on June 3–4, 1925.

As to the 2-5/8-inch or 3-inch bronze or silver medal, it can only be added that they were struck after November 27, 1925, and are triple silver plated on a copper-bronze planchet. Thirty, instead of 26 pieces, were presented to guests from Norway.

Also surfacing on the numismatic market—and previously unknown—are several excessively rare items. One was a die trial piece struck in solid silver of the 2-5/8-inch silver-plated medal. The following is a description by the medal-ist expert David T. Alexander: "This Norse piece is the 2-5/8-inch medal, as struck in bronze. The specimen is untrimmed, presenting a fully struck octagon on an unevenly scalloped planchet which appears to be solid silver, its edges rough, with no trace at any point of any other metal underneath the silver sur-face.

"The overall diameter is about 3 5/16 inches, darkened by toning, but spared handling by incurious years 'in a box.' The reverse die is the 'Authorized by Congress of the United States' type."

Concerning the potential of this trial specimen, Alexander believes "it has unique market potential because of the long association of the Norse Thick and Thin with America's commemorative coinage, creating unmatched appeal. As a U.S. Mint medal, as a work of James Earle Fraser, and as an untrimmed die trial in a precious metal, this piece will offer powerful appeal to 16,000 medal collectors!"

Vividly seen on this trial piece's obverse is the designer's initial F (Fraser), at the seven o'clock position on the boulder, below the ship's rear oar.

Also recently discovered by the dealer Richard Hertzog of Rockford, Illinois, was a trial 3-inch (or 2 5/8-inch) medal struck in nickel. Unlike the silver trial piece, the edges were trimmed, polished, and rounded. The specimen was auc-tioned through World Exonumia, and was sold for $4,600. Today it resides in the collection of the dealer Robert Rhue of Englewood, Colorado. Both these trial medals were struck for John Ray Sinnock and possibly presented to Kvale.

Neil Harris, former editor of *The Numismatist*, has been researching the life and works of Sinnock. "This chief engraver seemed to have a particular inter-est in nickel pieces, possibly because nickel was such a difficult and challenging metal to use. He might have liked to show his colleagues a large nickel medal." There are five nickel medals struck of the Nellie Tayloe Ross medal by Sinnock, but Harris's research thus far does not show any striking records of the Norse piece.

Another discovery, made by me, was an extremely rare brilliant proof trial piece. This double or triple struck medal's planchet weight is between that of the Thick and Thin (about 9.2 pennyweight), thus the medium weight Norse proof. Within the realm of the regular Thin issue, my friend, dealer and co-Norse explorer, Selby Ungar, discovered a double-die specimen, as well as pieces displaying a thin and fat (regular) horn on the helmet—along with a fat with almost full horn—aside from the normal striking. There are copper obverse and reverse trial pieces. I have seen proof trial pieces of the Thick and Thin issues.

There are approximately ten complete sets (all four strikings) in a special velvet and wood frame covered with a glass slide. These are very difficult to locate and always in demand.

Can this medal be graded BU or AU? I do not know of any other issues that have been, since I am not a medalist. However, being a true professional numismatist, I thought the grading should be done, for a quality medal is worth more than one that is almost uncirculated or slightly worn.

Obverse wear will first occur on the handle of the dagger, the central portion of the diagonal chest strap, and on the edge of the battle shield between the eight o'clock and nine-thirty positions. Crisscross friction lines, which will indicate a loss of metal and thus wear, will first appear on the reverse sloop's sail between the three o'clock and four-thirty positions on the right side (closest to the mast), as well as on the last three battle shields and the oar's blades below them. Thus, should your specimen show signs of lost metal or friction in these areas, your medal is somewhat abused.

The story does not end here. Kvale also was pushing for a commemorative stamp. It was to be explained by him to the Third Assistant Postmaster General, Warren Irving Glover, that, while the centennial was to especially observe the hundredth anniversary of the arrival of the *Restaurationen*, it also, in a broader sense, commemorates the arrival of the Vikings in AD 1000. Thus Kvale felt two stamps would be more proper than one. Political pressure—on the right people—resulted in the Postmaster General's issuing two commemorative stamps.

There is even more. Both stamps were to be issued in two colors (bicolor). This meant that they were the first commemorative stamps issued as such and the only two-color stamps then in circulation, with the exception of the $5 stamp (Scott catalogue of postage stamps reference #573–a beautiful issue depicting the Head of Freedom Statue, Capitol Dome, in dark blue ink, with borders or carmine [lake], issued on April 20, 1923). Some philatelists might be quick to mention that the Pan-American Exposition issue of 1901 consisted of six commemorative bicolor stamps (Scott #294-299). True, but, again, they were not in circulation on May 18, 1925, when the Norse American issue was released.

The 2-cent stamp (Scott #620), printed in carmine and black ink, pictures a reproduction of the sloop *Restaurationen*. Flanking it on the borders on each side are depicted the figures that adorned the prows of the ancient Viking ships and the battle shields used by the old chieftains.

The 5-cent stamp (Scott #621), printed in dark blue and black ink, depicts the actual Viking ship that sailed to America from Norway at the time of the World's Columbian Exposition in Chicago in 1893. This beautifully crafted romantic ship is flanked on the left by a Norse shield with the U.S. shield seen on the right.

The story behind this issue is not complete, for those few additional needles must and will be found in the haystack. In closing, I would like to express my sincere appreciation to the following who assisted me in locating the "found" needles: Frances D. Campbell, Jr., Lloyd Hustvedt, Roland Finner, Dr. Edward Lewis, John Lofgren, David F. Schmidt, Ruby Shields, Gloria Swiatek, and Selby Ungar. Credit is also due to the following institutions and societies for data and service: The National Archives, Washington, D.C.; The Minnesota Historical Society; and St. Olaf's College.

Future Potential of the Norse American Medal

When NGC and PCGS decided to grade the Norse Thick and Thin medallic issue in 2004 population figures were rather low at first in all grades up to MS-66, which caused values to rise. As collectors and dealers became more aware of the low populations they began submitting their holdings. These subsequent submissions caused an increase in the population figures in all grades up to MS-65. At the current price levels the Thick planchet is somewhat overvalued in all grades up to MS-65: buy it only for the joy of collecting.

Consider the MS-66 Thick planchet medal for acquisition.

If considering a Norse American medal for your collection, you should contemplate adding a Thin variety in grades MS-63 to MS-66 because of greater collector and dealer allure.

The Norse matte proof gold issue is sought by individuals with sufficient funds who like the issue for its rarity. Currently this issue is undervalued in all grades.

Population Figures

Date	Service	AU 58	MS 60	MS 62	MS 63	MS 64	MS 65	MS 66	MS 67	MS 68	MS 69
1925 Thick	NGC	11	0	72	148	264	154	26	2	0	0
1925 Thick	PCGS	25	3	41	149	309	182	33	0	0	0
1925 Thick	Combined	36	3	113	297	573	336	59	2	0	0

Date	Service	AU 58	MS 60	MS 62	MS 63	MS 64	MS 65	MS 66	MS 67	MS 68	MS 69
1925 Thin	NGC	5	0	44	62	114	34	8	0	0	0
1925 Thin	PCGS	7	2	41	99	111	36	3	0	0	0
1925 Thin	Combined	12	2	87	161	225	70	11	0	0	0

Date	Service	EF 40 BN	AU 58 BN	MS 60 BN	MS 62 BN	MS 63 BN	MS 64 BN	MS 65 BN	MS 66 BN	MS 67 BN	MS 68 BN	MS 69 BN
1925 Copper Die Trial	PCGS	1	0	0	0	1	0	0	0	0	0	0
1925 Copper Die Trial	NGC	0	0	0	0	2	0	0	0	0	0	0
1925 Uniface Die Trial	PCGS	0	0	0	0	0	1	0	0	0	0	0

Date	Service	PF 58	PF 60	PF 62	PF 63	PF 64	PF 65	PF 66	PF 67	PF 68	PF 69
1925 Gold	NGC	0	0	0	2	0	5	2	1	0	0
1925 Gold	PCGS	1	0	0	2	4	3	2	0	0	0
1925 Gold	Combined	1	0	0	4	4	8	4	1	0	0

1925 Stone Mountain Memorial

Reason for Issue:	To commemorate the commencement, on June 18, 1923, of carving a memorial to the soldiers of the South on Stone Mountain, Georgia, and in memory of President Warren Gamaliel Harding, during whose administration the work was begun.
Authorization:	Act of March 17, 1924, with a maximum of 5,000,000 pieces.
Issued by:	Stone Mountain Confederate Monumental Association
Official Sale Price:	$1

Production Figures

Date	Business Strikes	Assay Coins	Proofs	Melted	Net Mintage
1925	2,310,000	4,709	4	1,000,000	1,310,000

Current Market Values

Date	AU-58	MS-60	MS-63	MS-64	MS-65	MS-66	MS-67
1925	$60	$65	$80	$155	$240	$380	$1,200

DESIGNS BY GUTZON BORGLUM

Obverse

The equestrian figures of General Thomas J. ("Stonewall") Jackson (1824–63), facing the viewer, and of General Robert E. Lee (1807–70), in profile and wearing the hat of a Confederate high-ranking officer. In the lower left field are the words "STONE MOUNTAIN" and the date of issue, 1925. There are 13 stars in the upper field, one for each state in the Confederacy, plus Kentucky and Missouri, which had secessionist factions. Each state, by the way, is also represented by a star on the Confederate flag. The motto "IN GOD WE TRUST" is seen in the upper border. Located at the extreme right border near the horse's tail are the designer's incused initials (GB) for Gutzon Borglum, the famous American sculptor who created the Mount Rushmore carvings. Borglum was commissioned for the actual carving of Stone Mountain in northwest Georgia, but his plans were never fully carried out. A dispute arose between the sculptor and the Stone Mountain Confederate Monumental Association, and Borglum was dismissed. Augustus Lukeman was hired to complete the beautiful project.

Reverse

An eagle with wings stretched, standing on a mountain crag. In the center left field is the inscription "MEMORIAL TO THE VALOR OF THE SOLDIER OF THE SOUTH"; "UNITED STATES OF AMERICA" arcs above; "HALF DOLLAR" below. "E PLURIBUS UNUM" in small letters is in the upper left; "LIBERTY" is above "HALF DOLLAR". There are also 35 dimly visible stars on the field of this coin, and not 34 stars, which are supposed to represent the number of states in the Union before the Civil War.

Origins of the Stone Mountain

The Philadelphia Mint struck 2,310,000 Stone Mountain 50-cent pieces from January through March 1925, as well as 4,709 coins for assay purposes (the largest number of commemorative assay coins produced to date). The first 1000 pieces were produced on January 21, 1925, the 101st birthday of Stonewall Jackson. The approved authorization was a maximum coinage figure of 5,000,000. However, this issue encountered a great deal of flak from Northerners who believed a United States coin should not honor only Confederate leaders. To pacify the North, the phrase "and in memory of Warren G. Harding (1865–1923), President of the United States of America, in whose administration the work was begun," was added to the bill. In fact, the bust of Harding was considered as the main obverse design. However, there is no reference made to Harding on the coin itself: a total of nine changes were made to the obverse die design, one of which removed the inscription honoring the president. Harding was not destined to appear on this half dollar, nor on the 2½-cent and 7½-cent commemorative coins because the bills of February 16, 1925 and May 27, 1925 were not successful.

The coins were distributed through the Stone Mountain Confederate Monumental Association at $1 each. Several large institutions, such as the Baltimore and Ohio Railroad, the Southern Fireman's Fund Insurance Company, the Atlanta Coca-Cola Bottling Company, and many banks purchased huge quantities of these commemorative half dollars at the issue price and distributed them at face value.

Counter-stamped Coins

A number of Stone Mountain half dollars were counter-stamped with a numeral and an abbreviated state name. Dr. Charles R. Stearns of Lilburn, Georgia, an expert in this area, has presented me with the following valuable information to use in this work:

> A great distribution campaign extending from Virginia to Texas was initiated to sell the Stone Mountain issue at $1.00 each. The governors of the States of Virginia, South Carolina, Georgia, Florida, Alabama, Mississippi, Louisiana, Texas, Oklahoma, Arkansas, Kentucky and Tennessee served as campaign chairmen. (North Carolina joined the program later.) Each governor assumed a sales quota based upon population and bank deposits. The "Great Harvest Campaign," as it was called, probably would have succeeded had it not been for Borglum's abandonment of the carving project in March 1925. His subsequent arrest and ultimate departure provided bad publicity and put a heavy damper on the fund-raising project.

The Harvest Campaign administrators devised a plan to counter-stamp some Stone Mountain half dollars with numbers and letters to produce unique pieces. Lettering styles indicate there was one basic source, most probably the Confederate Monumental Association, for nearly all the counter-stamped coins. For example all A's are square-topped; periods were generally rectangular; and all 2's are square-based.

The most common coins are described as the "State and Number" coins: these feature an abbreviation of the state name and a serial number. There is some apparent continuity in the serial numbers within a given state, but some numbers appear more than once (Tenn. 102; Okla. 358; Va. 202). Three of this variety of coin are known to have had certificates of ownership issued when they were sold. The counter-stamped pieces were meant to be sold at public auction to raise additional funds above the normal profit level. A letter dated December 10, 1925 from J. Wilson Gibbs, Jr., executive secretary in charge of South Carolina auction coins, to Mrs. R.E. Shannon of Blastock, South Carolina, gives some insight into the plan. Mr. Gibbs reported that in South Carolina the auction prices varied from $10 to $110 with an average price of $23 realized. He recommended that a little speech be given prior to the coin being offered and thought that special mention might be made to the fact that a similar coin brought $1,300 in Bradenton, Florida. The Blastock coin is identified with counter-stamps "S.C." and "109." One specimen of this type of state and number counter-stamp is known with the number "42" and no state name; it appeared in Florida a few years ago.

Close examination of "Texas 182" and "Texas 242" yielded the letters "FLA" under the "EXA" of "TEXAS". This indicated that the demand in Florida was not as great as first projected and that the coins were stamped a second time to satisfy the demand in Texas.

Another type of counter-stamped coin differs from this first group in that the letters "S.L." also appear. One hypothesis is that these letters stand for "State Legislature." It has been suggested that these coins were presented to promi-nent legislators to promote the Harvest Campaign. A Florida piece stamped "G.L.": this might be an error or might stand for "General Legislature." Unfor-tunately, none of these coins has been traced back to its original owner, so the facts remain elusive.

A third type of counter-stamped coin is exemplified by some of the Tennes-see coins. The letters "U.D.C.," designating the United Daughters of the Con-federacy, and very high serial numbers are found. These higher serial numbers may be a membership or chapter number of the U.D.C.

The fourth and last group of counter-stamped coins is the "N" series. Only three specimens are accounted for at this time. "N-6" came from the estate of a Nashville bank employee in 1925. This series differs markedly from all the other coins: the coins are much more deeply stamped, and the letters are serif and much heavier in style.

A fortunate collector can sometimes acquire these counter-stamped coins in a mutilated condition. Unfortunately the pieces can be easily manufactured by anyone with a tool and die punch set. Collectors would be well advised to avoid purchasing a counter-stamped coin unless ownership can be traced back to the original purchaser or the coin is accompanied by an original certificate.

Several counter-stamped coins have recently come on the market, and arti-cles about them have raised interest among collectors hoping to cherry-pick them. However, most of these coins were initially purchased by non-collectors who were supporting a cause, and had the means to pay the premium auction price. Now, several decades after the sales campaign, these individuals have passed away and their estates are coming up for settlement. Since most were non-collectors, their coins probably rattled in a dresser drawer or served as a pocket piece or a memento. Most of the counter-stamped coins are not Uncir-culated or any grade even approaching that.

An "UGLY OKLA 192" graded VF brought $540 at a Heritage auction, January 10, 2004, while an OKLA 26 rated MS-60 sold for $345. At a January 10, 2004 Heritage auction, an LA 206 graded AU-58 sold for $1,100, and a cleaned TEX/VA 32 rated XF-40 brought $980. Value for these pieces will vary based on condition, demand, provenance, and current owner.

At Heritage's July 4, 2005 Bullet sale a piece graded ANACS NET40 brought $322. It was counter-stamped "80" and "TEXAS/VA". In Heritage's February 26, 2005 Signature Sale, a Stone Mountain featuring "222" and OKLA sold $690. It was a raw AU-50 coin. On January 15, 2005, an XF-40 piece, in a bezel, brought $1,150. It was counter-stamped ARK with the number 18 and the letters "SL" below.

For the next decade or so, these coins probably will continue to appear with some regularity and then slowly dry up in supply as their original owners' estates are dispersed.

When we speak of an officially documented piece with a number located between 1 and 50, we are speaking of an item in a different numismatic vein. A specimen of the 29th Stone Mountain struck by the Philadelphia Mint, with documentation, sold for $1,300 in 1937. What about the first piece struck? It was presented to President Coolidge, mounted on a plate of gold. The second was presented to Andrew W. Mellon, Secretary of the Treasury. One million coins were returned to the Mint by the Confederate Monumental Association, leaving us with a total mintage figure of 1,314,000. That's still a lot of coins.

The Stone Mountain Today

This issue, which Borglum referred to as the Federal Confederate or Memorial half dollar, is abundant in EF-AU condition. Its availability makes it a nice gift, especially for a youngster, as it might generate interest in the wonderful world of numismatics. Value spread is insignificant between grades MS-60 and MS-64; the coin is not difficult to locate in grades up to MS-66. Collectors should attempt to procure the flashier, eye-appealing coin, but only for the joy of collecting. Only the loftier grades are likely to increase in value.

Luster will range from blazing frosty, to frosty, to dull frosty. A weakness of strike on General Lee's thigh and the reverse eagle's breast can lower a coin's grade-value. However, the supply is so plentiful that a strongly struck specimen can be obtained with little challenge. The primary focal areas are the obverse and reverse devices. Bag marks, slide marks, and other elements of numismatic abuse attack these locations as well as their surrounding fields. Over the past 20 years, I have examined more than 1,450 Stone Mountains, struck from doubled dies. I would not label them even scarce, but they are fun to own for the joy of collecting. Should funds be available, collectors should focus on attractive MS-66 pieces.

Errors

To date, no error coinage has entered the marketplace.

Detecting Counterfeits

Bogus coins have a gray frosty luster, and the obverse has tool marks between both horses' hoofs and the rim at the six o'clock and six-thirty positions. Likewise a depression can be found on Lee's horse's tail. On the reverse look for a surface depression on the upper right vertical section of the letter "R" in "DOL-LAR", as well as on the rock below the eagle's right talon.

Is Your Stone Mountain Circulated or Mint State?

Obverse

Wear will first occur on the thigh and elbow of General Lee: look for a difference in metal texture or a dull grayish discoloration or slight friction.

Reverse

A metal loss will first be observed on the breast of the eagle.

Related Material

Some organizations sold the coins at a premium price in wooden boxes (similar to the Lexington issuing box) with a slide-off top on which there was a large paste-on foil Silver Star (15/16-inch) with the outline of a thin printed blue star within. Original boxes with the foil star may be valued in the $100 to $500 range, depending on the condition of the coin and the box.

Other coins were sold in a cellophane coin envelope stapled to a distributing holder listing the name of the United Daughters of the Confederacy and depicting a Confederate flag in color.

This item was housed in a Citizens and Southern National Bank envelope. Another was distributed in a white cardboard Christmas card (5 7/16 × 3 7/16 inches) with a coin cut-out covered on both sides by white gummed tape. Imprinted in black ink, one side notes that the coin is an emblem of peace and good will between the people of the North and the South, Compliments of ____, Address_____ with Christmas Greetings. The other side depicts the gigantic Stone Mountain frieze with a circular photo of Augustus Lukeman. This was placed in an envelope with the address "Stone Mountain Memorial Association, 900 Southern Building, Washington, D.C."

Stone Mountain Memorial
Half Dollar

From The Collection of
Bernard Baruch

Price
$3.25

Sold for The Benefit of
United Daughters of The
Confederacy

Sales Agent
The Citizens & Southern National Bank
Broad and Marietta Street Branch
Atlanta, Georgia

Stone Mountain envelope.

Stone Mountain holder—front.

Stone Mountain holder—back

Stone Mountain membership application.

Stone Mountain promotional tag.

The Retail Credit Company distributed coins in a cardboard holder with a circular insert for one coin. Black imprinting described the issue, occasion, etc., on both sides. The holder was then placed inside a sheet of heavy glossy paper, folded in thirds. Within is pictured Stone Mountain before and after (superimposed). The outer section notes it was given with compliments by the sponsoring company.

Additional coins were issued by the *Atlanta Journal* in a cardboard holder insert for one coin. Black imprinting describing the coin as a token of friendship and pledge of a united country, etc. The reverse pictures Stone Mountain, the largest body of granite in the world, before the carving. Beneath is a short description of what is to come. (A chip of granite from General Lee's figure was wrapped in tissue paper, placed in a small cardboard box, and sold by the Confederate Monumental Association as a souvenir: today it is worth $20 to $45.) Coins were also distributed in a gold-colored box with a cardboard inner support and a circular cut-out for one coin, with black imprinting on the cover. Many other unofficial distributing holders were issued by banks and other businesses.

Holders may be valued in the $100 to $500+ range, depending on the coin's condition.

An original white cardboard box has a cardboard insert for one coin, imprinted Life Insurance Co., Atlanta. Its inner lid has an inscription describing the issue. This brought $2,300 with an MS-63 coin enclosed at the American Numismatic Rarities auction on March 8, 2005. An original holder housing five coins, grading MS-64 to MS-66 and indicating the Coin Committee address (Hotel Roosevelt/50 East 46th Street) brought $2,990. The coins justified the price, not the holder ($75–$150).

Future Potential of the Stone Mountain Half Dollar

Population Figures

Date	Service	AU 58	MS 60	MS 62	MS 63	MS 64	MS 65	MS 66	MS 67	MS 68	MS 69
1925	NGC	131	0	278	860	2860	2139	633	141	10	0
1925	PCGS	0	43	497	2012	3566	2023	744	171	6	0
1925	Combined	131	43	775	2872	6426	4162	1377	312	16	0

This popular, high mintage issue is the fifth least expensive commemorative design available in circulated condition. The lowest priced is the Carver–Washington type coin, followed by the Booker T. Washington type coin, and the respective 1893 and 1892 Columbian issues.

Pieces grading EF-AU through MS-65 should be acquired only for the joy of collecting. They appear fairly priced in these grades, based on current supply and demand. The previous high dollar spread between the MS-64 and MS-65 Stone Mountains was approximately $600. That is no longer the case. I would lower the census between 22% and 25% for the MS-64 category, and I see average future possibilities for these ratings. Strictly graded flashy MS-66 pieces are somewhat undervalued at current levels. The former top price variance between MS-65 and MS-66 was $1,050; a promotional period would lead to a similar, but lesser, variance. I would lower the census by 21% to 26% for each grade, and see good to very good future potential. However, it is hard to determine what percentage of Stone Mountains residing in roll form (20 pieces) in Southern vaults will enter the marketplace in the 21st century. I know of several individuals who still own 60 of these original rolls in total: that's 1,200 half dollars.

Pieces grading MS-67 ($1,200) presently offer very good to excellent future potential, provided they possess that all-important flash or eye appeal. Should the coin border on MS-68, meaning it's an MS-67++ coin, collectors and dealers could pay much more for it. I have seen MS-68 pieces with amazing natural colored surfaces sell for $21,850 (NGC) and $28,000 (PCGS). Another sold for $28,750 (PCGS) at the February 2005 Heritage Long Beach, CA auction, as well as a much lower $8,050 at the August 2009 Los Angeles, CA US coin auction. Why? Have population figures risen? Such appears to be one answer. Let's not forget the eye-appeal of the coin.

Reason for Issue:	To commemorate the 150th anniversary of the signing of the Declaration of Independence.
Authorization:	Act of March 3rd, 1925, with a maximum of 1,000,000 for half dollars and 200,000 for the gold quarter eagles ($2.50).
Issued by:	National Sesquicentennial Exhibition Association
Official Sale Price:	Half dollars at $1 each and quarter eagles at $4 each.

Production Figures

Date	Business Strikes	Assay Coins	Proofs	Melted	Net Mintage
1926 50¢	1,000,000	528	4?	859,408	45,793
1926 $2.50	200,000	226	2?	154,207	45,793

Current Market Values

Date	EF 40	AU 58	MS 60	MS 63	MS 64	MS 65	MS 66
1926 50¢	$55	$75	$95	$135	$325	$2,800	$18,000

HALF DOLLAR DESIGNS BY JOHN RAY SINNOCK

Obverse

The accolated busts of George Washington and Calvin Coolidge, facing right. Around the top border, between two rosettes representing a badge of office, is the word "LIBERTY"; "UNITED STATES OF AMERICA" arcs below; "IN GOD WE TRUST" is in two lines just below Coolidge's chin. The incused designer's initials (JRS) appear on the truncation of Washington's bust.

Reverse

The Liberty Bell, which proclaimed liberty "throughout all the land unto all its inhabitants thereof" (Leviticus 25:10), rallying the Colonists to the cause of independence.

How was the Liberty Bell cracked? This famous crack occurred in 1835, as the bell tolled for Chief Justice John Marshall's funeral procession. The anniversary dates 1776 and 1926 are separated by the bell, which hangs from a beam. Around the raised border is the inscription "SESQUICENTENNIAL OF AMERICAN INDEPENDENCE"; "HALF DOLLAR" is in the bottom border; "E PLURIBUS UNUM" is at the top between the beam and the border inscription. An inscription is seen in the following form upon the Bell:

EOF LEV XXV FX PROCLAIM LIBERTY

OUSE IN PHILADA BY ORDER OF THE AS

PASS AND STOW

PHILADA

MDCCLIII

The complete inscription reads: PROCLAIM LIBERTY (throughout all the land unto the inhabitants thereof, LEV(iticus, chapter) XXV, (verse)X. By order of the AS(sembly of the Providence of Pennsylvania for the State H)OUSE IN PHILAD(elphi)A. PASS AND STOW, PHILAD(elphi)A. 1753.

Origins of the Sesquicentennial Coins

For a period of 150 years, the portrait of a living president of the United States had never appeared on United States coinage. While individuals such as Thomas E. Kilby, Governor of Alabama; Carter Glass, Secretary of the Treasury under President Wilson; and Senator Joseph T. Robinson of Arkansas had their portraits on United States commemorative coins, Calvin Coolidge, who was president at the time of the Sesquicentennial celebration in 1926, is the only president to have his portrait on a coin in his lifetime. George Washington was the first president to appear on a commemorative coin—the 1900 Lafayette dollar.

The Philadelphia Mint struck 1,000,000 half dollars, plus 528 assay coins, during May and June of 1926. It marked the first time that private advertising appeared on U.S. coinage. Sinnock's Liberty Bell design was also used on the 1948 Franklin half dollar, which is the first and only circulating coin with private advertising. The most recent coin with advertising is the 1999 Dolley Madison commemorative silver dollar. Tiffany & Company designed the coin, and their historic hallmark is present on it (see the Dolley Madison entry). The Mint also produced 200,000 gold $2.50 pieces, plus 226 assay coins in this same period. Since it was believed that the Sesquicentennial celebration would be viewed as one of major national importance, the full numismatic authorization was produced. Unfortunately, the National Sesquicentennial Exhibition Commission, selling the half dollars at $1.00 each, saw sales come to a halt well short of the goal and returned 859,408 half dollars and 154,207 quarter eagles to the Mint to be melted. With almost 6 million people attending the Exhibition, which opened June 1, 1926, and closed November 30, 1926, one wonders why more coins of each issue were not sold. In all likelihood many attendees could not afford either coin. The first half dollar, struck at noon by Philadelphia Mayor W. Freeland Kendrick at the May 19 striking ceremony, was presented to President Coolidge when he visited the Exhibition.

Aside from the half dollar and the quarter eagle, the original bill for these coins also requested the creation of a gold $1.50 coin. Unfortunately, this unusual new denomination was not approved by Secretary of the Treasury Andrew Mellon. The bill was amended, and only the half dollar and the quarter eagle were produced.

The Sesquicentennial Half Dollar Today

This coin is readily available in EF-AU condition: specimens can be obtained naturally worn or abused in some manner. MS-60 through MS-64 coins are also relatively easy to find, but should be bought only for the joy of collecting. Attempt to locate a lustrous MS-63+ coin without deep cuts, scratches, or detracting bag and slide marks on the primary focal areas. These areas are the obverse portraits, then the right field; on the reverse the Liberty Bell, then the surrounding fields.

Flashy, eye-appealing MS-64 coinage is undervalued when it looks like an MS-65 coin: the difference is between something worth $3,000 instead of $500. I have seen a few very alluring, flashy MS-64++ pieces sell for $900 to $1500. A long fine hairline scratch or two and/or a major surface negative not observed even by the normally astute will always keep the coin out of the MS-65 category. Strictly graded MS-65+ coins are rare. In MS-66 condition it is rarer than the Missouri coinage and the silver Grant Star.

Luster will range from a proof-like gloss, to a semi-proof-like gloss, to flashy brilliant frosty (not the norm), to frosty, to dull frosty. However, most specimens will lack that original brilliant mint lustrous look.

The issue possesses a soft strike because of its shallow relief. It also displays porous openings or minute holes located in the cheek area of Washington and Coolidge. To date, I have yet to encounter a Sesqui half dollar that does not exhibit at least a slight graininess or lack of metal fill in these locations.

The complete inscription, "PASS AND STOW, PHILADA, MDCCLIII" on the reverse is not often seen. Upon inspection, its letters will be flatly struck, or partially visible, or not apparent at all. Under magnification of ten power the inscription appears to have weathered over a long period of time. A specimen that possesses original brilliant mint luster, a smooth clean full strike with no porosity visible in the cheek area of Washington, and a completely legible inscription on the Liberty Bell, will be a major find.

The luster and strike problems, as well as surface-attacking negatives, make it easier to understand why strictly graded MS-64+ and higher graded coins are quite difficult to find.

Possibly four matte proof Sesquicentennial half dollars exist. These were double struck, then acid treated by the Mint for its Chief Engraver, John Ray Sinnock. One such specimen, the ex-King Farouk coin, appeared as Lot 2124 of the Stack's R.E. Cox, N.Y. Metropolitan Sale, 1962.

No error coinage or counterfeit 50-cent pieces have entered the market-place.

IS YOUR SESQUICENTENNIAL HALF DOLLAR CIRCULATED OR MINT STATE?

Obverse

A metal loss will first be observed on the cheekbone and shoulder of President Washington, the prime target for the coin doctors. Look for a difference in metal texture.

Reverse

Wear will first be noticed just below the central lower inscription on the Liberty Bell, as well as in the center section of the beam that supports it. This location also attracts doctoring.

Related Material

The half dollar was sold unprotected over the counter at the Exhibition itself. It was distributed in an envelope (4 1/4 × 2 5/8 inches) imprinted in blue "FRANKLIN TRUST COMPANY, PHILADELPHIA, PA.", "AT YOUR SERVICE DAY AND NIGHT," and other statements: "OFFICIAL SESQUICENTENNIAL SOUVENIR COINS" and "AMERICA'S LARGEST EXCLUSIVELY DAY AND NIGHT BANK." These envelopes make an occasional appearance, and may be valued at $25 to $100, if original.

Sesquicentennial envelope—front.

Sesquicentennial envelope—back.

The Sons of the American Revolution sold a 4 × 2 1/2-inch card as an official ticket to the Centennial Celebration; this contained a circulated half dollar issued between 1916 and 1923. Its thinner paper cover depicted the organization's logo and an American flag. Should such an item cross your path, check the date on the enclosed coin. It could be a 1919-S or 1921-D or 1921-S, all with values above par in the circulated grades.

Future Potential of the Sesquicentennial Half Dollar

Population Figures

To date, no Sesquicentennial has been graded higher than MS-66. None of the extremely rare matte proofs has been encapsulated to date.

Date	Service	AU 58	MS 60	MS 62	MS 63	MS 64	MS 65	MS 66	MS 67	MS 68	MS 69
1926	NGC	86	12	528	1264	1747	275	18	0	0	0
1926	PCGS	144	24	542	1457	1950	252	8	0	0	0
1926	Combined	230	36	1070	2721	3697	527	26	0	0	0

This half dollar is located with no difficulty in ratings EF-AU through MS-64; I suggest acquiring these grades simply for the joy of ownership. The coin is somewhat undervalued in MS-64+ condition, when it is very eye-appealing or flashy looking, but not all MS-64 encapsulations have these qualities. The real future for the issue begins with the very attractive MS-64+ half dollar or borderline MS-65 striking. One raw MS-64 coin was offered to me at $4,400; the MS-65 bid was $5,900. The coin possessed the most flash and blast that I have ever seen for the issue. Upon inspection, I saw a hairline scratch—not exactly the lightest—across the heads of both presidents. On their foreheads and in the field above were some light hairlines. I would have paid $800+ for the piece at the time because it was so lustrous and a marked exception to the normally found coin. The normal bid for an attractive MS-64 specimen is $425. No doubt it was submitted for slabbing many times by many owners, then returned MS-64 and thus cracked out of the holder. I found those scratches a bit beyond the acceptable limit. This seemed a high price for an over-graded "lure coin" aimed at catching the uneducated fish.

Coins like this were and are constantly resubmitted in the hopes of an upgrade. During the May 1989 high, there was a $1,700 price variance between MS-63 and MS-64 coinage, but that won't recur. Between the MS-64+ and the rarer MS-65 specimen, a colossal $7,000 was the norm, and may be once again. I can reduce census figures by 20% for 23% for the MS-64 category. There is an excellent future for accurately graded and captivating MS-64+ coinage.

A strictly graded flashy MS-65+ Sesquicentennial is rare. I have recently seen a great many pieces labeled MS-65 that I would not place in my collection, nor offer to clients. The population count can be reduced by 15% to 26%. The dollar spread during the last high between grades MS-65 and MS-66 was a gigantic $11,000. Should funds be available, this is a great coin to add to one's portfolio.

In the MS-66 category, this is a very rare coin. The past high was $20,000 in the grade; the current approximate asking price is $17,000+. In fact this is the only coin to hold near its value from the May 1989 high; it certainly has upside potential. None have been rated MS-67 as of this writing.

1926 SESQUICENTENNIAL OF AMERICAN INDEPENDENCE
$2.50 (OR QUARTER EAGLE)

Current Market Values

Date	AU 58	MS 60	MS 63	MS 64	MS 65	MS 66
1926 $2.50	$410	$425	$625	$1,450	$2,300	$10,000

GOLD $2.50 DESIGNS BY JOHN RAY SINNOCK, FROM ROUGH DRAWINGS BY JOHN FREDERICK LEWIS

Obverse

The figure of Liberty standing on a globe. She is holding the Torch of Freedom in her right hand and a scroll in her left hand, symbolic of the Declaration of Independence. In the field are the commemorative dates 1776–1926. "UNITED STATES OF AMERICA" arcs above; "LIBERTY" below.

Reverse

Independence Hall, Philadelphia, home of the Liberty Bell and the site where the Declaration of Independence was written. In the background are the sun's rays—these are not clear on all pieces. The inscription "SESQUICENTENNIAL OF AMERICAN INDEPENDENCE" runs around the upper border; the denomination "2 1/2 DOLLARS" appears at the lower border. Incused in small letters, above the right wing of Independence Hall, are the designer's initials (JRS). "IN GOD WE TRUST" is split by the spire of Independence Hall; "E PLURIBUS UNUM" is just below the base of the building.

The Sesquicentennial Gold $2.50 Today

This coin is not too difficult to locate in EF-AU condition, and in fact is the easiest to acquire of all commemorative gold coins produced from 1903 through 1926 in circulated condition. (The next easiest are the 1916 McKinley and 1915-S Panama–Pacific dollars.) Specimens will usually exhibit some form of abuse. I suggest considering pieces that may display a metal loss, but possess a natural, un-doctored surface—unless the price is right or you are simply acquiring the design in any condition for the joy of ownership.

The Sesquicentennial $2.50 gold piece can also be obtained with little difficulty in MS-60 through MS-65 grades. The best future is in coinage in at least MS-65+ condition. Should funds permit, attempt to locate flashy, eye-appealing examples with no obvious high-point friction on Liberty's breast or thighs.

Strictly graded, MS-65+ coins are quite undervalued. Should funds be available, consider buying one. In the loftier grades, this issue has excellent future potential.

Numismatic negatives plague the primary focal areas, which are the obverse figure and reverse building, and then surrounding fields.

Luster will range from a brilliant flashy frost (not the norm), to frosty, to dull frosty. This design was executed in low relief; it will lack sharpness in the details. Varying degrees of strike do exist, so you should attempt to locate a sharp strike. Strike will affect the coin's grade-value when Liberty displays weak definition on her head, cap, and upper body. The same applies to the reverse, causing Independence Hall to display very weak window and building detail. It should be noted that the designer did not add hands to the clock face, so no time is shown. On the 1936-S Bay Bridge, the time seen is twelve o'clock. Closely examining the 1976 Bicentennial half dollar, the time is three o'clock (on the back the current $100 bill it is 1:23).

One or possibly two extremely rare matte proof quarter eagles exist. This double-struck issue was over-acid-treated by the Mint employee who was following Sinnock's orders to matte surface the piece. Thus, the striking detail may not look double-struck. Procure this coin only if it has been encapsulated by a major service.

No error coinage has entered the marketplace.

Detecting Counterfeits

One of the better fakes has brilliant luster, but displays some weakness in strike. It will show a small raised piece of metal on the diagonal bar of the first letter "N" of "INDEPENDENCE" on the reverse. Another counterfeit will reveal depressions in the obverse field below the "A" of "STATES", as well as between "ER" of "AMERICA", plus a thin raised line running parallel to the rim, above Liberty's head, ending at the top vertical bar of the letter "F" of "OF".

Yet another example will reveal a depression on Liberty's torch, and raised tooling marks above the digit "2" of the date 1926. The surfaces of this fake will be more granular than a genuine coin's.

IS YOUR SESQUICENTENNIAL GOLD $2.50 CIRCULATED OR MINT STATE?

Obverse

Wear will first be noticed on Liberty's left thigh and breast, then on the bottom part of the scroll: these are the primary target areas for the coin doctors.

Reverse

A metal loss will occur on the center vertical section of Independence Hall.

Related Material

The Sesquicentennial $2.50 gold piece was distributed in the same envelope as described for the half dollar, as well as in a Christmas card issued by the Bethlehem National Bank, Bethlehem, Pennsylvania. This was imprinted with a

Liberty Bell, the anniversary dates, and "150 Years of Independence." Without the coin the card is worth between $150 and $275, depending on condition.

Future Potential of the Sesquicentennial Gold $2.50

Population Figures

Date	Service	AU 58	MS 60	MS 62	MS 63	MS 64	MS 65	MS 66	MS 67	MS 68	MS 69
1926 $2.50	NGC	324	28	1129	1384	2701	1100	80	3	0	0
1926 $2.50	PCGS	628	114	1329	2314	4303	1830	134	0	0	0
1926 $2.50	Combined	952	142	2458	3698	7004	2930	214	3	0	0

Date	Service	PF 58	PF 60	PF 62	PF 63	PF 64	PF 65	PF 66	PF 67	PF 68	PF 69
1926 $2.50	NGC	0	0	0	0	0	1	0	0	0	0
1926 $2.50	PCGS	0	0	0	0	0	0	0	0	0	0
1926 $2.50	Combined	0	0	0	0	0	1	0	0	0	0

There are also one or possibly two excessively rare matte proof strikings; this is the only commemorative gold coinage with this surface.

There were only two commemorative $2.50 gold pieces produced from 1892 through 2005. One is the rarer and more expensive Panama–Pacific striking. The other is the Sesquicentennial coin. While its population count is high for most categories, the issue is very popular and affordable. Pieces rated EF-AU and as high as MS-65, offer average future possibilities. Were I evaluating a similar issue with equal values and identical census figures—but one not nearly as popular with collectors—I would recommend its acquisition in grades EF-AU through MS-65 only for the joy of ownership. During the May 1989 high, the dollar spread among ratings were as follows: MS-62 and MS-63: $700; MS-63 and MS-64: $2,300; MS-64 and MS-65: $20,000.

I would reduce the census in MS-64 condition by 28% to 36%; in MS-65 condition between 18% and 23%. Be aware that when the market heat begins to decrease, the higher population issues will become more abundant, as collectors, dealers, and investors begin selling. Thus, values can decline rapidly. Again, beware of counterfeits usually offered at bargain prices, or even at going values by the unknowledgeable dealer.

Reason for Issue:	To commemorate the heroism of those who traversed the Oregon Trail to the Far West and to rescue the various important points along the Trail from oblivion.
Authorization:	Act of May 17, 1926, with a maximum of 6,000,000 for the entire issue.
Issued by:	Oregon Trail Memorial Association
Official Sale Price:	1926 • 1926-S • $1 1928 • 1933-D • 1934-D • $2 1936 • 1936-S • $1.60 1937-D • $1.60 or $1.65 by mail 1938 PDS set • $6.50 1939 PDS set • $7.50

Production Figures

Date	Business Strikes	Assay Coins	Proofs	Melted	Net Mintage
1926	48,000	30	4?	75	47,925
1926-S	100,000	55	4?	17,000	83,000
1928	50,000	28	4?	44,000	6,000
1933-D	5,250	5?	4?	242	5,008
1934-D	7,000	6	4?	0	7,000
1936	10,000	6	4?	0	10,000
1936-S	5,000	6	4?	0	5,000
1937-D	12,000	8	4?	0	12,000
1938	6,000	6	4?	0	6,000

Date	Business Strikes	Assay Coins	Proofs	Melted	Net Mintage
1938-D	6,000	5	4?	0	6,000
1938-S	6,000	6	4?	0	6,000
1939	3,000	4	4?	0	3,000
1939-D	3,000	4	4?	0	3,000
1939-S	3,000	5	4?	0	3,000

Current Market Values

Date	AU 58	MS 60	MS 63	MS 64	MS 65	MS 66	MS 67
1926	$150	$ 190	$205	$200	$ 310	$ 460	$925
1926-S	$150	$190	$205	$200	$290	$415	$1,400
1928	$225	$265	$295.	$300	$340	$445	$1,000
1933-D	$355	$350	$360	$370	$425	$510	$1,200
1934-D	$180	$205	$220	$230	$350	$550	$1,400
1936	$175	$195	$205	$225	$320	$410	$750
1936-S	$185	$200	$215	$225	$335	$450	$750
1937-D	$180	$215	$220	$240	$300	$340	$450
1938 PDS set	$450	$495	$585	$625	$870	$1,150	$1900
1939 PDS set	$1,400	$1,600	$1,615	$1,650	$2,200	$2,700	$2400

Designs

According to Mint reports, the wagon side is the obverse. According to the designers, the Indian side is the obverse. Although I tend to side with the majority of collectors, dealers, and numismatists who consider the Indian as the obverse (because it is the more eye-catching and artistic of the designs), the Mint appears to have the last word, and the official obverse is the wagon side.

Obverse by James Earle Fraser, modeled by Laura Gardin Fraser

A Conestoga wagon drawn over a hill by two oxen, guided by a figure holding a stick or branch. Within the wagon is the first *implied* baby or child depicted on U.S. coinage. (The first *suggested* infant appears on the 1936 Elgin reverse, while the first *defined* infant can be observed on the 1937 Roanoke reverse.) The figures are trekking westward toward the setting sun, whose rays extend across the upper field. The inscription "OREGON TRAIL MEMORIAL", with five small decorative stars below, appears in the field above the date of issue. "IN GOD WE TRUST" is in the upper border; the husband and wife designers' initials (JE / F / LG) are at the three o'clock position behind the Conestoga wagon.

Reverse by Laura Gardin Fraser

An American Indian, who appears to be signaling to an advancing person or group of individuals to stop—a gesture similar to a traffic policeman's. No particular tribe is represented. Facing to the right, he is wearing a long, feathered bonnet. He holds a bow in his right hand, and has a blanket draped over his left shoulder. Extending on both sides of the Indian is an outline map of the United States with a line of Conestoga wagons indicating the Oregon Trail. The inscription "United States of America" is superimposed on the map. The denomination "Half Dollar" appears in the lower border; the Mint mark—if the coin has one—is to the right of the "F" in "Half".

Origins of the Oregon Trail

What might have prompted the Mint to make the change of obverse–reverse? Previous branch Mint coins, such as the 1915 Panama–Pacific issues, displayed their S Mint mark next to the obverse date or displayed the year of striking on the obverse and Mint mark on the reverse. The 1923 Monroe had its mark below the date, on the obverse, while the 1925 California Jubilee displayed an obverse date and reverse Mint mark. However, with the Oregon Trail 1926-S issue, we have the first instance where a Mint mark created a *variety* within an *issue*. No problem might have arisen had the issue been struck only at Philadelphia, which used no Mint mark. Unaccompanied by a date, a Mint mark's place is on the reverse. Examining previous coins, such as the Columbian, Lafayette, or Maine Centennial, we can note that these issues are dated in some fashion on the reverse. Had the 1892 or 1893 Columbian half dollar been produced at two Mints during the same year, as were the 1926-P and 1926-S Oregon Trail coinage, would the Mint have called the figure of Columbus the reverse side because the ship side bears the date? The correct positioning of the Mint mark is next to the date or opposite the date side. It appears the Mint used its only option when labeling the Oregon Trail and changing the artist's reverse to the obverse—even though this meant the obverse looked like it was the reverse design.

The 1926 issue was later to be named the Ezra Meeker coin by the coin's sponsors. In 1907, at the age of 76, Meeker (1830–1928) left his home in Oregon with an ox team and covered wagon on a 15-month journey on the trail he had traversed in his youth. Meeker's objectives were to perpetuate the memory of the Old Trail, to honor those who had traveled it, and to kindle in the breast of the new generation a flame of patriotic sentiment. Meeker was president of the Oregon Trail Pioneer Memorial Association, until his death at the age of 98.

In September 1926, the Philadelphia Mint struck 48,000 coins, plus 30 pieces for assay purposes. One very rare matte proof was struck for John Ray Sinnock, Chief Mint Engraver, to study the coin's form. However, during the following two months, the San Francisco Mint struck 100,000 half dollars, plus 55 assay coins. Thus, we had the first instance, as previously noted, where a Mint mark (S) created a variety within an issue, such as the 2X2 of the Alabama issue or the Star of the Grant issue. These coins were distributed at $1 by the Oregon Trail Pioneer Memorial Association, but there was soon a sharp decline in sales.

There were 17,000 pieces of the S Mint coin melted, as well as 75 pieces from the Philadelphia Mint. Weakly struck rims were creating production problems, and many of the coins were destroyed before they left the Mint.

Although requested, no coins were struck in 1927, since the Mint had unpaid amounts of the 1926 San Francisco coin on hand. However, in June 1928 the Philadelphia Mint struck 50,000 pieces, plus 28 assay specimens, of the new 1928 Oregon Trail, later referred to as the "Jedediah Smith" coin. This production honored the man who pioneered the trails to California and the Pacific Northwest. Four years passed and this issue had still not been released. It was held back because the Treasury Department still had a supply of the 1926 striking and would not release the 1928 issue until the 1926 supply was purchased. Finally, the situation was resolved with the melting of 17,000 unsold 1926-S pieces. The 1928 Oregon Trail was released in 1933, along with the first commemorative coinage produced by the Denver Mint.

Scott Stamp and Coin Company of New York City was now to market the issue. In an effort to increase sales of the new coins, historical names were given to each issue. These special names, which are rarely referred to today, were not designated by government approval and ended with the 1936-S issue.

The 1928 coin was offered for sale at $2 each. However, most collectors refused to pay the asking price for this coin with its high mintage, since they could purchase the 1933-D low mintage piece (5,245) for $1.50. Sales were poor and 44,000 coins were returned to the Mint. The objective in melting them was to make the survivors rarer, leaving a net mintage of 6,000.

The Denver Mint produced 5,250 strikings plus five assay pieces in July 1933. These were referred to as the "Century of Progress Exposition" coin. With most of these pieces being purchased by collectors and speculators of the period, only 242 pieces were returned to the Mint, leaving a mintage figure of 5,008 coins.

In July 1934, the Denver Mint produced 7,000 half dollars, plus six pieces for assay, of the coin termed the "Fort Hall, Fort Laramie and Jason Lee" coin. The missionaries Jason Lee (1803–45) and Marcus Whitman (1802-47) founded missions that were to become centers of American settlement in the Oregon Territory. This issue sold well at $2 each and no coins were returned to the Mint.

No Oregon Trail coins were produced in 1935. However, the Philadelphia Mint struck 10,000 coins plus six assay pieces in May 1936, and the San Francisco Mint produced 5,000 pieces, plus six assay coins, of an issue named the "Whitman Mission" coin. None of these coins had to be returned to the Mint, since sales were excellent. Both were offered at $1.60 each. However, it was the S Mint coin that Scott Stamp and Coin Company sold out within 10 days after the announcement that only 5,000 coins would be produced. Several months later, the distributor was willing to repurchase the 1936-S issue at $10 each. The distributor sold and promoted the 1928 through 1936 strikings; they owned large quantities of these dates. The Memorial Association, which marketed the original 1926 issue, sold part of the 1936 production as well as the 1937, 1938, and 1939 issues.

The Denver Mint struck 12,000 pieces plus eight assay coins during February 1937. These coins were later offered by the Memorial Association at $1.60 each. The historical names applied to certain previous issues were finally discontinued. This was no great loss, since the entire coin's design remained the same, except for the Mint mark and date change.

In 1938, Oregon Trails from the three Mints were offered for the first time as a set, at $6.50. Each Mint produced 6,000 coins. Denver struck five assay coins, one fewer than the other Mints. The three Mints each produced 3,000 coins in 1939; the set was offered at $7.50; San Francisco minted an additional assay coin (five, not four).

The Oregon Trail Today

The 1926-P striking can be located with little difficulty in EF-AU condition. Many of the pieces will bear evidence of some form of abuse. It is also available in grades MS-60 through MS-64. The price spread is insignificant between these states, so collectors should look for an eye-appealing higher grade. Believe it or not, this issue in MS-65 condition is almost as equal in rarity to the popular 1933-D strikings, and possesses an average future. In MS-66+ condition it is underrated. Great coin rated MS-67 and higher. Luster will range from brilliant frosty (not the norm) to dull frosty. The majority of this issue will lack thumb and finger definition on the Indian's hand. Only the early strikes—from a new pair of dies that were put into production—will show this detail: you might think you are examining a 1937-D striking. There is a small die crack that extends upward from the head of the ox on this striking.

The 1926-S is the easiest of the series to locate in circulated EF-AU condition. A large percentage of the specimens I have examined display some form of cleaning, polishing, whizzing, etc. The value spread between MS-60 and MS-64 is small, so you should focus on the higher grades if funds permit. In MS-65 condition this coin is more common than the 1937-D. There really is a good future in the higher grades of this coin—especially in grade MS-67.

Luster will range from amazing proof-like (not the norm), to brilliant satiny, to dull satiny. The semi-proof-like coin offers amazing eye appeal, as well as die polishing marks in the field below part of the motto "IN GOD WE TRUST": it is a great coin to possess. Strike weakness in the letters of "STATES" can keep the coin out of the MS-65 category, unless the piece is otherwise impeccable.

The 1928-P production is not abundant in circulated condition. Most pieces I have seen were polished, cleaned, or abused in some way. There is little value spread between the MS-60 and MS-64 conditions, so why not look for a higher grade? Luster will range from brilliant frosty to dull frosty. Strike seldom affects the coin's grade or value. Oregon Trails dated 1933-D are certainly not abundant in circulated condition, and usually display some form of numismatic abuse. The value spread is smallish between the EF-AU and MS-64 categories, so aim for the higher grades, unless pure joy of ownership is your goal. The real future is in

MS-65+ and especially the higher, underrated states. Luster will range from brilliant satiny to dull satiny (not the norm). This coin tends to a weakness of strike on the pioneer leading the Conestoga wagon, but grade and value will not be affected, unless the figure and rear wagon frame canvas support are, respectively, extremely flat or rounded.

The 1934-D striking is not abundant in circulated condition, and examples are usually abused in some way. There is little value spread between ratings up to grade MS-64. The coin is definitely fairly valued in grade MS-64 and should be purchased for the joy of collecting. The real future lies in the MS-66 and, without question, in the higher states. Luster will range from brilliant frosty (not the norm) to dull frosty; attractive lustrous coinage will be hard to find. The second "T" of "STATES" can display a weakness of strike in these coins, affecting value. I have seen pieces with what I classify as a Class II Distorted Hub Doubling. Different hubs were used creating the die, resulting in a tripling on the bottom of "HALF DOLLAR", the coastline, and Baja California.

The 1936-P production is not too easily found found in circulated condition. There is little value spread between EF-AU and MS-64 conditions, so collectors should aim for the higher grades. The coin is available in all grades up to MS-66 at present. The future lies in the higher grades. Luster will range from brilliant frosty (not the norm) to dull frosty. Most of this issue lacks eye appeal, presenting a stainless-steel look. Strike normally presents no problem, though raised lines, which are die polishing marks, can be observed in the field at the sides of the Indian's head.

The 1936-S low mintage issue is also not abundant in circulated condition. It is usually the abused specimen that receives this label. The value spread between grades MS-60 and MS-64 is currently too low. Luster will range from brilliant frosty (not the norm) to dull frosty. Unfortunately, many examples lack eye appeal, again looking as if they were struck on stainless steel planchets. Strike itself seldom presents a grade-lowering problem.

The 1937-D coin offers all the attributes the collector could desire in the form of strike, luster, and overall beauty. It can be found will little difficulty in circulated condition, up to MS-67. There is little value spread between these states. This coin is the easiest to procure and the most abundant of the entire series in grades MS-65 through MS-68. Should one desire a stunning example of the Oregon Trail design for the pure joy of collecting, this is the coin. Luster will range from blazing frosty, to frosty, to dull frosty. Strike seldom presents a problem for the date.

The 1938 PDS sets which fall into the circulated category do so because of polishing, cleaning, whizzing, or some form of abuse. They are not abundant. Just buy for the joy of ownership. There is an average future in MS-66. Think coins graded loftier. Luster will range from brilliant frosty (not the norm) to dull frosty. The majority of the coins simply lack eye appeal. They too would make a numismatic neophyte believe stainless steel planchets were used during production. Strike seldom presents a problem for the issue.

The 1939 PDS set is the rarest (3,000 produced at each Mint) and most popular coinage of the series. When located in circulated condition or offered at less than MS-60 values, the individual coin or set has been polished or abused in some fashion. The value spread between MS-60 and MS-64 condition is small. The coins are not that available, and are definitely underrated. The best future lies in original eye-appealing specimens grading MS-65+ and loftier. Luster will range from semi-brilliant frosty (not the norm) to dull frosty. Many specimens will display an unimpressive stainless-steel look. Strike rarely presents a problem, as far as grade and value lowering is concerned.

On examination this issue shows a rim indentation on the sides of each coin's reeded edge. This is not a form of damage, but rather the result of the metal flow that was necessary to create the high relief on the back of the obverse Conestoga wagon.

The primary focal points, such as the Conestoga wagon and ox, as well as the reverse American Indian, are prime targets for those grade and value lowering numismatic villains named bag mark, reed mark, hairline scratch, slide mark, dig, etc.

Error Coinage

To date, no error coinage or counterfeit pieces have surfaced.

Is Your Oregon Circulated or Mint State?

Obverse

Wear will first be observed on the hip of the ox and thigh of the pioneer leading the Conestoga wagon.

Reverse

A metal loss will first be noticed on the thigh of the American Indian opposite the word "of", then on his hand. Look for a difference in metal texture and crisscross scratches in this location, as well as doctoring in the form of whizzing, buffing, or polishing.

Related Material

The coins were distributed in a cardboard holder with inserts for three coins. The holders housed a three-piece set, coins of two separate dates, or one coin. In the case of the latter, the holders were cut into thirds (to be thrifty). One type is imprinted with the Memorial Association's name and address, and the manufacturer, John H. Eggers, New York, while the other is plain with a note at the bottom that it was patented and sold by John W. Rogers, New York. The mailing envelope is imprinted with the Memorial Association's New York City address, 1775 Broadway.

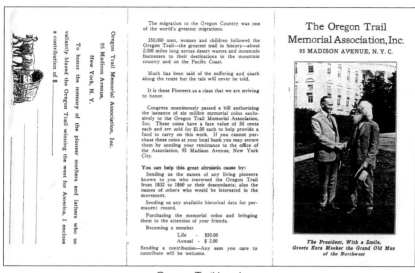

Oregon Trail brochure.

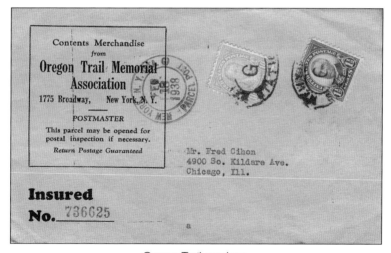

Oregon Trail envelope.

The envelope and holder together, if original, may be valued in the $100 to $150 range. Individual cards are worth $30 to $50. Material in support of the 1939 set can be worth a lofty $250 to $300. A Memorial Association membership application (10 × 6½ inches), folded in thirds and portraying President Coolidge shaking hands with Ezra Meeker, is worth between $100 and $150+, depending on condition.

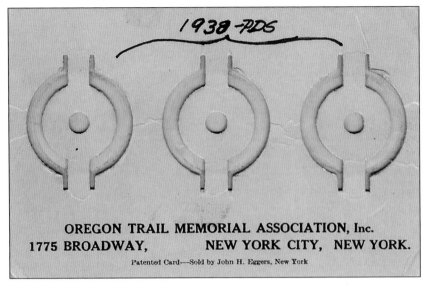

Oregon Trail coin holder (1175 Broadway, NY).

Oregon Trail coin holder (Bayside, Queens).

Future Potential of the Oregon Trail Half Dollars

Population Figures

Date	Service	AU 58	MS 60	MS 62	MS 63	MS 64	MS 65	MS 66	MS 67	MS 68	MS 69
1926	NGC	22	1	37	163	625	589	320	60	4	0
1926	PCGS	43	3	63	383	1072	750	392	62	3	0
1926	Combined	65	4	100	546	1697	1339	712	122	7	0

Date	Service	PF 58	PF 60	PF 62	PF 63	PF 64	PF 65	PF 66	PF 67	PF 68	PF 69
1926	NGC	0	0	0	0	0	1	0	0	0	0
1926	PCGS	0	0	0	0	0	0	0	0	0	0
1926	Combined	0	0	0	0	0	1	0	0	0	0

Date	Service	AU 58	MS 60	MS 62	MS 63	MS 64	MS 65	MS 66	MS 67	MS 68	MS 69
1926-S	NGC	26	1	33	145	671	841	601	193	11	0
1926-S	PCGS	53	6	117	552	1257	867	375	107	5	0
1926-S	Combined	79	7	150	797	1928	1708	976	300	16	0

Date	Service	AU 58	MS 60	MS 62	MS 63	MS 64	MS 65	MS 66	MS 67	MS 68	MS 69
1928	NGC	0	0	5	26	208	409	398	87	6	0
1928	PCGS	2	0	20	136	498	572	386	74	1	0
1928	Combined	2	0	25	162	706	981	784	161	7	0

Date	Service	AU 58	MS 60	MS 62	MS 63	MS 64	MS 65	MS 66	MS 67	MS 68	MS 69
1933-D	NGC	0	0	4	30	220	388	246	38	2	0
1933-D	PCGS	1	0	5	118	555	704	368	77	0	0
1933-D	Combined	1	0	9	148	775	1092	614	115	2	0

Date	Service	AU 58	MS 60	MS 62	MS 63	MS 64	MS 65	MS 66	MS 67	MS 68	MS 69
1934-D	NGC	1	0	3	42	391	523	219	21	0	0
1934-D	PCGS	3	1	15	229	837	768	338	52	0	0
1934-D	Combined	4	1	18	271	228	1291	557	73	0	0

Date	Service	AU 58	MS 60	MS 62	MS 63	MS 64	MS 65	MS 66	MS 67	MS 68	MS 69
1936	NGC	0	0	3	28	240	505	499	141	3	0
1936	PCGS	5	1	18	166	625	797	524	148	2	0
1936	Combined	5	1	21	194	865	1302	1023	289	5	0

Date	Service	AU 58	MS 60	MS 62	MS 63	MS 64	MS 65	MS 66	MS 67	MS 68	MS 69
1936-S	NGC	0	0	2	25	136	306	441	153	13	0
1936-S	PCGS	0	0	16	140	328	482	413	126	4	0
1936-S	Combined	0	0	18	165	464	788	824	279	17	0

Date	Service	AU 58	MS 60	MS 62	MS 63	MS 64	MS 65	MS 66	MS 67	MS 68	MS 69
1937-D	NGC	0	0	3	23	167	480	890	544	70	1
1937-D	PCGS	2	1	18	136	409	909	1144	576	40	1
1937-D	Combined	2	1	21	159	576	1389	2034	1120	110	2

Date	Service	AU 58	MS 60	MS 62	MS 63	MS 64	MS 65	MS 66	MS 67	MS 68	MS 69
1938	NGC	1	0	0	24	147	388	438	109	4	0
1938	PCGS	0	0	13	144	478	665	443	81	2	0
1938	Combined	1	0	13	168	625	1053	881	190	6	0

Date	Service	AU 58	MS 60	MS 62	MS 63	MS 64	MS 65	MS 66	MS 67	MS 68	MS 69
1938-D	NGC	1	0	1	12	117	332	524	243	59	2
1938-D	PCGS	0	0	6	115	326	640	589	199	34	2
1938-D	Combined	1	0	7	127	443	972	1113	442	93	4

Date	Service	AU 58	MS 60	MS 62	MS 63	MS 64	MS 65	MS 66	MS 67	MS 68	MS 69
1938-S	NGC	0	0	4	26	159	327	457	132	19	0
1938-S	PCGS	1	0	16	124	410	649	448	115	9	0
1938-S	Combined	1	0	20	150	569	976	905	247	28	0

Date	Service	AU 58	MS 60	MS 62	MS 63	MS 64	MS 65	MS 66	MS 67	MS 68	MS 69
1939	NGC	0	0	2	16	83	214	299	96	5	0
1939	PCGS	0	1	9	86	249	374	266	80	4	0
1939	Combined	0	1	11	102	332	588	565	176	9	0

Date	Service	AU 58	MS 60	MS 62	MS 63	MS 64	MS 65	MS 66	MS 67	MS 68	MS 69
1939-D	NGC	0	0	1	10	76	193	283	166	25	0
1939-D	PCGS	0	0	20	79	220	338	340	133	18	0
1939-D	Combined	0	0	21	89	296	531	623	299	43	0

Date	Service	AU 58	MS 60	MS 62	MS 63	MS 64	MS 65	MS 66	MS 67	MS 68	MS 69
1939-S	NGC	0	I	I	17	96	233	293	98	8	0
1939-S	PCGS	I	0	15	96	240	362	255	81	8	0
1939-S	Combined	I	I	16	113	336	595	548	179	16	0

Most available circulated Oregons are dated 1926-P and 1926-S, and, to a lesser degree, 1937-D. Other issues are usually cleaned or abused uncirculated pieces.

There are no major price spreads for most of this issue between MS-60 and MS-65. Therefore, we shall begin with and concentrate on MS-64 coinage.

The best bets at present are the undervalued 1939-D, 1939-S, 1939-P, 1938-D, and 1936-S issues. When looking for just a representative example of the series or a type coin that possesses extra flash or luster and has a strong strike, as well as good value, zero in on the 1937 Denver production. Acquire the 1926-P, 1926-S, and 1934-D pieces only for the joy of collecting.

I would estimate that between 26% to 39% of the MS-64 population was resubmitted for upgrade in the past, and their insert grading labels were thoughtlessly discarded. The price spreads during the May 1989 market high between the MS-64 and MS-65 category ranged from $270 to $670 for the common issues and from $380 to $1,575 for the 1934-D coin. (That is the reason for the constant resubmission.) Those most often resubmitted were the 1934-D, 1933-D, 1928-P, and the 1939 PDS set: these have average future potential.

Best bets for the MS-65 category are : 1939-D, 1939-S, 1939-P, and 1936-S. These are certainly undervalued as individual issues—if strictly graded. The population figures for this classification should be lowered by 26% to 37%. I see average to good future potential; many coins have been resubmitted in hopes of a higher grade. The price spreads were tremendous between the MS-65 and MS-66 categories during the 1989 high: there was once a $2,000 variance for the 1934-D issue. Dates to consider only for the joy of collecting are the 1937-D, 1926-P, 1926-S, and 1936-P.

The MS-66 issues that now offer the most potential and are extremely undervalued at current levels are the 1934-D, the 1939 issue, and the 1926-P strikings.

Dates offering average future possibilities are: 1926-S, 1936-P, 1938-S, 1936-S, and 1938-D. The 1937-D pieces should be acquired only for the joy of ownership. This coin has the fifth highest population in MS-66 (2,034), the third highest in MS-67 (1120) and the third highest in MS-68 (110). I would estimate that the population figures for this grade could be lowered between 16% and 23%.

In MS-67 condition, these undervalued dates can be difficult to locate: 1934-D, 1926-P, 1933-D, 1928-P, 1939-S, 1939-P, a very good to exceptional future here. I would estimate that most population figures could be decreased by 15% to 25% for this grade.

I recommend the aforementioned MS-67 issues and especially MS-68 acquisitions at present levels. I recently saw a 1928 Oregon Trail NGC MS-68 (star) encapsulation that was the best to cross my path since 1975. This outstanding gem coin was sold by a dealer for $18,500. Remember, a bargain can translate into being able just to own the issue—even when a premium has to be paid. Prices for NCG and PCGS MS-68 and MS-68 ★ (NGC only) or MS-68 + coinage can vary between $4,000 and $27,000+. The answer is the coin's total makeup. Feel free to contact me should you need assistance.

Reason for Issue:	To commemorate the 150th anniversary of the Battle of Bennington and the independence of Vermont.
Authorization:	Act of February 24, 1925, with a maximum of 40,000 pieces.
Issued by:	Vermont Sesquicentennial Commission
Official Sale Price:	$1 ($1.25 by mail)

Production Figures

Date	Business Strikes	Assay Coins	Proofs	Melted	Net Mintage
1927	40,000	34	4?	11,892	28,108

Current Market Values

Date	AU 58	MS 60	MS 63	MS 64	MS 65	MS 66	MS 67
1927	$195	$200	$210	$245	$575	$950	$3,000

DESIGNS BY CHARLES KECK

Obverse

Bust of Ira Allen, facing right. His name appears below his bust, with the inscription "FOUNDER OF VERMONT" in the lower border; "UNITED STATES OF AMERICA" arcs above. In 1777 Ira Allen helped formulate Vermont's declaration as an independent state. This Green Mountain Boy's primary objective was to free his land not only from the British soldiers, but also from those land grabbers of today's Empire State, New York.

Reverse

A catamount (short for a cat-a-mountain), or mountain lion, walking left. The original design incorporated Fay's Tavern, also known as the Catamount Tavern. Its name was derived from a stuffed member of the species exhibited atop a flagpole outside this historic meeting place of the Green Mountains Boys. However, the design showing the tavern was regarded as inartistic by the Federal Fine Arts Commission and rejected. The catamount was preferred. The words "Battle of Bennington" appear around the upper border, with "In God We Trust" and the anniversary dates 1777–1927 in the field above the cat. "Aug. 16" appears at the left, below the catamount's head. The Battle of Bennington (August 16, 1777) was a positive turning point for the Colonists.

Around the bottom border is "Half Dollar", with "E Pluribus Unum" just above it. The designer's initials (CK) are incused in the field located between the animal's left hind leg and tail.

Origins of the Vermont

The Philadelphia Mint produced 40,000 Vermonts plus 34 assay coins during January and February 1927. The original bill called for a gold dollar, as well as the 50-cent piece that was authorized almost two years prior to its creation. Distributed through the Bennington Battle Monument and Historical Association (Lock Box 432, Bennington, Vermont), the coins were offered for sale by local banks at $1 each and $1.25 by registered mail. Approximately 75 percent of this issue was sold and the remaining 11,892 pieces were returned to the Mint.

The Vermont Today

In EF-AU condition, these coins can be obtained with some effort. A large percentage will display the effects of numismatic abuse in the form of cleaning, light buffing, whizzing, or over-dipping. I recommend acquiring attractive pieces, exhibiting natural surfaces with little wear, unless all that is required is a representative example for the joy of collecting. In grades MS-60 through MS-65, the issue can be considered available. There is little value spread between the MS-60 and MS-64 categories, so collectors should seek out the higher grades. The future of this coin is in underrated, eye-appealing specimens grading MS-66 and higher.

Luster will range from proof-like, to semi-proof-like, to brilliant frosty (these are not the norm), to frosty, to dull frosty. Strike seldom presents a problem involving grade-value. Locating a specimen with sharp curl definition on the upper central section of Allen's periwig will not be an easy task, especially in MS-64 condition.

The primary focal obverse location is Allen's portrait, especially his exposed cheek, jaw, and forehead. On a small percentage of this issue, a characteristic die break, which resembles a small scratch, will be seen on the forehead, just above the eyebrow. Raised die polishing marks will appear in the obverse field above Allen's head, and below the animal's belly. Bag marks, slide marks, lack of metal fill marks, etc., plague the area. Smooth fields can be a target for large bag or reed marks. The reverse primary focal location is the cat, which can readily display the same numismatic wounds. When looking for a nice MS-63+ or MS-64 specimen, attempt to locate a flashy eye-appealing coin without major negatives in these key locations.

No error coinage or counterfeit coinage has entered the marketplace.

Is Your Vermont Circulated or Mint State?

Obverse

Wear first begins on the hair in the temple area of Ira Allen, then on his cheek. The portrait is a prime target for the coin doctors: wire-brushing will attempt to simulate the original Mint luster. Look also for an aluminum-like appearance as you slowly rotate the coin 360 degrees.

Reverse

Wear will first be apparent on the upper shoulder and cheek of the cat. Look for a difference in the texture of the metal.

Related Material

No official mailers from the Bennington Association have been seen to date. However, the issue was distributed by various Bennington banks, such as the County National Bank and First National Bank, in their own cardboard folded holders (4 × 2 7/8 inches). A cardboard insert for one coin is pasted within. Imprinted in green is "Vermont–Bennington Commemorative Half Dollar from" [bank's name], then "Bennington, Vt." The holder may be valued at $75 to $150+, depending on condition. A small flyer depicting the coin's obverse and reverse on the front cover can also be found; within is information about the coin and ordering instructions ($50). (See next page.)

Future Potential of the Vermont Half Dollar

Population Figures

Date	Service	AU 58	MS 60	MS 62	MS 63	MS 64	MS 65	MS 66	MS 67	MS 68	MS 69
1927	NGC	44	1	125	423	1246	759	189	19	2	0
1927	PCGS	82	9	246	979	1477	879	287	20	0	0
1927	Combined	126	10	371	1402	2723	1638	476	39	2	0

At current levels, this very popular single-year issue is somewhat undervalued in all ratings up to MS-65. I suggest that collectors buy for the joy of ownership. These grades have average to good possibilities for price increases. The past dollar high during the May 1989 market peak between grades MS-63 and MS-64 was a large $500; the difference in MS-64 and MS-65 ratings was $2,500; that

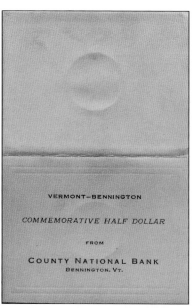

VERMONT–BENNINGTON

COMMEMORATIVE HALF DOLLAR

FROM

COUNTY NATIONAL BANK
BENNINGTON, VT.

Vermont coin holder—outside cover.   Vermont coin holder—inside

between MS-65 and MS-66 was a massive $5,000. Needless to say, population figures were lower at the time.

Pieces strictly evaluated as MS-66 are under priced at present levels. I would reduce the census count by 25% to 30% for the MS-65 category and by 20% to 25% for the MS-66 grade: these have very good to excellent future potential. MS-67 Vermonts are very much underrated: I would love to own the coin. Some collectors have told me they would prefer having three MS-66 pieces in their portfolios, instead of one MS-67 coin. That's a good point. One MS-67+ or high end Vermont sold for $5,000 while another sold for $15,000. The latter buyer possibly thought the coin could upgrade to an MS-68 rating. He was successful.

Reason for Issue:	To commemorate the 150th anniversary of the landing on the Hawaiian Islands by Captain James Cook, a British navigator, and for the purpose of aiding in the establishment of a Captain James Cook Memorial Collection in the archives of the Territory of Hawaii.
Authorization:	Act of March 7, 1928, with a maximum of 10,000 pieces.
Issued by:	Captain Cook Sesquicentennial Commission
Official Sale Price:	$2

Production Figures

Date	Business Strikes	Assay Coins	Proofs	Melted	Net Mintage
1928	10,008	8	50	0	9,950

Current Market Values

Date	AU-58	MS-60	MS-63	MS-64	MS-65	MS-66
1928	$1,600	$1,700	$2,100	$2,750	$4,300	$9,000

Designs by Juliette May Fraser, modeled by Chester Beach

Obverse

Bust of Captain James Cook, facing left. In the left field are the words "Capt. James Cook Discoverer of Hawaii". To the right of the word "Capt." is a compass needle. At the lower border are eight triangles symbolizing the eight largest islands of the Hawaiian chain. "In God We Trust" is in the upper right field; "UNITED STATES OF AMERICA" arcs above; "HALF DOLLAR" below. At the right base of the bust in relief are the artist's initials (CB): Chester Beach executed the design based on a sketch by Juliette May Fraser of Honolulu.

Reverse

Hawaiian warrior chief in full regalia, standing at the top of a hill, extending his right arm in welcome and holding an upright spear with his left hand. In the left field is pictured a village of grass huts at the foot of Diamond Head and Waikiki Beach. A coconut palm tree, representing romance, occupies the right and upper field. "E PLURIBUS UNUM" is in the lower left field, where the ocean meets the shore. The anniversary dates 1778–1928 appear in the lower border.

Origins of the Hawaiian

The Philadelphia Mint produced 10,000 Hawaiian half dollars plus eight for assay purposes in June 1928. They were sold at $2 each—the highest price asked for a commemorative half dollar to that date—by the Captain Cook Sesquicentennial Commission of Honolulu via the Bank of Hawaii Ltd. of Honolulu, starting on October 8, 1928.

Of the total mintage, 50 specimens were issued in the form of sandblast proofs and later presented to various officials and museums. Today, nine of these extremely rare pieces are in museums. There were also 400 pieces of the regular issue kept for special presentation purposes. Supposedly, half of the remaining coins were shipped to the Territory of Hawaii and the other half was distributed on the mainland.

Low mintage, unintentional numismatic abuse, and a wide distribution, makes the Hawaiian one of the more valuable silver commemoratives today. Most people who own the Hawaiian half dollar keep the coin in their possession. I personally believe that a wealthy family or group of investors in Hawaii acquired and still owns between 1,500 and 2,000 or more pieces in various Mint State grades. It is difficult for me to believe that a large number of "Islanders" so readily forked over four times face value for the half dollar. I was met with skepticism when I expressed the opinion that the Bank of Hawaii possibly possessed 500 of these coins. When inquiries were made to the bank by friends and clients in Hawaii, no one knew of their existence. However, on January 23, 1986, Bowers & Merena Galleries auctioned off 137 of the coins for the bank.

The Hawaiian Today

Specimens in the EF-AU category are usually seen lightly whizzed or doctored in some fashion. These $700 to $900 coins are the pieces forwarded by unscrupulous or unknowledgeable dealers to collectors who inform them that they can spend only up to $1,000 or $1,100 for an MS-62 coin or just ask for an MS-62 coin at $1,500. Collectors should acquire coins in this grade only if the price is too good to pass or you just would like a representative example. Original appealing coins exhibiting some natural wear can be difficult to locate and could easily bring close to MS-60 money. Strike seldom if ever will be detrimental to the coin's grade or value. Luster will range from flashy satiny (not the norm) to dull satiny. It is those bag marks, reed marks, hairline scratches, etc., that plague this issue in the primary focal areas: Captain Cook's face and head, as well as the Hawaiian warrior chief's body on the reverse. One deep hit in any of these areas can lower a coin's grade and value by $1,000 to $3,500.

The Hawaiian sandblast proof—which was referred to as a token (of appreciation) when presented to the Sesquicentennial Commission Chairman Col. C.P. Laukea by Edgar Henriques, its Executive Secretary, on June 6, 1928—is a rare item. Each double struck proof coin was individually sandblasted at the Philadelphia Mint; the coin dies were not sandblasted. At times, one of these coins is offered for sale at auction or at a coin show. Values can range from $7,500 upwards, depending on its rating. I suggest you examine this treasure and compare its surface and double-strike to the normal business strike. Beware of a business strike that was sandblasted outside the Mint. One of these can be inserted in place of the genuine proof within the purple coin case that possibly accompanied other documentation.

In 1982 I was asked by my friend Gerry Bauman, Senior Numismatist for Manfra, Tordella & Brookes (MTB), to authenticate such a coin. It was originally presented to a US Naval officer in 1928. The coin was being offered by a supposed family member. After examining the coin I declared the coin was not double-struck and the surface applied by some jeweler. The documentation as well as the coin case were genuine. This offered piece was switchd by some person who knew the value of the genuine item and wanted to make a score! Beware this offering should it cross your path.

The designer's original sketch, her cracked Wedgwood depicting Captain Cook, plus the proof coin and case given to her were offered for sale at $100,000. One must ask: How much is history worth? You decide. I later learned that this material purportedly sold for approximately $48,000 in a private sale.

To date, no error coinage has been reported.

Detecting Counterfeits

All known coins produced by the Philadelphia Mint have a raised die polishing mark extending from the upper part of the warrior's cap through the palm leaves, as well as a fine die polishing mark extending from his underarm into the coin's field. One counterfeit will exhibit a depression in the border design to the right of the second "A" in "AMERICA" on the obverse. Its reverse will display a small circular depression above the back part of the warrior's hand. There have been attempts to hide the counterfeit diagnostics by whizzing or polishing the coin. Another counterfeit displays a glossy luster and a semi-proof-like surface along with fuzzy details and sharp edge reeding. Examining the portrait of Captain Cook, we can observe a small raised line or spike protruding from his throat, extending into the field. The reverse bears an extra piece of raised metal near the rim, above the fuzzy palm leaves near the eleven o'clock position.

IS YOUR HAWAIIAN CIRCULATED OR MINT STATE?

Obverse

The rim of this coin offers its high points little protection. Therefore, at the slightest abuse Captain Cook's cheekbone and then the roll of hair over his ear will display a loss of metal. Should you observe a distinct difference in metal texture or the worn shiny or bright look when comparing the cheekbone to the bordering facial area, friction has occurred. If no difference is present, but small scratches are observed, this indicates only a lack of metal fill. In other words, when the planchet metal flowed cold as the coin was produced, there was not enough metal to fill in the cheekbone design and make it totally smooth. This location and Cook's face will be the primary target of the doctoring artists. Rotate the coin slowly 360 degrees, tilting it back and forth, attempting to detect their workmanship.

Reverse

Look for a metal loss in the form of a grayish white texture on the thighs, knees, sash, and left hand of the warrior chief.

Related Material

The very rare and desirable Hawaiian sandblast proof was distributed in an unmarked purple wooden box. Its inner top was made with a purple satiny material with purple velour lining the lower section. A metal push button is in the front lower section of the box. The few I have encountered possess a church-like incense aroma. They have sold for between $3,500 and $6,500.

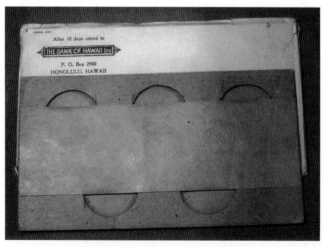

Hawaiian coin envelope and holder.

The business strike was mailed in a Bank of Hawaii Ltd. envelope (P.O. Box 2900, Honolulu, Hawaii), which contained a cardboard holder with openings for five coins. The coins were held in place by a piece of paper tape. On occasion, the enclosed coins will show some degree of captivating iridescent shades of green, greenish gold, red, and reddish brown. Higher graded specimens will bring greater monetary rewards.

Expect a value of $250 to $650+ for the original envelope and card, depending on condition.

Future Potential of the Hawaiian Half Dollar

Population Figures

Date	Service	AU 58	MS 60	MS 62	MS 63	MS 64	MS 65	MS 66	MS 67	MS 68	MS 69
1928	NGC	14	3	132	262	732	359	74	4	0	0
1928	PCGS	58	22	240	590	1023	457	73	2	0	0
1928	Combined	72	25	372	852	1755	816	147	6	0	0

Date	Service	PF 60	PF 61	PF 62	PF 63	PF 64	PF 65	PF 66	PF 67	PF 68	PF 69
1928	NGC	0	0	3	3	9	4	4	0	0	0
1928	PCGS	0	1	1	1	7	0	0	0	0	0
1928	Combined	0	1	4	4	16	4	4	0	0	0

Most circulated offerings of this, the king of commemoratives, are usually cleaned or whizzed and worth less than current levels. Un-doctored AU coinage is worth between $1,200 and $1,450. Collectors should buy for the joy of ownership. Attractive AU+ material will usually bring MS-60 money or more, depending on the coin's makeup. The Hawaiian is the most expensive commemorative half dollar in circulated condition. In grades MS-60 through MS-63, the Hawaiian is still, because of its strong allure, most desired. Attempt to procure a nice MS-63+ specimen, if available. In MS-64 condition, this very popular issue, depending on eye-appeal, is somewhat undervalued, and it is such coinage that has genuine future potential. The past price spread between MS-64 and MS-65 was $2,300. I would lower the population figures between 27% and 34%.

Pieces grading MS-65 are definitely undervalued at present—if strictly graded. The marketplace does have a fair quantity of Hawaiians that leave much to be desired. They lack eye appeal and are liberally rated. It is this kind of material that drives values downward. Were they to be cracked out and resubmitted, a degree of downgrading would certainly take place. Collectors should pass on the dull, dark and smoky unattractive coinage, even coins with iridescent or colored toning. When the right stuff makes its appearance, it almost always brings much more than these pieces. There is very good future potential here. The past price spread between this grade and the MS-66 rating was more than $10,000.

Presented here is an updated listing of the original roster of the 50 recipients of the rare 1928 Hawaiian Sandblast half dollar, as well as the current owners.

1. Edgar Henriques, Ex. Secy, Captain Cook Sesquicentennial Comm.
2. Bruce Cartwright, Jr. Chairman, Captain Cook Sesquicentennial Comm.: Robert van Dyke.
3. Dr. Albert E. Gregory, Commissioner
4. Albert Pierce Taylor, Commissioner
5. Bishop H. B. Restarick, Commissioner
6. Col. C.P. Iaukea, Commissioner; Anthony J. Swiatek
7. Prof. Ralph S. Kuykendall, private collection
8. Juliette Mae Frazer, Robert van Dyke, Alfred J. Ostheimer, Superior Galleries, private collection
9. Hon. Wallace R. Farrington
10. Ms. Marie von Holt
11. Hawaiian Historical Society
12. Bernice Pauahi Bishop Museum, 1355 Kalihi St., Honolulu
13. Hon. Gerald H. Phipps
14. Archives of Hawaii
15. B.C. Stewart
16. U.S. National Museum, "not delivered", now in Smithsonian Inst.
17. British Admiralty
18. Rt. Hon. S.M. Bruce
19. Hon. T.R. Bavin
20. The British Museum
21. President Coolidge, private collection
22. King George V of England. Presumably with the Royal Collections
23. Lord Sandwich
24. Andrew W. Mellon, Secretary of Treasury
25. Rear Admiral George S. Marvell, USN
26. Maj. Gen.Fox Conner, USA, his grandson, private collection
27. American Numismatic Assn.
28. Captain Leveson-Gower, R.N., D.S.O.
29. Captain Gerald Cartwell Harrison
30. Commodore ___ Swabey
31. Captain John Greenslade
32. Hon. Dwight F. Davis, Secretary of War under President Coolidge
33. Sir Joseph Carruthers
34. Sir Hnery Newbolt
35. Prof. Frank A. Golder
36. Judge F.W. Howay
37. Verne Blue, "not delivered"
38. Kauai Historical Society, Lihue, Kauai
39. James A. Wilder
40. Unassigned. Later given to Hon. Lawrence M. Judd
41. Theodore B. Pitman
42. Dr. Peter H. Buck
43. Hon. Maurice Cohen
44. The Right Hon. J.G. Coates
45. National Museum Wellington, New Zealand
46. Ho. John C. Lane
47. American Numismatic Society
48. Edward L. Caum, private collection, Mitchell Proctor (John Dean Coin Co.), Gary Filler (Chattanooga Coin Co.), James N. Anthony
49. J. Frank Woods
50. Commander Victor Stewart Kaleoaloha Houston, private collection

1934 Maryland Tercentenary

Reason for Issue:	The 300th anniversary of the founding of the Province of Maryland.
Authorization:	Act of May 9, 1934, with a maximum of 25,000 pieces.
Issued by:	Maryland Tercentenary Commission
Official Sale Price:	$1

Production Figures

Date	Business Strikes	Assay Coins	Proofs	Melted	Net Mintage
1934	25,000	15	4-6?	0	25,000

Current Market Values

Date	AU-58	MS-60	MS-63	MS-64	MS-65	MS-66	MS-67
1934	$115	$120	$130	$140	$230	$450	$1,350

Designs by Hans Schuler

Obverse

A three-quarter bust of Cecil Calvert, second Lord Baltimore (after whom the city is named); with Calvert's name below the bust. "United States of America" arcs above; "Half Dollar" below. "E Pluribus Unum" is in the left field; "In God We Trust" in the right.

Reverse

The coat of arms of the State of Maryland, adapted from the Calvert family's crest. This is one of two coins (the other being the York County, Maine) that depicts a cross (or crosses) as part of its design. The two reverse figures represent Labor (with the spade) and Fisheries (with the fish). Next to Labor's foot are the designer's initials (HS). The Italian motto, "FATTI MASCHII PAROLE FEMINE", means "Deeds are manly, words are womanly." The anniversary dates, 1634–1934, with decorative stars on each side, are in the lower field. The date 1634 represents the founding of St. Mary's City by more than 200 colonists, who were the first to settle after Calvert obtained a land grant from King Charles I. "MARYLAND TERCENTENARY" appears in the border.

Origins of the Maryland

After the striking of the Hawaiian half dollars by the Philadelphia Mint in June 1928, Congress approved no new issues until the Texas Centennial Coinage Act of June 15, 1933. The Maryland issue was approved on May 9, 1934.

The Texas issue was coined in October and November 1934. However, 25,000 Maryland half dollars plus 15 assay coins were struck during July 1934 at the Philadelphia Mint. Although the Texas issue was authorized earlier, the Maryland issue was the first authorized souvenir coin to be issued in the Roosevelt administration.

Beginning with this issue, the Director of the Mint was assigned the responsibility of minting commemorative coins. Previously, authorizing Acts—with several exceptions—referred only to the complete mintage allowed. However, in the case of the Maryland Tercentenary half dollar, a fixed production figure was given and the Director was made responsible. This Act was also the first to specify that the coin was to be sold at a price above face value; no previous Acts had referred to a selling price.

The Maryland issue was distributed by the Maryland Tercentenary Commission of Baltimore via Maryland banks at $1 each. However, almost 5,000 coins remained unsold. From the remaining coins, about 2,000 coins were sold at 75 cents each, the remainder was offered for sale at 65 cents per coin.

The Maryland Today

The issue is not exactly abundant in EF-AU condition. Most coins will exhibit some form of abuse in the form of polishing, whizzing (especially Calvert's portrait), or the effects of being kept as a souvenir coin. The value spread between EF and MS-64 is narrow: so why should collectors buy an MS-60 coin when an MS-63 or MS-64 piece can be procured for not much more money? Coins are available in the marketplace in these classifications and can be acquired for the joy of collecting. Luster will range from blazing satiny (not the norm), down to dull satiny.

The Maryland can be somewhat difficult to locate in eye-appealing gem MS-66+ condition because of excessive or heavy nicks, cuts, scratches, and lack of metal fill marks, especially on Calvert's portrait—including the nose, which always looks almost flat. Collectors should remember that this was a "rush job," as evidenced by the poor workmanship in the areas of the cheekbone and nose, and especially in the lower forehead area, which resembles giant eyebrows. I have not seen any coin where the degree of strike flatness would lower the grade or value.

When purchasing this issue, look for specimens displaying natural attractive lustrous surfaces, accompanied by a minimum of marks in critical locations: eye appeal is very important. Die abrasions are acceptable, provided they are not detracting or excessive. The reverse seldom presents a problem, although lack of fill marks of various sizes will make their presence known in the lower left quarter of the shield. There are possibly four to six matte proofs (double-struck, acid-dipped at the Mint). I know of one piece that was cleaned by its owner to make it bright and new looking: it is now numismatically impaired forever. I have personally examined two other such pieces: (1) Ex J.R. Sinnock estate, 1962 ANA Convention Sale, Lot 2053; (2) Ex J.R. Sinnock estate, 1962 ANA Convention Sale, Lot 2054.

To date, no error coinage or counterfeits are known to exist.

Is Your Maryland Circulated or Mint State?

Obverse
Wear first begins on Calvert's nose, jaw, and the left side of the hair above the temple area, down to the back jaw (opposite the word "UNITED"). The flat nose appearance was caused by the striking. Calvert's portrait is a target for whizzing and other forms of doctoring. Surface negatives in the unprotected fields can easily downgrade coin.

Reverse
A metal loss will first be observed on the drapery folds above the heads of the male figures, then in the crown. The primary focal area is the shield.

Related Material
Many of the Maryland half dollars mailed to subscribers were forwarded in a standard Dennison one-coin holder, with a green paper flap that held the coin in place. I personally would not pay more than $1 to $2 for these, simply because there is nothing special about them. In this case, be influenced by the coin, not the holder, even if it is accompanied by the mailing envelope. Other coins were mailed in tissue paper. There is four-line imprinting on the envelope: "1634–1934, Maryland Tercentenary Commission, 902 Union Trust Building, Baltimore, Maryland".

The original envelope and holder together, I would value at $75 to $125; the holder by itself, no more than $2.

Future Potential of the Maryland Half Dollar

Population Figures

Date	Service	AU 58	MS 60	MS 62	MS 63	MS 64	MS 65	MS 66	MS 67	MS 68	MS 69
1934	NGC	5	0	23	181	1099	1305	483	90	3	0
1934	PCGS	8	3	84	714	1781	1340	550	45	0	0
1934	Combined	13	3	107	895	2880	2645	1033	135	3	0

Date	Service	PF 50	PF 60	PF 62	PF 63	PF 64	PF 65	PF 66	PF 67	PF 68	PF 69
1934	NGC	0	0	1	0	1	0	0	0	0	0
1934	PCGS	0	0	0	0	0	0	0	0	0	0
1934	Combined	0	0	1	0	1	0	0	0	0	0

The Maryland is not exactly abundant in circulated condition, and most offerings are of the abused variety. The issue is fairly priced in grades EF-AU through MS-66. There is little price spread between grades MS-60 and MS-64. Collectors should attempt to acquire an attractive MS-64+ specimen, if funds permit.

The May 1989 high dollar spread between the MS-64 and MS-65 grades was $1,100: this is unlikely to recur. I would lower the census between 20% and 25%, but buy these grades only for the pride of ownership.

At current levels, the MS-65 specimen is also fairly priced, and may benefit from promotion. The past high between MS-65 and MS-66 graded pieces was $2,800, but this won't happen agani. I would lower population figures between 25% and 30%, and see average future potential in this category.

The Maryland half dollar is somewhat undervalued in MS-66 condition, but only if the coin has eye appeal. Pass on the unattractive offering. I would lower the census between 27% and 34%, and see good future potential. The real future lies in alluring Maryland pieces rated MS-67. If you are able to afford this item, you should but it: your reward will arrive with the next market heat.

In May 2006 at a Bowers & Marena auction held in Anaheim, CA, a coin with amazing eye-appeal sold for $19,309. Population was 2 at the time. At the February 2009 Long Beach Heritage coin auction #1122, an NGC MS-68 Maryland sold for $8,625.

1934–1938 Daniel Boone Bicentennial

Reason for Issue:	To commemorate the 200th anniversary of the birth of Daniel Boone.
Authorization:	Act of May 26, 1934, with a maximum of 600,000 pieces for all issues.
Issued by:	Daniel Boone Bicentennial Commission
Official Sale Price:	1934: $1.60 1935-D: $1.60 1935-S: $1.60 1936-D: $1.60 1936-S: $1.60 1935: $1.10 1935 with small 1934: $1.10 1936: $1.10 1935-D and 1935–S: small 1934 added: $3.70/pair 1937: only with 1937-D: $1.60; after May 1937: $7.25 set 1937-D; only with 1937: $7.25 set 1937-S: For 17 days, $5.15; afterwards in a 3-piece set at $12.40 1938 PDS: $6.50 set

Production Figures

Date	Business Strikes	Assay Coins	Proofs	Melted	Net Mintage
1934	10,000	7	4?	-	10,000
1935	10,000	10	4?	-	10,000
1935-D	5,000	5	4?	-	5,000
1935-S	5,000	5	4?	-	5,000
1935 (small 1934)	10,000	8	4?	-	10,000
1935-D (small 1934)	2,000	3	4?	-	2,000
1935-S (small 1934)	2,000	4	4?	-	2,000
1936	12,000	12	4?	-	12,000
1936-D	5,000	5	4?	-	5,000
1936-S	5,000	6	4?	-	5,000
1937	15,000	10	4?	5,200	9,800
1937-D	7,500	6	4?	5,000	2,500
1937-S	5,000	6	4?	2,500	2,500
1938	5,000	5	4?	2,900	2,100
1938-D	5,000	5	4?	2,900	2,100
1938-S	5,000	6	4?	2,900	2,100

Current Market Values

Date	AU 58	MS 60	MS 63	MS 64	MS 65	MS 66	MS 67
1934	$95	$100	$135	$150	$225	$345	$950+
1935 PDS set	$300	$325	$370	$450	$675	$1035	$5600+
1935 with small 1934	$825	$890	$970	$1075	$1900	$3200	$6100+
1936 PDS set	$300	$325	$370	$450	$675	$1035	$3400
1937 PDS set	$690	$775	$825	$890	$1250	$1790	$3000
1938 PDS set	$1000	$1075	$1150	$1200	$1600	$2800	$4500

DESIGNS BY AUGUSTUS LUKEMAN

Obverse

The bust of Daniel Boone, facing left. It is based on the frontispiece in *Collins' History of Kentucky* (1847 and 1848 editions) and the designer's conception the famed Indian fighter's appearance. It was accepted by the Daniel Boone Bicentennial Commission of Kentucky, when the *Lexington Herald*—a newspaper that according to Colonel William Boone Douglas, president of the Boone Family Association, had more knowledge about Boone than any other publication—

approved the designs. This settled previous disputes between the U.S. Commission of Fine Arts and the Bicentennial Commission. "UNITED STATES OF AMERICA" arcs above; "HALF DOLLAR" below.

Reverse

Daniel Boone holding a musket upright with his left hand and holding a peace treaty with his right hand, facing Chief Black Fish of the Shawnees, who is standing at right, holding a tomahawk. In the original design, the chief held a peace pipe. When the pipe was substituted with a tomahawk, the U.S. Mint Director Nellie Tayloe Ross suggested that Boone's scroll be removed and he be armed with a knife. The designer agreed, but lack of time prevented the change.

The men are depicted discussing the treaty that put an end to the nine-day siege of Fort Boonesborough (1778), which is in the background. "IN GOD WE TRUST" is in large letters at the top border; "E PLURIBUS UNUM" is in smaller letters just below. In the left field is "DANIEL BOONE BICENTENNIAL"; in the right field, within the rays of the rising sun, are the words "PIONEER YEAR". The issue date appears at the bottom border.

Beginning in 1935, a small "1934" was added to the design just above "PIONEER YEAR", creating two 1935 varieties. The small date 1934 is supposed to represent an anniversary date. I use the word "supposed" because the companion date 1734, the year of Daniel Boone's birth, is omitted entirely on this issue. Mint marks (D or S) will be found in the lower right field, to the right of Black Fish's ankle.

Boone was captain of a group of civilian soldiers during a salt-making expedition in February 1778, when he was captured by the Shawnees, and then taken to the British command center in Detroit. He was highly regarded as a hunter by the Native Americans, and his life was spared. Boone was adopted by the tribe, as a son of Black Fish—and named Big Turtle.

During Boone's three-month captivity, he overheard a conversation between a British agent and Black Fish. Their objective was to extend the campaign against the pioneers across the Alleghenies, and Fort Boonesborough was scheduled for attack. Escaping, Boone reportedly ran 160 miles to warn of the impending raid. During the nine-day siege, the Indians began digging a tunnel toward the citadel. Their goal was to place explosives beneath the fort's entrance and to blast their way in. Boone ordered an intercepting tunnel to be dug, and this too was filled with explosives. When Black Fish was informed about the countermine, he withdrew his force of 500 men. Boone's escapades caused Black Fish to claim he was supernatural.

Boone was the type of man who favored the rigors of field and forest over the enjoyments of home and cozy fireplace. Nevertheless, his final illness (in 1820, at age 85) was caused not by the great outdoors, but by an overindulgence in baked sweet potatoes. He was laid to rest in Missouri alongside his wife, Rebecca.

Twenty-five years later, it was claimed that Daniel and Rebecca had been reburied in Frankfort, Kentucky. However, a recent investigation claims that

Boone's place of burial in Kentucky, next to Rebecca, possibly holds the remains of a slave who was mistakenly exhumed instead of Boone. Until proven, the legendary hero may still rest in Defiance, Missouri, undisturbed.

Origins of the Boone

Public Law 258-73rd Congress authorized the Director of the Mint to issue 600,000 half dollars, a fixed amount. This meant that the total authorization was to be produced at one striking. The wording of the Act was not fully understood, however, because in October 1934 the Philadelphia Mint struck just 10,000 (plus seven for assay) coins.

The first piece struck was presented to President Franklin D. Roosevelt from the Daniel Boone Bicentennial Commission through Senator A.W. Barkley. The Superintendent of the Philadelphia Mint placed the coin in a specially marked envelope bearing his signature.

The Boone Today

Surfaces for the issue range widely from proof-like (PL), to semi-proof-like, to chrome-like, to dull satiny, to an unattractive dullish semi-matte (coins with the latter grainy surface have a loss-of-luster look). A 1937-S coin has a PL surface, as well as a frosty luster; a 1936-S specimen for the most part will display an attractive brilliant frosty look. There are also exceptions, with unappealing luster or chrome-like reverses (because of die polishing).

Strike for the entire series will present no problems that will influence the coin's value or grade. Inspection will reveal an insignificant weakness in the Chief's head and hand (which appears to be covering a split in his buckskin trousers). I have seen several 1936-P specimens whose reverses were produced from filled dies. In this case, some form of foreign matter clogged the incused area of the die. When the planchets were struck, a portion of Boone's hand and scroll were missing. This condition does lower the value of the affected coins.

Coins grading EF-AU can be found with little effort. Most of the time, they will exhibit some form of numismatic abuse, such as polishing, whizzing, etc. The most common issues are both 1935 Philadelphia varieties, the 1936-P, and, to a lesser degree, the 1937-P. Since price spread for these dates in conditions EF-AU through MS-65 is small, it seems most logical to acquire at least an MS-64 or MS-65 specimen, funds permitting. That is unless all that matters to you is to find a representative example in any grade.

The 1934 Boone was sold at $1.60 through the Bicentennial Commission, which widely distributed this issue, and prevented their return to the Mint. Luster will range from appealing satiny bright (not the norm), to very bright with little portrait–field contrast, to dull.

The 1934 Boone is not abundant in strict MS-66+ and better condition. It has an excellent future in the higher grades. The majority of the existing market supply falls into the not-so-choice categories (MS-60 through MS-63), because of numismatic abuse. In many cases in this issue, raw MS-64+ coins are offered at MS-65 prices. These are often fully original coins that were MS-65 by past standards, but that display surface detractions in the primary focal areas.

The Philadelphia pieces, struck in March 1935, were sold at $1.10; the Denver and San Francisco issues, produced in May, were sold at $1.60 each. There are obverse and reverse die trial pieces for this issue, in silver as well as copper, without a Mint mark. Today, only 5,000 sets of this issue can be assembled, with the 5,000 remaining Philadelphia pieces offered for sale as type coins. Luster will range from brilliant frosty (the norm) to just appealing. Nevertheless, locating top quality sets is not easy, because of past distribution and later numismatic abuse. A large number of the coins bear cuts, nicks, deep scratches, slide marks, bag marks, and abrasions that were overlooked by many from the early 1960s through the early 1970s, when the term BU (Brilliant Uncirculated) was heavily applied. In the mid-1970s, such coins were often considered gems because of blazing luster. Today, they are yesterday's gems: grading standards have become very strict. Collectors should beware of sellers who offer "bargains." If prices seem too good to be true, you can bet they are. The key date is the 1935 Denver issue in MS-65 condition and the San Francisco striking in MS-64.

In October 1935 the Philadelphia Mint produced 10,000 coins plus eight assay pieces with the added "small date 1934" above the words "Pioneer Year". Die trials of the P, D, and S strikings exist. However, in the following month, the branch Mints struck what amounted to be the lowest commemorative mintage ever created. Denver made 2,000 plus three assay pieces with the added "1934," while the San Francisco Mint produced 2,000 plus four assay pieces. Not a single coin of this issue was returned to the Mint. The D and S specimens sold in pairs for $3.70, while the remaining P issue was offered at $1.10. With mintages like these, every collector and speculator wanted a set, or whatever quantity of coins that could be purchased. Many orders were not filled, and the Bicentennial Commission was heavily criticized by those who did not receive the very rare Small Date issue. Congressional hearings resulted and brought to light the abuses of commemorative coin authorizations. Afterwards, larger mintages were authorized; the number of pieces that could be secured from the Mint was fixed and each new issue would be produced at one Mint only. Today if the U.S. Mint offered such low mintage pieces, they would be sold out within two hours—or less.

Eye-appealing brilliant frosty luster is the norm for the Philadelphia coin; some pieces will have a semi-brilliant surface. However, because of a late delivery to Denver and San Francisco (and hence lack of time) and ignorance of the appearance of the Philadelphia coin, no attempt was made to alter the original surfaces of the forwarded dies; they were used as received. Thus, the rare D and S issues of 1935 display a virtual matte-like finish, especially on the obverse. They will look dull or grainy instead of lustrous because the dies were not prepared in a manner similar to the Philadelphia dies.

Examining the obverse surface of this issue, we can observe die polishing marks in the field. These marks result from incomplete die polishing and from a residue from wire-brushing the dies. For whatever reason, the reverses of both issues were polished during a halt in production, creating a chrome-like appearance: no contrast between the coin's design and field can be observed. The Denver coin displays this condition less frequently than the San Francisco coin, and with much less chrome depth. Many of these coins were altered to increase brightness, with a resulting lowering of value. Some have been artificially toned in an attempt to hide the altered surfaces.

Collectors should make certain that your set has the Small Date "1934" above the words "PIONEER YEAR" in order to be classified the "rare date set." I have seen the 1935 set without the Small Date substituted in complete commemorative sets for the rare date issue. The higher mintage Philadelphia issue is not rare, and should sell at a type coin price. In other words, if an MS-65 set were to sell for $1,850 because of the low mintage D and S issues, the Philadelphia striking would be valued at $150. Should the coin be extra appealing, it would be worth more money.

I highly recommend the 1935 set with the added Small Date in all grades, as well as the individual rarer D and S specimens. The rarer pieces are not abundant. In MS-64 condition, the Denver coin is the rare issue; in MS-65 they are equally as rare. Rated MS-66 the San Francisco strike is rarer. When examining the D Mint mark, a shift in the "D" can be observed.

The 1936 Boone set will have a luster range between brilliant frosty (for the majority of the issue) to dull frosty (as seen on some Philadelphia coins). Buy only for the joy of ownership. For future price rises, collectors will have to seek 1936-D in MS-66 and loftier.

Another rare set was created in 1937 because coins were returned to be melted. In January 1937, the Philadelphia Mint produced 15,010 specimens, later offered at $1.60 each. Luster will range from deep mirror proof-like, to semi-proof-like (not the norm), to brilliant frosty, being similar in appearance to the 1935 No-Small Date specimens, the 1935-P with the addition, and the 1936 coins. Where are these beautiful proof-like coins hiding? It could be that many of those produced were bagged with the group returned for re-melting, while others reside in collections. I would apply same logic to the 1937-D and -S and the 1938 issues.

Five months after the Philadelphia issue, the Denver Mint produced 7,506 specimens. Both issues were offered as a pair at $7.25: the Denver issue was not sold individually. The San Francisco Mint produced 5,006 specimens in October 1937, which were sold at $5.15. Sets were made available, and the three coins sold for $12.40. Altogether, 1937 saw some strange pricing.

1937-D and -S surfaces will range from semi-proof-like, to brilliant frosty, to dull frosty. Die polishing marks or raised surface lines resembling fine scratches, but which do not scratch into the surface, will be conspicuous in varying degrees.

With 2,500 available sets, collectors should consider the acquisition of strict MS-64 and higher grade sets and of individual D and S specimens. The rare D and S pieces give the set its value and not the common Philadelphia issue, which should sell at type coin prices.

Fifty presentation pieces were supposedly struck from a set of highly polished dies at the San Francisco Mint. There is good future potential for these issues, especially in MS-66 and MS-67 condition. The San Francisco is the rarest of the three coins.

Possibly four 1937 Boone matte proof sets were made for the Chief Engraver of the U.S. Mint, John Ray Sinnock. The branch Mint specimens were struck in Philadelphia, before the shipment of dies to the branches. Each coin possesses a double strike with sharp squared letters and a matte surface. Remember, anyone can dip a coin in acid to attempt to duplicate this grayish finish, but they cannot create an extra blow from the coin press.

The Daniel Boone Bicentennial Commission stated that the Boone issues would end with the 1937 set, but nevertheless went ahead and obtained 5,000 sets dated 1938. Luster for all three coins will range from proof-like, down to a dull satiny.

Lack of sales meant that 2,900 coins from each Mint entered the melting pot, leaving only 2,100 available sets for 1938. These are a must to own in MS-64 and better condition—excellent future potential for all who possess or plan to acquire the set or the individual type coin. Again, the Denver is the rarest in grade MS-64, the Philadelphia issue in MS-65.

No error coinage or counterfeits for this issue are known at this time.

Is Your Boone Circulated or Mint State?

Obverse

A metal loss will first be observed on the cheekbone and hair above Boone's ear. The primary focal portrait is a target for the whizzing merchants.

Reverse

A loss of metal will first be noticed on the shoulder of Chief Black Fish (diagonally above "Unum"), as well as on his hand.

Related Material

Frank Dunn, Secretary of the Daniel Boone Bicentennial Commission, was responsible for the distribution of this issue. He had the 1934 half dollar forwarded to subscribers in a Dennison half dollar coin mailer. Later, coins were mailed in a Wedge Pocket coin holder, manufactured by the Lindly Box Company of Marion, Indiana. When supplies were temporarily exhausted, individual pieces and sets were placed in tissue paper or between cardboard, inserted into an envelope, and shipped. In order to save on expenses, two coins were placed in one Wedge Pocket and one in another, if a three-piece set was requested. If two coins were required, both were placed in this holder. The 1934 envelope and holder may be valued in the $50 to $100 range; the Dennison holder itself, $2. The Wedge Pocket coin holder has sold for between $25 and $50.

Boone acknowledgement postcard—front.

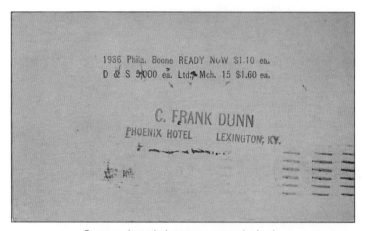

Boone acknowledgement postcard—back.

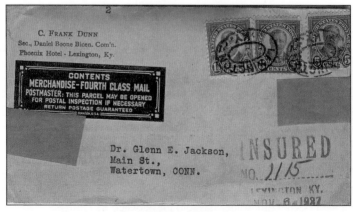

Boone mailing envelope.

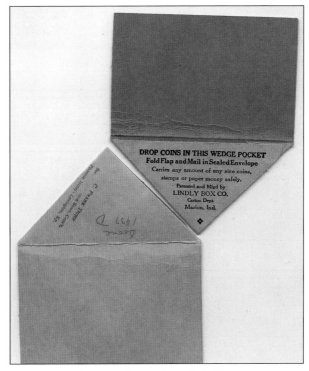

Boone mailing wedge coin holder.

Future Potential of the Boone Half Dollar

Population Figures

Date	Service	AU 58	MS 60	MS 62	MS 63	MS 64	MS 65	MS 66	MS 67	MS 68	MS 69
1934	NGC	0	0	7	43	252	425	163	22	1	0
1934	PCGS	3	0	33	155	436	557	213	31	1	0
1934	Combined	3	0	40	198	688	982	376	53	2	0

Date	Service	AU 58	MS 60	MS 62	MS 63	MS 64	MS 65	MS 66	MS 67	MS 68	MS 69
1935	NGC	0	0	14	58	313	464	162	31	2	0
1935	PCGS	2	3	33	240	500	536	187	37	0	0
1935	Combined	2	3	47	298	813	1000	349	68	2	0

Date	Service	AU 58	MS 60	MS 62	MS 63	MS 64	MS 65	MS 66	MS 67	MS 68	MS 69
1935 D	NGC	0	0	7	35	234	232	80	4	0	0
1935 D	PCGS	1	0	16	142	412	312	80	11	0	0
1935 D	Combined	1	0	23	177	646	544	160	15	0	0

Date	Service	AU 58	MS 60	MS 62	MS 63	MS 64	MS 65	MS 66	MS 67	MS 68	MS 69
1935 S	NGC	0	0	2	28	165	341	159	34	1	0
1935 S	PCGS	0	0	16	116	297	368	171	19	1	0
1935 S	Combined	0	0	18	144	462	709	328	53	2	0

Date	Service	PL 50	PL 60	PL 62	PL 63	PL 64	PL 65	PL 66	PL 67	PL 68	PL 69
1935 S	NGC	0	0	0	1	0	0	0	0	0	0

Date	Service	AU 58	MS 60	MS 62	MS 63	MS 64	MS 65	MS 66	MS 67	MS 68	MS 69
1935 with small 1934	NGC	1	0	4	48	336	516	245	46	1	0
1935 with small 1934	PCGS	0	0	26	201	625	641	229	36	2	0
1935 with small 1934	Combined	1	0	30	249	961	1157	474	82	3	0

Date	Service	AU 58	MS 60	MS 62	MS 63	MS 64	MS 65	MS 66	MS 67	MS 68	MS 69
1935 D with small 1934	NGC	0	0	2	20	112	151	116	63	6	0
1935 D with small 1934	PCGS	0	0	11	67	143	236	164	53	7	0
1935 D with small 1934	Combined	0	0	13	87	255	387	280	116	13	0

Date	Service	AU 58	MS 60	MS 62	MS 63	MS 64	MS 65	MS 66	MS 67	MS 68	MS 69
1935 S with small 1934	NGC	0	0	6	23	145	177	86	25	5	0
1935 S with small 1934	PCGS	0	0	18	75	214	192	97	14	2	0
1935 S with small 1934	Combined	0	0	24	98	359	369	183	39	7	0

Date	Service	AU 58	MS 60	MS 62	MS 63	MS 64	MS 65	MS 66	MS 67	MS 68	MS 69
1936	NGC	1	0	17	55	431	560	238	52	5	0
1936	PCGS	5	1	49	234	701	717	313	63	1	0
1936	Combined	6	1	66	289	1132	1277	551	115	6	0

Date	Service	AU 58	MS 60	MS 62	MS 63	MS 64	MS 65	MS 66	MS 67	MS 68	MS 69
1936 D	NGC	0	0	5	24	168	364	194	10	0	0
1936 D	PCGS	0	0	12	119	383	512	241	23	0	0
1936 D	Combined	0	0	17	143	551	876	435	33	0	0

Date	Service	AU 58	MS 60	MS 62	MS 63	MS 64	MS 65	MS 66	MS 67	MS 68	MS 69
1936 S	NGC	0	0	4	28	173	365	233	35	1	0
1936 S	PCGS	0	0	16	120	345	441	224	55	1	0
1936 S	Combined	0	0	20	148	518	806	457	90	2	0

Date	Service	AU 58	MS 60	MS 62	MS 63	MS 64	MS 65	MS 66	MS 67	MS 68	MS 69
1937	NGC	0	0	11	51	355	544	251	59	0	0
1937	PCGS	1	1	30	181	620	742	389	77	3	0
1937	Combined	1	1	41	232	975	1286	640	136	3	0

Date	Service	PL 50	PL 60	PL 62	PL 63	PL 64	PL 65	PL 66	PL 67	PL 68	PL 69
1937	NGC	0	0	0	0	2	3	1	0	0	0

Date	Service	AU 58	MS 60	MS 62	MS 63	MS 64	MS 65	MS 66	MS 67	MS 68	MS 69
1937 D	NGC	0	0	5	18	138	194	107	27	1	0
1937 D	PCGS	0	0	7	73	208	259	139	44	2	0
1937 D	Combined	0	0	12	91	346	453	246	71	3	0

Date	Service	PL 50	PL 60	PL 62	PL 63	PL 64	PL 65	PL 66	PL 67	PL 68	PL 69
1937 D	NGC	0	0	0	0	3	0	0	0	0	0

Date	Service	AU 58	MS 60	MS 62	MS 63	MS 64	MS 65	MS 66	MS 67	MS 68	MS 69
1937 S	NGC	0	0	3	19	108	197	138	28	4	0
1937 S	PCGS	0	0	15	71	187	220	122	31	2	0
1937 S	Combined	0	0	18	90	295	417	260	59	6	0

Date	Service	PL 50	PL 60	PL 62	PL 63	PL 64	PL 65	PL 66	PL 67	PL 68	PL 69
1937 S	NGC	0	0	0	3	54	42	26	3	0	0

Date	Service	AU 58	MS 60	MS 62	MS 63	MS 64	MS 65	MS 66	MS 67	MS 68	MS 69
1938	NGC	0	0	4	20	119	183	86	7	0	0
1938	PCGS	0	0	11	64	186	281	123	16	1	0
1938	Combined	0	0	15	84	305	464	209	23	1	0

Date	Service	AU 58	MS 60	MS 62	MS 63	MS 64	MS 65	MS 66	MS 67	MS 68	MS 69
1938 D	NGC	0	0	2	19	102	171	121	34	6	1
1938 D	PCGS	0	0	9	53	182	261	156	48	2	1
1938 D	Combined	0	0	11	72	284	432	277	82	8	2

Date	Service	AU 58	MS 60	MS 62	MS 63	MS 64	MS 65	MS 66	MS 67	MS 68	MS 69
1938 S	NGC	0	0	3	26	127	156	99	34	2	0
1938 S	PCGS	0	0	16	73	206	205	123	32	2	0
1938 S	Combined	0	0	19	99	333	361	222	66	4	0

Date	Service	PL 60	PL 62	PL 63	PL 64	PL 65	PL 66	PL 67	PL 68	PL 69
1938 S	NGC	0	0	2	5	1	0	0	0	0

There is little value spread between grades EF-AU and MS-64, for the generic issues. There are just too many pieces graded MS-64 and MS-65 of the now common, more available dates, such as both 1935-P issues, the 1936-P and D, and the 1937-P: acquire these only for joy of collecting. Type coins with possible good future potential are the 1935-D and 1935-S Small Date productions, as well as the 1937-D and the 1937-S coinage. All are undervalued. Collectors should attempt to procure attractive MS-64+ pieces. I would estimate that the MS-64 population figures can be reduced by 28%.

Values appear inexpensive for MS-65 Boones, but, unfortunately, too many pieces have been given this grade. In fact, the generic dated or high census coins are actually fairly priced. The 1935-D No Small Date is undervalued among the dates that are thought of as common. Other type dates highly recommended are the 1938-S, 1935-D and 1935-S Small Dates, the 1937-P, 1937-D, 1937-S, and the 1938 PDS pieces. Set-wise, collectors should seek the 1938 and 1935 with the small 1934 coinage. (Remember, the Philadelphia piece from the latter set is a common coin.) There is very good future potential here. I would lower the MS-65 population figures by 27% for the generic dates and 20% for the lower-census material. Again, purchase only eye-appealing pieces—and never purchase without seeing the coin first.

Present MS-66 values are just too low—for the specific dates I cite. Sleeper type dates are the 1935-D No Small Date, the 1935-S Small Date, and 1938-S production. The low mintage 1935 PDS Small Date set and the 1938 PDS set are wonderful coins to possess.

There is excellent future potential in the undervalued lofty grade of MS-67, especially for the 1935-D, 1938-P, 1935-S Small Date, and 1936-D coins. Also the MS-68 coinage: an MS-68 1935-S Small Date sold for $27,600, while a 1938-P brought $29,900. Please remember that values for pieces rated MS-68 are based on the coin's total makeup; market conditions, populations, and the number of buyers. This is why values can range from $7,800 to $30,000+.

To date, NGC and PCGS have each graded a single 1938-D Boone in MS-69.

Some Boone pieces were produced from polished dies. These are classified as proof-like (PL) by NGC. As of this writing, we can note that the following issues were granted such status: 1935-S, MS-63 (1); 1936-S, MS-64 (1); 1937-P, MS-64 (2), MS-65 (3), and MS-66 (1); 1937-D, MS-64 (3); 1937-S, MS-63

(3), MS-64 (54), MS-65 (42), MS-66 (26), and MS-67 (3); 1938-S, MS-63 (2), MS-64 (5), and MS-65 (1). The largest population is the 1937-S issue. These are desired by collectors and command double to triple sheet prices. Beware of the raw polished, cleaned, or doctored coin offered as a proof-like. I highly recommend pieces with a deeper proof-like mirrored surface but not one that is weak or questionable. Some dealers question the weak-looking proof-like status. Please review the requirements necessary for a coin to be labeled proof-like (see pages 22-25). Also beware of surface negatives, such as spit spots: they can lower value. Always get a 30-day return agreement in writing should you purchase such a coin—you might want it verified by an expert. There is excellent future potential in grades MS-64+ and higher, especially when the surface has a deeper proof-like look.

1934–1938 Texas Centennial

Reason for Issue:	The 100th anniversary in 1936 of the independence of Texas.
Authorization:	Act of June 15, 1933, with a maximum of 1,500,000 pieces for the series.
Issued by:	American Legion Texas Centennial Committee
Official Sale Price:	1934: $1 plus 15 cents postage 1935-1937: $1.50 per coin; $4.50 per set 1938: $2.00 per coin; $6.00 per set

Production Figures

Date	Business Strikes	Assay Coins	Proofs	Melted	Net Mintage
1934	205,000	113	4?	143,650	61,350
1935	10,000	8	4?	12	9,988
1935-D	10,000	7	4?	0	10,000
1935-S	10,000	8	4?	0	10,000
1936	10,000	7	4?	1,097	8,903
1936-D	10,000	7	4?	968	9,032
1936-S	10,000	8	4?	943	9,057
1937	8,000	5	4?	1,434	6,566
1937-D	8,000	6	4?	1,401	6,599
1937-S	8,000	7	4?	1,370	6,630
1938	5,000	5	4?	1,225	3,775
1938-D	5,000	5	4?	1,230	3,770
1938-S	5,000	6	4?	1,192	3,808

Current Market Values

Date	AU-58	MS-60	MS-63	MS-64	MS-65	MS-66	MS-67
1934	$105	$115	$125	$130	$275	$380	$1,400
1935 PDS set	$335	$355	$390	$415	$850	$1,300	$2,100+
1936 PDS set	$335	$355	$390	$415	$850	$1,300	$2,100+
1937 PDS set	$335	$355	$390	$430	$850	$1,350	$3,200+
1938 PDS set	$580	$725	$780	$850	$950	$1,300	$4,400+

DESIGNS BY POMPEO COPPINI

Obverse

Large American eagle facing left and superimposed on a five-pointed "Lone Star," symbolic of the state of Texas. Below the oak branch held by the eagle's talons is the date of issue. "UNITED STATES OF AMERICA" arcs above; "HALF DOLLAR" below. "IN GOD WE TRUST" is in the upper right field; "E PLURIBUS UNUM" in the left field.

Reverse

A winged and draped Victory holding an olive branch in her right hand, while resting her left hand on a representation of the Alamo. Appearing on a scroll above the figure's head is the word "Liberty"; in the same area are the six flags of Spain, France, Mexico, the Republic of Texas, the Confederacy, and the United States, which represent periods in the history of Texas.

The medallion portrait of General Sam Houston, the first president of the independent Republic of Texas, appears in the coin's left field; Stephen F. Austin, one of the founders of the state, is pictured in the right field. Their names are also presented in very small letters. Around the coin's border are the inscriptions "The Texas Independence Centennial" and "Remember the Alamo"; the designer's initials (PC) are placed at the right base of the Alamo. This issue's Mint marks (D or S) are located below the left knee of Victory. Coins struck at the Philadelphia Mint bear no Mint mark.

Origins of the Texas

Texas was to celebrate its centennial in 1936, but there are issues dated 1934 and 1935. In 1933, the American Legion Texas Centennial Committee of Austin believed that the planned Centennial Exposition, to take place in Dallas between June 6 and November 29, 1936, would be quite expensive. They asked for authorization to have coins produced prior to the opening of the Exposition in order to obtain the needed funds. An authorization of 1,500,000 coins was approved June 15, 1933.

On March 16, 1936, Texas Senator Tom Connally's secretary, R.M. Jackson, gave testimony before the Senate Committee on Banking and Currency in an attempt to have five different designs created: this proposal was rejected.

During October and November 1934, the Philadelphia Mint struck 205,000 pieces plus 113 assay coins of one of my favorite designs. Considering the mintage, which was considered large at the time, these coins sold rather well at $1 each. However, when sales declined, 143,650 pieces were returned to the Mint and melted, leaving a net mintage of 61,350 coins. The Treasury Department demanded that the 1934 coinage on hand be paid in full before any new varieties were produced. The Centennial Committee chose to return the coins, owe nothing, and obtain a new variety.

Each of the Mints struck 10,000 Texas Centennial pieces in November 1935. Only 12 Philadelphia coins were returned for melting. The coins were now distributed by the Texas Memorial Museum Centennial Coin Campaign at $1.50 each. Sales were excellent. In fact, a letter dated April 12, 1937, from Beauford Halbert Jester, general chairman of the Texas Memorial Museum, notified collectors that advance orders had reserved more than half of the 1937 Texas set, then being struck, and indicated that the 1935 set was completely sold out.

Each Mint struck 10,000 Texas commemorative half dollars in February 1936. The issue was distributed on April 3, 1936. Sales were a bit weak at $4.50 per set, and 1,097 Philadelphia, 968 Denver, and 943 San Francisco coins were returned to be melted.

During the months of April and May 1937 each Mint produced 8,000 Texas Centennial half dollars. Cost was $1.50 per coin or $4.50 per set. Sales were not up to expectations, and 1,434 Philadelphia, 1,401 Denver, and 1,370 San Francisco commemoratives were returned for melting.

Although the Centennial Exposition was over, in January 1938 the three Mints each struck 5,000 Texas half dollars. Collectors were notified that the coins would cost $2 each or $6 per set. They were later informed that the 1936 and 1937 sets were still available, but that as of November 1, 1938, no more orders would be accepted. Sales came to a halt, and 1,225 Philadelphia, 1,230 Denver, and 1,192 San Francisco half dollars were returned to be melted.

The Texas Today

The 1934 Philadelphia striking is the date within the series that is most common in EF-AU condition, it was treated as a souvenir and often abused.

Other issues can at times be obtained at or near circulated values because they were once over-cleaned, lightly polished, or whizzed or could simply display a natural metal loss. I suggest coins that have earned their wear naturally from circulation, instead of from numismatic abuse such as cleaning or polishing, unless all that is required by the collector is a representative example in any condition. Coins grading MS-60 through MS-65 can also be found without much difficulty. The value spread is small, so collectors should look for the higher grade. In fact, should funds be available, focus on MS-66 coinage. The luster will range from blazing satiny, to satiny, to dull satiny. Striking problems, especially on the reverse, can lower the grade and value of any coin within the entire series. Should you observe too much flatness or weakness of strike on the hand and knee of the Victory, your specimen possesses a weak strike. The primary focal areas are the obverse eagle, then the surrounding fields, and the reverse Victory. Numismatic villains such as bag marks, slide marks, hairline scratches, etc., can lower a coin's grade-value by appearing in the focal locations.

There is little value spread between grades MS-60 and MS-64 for the 1935 Texas set. The San Francisco striking is somewhat easier to locate than coins from the other two Mints. In MS-65 condition the set can currently be located without much difficulty. Sets were broken up in the past by collectors seeking to acquire the Denver Mint coin. The Philadelphia and San Francisco Mint are the lower census coinage of the three-piece MS-65 set. In MS-66 condition the lowest census is San Francisco. The other Philadelphia and Denver productions are about equally as rare in MS-67 condition. A collector's best bet is the San Francisco production in MS-66 condition.

Luster for the 1935 set is as follows:

- The 1935-P pieces are brilliant frosty (not the norm) to dull frosty. Too often the coin will lack eye appeal, having a chrome-like appearance.
- The 1935-D specimens can be found with a proof-like very early strike, to semi-proof-like, to brilliant satiny, to satiny. This is the most eye-appealing issue within the series. The reverse will look blazing satiny on the proof-like coins.
- The 1935-S issues can have a brilliant frosty (not the norm), to dull frosty, to dull chrome-like appearance. Too often the coin will lack eye appeal. Original Mint-struck specimens will have that over-dipped look.

Little value spread can be noted for the 1936 coins between grades MS-60 and MS-64, so collectors should aim for higher grades. The Denver coin is the rarest of the three in these grades; the Philadelphia is a bit more difficult to locate than the San Francisco. In MS-65 condition, the Denver coin has a slight rarity edge. The other two are about equal. The best future is in eye-appealing MS-66 and loftier states. In MS-66 condition, the San Francisco coin is more than 40% rarer than the Philadelphia, which is itself approximately twice as difficult to find as the Denver coin. Luster will range from flashy, to brilliant satiny, to satiny, to dull satiny. Aside from the flashy 1934-P and 1935-D strikings, flashy specimens from this issue make excellent, captivating acquisitions. Rarely will any of the remaining coins in the series equal the beauty of these.

In the 1937 issues, there is not much value spread between the MS-60 and MS-65 categories, so aim for at least MS-65, funds permitting. The future for this undervalued issue is in the loftier states. Collectors should prefer this lower-mintage set to the earlier issues, if they are attractive. Up to grades MS-64, the 1937-S set is the rarest of the group. In MS-65 condition, the Philadelphia striking is the slightly rarer coin; the Denver coin is somewhat more available. Eye-appealing specimens are not as abundant as many believe. Luster will range from brilliant satiny (not the norm), to satiny, to dull satiny.

The 1938 coins grading from MS-60 through MS-62 possess little eye appeal; these are fairly priced. There is little value spread between the MS-63 and MS-64 grades, so aim higher. Up to MS-63 the S Mint coin is rarer than the Denver issue, and the Philadelphia coin is the easiest to obtain. In MS-64 condition, the Denver and San Francisco strikings are close in rarity; the P Mint coin is, again, more available. However, Philadelphia coins in the undervalued MS-65 and loftier categories are rarer than the other two branch Mint strikings. The P Mint is rarer than the D and S Mint in MS-66 condition, and in the next loftier grade. In grades MS-64 and higher, the Philadelphia is the rarest set within the series and the most popular.

To date no error coinage or counterfeit pieces have entered the marketplace.

Is Your Texas Circulated or Mint State?

Obverse

A metal loss will first be observed on the breast of the eagle. You should examine this area for whizzing.

Reverse

Wear will first be observed on the head of the Victory as well as on her knee. Should her knee be flatly struck, examine it for a difference in metal texture and fine crisscross scratches.

Related Material

The 1934 issue was distributed through 314 banks in Texas, as well as banks outside the state. According to purchasers, some banks sold the coin at $1 each in a plain envelope, as well as without any container. Others were mailed in a plain dark green Dennison half dollar coin mailing card, with one insert and a gummed paper security flap.

The 1935 through 1938 issues were distributed in unprinted envelopes, as well as in unprinted cardboard coin mailers, with inserts for five coins.

Fifty gold foil presentation boxes with green velour interiors, housed only the early-struck, proof-like 1935 Denver strikings. (Should any other Texas issue be found in such a box, it was replaced.) The inner top cover is imprinted in black: "The Texas Independence Centennial, Compliments of E.H.R. Green"—he was the son of Hetty Green, known as the "Witch of Wall Street," and a famous collector of coins, railroad cars, and pornography.

Green also presented 50 three-piece sets in silver foil boxes with a black velour interior. These had the same black imprint as the gold foil box, with the addition of the date 1935 and P Mint, D Mint, and S Mint. A white folded piece

ORDER FOR TEXAS CENTENNIAL COINS

Date_____193____

THE TEXAS MEMORIAL MUSEUM
CENTENNIAL COIN COMMITTEE
AUSTIN, TEXAS

Please enter my order for the following Texas Centennial Half Dollars:

Number Wanted	Mint	Year	Cost	Total
_____	Philadelphia	1934	$1.15	$_____
_____	Denver	1936	1.50	$_____
_____	San Francisco	1936	1.50	$_____
_____	Philadelphia	1936	1.50	$_____
			Total - - -	$_____

Remittance Record

Amount Enclosed $_____

P. O. Order ☐   Check ☐

Money Order ☐

Name_____

Address (Street)_____

City_____ County_____ State_____

Texas order form.

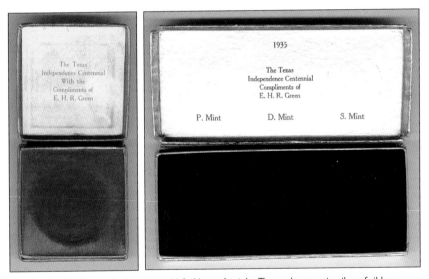

On the left: Texas single-coin gold foil box. *At right:* Texas three-coin silver foil box.

of tissue paper was placed on top the coins. These presentation items are very difficult to acquire.

The envelope may be worth $25. Green's boxes are worth $350 to $450 without the coin enclosed. With enclosed coins, it has sold for between $3,000 to $4,000, depending on condition and the seller. A three-piece box without coins sells for upwards of $350 to $800.

Future Potential of the Texas Half Dollar

Population Figures

Date	Service	AU 58	MS 60	MS 62	MS 63	MS 64	MS 65	MS 66	MS 67	MS 68	MS 69
1934	NGC	15	0	38	132	657	838	395	47	1	0
1934	PCGS	44	1	65	401	1385	1182	388	40	2	0
1934	Combined	59	1	103	533	2042	2020	783	87	3	0

Date	Service	AU 58	MS 60	MS 62	MS 63	MS 64	MS 65	MS 66	MS 67	MS 68	MS 69
1935	NGC	0	0	2	17	131	441	605	222	13	0
1935	PCGS	2	0	11	119	410	778	766	204	5	0
1935	Combined	2	0	13	136	541	1219	1371	426	18	0

Date	Service	AU 58	MS 60	MS 62	MS 63	MS 64	MS 65	MS 66	MS 67	MS 68	MS 69
1935 D	NGC	0	0	1	15	163	464	661	165	6	0
1935 D	PCGS	1	0	20	105	384	877	720	199	4	0
1935 D	Combined	1	0	1	120	547	1341	1381	364		0

Date	Service	AU 58	MS 60	MS 62	MS 63	MS 64	MS 65	MS 66	MS 67	MS 68	MS 69
1935 S	NGC	1	1	4	23	192	491	422	79	2	0
1935 S	PCGS	3	3	22	163	496	818	347	98	1	0
1935 S	Combined	4	4	26	186	688	1309	769	177	3	0

Date	Service	AU 58	MS 60	MS 62	MS 63	MS 64	MS 65	MS 66	MS 67	MS 68	MS 69
1936	NGC	1	0	1	19	167	518	490	130	8	1
1936	PCGS	0	0	15	115	471	847	603	121	6	0
1936	Combined	1	0	16	186	638	1365	1093	251	14	1

Date	Service	AU 58	MS 60	MS 62	MS 63	MS 64	MS 65	MS 66	MS 67	MS 68	MS 69
1936 D	NGC	1	0	5	17	158	402	674	258	10	0
1936 D	PCGS	1	0	13	90	341	681	916	307	14	0
1936 D	Combined	2	0	18	107	499	1083	1590	565	24	0

Date	Service	AU 58	MS 60	MS 62	MS 63	MS 64	MS 65	MS 66	MS 67	MS 68	MS 69
1936 S	NGC	0	0	4	21	167	489	485	64	4	0
1936 S	PCGS	2	3	15	96	459	849	452	63	1	0
1936 S	Combined	2	3	19	117	626	1338	937	127	5	0

Date	Service	AU 58	MS 60	MS 62	MS 63	MS 64	MS 65	MS 66	MS 67	MS 68	MS 69
1937	NGC	0	0	4	23	218	426	347	72	7	0
1937	PCGS	2	0	19	121	426	629	345	87	2	0
1937	Combined	2	0	23	144	644	1055	692	159	9	0

Date	Service	AU 58	MS 60	MS 62	MS 63	MS 64	MS 65	MS 66	MS 67	MS 68	MS 69
1937 D	NGC	0	0	2	19	135	413	431	95	5	0
1937 D	PCGS	0	0	20	90	345	671	487	122	2	0
1937 D	Combined	0	0	22	109	480	1084	918	217	7	0

Date	Service	AU 58	MS 60	MS 62	MS 63	MS 64	MS 65	MS 66	MS 67	MS 68	MS 69
1937 S	NGC	0	1	4	16	160	424	431	95	5	0
1937 S	PCGS	0	0	14	107	351	607	434	81	0	0
1937 S	Combined	0	1	18	123	511	1031	865	176	5	0

Date	Service	PL 58	PL 60	PL 62	PL 63	PL 64	PL 65	PL 66	PL 67	PL 68	PL 69
1937 S	NGC	0	0	0	1	2	4	1	0	0	0

Date	Service	AU 58	MS 60	MS 62	MS 63	MS 64	MS 65	MS 66	MS 67	MS 68	MS 69
1938	NGC	0	0	3	22	159	311	216	49	2	0
1938	PCGS	0	1	19	147	356	378	186	38	1	0
1938	Combined	0	1	22	169	515	689	402	87	3	0

Date	Service	AU 58	MS 60	MS 62	MS 63	MS 64	MS 65	MS 66	MS 67	MS 68	MS 69
1938 D	NGC	0	0	2	18	107	287	287	109	6	0
1938 D	PCGS	1	0	16	114	248	273	273	73	0	0
1938 D	Combined	1	0	18	132	355	560	560	182	6	0

Date	Service	AU 58	MS 60	MS 62	MS 63	MS 64	MS 65	MS 66	MS 67	MS 68	MS 69
1938 S	NGC	0	0	2	19	118	306	258	76	13	0
1938 S	PCGS	0	1	19	99	292	418	282	51	1	0
1938 S	Combined	0	1	21	118	410	724	540	127	14	0

This beautiful coin appears to have come out of the numismatic woodwork since the last May 1989 market high. It has now entered the realm of the common—up to MS-66 condition—for the most part. There is no major price variance for coins rated EF-AU through MS-66: these should be acquired for the joy of collecting, and have fair to average possibilities for increasing in value. Type pieces and sets will certainly be promoted during the next hot market. Values will rise, but will return to previous levels when the scene begins to cool. The best bets for coins in MS-64+ condition are the 1938-D and S issues, as well as the complete set. There is average future potential for this and the MS-65 category. Too many pieces have been slabbed MS-65: average potential here. Best bet again is the 1938 P, D and S strikings, and the complete set. Just remember that this date's luster is almost always chrome-like in appearance, and that not too many pieces will display the appealing silver-white look.

In MS-66 condition, the coins that are underrated and offer the best future are: the 1938-P, 1938-S, 1938-D, and 1937-P. We can expect very good to excellent future potential from these—especially the 1938 Philadelphia issue. The remaining coins offer average to good possibilities for tomorrow. The census can be reduced by 27% and 30% for each date. If demand intensifies, prices will climb beyond these expectations—for a while.

In MS-67 condition the most undervalued are the 1938-P, 1934-P, 1938-S, and 1936-S coins. Type coin prices reflect the higher population 1935-P, 1935-D, and 1936-D strikings. All other dates are somewhat undervalued as individual issues. A coin with the same grade and a census of 176 pieces should not be worth $150 more than one with 357 encapsulated coins. Such anomalies are caused by a combination of the present economic situation, limited and careful spending (at present) by collectors, and a large population count for a date or dates within an issue. A large population especially dampens interest in the real sleeper pieces, as most collectors see their values as being very close to those of the higher-census coins. The astute are those who attempt to locate an accurately graded specimen; once bought such coins are placed in collections, waiting to reap future mental and monetary rewards. What will help bring about a change? Awareness, desire to acquire, and demand. More and more people are becoming aware of the value of semi-scarce and better low population issues. As the marketplace begins to heat up and more money enters the numismatic scene, purchases will follow. These issues, accurately graded, are very difficult to obtain in a slow market. The new demand will cause a justifiable rise in values to deserving new highs, leaving behind the higher-census pieces. (Collectors should apply these principles to the entire U.S. commemorative series, as well as to most U.S. coinage.) There is excellent future potential for the individual issues just mentioned. MS-68 rated pieces are quite undervalued. These dates have sold at auction for the indicated prices: 1935-P ($3,220, September 2008), 1935-S ($5,175, May 2007), and 1936-D ($5,462, August 2009).

1935 Connecticut Tercentenary

Reason for Issue:	The 300th anniversary of the founding of the Colony of Connecticut.
Authorization:	Act of June 21, 1934, with a maximum of 25,000 pieces.
Official Sale Price:	$1
Issued by:	Connecticut Tercentenary Commission

Production Figures

Date	Business Strikes	Assay Coins	Proofs	Melted	Net Mintage
1935	25,018	18	4	0	25,000

Current Market Values

Date	AU-58	MS-60	MS-63	MS-64	MS-65	MS-66	MS-67
1935	$205	$250	$260	$305	$360	$650	$2,000+

Designs by Henry G. Kreiss

The eagle side of the coin was referred to as the obverse in a letter dated December 6, 1934, discussing design revisions, sent to Henry Morgenthau, Secretary of the Treasury, by Charles Moore, Chairman of the U.S. Commission of Fine Arts. Most collectors and dealers refer to the eagle side as the reverse even today. However, Mint officials chose the Charter Oak as the official obverse side.

Obverse

The Charter Oak, taken from the original painting by Charles De Wolf Brownell. Connecticut received a royal charter in 1662. In 1687 its administrator, Sir Edmund Andros, attempted to revoke the charter under orders from the King of England, James II (James VII of Scotland). It is traditionally believed that while a discussion was in progress concerning the royal charter, the candles were extinguished in the meeting room and the charter was removed and later hidden in a cavity in a large oak tree, which is now known as the Charter Oak. The words "THE CHARTER OAK" appear in the lower right field, below the tree branches. In the lower border are the word "CONNECTICUT" and the anniversary dates 1635–1935. "IN GOD WE TRUST" is in small letters at the upper left border; "LIBERTY" in small letters at the upper right border.

Reverse

A bold, standing eagle, facing left. "UNITED STATES OF AMERICA" arcs above; "HALF DOLLAR" below; "E PLURIBUS UNUM" is in the lower left field.

Origins of the Connecticut

This issue was produced at the Philadelphia Mint during April and May 1936. It possesses a mintage of 25,000, plus 18 coins for assay purposes. Public Law 466-73rd Congress states "the United States shall not be subject to the expense of making the models for master dies or other preparations for this coinage." However, the coins were financed through a Public Works Administration project. The Connecticut Tercentenary Commission did a fantastic job in distributing a large percentage of this issue to Connecticut residents. They were "circulated" in six different cardboard boxes via banks within the state, as well as through the U.S. mail system.

The Connecticut Today

As noted, the Connecticut was well distributed to many state residents. It was admired as a beautiful souvenir coin and received some degree of unintentional abuse.

Today, specimens in the EF-AU category are not abundant and are usually cleaned, whizzed, or polished to some degree. The majority of the issue grading between MS-60 and MS-64 shows granular surfaces that display little to no originality—because of over-dipping in a tarnish-removing solution—to partial or complete originality. Luster, when original, ranges from almost always dull satiny, resembling a light talcum-powdery white look, to semi-flashy brilliant (similar to a flashy Bay Bridge obverse). Strike rarely poses a detriment to the coin's grade or its worth. What does affect the value is the presence of numismatic negatives in varying degrees, such as bag marks, reed marks, slide marks, hairline scratches, etc., especially located on the reverse primary focal area. This is the eagle's main body, especially that smooth wing, which seems to act as a magnet for these undesirables. I suggest acquiring MS-63+ and MS-64+ coinage that is fully original and eye-appealing, for the joy of ownership. Connecticuts in MS-65 and MS-66 condition are not hard to find.

Flashy MS-66 pieces, however, are somewhat elusive. Collectors who can afford higher grade material, should not hesitate to add such a coin to their collections.

Four to six double-struck matte proofs were produced for John Ray Sinnock, the Chief Mint Engraver. One appeared as Lot 2055 in the 1962 American Numismatic Association Convention auction.

No error coinage for this issue has yet surfaced.

Is Your Connecticut Circulated or Mint State?

Obverse

Examine the base of the Charter Oak, above the letters "ON" and "TI" in "Connecticut". At times the tree trunk shows a large hit or reed mark. A small buffing tool is used in an attempt to conceal such a mark.

Reverse

Look for wear or a difference in metal texture on the upper part of eagle's front wing, just below neck. Doctoring in the form of light whizzing is usually found in this area and can be observed by its aluminum look when the coin is rotated slowly 360 degrees.

Related Material

Banks in the Connecticut distributed this coin in several different small cardboard boxes:

- Silver foil covered paper hinged box. State coat of arms in blue ink on top cover with royal blue velour interior. Plain bottom, no slit pouch to hold coin in place. The most common of the boxes: may be valued at $50 to $100.
- Silver gray embossed slip-out box. "Hartford National Connecticut Trust Company Old State House Square" imprinted on top. Navy blue velour interior with slit pouch to hold coins. Small silver-colored ribbon at bottom to help slip out section and view coin. Very difficult to locate.
- Red circular embossed design covered box. Imprinted on the inner cover "The New Haven Savings Bank, New Haven, Conn." Celery green velour interior with slit pouch. Red pull tab or ribbon at bottom of box was intended for a planned slip-out box. Very difficult to locate.

Silver foil covered paper hinged box.

Red circular embossed design covered box.

Silver grey and white cube design box.

Silver and white marble grain design box.

- Red circular embossed design. The same as the Red circular embossed design covered box, except imprinted on top. Exactly the same interior as the Silver gray embossed slip-out box, except for the celery green interior. Very difficult to locate.
- Gold fine embossed covered box. Imprinted on inner cover "Hartford National Bank and Trust Co., Hartford, Connecticut." Moss green velour interior with slit pouch. Extremely difficult to locate.
- Gold cardboard box with green (background) and gold (depictions) adhesive label with the words "The Hartford Connecticut Trust Company." Within border on label is a street scene depicting the Trust Company building, parked cars, and trees. Olive green interior with slit pouch. Extremely difficult to locate.
- Silver gray and white cube design box. "Hartford National Connecticut Trust Company Old State House Square" imprinted on top. Navy blue velour interior with slit pouch. Winter-white ribbon at bottom to slip out section and view coin. Extremely difficult to locate. Boxes other than the foil may be valued at $100 to $350+,

Red circular embossed design—detached box.

Gold cardboard box with green (background) and gold (depictions).

depending on condition and rarity. The Silver foil covered paper hinged box is the most common. All others are difficult to locate.
- Silver and white marble grain design box. All other features are identical to the Silver gray and white cube design box. (See page 246.)

Future Potential of the Connecticut Half Dollar

Population Figures

Date	Service	AU 58	MS 60	MS 62	MS 63	MS 64	MS 65	MS 66	MS 67	MS 68	MS 69
1935	NGC	21	1	74	259	1092	1222	437	72	1	0
1935	PCGS	50	14	179	783	1477	1151	442	40	1	0
1935	Combined	71	15	253	1042	2569	2373	879	112	2	0

Date	Service	PF 58	PF 60	PF 62	PF 63	PF 64	PF 65	PF 66	PF 67	PF 68	PF 69
1935	NGC	0	0	0	0	0	1	0	0	0	0
1935	PCGS	0	0	0	0	0	0	0	0	0	0
1935	Combined	0	0	0	0	0	1	0	0	0	0

There is little price spread between pieces grading EF-AU and MS-64. The limited number of circulated offerings are usually cleaned or abused in some form. Collectors should aim for the higher grades, preferably an original flashy MS-64+ coin, should funds be available. The price spread between grades MS-64 and MS-65 during the May 1989 market high was $1,600. I would lower the population count between 20% and 25%.

Attractive MS-65 strikings of this coin should be bought for the joy of collecting: it is a popular issue with a high population figure. The price spread between this and the MS-66 rating was $2,000+, during the May 1989 high. I would lower the census count by 20%.

Connecticuts grading MS-66 are somewhat cheap at present levels for a single-year type coin. Examine the eagle's wing for hairline scratches: it should be virtually clean for an MS-66 rating. I would deduct 20% from the slabbed figures given above. There is excellent future potential for this coin in MS-67 condition. An NGC MS-68 Connecticut has sold for almost $9,500. The other example, which is reported to be more atractive, could bring $15,000.

1935 Hudson, New York, Sesquicentennial

Reason for Issue:	To commemorate the 150th anniversary of the founding of the city of Hudson, New York.
Authorization:	Act of May 2, 1935, with a maximum of 10,000 pieces.
Issued by:	Hudson Sesquicentennial Committee
Official Sale Price:	$1

Production Figures

Date	Business Strikes	Assay Coins	Proofs	Melted	Net Mintage
1935	10,008	8	4?	0	10,000

Current Market Values

Date		AU-58	MS-60	MS-63	MS-64	MS-65	MS-66	MS-67
1935		$680	$825	$1,080	$1,375	$1,850	$2,650	$8,000+

Designs by Chester Beach

Obverse

Henry Hudson's flagship, the famous *Half Moon*, a small but sturdy merchant ship, sailing to the right. Located in the field is a fancifully stylized quarter moon. "UNITED STATES OF AMERICA" arcs above; "HALF DOLLAR" below; "IN GOD WE TRUST" is in smaller letters above the ship. Below the ship, on the wave and field, is the word "HUDSON". The designer's monogram (CB), is at the lower border.

Reverse

An adaptation of the seal of the City of Hudson, with Neptune riding backwards on a spouting whale while holding a trident in his right hand. In the left background is a triton or mermaid blowing a conch shell. The inscription "CITY OF HUDSON N.Y." appears in the upper border; the city's motto "ED DECUS ET PRETIUM RECTI" ("Both the honor and the reward of the righteous") is on a scroll below the border inscription. In the lower border are the anniversary dates 1785–1935, with the motto "E PLURIBUS UNUM" directly above.

Origins of the Hudson

In June 1935 the Philadelphia Mint struck 10,000 pieces, plus eight coins for assay purposes, for an issue that honored the city founded in 1785, and named for Henry Hudson, who explored the area in 1609. Obverse and reverse hub trial pieces exist in copper. The Mint delivered the souvenir issue on June 28, 1935, to the First National Bank and Trust Company of Hudson. This bank was selected by the mayor, as required in the authorizing legislation, to receive delivery on behalf of the Hudson Sesquicentennial Committee. Orders were received by John R. Evans at the bank. Delivery cost $1 per coin, plus 18 cents for registry fee and 3 cents for each two coins mailed. Thus, one Hudson would have cost $1.21. A great deal of criticism developed shortly thereafter, because only a small number of collectors were able to obtain this issue, which was said to be "sold out" five days after delivery.

Evans advised the infuriated collectors that the situation arose because people pre-ordered the issue in early May, and demand was so great that the authorization was sold out. One month later a retail high of $12.50 was asked for the coin. Who bought all the coins? It is believed that Julius Guttag of Guttag Brothers, New York City, acquired approximately 7,500 pieces at 95 cents each, and that Hubert W. Carcabla of St. Augustine, Florida, purchased 1,000 Hudsons at the same price. The coins were abundant in the marketplace several months after Evans's announcement—at between $4.50 and $7.00 each. However, large numbers were purchased by many individuals at these new levels, thus becoming genuinely well distributed and valuable. The Spanish Trail, with a similar mintage, is not as rare in MS-65 condition as the Hudson because it did not receive as much numismatic abuse. It is rarer, however, in MS-60 through MS-64 condition.

The Hudson Today

This issue is not readily available in EF-AU condition. When spotted, it will usually display some form of cleaning or doctoring. The coin is not that difficult to obtain in MS-60 through MS-64 condition, but numismatic abuse in the form of bag marks, reed marks, hairline scratches, over-dipping, etc., places much of the issue in this category. For the joy of collecting, look for specimens in these grades that possess eye appeal. The primary focal points are the whale and the *Half Moon*. Attractive MS-64+ specimens offer the collector the chance to own a more valuable coin in the future. Specimens grading strict MS-65+ and higher are not exactly abundant and should be sought by collectors, if funds permit.

Surface luster will range from brilliant frosty (not the norm) to dull frosty. On a very rare occasion, strike will be a detriment to grade or value. The definition of the design was not meant to be crisp or sharp; for example, the ship's main sail definition (ribbing) will rarely display completeness. What minute definition was present on the dies was quickly lost after a small number of coins was struck.

No error coinage is known.

Detecting Counterfeits

A counterfeit specimen will show raised obverse tool marks resembling spikes or spears by the letter "F" of "HALF" and "AR" of "DOLLAR" protruding into the field, as well as a depression in the second "A" of "AMERICA". The reverse will exhibit a re-tooling of Neptune's face—by an unknown numismatic plastic surgeon—plus two depressions above the "P" of "PRETIUM".

IS YOUR HUDSON CIRCULATED OR MINT STATE?

Obverse

A metal loss will make its ugly appearance just below the center of the mainsail: a difference in metal texture, a grayish white color, and fine crisscross scratches will be apparent. In an attempt to conceal the wear, the coin may have been polished or whizzed, or had this small area surface textured.

Reverse

The first location to show the negative effects of friction will be the motto "Ed Decus et Pretium Recti"—which usually appears softly struck. Add to this location Neptune's thigh and his shoulder directly above the thigh.

Related Material

Orders were mailed to lucky subscribers by the First National Bank and Trust Company, Box 148, Hudson, N.Y. in their craft-type envelope and housed in an unmarked cardboard holder with a plain blue backing. A red wax seal was used by the bank on the back of these very hard to locate items. The holder itself may be valued at $75 to $150; with the original envelope, $200 to $500 depending on condition.

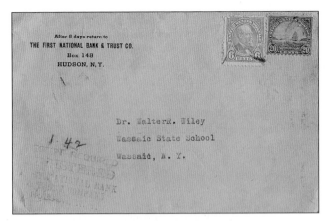

Hudson coin mailing envelope—front.

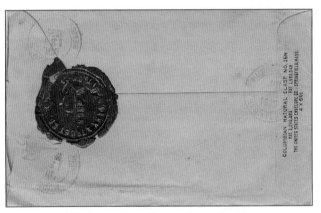

Hudson coin mailing envelope—back.

Future Potential of the Hudson Half Dollar

Population Figures

Date	Service	AU 58	MS 60	MS 62	MS 63	MS 64	MS 65	MS 66	MS 67	MS 68	MS 69
1935	NGC	23	1	65	248	813	498	152	29	0	0
1935	PCGS	32	12	162	636	1185	637	196	7	0	0
1935	Combined	55	13	227	884	1998	1135	348	36	0	0

Most circulated offerings will be of the cleaned and abused variety. They are worth much less than current bid levels. MS-60 coinage is usually not attractive, so aim for MS-63, should funds permit. The very popular single-year type coin is somewhat undervalued at current levels in MS-60 through MS-64 condition. The past value spread between MS-64+ and MS-65 during the May 1989 high

Hudson coin holder.

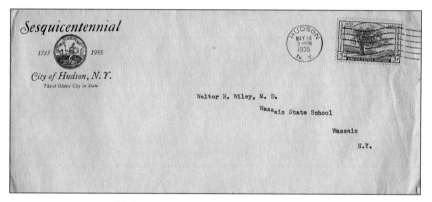

Hudson correspondence mailing envelope.

was $3,700. I would lower the census between 25% and 30%. I expect this issue to be promoted when the bull market arrives, and see a good to very good future potential.

The real future for this issue is in the eye-appealing, strictly graded MS-65+ coin. This popular coin offers good potential and is recommended. The value spread between this grade and MS-66, during the market high was $5,200. Population figures can be reduced between 20% and 25%. In the loftier grades the Hudson is undervalued and offers excellent future potential, to those who can afford such a rating. The same applies to MS-67. This rating has sold for $3450, $5,700, $6,900, $14,000, and $31,050 since July 30, 2002. Those who paid the latter two figures rated the beautiful Hudson MS-67++ coins. They had hopes of an upgrade to an MS-68 coin, but the population for that rating is still zero. The first two noted sale prices were believed to be low-end MS-67 pieces, solid for the grade by their buyers.

Reason for Issue:	To commemorate the 400th anniversary of the expedition of Cabeza de Vaca and the opening of the Old Spanish Trail.
Authorization:	Act of June 5, 1935, with a maximum of 10,000 pieces.
Issued by:	El Paso Museum Coin Committee
Official Sale Price:	$2, plus 10 cents postage

Production Figures

Date	Business Strikes	Assay Coins	Proofs	Melted	Net Mintage
1935	10,000	8	4?	0	10,000

Current Market Values

Date	AU-58	MS-60	MS-63	MS-64	MS-65	MS-66	MS-67
1935	$ 1,080	$ 1,100	$ 1,275	$ 1,300	$ 1,350	$ 1,775	$ 2,925

DESIGNS BY L.W. HOFFECKER, MODELED BY EDMUND J. SENN

Obverse

The head of a cow, but not the head of the 16th-century explorer Alvar Nuñez Cabeza de Vaca. Since there is no known portrait of this individual and because Cabeza de Vaca means "head of a cow," the cow's head was selected for the obverse. Below the animal is the explorer's name; "UNITED STATES OF AMERICA" arcs above; "HALF DOLLAR" below. "E PLURIBUS UNUM" and "LIBERTY" are above and between the cow's horns.

Reverse

A yucca tree in full bloom is superimposed on a map of the Old Spanish Trail, the supposed route Cabeza de Vaca took through the present states of Florida, Alabama, Mississippi, Louisiana, and Texas. The sites of those cities though which the expedition passed—St. Augustine, Jacksonville, Tallahassee, Mobile, New Orleans, Galveston, San Antonio, and El Paso—are represented by dots. Since the trail ended at El Paso, the city's name appears in left field. In the upper border is the inscription "OLD SPANISH TRAIL". "IN GOD WE TRUST" appears in the lower right field; the anniversary dates 1535–1935 are in the lower border. The designer's initials (LWH) are faintly visible at the lower right border, near the edge.

As mentioned, Cabeza de Vaca's route as shown on the coin misrepresents the historical record. He did not travel overland, but sailed along the Gulf Coast. What Cabeza de Vaca did accomplish was the encouragement of Spanish exploration through his tales of cities of gold.

Origins of the Spanish Trail

The Philadelphia Mint struck 10,000 pieces, plus eight assay coins in September 1935. These were distributed by the El Paso Museum Coin Committee at $2 each plus 10 cents postage; the profits to help further the work of the museum. The chairman of this committee was L.W. Hoffecker, a famous numismatist who was elected President of the American Numismatic Association in 1939. (I was elected the same organization's 50th President in 1997.) Hoffecker's goal was to keep this issue out of the hands of speculators; this was accomplished through a fair and wide distribution. [I would like gratefully to acknowledge and thank the ANA's Numismatic Researcher David Sklow for his efforts in uncovering the long obscured meaning of L.W.'s initials. We now know these represent Lyman William.]

The Spanish Trail Today

Coins in the circulated category will usually exhibit some maltreatment, in the form of light polishing or whizzing to hide natural wear on those used as pocket pieces. Specimens naturally grading EF-AU are seldom seen. In these grades, the Old Spanish Trail is the second most expensive single issue silver design, after the Hawaiian. What makes an example worth less than current values is the type and amount of numismatic abuse: how heavily is it polished or whizzed? Thus, the coin in question might be worth only half the trend value. Collectors should look for a coin with original surfaces, and one that has no deep cuts, scratches, and large bag marks unless all you require is a representative example of the design, with condition being unimportant.

It will be difficult to obtain Spanish Trails encapsulated by the major third-party grading services (NGC and PCGS) in grades MS-60 up to MS-62, since few are submitted. The value spread is not significant in grades MS-60 through MS-65 at present. If funds are available, look for higher grades. This popular coin is available in the MS-64 and MS-65 grades, and the future lies in these and in loftier levels strictly rated MS-66+ and higher. The Old Spanish Trail is not as rare in these grades as the Hawaiian or Hudson, since the latter two received more numismatic abuse from non-collectors. Population figures have heavily increased, rated MS-64 through MS-66. Luster will range from very brilliant satiny (not the norm), to brilliant satiny, to dull satiny. Strike seldom causes a problem for the issue. What does cause problems, however, are those bag marks, slide marks, etc., that attack the primary obverse focal location of the cow's head, and then the surrounding fields, as well as the reverse unprotected field design and field.

No error coinage has entered the marketplace to date.

Detecting Counterfeits

Counterfeits do exist. One example displays a field depression, just above the cow's right horn, directly below the "M" of "Unum" on the obverse, as well as in the reverse field opposite the "D" of "God" (just off Florida's west coast). The coin will look grayish and can display sharp reeding if un-doctored. Another fake will show small raised pimples on the right side of the cow's head, where this part of the design and field meet. On its reverse, look for field irregularity, or unevenness, especially below the words "Spanish Trail". The irregularity

Counterfeit Spanish Trail coin—note pit/depression at base of tree.

resembles an area of soil that has recently been raked. Do not confuse the latter with fine field die polishing marks. These raised lines are the result of the dies being steel brushed at the Mint. Genuine strikings do not have semi to proof-like fields, as recent fakes exhibit.

Is Your Spanish Trail Circulated or Mint State?

Obverse
Wear will first develop on the top of the cow's head opposite the horns, then in the center of its face. This location is a prime target for the coin doctors.

Reverse
A metal loss will first be observed on the central lower section of the yucca tree.

Related Material
The issue was distributed in an unprinted cardboard holder, having inserts for five and for six coins; "L.W. Hoffecker, 1514 Montana St., El Paso, Texas" is printed on the plain front cover. These were the same coin mailing vehicles Hoffecker used to deliver the Elgin half dollar. The holders are valued at $20 to $25; with original envelope, $50 to $125. A plaster model of the obverse and reverse sold for $4,400.

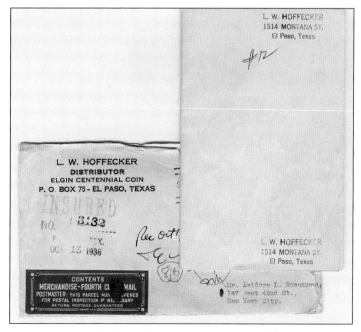

Spanish Trail mailing envelope and coin holder.

Future Potential of the Spanish Trail Half Dollar

Population Figures

Date	Service	AU 58	MS 60	MS 62	MS 63	MS 64	MS 65	MS 66	MS 67	MS 68	MS 69
1935	NGC	1	0	12	68	419	634	427	99	7	0
1935	PCGS	1	1	46	272	1010	1266	573	95	2	0
1935	Combined	12	1	58	340	1429	1900	1000	194	9	0

This beautiful and very popular coin is currently the second most expensive circulated U.S. commemorative single-year design produced between 1892 and 1954. The Hawaiian takes first-place honors, followed by the Hudson and Grant Star half dollar. The limited number in the circulated state are usually whizzed to some degree or abused, and are worth less. There is little price spread between grades EF-AU and MS-65, so collectors should aspire to the latter rating if possible.

There is average potential in the EF-AU to MS-65 classifications. I would lower the census between 25% and 30% for the MS-65 and MS-66 categories.

The previous dollar variation between grades MS-64 and MS-65, during the 1989 market peak was $1,600. The MS-65 and MS-66 differential was a lesser $1,500. There is good future potential in grade MS-66+, and excellent possibilities for coinage rated MS-67 and higher. These grades are definitely undervalued at present. Nine pieces have been rated MS-68.

Between February 2005 and August 2008, four pieces sold between $10.300 and $25,300. The latest MS-68 Spanish Trail sold at the Heritage January 2010 Orlando, FL FUN auction (#1136, lot 2639) for $17,250. We have previously discussed in other chapters the reasons for these price differentials.

Reason for Issue:	To commemorate the ideals and purpose of the California–Pacific International Exposition held at San Diego.
Authorization:	Act of May 3, 1935, with a maximum of 250,000 to be issued in 1935 and a maximum of 180,000 to be issued in 1936.
Issued by:	California–Pacific International Exposition Company
Official Sale Price:	1935-S $1 1936-D $1.50

Production Figures

Date	Business Strikes	Assay Coins	Proofs	Melted	Net Mintage
1935-S	250,000	132	4?	180,000	70,000
1936-D	180,000	92	4?	150,000	30,000

Current Market Values

Date	AU-58	MS-60	MS-63	MS-64	MS-65	MS-66	MS-67
1935-S	$90	$95	$100	$110	$135	$205	$1,125
1936-D	$90	$110	$115	$130	$140	$250	$1,000

DESIGNS BY ROBERT I. AITKEN

Obverse

Minerva, goddess of wisdom, seated and looking to her left. This image was adopted from the arms of the State of California. Minerva is wearing a crested helmet and holding a spear with her right hand. Her left hand has a firm grip on a shield that bears the head of Medusa, who could turn a beholder into stone with her glance. Above Medusa's head is the word "EUREKA", a word shouted by Archimedes when he discovered a method for determining the purity of gold, and an exclamation used to express triumph on a discovery by us today. It is also the state motto of California. Resting against the shield is a cornucopia (a carved goat's horn overflowing with fruit and ears of grain), symbolizing the state's abundance.

A bear facing left who appears to be looking at a lightly struck miner with pickaxe is at Minerva's side. Also appearing lightly struck in the field is a three-masted sailing ship; mountains are outlined in the coin's upper background. The artist's initials (RA) are at the extreme left border. "UNITED STATES OF AMERICA" arcs above; "HALF DOLLAR" below; "LIBERTY" appears just below Minerva's throne.

Reverse

Two structures from the Exposition grounds: the California Tower (right) and the St. Francis Chapel (left) of the State of California Buildings. At the base of the buildings is the motto "IN GOD WE TRUST". Below the first "T" in "TRUST" is the Mint mark. Above the chapel in the left field is "SAN DIEGO"; the date of issue appears in the right field. A simple design device is in the upper field. Encircling the coin is the inscription "CALIFORNIA PACIFIC INTERNATIONAL EXPOSITION".

Origins of the San Diego

The San Francisco Mint produced 250,000 plus 132 assay coins, in August 1935. A die trial piece struck on an undersized planchet exists in copper. The coins, bearing the date 1935 and the S Mint mark, were sold in San Diego during 1935 and 1936 by the California–Pacific International Exposition Commission, at $1 each. Tremendous efforts to sell this issue were made and supposedly 68,132 specimens were sold in 1935. It was at this time that interest in the commemorative series was just beginning to gain momentum; but this was also the time when the collector, dealer, and farsighted investor viewed such an issue—with its large mintage—with little enthusiasm. Their reasoning was that this coin would take a decade to be sold, since a large quantity would be available for too long a period of time, preventing any significant monetary gains in a reasonable span. The Exposition Commission was conscious of the coin professional's rationale concerning large mintage figures, and were aware that the sales of 1935-S San Diegos were coming to a standstill. The Commission was able to have Congress pass a bill (May 6, 1936) that gave birth to the 1936-D San Diego issue. The authorizing Act stated that "the coins shall be of the same design, bear the 1936 date irrespective of the year in which they are minted or issued, and shall be coined at one of the Mints of the United States." This issue's maximum authorization was not to exceed 180,000, and no coins were permitted to be issued later than one year after the date of the Act.

A whopping 180,000 1935-S specimens were returned to the Mint to be melted. "Reincarnation" occurred, and 180,000 new San Diegos, plus 92 assay coins were reborn at the Denver Mint, bearing the date 1936 and the D Mint mark. They were sold at $1.50 each. Thus, a total of 430,224 souvenir half dollars were produced at two Mints, via two authorizations. The San Diego was the only commemorative coin produced at two different branch Mints (and not the Philadelphia Mint) between 1892 and 1954. The following year, the Exposition Commission decided to sell both issues at $3 per coin, in order to create the appearance of demand and future rarity. This didn't work.

You might ask: "Where did they obtain the additional 1935-S pieces if they were reincarnated?" Answer: All were not destroyed. The members of the Exposition Commission envisioned a later demand for the 1935 issue once the 1936 coin had appeared, and vaulted 2,000 pieces, rather than returning them to the Mint for melting. One other individual owned between 15,000 and 16,000 pieces, and with fantastic foresight left them to a future family member.

In 1938 Emil Klicka, Treasurer of the Exposition, endeavored to sell the 1936-D issue at $1 each, placing a limit of 10 coins per order. How many orders under a brother, sister, or friend's name do you think would have been accepted, especially when sales for both issues had virtually ceased? Large hoards of both dates remained in San Diego.

The San Diego Today

The 1935-S issue is readily available in EF-AU condition on up to MS-66; so is the 1936-D striking, up to MS-66. Since there is little value spread between these conditions, collectors should aim for the highest grade. The ideal should be a flashy or lustrous MS-66, should funds permit, unless any grade will do. The 1936-D coin is underrated, when compared to the 1935-S issue, in MS-66 condition. The problem is that there are too many of each issue. Some 10,000 1935-S and 5,000 to 6,000 1936-D coins were acquired at face value; they were eventually sold, and many were graded by PCGS. A promotion will bring about a quick value increase, but afterwards values will return to the previous low realistic levels. The future for this beautiful issue is in the MS-66 category only, especially the Denver coin, which is more than three times as rare as the San Francisco striking. Luster will range from blazing frosty, to frosty, to dull frosty.

Strike at times can affect the grade-value especially for the 1936 issue. Locating 1936-D specimens that are fully struck or equal in strike to a sharply struck 1935-S piece must be considered the impossible dream, at present: after 40 years, I'm still searching!

The California Tower is flatly struck on the upper right corner of the building, beginning with the section opposite the "1" in the date 1936 (center right field) and working up two sections, appearing to be marked off by the design's inverted right angle (below the letters "IA" in "CALIFORNIA"), which appears to be part of the building at first glance. It is possible that virtually all the coins that displayed a sharp strike were melted. What remains are those pieces produced with a worn reverse die or struck with less pressure to save die wear from an over-polished die, eliminating design definition. Grade-value is lowered when this location displays too much strike softness or lack of detail. There have been instances where the S Mint mark on the 1935 issue appears as a blob of metal. If you look carefully, part of the "S" will be visible. Locating specimens of this issue with a fully defined "S," or fully struck Mint mark will be a find, since many pieces have this blob-like characteristic. The Mint mark will cause no grade-value lowering.

Bag marks, reed marks, lack of metal fill marks, slide marks, etc., make their presence felt on the obverse portrait, the primary focal area. They especially attack the sensitive smooth surfaces of Minerva's knee and long dress. The reverse primary focal location, the California Tower and the surrounding smooth fields, are not immune to these numismatic negatives.

So-called satin finish proofs are no more than lustrous sharply struck—*not double struck*—specimens that received angelic protection. In other words, true satin finish proofs do not exist.

No error coinage or counterfeits is known for either date.

IS YOUR SAN DIEGO CIRCULATED OR MINT STATE?

Obverse
A metal loss will first be detected on the breast and knees of Minerva, as well as the on back of the bear's head.

Reverse
Examine for a difference of metal texture on the right edge of the California Tower; crisscross scratches indicate a metal loss, if accompanied by a grayish-white metal color.

Related Material
This issue was distributed in a plain white coin envelope and in two types of heavy unprinted holders, with an insert for one and three coins. They were contained by a gummed paper cover. There were superior mailing vehicles with three different types of folder holders (3 7/16 × 2 3/8 inches), with a cut-out for one coin, glued to a piece of thin cardboard backing (4 1/2 × 3 3/8 inches). At times, cellophane tape was added to contain the coin. The front cover on one portrays the issue's two reverse buildings in silver and blue ink. Another features "Merry Christmas" in blue lettering and silver background. Both have thin royal blue

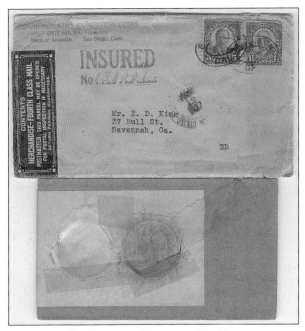

San Diego envelope and coin holder.

San Diego correspondence envelope.

velour interiors. The third is also a Christmas card, with green and red lettering, red poinsettia and green velour interior. This is the nicest of the holders. All orders were accompanied by a golden-yellow Exposition paper advertising insert (5 11/16 × 3 3/8 inches), printed in blue ink. Most were folded in some manner.

Collectors should value regular holders with mailing envelope at $40 to $85; the decorative holders at $95 to $200, or $175 to $225 with mailing envelope, depending on condition.

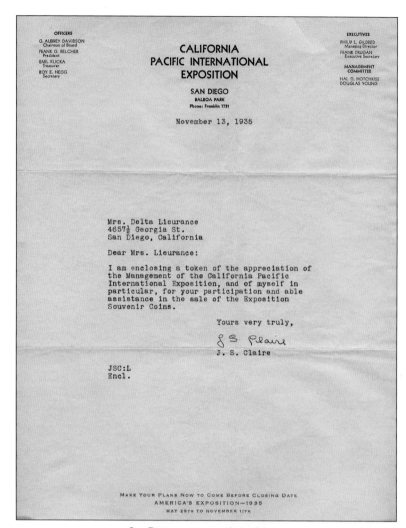

San Diego correspondence letter.

San Diego Christmas coin holder.

San Diego Exposition season pass—exterior.

San Diego Exposition season pass—interior.

Future Potential of the California–Pacific Exposition (San Diego) Half Dollar

Population Figures

Date	MS-63	MS-64	MS-65	MS-66	MS-67	MS-68
1935-S	728	3090	7169	1503	127	6
1936-D	335	2190	6125	749	69	1

Date	Service	AU 58	MS 60	MS 62	MS 63	MS 64	MS 65	MS 66	MS 67	MS 68	MS 69
1935 S	NGC	6	0	28	139	929	2549	635	105	6	0
1935 S	PCGS	21	4	76	643	2554	5653	1580	115	3	0
1935 S	Combined	27	4	104	782	3483	8202	2215	220	9	0

Date	Service	PL 50	PL 60	PL 62	PL 63	PL 64	PL 65	PL 66	PL 67	PL 68	PL 69
1935 S	NGC	0	0	0	0	0	0	6	0	0	0

Date	Service	AU 58	MS 60	MS 62	MS 63	MS 64	MS 65	MS 66	MS 67	MS 68	MS 69
1936 D	NGC	0	0	4	44	620	1442	423	56	2	0
1936 D	PCGS	4	1	26	300	1746	4013	773	73	0	0
1936 D	Combined	4	1	30	344	2366	5455	1196	129	2	0

These coins have the highest population figures for MS-66 strikings, as individual and series coin totals, so collectors should procure EF-AU through MS-66 pieces only for the joy of owning a beautifully designed coin. The price spread between EF-AU and MS-66 rated pieces is almost nonexistent. The coins are definitely a promotional candidate, when the numismatic scene heats up, but remember that as any market high runs its course it will return to pre-high value levels.

Each striking now has the highest encapsulation figure in MS-65 condition. Part of a large hoard that entered the marketplace in the recent past is responsible: thousands of pieces of each date from the stockpile were submitted for slabbing. Their owners were in at face value or close to it. During the past market peak, the price variation between the MS-64 and MS-65 San Diego was $350 for the 1935-S production and $490 for the 1936-D coin. Between the MS-65 and MS-66 classification the spread was $1,870 and $2,500 for the respective dates. We should never say "never," but I'll say that for this situation: it will never recur. Population figures can be reduced by 16% to 20% for MS-65 coinage, but who really cares, in this case?

In MS-66 condition, obviously choose the 1936 Denver coinage. This has average future potential. I do not believe that those hoard coins will inflate the census. I would reduce the population count by 19% to 23%, for each issue. Both strikings are also undervalued at MS-67, and there is excellent future potential for each. One of the 1935-S MS-68 pieces, which looks to me like it should grade MS-69, brought $18,400. An MS-68 1936-D coin that looks like it won't rate any higher was sold for $6,600. With the MS-69 look, it too might have sold for $18,000.

1935–1939 ARKANSAS CENTENNIAL

Reason for Issue:	To commemorate the 100th anniversary of the 1836 admission of Arkansas into the Union.
Authorization:	Act of May 14, 1934, with 500,000 total for the issue.
Issued by:	Arkansas Centennial Commission
Official Sale Price:	1935, 1936 issues: $1 per coin 1937, 1938 sets: $8.75 1939 set: $10

Production Figures

Date	Business Strikes	Assay Coins	Proofs	Melted	Net Mintage
1935	13,000	12	4	-	13,000
1935-D	5,500	5	4	-	5,500
1935-S	5,500	6	4	-	5,500
1936	10,000	10	4	350	9,650
1936-D	10,000	10	4	350	9,650
1936-S	10,000	12	4	350	9,650
1937	5,500	5	4	-	5,500
1937-D	5,500	5	4	-	5,500
1937-S	5,500	6	4	-	5,500
1938	6,000	6	4	2,850	3,150
1938-D	6,000	5	4	2,850	3,150
1938-S	6,000	6	4	2,850	3,150

Date	Business Strikes	Assay Coins	Proofs	Melted	Net Mintage
1939	2,100	4	4	-	2,100
1939-D	2,100	4	4	-	2,100
1939-S	2,100	5	4	-	2,100

Current Market Values

Date	AU-58	MS-60	MS-63	MS-64	MS-65	MS-66	MS-67
1935 PDS set	$240	$250	$320	$355	$655	$1,300	$7,000
1936 PDS set	$240	$250	$320	$355	$655	$1,300	$8,800
1937 PDS set	$270	$280	$335	$380	$800	$2,100	$13,000
1938 PDS set	$425	$490	$500	$580	$1,700	$2,600	$22,500
1939 PDS set	$900	$1.050	$1.150	$1.250	$2,800	$5,400	$31,000
Type coin	$90	$95	$100	$110	$190	$525	$2,400

DESIGNS BY EDWARD EVERETT BURR, MODELED BY EMILY BATES

Obverse

An eagle with outstretched wings facing right, positioned atop a sun (representing enterprise) with rays extending across the entire background of the coin. The eagle holds in his beak a scroll bearing two mottoes: on the left, "IN GOD WE TRUST"; on the right "E PLURIBUS UNUM". "UNITED STATES OF AMERICA" arcs above. The three stars located directly above the eagle are symbolic of Arkansas being the third state created from the Louisiana Purchase, and also represent the three flags that have flown over Arkansas: Spain, France, and the United States. The single star above the word Arkansas commemorates the state's participation in the Confederacy. The eagle also shows that the flag remained under the protection of the United States. Above the eagle is a diamond shape, taken from the state flag, which was originally adopted because Arkansas was then the only state that produced diamonds. This symbol is studded with 13 stars. The lower half of the diamond, shape bearing the remaining 12 stars, totaling 25—indicative that Arkansas was the 25th state to be admitted into the Union—is not shown.

On the sun is the inscription "HALF DOLLAR" and the date of issue. (The letter "R" in "DOLLAR" is larger than the rest of the letters, which is characteristic of the issue.) The Mint mark is at the five o'clock position, on the first right ray near the sun.

Reverse

The left-facing accolated heads of a Native American Chief wearing a feathered headdress, and an allegorical Liberty wearing a Phrygian cap with a band and a wreath of cotton leaves.

The Chief is most likely a Quapaw, since his tribe inhabited much of the area that became the territory of Arkansas. The word "Liberty" appears above the wreath. In the left and lower left field appear the centennial dates 1836–1936— and not the date of striking; around the lower border are the words "Arkansas Centennial". The second "S" of "Arkansas" is closely spaced to the letter "A", which is a design characteristic.

Origins of the Arkansas

The original sketches created by Edward Everett Burr of Little Rock and modeled by Emily Bates were rejected because the U.S. Commission of Fine Arts thought the original reverse eagle resembled designs reminiscent of the unimpressive eagles that were commonly used in commercial advertisements at the time. In fact, the U.S. Mint Director Nellie Tayloe Ross was later to suggest that Bates should be replaced with a medalist with more experience. The Arkansas Centennial Commission, however, opposed Bates's dismissal.

Based on sketch suggestions by Lee Lawrie, sculptor member of the Commission of Fine Arts, the issue was modeled by Bates, under the supervision of Illinois sculptor Larado Taft, an intermediary between the creators and the Commission. On December 5, 1934, the new sketch was returned to Burr with the addition of the date 1935. Models were prepared. On February 7, 1935, Lawrie informed Fine Arts Secretary H.P. Caemmerer that the finished plaster model of the original eagle reverse had an unprofessional look. The anniversary dates (1836–1936) were the only dates intended to appear on the original obverse in the lower field. Lawrie's suggestions and criticisms were presented hurriedly in order to get the coin into production. The eagle side, which was originally supposed to be the reverse, was suddenly referred to as the "United States side," while Liberty and the Indian Chief were labeled the "Centennial side." Thus, the United States side—with the eagle—was designated the obverse, with the date of issue now seen in the lower border.

Why the quick change from the artist's obverse to reverse? The obverse–reverse customs that applied to regular circulating coinage did not apply to commemoratives. The Alabama Centennial commemorative was the first to possess three dates—its year of production (1921) on the obverse and the Centennial dates (1819–1919) on the reverse. The 1934 Texas issue was the second coin to do likewise. The third coin scheduled to bear three dates was the Arkansas. The pressure was on the Mint to produce a coin as quickly as possible. With the addition of the 1935 date to the design it was decided simply to follow the Alabama–Texas three-date pattern. The obverse is determined by the year in which a coin was minted, while the celebration or anniversary dates grace the reverse.

The Arkansas Centennial anniversary occurred in 1936, but the first coins struck to commemorate that event were produced in 1935. The gentlemen in

Max Mehl

charge of the Arkansas Centennial did not want to be outdone by other commemorative committees. They wanted their commemorative coins struck and issued as soon as possible. Hence, 10,000 pieces were created at Philadelphia during May 1935.

By September of that year, all the coins had been sold through the Arkansas Centennial Commission of Little Rock at $1 each. Since requests for the coin were still being received, the Centennial Commission decided it might be wise to have a small additional quantity struck. They enlisted the aid of the coin dealer B. Max Mehl of Fort Worth, Texas.

I would like to bring to light some recently discovered information concerning a special request made to Mint Director Ross. After the discussion with Mehl, A.W. Parke, the Centennial Commission's Secretary, sent a letter to Ross about the authorized purchase of the Arkansas 1935 issue, to be struck at the Mints. Parke requested that an oversized Mint mark be used to make it more distinguishable than the customary small D and S. In addition, Parke also requested that half of the total branch Mint production bear the Mint mark on the obverse and half on the reverse.

His request was denied on the grounds that it would involve additional expenses for which the Mint could not be reimbursed, since there was no provision in the law permitting these features, plus the fact that the alterations would involve a change in policy that the Mint did not feel justified in making.

However, some of Mehl's advice was followed and an additional 3,000 commemorative halves were struck at Philadelphia. In November, 5,500 pieces were produced at each of the branch Mints. Few were actually sold at $1, since Mehl himself purchased most of these coins. In January 1936, Mehl offered the 1935-D and 1935-S issues at $2.75 each and the 1935-P at $2. If you already owned the

Philadelphia coin, you could get the other two for $5. Approximately 11 years later, the lower mintage coins were offered separately from the higher production issue. A characteristic of this coin is that the digit 5 is slightly tilted to the right. There are silver and bronze obverse and reverse die trials for the issue.

In the actual centennial year (1936) 10,000 coins were struck at each Mint and were offered at $1 per coin. After January 31, 1936, they were selling for $1.50 per coin. Later they sold for $6.75 per set. After the year's end, the Centennial Commission had no desire to direct the retail disposal of the coins: they wanted to sell out the remaining stocks to the highest bidder. Many of the coins were sold, in lots, to dealers, for resale in other states. These conditions combined to make the series obtainable anywhere—except in Arkansas. Accordingly, the series soon came to be known as the "Orphan Issue."

According to additional correspondence from Parke, we can assume the 1937 strikings were produced by the Mints in late March or early April. The 5,500 production by each facility was offered as a three-piece set for $8.75. No coins were returned for melting. During January 1938, each of the three Mints produced 6,000 Arkansas commemorative half dollars for collectors and investors; they were offered at $8.75 per set.

However, the so-called commemorative bubble had burst by late 1937. Prices dropped in varying degrees, as the value of commemoratives fell from their previous levels. Because of the decline of interest in commemoratives in general, only slightly more than half of the 1938 Arkansas issue was sold. The balance was returned to the Mints to be melted, leaving a very low 3,150 mintage.

It appears that in January 1939, Philadelphia and Denver each struck 2,104 coins; 2,105 were struck at San Francisco. The actual delivered quantity was 2,100 pieces from each Mint, those 13 extra coins being used for assay purposes. One year later, the set was being advertised for $20.

The Arkansas Today

A small percentage of these Arkansas Centennial halves saw actual circulation. Those that grade less than EF-AU, do so because they were truly used as long-term pocket pieces. Pieces that are sold below the MS-60+ price range almost always have been cleaned, whizzed, over-dipped, or heavily marked—or just lack eye appeal. They should be purchased only if the price is very right. Such a coin could be presented to a youngster for his or her collection and an avid collector and preeminent numismatist might result. The dates most often encountered are the 1935 and 1936 Philadelphia issues. There is little value spread between all sets produced from 1935 through 1937 in MS-60 up to MS-64 condition. Should funds be available, collectors should aim for a higher MS-64 acquisition; the best dates are 1937-S and 1937-D. You should be aware that eye-appealing coins are not easy to find.

The 1938 and 1939 set productions are excellent buys in all grades from MS-60 through MS-67. Eye-appealing sets or individual pieces of these issues are not plentiful. At times the coins would have been polished, whizzed, or otherwise abused: their worth depends on the extent of the damage. Collectors should aim for a minimum of MS-64+, if debating purchase; the future lies at this level and upwards. In MS-63 condition, the 1939-S, 1939-P, and 1938-D will be the hardest to locate. In MS-64 condition, all 1939 coins are almost equal in rarity, but are harder to find than the 1938 production. The relatively low mintage of most issues contributes to the difficulties in locating pristine specimens.

The physical characteristics of the dies themselves contributed even more to the difficulty of obtaining a quality specimen from the Mint. Many of the issues struck from 1935 through 1939 appear to be dull or have little lustrous life or little Mint luster. Luster will range from brilliant frosty, to brilliant satiny (not the norm), to unattractive dull. Some coins are plagued by lack of metal fill marks caused by not enough striking pressure in the affected location or even planchet handling damage. Also numismatic abuse has taken its toll, especially on the reverse primary focal locations, which are the portraits of Liberty and the Quapaw Chief. Pay special attention to the lady's cheek and the man's jaw. On the obverse the eagle's neck is the primary focal area. Silver white or pristine or naturally lustrous individual pieces, as well as sets, should be purchased immediately. However, they must not possess excessive bag marks, slide marks, cuts and scratches, as are frequently seen on the coin's reverse. Naturally, such coins will not grade MS-65 or MS-64+; this is the type that can be offered unslabbed, and can grade from MS-64 down to MS-60.

Do not expect the obverse of this issue to be equal in strike to the 1936 Arkansas–Robinson coin. The latter's die engraving was deeper and sharper, giving the finished product more relief. In many years of researching U.S. commemorative coins, I have seen but very few examples of the Arkansas Centennial with a fully struck twisted scroll across the eagle's breast. On most of them, the twist at that point will look as though it had been flattened to various degrees. Picture a hot liquid turning into a solid that did not fully cool. Something was placed on top of it, slightly flattening part of the design. This is true especially of the Denver and San Francisco strikings during the years 1935–38. The Philadelphia strikings of 1935 and 1936 have an even greater percentage with this worn appearance. By contrast, almost all of the 1939 issue from all Mints were well struck. Strike will thus range from sharp to very weak. When the eagle's breast feathers and the central ribbon begin to lose detail, you lose grade and value. Specimens that are graded to a strict MS-65 and higher offer exceptional future value, especially all dated complete sets (1935–1939).

Few Arkansas specimens will accurately grade MS-66+ or MS-67; locating individual coins of such magnitude will be a formidable task, let alone finding a three-piece set. At times, I am asked which individual dates are the seven rarest issues in MS-64, MS-65, and MS-66 condition. Rated 64 are: 1939 PDS, 1938 PDS, 1937-D, and the 1937-S. Rated MS-65 are: 1939-P, 1938-S, and 1938-D. Rated MS-66 are: 1939-P, 1938-S, 1937-S, and 1939-D. Simply because an issue is in ninth place in population does not mean it will be easy to find, especially attractive coins. However, the chances of acquiring an Arkansas occupying 12th through 15th places, per population figures, will be greater.

Proof coins do exist for this issue. Before the dies destined to be sent to the Denver and San Francisco Mints were shipped, John Ray Sinnock, Chief Mint Engraver, ordered struck (each year) a few sets of the extremely rare and beautiful matte proof (double-struck, acid-treated) coinage. (Their respective Mint marks were "punched in" at the Philadelphia Mint.) To date, a 1938-P (PF-63), a 1938 and 1938-S (both PF-64) have been encapsulated by NGC. Coins can be acid-treated or sandblasted (as was the case of the Hawaiian issue) after they leave the Mint. However, what cannot be added is an additional striking. Upon side by side inspection with a business strike, the difference is easy to see. Should a possible proof candidate cross your path, send it to me for a free evaluation. I would personally pass on any specimen offered as a satin finish proof. In my opinion they were never created at any of the Mints. If you cannot resist the offering, you must attempt to have it graded by NGC or PCGS for your own protection.

No error coinage or counterfeits are known.

Is Your Arkansas Circulated or Mint State?

Obverse

Wear will first make its appearance on the primary focal area of the eagle's neck feathers, then on its head and upper right wing as we view the coin.

Reverse

Look for wear on the primary focal area of Liberty's cheek. A loss of metal will next be observed on the band of her cap, directly behind her eye. This is the primary target for the whizzers.

Related Material

Unprinted one-piece coin holders with inserts for five half dollars were used to distribute the 1935 and 1936 Arkansas Centennial coinage. Attempt to acquire a holder with the 1936 stamped mailing envelope from the Centennial Commission: this is seldom seen. The back of the envelope has a colorful red, white and blue Centennial stamp and 1936 date. At times, individual coins of the first two issues are seen housed in B. Max Mehl's coin envelopes, but these have no real extra value.

Stack's of New York City distributed the 1937 sets at $8.75 per set of three. The coins were encased in a black velvet rectangular case. The date 1937 appeared in the upper left corner of the outer top with "Arkansas Commemorative Half Dollars" in gold letters across the central part of the rectangular holder. Within, there appears the name of the official distributors as well as a blue Stack's advertising insert, which all too often does not accompany the case when offered for sale today: most were thrown away.

Stack's also offered the 1938 sets, again at $8.75 per set, in the same type of cases as the 1937 sets. (The 1937 date was removed.)

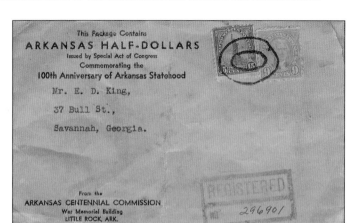

Arkansas mailing envelope—front.

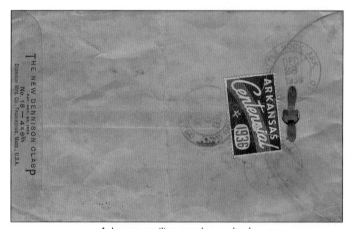

Arkansas mailing envelope—back

Arkansas coin holder.

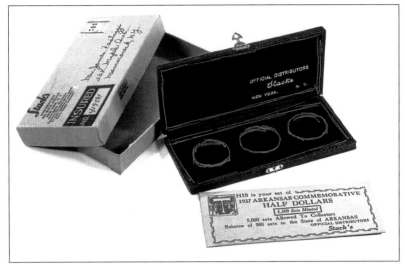

Stack's coin case, mailing box, and insert.

When the existing supply of the black cases ran out, and before all of the 1938 sets were distributed, a different 4 × 5-inch holder was substituted. The outer case and the inner top was made from a fine looking, light tan, imitation wood-grained paper. Velour (either black or green) covered the inside of the bottom section, which had slots for the three coins, arranged in a triangle. This holder was also used to distribute the 1939 issue by Stack's, at $10 per set. Orders were accepted in the fall of 1938. Demand was so great that this issue was sold out before it was struck. For the 1935 envelope with insert, value is $35 to $75; the black case for the 1937 set is valued at $75 to $150; the blue advertising insert, $15 to $50; the wood-grained type, $50 to $100.

Future Potential of the Arkansas Half Dollar

Population Figures

Date	Service	AU 58	MS 60	MS 62	MS 63	MS 64	MS 65	MS 66	MS 67	MS 68	MS 69
1935	NGC	2	1	20	114	437	366	82	7	1	0
1935	PCGS	1	0	52	291	602	489	152	12	0	0
1935	Combined	3	1	72	405	1039	855	234	19	1	0

Date	Service	AU 58	MS 60	MS 62	MS 63	MS 64	MS 65	MS 66	MS 67	MS 68	MS 69
1935 D	NGC	0	2	4	48	266	325	98	34	2	0
1935 D	PCGS	0	0	19	168	448	389	192	42	0	0
1935 D	Combined	0	2	23	216	714	714	90	76	2	0

Date	Service	AU 58	MS 60	MS 62	MS 63	MS 64	MS 65	MS 66	MS 67	MS 68	MS 69
1935 S	NGC	1	0	9	51	275	333	105	13	0	0
1935 S	PCGS	0	0	29	161	435	406	160	17	0	0
1935 S	Combined	1	0	38	212	710	739	265	30	0	0

Date	Service	AU 58	MS 60	MS 62	MS 63	MS 64	MS 65	MS 66	MS 67	MS 68	MS 69
1936	NGC	0	0	20	107	417	256	56	7	0	0
1936	PCGS	4	1	57	259	533	279	88	7	0	0
1936	Combined	4	1	77	366	950	535	144	14	0	0

Date	Service	AU 58	MS 60	MS 62	MS 63	MS 64	MS 65	MS 66	MS 67	MS 68	MS 69
1936 D	NGC	0	3	11	70	345	323	80	13	2	0
1936 D	PCGS	3	1	36	261	569	406	188	21	0	0
1936 D	Combined	3	4	47	331	914	729	268	34	2	0

Date	Service	AU 58	MS 60	MS 62	MS 63	MS 64	MS 65	MS 66	MS 67	MS 68	MS 69
1936 S	NGC	0	0	17	70	337	352	72	8	0	0
1936 S	PCGS	3	4	40	245	503	347	121	9	0	0
1936 S	Combined	3	4	57	315	840	699	193	17	0	0

Date	Service	AU 58	MS 60	MS 62	MS 63	MS 64	MS 65	MS 66	MS 67	MS 68	MS 69
1937	NGC	0	0	8	74	331	204	47	3	0	0
1937	PCGS	0	1	39	213	436	245	95	5	0	0
1937	Combined	0	1	47	287	767	449	142	8	0	0

Date	Service	AU 58	MS 60	MS 62	MS 63	MS 64	MS 65	MS 66	MS 67	MS 68	MS 69
1937 D	NGC	0	0	6	62	262	296	76	10	0	0
1937 D	PCGS	0	1	26	184	401	348	123	15	1	0
1937 D	Combined	0	1	32	246	663	644	199	25	1	0

Date	Service	AU 58	MS 60	MS 62	MS 63	MS 64	MS 65	MS 66	MS 67	MS 68	MS 69
1937 S	NGC	0	0	2	76	301	170	29	3	1	0
1937 S	PCGS	0	1	49	216	407	206	58	3	0	0
1937 S	Combined	0	1	51	292	708	376	87	6	1	0

Date	Service	AU 58	MS 60	MS 62	MS 63	MS 64	MS 65	MS 66	MS 67	MS 68	MS 69
1938	NGC	0	0	6	62	212	145	39	0	0	0
1938	PCGS	2	0	27	154	292	200	73	7	0	0
1938	Combined	2	0	33	216	504	345	112	7	0	0

Date	Service	AU 58	MS 60	MS 62	MS 63	MS 64	MS 65	MS 66	MS 67	MS 68	MS 69
1938 D	NGC	2	0	16	52	195	160	42	24	2	0
1938 D	PCGS	1	1	30	130	284	200	108	19	0	0
1938 D	Combined	3	1	46	182	479	360	150	43	2	0

Date	Service	AU 58	MS 60	MS 62	MS 63	MS 64	MS 65	MS 66	MS 67	MS 68	MS 69
1938 S	NGC	0	0	16	58	200	166	34	3	0	0
1938 S	PCGS	1	1	30	138	282	206	57	0	0	0
1938 S	Combined	1	1	46	196	482	372	91	3	0	0

Date	Service	AU 58	MS 60	MS 62	MS 63	MS 64	MS 65	MS 66	MS 67	MS 68	MS 69
1939	NGC	0	0	10	53	203	111	21	1	0	0
1939	PCGS	0	1	40	149	243	144	28	1	0	0
1939	Combined	0	1	50	202	446	255	49	2	0	0

Date	Service	AU 58	MS 60	MS 62	MS 63	MS 64	MS 65	MS 66	MS 67	MS 68	MS 69
1939 D	NGC	0	0	6	45	192	142	33	9	0	0
1939 D	PCGS	0	1	21	152	232	182	71	6	1	0
1939 D	Combined	0	1	27	197	424	324	104	15	1	0

Date	Service	AU 58	MS 60	MS 62	MS 63	MS 64	MS 65	MS 66	MS 67	MS 68	MS 69
1939 S	NGC	0	0	11	49	168	168	54	3	0	0
1939 S	PCGS	0	0	40	117	218	218	89	5	0	0
1939 S	Combined	0	0	51	166	386	386	143	8	0	0

Circulated type coins are usually those with higher mintage strikings. There is little price spread between such material graded EF-AU and MS-64: it is that abundant and offers at best average eye appeal. The same can be said for many of the 1935–1937 three-piece sets grading MS-60 to MS-63, as well as unattractive MS-64 sets. These should be acquired only for the joy of ownership.

Should one desire an MS-64 type coin of this issue, focus only on the low-census, attractive coinage, for any real future potential. I highly recommend the 1938 and 1939 P, D, and S coinage—especially the 1939-S striking. As far as three-piece sets are concerned, attempt to locate at least MS-63+ material. If there is any chance of progress in the coming years, this is where it is. Concentrate on the 1938 and 1939 sets, if funds permit. Otherwise, just acquire an attractive type coin for the pleasure of ownership.

In the MS-64 category, eye-appealing 1938 and 1939 examples are under priced. Unfortunately for the 1937 set, interest is lacking, although these coins are rarer than the earlier 1935 and 1936 sets. The real future lies in alluring 1938 and 1939 sets. Add to this list any set that can be labeled MS-64+.

During the last market high of May 1989, the price for an Arkansas MS-65 type coin was $1,450. It has now fallen to $190. What happened? When all examples are combined, the population figure is high for the generic dates, so the value is realistic. Knowing how difficult accurately graded and appealing pieces are to come by, my response, based on 40-plus years of battlefield experience, is that all is dependent on the particular coin being examined. When it lacks drawing power, and/or possesses surface negatives where they should not be, or the grade is very questionable, I couldn't care less what the grading label insert indicates. To me, it might be an MS-64.0 or MS-64.5 or MS-64.9 coin (if such granular decimal grades were offered by the major grading services) in an MS-65 holder. Real quality, when offered, will usually bring much more money, but all is contingent on the buyer. Most dealers, however, will pay more for quality—especially in a hot market. Thus, the bad drives the good into hiding. A quantity of lesser material in the marketplace keeps prices from rising. I suggest never buying sight-unseen: you must see what you are acquiring. Given these factors and combined with grading-label discarding, I would reduce the population figures for the generic and semi-common dates by 38% or more, and would lower the census by 35% or more for the rarer dates.

I highly recommend the following type dates in MS-65 condition for tremendous future potential: 1939-P, 1938-S, 1939-D, 1938-P, and 1938-D. For sets, focus on the 1938 and 1939 productions: all are extremely undervalued.

The same can be said for coins rated MS-66, such as the 1939-P, 1938-P, 1938-S, 1937-S, and 1939-D issues. Even the higher 1937-P, 1936-P, and 1936-S census dates are undervalued at these levels—if accurately graded. You can bet that few pieces rated at this level have been resubmitted in the past. There is an exceptional future here for all dates, especially the lower-census issues.

MS-67 coinage can be difficult to locate, depending on the issue. The coins should be virtually hairline-free and not have any large bag marks. The highest population issues are the 1935-D (76) at $1500, 1938-D (43) at $4200, 1936-D (34) at $2200, and 1937-D (25) at $2900. That's minute in my book. I wish I owned a few. There is tremendous potential in this grade. Values can range from $1500 to $12000. Populations for MS-68 coinage are very small.

Reason for Issue:	To commemorate the 250th anniversary of the founding of the city of Albany, New York.
Authorization:	Act of June 16, 1936, with a maximum of 25,000 pieces.
Issued by:	Albany Dongan Charter Coin Committee
Official Sale Price:	$2

Production Figures

Date	Business Strikes	Assay Coins	Proofs	Melted	Net Mintage
1936	25,000	13	4?	7,342	17,658

Current Market Values

Date	AU-58	MS-60	MS-63	MS-64	MS-65	M7-66	MS-67
1936	$260	$275	$285	$290	$355	$480	$1,200+

Designs by Gertrude K. Lathrop

Obverse

An American beaver, facing right, is gnawing on a branch of maple, the New York state tree. (A beaver is also on the Albany city seal.) "UNITED STATES OF AMERICA" and "HALF DOLLAR" encircle the obverse, separated by two maple keys, which represent growth and fertility, at about the four and seven o'clock positions. "E Pluribus Unum" is to the left of the beaver; "In God We Trust" to the right.

Reverse

Governor Thomas Dongan bidding farewell to Robert Livingston, his secretary, and Peter Schuyler, the first Mayor of Albany, holding the newly acquired Albany City charter of July 22, 1686 (the charter is now housed in the Manuscript Room of the State Library in Albany). Over the group is an eagle with outstretched wings. The word "Liberty" can be noted in minute letters above the eagle. Encircling the coin is the inscription "Settled 1614 Chartered 1686 Albany NY", separated by two pine cones in the same position as the maple keys on the obverse. Incused in very small letters beside Dongan's foot are the designer's initials (GKL). The date of striking, 1936, is located in the lower field.

Origins of the Albany

The Albany Dongan Charter Coin Committee, which was responsible for distribution, sold approximately 72 percent of the entire issue (25,000 pieces; there were 13 coins struck for assay purposes) produced in October 1936 by the Philadelphia Mint: 17,658 specimens were purchased. When the commemorative boom of 1937 passed, the Coin Committee got tired of holding meetings to account for sales of a dozen pieces. The decision was made in 1943 to return all 7,342 coins being held to the Mint for melting. Between 1,600 and 2,400 undistributed pieces were supposedly in the possession of the State Bank of Albany in 1954. All were said to have been purchased at $2 per coin by dealers and collectors; their market value was $8.

According to Lee F. Hewitt of Florida, his "brother accumulated 638 of these low mintage souvenirs over the years (that equates to nearly 32 rolls). In February 1979, the safe deposit boxes where these estate coins were housed were burglarized. The coins were in rolls in a box marked 'half dollars.' At the same time they were taken, these thieves threw a complete type set of commemoratives contained in their Lucite holders on the floor, not knowing what they were! Silver at the time was on the road to higher and higher prices. Is it possible that the 638 Albanys were melted?" Based on $350 per coin, at the time, I derive a total market value of $223,300—a considerable loss, if the coins really were melted.

The Albany Today

Since the coin is available in most grades, it makes most sense for collectors to look for higher grades, if funds permit. Albanys rated MS-65 are not hard to find. The key is to acquire flashy eye-appealing specimens, primarily for the joy of ownership. Avoid examples with beaver hip rub or slide marks: these are not MS-65 coins. The real future lies in loftier graded coins (MS-66+).

Luster will range from blazing, brilliant frosty, to dull frosty. At times, when comparing both sides of a coin, I have noticed the obverse showing more intensity. The uninformed or unscrupulous will "dip" (in a tarnish-removing solution) the reverse side, in an attempt to duplicate the luster intensity. Because of the die preparation and surface, this procedure will not work: the surface is "hurt" and the coin's grade-value lowered. Strike rarely causes the Albany any problems.

Over the past six years or so, when an eye-appealing, blazing lustrous coin was purchased by a dealer or collector, a bag mark or two on the primary focal areas (the obverse beaver or the reverse coat of the Governor or on what appears to be one large coat housing both Robert Livingston and Peter Schuyler) fazed virtually no one, unless it really was detracting. These coins—and almost every other issue—were continuously bought and sold at gem or MS-65 levels. But today, as most of us are now aware, to solidify the grade it takes—in most cases—more than flash or eye appeal. Detracting marks in the primary focal areas are no longer accepted. Consequently, fewer Albanys make the grade and higher prices result from demand and low mintage. This applies to American numismatics generally.

To date, no error coinage has surfaced.Detecting Counterfeits

Counterfeit Albanys display a washed-out luster. The surface color is dull gray, and the lettering is not sharp. Look for a depression near the center of the "D" in "Dollar" at the obverse six o'clock position, as well as raised lumps of metal in the field adjacent to the top of Peter Schuyler's head, down to his coat's cuff on the coin's reverse.

Is Your Albany circulated or Mint State?

Obverse

Wear will first be observed on the hip of the beaver, causing the metal texture to appear grayish-white. Even slight abuse will bring this about because of the area's high relief. Collectors should examine the beaver closely for some form of doctoring, especially whizzing, intended to hide a slight metal loss or, at times, slide marks.

Reverse

The reverse design is better protected from wear than the obverse. However, a metal loss will first be observed on the sleeve of Governor Dongan.

Related Material

Many of the coins were offered for sale at $2 each in an official original holder, which pictures the obverse and reverse of the coin, plus the word "Albany" centered above the photographs. Page two of the holder presents a short history of Albany, and page three contains five slots in which one to five coins were placed when filling an order. Page four or the back of the holder was blank.

The official mailing envelope is imprinted: "Albany Dongan Charter Committee, 60 State Street, Albany, N.Y." Rarer are the cardboard boxes that housed

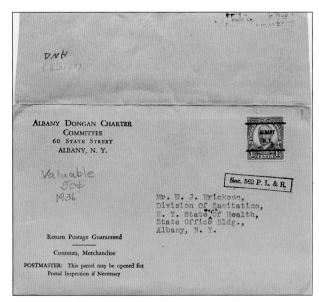

Albany mailing envelope with top flap.

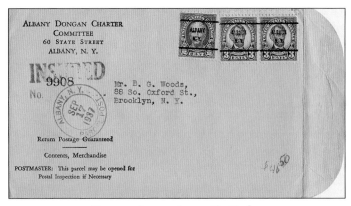

Albany mailing envelope with side flap.

a single coin. These were distributed by and imprinted with "The National Commercial Bank and Trust Company of Albany" in a red box with a red velour interior and a slit pouch for the coin. The bank's coat of arms is imprinted in gold ink on the top cover, as well as on a white box with a blue velour interior (in blue ink). Today, it is this special type of holder that determines the worth of a coin-holder offering. The above boxes housing an MS-64 and an MS-65 coin brought $4,370 as a pair in the American Numismatic Rarities auction on March 8, 2005. Holders can be valued at $75 to $125; with the original official mailing envelope, $125 to $175. The rarer boxes have brought between $350 and $1,000. In all cases, value is based on condition.

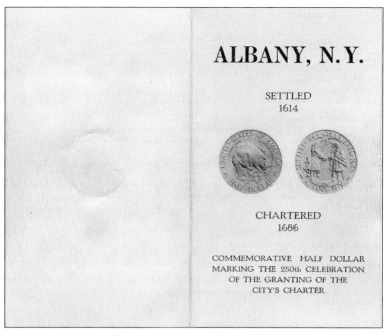

ALBANY, N.Y.

SETTLED
1614

CHARTERED
1686

COMMEMORATIVE HALF DOLLAR
MARKING THE 250th CELEBRATION
OF THE GRANTING OF THE
CITY'S CHARTER

Albany mailing coin holder—outside.

ALBANY, N. Y.

The history of Albany began with a settlement of adventurous seekers of new commercial fields in 1614.

For 322 years it has had a continuing existence.

Within its borders and in the territory it has served as a center of Commerce, of Education and of Transportation and Communication. It has taken a leading part in the birth and building of America and its institutions.

In 1686 it was chartered as a city.

On the obverse of the Commemorative Half-dollar marking the 250th Anniversary of the granting of its charter is shown the beaver and the maple leaf. The beaver became the base of a fur trade upon which the life of the colony depended. Recognition of the importance of the busy little animal came early in the history of Albany. It was pictured on the Colony's seal and is today part of the City's official seal.

The Maple is New York State's tree.

On the reverse of the Commemorative coin is pictured the presentation of the City's charter on July 22, 1686, by Governor Thomas Dongan to Albany's representatives, Pieter Schuyler, the first mayor, and Robert Livingston, secretary.

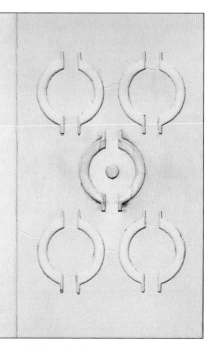

Albany mailing coin holder—inside.

Future Potential of the Albany Half Dollar

Population Figures

Date	Service	AU 58	MS 60	MS 62	MS 63	MS 64	MS 65	MS 66	MS 67	MS 68	MS 69
1936	NGC	4	1	32	128	795	1130	501	143	7	0
1936	PCGS	7	1	81	528	605	1419	746	85	1	0
1936	Combined	11	2	113	656	2400	2549	1247	228	8	0

The Albany is not abundant in circulated condition. Cleaned or whizzed (wire-brushed) pieces that hide actual metal loss on the obverse beaver's hip are the most frequently seen coins. There is little price difference between material graded EF-AU and MS-66 at present. These grades offer average potential so acquire these only for the joy of ownership or to possess an Albany as part of the 50-piece type set or 144-piece date-and-mint commemorative set. I would estimate that population figures for grades MS-64 and MS-65 can be lowered by as much as 28%, because of crack outs and the non-return of grading labels. That still leaves us with high population figures.

The future for this coin is in attractive MS-66+ and loftier grades. I would consider a 20% census deduction from the given population figures. I know of 11 MS-67 Albanys that were cracked out from the slabs, in hopes of the wonder MS-68 grade (I wonder how many of the insert labels have been destroyed and not returned?). Be certain your offering is a knockout coin. To qualify, it should have beautiful color, possess tremendous eye appeal, and show no obvious marks. A coin like this can bring multiples of the current value because it totally outclasses other coins of the same grade.

At the January 2011 Tampa FUN coin auction (#1155, lot 5702) a PCGS MS-68 encapsulation brought $19,550. Earlier (2004-2008) NGC and PCGS examples have sold at auction between $5,750 and $20,000.

Reason for Issue:	To commemorate the 100th anniversary of the admission of Arkansas into the Union.
Authorization:	Act of June 26, 1936, with a 25,000 minimum and a 50,000 maximum.
Issued by:	Stack's, New York City
Official Sale Price:	$1.85

Production Figures

Date	Business Strikes	Assay Coins	Proofs	Melted	Net Mintage
1936	25,250	15	8	0	25,250

Current Market Values

Date	AU-58	MS-60	MS-63	MS-64	MS-65	MS-66	MS-67
1936	$95	$100	$150	$190	$275	$600	$1,700

Designs

According to Public Law No. 831–74th Congress, the reverse of this issue bears the new design, since the side bearing the date—as stated in the Act—is referred to as the obverse. However, from a numismatic point of view, the portrait side of regular U.S. coinage is usually the obverse.

Obverse by Edward Everett Burr, modeled by Emily Bates

Same as the Arkansas Centennial, 1935–39.

Reverse by Enid Bell, modeled by Henry G. Kreiss

The bust of Senator Joseph T. Robinson, past Governor of Arkansas (1913), and Majority Leader in the Senate from 1933 to 1937, facing right. Around the upper border is the inscription "Arkansas Centennial 1836–1936". Below the Senator's chin, in the lower right field, is his name in two lines; "Liberty" is at the left, just behind Robinson's neck.

Henry Kreiss, who was responsible for the Bridgeport and Connecticut commemorative coins, prepared the model from a rough drawing made by Enid Bell. Since it is the final product that counts, his initial (K) appears near Robinson's shoulder, touching the coin's rim.

Origins of the Robinson

In 1936 the Texas Centennial Commission introduced a bill in Congress which, if successful, would have allowed for the creation of not one but five new reverses beautifying their beloved issue. Immediately the Arkansas group acted, calling for three new reverse designs. The Texas bill failed, but a single alteration was authorized for the Arkansas. Originally, the Arkansas Centennial Commission considered the portrait of a Native American woman and Hernando de Soto, who explored the territory that was to become Arkansas. After some outside pressure, however, it was decided that a well-known politician would be a better choice. Senator Robinson's portrait was selected and the design was quickly approved by the U.S. Commission of Fine Arts on December 23, 1936.

A long-standing debate in numismatic circles is whether it was illegal for the likeness of a living person to be placed on U.S. *coinage*, since a law prohibits portraits of living persons on U.S. *currency*. Whether legal tender coins, particularly commemoratives, qualify as "currency"—literally "current monetary instruments"—or whether the term should be restricted to its more common reference to paper money, is the crux of the debate. At least one researcher, a coin collector and a New Jersey attorney, claims the intent of the legislators at the time was that the law was to refer to paper money only. The pertinent statutory provision, now codified as 31 USC 5114 (b) says: "Only the portrait of a deceased individual may appear on United States currency and securities. The name of the individual shall be inscribed below the portrait." So it would seem that the statute does not apply to coinage. If it does, the Treasury Secretary must answer why the names of Lincoln, Jefferson, Roosevelt, and Washington, et al., are not properly inscribed below their portraits on the circulating coinage.

The supplementary Act authorizing the design change specified the minimum amount of coins that could be struck. It also had a date clause specifying that the coin must bear the date 1936, irrespective of the year in which it was minted or issued. Although a maximum of 50,000 pieces had been authorized in two allotments of 25,000 each, only 25,250 Robinsons plus 15 assay coins were minted in January 1937, in Philadelphia. Thus, because of the Act's dating clause, for the first time coins were produced in a year other than the indicated date. The Senator died just over six months later, on July 14, 1937, at the age of 64. He was the fourth living person to be depicted on U.S. coinage.

Stack's of New York City distributed the issue at $1.85 each. The commemorative coin bubble had burst, but none of the 25,250 coins was returned to the Mint. Abe Kosoff, a great professional numismatist whose name is known the world over, purchased 8,000 Arkansas–Robinson pieces sometime after a major decline in sales of this issue occurred.

The Robinson Today

Nearly the entire mintage of the Arkansas–Robinson exists today in Mint State. Coins offered at EF-AU values are almost always abused in some fashion or are unattractive dipped-out UNCs. The issue is abundant in grades up through MS-65; there is not much value spread between grades, so collectors should aspire to at least an eye-appealing MS-64+, should funds permit.

Luster can vary from brilliant frosty to dull frosty; look for the most eye-appealing brilliant or naturally toned coin. Strike presents no problem whatsoever. You should not compare these coins with the Arkansas Centennial obverse: its die design was not as deeply engraved. Lower grades are caused by bag marks, slide marks, nicks, cuts, scratches, and lack of fill marks. The smooth clean surfaces of the Senator's cheek and jaw are susceptible to damage, and, as a consequence, few coins can honestly be labeled MS-65 or higher.

The official distributor has no record of handling the proofs. However, it is known that the Arkansas Centennial Commission did present Wayte Raymond, a leading numismatist, with four satin finish proof specimens. Four others were also struck. A satin finish proof does not have the mirror-like surface of a Proof coin. Its surface looks like a cross between the 1909 Lincoln cent Proof and the 1909 Roman Finish gold Proofs. This is a difficult comparison for the neophyte to understand—this seldom-used surface is virtually identical to the finish on a satiny surfaced coin. Even astute numismatists of the past who examined the genuine item claimed they could not see the difference between the Proof and the regular issue.

After closely examining the striking characteristics of more than 1500 Arkansas–Robinson commemorative half dollars, I have reached the following conclusions concerning the Satin Finish coin, based on one that I once possessed. (It was stolen! Should you know of its whereabouts, kindly advise the author.)

- The eight coins given this special finish were produced with some extra striking pressure—but not via two blows from the press.
- Coins that were struck after the "special eight" were struck with somewhat less striking pressure.
- Since the identical, deeply engraved new obverse and reverse dies were used, a number of pieces (possibly 35 to 50 or more) that were

produced after the Satin Proofs will be observed with a close corresponding sharpness of strike. This will be evident in the upper and
middle parts of the Senator's hair and ear. In fact, the ear can appear
so raised that it seems possible to peel the outer part of the ear off
the coin.

The raised ear effect will intensify according to the amount of oxidation
present on the surface: the heavier the tone, the greater the enhancement.
Should toning be too heavy or dark, it will be extremely difficult to determine
whether the coin in question is the real thing, because the oxidation has now
become part of the surface: its originality can never be viewed again. Lost within
is that specially applied Satin Finish, which was difficult to appreciate even
when fully original, since it resembles the normal satiny surfaced coin. Dipping
in a tarnish-removing solution will certainly not help the situation.

Unless unquestionable U.S. Mint or a coin designer's documentation accompanies an offered coin, I suggest that collectors avoid. Having such a coin graded
by a third party is very important, since it is quite possible that the offered coin
and documentation might not be related.

No error coinage or counterfeit pieces have surfaced to date.

Is Your Robinson Circulated or Mint State?

Obverse

Wear will first make its appearance on the primary focal area of the eagle's neck
feathers, then on its head and upper right wing as we view the coin.

Reverse

Senator Robinson's cheekbone will be the first area to display any loss of metal.
The prime target for the whizzing doctors is the portrait, which is also the primary focal area.

Related Material

Stack's of New York City distributed this coin in a buff-colored cardboard presentation holder. On the front cover is printed in black ink the following: "Senator Joseph T. Robinson, Commemorative Half Dollar; a New Design Issued by
the Arkansas Centennial Commission: Authorized by Special Act of Congress
June 26, 1936; Official Distributors: Stack's, 690 Sixth Ave., New York, NY."
The inner front cover presents a photograph of the Senator, which is signed:
"Sincerely yours, Joseph T. Robinson." Beneath this photograph is the following
inscription: "This coin is issued in recognition of the remarkable services that
the honorable Jos. T. Robinson has rendered to the State of Arkansas". Page
three, or the back inner cover, has slots for five coins; while on the back cover is
printed the official distributor's advertisement. While not rare, this holder is not

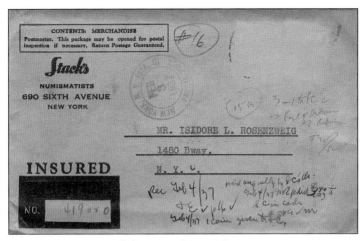

Robinson mailing envelope.

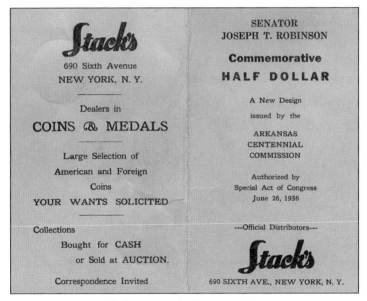

Robinson coin holder—outside.

abundant. Value the original envelope with holder at $100 to $275; the holder alone at $50 to $100, depending on its condition.

There is also a 10-coin holder where the interior picture is replaced with slots for an additional five coins.

The eight satin finish proofs were each placed in a black leather-grained looking box, measuring 3 × 3 inches. The top cover is stamped in gold lettering,

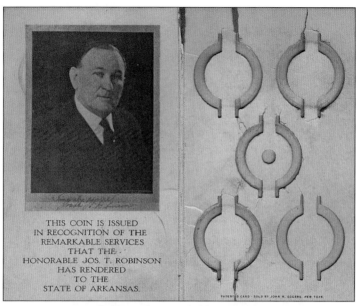

THIS COIN IS ISSUED
IN RECOGNITION OF THE
REMARKABLE SERVICES
THAT THE
HONORABLE JOS. T. ROBINSON
HAS RENDERED
TO THE
STATE OF ARKANSAS.

Robinson five-coin holder—inside.

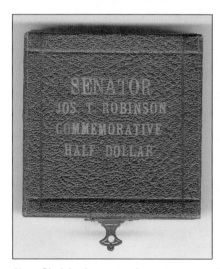

Above: Black leather-grained exterior.

At Right: Black leather-grained interior.

reading "Senator Jos.T. Robinson Commemorative Half Dollar". The lettering appears to float or be etched in glass inserted into a depression on the top cover. Opening the front bronze latch will reveal a cerise-colored velour coin holder. The box without the coin has sold for $4,400.

Future Potential of the Arkansas–Robinson Half Dollar

Population Figures

Date	Service	AU 58	MS 60	MS 62	MS 63	MS 64	MS 65	MS 66	MS 67	MS 68	MS 69
1936	NGC	1	0	62	290	1097	763	198	31	0	0
1936	PCGS	7	7	148	856	1807	1035	409	61	1	0
1936	Combined	8	7	210	1146	2904	1798	607	92	1	0

This is another issue in the generic realm, up to grades MS-65. Acquire only for the joy of collecting. There is no major price spread between pieces grading EF-AU through MS-65. Pieces rated MS-64 are fairly valued at present. The past dollar variation between MS-64 and MS-65 coinage was $1,500; this range will recur, but not as dramatically. The issue is also common in MS-64 condition, but not as easily located in the higher grades. I would reduce the census between 25% and 30%. President Clinton was not a catalyst for Arkansas and Arkansas–Robinson dealer promotion.

I have seen a bit too many pieces that would not have been rated MS-65 during the 1989 market high. These half dollars lack eye appeal or possess reverse facial negatives that would never have qualified them for the past high $1,800 bid. The previous dollar spread between grades MS-65 and MS-66 was a huge $3,100, but that will not recur: population figures were much lower at the time. I would reduce the census between 25% and 30%. There is average future potential for the strictly graded piece. Robinsons grading MS-66—if strictly graded—are undervalued at present levels; this would be a great coin to own. I would lower the census count by 20% to 27%, and see excellent future potential. This issue is quite underrated in the MS-67 category; should funds be available, procure one. To date, only one coin has been rated MS-68; this sold for $14,375.

1936 Battle of Gettysburg

Reason for Issue:	To commemorate the 75th anniversary of the Battle of Gettysburg.
Authorization:	Act of June 16, 1936, with a maximum of 50,000 pieces.
Issued by:	The Pennsylvania State Commission
Official Sale Price:	$1.65 (later raised to $2.65)

Production Figures

Date	Business Strikes	Assay Coins	Proofs	Melted	Net Mintage
1936	50,028	28	4?	23,100	26,900

Current Market Values

Date	AU-58	MS-60	MS-63	MS-64	MS-65	MS-66	MS-67
1936	$375	$420	$480	$570	$875	$1100	$1,800+

Designs by Frank Vittor

Obverse

The accolated busts of a Confederate and a Union soldier in uniform facing right. "United States of America" and "Blue and Gray reunion" form the outer border; "Liberty" is widely spaced above the soldiers; "E Pluribus Unum" appears in the top field.

Reverse

The shields of the Union and Confederate armies, divided by a double-bladed fasces. Below and at the side of the shields are oak and olive branches, which symbolize war and peace. "IN GOD WE TRUST" appears divided above each shield; the coin's date 1936 and denomination appear in the lower field. On the outer border on a raised rim is the inscription "1863 75TH ANNIVERSARY 1938 BATTLE OF GETTYSBURG".

Origins of the Gettysburg

In June 1937 the Philadelphia Mint struck 50,000 half dollars, plus 28 coins for assay purposes. This issue is associated with several dates: it was, like the Delaware, authorized in and dated 1936, and minted in 1937 for the Blue and Gray Reunion celebration, which took place July 1, 1938.

The Gettysburg was distributed by the Pennsylvania State Commission in Gettysburg at $1.65 each. Paul L. Roy, executive secretary of the State Commission, was a tireless, not entirely truthful promoter of the coin. He counted on three Mints striking the issue, but when it became clear that this would not happen he failed to make the situation clear to potential buyers. Purchasers were hesitantly informed that three coins from the Philadelphia Mint would be delivered, unless a refund was desired. By mid-May of 1937 he informed all on his mailing list that the maximum authorization of 50,000 pieces was oversubscribed—another fabrication that may have worked were it not for the declining interest in the commemorative coin market. Thirteen months later, the coins in inventory were delivered to the American Legion, Department of Pennsylvania, with the hope that the Legion could distribute the issue at $2.65. The "rarity lure" did not work: the commemorative mania bubble had already burst.

The Gettysburg Today

In the non-abundant grade of EF-AU specimens will usually be cleaned or abused in some manner. Their retail worth is close to Mint State coinage. Collectors should acquire only when the price is very right or if the About Uncirculated (AU) coin possesses more eye appeal than an MS-60 to MS-62 specimen. The majority of this very popular issue is in the MS-63 through MS-66 grades. Collectors should attempt to concentrate the on the higher graded MS-64 coin for the joy of collecting. Luster will range from brilliant frosty to unappealing dull. Strike offers no problems for the Gettysburg. However, the same cannot be said about surface negatives such as bag marks, reed marks, scratches, etc., which are drawn to the reverse smooth shields as if they were magnetized.

To date, no error coinage or counterfeit pieces have entered the marketplace.

Is Your Gettysburg Circulated or Mint State?

Obverse

Wear can be first noticed of the cheekbones of the soldiers, the primary focal area; coin doctoring usually is performed here.

Reverse

Crisscross scratches and a difference in metal color or texture (all signs of wear), if present, will be discerned on the three ribbons that bind the fasces.

Related Material

The issue was mailed in an unprinted coin mailer with inserts for three coins; the accompanying mailing envelope and stationery are attractive. When offered as a pair, along with the documentation, this material has sold for between $200 to $475, depending on condition.

Gettysburg order acknowledgement postcard—front.

Dear Sir:

Gettysburg, Pennsylvania

The Pennsylvania state commission will handle sale and distribution of the Gettysburg commemorative half-dollars.

The price is $1.65 per coin. We do not have order blanks and there will be no C. O. D. shipments.

The commission has requested 20,000 coins from the Philadelphia mint, 15,000 from the Denver mint and 15,000 from the San Francisco mint.

We will deliver coins as soon as they are minted which we hope will be within several months. We are accepting orders.

Pennsylvania State Commission,

Paul L. Roy, Executive Secretary.

You have ordered _____6___ coins.

We acknowledge receipt of $ _9.90__ from you.

Gettysburg order acknowledgement postcard—back.

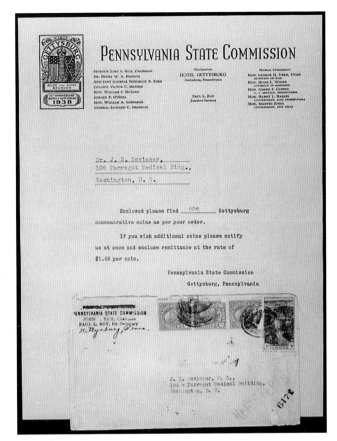

Gettysburg mailing envelope and order receipt letter.

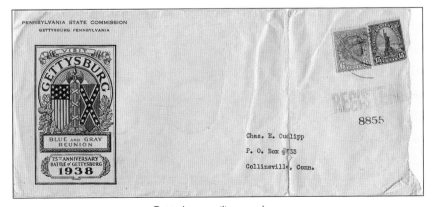

Gettysburg mailing envelope.

Future Potential of the Gettysburg Half Dollar

Population Figures

Date	Service	AU 58	MS 60	MS 62	MS 63	MS 64	MS 65	MS 66	MS 67	MS 68	MS 69
1936	NGC	14	0	76	207	1141	1211	303	61	3	0
1936	PCGS	32	3	125	709	1929	1521	624	85	2	0
1936	Combined	46	3	201	916	3070	2732	927	146	5	0

At present there is not much price spread between EF-AU and MS-64. When available, circulated offerings are usually cleaned or souvenir-abused UNC.

For the Gettysburg, any future potential begins with attractive pieces grading MS-65+. During the 1989 market high, there was a $1,500 difference between coins rated MS-64 and MS-65. I would lower the census count between 10% and 15%. At current levels, the eye-appealing MS-65 specimen is fairly priced at present. During the market high, there was a spread of $4,000 between the MS-65 and MS-66 categories: as usual, this is unlikely to recur.

In MS-66 condition, the coin is undervalued, especially captivating specimens. To be worthy of this grade, the reverse shields can exhibit only a few minute marks. I would lower population figures between 18% and 23%. There is excellent future potential at this level and for Gettysburgs rated MS-67 and loftier.

Reason for Issue:	To commemorate the 100th anniversary of the incorporation of Bridgeport, Connecticut.
Authorization:	Act of May 15, 1936, with a 25,000 minimum and an unlimited maximum.
Issued by:	Bridgeport Centennial, Inc.
Official Sale Price:	$2

Production Figures

Date	Business Strikes	Assay Coins	Proofs	Melted	Net Mintage
1936	25,000	15	4?	-	25,000

Current Market Values

Date	AU-58	MS-60	MS-63	MS-64	MS-65	MS-66	MS-67sa
1936	$120	$135	$170	$180	$250	$420	$2,100

DESIGNS BY HENRY G. KREISS

Obverse

The head of the one-time Mayor and best known showman of Bridgeport, Connecticut, Phineas Taylor (P.T.) Barnum, facing left. Around the coin's border is the inscription "BRIDGEPORT CONNECTICUT CENTENNIAL 1836–1936". Above the centennial dates is the name "P.T. BARNUM".

Reverse

A modernistic, stylized eagle, thrusting and metallic, with wings upraised and standing atop a ledge, facing right. (Inverted, it resembles a shark.) Below the ledge is the denomination; in the lower right field are "IN GOD WE TRUST", "E PLURIBUS UNUM", and "LIBERTY". Around the upper border is the inscription "UNITED STATES OF AMERICA". Slight die doubling can be noted in this location on some specimens. The letters "AM" of "AMERICA"are partly covered by the eagle's right wing. In the lower right field near the border is the designer's incused initial (K). The eagle's beak, as well as some of the reverse lettering, outstretch into the raised rim.

Origins of the Bridgeport

According to Bridgeport Centennial, Inc., Barnum's portrait appears on this half dollar because of his character as a showman, citizen, Mayor, and philanthropist. He laid the streets and lined them with trees, and reserved for public use a grove of eight acres, now known as Washington Park. The organization believed in 1936 that Barnum's improvements were the beginning of industrial development in their city, which had by then grown to great proportions.

Barnum (1810–91), possibly the most innovative and celebrated showman ever to thrive in this country, began his career in 1835. One of his first ventures was the purchase and exploitation of a black woman, Joice Heth, alleged to have been the nurse of the infant George Washington. Barnum claimed she was 161 years of age. After a short, successful exhibition period, Miss Heth died. It was proven on her death that she was closer to 80 years old. Barnum also presented the famous 25-inch midget, Charles S. Stratton, ballyhooed as General Tom Thumb, who helped the promoter sell 20 million tickets to his museum. The Feejee Mermaid had a human head and the finned body of a fish. Yes, the legendary sea creature was proven to be a fake. Barnum engaged Jenny Lind, the soprano dubbed the "Swedish Nightingale," to sing in the U.S. Barnum, Bailey and Hutchinson's circus was "The Greatest Show on Earth," and featured Jumbo, the huge elephant purchased for $10,000.

The Philadelphia Mint struck the minimum allowance of 25,015 coins during September 1936. The Act that approved this issue stated that there would be no limit to the number of pieces that could be minted: this issue could be struck indefinitely, provided that each coin was dated 1936—the Act listed no expiration date. Have you seen the 1915 Austrian Corona or the 1947 Mexican 50-peso gold bullion restrike pieces? Imagine a 1936 Bridgeport commemorative half dollar struck in 1993. Fortunately, an Act was passed on August 5, 1938 prohibiting the further issuance of commemorative coins authorized before March 1, 1939.

An attempt was made to distribute this coin widely and to limit the sale to five coins per buyer, but almost 1,000 pieces remained unsold. During the late 1950s most of this supply came on the numismatic market and was purchased by Allen Johnson, son of Toivo Johnson, a well-known coin dealer from East Holden, Maine. Allen sold most of this hoard to Joe Flynn, Sr., a Kansas City dealer, and the remainder to First Coinvestors, Inc., of Albertson, New York.

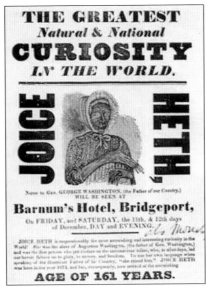

Joice Heth poster.

The Bridgeport Today

Most of the circulated specimens offered for sale are either lightly cleaned, polished, whizzed, or dipped-out bright (which can look better than new to the neophyte). On occasion, a pocket piece or good-luck piece will make its appearance.

The Barnum coin is easily obtainable in grades MS-60 through MS-66. Because of their easy accessibility, collectors should consider procuring only for the pride of ownership: such grades are at times targeted by promoters who buy low and sell high. When the promotion ceases, so does the price increase. Thus, acquire only if the price is very right in your favor.

Why are most of the Bridgeports in these lower levels? Because all that exposed smooth area on Barnum's portrait and on the large modernistic reverse wing simply act as huge magnets attracting all forms of numismatic abuse. Bag marks, reed marks, slide marks, hits, cuts, scratches, etc., just have an affinity for the cheek, lower jaw, and bald reverse wing. These are the primary focal areas.

By current grading standards, it's the bag mark, several small marks, or hairline scratches that are viewed as a bit too large that keep the coin out of the MS-65 category, especially if the faults are in the primary focal areas. Eye-appealing MS-67 Bridgeports will be hard to find—but, if found, are recommended for purchase. They have excellent future potential.

Bridgeport surfaces will vary from semi-proof-like, to flashy satiny, to semi-dull satiny (the norm), to dull satiny. The grainy appearance observed on this issue is the result of a turbulent metal flow that caused grainy wear of the dies: coin surfaces resemble the die surfaces. Raised lines seen in the fields were created when a steel wire brush was used to polish the dies. Fine scratches that cut into the die's metal become fine raised lines on the coin's surface. In most cases, this should not influence the price or grade. However, lack of metal fill, which can resemble small cuts or scratches, can lower a specimen's worth, depending on size, location, and number.

To date, no error coinage or counterfeit pieces have made their presence known.

Is Your Bridgeport Circulated or Mint State?

Obverse

The coin's rims offer this issue's lower relief designs excellent protection. Therefore, a loss of metal or rubbing will first be seen on the rims, and does not at all affect the grade. When a difference in metal texture does make its presence known, it will do so on Barnum's cheekbone and on his hair, diagonally above the ear, directly below the vertical bar of the second letter "T" of "Connecticut".

Reverse

A loss of metal will be evident on the central part of the eagle's wing tip, inwards, between the "AM" of the word "America" and the beak. The modernistic eagle is a prime target for the whizzing doctors.

Related Material

Local residents could purchase up to five coins from their bank. Out-of-state requests were handled by the First National Bank and Trust Company. The item was distributed in a dark blue and gold cardboard presentation box, housing

Above: Outside of mailing box—front.

At Right: Outside of mailing box—back.

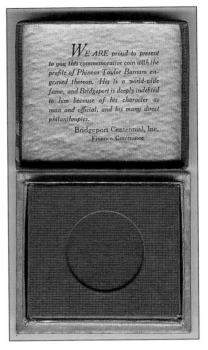

Above: Bridgeport single-coin holder—
exterior.

At Right: Bridgeport single-coin holder—
interior.

Above: Bridgeport three-coin holder—
exterior.

At Right: Bridgeport three-coin holder—
interior.

either one or three pieces. Depicted in gold ink on the cover is the city coat of
arms and two gold diagonal bands. The inner covers present an inscription about
Barnum. I have seen both holders marketed in the $30–$100 range, depending
on condition and demand. Possibly 500 single and 200 three-piece boxes exist
today. This is the second most available coin mailer or holder after the genuine
Lexington wooden box. However, if accompanied by its stamped mailing box, it
becomes worth at least $200 more.

Future Potential of the Bridgeport Half Dollar

Population Figures

Date	Service	AU 58	MS 60	MS 62	MS 63	MS 64	MS 65	MS 66	MS 67	MS 68	MS 69
1936	NGC	2	0	28	177	1035	1160	360	29	1	0
1936	PCGS	8	7	107	541	1798	1582	641	57	0	0
1936	Combined	10	7	135	718	2833	2742	1001	86	1	0

There is little price spread between grades EF-AU and MS-64. The Bridgeport is a very common coin up to MS-65 condition, and collectors should acquire it only for the pure joy of ownership; I advise aiming for a flashy MS-64+ coin. During the 1989 market high, the price spread between MS-64 and MS-65 was more than $1,100. I would lower the population figure between 30% and 35% for this grade. The population figure for the MS-65 category should be lowered by the same percentage, but too many Bridgeports graded MS-65 possess reverses that grade to some degree of MS-64 or MS-64+, because of numismatic negatives and lack of metal fill marks. (Collectors should carefully examine the modernistic eagle.) The only MS-65 pieces that are on grade and recommended are those that have flash or real eye appeal. The price spread between MS-65 and MS-66 during the 1989 market high was more than $4,200, which encouraged much resubmission. When the market heats up, so will the accurately graded Bridgeport, although the population count, and the coin's comparatively unpopular design, may hold down the value of the issue.

Real future potential lies in the MS-66+ grade and loftier: these coins are certainly under priced and are recommended. I would lower the population figures between 10% and 15%. Collectors should focus on attractive pieces, staying away from any dark and unattractive specimens. To date, only 86 Bridgeports have been graded MS-67. One was rated MS-68 by NGC.

1936 CINCINNATI MUSIC CENTER

Reason for Issue:	To commemorate the 50th anniversary of Cincinnati, Ohio, as a center of music and its contribution to the art of music.
Authorization:	Act of March 31, 1936, with a maximum of 15,000 pieces.
Issued by:	Cincinnati Musical Center Commemorative Coin Association
Official Sale Price:	$7.75 per set

Production Figures

Date	Business Strikes	Assay Coins	Proofs	Melted	Net Mintage
1936	5,000	5	4?	-	5,000
1936-D	5,000	5	4?	-	5,000
1936-S	5,000	6	4?	-	5,000

Current Market Values

Date	AU-50	MS-60	MS-63	MS-64	MS-65	MS-66	MS-67
1936 PDS set	$800	$845	$895	$1525	$2,700+	$7,000+	$25,000+
1936-P	$280	$290	$300	$350	$460	$835	$10,000+
1936-D	$280	$290	$300	$335	$475	$525	$3,300

DESIGNS BY CONSTANCE ORTMAYER

Obverse

An idealized, almost unrecognizable bust of the popular composer and song-writer Stephen Foster. Foster was born on July 4, 1826, in what is now part of Pittsburgh. He wrote the songs "Oh Susannah," "Old Kentucky Home," and "Old Black Joe," among many others. "STEPHEN FOSTER AMERICA'S TROUBA-DOUR" appears below the bust (the origin of this expression cannot be traced). "UNITED STATES OF AMERICA" arcs above; "HALF DOLLAR" below. In the left field in a direct line with the "U" in "UNITED" and the nape of the neck in faint relief are the designer's initials (CO), in monogram. On some coins, the initials are almost impossible to make out.

Reverse

A female figure, representing music; she is on one knee, and is playing a lyre that she holds with both hands. In the lower right field is one anniversary date, 1936; in the upper left field is the other, 1886. This date was chosen on the basis of no historical event whatever, but a suitable year was needed to con-vince Congress to authorize a 50th anniversary coin. The Denver (D) or San Francisco (S) Mint mark is below the date 1936 on the respective issues. The Philadelphia Mint uses no identifying mark on this issue. Below the kneeling figure are the inscriptions "IN GOD WE TRUST", and "E PLURIBUS UNUM", AND "LIBERTY." Around the coin's border is the inscription "CINCINNATI A MUSIC CENTER OF AMERICA". The word "OF" appears somewhat weakly struck: this is a design characteristic.

Origins of the Cincinnati

False claims on behalf of this commemorative were at once used as grounds for rejection of the designs by the U.S. Commission of Fine Arts, whose Chair-man, Charles Moore, wrote on May 13, 1936, complaining about them to Mint Director Nellie Tayloe Ross. First of all, Stephen Foster had no association with the musical life of Cincinnati: his only relevance to the city was that he worked there as a bookkeeper in his brother's firm for three years in the 1840s. Foster lived his life in Pittsburgh and New York. In addition, Moore pointed out, Cin-cinnati first became the locale for a musical festival back in 1873, with the May Festival Association, organized by George Ward Nichols, and conducted by the illustrious Theodore Thomas, using a chorus of more than 1,000 voices assem-bled from 35 midwestern musical societies. Nichols became director (1878–81) of the newly founded Cincinnati College of Music, and in later years acquired the title of "Musical Missionary" by taking the Cincinnati Symphony Orchestra (itself an outgrowth of the biennial festivals) on nationwide tours, gradually cre-ating an appetite in audiences from Massachusetts to California for symphonic music, at a time when most people's musical experience consisted of village band concerts, singing around the parlor piano, or watching song-and-dance

Theodore Thomas.

routines done in blackface minstrel shows. Thus, a commemorative coin struck to preserve the remembrance of Cincinnati's immense contribution to American's cultural life should have possessed the dates 1873–1923 and should have portrayed Theodore Thomas.

Unfortunately for rationality and historical accuracy, the Cincinnati Musical Center Commemorative Coin Association (unknown to any of the Cincinnati musical groups then or later) put pressure on the Treasury to overrule the Commission of Fine Arts, and the initial design was adopted.

There were neither local celebrations nor any attempts to coordinate publicity for the coin with any musical event in Cincinnati. In fact, as it was an even-numbered year, there was not even a Festival to tie in with publicity for the coins, let alone to justify the act's wording. But all of these complaints proved ineffective.

The Mints each produced 5,000 specimens of this issue. San Francisco struck six rather than five coins for assay purposes. Thomas G. Melish, Treasurer of the Cincinnati Musical Center Commemorative Coin Association, as well as Treasurer of the Cleveland Centennial Commemorative Coin Association, was a coin collector, as well as a businessman. He originally attempted to have the Philadelphia Mint strike 10,000, Denver 2,000, and San Francisco 3,000 pieces. Melish was unable to pull this off, but he did have the influence to have the first 200 pieces struck of each issue caught by an operator wearing a soft glove (to avoid any nicks or scratches). Each piece was then placed in a specially marked envelope (at each Mint) in the order of each coin's striking.

After the specially marked envelopes were received by the Cincinnati Association, the specimens were taken from their containers and placed in black cardboard holders, which had slots for each Mint's issue. A celluloid strip

Cincinnati Musical Center, c.1910.

covered the exposed set of coins. On the back of these holders there is pasted official documentation (now much desired) that states the numbered set of coins enclosed. If you had a numbered holder stating that the enclosed coins are the sixth piece struck at each Mint, this is what should be contained, unless a coin was substituted. The signature of a notary public, his seal, and Melish's signature are also on the document. An accompanying letter was mailed with each numbered set of coins—sealed in cellophane—to prominent individuals, including the President Roosevelt, some U.S. senators, and to Melish's close friends. These specimens exhibit no special surface.

Ordered sets were forwarded by the Cincinnati Association to buyers in the same type of holders—but without official documentation—at $7.75 each. The buyers were most fortunate, because the issue was oversubscribed before the sets were released.

This Cincinnati set was mailed during the height of the commemorative speculation mania, a time when many were attempting to invest as much as possible in an issue, thereby decreasing its availability to bona fide collectors who would be forced to pay a prohibitive price. Cartoons of the time depicted a scene showing speculators buying commemorative coins for $5 and selling them to the rushing collector for $10.

In August 1936, when the low-mintage set was released, the asking price to the "late bids," or those who were fortunate to be classified "an over-subscriber," was $45. This was because of both great demand and good distribution, plus the fact that few owners wanted to part with their sets at any price. In fact, the set was later offered for sale at $75, or almost $700 today's values. The Cincinnati Association attempted to have a 1937 issue minted, but the bill was killed.

The Acts of Congress that authorized the various issues during this period specify that the issues will be coined by the Director of the Mint. Melish was able to pull a few political strings and had the phrase "at the Mints" inserted, which permitted this small authorization (15,000) to be divided among "the Mints." However, this was the last time this phrase was to be inserted during the 1930s.

The Cincinnati Today

Virtually all coins offered at circulated values are of the polished, whizzed, or doctored variety. Since the value spread between the EF-AU and MS-64 categories is at present insignificant, collectors should focus on the highest grade of coin. Bag marks and numismatic abuse place a large number of this issue in the MS-60 to MS-63 categories. In the latter grade, the Denver striking is harder to locate, at present, than the Philadelphia and San Francisco coinage. However, in MS-64, the Philadelphia is the rarest issue followed by Denver. In strict MS-65 condition, the San Francisco striking is the most difficult to obtain: it is almost 2½ times as rare as the Denver piece, and is also considerably rarer than the Philadelphia issue.

Cincinnati Musical Center today.

It is an outright score for a collector or dealer to acquire a strictly graded 1936-S slabbed MS-65 Cincinnati for a type coin value. Each mint striking has its own value, especially in grades MS-64+ and higher. Please remember that the coin with the higher population or census figure, which is the Denver striking for this issue, reflects the type coin price. Luster will range from brilliant frosty, to dull frosty, and to chrome-like (not the norm) for Philadelphia coinage. Luster is brilliant frosty to dull frosty for the Denver production and brilliant satiny (not the norm) to dull satiny for the San Francisco coins. This issue was designed to exhibit soft detail. On occasion, a too soft of a strike can lower a coin's grade and value, especially if the hair detail above Foster's ear displays too much flatness or the head of the reverse female does likewise.

True MS-65 sets can be difficult to find, as can MS-66 coinage, especially the 1936-S and 1936 Philadelphia strikings. A set at this grade should possess full original mint luster, no detrimental bag marks, and be fully struck (for the issue). A specimen can possess almost all these qualities—and a fair number do—but what might spoil the piece is a large bag mark or slide marks on Foster's portrait, or similar marks located somewhere on the reverse female—your primary focal points—or field. On occasion, should a coin be so spectacular or eye-appealing, the surface negative is overlooked and the coin is graded MS-65. But, to be persuaded, collectors should be sure they know how to grade.

Set No. 134 is still housed in its holder and sealed in the original cellophane. Upon inspection, the San Francisco Mint coin has a large bag mark on the female's arm. The coin was removed by hand from the coining press—but appears to have been dropped. However, for some reason, the Denver Mint specimens received a little more care. They are usually found in better shape, followed by the Philadelphia and San Francisco issues, in terms of the depth of strike, surface luster, and surface negatives.

Should you observe scratches behind Foster's head near the letters "TED" in the word "UNITED", do not panic: these raised lines are die scratches. Remember, it is the scratches that scratch into the surface that one should be concerned about. Also be alert for those fine hairline scratches resulting from improper drying with a cloth or towel. Tilt the coin back and forth, to observe if these are present. Long or large hairline scratches, if present in primary focal areas, can quickly lower a coin's grade from MS-65 to MS-64.

To date, no error coinage has entered the marketplace.

Detecting Counterfeits

Cast counterfeits are high quality coins made from a genuine specimen. Aside from the strange surface (which is unlike ordinary mint bloom), the Cincinnati examples show raised granular defects, especially on Foster's cheek and in the field near the word "TROUBADOUR". On the reverse, there are raised die file marks at "CINCINN", and more of the same kind of granular raised "bubbles" around the dates and mottoes.

A more recent counterfeit will reveal what resembles minute pinholes above the ear and temple area of Foster and a metal spike under the "A" of the

Counterfeit coin.

word "HALF". The reverse design will reveal thin file marks between the letters "AMER" of "AMERICA", "ATI" of "CINCINNATI" and "NT" of "CENTENNIAL". The coin's rim is rounded.

Another counterfeit coin will exhibit pock marks above and below the word "LIBERTY" and to the right and left of the "S" on "PLURIBUS" on the reverse of the coin.

IS YOUR CINCINNATI CIRCULATED OR MINT STATE?

Obverse
Metal loss will first be noticed in the temple area and cheekbone of Foster; the portrait is a prime target for the whizzing merchants. Collectors should look for that aluminum appearance as you slowly rotate the coin.

Reverse
Examine the female's breast for a difference in metal texture and crisscross scratches, as well as her thigh opposite the date 1936: both areas are prime targets for coin doctors.

Related Material
This issue was distributed to 200 lucky people in the holder described above, with its notarization notice pasted on the back. Also included were three manila coin envelopes. The paper container that housed the Denver coin had the following typed: "The enclosed coin is no. 134 of the first 200 half dollars struck at the Denver Mint for the Cincinnati Music Center Commemorative Coin Association. Mark A. Skinner, Superintendent, by Acting Superintendent". The number (134) is also stamped on the envelope. The accompanying two envelopes are blank except for the stamped number. One was pencil-marked "P" and the other "S," most likely by Melish. The same Wynne black leatherette

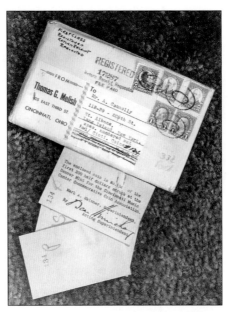

Set #134 mailing envelope and coin holders.

Front of PDS set #134 coin holder.

Back of PDS set #134 coin holder showing notary's seal and signature

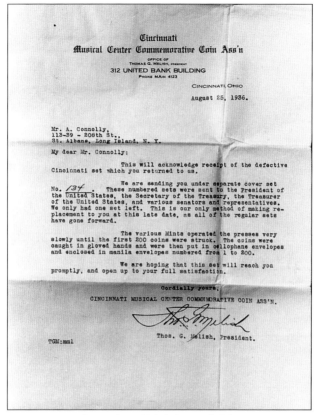

Letter from Melish for set #134.

holder without back notarization and imprinted "Cincinnati, Musical Center Golden Anniversary, Commemorative Half Dollars", "P", "D", "S" (both small and large) housed the coin set, mailed from "Thomas G. Melish, 105 East, Third Street, Cincinnati, Ohio."

Original numbered holders can be valued in the range of $250 to $500 depending on their condition. In the same state as #134 above, $459 to $700+ without the coins. With coins contained, all is dependent upon the coins' condition, since they may have been cleaned by a past owner. Of course, the buyer's desire to own the item must also be factored in.

A notarized set (#73) grading MS-64+, with accompanying documented coin envelopes from the three Mints and a mailing envelope from Melish, brought $5,000 in the American Numismatic Rarities auction on March 8, 2000: there is no doubt that the complete package sells. Another notarized set (#110) housing three MS-64+ coins brought $3,680. A MS-64 condition set can sell between $1,150 and $1,400. Those enclosed coins had claims to MS-65; were they to slab as such, they would be valued between $2,300 and $2,800. Again, value is based on the variables mentioned above.

Future Potential of the Cincinnati Half Dollar

Population Figures

Date	Service	AU 58	MS 60	MS 62	MS 63	MS 64	MS 65	MS 66	MS 67	MS 68	MS 69
1936	NGC		1	12	72	390	252	62	4	0	0
1936	PCGS	0	1	41	255	612	419	102	3	0	0
1936	Combined	0	2	53	327	1002	671	164	7	0	0

Date	Service	AU 58	MS 60	MS 62	MS 63	MS 64	MS 65	MS 66	MS 67	MS 68	MS 69
1936 D	NGC	0	3	8	39	343	508	234	32	2	0
1936 D	PCGS	1	0	27	164	634	577	271	31	1	0
1936 D	Combined	1	3	35	203	977	1085	505	63	3	0

Date	Service	AU 58	MS 60	MS 62	MS 63	MS 64	MS 65	MS 66	MS 67	MS 68	MS 69
1936 S	NGC	0	0	22	114	499	174	18	3	0	0
1936 S	PCGS	0	0	51	270	700	251	51	1	0	0
1936 S	Combined	0	0	73	384	1199	425	69	4	0	0

Date	Service	PL 58	PL 60	PL 62	PL 63	PL 64	PL 65	PL 66	PL 67	PL 68	PL 69
1936	NGC	0	0	0	0	2	0	0	0	0	0

There is little price spread in grades EF-AU through MS-64. The limited number of circulated coins are usually cleaned or abused in some fashion. Collectors should focus on MS-63+—as well as MS-64 coinage, strictly for the joy of ownership. During a hot market, prices will rise for a short time, then retreat to previous levels. Attractive specimens not plagued by excessive bag marks and other surface negatives, especially on the devices, are highly recommended. The San Francisco striking is the highest census issue among the three productions, but it is not the nicest looking or flashiest of this issue. I would estimate that between 18% and 25% have been resubmitted in attempts to acquire a better grade. Figure about 15% crack-out for the other Mints (Denver and Philadelphia) in this grade—with most of these grading labels cast into the garbage pail. There are a number of dealers who purposely destroy these inserts; their objective is to inflate the grading service census figures, in order to make an issue appear more available than it actually is. Type price spread between MS-64 and MS-65 during the May 1989 market high was about $2,000. In truth, much of the MS-64 Cincinnati material that I examined for higher grade possibilities never had a chance. Any hope for future potential lies in alluring MS-64+ and higher graded pieces.

Currently in this marketplace are a number of MS-65 encapsulations as well as MS-66 pieces with grade assignments that should make the astute grader exclaim "How can this be?" The coins are not attractive and the grade is very questionable: pass on these. The Denver coin is the flashiest of the three, as well as the easiest to obtain. I would lower its census figures by 29% and reduce the others between 15% and 20%. The difference between MS-65 and MS-66 type coin value during the market high was approximately $6,000. There is excellent future potential, especially for the Philadelphia and San Francisco coins, which are quite undervalued and difficult to locate. Collectors should be sure to look at the listed populations. Owning an MS-67 might make you believe you are hearing the music of Stephen Foster: these are rare coins. As of this writing only four San Francisco coins have been encapsulated with a grade of MS-67 and seven Philadelphia coins.

The only MS-68 creations that currently exist were struck at the Denver Mint. They are encapsulated by NGC. Estimated value, which is dependent upon the coin's makeup and the buyer, might range between $19,000 and $30,000.

Reason for Issue:	To mark the 100th anniversary of the incorporation of the city of Cleveland, Ohio.
Authorization:	Act of May 5, 1936, with a minimum of 25,000 pieces and a maximum of 50,000 pieces.
Issued by:	Cleveland Centennial Commemorative Coin Association
Official Sale Price:	$1.50

Production Figures

Date	Business Strikes	Assay Coins	Proofs	Melted	Net Mintage
1936	50,000	30	4?	0	50,000

Current Market Values

Date	AU 58	MS 60	MS 63	MS 64	MS 65	MS 66	MS 67
1936	$90	$95	$100	$115	$145	$340	$1,425

DESIGNS BY BRENDA PUTNAM

Obverse

The bust of Moses Cleaveland (1754–1806), a lawyer, Revolutionary War general, and later state congressman from Canterbury, Connecticut, facing left and wearing a wig of his period. Cleaveland became one of the directors and surveyors for the Connecticut Land Co., which bought 3,267,000 acres of the Western Reserve area in what is now northeastern Ohio. "UNITED STATES OF AMERica" arcs above; "Half Dollar" below. Paralleled within is the name "Moses Cleaveland". The word "Liberty" is in the left field; in the field below the bust of Cleaveland are the incused initials (BP) of the coin's artist, Brenda Putnam of New York City.

Reverse

Map of the Great Lakes region, with a compass pointing to the city of Cleveland and the other end encircling the Great Lakes. There are nine five-pointed stars: the largest represents Cleveland. The other eight also represent the cities on the Great Lakes; from left to right (west to east on the map): Duluth, Milwaukee, Chicago, Toledo, Detroit, Cleveland, Buffalo, Toronto, and Rochester. "In God We Trust" is in the upper field, "E Pluribus Unum" in the upper left, and the inscription "1836 Great Lakes Exposition 1936 Cleveland Centennial" circles the coin. The city was incorporated in 1836.

Origins of the Cleveland

The Cleveland Centennial and Great Lakes Exposition was held from June 27 to October 4, 1936, on a 125-acre lakefront site. "A Glamorous Spectacle of Supreme Significance ... Presenting Outstanding Attractions Worthy of a World's Fair ... presenting achievements of the Arts and Science in understandable ways ... portraying the drama of Industry and Commerce in fascinating and colorful manners ...unfolding the romance of Iron and Coal in impressive methods..." to quote puffery for the $25 million event. This provided Thomas G. Melish, a coin collector, with another chance to request that Congress strike a commemorative coin. This was duly approved, "to commemorate Cleveland's contribution to the industrial progress of the United States for a century," in the orotund phrases of the Act of May 5, 1936.

The Cleveland issue was minted in connection with a legitimate celebration, and Melish's sales strategy was aimed at the Exposition visitors and the general public; coins were sold at $1.50 each. As soon as the U.S. Commission of Fine Arts approved the design, on June 2, 1936, the Medallic Art Company of New York reduced Putnam's models to half dollar size and shipped them to the Philadelphia Mint, where 25,000 were struck in July 1936 (with an extra 15 reserved for assay). Sales were excellent. Thus, in February 1937, the Philadelphia Mint struck 25,015 more Clevelands. Under the coinage laws of the United States, these coins must bear the date of the year in which they were manufactured. However, the Act that created this commemorative required the entire issue to be dated 1936. The result is one date and one type of issue, and a total mintage of 50,030 coins, including assay coins.

As with the special 200 Cincinnati sets, Melish arranged with the Philadelphia Mint to have the first 201 coins struck and placed in specially marked envelopes in the order of the coins' striking. The first coin struck was placed in a separate envelope so marked until the 201st striking was reached. From that point on it was business as usual for the Mint operator.

When comparing the 6th, 14th, 32nd, and 33rd pieces struck of the Cleveland with other gem or original pieces, I noted that the dies used for this issue were not highly polished: the early presentation pieces are not proof-like in appearance. However, these coins possess a much sharper strike and their fields have a shiny smooth aluminum-looking finish, as compared to the satiny finish of the regular issue. Early numbered holders, possessing one coin, have sold for between $750 and $2,000 depending on the condition of the enclosed coin. Collectors should just be certain that the coin you are examining wasn't switched.

After receiving the first 201 coins from the Mint, Melish had these selected specimens taken from their numbered envelopes and placed in specially numbered black cardboard holders that had a slot for one coin, or, in some cases, two coins, protected by a celluloid strip that covered the slot. I saw the holder housing the 200th and 201st striking that a collector owned. On the back of these rare holders there is pasted that much-sought official documentation stating the number of the enclosed coin, and also including the signature of a notary public, his seal, and the signature of Exposition Treasurer Thomas G. Melish.

These holders, along with an accompanying letter, were mailed to prominent individuals and some of Melish's close friends.

At the Exposition, the coins were issued in the same cardboard holder minus any documentation, as well as in a small paper envelope, with an ink-stamped inventory number. Ohio banks also sold the commemorative half dollar.

Counter-stamped Coins

The Western Reserve Numismatic Club of Cleveland celebrated its 20th anniversary in 1941. It was during this event that 100 Cleveland half dollars were counter-stamped with an obverse die having a portrait of Moses Cleaveland, the club's name, the date 1921 and the words Cleveland, Ohio below the portrait. The reverse die bears the inscription "20th Anniversary" and the dates 1921–41. After the 100th counter-stamp, the dies were destroyed. The Club later requested, via a letter, that these coins be returned by their owners. Why? The Secret Service at the time felt the coins should not have been issued. Most owners obliged. A gentleman who was a member of the Cleveland Club was present at a lecture I gave at the Demorest (New Jersey) Coin Club in the early 1980s. He informed me that 75 of the 100 counter-stamped pieces were returned to the U.S. Secret Service. These pieces have sold for between $660 (cleaned) to $3,500 depending on the coin's condition. I would estimate that 25 pieces are extant. The Secret Service should present collectors with no problem today.

To celebrate their 50th anniversary, the Western Reserve Numismatic Club of Cleveland had counter-stamped only 13 Cleveland half dollars when the die was apparently destroyed. (I say apparently, because a few too many pieces have entered the marketplace in the last two years. However, anything is possible.) The obverse die shows a portrait of Moses Cleaveland, facing the words "Fifty Years 1971". Below the bust the name is spelled incorrectly, with the letter "a" is missing from his name. Around the border is the inscription "Western

RESERVE NUMISMATIC CLUB" and the date 1921. No reverse die was used. The coin caused no problem with the government.

Celebrating the 75th anniversary in 1996, the Western Reserve Numismatic Club of Cleveland counter-stamped approximately 400 items with an obverse and reverse 11-millimeter die. Of this number, 21 Cleveland half dollars grading between MS-63 and MS-65 (which were removed from their respective NGC encapsulations) were impressed with the counter stamp. The procedure was performed by Ron Landis, creator of the dies, at the Gallery Mint. One of the 21 pieces was struck with a reverse die rotation.

Today's city of Cleveland was originally named Cleaveland, honoring the man who conducted the first territorial survey. However, when the area's first newspaper, the *Cleveland Advertiser*, was founded in the 1830s, the letter "a" was removed to save space on the masthead. This revision was readily approved by the people of the area, and thus we have today's spelling.

The Cleveland Today

The issue is quite available in circulated EF-AU condition. Most such pieces will display original surfaces with some metal loss, as well as numismatic abuse. The value spread between MS-63 and MS-65 is quite small, so collectors should aim for MS-65+, since the common Cleveland is readily attainable.

Luster will range from brilliant frosty to dull frosty. Strike will rarely be responsible for a grade-value lowering. Bag marks and other surface negatives can plague the obverse portrait and the reverse compass, plus its surrounding fields, thereby removing many coins from the MS-65 category.

To date, no error coinage or counterfeit pieces have entered the marketplace.

IS YOUR CLEVELAND CIRCULATED OR MINT STATE?

Obverse

Wear will first be observed on the cheekbone and the hair at the in back of Cleaveland's ear. At times, the portrait will display the effects of doctoring.

Reverse

A metal loss will first occur on the compass top; this area should be examined for a difference in metal texture.

Related Material

The first 201 coins were distributed in Wynne leatherette single and double coin holders, with notarization on the back. Coins sold by mail order were housed in these holders without notarization ($20), as well as a cardboard holder (4 × 3 inches) with an inverted triangular pocket (4 3/8-inch base; 3 1/16 -inch sides), in which one or two Clevelands were inserted unprotected. These hold-

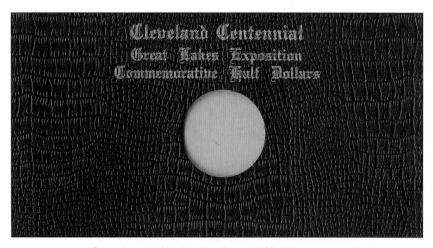

Special coin holder housing the sixth Cleveland struck.

Notary's seal certifying the coin's authenticity.

ers were imprinted with Melish's mailing address ($75 to $125). This coin was also sold at the Exposition in a 3 1/2 inch × 2 inch coin envelope, imprinted "Great Lakes Exposition, Cleveland Centennial, Commemorative Half Dollar" and accompanied by a blue stamped inventory number ($25–$100).

A single-coin notarized holder (#28), housing an MS-65 coin, sold for $747 at the American Numismatic Rarities auction on March 8, 2005. One double notarized coin holder containing two MS-64 coins, supposedly #49 and #51 as struck by the Philadelphia Mint, brought $2,070 at the same auction. Another

Cleveland triangular pocket holder

Cleveland coin envelope with inventory number 738.

single-coin notarized holder housing the 14th coin struck with an original Thomas Melish letter brought $2,300. The enclosed coin was graded About Uncirculated (AU).

Notarized empty holders may be valued from $400 to $750, depending on condition. Remember that an MS-64 Cleveland is currently worth around $115, and can be substituted for the genuine item.

Future Potential of the Cleveland Half Dollar

Population Figures

Date	Service	AU 58	MS 60	MS 62	MS 63	MS 64	MS 65	MS 66	MS 67	MS 68	MS 69
1936	NGC	5	2	54	310	1595	1971	522	57	5	0
1936	PCGS	33	18	308	1305	2750	2083	613	40	1	0
1936	Combined	38	20	362	1615	4345	4954	1135	97	6	0

There is little price range currently between grades EF-AU and MS-66. Collectors should consider acquiring coins in these grades only for the pride of ownership: I suggest MS-65+ specimens. During the May 1989 market high, the price spread between the MS-64 and MS-65 ratings was almost $1,500, but this will never happen again. This coin is a very promotable item; it seems to have come out of the woodwork. I would reduce the population figures between 25% and 30%, but this adjustment still makes no real dent in the figures.

The only genuine hope of future potential for this coin lies in eye-appealing MS-66+ pieces. A $3,200 spread existed during the 1989 high between MS-65 and MS-66 material; that is not to be duplicated. I would reduce the census count by 30%. The coin is undervalued in MS-66+ condition, and there is excellent future potential in the MS-67 state. Six pieces have been encapsulated MS-68 (five NGC, one PCGS). An NGC example sold for $9,200 at ANR's New York Connoissuer's Collection in March 2006.

An MS-66 example housed in an old NGC holder brought $1,610 at the August 2011 Heritage Chiago coin auction #1158. Current approximate value for an MS-66 Cleveland is $340. What gives? The piece posessed amazing eye-appeal and color. It was definitely an MS-67+ coin in an MS-66 hlder! Thus the deviation from the norm.

1936 Columbia, South Carolina, Sesquicentennial

Reason for Issue:	To commemorate the sesquicentennial of the founding of Columbia, South Carolina.
Authorization:	Act of March 18, 1936, with a maximum of 25,000 pieces.
Issued by:	Columbia Sesquicentennial Commission
Official Sale Price:	$6.45 per set; $2.15 each

Production Figures

Date	Business Strikes	Assay Coins	Proofs	Melted	Net Mintage
1936-P	9,000	7	4?	-	9,000
1936-D	8,000	9	4?	-	8,000
1936-S	8,000	7	4?	-	8,000

Current Market Values

Date	AU-58	MS-60	MS-63	MS-64	MS-65	MS-66	MS-67
1936 PDS set	$650	$710	$735	$770	$850	$1,150	$3,300+
1936 single	$215	$225	$235	$245	$285	$365	$750+

Designs by Abraham Wolfe Davidson

Obverse

Justice, standing and holding a sword in her right hand, pointed downward with "scales" in her left hand. (Where is the blindfold?) In the right background is the new South Carolina State Capitol building, with the anniversary date

1936 below it. The Old State House is in the left background, with the date 1786 appearing below it. Above this structure in the upper left field is the word "Liberty". The inscription "Sesquicentennial Celebration of the Capital Columbia South Carolina" appears between an outer and inner border encircling the obverse.

Since three Mints produced this issue, the Mint mark for the Denver coin (D) or the San Francisco coin (S) is located at the base of Justice. The Philadelphia Mint used no Mint mark during this period.

Reverse

A palmetto tree, the state emblem of South Carolina, with oak branches at its base. Barricades of this soft tree were constructed to offer protection to South Carolina's batteries on Sullivan's Island, in Charleston Harbor, against shells fired by the ships of the British Navy in its attempt to capture Charleston during the Revolutionary War. Most British missiles just buried themselves into the soft trees and caused little damage, even after a 12-hour bombardment. By the end, 12 colonists and more than 200 British lost their lives. The British wooden ships also suffered much damage from Fort Moultrie's shells, and Charleston was not captured. The crossed arrows tied to the palmetto tree refer to this battle. (In December 1936 some people referred to the palmetto side of the coin as the obverse: this was a manifestation of local pride, based on state symbolism.) The broken oak branches at the base of the tree symbolize the defeat of the British Navy's ships. A semicircle of 13 five-pointed stars symbolizes the original 13 states. "United States of America" arcs above; Half Dollar below. "E Pluribus Unum" is just above the palmetto; "In God We Trust" is in the right central field. Davidson's initials do not appear on his creation.

Origins of the Columbia

This issue was produced at the three U.S. Mints for the most part in September 1936. When the final tally was taken, the Philadelphia Mint struck 9,000 specimens; Denver and San Francisco 8,000 each. The wording of the Act made the use of three Mints possible. This issue was distributed by the Sesquicentennial Commission of Columbia, which was appointed by the city's mayor. They pledged that these coins would receive the widest distribution possible, thereby keeping them out of the hands of speculators and placing them into the hands of true collectors, who would not be required to pay a large premium for their acquisition.

The Columbia 50-cent pieces were not delivered to the Sesquicentennial Commission in one complete shipment from the Mint; it was decided that the mailings would begin only when all three varieties had been received.

The Columbia Today

Circulated specimens are not plentiful. Those usually encountered have been polished or wire-brushed (whizzed) to some degree, hurting their numismatic value.

Fort Moultrie in 1861

Concerning this issue's luster, the obverse coin surfaces will range from semi-proof-like (early strikes), to brilliant, to satiny, to dull-satiny. On the coin's reverse, surfaces will display a reflecting quality that can appear satiny, or dull satiny, or just unappealing dull. Die polishing marks can be observed at times in the obverse fields, especially on the sides and above the head of Justice. What appears to be a depression behind her head may be the result of minor hub damage, and is characteristic for the issue. Where the reverse die has been steel brushed, expect to see small, raised hairline swirls.

Strike seldom presents a problem: the majority of this issue possesses a strong strike. However, because of slight die wear, later strikings from all Mints can exhibit some trivial weakness on the rim of the inner circle opposite the letters "PITA" in the word "Capital". A slight loss of detail can also be detected by the knowledgeable on the palmetto trunk, leaves, etc.

Based on current grading standards, MS-65 specimens cannot posses any detracting marks on the main devices or fields – unless the coin possesses amazing eye appeal. If anything minute is present, it should be hidden in the coin's design; the same applies to the reverse palmetto or field. MS-64 coins must be fully original, though they can have a mark or two in critical locations. A pinhead-sized dig hurts. The primary focal areas are Justice, the palmetto tree, and the surrounding fields.

No error coinage or counterfeit examples have entered the marketplace.

Is Your Columbia Circulated or Mint State?

Obverse

Wear or a loss of metal will make its presence known as a difference in metal texture on the breasts of Justice. (It actually begins on her left breast, as you view in the coin, which is slightly higher.) Wear can also be observed on the central fold of her dress, which is not equal in height to the breast location just mentioned. How is that possible? Coins were housed in albums with moveable celluloid strips. At times, the strip was stuck and became very difficult to move. Some individuals would push down and sideways with a thumb or a finger against the celluloid window, pushing the window into contact with the coin's surface, in an attempt to free the coin. The area abused could have been the central fold or Justice's breasts. If only the breasts display the loss of metal, the cause (if the coin is in the album) would be too much back-and-forth movement of the strip in order to examine the coin. Some coins with slight wear can appear new and very lustrous or toned. These coins would grade Almost Uncirculated (AU) or slider AU+, depending on surface marks, eye appeal, etc., because of their actual condition. But such AU coins can be lightly wire-brushed by unscrupulous dealers or collectors in order to hide the loss of metal and to deceive the unknowledgeable and be offered as Mint State.

Reverse

When a metal loss does occur, it will be observed at the top of the palmetto tree. However, before this happens, the obverse Justice would lose one-fifth of her breast design; her relief is much higher than the reverse high point.

Related Material

The issue was distributed in a cardboard holder with inserts for three coins, manufactured by John H. Eggers. The holder was imprinted with: "1786–1936 Half Dollar Commemorating the Sesquicentennial of the Founding of Columbia as the Capital of South Carolina". It was mailed in Karolton Klasp 33/8 × 6-inch envelope imprinted with a representation of the coin's obverse in dark ink. The holder may be valued at $50 to $100; with original mailing envelope, $125 to $200.

Thin balsa wood flats or certificates were issued to sesquicentennial. They were redeemable at face value for cash on or before March 31, 1936 at the office of the Columbia Chamber of Commerce.

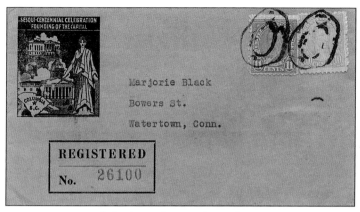

Columbia mailing envelope – front.

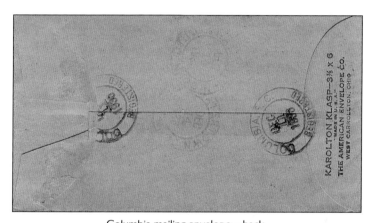

Columbia mailing envelope – back.

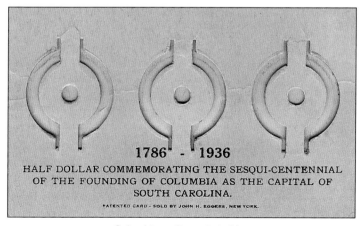

Columbia mailing coin holder.

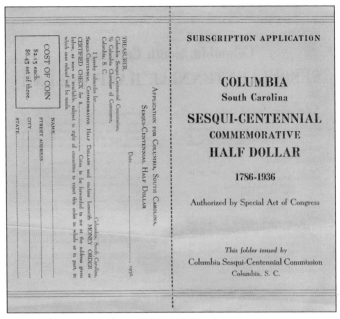

Columbia subscription form.

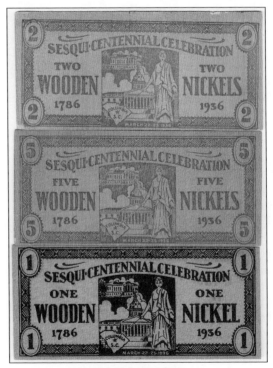

Columbia nickel flats.

Future Potential of the Columbia Half Dollar

Population Figures

One MS-68 Denver striking with exceptional eye appeal sold for $26,450. The piece was an MS-68++ coin. The buyer believed it to be an MS-69 example. To date, no Columbia striking has been graded that lofty.

Date	Service	AU 58	MS 60	MS 62	MS 63	MS 64	MS 65	MS 66	MS 67	MS 68	MS 69
1936	NGC	0	0	3	27	238	579	496	75	1	0
1936	PCGS	0	0	24	142	581	829	413	57	0	0
1936	Combined	0	0	27	169	819	1408	909	132	1	0

Date	Service	AU 58	MS 60	MS 62	MS 63	MS 64	MS 65	MS 66	MS 67	MS 68	MS 69
1936 D	NGC	0	0	3	16	169	418	636	220	46	0
1936 D	PCGS	0	0	15	142	427	649	548	159	19	0
1936 D	Combined	0	0	18	158	596	1067	1184	379	65	0

Date	Service	AU 58	MS 60	MS 62	MS 63	MS 64	MS 65	MS 66	MS 67	MS 68	MS 69
1936 S	NGC	0	0	1	16	187	521	599	120	6	0
1936 S	PCGS	0	0	19	175	527	685	481	74	4	0
1936 S	Combined	0	0	20	191	714	1206	1080	194	10	0

There is little price differential between grades AU-58 to MS-66. The limited number of circulated offerings are those UNCs that have been cleaned or abused in some fashion. The lowest census issue in MS-64 and MS-65+ condition is the Denver coin. This issue is fairly priced at present up to the MS-66 category, and, in fact, is slightly under-rated. It is a great candidate for a future promotion, as is the MS-66 coin. During the May 1989 market high, there was a $400 difference between the MS-64 and MS-65 ratings. From MS-65 to MS-66, the differential was $1,000. There is future potential in eye-appealing Philadelphia pieces grading MS-66+. I would reduce the census figures between 25% and 30% for the MS-64 and MS-65 categories.

In MS-66 condition, the Philadelphia coin is somewhat undervalued. I would deduct between 15% and 20% from the population figures. The Denver MS-67 Columbians are somewhat under priced at present levels. The best bets are the lower mintage Philadelphia and San Francisco coins, especially if they can be had at a type coin price. Price levels will vary depending upon the coin's eye appeal. I would eliminate 15% of their census figures. Who would not want to own a slabbed MS-68 Columbia? During a hot market, their asking price has to skyrocket.

1936 DELAWARE TERCENTENARY

Reason for Issue:	To commemorate the 300th anniversary of the founding of a Swedish community in Delaware.
Authorization:	Act of May 15, 1936, with a maximum of 20,978 pieces.
Issued by:	Delaware Swedish Tercentenary Commission
Official Sale Price:	$1.75

Production Figures

Date	Business Strikes	Assay Coins	Proofs	Melted	Net Mintage
1936	25,015	15	?	4,022	20,978

Current Market Values

Date	AU-58	MS-60	MS-63	MS-64	MS-65	MS-66	MS-67
1936	$210	$235	$245	$260	$375	$600	$1,250+

DESIGNS BY CARL L. SCHMITZ

According to Mint records, the obverse is the Old Swedes Church. Some collectors and dealers refer to the ship side as the obverse.

Obverse

The Old Swedes Church at Wilmington, which was dedicated in 1699 and is still standing near "The Rocks." It is claimed to be the oldest Protestant church building in the U.S. still used for worship. It was also near this location that the *Kalmar Nyckel* finally anchored. Above the church the sun's rays are piercing the clouds. Below the church is the motto "IN GOD WE TRUST"; the authorization date 1936 is below the motto, with the denomination appearing in the lower border. "UNITED STATES OF AMERICA" is around the upper border.

Reverse

The *Kalmar Nyckel*, the ship that carried the first Swedish colonists, who left Gothenburg in 1637 and arrived in Delaware Bay in March 1638. Others left on the *Fogel Grip*, which is not depicted. The ship design was made from a model made in Sweden, which is a copy of the authentic model of the actual ship now in the Swedish Naval Museum. "Kalmar Nyckel" means the Key of Kalmar (a skeleton key was positioned on the rim of the rejected bronze-colored [reverse white] 10 3/4 -inch diameter and 1 1/8 -inch thick plaster model reverse design by Adam Pietz). Kalmar is a port city in southeast Sweden.

Incused in small letters at the right of the ship are the designer's initials (CLS). Around the upper border is the inscription "DELAWARE TERCENTENARY"; "E PLURIBUS UNUM" and "LIBERTY" appear below the waves in the lower field. At the lower border are the anniversary dates 1638–1938, with three diamond-shaped figures appearing on the sides and in between the dates, symbolizing the state's size, its fertile soil, and its three counties of Kent, New Castle, and Sussex. Delaware is at times called the Diamond State.

Origins of the Delaware

This issue, along with the Bridgeport and Wisconsin issues, were approved on May 15, 1936. Because of the minimum coinage clause all these issues could be produced in any quantity desired, until the expiration date was reached. During March 1937 the Philadelphia Mint struck 25,000 pieces, plus 15 assay pieces. This issue had to bear the 1936 date of authorization according to the Act, although the anniversary celebration took place in 1938. Thus we have an issue that was authorized in and dated 1936, and struck in 1937 for a commemoration in 1938. (The same applies to the Gettysburg.)

In 1938 Sweden struck a 2-kronor coin in conjunction with the 1936 Delaware commemorative coin. The Swedish coin depicted King Gustaf V and the *Kalmar Nyckel* on its reverse. Mint State examples of the Swedish coinage retail between $17 and $20, while AU pieces can be worth $8 to $10. These coins were offered in a blue-printed heavy paper holder, depicting and describing the coin and its history.

The Delaware was distributed by the Delaware Swedish Tercentenary Commission at $1.75 through the Equitable Trust Company of Wilmington. Unfortunately, 4,022 coins remained unsold and were returned to the Mint to be reincarnated into some other coinage.

The Delaware Today

Luster for the issue will range from proof-like, to semi-proof-like, to brilliant frosty, to dull frosty. Proof-like pieces will be the most difficult to locate. Coins displaying semi-proof-like strikings on both sides will also be hard to find. Specimens in the EF-AU category usually display the effects of cleaning, polishing, or some degree of whizzing. Most of the issue is in the MS-60 through MS-64 categories, and currently there is little value spread between these grades. Collectors should take advantage of this situation: why buy an MS-60 coin when an MS-64 specimen can be had for just $50–$70 more? In these categories, this coin should be bought only for the joy of collecting.

Numismatic abuse, in the form of nicks, cuts, hits, bag marks, reed marks, and especially lack of the metal fill marks, keeps many coins out of the MS-65 category.

If Proofs exist, and I believe they do, they are in matte proof condition—not in satin finish. Satin finish specimens are simply those early-struck coins produced from a new die that were struck with one blow of the press, with possible extra striking pressure. They are certainly seldom encountered and are worth as much as potential owners want to pay. Beware of a polished coin being offered as proof-like or semi-proof-like.

Strike rarely affects the grade or value for this issue. Locating specimens with a clean-surfaced center sail or the sail located in the exact center of the coin's reverse, plus an obverse with a fully struck triangular top section above the door's entrance (which resembles a wide arrowhead pointing to the clouds above) will be a real find. Most issues show a flatness because of striking in this area on the reverse, while the sail usually has slide marks, fine scratches, or lack of fill marks, also created by the striking process. At times the triangular section and the sail can have the appearance of being battle-scarred.

No error coinage or counterfeit pieces have entered the marketplace to date.

Is Your Delaware Circulated or Mint State?

Obverse

The design is well protected by the coin's rim. Wear will first begin in the central section of the church roof directly above the triangular section of the door.

Reverse

The design will first display a loss of metal on the central or lower middle sail. Look for a difference in metal texture and fine crisscross scratches in this area.

Related Material

The Equitable Trust Company distributed these coins at $1.75 each in a thick paper holder that had inserts for five coins. This holder's outer cover shows the coin's obverse and reverse, gives the name of the issue, and states the event

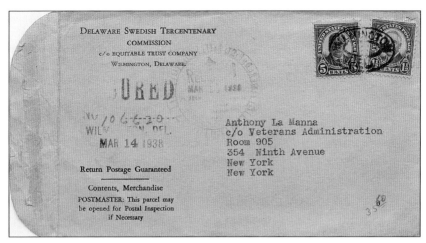

Delaware mailing envelope.

commemorated. The inner cover offers a small history of Delaware plus a description of the coin. The back cover is blank. Holders may be valued at $75 to $125; with original mailing envelope they are worth $125 to $200, depending on condition.

There exists a plaster model of a rejected design for this issue that sold around 2005 for $6,000. The consensus among knowledgeable collectors and dealers is that this price was too high. If the model is offered to you, consult with several commemorative experts before committing financially.

Future Potential of the Delaware Half Dollar

Population Figures

Date	Service	AU 58	MS 60	MS 62	MS 63	MS 64	MS 65	MS 66	MS 67	MS 68	MS 69
1936	NGC	7	1	25	170	877	1045	462	127	5	0
1936	PCGS	8	4	123	560	1421	1354	624	74	0	0
1936	Combined	15	5	148	730	2298	2399	1086	201	5	0

Date	Service	PL 58	PL 60	PL 62	PL 63	PL 64	PL 65	PL 66	PL 67	PL 68	PL 69
1936	NGC	0	0	0	2	9	5	2	0	0	0

There is no major price spread between the EF-AU and MS-65 ratings. The limited supplies of circulated offerings are usually abused. Future potential, should that be your concern, begins with attractive pieces rated MS-66+. The price difference between the latter grade and MS-65 was almost $1,400 during the

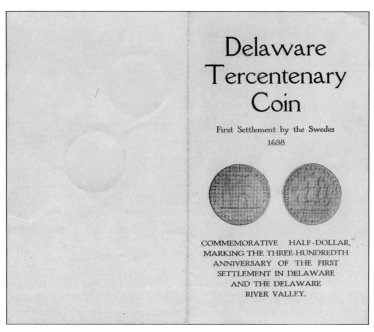

Delaware mailing coin holder—outside.

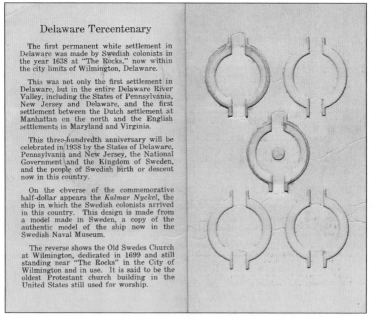

Delaware mailing coin holder—inside.

KM-571 obverse

KM-571 reverse

names below, the Swedish salute was given by the guns of the Kalmar Nyckel and the coat of arms of Sweden was erected on the shore as a sign that the territory was a Swedish possession.

Thus was the beginning of the permanent settlement by Swedes in the Delaware. They called the colony New Sweden.

New Sweden Tercentenary Celebration June 27-30, 1938

This year, the founding of New Sweden will be observed by the three states within whose present boundaries the first Swedish settlers made their homes, built their churches and organized law-abiding communities. The states of Delaware, Pennsylvania and New Jersey will receive as their guests a large official delegation from Sweden, headed by His Royal Highness Crown Prince Gustaf Adolf and Crown Princess Louise. Americans of Swedish birth and extraction from all parts of the United States will visit Wilmington, Philadelphia and Salem, N. J., to participate in the celebration which will continue from June 27 to June 30.

SWEDISH AMERICAN TERCENTENARY ASSOCIATION, Inc.

630 Fifth Avenue, New York, N.Y.

624 South Michigan Avenue, Chicago, Ill.

Patented Card—Sold by John H. Eggers, New York

SWEDISH TWO KRONOR
TERCENTENARY
MEMORIAL COIN

In commemoration of the 300th Anniversary
of the founding of New Sweden
in 1638.

KM-571 mailing coin holder—outside.

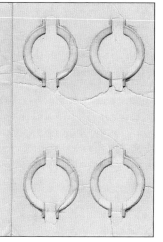

The Founding of New Sweden

It was late in the year 1637 that the first Swedish expedition to the New World set sail from Gothenburg, Sweden. It consisted of two ships: Kalmar Nyckel (the Key of Calmar) and Fogel Grip (the Bird Griffin). After a long and perilous journey across the Atlantic the expedition arrived in Delaware Bay about the middle of March and proceeded up the river. Turning into Minquas Kill, now called Christina River, the two vessels dropped anchor opposite a rocky ledge almost below the present site of Old Swedes Church in Wilmington, Delaware.

The colonists landed and their leader, Peter Minuit, established friendly connections with the Indians. On March 29, (April 8, new style) 1638, five chiefs went aboard the Kalmar Nyckel and in a cabin of this ship sold the first land to the Swedes. It comprised land which extended from the Cape to the Schuylkill River. Deeds were drawn up and presents were given to the Indians on behalf of the government of Stockholm. When the Indian chiefs had placed their scrawling marks on the deeds and the officers of the New Sweden Company had signed their

KM-571 mailing coin holder—inside.

Delaware medals in pewter and bronze—obverse.

Delaware medals in bronze and pewter— reverse.

May 1989 high. I would remove between 20% and 25% from current population figures.

Currently a strictly graded MS-66, eye-appealing Delaware can only be declared undervalued. However, continued population growth can have a future negative effect on the issue and its value: only time will tell. Collectors should avoid rainbow-toned or flashy coins that exhibit too many surface negatives in the primary focal areas, unless the price is right. I would lower the census figures by 30%. There is excellent future potential in the rarer MS-67 category. Pieces have sold for between $1,800 and $2,900. Value is based on the coin's total makeup, the possibility of an upgrade, the colored toning, and, of course, the buyer. Two NGC MS-68 pieces sold between $5,750 (2007) and $7,475 (2008). Were they more eye appealing, prices would be loftier.

1936 Elgin, Illinois, Centennial

Reason for Issue:	To commemorate the 100th anniversary of the (1835) founding of the city of Elgin, Illinois, and the construction of the heroic Pioneer Memorial.
Authorization:	Act of June 16, 1936, with a maximum of 25,000 pieces.
Issued by:	Elgin Centennial Monumental Committee
Official Sale Price:	$1.50

Production Figures

Date	Business Strikes	Assay Coins	Proofs	Melted	Net Mintage
1936	25,015	15	4?	5,000	20,000

Current Market Values

Date	AU-58	MS-60	MS-63	MS-64	MS-65	MS-66	MS-67
1936	$195	$210	$220	$240	$300	$420	$975+

Designs by Trygve Andor Rovelstad

Obverse

The head of a bearded pioneer wearing a fur cap, facing left. Widely spaced in the upper border is the word "Pioneer". The designer's monogrammed initials (TAR) are placed in the field below the beard; in the lower field is the motto "In God We Trust".

Below the pioneer are the commemorative dates, separated by a star. Elgin, a city on the Fox River some 29 miles northwest of Chicago, celebrated its 100th anniversary in 1935. The dates that appear on this issue (1673–1936) have no connection with Elgin. The first refers to the year in which the French explorers Joliet and Marquette first entered the territory, a section of which today is Illinois. The date 1936 refers to the date of striking. The actual centennial of the city was 1935.

Reverse

A group of five pioneers. Can you count the five? At the left is a pioneer holding a rifle in a horizontal position; his is the head depicted on the coin's obverse, and was based on a figure from the Pioneer Memorial. There is also a standing boy holding a stick and another male in the background. The baby being held in the mother's arms is the fifth pioneer.

The Elgin is the very first issue to depict a "suggested" infant on U.S. coinage. The baby is faceless and you almost do not realize what the woman pioneer is holding (this is why mint designers label it "suggested"). The first "defined" infant is on the 1937 Roanoke half dollar; the first "implied" baby appears within a Conestoga wagon on the 1926 Oregon Trail issues.

Around the upper border is "UNITED STATES OF AMERICA"; directly below is the legend "LIBERTY" (barely visible). In the lower field is "E PLURIBUS UNUM" and the coin's denomination. In the left field is the inscription "PIONEER MEMORIAL"; in the right field the inscription "ELGIN, ILLINOIS".

Origins of the Elgin

The Philadelphia Mint struck 25,000 coins plus 15 pieces for assay purposes in early October 1936. This issue was well distributed by the Elgin Centennial Monumental Committee through L.W. Hoffecker—the anti-speculator—of El Paso, Texas, who designed the Spanish Trail issue.

By November 16, 1936, only 170 coins had been sold at $1.50 each. By July 1937, it appears that all in numismatic circles who desired the issue had made their purchase. The general public had little interest. W.A. Schneider, an Illinois numismatist who was listed in Rovelstad's record book as desiring 6,000 pieces and who purchased only five coins, was not excited about the possibility of acquisition at a lower rate. Rovelstad and the Monumental Committee decided to return 5,000 coins to the Mint to be melted. Hoffecker requested that he be sold 500 to 1,000 of these coins at face value, based on his fantastic job in distributing the coins, but this never happened. I knew Trygve Rovelstad personally, and everything in his character indicates that he didn't think much of Hoffecker's idea.

The Elgin Today

A small number of Elgins are found in the EF-AU state. Those I have encountered over the years have been cleaned or abused in some manner. The retail

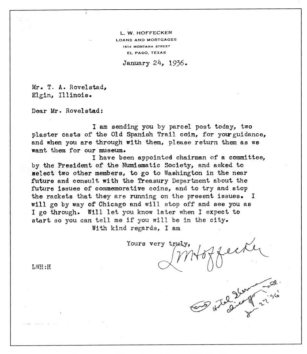

Letter to Rovelstad from Hoffecker.

worth is close to uncirculated values. Collectors should seek out Mint State coins, unless the price is far below Trends. Virtually all of the issue is in the MS-60 through MS-66 categories. Bag marks, reed marks, lack of fill marks, slide marks, etc., and lack of surface allure are responsible for these grades. There is currently little value spread between these grades, so collectors should look for an eye-appealing MS-64 acquisition, when possible, or even an MS-65—but only for the joy of ownership. The past value history for this issue will never repeat itself in grades MS-64 and MS-65, because of the wide availability. Luster will range from a flashy brilliant satiny (not the norm) to unattractive matte-like dull. Typical examples along this spectrum will offer little device–field contrast. Examining the reverse with its granular field, you should be able to observe a die polishing mark located below the first "A" in "AMERICA" (this is on most of the pieces I have seen). This characteristic does not take away from the coin's value or grade. The issue was not designed to offer sharpness of detail—especially on the reverse. Many specimens will display varying degrees of weakness, in the facial detail of the pioneer mother, as well as in the child (Tryvge later named her Gloria, upon my suggestion during a visit to his studio in 1982) whom she holds. I have found that strike will seldom affect the value and grade for specimens labeled up to MS-65. However, it can make a difference for grades of MS-66 or higher—unless there is otherwise something special about the coin, such as amazing natural color or iridescent toning. The real future potential for this issue lies in MS-66 and higher graded coins.

The 12 early strikings received from the Mint by the designer do not have the die polishing mark. Today some of those pieces are toned, others are brilliant. They do not blaze with flash, since the dies were not polished to any great extent. In fact, one of these specimens has a matte surface: the Chief Mint Engraver John Ray Sinnock had had it acid-treated. Also, it was given only one strike from the press (a Proof coin must be given two or even three strikings to show all the required details). The coin was sent to the three major grading services, and was returned by each with the notation "altered surfaces." I personally would not grant it a matte proof status: unfortunately, it resembles a regular issue that was properly acid-dipped by the Philadelphia Mint. It is possible that Sinnock later had a piece or two double struck and acid-treated. Only time will tell what the true story is regarding these pieces.

Elgins housed in a promoted hard plastic holder—exactly as the Bay Bridge issue—are worth the coin's grade plus $20 for the holder. The number assigned to this insert has no relationship to the order in which the coin was struck at the Mint. Both Rovelstad and the Bay Bridge designer, Jacques Schnier, received $5 for each cardboard coin holder they autographed; these autographed holders were placed in sealed cases by the dealers selling the respective issues.

To date no error coinage or counterfeit pieces are known to exist.

Is Your Elgin Circulated or Mint State?

Obverse

Wear or a difference in metal texture will first be noticed on the cheekbone of the pioneer. I suggest looking for surface doctoring such as whizzing in this area, since only a limited number of Elgins exhibit real wear. The primary focal location is the pioneer's face. A detracting mark here will hurt the coin's grade and value.

Reverse

Metal loss will make its appearance on the left shoulder (to the right as you view the coin) of the pioneer holding the rifle with both hands. The primary focal point is the smooth surface of the woman's dress. The presence of a reed mark, large bag mark, or large lack of fill mark will quickly remove this coin from the MS-65 category.

Related Material

The Elgin Centennial half dollar was mailed to subscribers in a plain off-white coin holder with inserts for five and for six coins. The front cover was rubber stamped once or twice with "L.W. Hoffecker, 1514 Montana St., El Paso, Texas"; in other instances it was forwarded unstamped, as received from the supplier. In the latter case, the coin should be accompanied by the postal mailing envelope

Elgin order confirmation postcard—front.

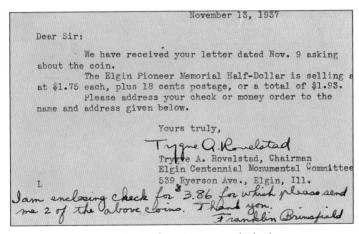

Elgin order confirmation postcard—back.

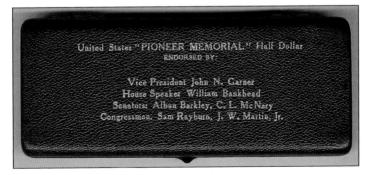

Extremely rare Elgin presentation case—top.

Elgin presentation case—inside.

Elgin presentation case—bottom.

and canceled stamps. The envelope will note Hoffecker's name, and details of the distributor, Elgin Centennial Coin, P.O. Box 75, El Paso, Texas. Collectors should value these holders at $20 to $25; with original stamped envelope, $50 to $200.

Rovelstad had a single three-piece coin case made by Medallic Art Co. of New York, gold-stamped on top, with the names of the politicians who helped make the coin a reality. I purchased this unique case from his late wife Gloria for $2,000, as well as the actual drawing of the issue ($5,000) housed in a frame 2 × 1 1/2 inches. Rovelstad forwarded this drawing to the U.S. Mint. He was advised (via a Western Union telegram) to change his three-quarters profile of the pioneer to what we observe on the current design.

Trygve sold me four plaster models or original castings (#2 through #5) of the obverse and reverse design on November 17, 1982. The first casting was sent

Rovelstad with plaster casts of the Elgin commemorative coin.

Left to right: the author, Gloria Ann Rovelstad, and Trygve Rovelstad examine plaster casts of the Elgin commemorative in the artist's studio.

The author modeling Trygve Rovelstad's artwork.

to the Philadelphia Mint to create the coin dies. Each pair was placed within a "plaster frame" for display. After Trygve's passing, his daughter Gloria Ann Rovelstad created copies of these for sale, which display a somewhat weaker definition than the originals: only the originals possess Trygve's special markings. These have sold for between $3,000 and $4,000 each. The second "copies" sell in the $800–$1,200 range.

Future Potential of the Elgin Half Dollar

Population Figures

Date	Service	AU 58	MS 60	MS 62	MS 63	MS 64	MS 65	MS 66	MS 67	MS 68	MS 69
1936	NGC	0	0	10	96	706	1281	729	110	6	0
1936	PCGS	5	0	52	472	1703	1922	988	110	3	0
1936	Combined	5	0	62	568	2409	3203	1717	220	9	0

There is not much dollar spread between grades EF-AU and MS-65. A limited number of circulated coins are abused UNCs. During the May 1989 market high, the Elgin was bid at $1,550; some pieces were selling at $1,700+. Over the last couple of years, these coins seem to have come out of the woodwork, now placing them within the generic or common category. I would acquire an attractive specimen only for the joy of ownership. Based on its past value—which will never be attained again, unless massive inflation develops—it certainly is a great promotable item. Collectors should sell when values rise, during our next bull market. If there is any real future potential, it will begin with strictly graded eye appealing MS-66+ material. Think attractive MS-67, if funds are available. Values will vary between $700 and $1,500+ depending on the coin's makeup. MS-68 rated pieces have sold between $7,000 and $11,000.

I suggest that you avoid the satin finish proof Elgin: it is nothing more than an early strike, and is too controversial. I also suggest that you ignore accompanying documentation letter.

1936 Long Island Tercentenary

Reason for Issue:	The 300th anniversary of the first European settlement on Long Island, New York.
Authorization:	Act of April 13, 1936, with a maximum of 100,000 pieces and a minimum of 5,000.
Issued by:	Long Island Tercentenary Committee
Official Sale Price:	$1

Production Figures

Date	Business Strikes	Assay Coins	Proofs	Melted	Net Mintage
1936	100,000	53	4?	18,227	81,773

Current Market Values

Date	AU 58	MS 60	MS 63	MS 64	MS 65	MS 66	MS 67
1936	$85	$90	$105	$115	$280	$750	$3,500+

Designs by Howard Kenneth Weinman

Obverse

The accolated heads of a Dutch settler and an Algonquin Indian, facing right. The settler symbolizes the Dutch settlement at Jamaica Bay in 1636, which was named *Breuckelin*, after a town in the Netherlands. This name was later changed to one that almost everyone has heard of: Brooklyn, once home of the famous Brooklyn Dodgers baseball team. The Indian symbolizes the 13 tribes of Algonquin Indians who lived on the island when Henry Hudson landed there in 1609. "LIBERTY" is at the upper border; "E PLURIBUS UNUM" in the lower border. Below the Indian's chin is the designer's monogram (HW), in relief.

Howard Kenneth Weinman is the son of A.A. Weinman, creator of the famous Walking Liberty half dollar and Winged Liberty dime, more commonly known as the Mercury dime.

Reverse

A Dutch three-masted ship, sailing to the right. "IN GOD WE TRUST" is incused on the waves below the ship; the date 1936 appears below the motto; the inscription "LONG ISLAND TERCENTENARY" is below the date in the lower border. Around the upper border is "UNITED STATES OF AMERICA" AND "HALF DOLLAR".

Origins of the Long Island

Section Two of the Act that approved this issue on April 13, 1936, stated the following: "The coins herein authorized shall bear the date 1936 irrespective of the year in which they are minted or issued; not less than 5,000 coins shall be issued … at any one time and no such coins shall be issued after the expiration of one year after the date of enactment of this Act." A previous section also states that "there shall be coined at a mint of the United States and not the mints," thus doing away with any hope of having the branch Mints create "mint varieties" of the same issue.

In the case of this issue, with a maximum authorization of 100,000 pieces, a required single date prevented this coin from being minted in 1936, 1937, 1938, etc. The minimum number of coins also stated in the Act prevents the possibility of small-mintage issues.

The Philadelphia Mint produced 100,053 coins in August 1936 for the tercentenary celebrations which, unfortunately, had taken place several months earlier. This issue was sold by the Long Island Tercentenary Committee and distributed through banks on Long Island at $1 each. It was originally delivered by armored truck to the National City Bank, 181 Montague Street, Brooklyn. The coins were called for by the bank's Vice President and Long Island Tercentenary Committee Treasurer Dewitt A. Forward and received by Louis C. Wills, Chairman, and John W. Smith, Secretary of the Committee.

Advance sales amounted to almost 19,000 pieces. Approximately 50,000 of these coins were designated for sale near my birthplace in Brooklyn via an office at the *Brooklyn Eagle* newspaper. One half of that figure would be aimed at potential sales in the Borough of Queens, 15,000 at Nassau County, and 10,000 at Suffolk County. When sales came to a standstill, 18,227 pieces were returned to the Mint and melted, leaving us with a total mintage of 81,826.

The Long Island Today

This issue is quite available in EF-AU condition. Collectors should attempt to acquire an un-doctored, appealing specimen, even if funds are limited. There is no problem in finding specimens graded MS-60 through MS-65. The current value spread between MS-60 and MS-64 is small, so collectors should target an attractive MS-64+ coin. Surface negatives, on the primary focal areas of the issue (obverse portraits and reverse ship) keep many coins out of the MS-65 category. Lack of metal fill may be responsible for what appears as very small scratches on the ship's center sail, but these are different from the fine hairline scratches caused by numismatic abuse or improper handling. The real future of the issue is in MS-66+ and higher grades. Luster will range from brilliant flashy to dull satiny. Strike rarely, if ever, affects grade and value.

To date, no error coinage or counterfeit pieces have entered the marketplace.

Is Your Long Island Circulated or Mint State?

Obverse

Wear will first be noticed on the Dutch settler's cheekbone. Examine this for a difference in metal texture and fine crisscross scratches. Also be aware of doctoring on the portraits.

Reverse

Metal loss first occurs in the center of the ship's mainsail. Lack of metal flow marks, which resemble small scratches and digs, can be present. They could detract from the specimen's eye appeal—and value—depending on their location as well as their size. The sails are the prime target for whizzing and doctoring of some form to make coin appear better than it actually grades.

Related Material

The issue was distributed in a Dennison unprinted cardboard holder with inserts for five pieces. The mailing envelope is imprinted with the Tercentenary Committee's name, in care of the National City Bank. There are also teal blue rectangular hinged presentation cases with gold peripheral trim design and embossed "Long Island Tercentenary Committee [presented] to" and the individual's name—but these seldom surface.

Subscription forms have appeared in two formats: a thin white, almost tissue-like, paper variety and one in sturdier yellow paper.

Original holders may be valued at $75 to $150, with envelope, and, at times, with the actual invoice, $150 to $500. The presentation case—if genuine—$500 to $750. The value of the coin(s) included should be based on grade and eye appeal.

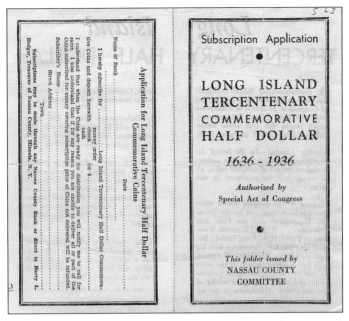

Long Island (Nassau County) Commemorative subscription form—outside.

Long Island
TERCENTENARY HALF DOLLAR

A commemorative HALF DOLLAR has been authorized by a Special Act of Congress to be issued in connection with the Long Island Tercentenary, which marks the first white settlement on Long Island in June, 1636.

Number Limited—To Be Issued by One Mint • The Congress has authorized the issuance of 100,000 coins, all of which will be produced in one mint.

Sculptor • The sculptor whose selection has been approved by the Treasury Department and the Fine Arts Commission is Howard Kenneth Weinman of Forest Hills, Long Island. Mr. Weinman has been associated with his father, Adolph Alexander Weinman, who has designed several of the coins in use by the United States Government and many important works of art and pieces of sculpture in the na-

tion's Capitol, together with notable public memorials and other works.

By Subscription Only • The coins will be sold by subscription only and applications will be limited to five (5) coins to a single subscriber.

Nassau County's allotment is 15,000, and its population is approximately 350,000 and as many of the citizens of this area will undoubtedly wish to have a lasting memento of this historic event, the Committee anticipates the authorized issue will be promptly subscribed.

If the experience of collectors with other special coins is any criterion, then it is fair to assume that this Half Dollar will have an increasing value with the passage of time.

(Tear off Subscription Blank, reverse side)

Long Island (Nassau County) Commemorative subscription form—inside.

LONG ISLAND TERCENTENARY HALF DOLLAR

A special Act of Congress has authorized the minting of one hundred thousand (100,000) commemorative coins to provide the people of this country with a physical reminder of this celebration of the founding of the first white settlement on Long Island. The coins are now being minted at the Philadelphia Mint and will be available for distribution by August 10th. Subscriptions are being received NOW so that everyone interested in having one or more of these coins will have the opportunity to subscribe. Subscriptions are limited to five coins per purchaser.

Howard Kenneth Weinman, noted sculptor of Forest Hills, Long Island, has designed the coin which is described as one of the most beautiful of the commemorative coins.

Value — Other commemorative issues have increased in value as the years pass and it is expected that these coins will too increase in value. Similar issues are now quoted at many times their original value.

HOW TO SUBSCRIBE—Fill in the application blank, retaining the stub as your receipt. Amounts are quoted on the reverse side, and the coins, as soon as received from the mint, will be sent by registered mail. ACT QUICKLY as the supply is limited.

Long Island Tercentenary of Queens County
Station Square, Forest Hills, L. I.
Louis C. Gosdorfer, Chairman

Application for Long Island Tercentenary Half Dollar

(Bank Stamp Here) Date..............1936

I hereby subscribe for.............Long Island Tercentenary Half Dollars at the prices indicated on the reverse side of this blank, and attach herewith money order or check in the sum of $............ I understand that the issue is limited and in the event that it is oversubscribed my remittance will be returned to me.

NAME..............

STREET ADDRESS..............

CITY.............. STATE..............

Note: Subscriptions limited to five (5) coins per purchaser.

Long Island (Queens County) Commemorative subscription form—outside.

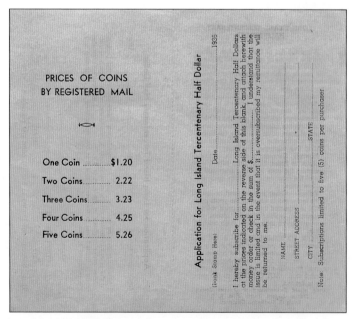

Long Island (Queens County) Commemorative subscription form—inside.

Long Island shipping statement.

Future Potential of the Long Island Half Dollar

Population Figures

Date	Service	AU 58	MS 60	MS 62	MS 63	MS 64	MS 65	MS 66	MS 67	MS 68	MS 69
1936	NGC	17	3	153	502	1769	1103	322	69	3	0
1936	PCGS	79	86	347	1247	2212	1161	380	27	0	0
1936	Combined	96	89	500	1749	3981	2264	702	96	3	0

The issue is not tough to obtain in less than Mint State condition; try to procure a nice looking coin with un-doctored, original surfaces. There is not much price variance between pieces rated EF-AU and MS-65. Should funds be available, buy coins in grades MS-64 and higher, but only for the pleasure of ownership. The price spread between MS-64 and MS-65 during the May 1989 high was $2,000, but that is no longer the case. I would lower the census by 20% to 25%. Accurately graded and flashy MS-65 coins are a nice item for a collector who can't afford more at present. The past price spread between MS-65 and MS-66 coinage was $3,100: that is also past history. I would deduct between 25% and 30% from the population count.

Eye-appealing Long Islands grading MS-66 are somewhat undervalued at present levels. I would reduce the census between 20% and 23%. There is good future potential for this grade, and excellent future potential for MS-67 coins. Three Long Islands have been granted the lofty MS-68 rating. Value can range between $13,000 and $21,000 depending on the coin's makeup.

1936 Lynchburg, Virginia, Sesquicentennial

Reason for Issue:	To commemorate the 150th anniversary of the issuance of a city charter to Lynchburg, Virginia.
Authorization:	Act of May 29, 1936, with a maximum of 20,000 pieces.
Issued by:	Lynchburg Sesquicentennial Association
Official Sale Price:	$1 (plus 25 cents per order).

Production Figures

Date	Business Strikes	Assay Coins	Proofs	Melted	Net Mintage
1936	20,000	13	4?	0	20,000

Current Market Values

Date	AU-5 8	MS-60	MS-63	MS-64	MS-65	MS-66	MS-67
1936	$210	$215	$250	$260	$315	$460	$1400+

Designs by Charles Keck

Obverse

Portrait of Senator Carter Glass of Virginia, facing left. His name is in the lower border. "United States of America" arcs above; "Liberty" is at the lower left, beneath Glass's chin, and "In God We Trust" is at the right, behind his neck.

Charles Keck (1875–1951)

Reverse

The standing figure of Liberty, with hands outstretched, symbolizing "You are welcome here." Located in the right background is part of the Monument Terrace and the old Lynchburg Courthouse. Placed in front of the Courthouse is the Confederate Monument. Around the upper border are the words "LYNCH-BURG VIRGINIA SESQUICENTENNIAL". The first letter "I" of "SESQUICENTENNIAL" is partially covered by Liberty's hand; this is not a Mint error. The motto "E PLURIBUS UNUM"—with the "S" of "PLURIBUS" located partly behind the standing Liberty—is in the left field, with the anniversary date 1786 below it. The other half of the commemorative date, 1936, is in the right field; the denomination is below the standing figure. Charles Keck also designed the Vermont and the Panama–Pacific gold dollar.

Origins of the Lynchburg

Senator Carter Glass, Secretary of the Treasury in the Wilson administration, vigorously protested against having his portrait appear on the Lynchburg commemorative 50-cent piece, which was honoring his home city. In fact, he called the Philadelphia Mint to determine if there was a law against the profile of a living person appearing on a coin. Informed there was not, Glass replied, "I had hoped there would be an avenue of escape." This particular prohibition applied to paper currency only. Glass was chosen because no likeness of the city's founder, John Lynch, could be located. Glass, who died in 1946, was the third living person to appear on U.S. coinage. Governor Thomas E. Kilby of Alabama was the first (1921); President Calvin Coolidge was the first president and second living person to be portrayed (1926); Senator Joseph Robinson was the fourth (1937); and Eunice Kennedy Shriver, who died in 2009, was, to date, the last (1995).

Glass was elected honorary president of the Lynchburg Sesquicentennial Association, which sold the coins from September 21, 1936—three weeks before the celebration—at $1 each plus 25 cents postage per order. There were 20,000 pieces plus 13 assay coins produced at the Philadelphia Mint in September 1936.

Fred W. McWane, Secretary of the Sesquicentennial Association, which was headquartered at the Virginian Hotel, informed potential buyers by September 2 that the issue was sold out—including the balance of 5,000 pieces allotted to the Association. The Confederacy receives prominent recognition on this coin—as it does on the 1925 Stone Mountain coin.

The Lynchburg Today

This issue is not abundant in EF-AU condition. Specimens I have seen are usually cleaned or doctored in some fashion. The issue is available in all grades from MS-60 through MS-65. There is not much price spread in these grades, so collectors should aim for MS-65. Should funds be available, go for a higher MS-65 coin, one with eye appeal and a strong strike. Luster will range from semi-prooflike, to brilliant satiny, to dull satiny. Strike at times can be responsible for lowering a coin's value and preventing it from grading MS-65+ or even MS-64. In this case, obvious flatness will be noticed on Liberty's head and thigh, next to the motto "E Pluribus Unum".

To date, no error coinage or counterfeit pieces have come to the light, though many doctored examples do exist.

Whizzed coin example

Common areas to look for doctoring are highlighted by the arrows in the picture below. Note the key areas, especially the hair-lined field, in the "whizzed" example on page 345.

IS YOUR LYNCHBURG CIRCULATED OR MINT STATE?

Obverse

Wear will first be noticed on the cheekbone and area above the ear of Carter Glass. A softness of strike can also be seen here, but should not affect grade, unless the upper ear details look flattened.

Reverse

Wear begins on knee and head, then on the breasts of Liberty. Should the high points be flat because of die wear or low striking pressure, look for difference in metal color and fine crisscross scratches to determine wear.

Related Material

The Lynchburg was distributed in a buff-colored cardboard holder with inserts to hold five coins, manufactured by J.N. Spies Mfg. Co. of Watertown, New York. The front page of the holder is imprinted with the following: "Lynchburg in Old Virginia is celebrating its 150th Birthday with the issuance of this Commemorative Half Dollar and Pageants, Parades, Booklets, Museum, Art Exhibit and Exhibition Hall" and the dates October 12–16, 1936. Pages 2 and 4 are blank; page 3 contains slots for five coins. The holder may be valued at $50 to $100, or, with original mailing envelope, $125 to $200: price is based on condition.

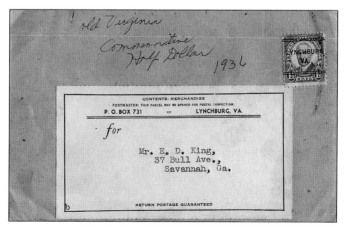

Lynchburg mailing envelope.

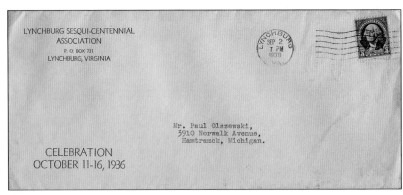

Lynchburg correspondence mailing envelope.

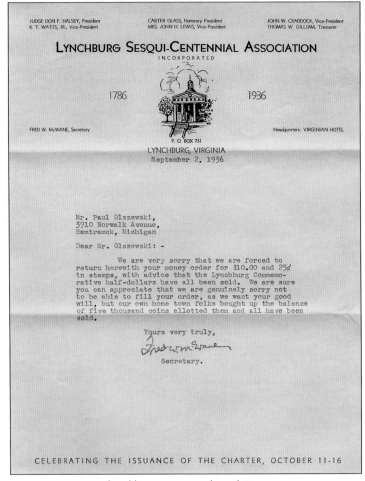

Lynchburg correspondence letter.

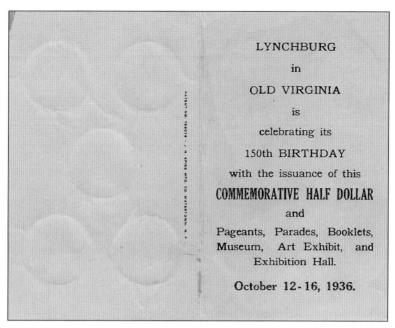

Lynchburg mailing coin holder—outside.

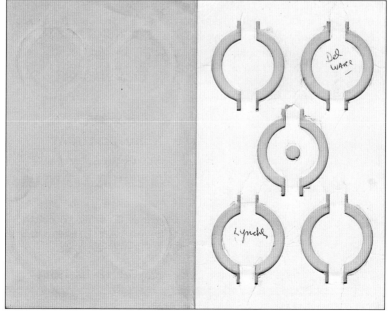

Lynchburg mailing coin holder—inside. One collector included
a 1936 Delaware half dollar in this Lynchburg holder.

Future Potential of the Lynchburg Half Dollar

Population Figures

Date	Service	AU 58	MS 60	MS 62	MS 63	MS 64	MS 65	MS 66	MS 67	MS 68	MS 69
1936	NGC	4	0	24	151	712	973	430	108	6	0
1936	PCGS	9	2	71	488	1290	1264	574	58	0	0
1936	Combined	13	2	95	639	2002	2237	1004	166	6	0

Of the limited number of coins in the circulated category, most are abused or doctored UNCs. There is only a small price spread between EF-AU and MS-65 coinage. Examples should be acquired for the joy of collecting. Should future potential be of concern, collectors should aim for eye-appealing MS-64+ specimens. The May 1989 market high spread between this grade and the MS-65 rating was $1,100; a repeat is unlikely. I would reduce the population figures between 25% and 30%.

In MS-65 condition, the Lynchburg appears fairly priced at current levels. Should you possess such a coin, I strongly recommend its sale when the issue is promoted in grades MS-64 and higher. The past high price range between the MS-65 and MS-66 ratings was $2,500, but this won't occur again. The census can be reduced between 20% and 25%.

The real potential is in alluring coinage rated MS-66+; it can be flashy or possess beautiful natural colored toning. I would lower the population figures between 20% and 25%. In MS-67 condition, a Lynchburg is an excellent acquisition. Recent auction sales have brought between $975 and $1,850. All is related to the coin's total makeup. At the January 2008 Orlando, FL FUN Heritage auction #454 (Lot #2346) an NGC MS-68 encapsulation sold for $4,830.

1936 NORFOLK, VIRGINIA, BICENTENNIAL

Reason for Issue:	To commemorate the 300th anniversary of the original Norfolk land grant (1636) and the 200th anniversary of the establishment of the city of Norfolk as a borough (1736).
Authorization:	Act of June 28, 1937, with a maximum of 25,000 pieces.
Issued by:	Norfolk Advertising Board, Norfolk Association of Commerce
Official Sale Price:	$1.50 locally; $1.65 by mail for first coin; $1.55 for additional coins

Production Figures

Date	Business Strikes	Assay Coins	Proofs	Melted	Net Mintage
1936	25,000	13	4?	8,077	16,923

Current Market Values

Date	AU-50	MS-60	MS-63	MS-64	MS-65	MS-66	MS-67
1936	$390	$400	$420	$450	$500	$570	$600

DESIGNS BY WILLIAM MARKS SIMPSON AND MARJORIE EMORY SIMPSON

Obverse

The official seal of the City of Norfolk, Virginia. A three-masted ship in stylized waves sails to the right; below is a plow and three sheaves of wheat; underneath is the word "Crescas", meaning "may you prosper." Above the ship is another motto, "Et Terra et Mare Divitiae", meaning "both land and sea are your riches." Within the cable border is "Town 1682 Borough 1736 City 1845 City of Norfolk Virginia". The outer border displays the anniversary date 1936 (coin was actually struck in 1937) between two scallop shells; "Borough of Norfolk Bicentennial" is placed within this border.

Reverse

The Royal Mace, with the British crown on its top. Norfolk received the only Mace presented to an American city during Colonial times. The date of the original land grant (1636) has sprigs of dogwood on each side. "In God We Trust" and "E Pluribus Unum"appear on either side of the mace handle, with denomination and designers' monograms above the "LL" in "Dollar". "Liberty" is in the lower left field; "United States of America" forms the upper border; "Norfolk Virginia Land Grant" is spaced to either side of the mace head.

Origins of the Norfolk

This coin was authorized in 1937 for a 1936 celebration. The reason given to the numismatic world for this centered on an unsuccessful 1936 bill that apparently created confusion as to whether a medal or coin should be produced. The Philadelphia Mint in September 1937 struck 25,000 Norfolks plus 13 assay coins dated 1936, as required by the Act.

These coins were distributed locally by the Norfolk Advertising Board at $1.50 per coin. A limit was set at 20 coins per order; the limit was later rescinded to allow bulk sales to dealers at a slightly lower price.

Mail orders cost $1.65 for the first coin, and $1.55 for each additional specimen. Sales came to a halt, and 5,000 pieces were returned to Philadelphia. Later on, another 3,077 were sent back for reincarnation into other coinage. Five dates appear on the coin: 1636 (original land grant); 1682 (town); 1736 (borough); 1845 (city); 1936 (anniversary year)—but not the date of actual striking (1937). The Norfolk commemorates a Bicentennial as well as Tercentenary celebration.

The Norfolk Today

The coin is certainly not abundant in circulated condition. Specimens will usually show some sort of abuse, such as cleaning and at times whizzing of the obverse ship, to hide a dig or slight wear on the sail. At present there is no major value spread between coins in EF-AU and MS-66 condition. This is very unusual, so it makes sense for collectors to aim for eye-appealing coins in the higher grades. The Norfolk often seems to have received angelic protection. Actually, its cluttered design plays an important role by protecting the design and fields from bag marks, etc. Luster will range from blazing satiny to dull satiny. I have yet to examine a specimen where strike would affect the value or grade.

To date, no error coinage or counterfeit pieces have entered the market-place.

Is Your Norfolk Circulated or Mint State?

Obverse
A metal loss will first be observed on the first and second lower rear sails of the ship. At times this area is doctored to hide wear: look for that buffed or aluminum appearance, telling you that doctoring has occurred.

Reverse
Wear will first be noticed on the central upper section, just below the base of the British crown. Look for a difference in metal texture.

Related Material
The coins were mailed by the "Norfolk Advertising Board, Affiliated with the Norfolk Association of Commerce," 107 West Main Street, Norfolk, in a light lime-green imprinted paper mailer with cardboard inserts for five coins.

Within a rectangular black border on the front cover is the name of the issue, reason for commemoration, sponsor and affiliated groups. For whatever

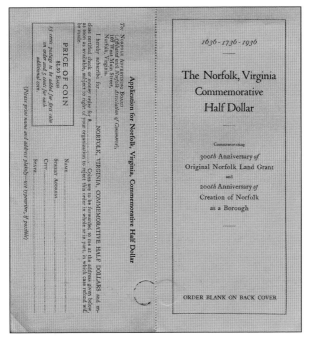

Norfolk order form—outside.

Norfolk order form—inside.

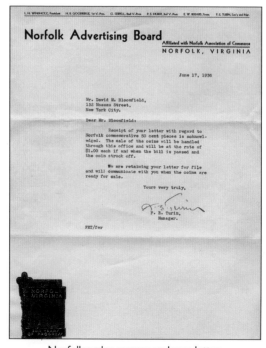

Norfolk order correspondence letter.

NORFOLK - VIRGINIA

A thousand tongues and a thousand songs
 Could never tell the world
The wondrous beauties a Generous God
 In all His love unfurled
And left at our feet, to have and hold
 Until the world shall cease,
A land where the angels come to find
 Their moment of perfect peace.

You'd learn to love this garden spot
 Its endless ocean-strand,
The forest deep, the fern-clad paths
 That make this wondrous land,
The sun-kissed shores, the lacy waves
 That move in a joyous sweep,
Bringing the purple of restless seas
 Out of the boundless deep.

Traditions ride through this hallowed land,
 So rich with history's lore,
And the hand of welcome waits to greet
 The stranger at its door.
So come to my land and find the joy
 That the Southland holds for you,
The spirit of hospitality
 That will live 'til time is through.

—CHARLES DAY.

THE NORFOLK COMMEMORATIVE HALF DOLLAR

Designed by William Marks Simpson

———

Commemorating

300th Anniversary of the Original Norfolk Land Grant in 1636 and the 200th Anniversary of the Creation of Norfolk as a Borough in 1736.

———

Sponsored by
NORFOLK ADVERTISING BOARD
Affiliated with
Norfolk Association of Commerce
NORFOLK, VIRGINIA

Norfolk coin holder—outside.

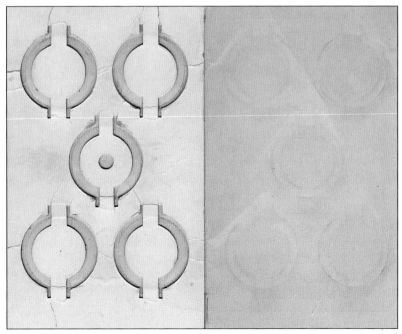

Norfolk coin holder—inside.

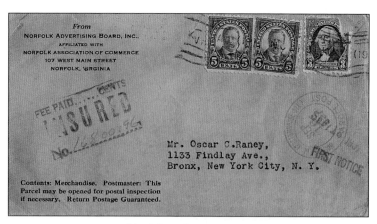

Norfolk mailing envelope.

reason, the front cover lists William Marks Simpson as the designer, but omits mention of his wife, Marjorie. The back cover presents a poem by Charles Day. The holder is not abundant, but neither is it rare. Value the holder at $50 to $75; $75 to $175 with original mailing envelope. However, the golden-orange original application for the issue is very difficult to locate; a few have sold for between $175 and $350.

Future Potential of the Norfolk Half Dollar

Population Figures

Date	Service	AU 58	MS 60	MS 62	MS 63	MS 64	MS 65	MS 66	MS 67	MS 68	MS 69
1936	NGC	0	0	2	22	196	561	1049	648	89	1
1936	PCGS	1	0	30	164	618	1113	1592	959	157	0
1936	Combined	1	0	32	186	814	1674	2641	1607	246	1

The small quantity of existing circulated coins usually turns out to be of the cleaned or abused variety. There is currently not much dollar spread between coins in EF-AU and MS-67 condition, and these are fairly priced. Acquire all for the pure joy of collecting. The Norfolk was another coin that came out of the numismatic woodwork: it has fair future potential. I would reduce the population figures in grades MS-64 through MS-66 by 30% to 31%. This is the only commemorative with more coins slabbed MS-66 than MS-65. The only real tomorrow for the Norfolk appears to be in the MS-67+ category. These are great promotional candidates, as will be the MS-65 and MS-66 coins. A very colorful or beautifully toned MS-68 Norfolk is worth much more than a silvery white or unattractive MS-68. With a high population for the grade, examples have recently sold at auction between $1,300 and $1,600.

1936 PROVIDENCE, RHODE ISLAND, TERCENTENARY

Reason for Issue:	To commemorate the 300th anniversary of the founding of Providence, the first settlement in Rhode Island.
Authorization:	Act of May 2, 1935, with a maximum of 50,000 pieces.
Issued by:	Rhode Island and Providence Plantations Tercentenary Committee
Official Sale Price:	$1 per coin, $1.50 by mail

Production Figures

Date	Business Strikes	Assay Coins	Proofs	Melted	Net Mintage
1936	20,000	13	4?	0	20,000
1936-D	15,000	10	4?	0	15,000
1936-S	15,000	11	4?	0	15,000

Current Market Values

Date	AU-58	MS-60	MS-63	MS-64	MS-65	MS-66	MS-67
1936	$90	$100	$125	$135	$225	$325	$1,600+
1936 PDS set	$270	$300	$375	$365	$775	$1,500	$6,500+

DESIGNS BY JOHN H. BENSON AND ARTHUR G. CAREY

Obverse

Roger Williams, often called the father of Rhode Island, kneeling in a canoe, with his right hand raised, holding the Bible with his left hand, and being welcomed in friendship by an Indian at State Rock. In the left background is a stalk of maize, symbolic of the many contributions given to the early colonists by the Indians. Beneath the stalk will appear the D or S Mint mark. Located in the center background is the sun, with extending rays, symbolic of religious liberty: Rhode Island was the first colony to have this right. The word "LIBERTY" appears within the rays; "IN GOD WE TRUST", the anniversary dates, and the words "RHODE ISLAND" appear between the thin inner and outer border; "LIBERTY" is in small letters just inside the inner border.

Reverse

The shield of Rhode Island, which consists of the anchor of Hope, with a mantle in the background. Above the shield is a ribbon bearing the word "HOPE". "UNITED STATES OF AMERICA" arcs above; "HALF DOLLAR" below. The denomination is in the lower field; the motto "E PLURIBUS UNUM" is on the mantle above.

Origins of the Rhode Island

The Act that authorized this issue was combined with the Act authorizing the Hudson Sesquicentennial half dollar. Three Mints produced the Rhode Island, with a maximum authorization of 50,000 pieces.

The Philadelphia Mint produced 20,000 coins plus 13 assay pieces, during January 1936. In the following month, the Denver and San Francisco Mints each struck 15,000 coins, plus 10 and 11 assay coins, respectively.

This issue was distributed by the Rhode Island and Providence Plantations Tercentenary Committee, Inc. at $1 each and Grant's Hobby Shop of Providence, Rhode Island, at $1.50 each. The Rhode Island Hospital National Bank, acting as depository and banking distributor of the coins, had exhausted its supply by noon March 5, 1936, and was unable to fill repeat orders. Arthur L. Philbrick, Treasurer of the Committee, thereafter claimed that approximately 45,000 pieces of the maximum authorization (50,000) was disposed of in 30 banks throughout the state, with most being sold before noon on March 5, 1936. He also noted that the residents received their coins before the mail orders were filled. Horace M. Grant of Grant's Hobby Shop originally received 6,750 pieces and had to request an additional 5,000 coins to fill the 11,500 orders he had received from almost all 48 states, Canada and other countries, as well as all the additional orders he would receive by March 6, 1936.

With the available supply rapidly decreasing, orders were scaled down by the banks. By 11:00 a.m. people who had ordered six to ten coins were given a smaller number. Depending on your location, you received from one to three coins. Did this situation develop because of a tremendous advertising campaign? The Committee apparently wanted distribution to be as wide as possible. Some people, however, thought the shortage had another cause and claimed that an influential banker owned more than 1,000 sets of this issue and was selling them in lots of five or ten at the highest market price. Others claimed that for a small premium they had access to 450, and so on. These claims now appear to be valid. The Committee had the first 100 coins produced at the Mints placed in numbered envelopes in order of striking and accompanied by Mint documentation. According to a notice dated June 24, 1936, the three-piece numbered sets would be sold to the highest bidders before the close of business on July 13, 1936. The orders would be handled by a special three-man subcommittee, consisting of Ira L. Letts (Committee Chairman), A.P. Monroe, and A.L. Philbrick. All three enclosed coins should display original captivating proof-like surfaces. To date, I have never seen such coinage.

The Rhode Island Today

The three-Mint issue is available in EF-AU condition. Coins can be found displaying lightly circulated natural surfaces, as well as in abused condition. The Philadelphia coin bears no Mint mark. Because of its design, this coin is not one of the popular commemoratives. A 1989 survey by the Society for United States Commemorative Coins (SUSCC)—I am currently its President—voted this issue the second-worst design after the Carver–Washington.

Luster will range from proof-like, to semi-proof-like (not the norm), to brilliant frosty, to dull frosty. Strike will rarely present a problem.

Numismatic negatives in the form of bag marks, slide marks, etc., gravitate toward the primary focal locations. These are the canoe and the two men, as well as the reverse anchor and surrounding fields. Such negatives lower the grade-value of many coins within the issue.

Collectors should beware of polished or slightly buffed pieces that are offered as proof-like pieces. If the genuine article makes its appearance, especially in grades MS-63+ and higher, acquire it. A small number of pieces were produced from rusty dies, which should have been rejected by Mint quality control. Die pits caused surface lumps, which can be observed on both sides of this issue.

To date no error or counterfeit pieces have surfaced.

Is Your Rhode Island Circulated or Mint State?

Obverse

Wear will first be observed on the tip of the canoe and upper shoulder of the Indian.

Reverse

A metal loss will first occur on the lower vertical section of the Anchor of Hope, the coin's highest area of relief, and a prime target for the coin doctors.

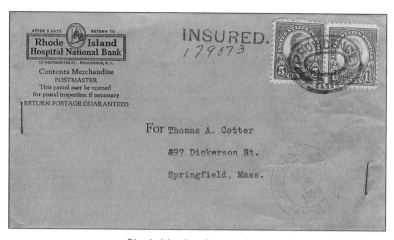

Rhode Island mailing envelope

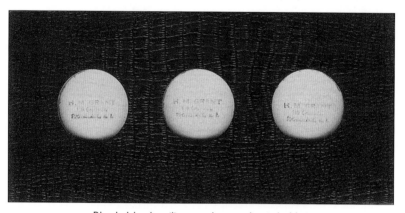

Rhode Island mailing envelope and coin holder.

Related Material

The issue was distributed unprotected by the banks or placed in a white plain paper coin envelope. Other orders were wrapped in plain tissue paper or placed in an unprinted five-coin insert cardboard holder, then mailed in a light tan envelope (6 × 35/16 inches), imprinted: "Rhode Island Hospital National Bank, 15 Westminster St., Providence, R.I." and a logo. Other coins were mailed in the same manner, but in an envelope imprinted: "Grant's Hobby Shop, Horace M. Grant, Prop. 109 Empire St., Providence, R.I." Housed within was a black cardboard three-coin holder with "H.M. Grant" and the address rubber-stamped in each of the three-coin slots.

Original mailing envelopes may be valued at $100 to $475. The Rhode Island and Providence Plantations Tercentenary Committee, Inc. distributed

Welcome to Rhode Island

MAY 4, 1936, the 160th anniversary of the Rhode Island Declaration of Independence, which preceded by two months similar action taken by the Continental Congress at Philadelphia, marks the official opening of the State celebration of the 300th anniversary of the founding by Roger Williams, at Providence Plantations, of what became the State of Rhode Island and Providence Plantations.

Throughout the State, pageants and special events commemorating its unique Colonial history, exhibits of the work of old Rhode Island silversmiths, cabinet makers, painters and others, will recall early days and mark the progress of three centuries.

Rhode Island this year more than ever invites citizens from other Commonwealths to visit a land of rare beauty, combining four hundred miles of coastline, world-famed beaches and summer resorts, with the charm of the hill country of old New England. It is a vacation land with splendid roads, beautiful Narragansett Bay and the broad Atlantic for sailing, some of the best fishing in America, salt water or fresh, storied spots and historic places, excellent golf courses, hotels, inns, camps—a place for every purse, a vacation for every desire.

Come to Rhode Island this Tercentenary year and enjoy Old New England at its best. Any information you may need will be furnished by addressing: RHODE ISLAND TERCENTENARY COMMISSION, State House, Providence.

© 1936, Rhode Island and Providence Plantations Tercentenary Committee, Inc.

THE
RHODE ISLAND TERCENTENARY
· HALF DOLLAR ·
Issued in commemoration of
RHODE ISLAND'S 300TH BIRTHDAY

Beige flyer—outside.

The Rhode Island Tercentenary Half Dollar

THE Rhode Island Tercentenary half dollar was issued in 1936 by the United States Government in commemoration of the 300th anniversary of the founding of the State of Rhode Island and Providence Plantations by Roger Williams. The Act of Congress providing for the issuance of 50,000 of these half dollars was passed in 1935. 20,000 of these were minted in Philadelphia, 15,000 in Denver, and 15,000 in San Francisco. The design is the result of the joint efforts of Mr. John Howard Benson and Mr. Arthur Graham Carey, both of Newport, Rhode Island. The requirements of the United States Mint provide that the coin have on the obverse, the words, "Liberty," "In God We Trust," and the date, "1936;" and on the reverse, the words, "United States of America," "E Pluribus Unum," and "Half Dollar."

The arrival of Roger Williams at the site of Providence seemed to be an excellent symbol of liberty. The gesture of the Indian, the hand extended palm down, is the sign for "Good" in the Indian sign language, while Roger Williams' raised hand is the white man's salutation of friendship. Behind the Indian stands a plant of Indian corn symbolic of the native contribution to the new American civilization and one particularly characteristic of Rhode Island, while Roger Williams carries in his hand the Bible, symbolic of the European contribution. Behind both rises the sun of religious liberty, which was established by Roger Williams in Rhode Island, the first time that a political power conceded to human beings the right to possess religious beliefs, and to worship God in a manner dictated by personal preference rather than by the governmental ordinance.

On the reverse is the shield bearing the anchor of Hope, which is taken from the Seal of the State of Rhode Island and Providence Plantations, and the ribbon above it bearing the word, "Hope" stands for the authority of the State; while behind, representing the authority of the nation, is the mantling with the motto, "E Pluribus Unum."

The cost of the coin with handling charges is $1.15 for the first one, and $1.05 for each additional coin. This price is subject to change without notice. Address all orders and correspondence regarding the memorial coin to

RHODE ISLAND AND PROVIDENCE PLANTATIONS TERCENTENARY COMMITTEE, INC.
634 Hospital Trust Building, Providence, R. I.

Beige flyer—inside.

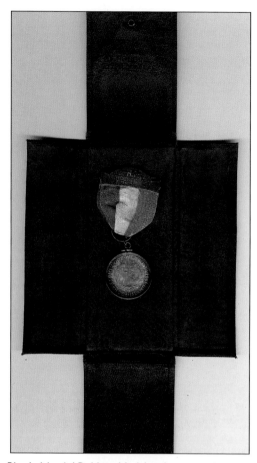

Rhode Island / Robbins Medal and presentation case.

a beige flyer describing the coin and the Tercentenary, and promoting Rhode Island as a place to visit. Few of the flyers have surfaced: they are valued between $25 and $100, depending on condition.

An extremely rare black leather presentation case, 2 1/4 × 5 1/4 inches, was manufactured by the"Robbins Co. of Atteboro Massachusetts". The four-flap holder houses a special badge inscribed: "1636 R.I. 1936 / Tercentenary / Special". The connecting ribbon is red, white, and blue with a Rhode Island coin mounted in a bezel. Reportedly, three such cases were produced. One holder is known to have realized $1,207.50 in the August 2004 Pennsylvania Heritage Signature Sale; it was resold for $2,000 three weeks later, then for $2,600 at the 2008 ANA Baltimore Convention, and most recently for $2,950 in March 2010.

Future Potential of the Rhode Island Half Dollar

Population Figures

Date	Service	AU 58	MS 60	MS 62	MS 63	MS 64	MS 65	MS 66	MS 67	MS 68	MS 69
1936	NGC	0	0	15	98	702	987	316	30	1	0
1936	PCGS	8	4	51	392	1104	1134	478	22	0	0
1936	Combined	8	4	66	490	1806	2121	794	52	1	0

Date	Service	PL 58	PL 60	PL 62	PL 63	PL 64	PL 65	PL 66	PL 67	PL 68	PL 69
1936	NGC	0	0	0	6	30	42	11	0	0	0

Date	Service	AU 58	MS 60	MS 62	MS 63	MS 64	MS 65	MS 66	MS 67	MS 68	MS 69
1936 D	NGC	0	0	19	81	549	744	245	36	3	0
1936 D	PCGS	2	3	48	333	899	880	448	45	0	0
1936 D	Combined	2	3	67	414	1448	1624	693	81	3	0

Date	Service	AU 58	MS 60	MS 62	MS 63	MS 64	MS 65	MS 66	MS 67	MS 68	MS 69
1936 S	NGC	2	2	25	73	513	592	186	20	0	0
1936 S	PCGS	6	3	56	383	857	703	210	17	0	0
1936 S	Combined	8	5	81	456	1370	1295	396	37	0	0

Date	Service	PL 58	PL 60	PL 62	PL 63	PL 64	PL 65	PL 66	PL 67	PL 68	PL 69
1936 S	NGC	0	0	0	1	1	0	0	0	0	0

Among commemorative coin designs produced between 1892 and 1954, this issue's obverse does not rate very high among collectors. The image of Roger Williams has the look of a robot from the old *Flash Gordon* serials. There is currently no major dollar spread between grades EF-AU and MS-66 for the higher-census Philadelphia and Denver type coins in grades MS-65 and MS-66. Collectors should look for the San Francisco striking, and acquire for the joy of ownership. The Philadelphia striking is the most abundant. Census figures reflect the true rarity for each Mint. Should a type coin be desired, I recommend the branch mint strikings. The past peak dollar variance between grades MS-64 and MS-65 was approximately $600 for the type coin and $1,600 for the set. I would lower population figures by 25% to 30%. There is good to very good potential for the proof-like NGC encapsulations.

In strict MS-65 condition, all the coins appear fully priced at present levels. Their combined population is not exactly small and the issue would not win a popularity contest. I would rate their future possibilities as fair. The price spread between the MS-65 and MS-66 ratings was a large $1,300 for the type coin and a whopping $11,000 for the three-piece set. I would reduce population numbers between 23% and 32%. .

In MS-66 condition, the issue is definitely undervalued, especially the San Francisco coin, which is the rarest of the three-piece sets. There is always the chance that one of these could be procured at the type coin price, from the un-alert seller. I would rate the potential of coins from the other Mints as good. To date, eleven Philadelphia proof-like pieces have been rated MS-66. Rhode Islands graded MS-67 are in demand—especially the rarest San Francisco coin; all are great to own.

Appealing Philadelphia and Denver issues reside in the $800 to $1,600 value range, with the rarer west coast issue in the $1,600 to $2,300 range. Yes it is true that a dealer paid $16,100 for a Rhode Island PCGS MS-67 creation. Would I? Don't think so! An NGC MS-68 example sold in 2007 for $5,750.

1936 San Francisco–Oakland Bay Bridge

Reason for Issue:	To commemorate the opening of the San Francisco–Oakland Bay Bridge.
Authorization:	Act of June 26, 1936, with a maximum of 200,000 pieces.
Issued by:	Coin Committee / Coin Division of the San Francisco–Oakland Bay Bridge Celebration
Official Sale Price:	$1.50; $1.65 by mail

Production Figures

Date	Business Strikes	Assay Coins	Proofs	Melted	Net Mintage
1936-S	100,000	55	4?	28,631	71,369

Current Market Values

Date	AU-58	MS-60	MS-63	MS-64	MS-65	MS-66	MS-67
1936-S	$145	$160	$195	$205	$350	$475	$1,300+

Designs by Jacques Schnier

Obverse

A large California grizzly bear, the emblem of the State of California. However, the bear's presence on this issue was highly criticized by numismatists, since Monarch II (considered the "model bear") was confined for 26 years of his life in a cage in Golden Gate Park. According to the Romanian designer, it is not

Jacques Schnier (1898–1988)

Monarch II portrayed on the obverse, but rather a composite of various bears from the Oakland and San Francisco zoos. Is this symbolic of freedom and liberty? The grizzly bear also symbolizes California's freedom from Mexico and appeared on the flag of the Republic of California.

Located near the animal's paw is the Mint mark S. The designer's monogram (JS) is in the upper right field. Below the bear is "LIBERTY" and the denomination; in the left field is the motto "IN GOD WE TRUST". Around the upper border is "UNITED STATES OF AMERICA"; four decorative stars appear around the lower border.

Reverse

An emblematic—rather than documentary—image depicts the Bay Bridge stretching from a point over the Embarcadero with the celebrated ferry tower seen in the foreground. (The opening of the bridge rendered obsolete the ferry traffic to Yerba Buena Island.) "SAN FRANCISCO–OAKLAND BAY BRIDGE" circles above.

The present Treasure Island is not shown because it is an artificial island that had not yet been completed. The next section of the bridge leads towards the Emeryville, Oakland, and Berkeley areas. Two steamships are passing the ferry tower.

In 1936 the cost of the bridge proper and its interurban car installation plus approaches was estimated at $77,200,000. It was financed entirely without taxation via the sale of 4.75% bonds, issued against protective revenues. Some

15,000 men and women labored on the bridge project, and 24 men died in its construction. Painting the bridge requires 200,000 gallons of paint—and when the job is finished, it's time to begin once again.

Origins of the Bay Bridge

Jacques Schnier, a local artist, sculptor, and designer, is the reason collectors can today enjoy this lovely coin. At the suggestion of Lee Lawrie, a sculptor member of the U.S. Commission of Fine Arts, the only design changes were the remodeling of the bear's snout and replacing the legend "E PLURIBUS UNUM" with "IN GOD WE TRUST".

Though the authorizing Act of June 26, 1936, had specified a maximum of 200,000 to be coined, only 100,000 (plus 55 assay coins) were produced (on November 4, 1936) at the San Francisco Mint. This amount was struck to discourage speculation. The San Francisco–Oakland Bay Bridge Celebration Coin Committee offered the coins for $1.50 each, with some being offered via the Clearing House Association. Others could be acquired at kiosks near the Bay Bridge entrances, so that motorists did not have to leave their vehicles. According to clients who had this experience on and from November 20, these small booths resembled newspaper stands. A large number of coins were sold after the official celebrations of November 12–14 had ended.

When sales came to a standstill in 1937, some 28,631 pieces of the minting were returned to the Mint for melting, leaving a total of 71,369 as the net mintage.

The Coin Committee Chairman Frank R. Havenner requested that the Mint place the first 200 strikings in numbered envelopes, accompanied by official documentation. The first 100 impressions of this issue—produced as normal coinage—were placed in numbered coin envelopes. Twenty-two of these specimens, numbering from the mid-50s, were never officially presented and became available. They were offered for sale with documentation in attractive Capital holders. These specimens were not struck from highly polished dies, nor is there anything special about their surface features. However, these fully original coins will grade at least MS-65 today. To assist with a dealer promotion, Schnier in 1980 autographed approximately 500 cards—for $5 each—that pictured him holding his creation. These cards have a cutout for the half dollar; they were placed in sealed hard plastic holders, accompanied by pieces grading AU-55 through MS-63. I would base acquisition on the coin's grade, plus $20 for the holder. The same applies to the promoted Elgin coin, which is housed in exactly the same sealed plastic holder.

The Bay Bridge Today

The issue can be located without much difficulty in EF-AU condition. Specimens usually reveal numismatic abuse. There is little price spread between the EF-AU and MS-64 categories, so collectors should concentrate on very attractive MS-64 pieces, if possible, unless they are purely buying for the pride of ownership. Bay Bridges grading MS-65 can now be found without much effort. The greater the eye appeal, the greater the specimen's future price performance. Long hairline scratches, slide marks and deep nicks, or ugly bag marks hurt the coin's grade and value. One major detracting mark on the bear, a primary focal area, will place a coin in the MS-64 category.

The obverse, with its granular die surface, is very vulnerable to the problems mentioned above. This is where I begin my visual inspection when attempting to purchase quality Bay Bridges for myself. The reverse is seldom affected because of its surface design, which can hide all but severe negatives. A bad hit on the ferry tower, however, can lower the grade.

Luster will range from intense satiny (not the norm) down to dull satiny. At times, the reverse will appear less lustrous than the obverse, because of die preparation and wear. However, this luster variation will not be as obvious as it is on the Albany issue.

Strike rarely presents a problem. I have at times encountered specimens with poor snout detail or steamship detail, but these problems are exceptions. The bear's right eye, as you observe the coin, will appear not strongly struck; this is characteristic for the issue. The strongest definition will appear only on the earlier strikings.

No error coinage or counterfeits have entered the marketplace.

IS YOUR BAY BRIDGE CIRCULATED OR MINT STATE?

Obverse
A metal loss will first occur on the bear's left shoulder (the right one as you examine the coin). This area is a prime target for the coin doctors.

Reverse
On this lower relief design, wear will be observed on the vertical steel bridge support (directly between the "AN" of the word "OAKLAND" and on the hills below the "O" of "OAKLAND".

Related Material
Coins were distributed in a thick cardboard holder with openings for six coins, accompanied originally by an unattached folder cover. Individual coins were wrapped in tissue paper and also enclosed in a mailing envelope. Imprinted on the envelope is "San Francisco–Oakland Bay Bridge Celebration, room 615 - 625 Market Street, San Francisco". The holder has no real value without the mailing envelope; with it, put it in the $75 to $175 range, based on its condition. The grade of the coin that accompanies the holder is what determines value.

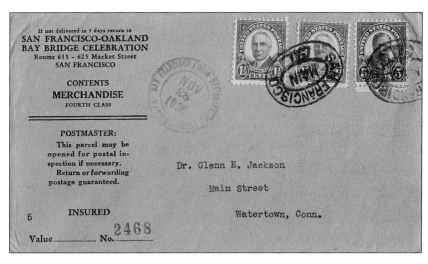

Bay Bridge mailing envelope.

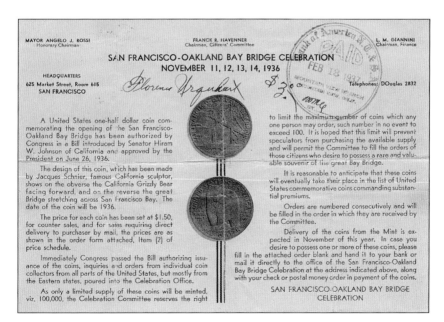

Advertisement/informational part of the subscription form
used as receipt for a Bay Bridge order.

Future Potential of the Bay Bridge Half Dollar

Population Figures

Date	Service	AU 58	MS 60	MS 62	MS 63	MS 64	MS 65	MS 66	MS 67	MS 68	MS 69
1936 S	NGC	17	1	63	200	1012	1336	560	67	10	0
1936 S	PCGS	43	21	208	776	1827	1636	775	121	9	0
1936 S	Combined	60	22	271	976	2839	2972	1335	207	19	0

There is no major price difference between grades EF-AU and MS-66, and the coin can be obtained in all these grades with little difficulty. Acquire coinage in grades MS-66 and below for the joy of collecting only. For those who would like to see their silver bear rise moderately in value, I suggest aiming for a very lustrous and eye-appealing MS-66+ specimen. I would reduce this grade's census figures by 20%. Bay Bridges are somewhat undervalued in the MS-66+ category, and I would definitely recommend acquiring a captivating specimen, if it crosses your path.

The same applies to the lofty MS-67 grade: this is also very undervalued and highly recommended, should funds permit. Price range can vary between $750 and $2,760. All is dependent on the coin's makeup, buyer, etc. I know of 16 grading inserts that were cast to various garbage containers in the past, in unsuccessful hopes of the elusive MS-68 grade. With its population of 19, MS-68 coins *would* be wonderful to own.

1936 Wisconsin Territorial Centennial

Reason for Issue:	The 100th anniversary of the establishment of the Territory of Wisconsin.
Authorization:	Act of May 15, 1936, with a maximum of 25,000 pieces.
Issued by:	Wisconsin Centennial Coin Committee
Official Sale Price:	$1.50; lots of 10 or more, $1.25 each

Production Figures

Date	Business Strikes	Assay Coins	Proofs	Melted	Net Mintage
1936	25,000	15	4?	0	25,000

Current Market Values

Date	AU 58	MS 60	MS 63	MS 64	MS 65	MS 66	MS 67	MS 68
1936	$190	$200	$230	$235	$320	$395	$800	$5,000

Designs by Benjamin Hawkins, originated by David Parsons

Obverse

A badger, the Wisconsin state animal, facing left, standing on a log. Below this log in relief is the designer's initial (H). Behind the badger are three arrows that represent the war between the settlers and the Black Hawk Indians. On the right side of the badger is an olive branch, representing the peace that paved the way for the creation of the Territory of Wisconsin. "United States of America" arcs above; "HALF DOLLAR" below. "E PLURIBUS UNUM" and "LIBERTY" are in smaller letters inside the other legends; "IN GOD WE TRUST" is wedged between the arrows and the olive branch.

Reverse

The Wisconsin Territorial seal (not reproduced exactly) and a miner's right forearm with his sleeve rolled up to the elbow, holding a pickaxe. In the background is a pile of lead ore and soil. Below this is the inscription "4TH DAY OF JULY ANNO DOMINI 1836", indicating the day when Henry Dodge, the first Governor of the Wisconsin Territory, took office. Around the border is the inscription "WISCONSIN TERRITORIAL CENTENNIAL". The date 1936 appears at the six o'clock position, between two five-pointed stars.

Origins of the Wisconsin

The original models of the Wisconsin were prepared by David Parsons, an art student at the University of Wisconsin. However, Benjamin Hawkins, a New York artist, made extensive changes in the designs and inscriptions in order to meet various Mint specifications. Thus Hawkins is credited with the finished creation and his initial appears on the coin. During July 1936, 25,000 coins were produced at the Philadelphia Mint. The additional 15 pieces were struck for assay purposes.

The Act for this issue did not limit the number of coins that could be manufactured by the Mint. However, Fred W. Harris, a coin collector who was Director of the Coinage Committee of the Wisconsin Centennial, believed the 25,000 pieces received from the Mint were sufficient. The coins were distributed at $1.50 each, plus 7 cents postage for the first piece and 2 cents for additional half dollars. As noted in a letter from L.M. Hanks, Treasurer of the Wisconsin State Historical Society, Harris was correct, since one could still purchase this issue in lots of ten or more for $1.25 per coin as late as March 7, 1945. In fact, one could acquire the coin for $3.00 plus 7 cents postage seven years after that.

The Wisconsin Today

The Wisconsin is not abundant in EF-AU condition. Specimens will usually be cleaned, have a slight metal loss from mishandling, or show some doctoring: a coin's value is dependent on the type and extent of abuse. It can be worth as much as an MS-60 coin or less than EF-AU values. The Wisconsin can be acquired with little effort in MS-60 through MS-66 condition. Collectors should look for flashy, attractive "badgers," with no ugly digs, hits, slide marks, or too many hairline scratches. Acquire for the pure joy of collecting. (This issue, as well as the York, Elgin, Roanoke, Stone Mountain, Iowa, Rhode Island [Philadelphia Mint strikings], and the San Diego [1935-S and 1936-D], have entered the marketplace in large numbers over the last eight years.) In MS-65 condition, the Wisconsin has the fifth highest population; rated MS-66, it is fourth; and rated MS-67, fifth. Luster will range from blazing satiny, to satiny, to dull satiny. Strike rarely presents a problem for the issue. Surface negatives, such as slide marks and bag marks, are attracted to the obverse badger, and the reverse forearm and surrounding fields.

To date, no error coinage or counterfeit pieces have entered the market-place.

IS YOUR WISCONSIN CIRCULATED OR MINT STATE?

Obverse

A metal loss will first occur on the badger's ribs, then shoulder: these are the primary targets for the coin doctors.

Reverse

Wear will first be noticed on the hand holding the pickaxe.

Related Material

The issue was distributed in a three-piece, as well as a plain five-piece cardboard holder with inserts for five coins. One- to two-coin orders were wrapped in

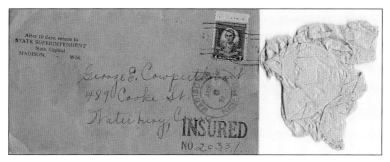

Wisconsin coin packaging material.

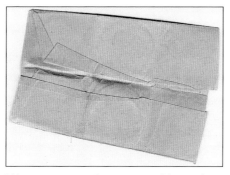

Wisconsin coin packaging material (note: there are no markings and original quality varies).

tissue paper and mailed in an envelope imprinted "L.M. Hanks, First National Bank Building, Madison, Wisconsin" or rubber-stamped: "After 10 days return to State Superintendent, State Capitol, Madison, Wis." These stamped envelopes can be valued at $50 to $75.

Wisconsin mailing envelope from 1945.

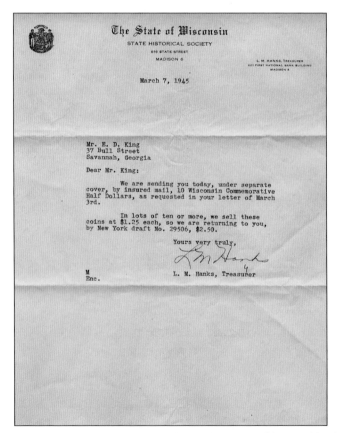

Wisconsin mailing letter that accompanied coins that were still being sold in 1945.

Future Potential of the Wisconsin Half Dollar

Population Figures

Date	Service	AU 58	MS 60	MS 62	MS 63	MS 64	MS 65	MS 66	MS 67	MS 68	MS 69
1936	NGC	1	0	18	65	641	1289	1206	373	31	0
1936	PCGS	6	0	46	307	1290	2195	1503	397	25	0
1936	Combined	7	0	64	372	1931	3484	2709	770	56	0

With population figures like these, I suggest procurement only for the joy of collecting. The coin has the fourth highest population figure in MS-65, and the third most abundant in MS-66, for an individual design. (The Iowa holds MS-66 first-place honors.) There is currently no major price spread between coins in EF-AU and MS-66 condition. During the 1989 market peak, there was a price difference of $700 between MS-64 and MS-65 coinage and $1,100 between the MS-65 and MS-66 ratings. The Wisconsin was heavily promoted in these grades during the last market heat, and pieces appear to have come out of the numismatic woodwork. When the next hot market arrives, expect the coin to be pushed. The astute can profit from this situation—but only if astute, not greedy: don't hold on too long. When the temperature begins to drop, so will this issue's value. I would reduce the census count by 30% to 35%, in grades MS-64 through MS-66. There is average future potential in the grade MS-66. The coin is somewhat undervalued in MS-67 condition. Collectors should pass on any MS-68 offering that looks ugly. The MS-68 has sold for $3,700 to $29,900 depending on the coin, it's buyer, etc.

1936 York County, Maine, Tercentenary

Reason for Issue:	The 300th anniversary of the founding of York County, Maine.
Authorization:	Act of June 26, 1936, with a maximum of 30,000 pieces.
Issued by:	York County Tercentenary Commemorative Coin Commission
Official Sale Price:	$1.50 local; $1.65 out of state.

Production Figures

Date	Business Strikes	Assay Coins	Proofs	Melted	Net Mintage
1936	25,000	15	4?	0	25,000

Current Market Values

Date	AU-58	MS-60	MS-63	MS-64	MS-65	MS-66	MS-67	MS-68
1936	$200	$210	$220	$265	$300	$385	$460	$2,500+

Designs by Walter H. Rich

Obverse

A stockade representing Brown's Garrison, once located on the Saco River at approximately the site of the present-day city of Saco, Maine. In the foreground are four sentries, one mounted. Seen above the stockade is the rising sun, with the word "LIBERTY" resting on the rays; "E PLURIBUS UNUM" is below the stockade; "United States of America" and "Half Dollar" form the border. Located below the "IBUS" in "Pluribus" are the designer's initials (WHR).

Reverse
The seal of York County, Maine, composed of a cross on a shield. This is one of two U.S. coins that depict a cross as part of the design (the other is the 1934 Maryland Tercentenary issue). In its upper quarter is a pine tree, symbolizing the state of Maine. The anniversary dates are at the sides of the shield, with "In God We Trust" in curved letters at the lower inner border; around the outer border is the inscription "York County First County in Maine", with decorative stars.

Origins of the York
The Philadelphia Mint produced 25,000 coins plus 15 assay pieces during August 1936. This issue was distributed by the York County Tercentenary Commemorative Coin Commission, Saco, Maine.

By not requesting the maximum 30,000 pieces permitted by the Act, the Coin Commission was unable to obtain the additional 5,000 Yorks. It was explained to the Commission that it had to secure the full authorization at one time—but not less than 25,000 coins. Any difference would be their loss. Two-fifths of this issue was put aside for the residents of York County and of Maine at $1.50 per coin. However, this amount had to be increased, since the demand was greater than the allotted supply. All out-of-state orders required an extra 15 cents to cover handling and shipping charges. When sales came to a halt, approximately 18,500 of this issue had been sold. Instead of returning the remaining coins to the Mint, the Coin Commission vaulted and later offered them for sale, in the late 1950s, in a half-roll minimum (10 coins) for $15.50.

The York Today
This coin is not plentiful in EF-AU condition. Coins will usually be cleaned, lightly mishandled, or display some form of doctoring. An example may have the value of an MS-60 coin or an EF-AU specimen: all is determined upon the kind and extent of mistreatment. There is currently a small value spread between coins grading MS-60 through MS-66. If funds are available, collectors should aim for the highest grade. The York can be obtained easily in grades MS-60 through MS-67; acquire only for the joy of collecting.

Luster will range from blazing satiny, to satiny, to dull satiny. Strike will not cause a problem with this issue. Numismatic negatives such as slide marks and bag marks will especially attack the reverse seal of York County, the primary focal point, and the surrounding fields. The obverse stockade and the field below is the primary focus.

No error coinage or counterfeits have entered the marketplace.

Is Your York Circulated or Mint State?

Obverse
Wear will first develop on the mounted sentry and right section of the stockade.

Reverse
A metal loss will first occur on the pine tree in the upper left quarter of the symbolic design. This seal is a target area for the coin doctors.

Related Material
The issue was distributed in a paper holder depicting on the front cover black and white sketches of Brown's Garrison and the York National Bank of Saco.

Page two, or the inner front cover, states the following:

> In the early days of York County probably most transactions were carried on by barter and it was not until 1803 that the business of the county had become complex enough to require a bank. It was then one hundred and thirty three years ago that our bank was chartered and as York County is the "First County of Maine" so The York National Bank is the "First Bank in Maine." On the day of its opening and until 1831, all the entries were made by a stocky gentleman with a serene and self confident countenance wearing long black silk stockings, short trousers, shoes with large silver buckles, and a stock, predecessor of the collar. He took great pride in the fact that he served for a brief period for General Washington as his clerk.
>
> There are many other interesting historical facts in the records of the bank and we take particular pride in the fact that we have stood the test of time and are an active, strong bank today servicing the entirely changed requirements of the public.
>
> —YORK NATIONAL BANK

Page three has slots for five coins; the back cover is blank. Within the accompanying mailer a tissue paper insert stated:

> We thank you for your interest in our commemorative Half Dollar, and extend to you the hospitality of York County, Maine.
>
> —York County Commemorative Coin Commission.

Envelopes were imprinted "York County Tercentenary, Commemorative Coin Commission, York National Bank, Saco, Maine" and "After 5 days, return to Clerk of Courts, Alfred, Maine". On the back of some envelopes was a red-orange paper seal. The envelope and mailer are worth between $50 and $125, depending on condition; with tissue insert, $50 to $150.

York coin holder folder—outside.

The first 100 Yorks minted were mounted in the lower right corner cutout of an attractive map of "Olde York County Maine." Below the coin and outside the map border was printed: "This Coin is no. ___ of the Issue". I do not know when or by whom the coin striking number was written; I have examined sealed frames that did not indicate a number. Any person can write a number on the frame's paper backing. Framed under glass, these strikings, which possess no proof-like or special Mint-produced surface, were presented to those who helped make the Tercentenary celebration a success in their communities. It was referred to as a token (of appreciation) by Ralph W. Hawkes, Secretary and Treasurer of the York County Tercentenary Commemorative Coin Commission. In the early 1980s, a Massachusetts dealer

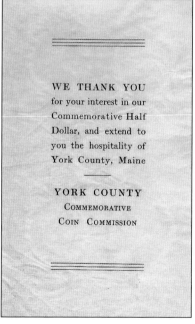

WE THANK YOU
for your interest in our
Commemorative Half
Dollar, and extend to
you the hospitality of
York County, Maine

YORK COUNTY
COMMEMORATIVE
COIN COMMISSION

York coin holder folder insert.

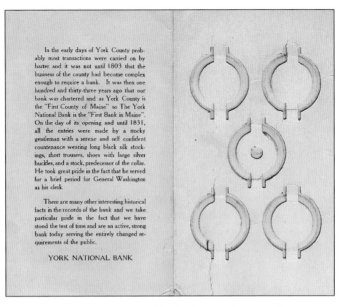

In the early days of York County probably most transactions were carried on by barter and it was not until 1803 that the business of the county had become complex enough to require a bank. It was then one hundred and thirty-three years ago that our bank was chartered and as York County is the "First County of Maine" so The York National Bank is the "First Bank in Maine". On the day of its opening and until 1831, all the entries were made by a stocky gentleman with a serene and self confident countenance wearing long black silk stockings, short trousers, shoes with large silver buckles, and a stock, predecessor of the collar. He took great pride in the fact that he served for a brief period for General Washington as his clerk.

There are many other interesting historical facts in the records of the bank and we take particular pride in the fact that we have stood the test of time and are an active, strong bank today serving the entirely changed requirements of the public.

YORK NATIONAL BANK

York coin holder folder—inside.

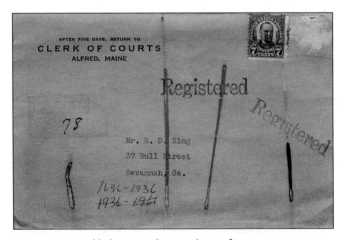

AFTER FIVE DAYS, RETURN TO
CLERK OF COURTS
ALFRED, MAINE

Registered

Registered

78

Mr. E. D. King
37 Bull Street
Savannah, Ga.

1636-1936
1936-1961

York coin mailing envelope—front.

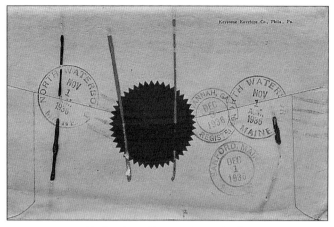

York coin mailing envelope—back.

York County commemorative display frame.

acquired the item below, with its beautifully colored toned York (lower right) in a frame, at a flea market for $75. He turned down my $2,500 offer. These coins have sold in the past in the $2,500 to $4,000 range. Collectors should beware of switched coins in these frames, should the original backing seem to have been tampered with.

Future Potential of the York Half Dollar

Population Figures

Date	Service	AU 58	MS 60	MS 62	MS 63	MS 64	MS 65	MS 66	MS 67	MS 68	MS 69
1936	NGC	1	1	13	64	434	1040	1235	386	31	0
1936	PCGS	2	2	58	364	1171	1866	1449	509	22	0
1936	Combined	3	3	71	428	1605	2906	2684	895	53	0

With census figures as indicated, a collector should simply buy this issue because you like it and want to own it. The York is now the fifth most encapsulated 1892–1954 commemorative half dollar in MS-65 condition, and second to the Norfolk and third to the Iowa when rated MS-66. It is fourth highest rated MS-67 and MS-68. There is currently no major price spread between the EF-AU and MS-66 classifications. During the last hot market of 1989, there was an approximate $800 difference between the MS-64, MS-65, and MS-66 grades. I would lower the census by 27%–31% for these levels. Unfortunately, the York coins have come out in droves from the numismatic woodwork, so there is only fair to average potential in all grades. Nonetheless, expect the issue to be promoted again in the future. Gains can be made by the astute, as long as they don't hold their hoard of Yorks too long or become greedy, awaiting the peak. Where will the buyers be for this very common issue, at these inflated population levels, should the market begin to slip or start losing some momentum? The same applies to other similar coins, such as the Iowa, San Diego, Wisconsin, Cleveland, etc. Strictly graded MS-67 coins are somewhat undervalued. Yorks are undervalued in MS-68 condition, but please remember—as I have said throughout this book—that value is dependent on the coin's eye appeal and its total makeup. Captivating pieces will bring much more than an unimpressive looking coin. As of this writing, values range from $1,100 to $3,200.

1937 Battle of Antietam

Reason for Issue:	To commemorate the 75th anniversary of the Battle of Antietam on September 17, 1862. This was the bloodiest one-day battle of the Civil War; 25,000 soldiers lost their lives near Sharpsburg, Maryland.
Authorization:	Act of June 24, 1937, with a maximum of 50,000 pieces.
Issued by:	Washington County Historical Society
Official Sale Price:	$1.65

Production Figures

Date	Business Strikes	Assay Coins	Proofs	Melted	Net Mintage
1937	50,000	28	4?	32,000	18,000

Current Market Values

Date	AU-58	MS-60	MS-63	MS-64	MS-65	MS-66	MS-67
1937	$625	$680	$700	$730	$950	$1,025	$1,400+

Designs by William Marks Simpson

Obverse

The profiles of General George B. McClellan, the Union Army's exceptional organizer and trainer of troops, and the distinguished Confederate General Robert E. Lee, in uniform, facing left. Below their busts are their ranks and names.

389

"United States of America" arcs above; "Half Dollar" below. "In God We Trust" is under McClellan's chin; "Liberty" is behind Lee's neck. To the right of the words "Half Dollar" are three stars representing Lee's rank as General in the Confederate Army; to the left are two stars representing McClellan's rank as Major General in the Union Army. Near Lee's shoulder and partly in the field are the designer's initials (WMS), in monogram and in relief.

Reverse

Burnside Bridge over Antietam Creek. It was constructed in 1836 by John Weaver at a cost of $2,300. The fury of the Battle of Antietam centered on the bridge; it was later named after General Burnside of the Union Army. This bridge was the central point for the Union troops' flanking attack on the southern edge of Sharpsburg. When Burnside's men finally crossed the bridge (with its 12-foot-wide road bed) the important high ground looking down on the town was eventually won. Below the bridge in small letters is: "The Burnside Bridge, September 17 1862". At the left of the bridge is a group of trees; a single tree is to the right. Above the trees is "E Pluribus Unum". Encircling the border in large letters interspersed by small triangles is the inscription "Seventy Fifth Anniversary Battle of Antietam". At the six o'clock position is the date 1937.

Origins of the Antietam

A leaflet that contained a description of the Antietam commemorative half dollar, a short history of the battle, and an application for purchasing the coins at $1.65 each, was distributed by the Washington County Historical Society of Hagerstown, Maryland. Park W. T. Loy, Chairman of the Society and Secretary of the United States Antietam Celebration Commission, believed the issue was appropriate because of the worldwide fame of General Lee and the honored place of General McClellan in U.S. history.

It was the objective of the sponsoring agency to have the Antietam commemorative pass directly into the hands of interested citizens and private collectors, thereby avoiding the possibility of speculation. Anticipating that the half dollar would be ready for distribution on or before August 1, 1937, the Historical Society was disappointed when the 50,028 half dollars were not produced at the Philadelphia Mint until some 10 days later. The first piece struck was given to President Roosevelt on August 12, according to *The Washington Post*.

Although, as noted, the Washington County Historical Society wanted to avoid the possibility of speculation, any individual could purchase whatever quantity of the Antietam desired, as long as the correct payment was enclosed. Unfortunately, it was just at this time that the sharp decline in the market for commemoratives became evident. The Antietam issue was not sold out; 32,000 pieces were returned to the Mint for melting, leaving us with a total mintage of only 18,000 coins.

The Congressional Act that authorized the Antietam striking has the distinction of being the only such Act approved in 1937 for which there is an issue dated 1937 and produced in that year. (The Roanoke commemorative is also dated 1937, but it was authorized on June 24, 1936.)

The Antietam Today

Since few Antietams were used as pocket pieces, collectors of such circulated coins will have a difficult time obtaining them. This accounts for the coin's prices in AU-58 condition. Issues that are fully lustrous, but have slight friction on the high points, are usually offered as MS-65 (if mark free). These are known as "FLS" on dealer computer systems, or fully lustrous sliders (AU-58). A good profit can be made with these, and at bargain prices. Whizzed coins are worth less: collectors should carefully examine the portraits for whizzing, and avoid affected coins unless the price is very right.

Luster will range from flashy or intense satiny (desirable), to the dull satiny (DS). It is best to avoid examples of the latter, unless it is offered at a real bargain price. There is no way to make this kind of surface naturally alive or eye-appealing. Dipping, etc., will not achieve the desired result, but instead will create an unnatural shiny metal disk: the film on the coin's surface—obverse and/or reverse—cannot be removed without making it look unnatural. The end result is a lowering of the coin's grade and value. Nevertheless, there are those who prefer this condition to a dull Antietam.

Strike seldom, if ever, will affect the grade-value. Remember that an Antietam's primary focal areas should show no severe imperfections. This applies especially to the faces of Lee and McClellan. Only a few barely noticeable marks can be present if the coin is to be labeled MS-65. This grade also requires an original luster, a strong strike, and no fine hairlines. Neither the Generals nor the bridge should show battle scars. Be concerned with the location and size of numismatic negatives on both sides of the coin, and their influence on the coin's seductiveness.

To date, no error coinage has entered the marketplace.

Detecting Counterfeits

There are counterfeits of this issue. Such pieces will have a dull grayish look or color. Surfaces will appear as if they were submerged in a tarnish-removing solution for an extended length of time, or just too many times, creating that washed-out lustrous look.

When I examine a questionable Antietam commemorative half dollar, the first area I target is the word "ANNIVERSARY", on the reverse. Should there be a raised metal line extending through the letters "ERSAR", I know immediately that the coin is counterfeit. On the obverse, a similar raised metal line will be seen piercing the letters "TES" of "STATES", diagonally to the eight o'clock position of Lee's cheek and on the lower shaft of the letter "D" in "UNITED". On the reverse, small depressions can also be noted above the "E" of "THE" and the "R" of "BURNSIDE" above the creek, as well as near the center, on the right arch of the bridge.

Is Your Antietam Circulated or Mint State?

Obverse

This issue will show a trace of wear on the cheekbone of General Lee: look for possible crisscross scratches. The portraits of Lee and McClellan are a primary target for the whizzing specialists; beware of the "aluminum-like" appearance here.

Reverse

Wear will first be observed on the leaves in the upper central area of the single tree in front of the bridge. Simply draw a mental line across from the dot located to the right of the letter "M" in "Unum" to find the crucial area.

Related Material

The coin was distributed in a coin mailer manufactured by J. N. Spies of Watertown, New York. The front page is imprinted with: "75th Anniversary of the Battle of Antietam Commemorative Half-Dollar", as well as the sponsor and the names of the sponsor's coin committee. Pages 2 and 4 are blank; page 3 is the five-coin insert. Value the holder alone at $75 to $125; with mailing envelope, $125 to $250, depending on condition.

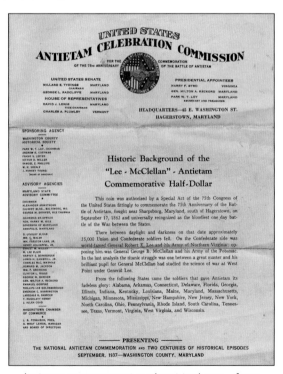

Antietam commemorative advertising letter—front.

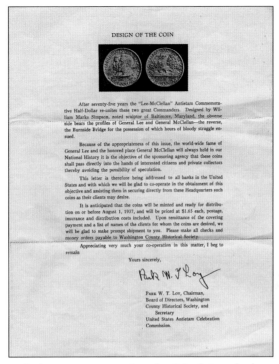

DESIGN OF THE COIN

After seventy-five years the "Lee-McClellan" Antietam Commemorative Half-Dollar re-unites these two great Commanders. Designed by William Marks Simpson, noted sculptor of Baltimore, Maryland, the obverse side bears the profiles of General Lee and General McClellan—the reverse, the Burnside Bridge for the possession of which hours of bloody struggle ensued.

Because of the appropriateness of this issue, the world-wide fame of General Lee and the honored place General McClellan will always hold in our National History it is the objective of the sponsoring agency that these coins shall pass directly into the hands of interested citizens and private collectors thereby avoiding the possibility of speculation.

This letter is therefore being addressed to all banks in the United States and with which we will be glad to co-operate in the obtainment of this objective and assisting them in securing directly from these Headquarters such coins as their clients may desire.

It is anticipated that the coins will be minted and ready for distribution on or before August 1, 1937, and will be priced at $1.65 each, postage, insurance and distribution costs included. Upon remittance of the covering payment and a list of names of the clients for whom the coins are desired, we will be glad to make prompt shipment to you. Please make all checks and money orders payable to Washington County Historical Society.

Appreciating very much your co-operation in this matter, I beg to remain

Yours sincerely,

Park W. T. Loy, Chairman,
Board of Directors, Washington
County Historical Society, and
Secretary
United States Antietam Celebration
Commission.

Antietam commemorative advertising letter—back.

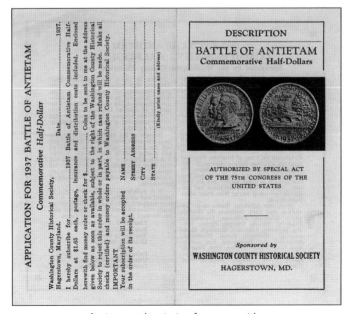

DESCRIPTION

BATTLE OF ANTIETAM
Commemorative Half-Dollars

AUTHORIZED BY SPECIAL ACT
OF THE 75TH CONGRESS OF THE
UNITED STATES

Sponsored by
WASHINGTON COUNTY HISTORICAL SOCIETY
HAGERSTOWN, MD.

APPLICATION FOR 1937 BATTLE OF ANTIETAM
Commemorative Half-Dollar

Washington County Historical Society,   Date_____, 1937.
Hagerstown, Maryland.

I hereby subscribe for_____1937 Battle of Antietam Commemorative Half-Dollars at $1.65 each, postage, insurance and distribution costs included. Enclosed herewith find money order or check for $_____. Coins to be sent to me at the address given below as soon as available, subject to the right of the Washington County Historical Society to reject this order in whole or in part, in which case refund will be made. Make all checks (certified) and money orders payable to Washington County Historical Society.

IMPORTANT
Your subscription will be accepted in the order of its receipt.

NAME_____
STREET ADDRESS_____
CITY_____
STATE_____
(Kindly print name and address)

Antietam subscription form—outside.

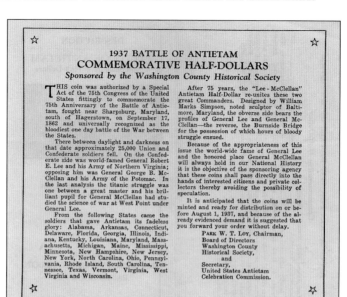

1937 BATTLE OF ANTIETAM
COMMEMORATIVE HALF-DOLLARS
Sponsored by the Washington County Historical Society

THIS coin was authorized by a Special Act of the 75th Congress of the United States fittingly to commemorate the 75th Anniversary of the Battle of Antietam, fought near Sharpsburg, Maryland, south of Hagerstown, on September 17, 1862 and universally recognized as the bloodiest one day battle of the War between the States.

There between daylight and darkness on that date approximately 25,000 Union and Confederate soldiers fell. On the Confederate side was world-famed General Robert E. Lee and his Army of Northern Virginia; opposing him was General George B. McClellan and his Army of the Potomac. In the last analysis the titanic struggle was one between a great master and his brilliant pupil for General McClellan had studied the science of war at West Point under General Lee.

From the following States came the soldiers that gave Antietam its fadeless glory: Alabama, Arkansas, Connecticut, Delaware, Florida, Georgia, Illinois, Indiana, Kentucky, Louisiana, Maryland, Massachusetts, Michigan, Maine, Mississippi, Minnesota, New Hampshire, New Jersey, New York, North Carolina, Ohio, Pennsylvania, Rhode Island, South Carolina, Tennessee, Texas, Vermont, Virginia, West Virginia and Wisconsin.

After 75 years, the "Lee-McClellan" Antietam Half-Dollar re-unites these two great Commanders. Designed by William Marks Simpson, noted sculptor of Baltimore, Maryland, the obverse side bears the profiles of General Lee and General McClellan—the reverse, the Burnside Bridge for the possession of which hours of bloody struggle ensued.

Because of the appropriateness of this issue the world-wide fame of General Lee and the honored place General McClellan will always hold in our National History it is the objective of the sponsoring agency that these coins shall pass directly into the hands of interested citizens and private collectors thereby avoiding the possibility of speculation.

It is anticipated that the coins will be minted and ready for distribution on or before August 1, 1937, and because of the already evidenced demand it is suggested that you forward your order without delay.

PARK W. T. LOY, Chairman,
Board of Directors
Washington County
Historical Society,
and
Secretary,
United States Antietam
Celebration Commission.

Antietam subscription form—inside.

Antietam mailing envelope.

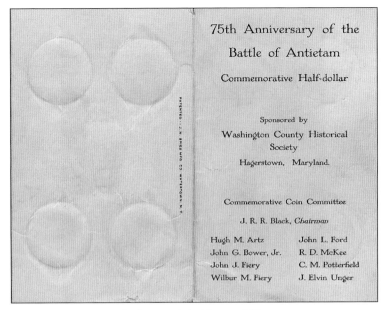

75th Anniversary of the

Battle of Antietam

Commemorative Half-dollar

Sponsored by

Washington County Historical
Society

Hagerstown, Maryland.

Commemorative Coin Committee

J. R. R. Black, *Chairman*

Hugh M. Artz	John L. Ford
John G. Bower, Jr.	R. D. McKee
John J. Fiery	C. M. Potterfield
Wilbur M. Fiery	J. Elvin Unger

Antietam coin holder—outside.

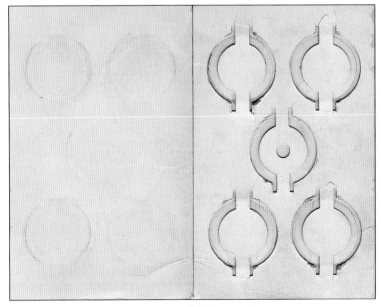

Antietam coin holder—inside.

Antietam commemorative multi-fold brochure—outside.

Antietam commemorative multi-fold brochure—inside.

Future Potential of the Antietam Half Dollar

Population Figures

Date	Service	AU 58	MS 60	MS 62	MS 63	MS 64	MS 65	MS 66	MS 67	MS 68	MS 69
1937	NGC	4	5	24	101	509	941	702	171	16	2
1937	PCGS	10	2	50	358	1108	1493	1191	237	14	0
1937	Combined	14	7	74	459	1617	2434	1893	408	30	2

Few Antietams saw actual circulation. Coins offered in this grade are usually cleaned or have whizzed surfaces. There is no major price spread between coins in EF-AU and MS-65 condition. Even if the population deductions (an estimated 30% in grades MS-64 and MS-65; 22% in MS-66) were right on the money—because of resubmissions and grading label throwaways—the issue must be classified as common in these grades. The slabbing census now makes this quite apparent. Collectors should buy these ratings only for the joy of collecting. However, continuous demand for the MS-66 coin will make its values rise.

At present, the MS-67 specimen offers real future potential. And who would not love to own one of those MS-68 pieces? Should you be able to afford this coin, it is highly recommended. Prices have ranged between $5,750 and $19,550. Personally, I thought the latter coin was a bit too dark, but its owner thought it was fantastic—and that's what counts.

Reason for Issue:	To commemorate the 350th anniversary of the founding of the "Lost Colony" on Roanoke Island, North Carolina, and the birth of Virginia Dare, the first child of English parents born on the American continent.
Authorization:	Act of June 24, 1936, with a 25,000-piece minimum and an unlimited maximum.
Issued by:	Roanoke Colony Memorial Association
Official Sale Price:	$1.65

Production Figures

Date	Business Strikes	Assay Coins	Proofs	Melted	Net Mintage
1937	50,000	30	4?	21,000	29,000

Current Market Values

Date	AU-58	MS-60	MS-63	MS-64	MS-65	MS-66	MS-67
1937	$200	$215	230	$240	$350	$400	$675

Designs by William Marks Simpson

Obverse

Facing left, the bust of Sir Walter Raleigh, the explorer, poet and historian. Raleigh is wearing a ruffled collar, an earring, and a hat with a showy feather. Below his shoulder is his name; in relief is the artist's monogram (WMS).

"United States of America" arcs above; "Half Dollar" below. "E Pluribus Unum" and "Liberty" form an inner border with "Sir Walter Raleigh". The date 1937 is in the lower left field.

Reverse

Eleanor Dare, dressed in a costume of her time, holds Virginia Dare in her arms. Virginia is the very first—defined—infant depicted on U.S. coinage. (The infant, who is virtually faceless, portrayed on the 1936 Elgin issue is "suggested," not "defined.") In the right and left center fields are two English sailing ships. Around the outer border are the words "The Colonization of Roanoke Island North Carolina". At the six o'clock position are the commemorative dates, 1587–1937. Virginia Dare was the first Christian born in America, on August 18, 1587.

The motto "In God We Trust" is in the lower left field; the inscription "The Birth of Virginia Dare" is located at the sides of her mother.

Origins of the Roanoke

The Philadelphia Mint produced 25,000 Roanoke half dollars plus 15 assay pieces in January 1937. Since the Act stated that "not less than twenty-five thousand silver 50 cent pieces shall be coined," an additional 25,000 plus 15 assay coins were struck in June, just days before the coinage rights expired on July 1, 1937. This, by the way, was the first time that a specific expiration date was stated in an Act irrespective of the year of coining. Also the Roanoke was the only issue authorized in 1936 that was minted in 1937 and displays the actual year of minting.

The Roanoke started out as one of those postdated "cousins," like the Delaware and New Rochelle issues, authorized in 1936, but coined in 1937. These two coins, however, carried the date 1938, in anticipation of an anniversary to occur in that year. Fortunately, they are the only two issues that fell into this chronological mess.

However, would you believe that the man commemorated on this issue had his name spelled incorrectly? Despite the documentary evidence cited by the designer, William Marks Simpson, that Sir Walter used only one spelling from June 9, 1584, until his death in 1618, that being "Ralegh," the U.S. Commission of Fine Arts was simply unwilling to yield. The models were approved only after the artist inserted the "i" in the name Raleigh.

The Roanoke Colony Memorial Association sold these coins for $1.65 each ($1.50 each plus 15 cents handling). Only 29,000 coins were sold, and after an almost total halt in interest, it was decided to return the balance of 21,000 coins to the Mint to be reincarnated into other coinage.

The Roanoke Today

The limited number of specimens in the EF-AU category for the most part have received some form of numismatic abuse.

Concerning this issue's luster, both obverse and reverse surfaces will range from proof-like (early presentation strikings), to semi-proof-like, to brilliant, to satiny, and to dull satiny. Needless to say (for this issue), the flashier the better. A collector's decision to purchase should also be based on the number of bag marks, cuts, nicks, scratches, abrasions, and any other numismatic negatives present.

Strike seldom presents a problem. On occasion, weakness can be observed on Raleigh's hat brim and ear, as well as the head of Eleanor Dare. Numismatic negatives are attracted to the primary focal areas such as the obverse portrait and reverse mid- to lower section of Eleanor Dare's long skirt.

In my opinion, brilliant proofs or satin finish proofs of this issue do not exist. The first example is nothing more than a bewitching early-struck Roanoke with proof-like surfaces. It possesses a very sharp strike without any field die polishing marks. Somewhere along the way, a die was re-polished. Its fields will display proof-like surfaces, accompanied by die polishing marks. However, it will not be equal in strike when compared with these early-struck pieces.

The so-called satin finish proof is nothing more than a captivating, early-struck specimen, of high grade, with a strong strike and angelically protected surfaces. Both are worth much more than an average MS-65 or higher graded specimen, based on their appearance and numismatic charm.

The only error coinage that has surfaced to date is a piece that shows no reeding and has wider rims. This sold for $3,500 in 1988 and has not surfaced since. Counterfeit pieces are not known.

Is Your Roanoke Circulated or Mint State?

Obverse
Wear will first occur on the brim of Raleigh's hat, as well as his cheekbone: both are prime target areas for the coin doctors.

Reverse
A metal loss will first be noticed on the head and upper left arm of Eleanor Dare, as well as on the length of her skirt covering her left hip down to her knee. That is directly above the 9 in the date 1937. This is also the prime doctoring area.

Related Material
The Roanoke was distributed in a thick paper holder, which pictures the coin's obverse and reverse and the dates 1587–1937 on the front cover; it also features a short history of the first English settlements in America and a description of the coin on the inner cover. Inserts for the placement of five coins are on the back inner cover.

The light tan mailing envelopes were imprinted with: "Roanoke Colony Memorial Association of Manteo, Manteo, N.C." The words "value ____ and no.____" are located in the lower left corner. A dab of dark red sealing wax was applied to the back flap. The holder can be valued at $75 to $125; with original mailing envelope, $175 to $275.

Future Potential of the Roanoke Half Dollar

Population Figures

Date	Service	AU 58	MS 60	MS 62	MS 63	MS 64	MS 65	MS 66	MS 67	MS 68	MS 69
1937	NGC	0	2	14	88	731	1459	933	256	27	0
1937	PCGS	5	0	61	380	1677	34	1137	269	12	0
1937	Com-bined	5	2	75	468	2408	1493	2070	525	39	0

Date	Service	PL 58	PL 60	PL 62	PL 63	PL 64	PL 65	PL 66	PL 67	PL 68	PL 69
1937	NGC	0	0	0	2	19	34	9	2	0	0

This coin has to be considered common. At present, there is not much price spread between grades EF-AU and MS-66. Up to grade MS-66, collectors should acquire only for the pride of ownership. The past dollar variance between the MS-64 and MS-65 ratings was $550. Between MS-65 and the MS-66 classification, there was once a $1,400 difference, but that won't happen again. This issue, like the Elgin, Iowa, and San Diego, appears to have emerged from the numismatic woodwork in droves. I would reduce the census figures in grades MS-64 through MS-66 between 18% and 24% and see fair to average potential in these grades.

In MS-66 condition, Roanoke population figures are high for the rating. Nonetheless, there was only one year of production. This is a grade desired by many who could not afford or chose not to spend the required $2,300 during the May 1989 high. Promotion and demand should offer this grade at least average future potential. The lofty MS-67 specimen boasts the sixth highest population in MS-67 condition. Despite this, there is very good potential here and in MS-68 condition. During the last market heat, bid was at $5,000, although the census was much lower. Historical repetition doesn't appear likely—but you can bet the issue will be promoted. Pieces rated MS-67 have sold for between $720 and $2,900. Rated MS-68, they have sold for between $2,250 and $46,000. As always, the price is dependent on the coin's makeup, the chance for an upgrade, and the buyer. At times, I wonder if the buyer has a client's open checkbook or there is a hallucinogenic "make me bid more" substance on the relevant catalogue page. Some of these prices could have been paid by a registry set buyer or by someone who wanted to assemble the highest graded set or envisioned an MS-69 grade, and went all out to own the coin. Collectors should remember: one procurement does not mean that all coins of the same grade are almost equal in value.

Reason for Issue:	To commemorate the 250th anniversary of the founding and settlement of New Rochelle, New York.
Authorization:	Act of May 5, 1936, with a maximum of 25,000 pieces.
Issued by:	New Rochelle Commemorative Coin Committee
Official Sale Price:	$2; $2:18 by mail; 5 pieces for $10.27

Production Figures

Date	Business Strikes	Assay Coins	Proofs	Melted	Net Mintage
1938	25,000	15	4–10?	9,749	15,251

Current Market Values

Date	AU-58	MS-60	MS-63	MS-64	MS-65	MS-66	MS-67
1938	$400	$430	$440	$465	$500	$780	$1,300

Designs by Gertrude K. Lathrop

Obverse

John Pell, Lord of Pelham Manor, dressed in the style of his period, holding a protesting "fatt calfe" on a rope.

When the French Huguenots purchased 6,000 acres of land in 1688 from John Pell, various provisions concerning the transfer of title were agreed upon. One such consideration required that the new inhabitants deliver to the lord, his heirs and assigns one fatted calf yearly every June 24, the Festival of St. John the Baptist, forever, if demanded. Thus, the calf.

Around the coin's upper border is the inscription "SETTLED 1688 INCORPORATED 1899"; around the lower border is "NEW ROCHELLE NEW YORK". In the lower right field, opposite the "Y" in "YORK" in relief are the designer's initials (GKL). Gertrude K. Lathrop also designed the Albany commemorative half dollar.

Reverse

A fleur-de-lis, symbolic of France; it also appears on the coat-of-arms of La Rochelle, France, in the area from which the Huguenots came. It is also a quarter part of the shield of the city of New Rochelle. Above the denomination in the lower field is the date 1938. "E PLURIBUS UNUM", "LIBERTY", and "IN GOD WE TRUST" surround the fleur-de-lis. "UNITED STATES OF AMERICA" arcs above; "HALF DOLLAR" below.

Origins of the New Rochelle

On March 12, 1937, the Treasury Department received $300 to make dies for the issue. Three weeks later, $12,500 was forwarded to pay for the 25,000 coins to be minted.

In April 1937 the Philadelphia Mint struck 25,000 New Rochelle commemorative 50-cent pieces, the maximum amount permitted by the authorizing Act, plus 15 coins for assay purposes. The Act further stated that the date 1938 must appear on this issue, regardless of the year in which the coin was minted. This issue was authorized in 1936, produced in 1937, and dated 1938, for the 250th anniversary celebration of a local event that began on June 10, 1938, and lasted 10 days. Coins were sold at $2 each through the mail by the New Rochelle Commemorative Coin Committee. The very first coin created was given to Committee Chairman Pitt M. Skipton; the second piece struck was sent to President Roosevelt. Coins three through eight were sent to the U.S. Ambassador to France, the Mayor of La Rochelle, the Governor of New York, the Consul-General of the French Consulate in New York City, New Rochelle Mayor Harry Scott, and William Dewey of the American Numismatic Association. The six people in charge of packaging were instructed by Skipton on the proper way to handle coins and to cull heavily scratched or marred pieces. Only two out of 4,859 mail orders were returned for exchange. Coins were also sold through banks and other distribution locations. When sales came to a standstill, some members of the Westchester County Coin Club (WCCC)—of which I'm a member—purchased hundreds of coins at face value, according to Skipton.

Unfortunately, this issue was not completely sold out, and 9,749 pieces were returned to the Mint and destroyed, leaving a total mintage of 15,251 pieces (the original request was for an authorization of 20,000 coins). The Committee's Executive Secretary was Pitt Skipton's wife, Amy; her book, *One Fatt Calfe*, was published by the Committee and tells the story of the coin.

The New Rochelle Today

Most New Rochelles offered at circulated prices—and there are not many—have received some form of abuse, such as light cleaning, polishing, or whizzing, especially the reverse fleur-de-lis. Luster will range from proof-like, to semi-proof-like, to brilliant frosty. Strike will rarely present a problem. Surface negatives such as slide marks, hairline scratches, bag marks, and reed marks gravitate toward the fatt calfe and fleur-de-lis, the primary focal areas. These negatives lower a coin's grade, as do field abrasions.

Fifty pieces were struck on proof planchets, receiving one blow from the press. They possess deep proof-like surfaces and a strong strike. The Numismatic Guaranty Corporation (NGC) in the past labeled one such coin "specimen," but no longer uses that designation. Not all such New Rochelle strikings are presentation coins, and may display a lack of contrast between the main designs. One genuine matte proof came from the estate of John Ray Sinnock, by way of lot 2056 at the 1962 American Numismatic Association Convention auction. NGC has encapsulated this specimen PF-61. The New Rochelle is the last U.S. coin to bear dentils (or denticles), or what resembles a beaded border. It was produced after such features were removed from the circulation denominations.

To date, no error coinage or counterfeit examples have entered the numismatic scene.

IS YOUR NEW ROCHELLE CIRCULATED OR MINT STATE?

Obverse

Wear will first be seen on the hip of the "fatt calfe". Areas of graininess, coarseness, or light striking can be seen on the hip and should not be mistaken for wear. Examine coins for crisscross scratches and a difference in metal texture.

Reverse

Metal loss will begin on the main vein of the central petal and the left edge of the flower. Because of die wear, light strike, or surface graininess or coarseness, this area can look worn. Again, examine for wear: this location is a prime target for the whizzing merchants.

Related Material

The special 50 proof-like coins were presented to various dignitaries, members of the Coin Committee, and selected members of the WCCC, in small dark red boxes with an inner red velvet coin slot for the specimen. These coins were accompanied by a popular sterling silver medal that depicted the city seal, the words "250th Anniversary", the dates 1688–1938, and the city incorporation date, 1899. The reverse informs the beholder that it was presented to the WCCC, by the 250th Anniversary Committee with the date June 1938. The underside of the gold paper box that housed this medal is imprinted with italic

 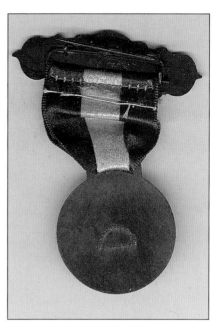

Whitehead & Hoag guest medal—front and back.

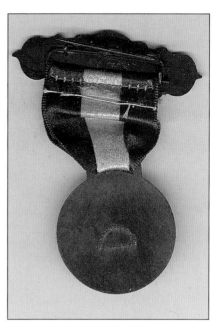

Whitehead & Hoag guest medal card—back.

type: "In recognition that the idea of a New Rochelle Half Dollar originated with the Westchester County Coin Club, New Rochelle, NY, October 18th, 1938." The medal was said to have been made by Tiffany & Company, but without their famous hallmark; it can be valued at $300 to $450. There are a few error medals with the Latin word under the seal misspelled "NUMQUAM" instead of "NUNQUAM". I haven't seen one since 1970.

There is also a badge depicting the obverse coin design with a red, white and blue ribbon and the word "Guest" on the upper plate ($425). Another badge has a red, white and blue ribbon, gold printed with "250th Anniversary, New Rochelle June 12th–18th, 1938" worn by the General Committee ($275).

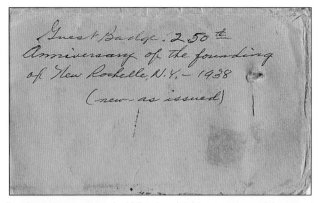

Envelope that contained a Whitehead & Hoag guest medal on card.

Whitehead & Hoag General Committee ribbon—front and back.

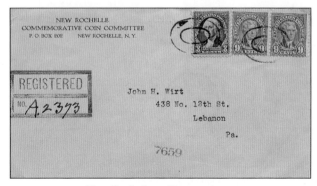

New Rochelle mailing envelope.

YOUR OWN
NEW ROCHELLE
HALF DOLLAR

is now for sale at all local banks, at
two dollars each.

We are sure YOU, as a resident of
the City, will want to help, by purchasing one or more of these coins, to
finance a gala celebration June twelfth
to eighteenth when New Rochelle will
celebrate her 250th Birthday by a huge
party which YOU are invited to attend.
The proceeds are for this purpose.

The issue is limited.

NO more coins will be minted.

These lasting souvenirs will increase
in value.

BUY NOW

NEW ROCHELLE
COMMEMORATIVE COIN
COMMITTEE

20 SUMMIT AVENUE, NEW ROCHELLE, N. Y.

NEW ROCHELLE CELEBRATING

ITS 250th BIRTHDAY

NEW ROCHELLE

COMMEMORATIVE

COIN COMMITTEE

MAYOR HARRY SCOTT	*Honorary Chairman*
PITT M. SKIPTON	*Chairman*
ERNEST H. WATSON	*Treasurer*
JERE MILLEMAN	*Secretary*

New Rochelle advertising flyer—outside.

NEW ROCHELLE
NEW YORK.

★   ★   ★   ★   ★   ★   ★   ★

In 1688 a small group of Huguenot
refugees from La Rochelle, France,
landed on what is now Bonnefoi Point,
New Rochelle, N. Y., later purchasing
through their agent, Jacob Leisler, one-
time Governor of New York State, a
tract of 6,000 acres from John Pell,
Lord of Pelham Manor, one of the considerations being the delivery of *"one
fatt calfe"* on the festival of St. John
the Baptist to Pell, his heirs and assigns, forever, if demanded. In 1698
the first census showed a total of "231
souls ---- men, women and children,
white and colored, free and bond."* By
1704 New Rochelle had become a community of importance in the New
Country and in 1857 became a Village,
with its incorporation as a City in 1899.

This is New Rochelle of to-day—
"Queen City of the Sound"—then the
haven in the wilds of the New World
of those brave Huguenots, few in number but great in courage and faith—
now a city of about 60,000.

In 1936 Congress saw fit to recognize the historical significance of this
settlement and passed a bill which the
President later signed directing the
United States Treasury to issue a
specially designed half dollar commemorating in 1938 the 250th Anniversary of the settlement and founding
of this City.

Gertrude K. Lathrop, sculptor, of
Albany, N. Y., a member of The National Academy of Design and of The
National Sculpture Society, is the designer.

The obverse of the coin shows Lord
Pell receiving the protesting "fatt
calfe," while the reverse bears a
conventionalized fleur-de-lis, flower of
France, which appears on the coat-of-
arms of old La Rochelle and on the
seal of modern New Rochelle.

New Rochelle advertising flyer—inside.

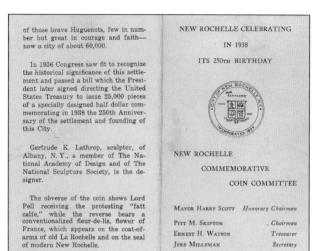

New Rochelle coin holder—single coin, outside.

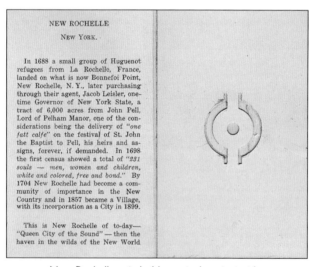

New Rochelle coin holder—single coin, inside.

This coin was mailed in a distribution holder with inserts for one, two, five, or 10 coins. The 10-coin holder is seldom seen. Page one presents a picture of the seal of the City of New Rochelle, an inscription, and the names of the following individuals: Mayor Harry Scott, Honorary Chairman; Pitt M. Skipton, Chairman; Ernest H. Watson, Treasurer; and Jere Milleman, Secretary.

The inner front page offers a short history of the city, as well as some information about the coin and its designer; the inner back page has the coin inserts. Value these inserts at $75 to $100; $100 to $200 with mailing envelope. Amy

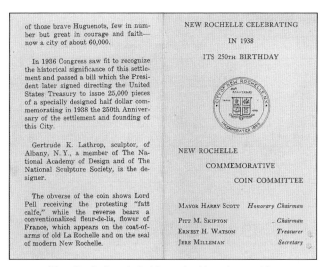

of those brave Huguenots, few in number but great in courage and faith—now a city of about 60,000.

In 1936 Congress saw fit to recognize the historical significance of this settlement and passed a bill which the President later signed directing the United States Treasury to issue 25,000 pieces of a specially designed half dollar commemorating in 1938 the 250th Anniversary of the settlement and founding of this City.

Gertrude K. Lathrop, sculptor, of Albany, N. Y., a member of The National Academy of Design and of The National Sculpture Society, is the designer.

The obverse of the coin shows Lord Pell receiving the protesting "fatt calfe," while the reverse bears a conventionalized fleur-de-lis, flower of France, which appears on the coat-of-arms of old La Rochelle and on the seal of modern New Rochelle.

NEW ROCHELLE CELEBRATING

IN 1938

ITS 250TH BIRTHDAY

NEW ROCHELLE

COMMEMORATIVE

COIN COMMITTEE

MAYOR HARRY SCOTT   *Honorary Chairman*

PITT M. SKIPTON   *Chairman*

ERNEST H. WATSON   *Treasurer*

JERE MILLEMAN   *Secretary*

New Rochelle coin holder—double coin, outside.

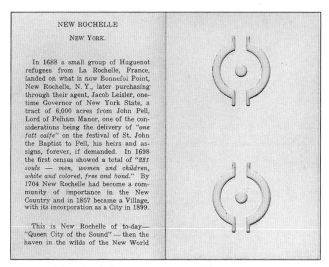

NEW ROCHELLE

NEW YORK.

In 1688 a small group of Huguenot refugees from La Rochelle, France, landed on what is now Bonnefoi Point, New Rochelle, N. Y., later purchasing through their agent, Jacob Leisler, onetime Governor of New York State, a tract of 6,000 acres from John Pell, Lord of Pelham Manor, one of the considerations being the delivery of "*one fatt calfe*" on the festival of St. John the Baptist to Pell, his heirs and assigns, forever, if demanded. In 1698 the first census showed a total of "*231 souls — men, women and children, white and colored, free and bond.*" By 1704 New Rochelle had become a community of importance in the New Country and in 1857 became a Village, with its incorporation as a City in 1899.

This is New Rochelle of to-day—"Queen City of the Sound"—then the haven in the wilds of the New World

New Rochelle coin holder—double coin, inside.

C. Skipton's book *One Fatt Calfe* (1939, ASIN: B000088I2Z4, 123 pages) sells for $175.

At least six plaster models of the rejected New Rochelle design by sculptor Lorrilard Wise are known. The obverse model featured the interesting scene of a crouching Native American overlooking a sailing ship in the Hudson River, with a sunrise (or sunset?) on the horizon. Five models feature the word "Liberty" inscribed in the center of the sun and the sixth has "Liberty" in the grass near the Native American. The reverse depicts the seal of the City of New Rochelle. These models sold in private sales for $2,000 to $2,500 in 2009.

Future Potential of the New Rochelle Half Dollar

Population Figures

Date	Service	AU 58	MS 60	MS 62	MS 63	MS 64	MS 65	MS 66	MS 67	MS 68	MS 69
1938	NGC	1	0	9	69	512	964	514	120	18	0
1938	PCGS	0	0	36	272	1251	1489	880	158	2	0
1938	Combined	1	0	45	341	1763	2453	1394	278	20	0

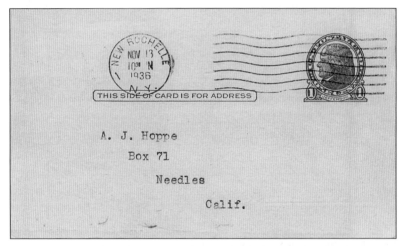

New Rochelle order acknowledgement postcard—front.

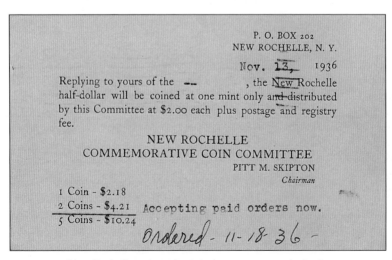

New Rochelle order acknowledgement postcard—back.

Date	Service	PF 58	PF 61	PF 62	PF 63	PF 64	PF 65	PF 66	PF 67	PF 68	PF 69
1938	NGC	0	1	0	0	0	0	0	0	0	0
1938	PCGS	0	0	0	0	0	0	0	0	0	0
1938	Combined	0	1	0	0	0	0	0	0	0	0

Date	Service	PL 58	PL 60	PL 62	PL 63	PL 64	PL 65	PL 66	PL 67	PL 68	PL 69
1938	NGC	0	0	1	8	46	53	58	15	1	0

I am often asked: "If there were only 50 special presentation pieces struck for the Westchester County Coin Club, why have 181 pieces been granted proof-like (PL) status by NGC? The answer: not all proof-likes were presentation pieces. Those coins possessing a lesser deep mirrored field are the proof-like coins—struck after the special production. Their count is combined with the deeper mirrored presentation New Rochelles—which for a short period, as I have said, were labeled "specimens" by NGC. The only known proof New Rochelle is the Matte Proof-61 piece that I sold in 2006. Those labeled otherwise are not brilliant proofs, but the earliest struck of the proof-like strikings. Digressing, those proof-like coins that I sold before slabbing should be accompanied by a photo of the identical coin. Those without a photo could be considered suspect. Also add to this total the crack-out labels, which were discarded and not deleted. Personally, I would not pay $25,000 for an MS-67 specimen. Recently, an NGC MS-67+ PL sold for $6,325 while an MS-67 strike sold for $4,900. I have examined MS-66 proof-like pieces that looked better. I would pass on those proof-like coins exhibiting only weak to average surface proof-like reflectivity.

A limited number of circulated offerings are abused or doctored UNCs. There is not much price spread between pieces rated EF-AU and MS-65. The issue appears fairly priced, at present, in grades MS-60 through MS-65. I recommend acquiring the eye-appealing New Rochelle—ideally in MS-65+ condition—only for the joy of collecting. Avoid dull, dark, and unattractive coins—unless the price is very right and all that you need is a representative example. Apply the same logic throughout the series. The MS-64 and MS-65 census can be lowered between 25% and 30%: coins in these grades have a fair future potential, even though it seems as if such coins have come out of the woodwork. In strict MS-66+ condition, the issue is somewhat undervalued. Any real future is in this rating. I would reduce the population figures by 20% and 25%. New Rochelles are underrated in the celebrated MS-67 category, value range $750 to $2,900. There is very good future potential for these, and for the MS-68 coins. Two recently sold for $3,400 and $4,000 respectively.

1946 Iowa Statehood Centennial

Reason for Issue:	To commemorate the 100th anniversary of the admission of Iowa into the Union.
Authorization:	Act of August 7, 1946, with a maximum of 100,000 pieces.
Issued by:	Iowa Centennial Committee
Official Sale Price:	$2.50 for Iowa residents, $3.00 to others; after January 16th, 1947, $3 to all

Production Figures

Date	Business Strikes	Assay Coins	Proofs	Melted	Net Mintage
1946	100,000	57	?	0	100,000

Current Market Values

Date	MS-60	MS-63	MS-64	MS-65	MS-66	MS-67	MS-68
1946	$105	$110	$125	$145	$190	$350	$1,300+

Designs by Adam Pietz

Obverse

The Old Stone Capitol in Iowa City with a cloud formation in the background. Below this structure is the inscription "THE OLD STONE CAPITOL IOWA CITY". Near the building's lower right corner are the artist's initials. In the upper field is the motto "IN GOD WE TRUST"; "LIBERTY" and the denomination are in the lower field and the lower border area; the words "UNITED STATES OF AMERICA" arc above.

Reverse

An eagle holding a ribbon in his beak, bearing the inscription: "OUR LIBERTIES WE PRIZE AND OUR RIGHTS WE WILL MAINTAIN". Below this inscription is the motto "E PLURIBUS UNUM"; between the upper portions of the eagle's wings are 29 stars indicating that Iowa was the 29th state admitted into the Union. The inscription outside of the beaded circle reads "IOWA STATEHOOD CENTENNIAL 1846–1946".

Origins of the Iowa

President Franklin D. Roosevelt wanted to put an end to the minting of commemorative coins because of the speculation and other abuses connected with them. He had corresponded on several occasions with the Committee of Banking and Currency in order to express his disdain. On August 5, 1939, an Act was passed that prohibited any further commemorative minting and prohibited the issuance of any commemorative coins that were authorized prior to March 1, 1939. Thus, this Act put an end to those issues with large authorizations, such as the Oregon Trail (6,000,000), the Texas (1,500,000), the Boone (600,000), and the Arkansas (500,000). Note the total quantity minted for each issue—the Oregon Trail (264,419), the Texas (304,193), the Boone (108,603), and the Arkansas (94,901). Also, the final mintage figures for each issue was becoming smaller and smaller as the years progressed, because of lack of interest in the series. We can use as an example the Arkansas 1938, with its 3,155 sets available, and the 1939 striking with 2,104 sets, to illustrate the continuation of annual small issues. Because of the original large authorizations, such small issues could have continued for up to 30 years, were it not for the new Act.

In 1945, Iowa led the vanguard for a centennial commemorative coin. On July 2, 1946, the Coins, Weights and Measures Committee met to consider the creation of the Iowa, the Booker T. Washington, and the Will Rogers commemorative half dollars. The latter issue never progressed past the committee stage. The first two issues were passed by the House on July 15, 1946. Three weeks later, on August 7, 1946, Harry S. Truman gave his approval for the issuance of the Iowa Statehood Centennial half dollar, as well as the Booker T. Washington issue.

On November 20, 1946, beginning at 10:12 a.m., the Philadelphia Mint struck 100,000 Iowa commemoratives plus 57 assay coins in approximately 24 hours. They were promptly shipped via the Railway Express Agency (REA) overnight, in REA's familiar green trucks.

Die manufacturing cost $545. These pieces were handled through the Iowa Centennial Committee in Des Moines, which made considerable effort to insure a proper distribution to the general public. The Centennial Committee

A Railway Express Agency truck.

was thereby able to avoid the main type of abuse against the previous souvenir half dollars—unjust distribution—which inevitably led to market speculation.

Local residents were the first to be given the opportunity to purchase their state's coin—as a memento of a century of progress and a share in creating a Centennial Memorial Fund—at $2.50 each. The coins were apportioned by county and population and sold through banks via a lottery system. If you wanted to purchase this issue you would select a numbered ticket. After a drawing, you would present the ticket to the distributing bank, giving you the right to make a purchase if you had the selected number. Unfortunately, this did not guarantee one the right of obtaining a coin. If that particular bank's allotment was exhausted before you received your coin, you were possibly out of luck until more commemorative half dollars were shipped from another bank that had not been able to sell its allotment. It was reported by the Committee Executive Secretary Edith W. McElroy on March 12, 1947, that 85,000 of the 90,000 Iowas were sold under their distribution plan during a 30-day campaign—a considerable achievement.

Five percent (or 5,000 specimens) were reserved, plus the total amount of unsold pieces, for out-of-state sales at $3 per coin. No great speculative market developed for this issue because of its excellent sales, fair distribution practices, and the fact that 100,000 coins were considered a large enough amount to dampen speculation. By the end of March 1947, all available pieces were sold out.

For the state's Sesquicentennial in 1996, and for its bicentennial in 2046, one thousand coins were set aside. Half this amount was (or is to be) presented to individuals during the celebration dates via an order of the Governor and the Centennial Committee. However, the State of Iowa began sales of the 1996 allotment in 1992 (see Future Potential section). The commemorative half dollars are kept at the Norwest Bank, 666 Walnut Street, Des Moines.

Adam Pietz, the coin's designer, had personally spent $25 on associated work photographs. He suggested he be paid in commemorative coins. His proposition met with success, and the State Treasurer, John M. Grimes, mailed him 25 Iowas in appreciation for services performed—aside from the reimbursed $25 expenses—in compliance with a request from Governor Robert D. Blue and Ralph Evans, Sub-Committee Chairman on Stamp and Coin.

The Iowa Today

Specimens in the circulated category are usually abused in some manner, or cleaned. The issue is abundant in grades ranging from MS-60 through MS-67. Over the last eight years, these grades came out of the numismatic woodwork. There is little value differential between the MS-60 and MS-67 categories, so collectors should zero in on the higher graded piece. Even a lofty MS-66 grade is quite attainable. Unless you are contemplating an MS-68 coin, buy only for the pure joy of collecting. Luster will run the gamut from brilliant satiny to dull satiny. The reverse eagle's head and part of its neck can display a weakness of strike. If pronounced, weak strike will affect the coin's grade and value. MS-66 coinage should show a strong strike. The obverse primary focal area is the upper section of the Capitol building and the field above. A die clash mark can be seen in the left cloud mass on part of the issue, but will not affect the grade. The reverse eagle is the main target for bag marks, etc. Presentation coins that have a "chrome look" or appear as if they were over-dipped in a tarnish-removing solution were provided to select individuals.

One such coin that I once owned and sold—not as a proof—had been given to John M. Grimes, the State Treasurer, for his assistance in distributing the Centennial half dollar, by Governor Robert D. Blue, on January 4, 1949. These early strikes were given one blow from the striking press. Those of you who purchased these coins for more than $20,000 each will be in for a surprise when you send them to NGC or PCGS for encapsulation. Your letter of accompanying dealer documentation should prove meaningless, in my opinion. Proof coinage must display the results from that second strike. All so-called satin finish proofs that I have examined to date were lovely coins—but were not double struck. They are worth more than the regular issue, but collectors should not go overboard: seek the advice of the knowledgeable.

No error coinage or counterfeit pieces have yet entered the marketplace.

Is Your Iowa Circulated or Mint State?

Obverse

A metal loss will first be observed on the cloud mass, directly below the words "IN GOD" of the motto, as well as on the columns of the Old Stone Capitol building.

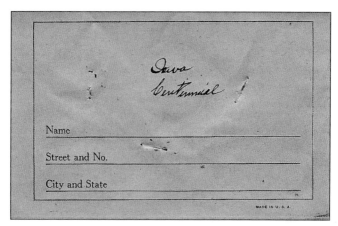

Iowa coin holder—outside.

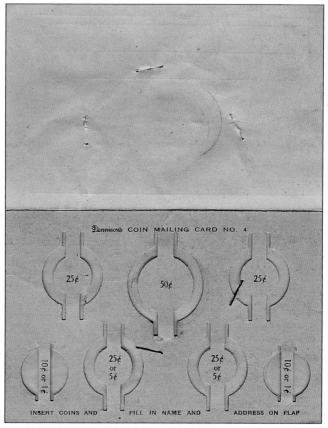

Iowa coin holder—inside.

Reverse

Wear will occur on the head and neck of the eagle. Since this area at times will display a weak strike, examine for the barest trace of metal loss.

Related Material

The regular issue was distributed in paper coin envelopes by the distributing banks such as the Farmers State Bank, Jesup, Iowa, as well as in a plain three-coin cardboard insert-type holder ($250) or in Dennison Coin mailing #4 cards.

Future Potential of the Iowa Half Dollar

Population Figures

Date	Service	AU 58	MS 60	MS 62	MS 63	MS 64	MS 65	MS 66	MS 67	MS 68	MS 69
1946	NGC	2	2	14	79	591	1727	2253	730	56	2
1946	PCGS	15	3	91	523	1841	3059	2515	712	61	0
1946	Combined	17	5	105	602	2432	4786	4768	1442	117	2

The Iowa Centennial half dollar—be it raw or slabbed—should be acquired only for the joy of collecting. In MS-65 condition, it has the third highest encapsulation population (4,786) behind the San Diego issues. Rated MS-66, it is number one (4,768). It ranks number two graded MS-67 (1,442) and MS-68 (117). There is no major price spread between the EF-AU and MS-67 categories. Future potential does not look promising for this lovely coin. Collectors should aim for an MS-67 coin, since it can be had much more cheaply than ever in the past and will make any owner feel proud. The exception is the MS-68 grade, if funding permits.

Should you buy one of the 500 commemorative half dollars offered by the State of Iowa? These sets were set aside in 1946 for a scheduled sale in 1996, when they were offered in a specially sealed plastic case for $510. I would recommend procuring from a dealer a sealed plastic case example of this coin only for the joy of owning a piece of U.S. commemorative history. The 1996 state sale pedigree brings no major numismatic value. It is just too expensive and appears to offer little if any future potential. In all fairness, this $510 tab was set when bid levels fluctuated in the $500–$510 range for MS-65 coinage and $900 for pieces grading MS-66. Since that period, values have plummeted. Moreover, each of the historical coins (as well as the extra 500 pieces set aside for sale in the year 2046) are coated with "Egyptian lacquer," which can hide surface negatives such as hairline scratches, small nicks or hits, etc. According to a numismatic staff member at the Smithsonian Institution, even boiling the coin in hot water—as suggested in the removal instructions of the person who coated these 1,000 coins in 1946—will not eliminate 100% of this glossy surface coating. Others who have experimented with or used this substance claim your coin can turn dark. This appears to be the reason why the major slabbing services would not encapsulate these coins. Possibly they can be conserved by the Numismatic Conservation Services (NCS). If the asking price were lowered to $200–$250 instead of $510, thereby adjusting to current market and economic conditions, chances of a sellout would seem more likely.

Coins graded MS-67 and MS-68 are worth looking for. Remember that a beautifully colored and toned encapsulated piece is always worth more than a white coin slabbed MS-68. MS-68 examples have sold for between $1,300 and $4,600. A MS-68+ PCGS example sold for $6,900 at the June 2011 Long Beach, CA Heritage auction #1156 (lot 239). Again, it is the coin's makeup, or the buyer, or the belief that the piece can upgrade that determines a coin's worth to the buyer.

1946–1951 Booker T. Washington

Reason for Issue:	To perpetuate the ideals and teachings of Booker T. Washington, and to raise funds to purchase, construct, and maintain memorials to his memory.
Authorization:	Act of August 7, 1946, with a maximum of 5,000,000 pieces.
Issued by:	Booker T. Washington Birthplace Memorial Commission
Official Sale Price:	1946: $1 plus 10 cents postage per coin 1946-D, -S: $1.50 each 1947 PDS: $6.00 set, plus 30 cents postage 1948 PDS: $7.50 set, plus 30 cents postage 1949 PDS: $8.50 set, plus 30 cents postage 1950 PDS: $8.50 set, plus 30 cents postage; $1 for S-Mint coin 1951 PDS: $8.50 set, plus 30 cents postage; $3 each

Production Figures

Date	Business Strikes	Assay Coins	Proofs	Melted	Net Mintage
1946	1,000,000	546	4?	500,000*	500,000*
1946-D	200,000	113	4?	100,000*	100,000*
1946-S	500,000	279	4?	180,000*	320,000*
1947	100,000	17	0	90,000*	10,000*
1947-D	100,000	17	0	90,000*	10,000*
1947-S	100,000	17	0	90,000*	10,000*
1948	20,000	5	0	12,000	8,000
1948-D	20,000	5	0	12,000	8,000
1948-S	20,000	5	0	12,000	8,000

Date	Business Strikes	Assay Coins	Proofs	Melted	Net Mintage
1949	12,000	4	0	6,000	6,000
1949-D	12,000	4	0	6,000	6,000
1949-S	12,000	4	0	6,000	6,000
1950	12,000	4	0	6,000	6,000
1950-D	12,000	4	0	6,000	6,000
1950-S	512,000	91	0	235,000*	277,000*
1951	510,000	82	0	230,631*	279,369*
1951-D	12,000	4	0	5,000	7,000
1951-S	12,000	4	0	5,000	7,000

* Estimate

Current Market Values

Date	AU-58	MS-60	MS-63	MS-64	MS-65	MS-66
1946 single	$19	$20	$23	$30	$85	$175
1946 PDS set	$60	$70	$90	$100	$220	$560
1947 PDS set	$100	$110	$200	$210	$280	$2,000
1948 PDS set	$135	$190	$240	$250	$280	$1,150
1949 PDS set	$200	$230	$265	$305	$325	$700
1950 PDS set	$120	$160	$175	$180	$235	$1,475
1951 PDS set	$110	$150	$200	$210	$220	$985

DESIGNS BY ISAAC SCOTT HATHAWAY

Obverse

The bust of the leading American educator Booker Taliaferro Washington (1856–1915), facing three-quarters to the right. His name is in the lower border; "UNITED STATES OF AMERICA" is around the upper border. Washington appears to be looking at the inscription "E PLURIBUS UNUM", in two lines in the right field; in the left field are the words "HALF DOLLAR". Appearing above the denomination is the date of issue, which can be any year from 1946 through 1951.

Reverse

The Hall of Fame for Great Americans, a domed structure with a pediment and arcaded base, constructed 1892–1912. The colonnade houses many busts and tablets honoring famous Americans. It was built as part of New York University's Bronx campus; the site is now part of Bronx Community College. Above the legend "LIBERTY" in the lower border is the first residence of Washington—

Isaac Scott Hathaway

a slave cabin. The Mint mark (D or S) is below. In the left field are the words "FRANKLIN COUNTY, VA." (in three lines), Washington's birthplace. Between the two structures is the inscription "FROM SLAVE CABIN TO HALL OF FAME"; encircling almost 80 percent of the border area is the inscription "BOOKER T. WASHINGTON MEMORIAL". The motto "IN GOD WE TRUST" is in the lower left field. This issue was created by Isaac Scott Hathaway, who also created the George Washington Carver–Booker T. Washington commemorative half dollars.

Origins of the Booker T. Washington (B.T.W.)

The Coins, Weights and Measures Committee met on July 2, 1946, to consider several House resolutions, including the possible creation of the Iowa, B.T.W., and Will Rogers commemorative half dollars. For whatever reason, the Will Rogers bill (HR-98 and HR-1281) was never reported out of committee. The other two half-dollar bills (HR-6528 and HR-2377) were unanimously passed on July 15, 1946, after just 31 minutes of discussion. Congressman John William McCormack of Massachusetts commented that he had never seen a bill acted on so quickly (except for emergency legislation) after it was reported out of committee. Less than one month later, on August 7, 1946, President Truman authorized their minting. The B.T.W. Act stated that the issue could be produced by the Mints, but for not more than a five-year period.

The well-known artist Charles Keck had previously designed the Lynchburg, Vermont, and Panama–Pacific ($1) commemorative coinage. He was solicited to create an appropriate representation for the B.T.W. Keck's models were accepted by the U.S. Commission of Fine Arts and by Dr. Sidney J. Phillips, President of the Booker T. Washington Birthplace Memorial of Rocky

Mount, Virginia. Suddenly an obscure black designer by the name of Isaac Scott Hathaway (1872–1967) entered the scene. Hathaway possessed the only existing life mask of Washington—and offered to prepare models free of charge. The Commission of Fine Arts recommended Hathaway's work, thereby offending Keck. Keck was paid for his work and bid farewell. The reverse drawing was provided by a nameless Commission of Fine Arts member.

The issue was marketed under the direction of Dr. Phillips, who was quite influential among the Baptists and black Elks. He claimed that a sell-out of the entire mintage would take only three months. Great expectations! Production began at the Mints in December 1946. I am often asked: "Was the B.T.W. or Iowa struck first?" The Iowa was first struck on November 20, 1946. On the 14th of that month, the Booker T. Washington Birthplace Memorial Commission began taking orders. However, sales were disappointing. In February 1947, Stack's of New York City was appointed authorized agent. In November, the Philadelphia Mint produced 100,000 coins; the following month, the branch Mints did likewise. Sales for this issue were not up to expectations, because the mintage figure was high and the issue was not of a new design. It sold as a set for $6, plus 30 cents postage.

In May 1948, each of the three Mints produced 20,000 coins. The set was distributed by Stack's, Bebee's of Omaha, and the Birthplace Memorial Commission. However, Bebee's advertised itself as the exclusive distributor for $7.50 per set. To help protect the design from bag marks, etc., Bebee's had the Mints place each coin in a cellophane envelope; the charge for this was 50 cents per coin. Collectors should note that the pieces were made using high-speed presses. After they bounced off each other and were stored in a bin, they were put in the envelopes. Special handling cannot prevent lack of fill marks on Washington's portrait: they resemble small cuts and scratches and are a characteristic of the striking.

During January 1949, the Mint facilities each produced 12,000 of these commemorative half dollars. They were sold at $8.50 per three-piece set, but, again, sales were not up to expectations.

In January 1950, Philadelphia and Denver each struck 12,000 coins. The San Francisco Mint, however, struck 512,000 half dollars, supposedly designated for building schools and hospitals. (To date no evidence has been found that proves any were built through promotions of the 1950 and 1951 issues.) This set also sold for $8.50.

In January 1951, the Philadelphia Mint struck 60,000 B.T.W. coins, while the branch Mints produced 12,000 each. In August, a needless 450,000 pieces were struck at Philadelphia. The three-piece set was sold for $10. (Examine the tabulation at the beginning of the entry for all issues returned for melting and used for assay purposes.)

The hopes of Dr. Phillips about selling out the entire authorization were never justified.

The B.T.W. Today

In circulated condition, the higher mintage dates, especially the 1946 coinage and the 1950-S and 1951-P pieces, are the easiest to locate. They also are the least expensive of all the commemorative coinage produced from 1892 through 1954, except for the common date (1952 Philadelphia) Washington–Carver issue, which is equally priced.

The value spread for the common dates grading EF-AU up to MS-64 is so little that collectors cannot afford to aim for anything but MS-64.

Luster will range for the entire issue from proof-like (re-polished dies), to semi-proof-like, to brilliant satiny, to satiny, to dull satiny. Strike will seldom lower grade-value. However, numismatic villains in the form of bag marks, lack of metal fill marks (resembling small scratches or cuts), reed marks, abrasions, slide marks, and hairline scratches, plague the obverse portrait, which is the primary focal area. The surrounding field also takes its share of hits. The design on the reverse offers more protection. The reverse primary focal area is the log cabin and surrounding field. When acquiring this issue, attempt to locate a flashy looking coin with a portrait as free of negatives as possible.

To date, some error coinage has been reported, but I have not examined any. On some coins of the 1946-P issue, a depression can be observed in the area of Washington's cheekbone, as can concentric marks that were transferred to the die from the hub that created the coin. These marks were made by the Janvier lathe's pointed engraving tool, and should have been removed via polishing at the Mint. To date, no counterfeits have entered the marketplace.

Is Your B.T.W. Circulated or Mint State?

Obverse

Wear will first develop on the cheekbone of Washington. Should his portrait look exceptional, examine any raw or unslabbed coin for possible doctoring.

Reverse

Wear will be observed on coin's central inscription, "From Slave Cabin…" and on the lower, horizontal section of the Hall of Fame.

Related Material

The 1946 issue was distributed in plain paper envelopes and several types of black leatherette cardboard holders. These have openings for three coins, contained by a movable celluloid strip. Value these holders at $50 to $75. Stack's holders (6 × 3 1/8 inches) are imprinted in silver with their name and New York City at the bottom. The Birthplace Memorial Commission's New York headquarters (261 W. 125th St., N.Y. 27, N.Y.) distributed the three-coin set in a similar holder (6 × 3 inches) with their 12-line blue imprinted advertisement glued to the reverse. Imprinted in gold ink on the upper front part is "Booker

Real United States Money

THE BOOKER T. WASHINGTON MEMORIAL HALF DOLLAR

"A Symbol of Democracy"

This coin should be in every American Home. The life story of Booker T. Washington inscribed on the reverse side. Philadelphia and San Francisco Coins, $1.00 each. Denver Coins, $1.50 each. Add 10c Postage for each coin up to 3 coins; 1c to each coin thereafter.

Proceeds to be used in establishing an INDUSTRIAL TRAINING PROGRAM FOR NEGRO YOUTH.

Send Your Order Today!

Booker T. Washington Birthplace Memorial

BOOKER WASHINGTON BIRTHPLACE, VA.

Price $1.00 and $1.50

GEMS OF WISDOM

Thoughts From Booker T. Washington's Philosophy That Have Rendered Invaluable Service To Mankind

1856   1915

Booker T. Washington Birthplace Memorial

Booker Washington Birthplace, Virginia

S. J. PHILLIPS, President
EMMETT J. SCOTT, Secretary
PEOPLES NATIONAL BANK, Treasurer

B.T.W. advertising flyer—outside.

Helpfulness Toward Others:

"The highest test of the civilization of any race is in its willingness to extend a helping hand to the less fortunate. Those who would help the Negro most effectually during the next fifty years can do so by assisting in his development along scientific and industrial lines in connection with the broadest mental and religious culture."

Success and Education:

"The end of all education, whether of head or heart, is to make an individual good, to make him useful, to make him powerful; is to give him goodness, usefulness and power in order that he may exert a helpful influence upon his fellows. The Negro should be taught book learning, yes, but along with it he should be taught that book education and industrial development must go hand in hand. No race which fails to do this can ever hope to succeed."

Friendship and Good Will:

"There is no permanent safety for any of us or for our intitutions except in the enlightenment of the whole peopie, except in continuing to educate until people everywhere be too big to be little, too broad to be narrow, be too high to stoop to littleness and meanness. The man is unwise who does not cultivate in every manly way the friendship and good will of his next door neighbor, whether he be black or white."

Glorifying and Dignifying Labor:

"We shall prosper in proportion as we learn to glorify and dignify labor and put brains and skill into the common occupations of life. We shall succeed not by abstract discussion, not by depending upon making empty demands, not by abuse of some other individual or race, but we will succeed by actually demonstrating to the world that we can perform the service which the world needs."

Everyday Christianity:

"I will allow no man to drag me down so low as to make me hate him."

Your PURCHASE of the Booker T. Washington Memorial half dollar or your CONTRIBUTION will aid in the development of a program which will make possible the widespread teachings of the sane philosophy expressed above. Such a program will not only help America today but will contribute to the well-being of FUTURE GENERATIONS.

Please address all correspondence to:

Booker T. Washington Birthplace Memorial
Incorporated
Booker Washington Birthplace, Virginia

B.T.W. advertising flyer—inside.

T. Washington Memorial Half Dollar". Beneath the coin openings are the Mint marks and at the bottom, "Struck at Three United States Mints" ($100–$150)). The coin was also forwarded in the same holder, but without the reverse promotion ($35–$50).

Christmas cards with two different scenes housed one coin, and a mailing card entitled the "Gems of Wisdom" had a coin taped to its inner right center

B.T.W. Christmas card mailing envelope.

B.T.W. Christmas card with coin.

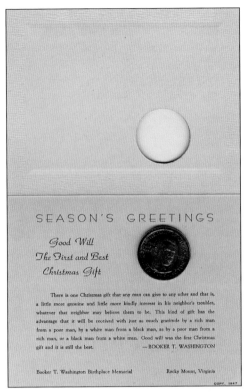

B.T.W. "peek-a-boo" Christmas card with coin.

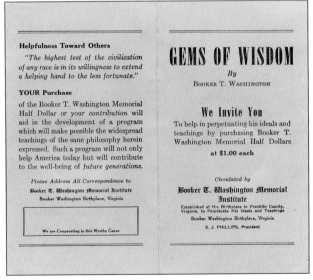

B.T.W. coin holder—outside.

spread. Other B.T.W.s were sold as prizes in a colorful, 10-coin punch board. Christmas holders can be worth $350 to $575. Another rare item is the Booker T. Washington Memorial contest certificate, which is a facsimile of a $3,500 check. If your name was selected first—and $12 were donated—you were the winner. These items have sold for between $350 and $550, when available.

Sets dated 1947 through 1951 were housed in cellophane envelopes, then placed inside a paper envelope. Bebee's also offered a single piece in a brown coin envelope (2 × 2 inches) as an official souvenir of the 1947 New Orleans Mardi Gras. It was imprinted with black ink on the back flap, with Bebee's address and the sale price of $1.25. As these envelopes are quite easily duplicated, they are worth only $1 to $3.

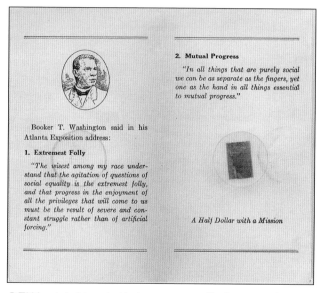

B.T.W. coin holder—inside (note tape to affix the coin to holder).

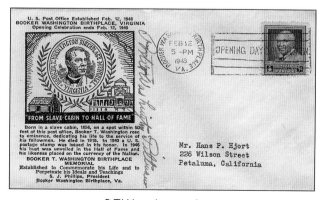

B.T.W. mailing envelope.

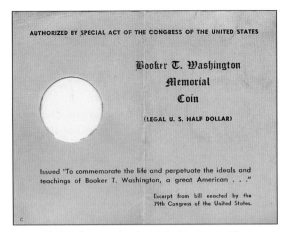

B.T.W. "peek-a-boo" coin holder—outside.

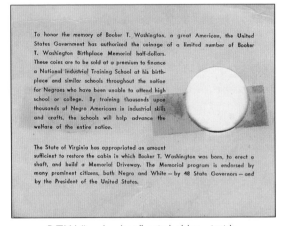

B.T.W. "peek-a-boo" coin holder—inside.

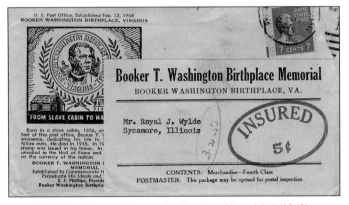

B.T.W. mailing envelope with adhesive address label (1948).

B.T.W. mailing envelope with adhesive address label (1956).

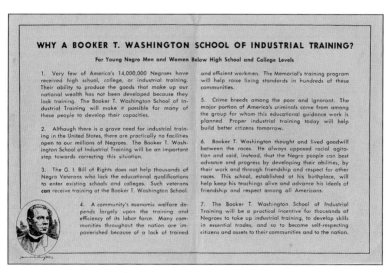

B.T.W. mailing envelope insert.

Future Potential of the Booker T. Washington Half Dollar

Population Figures

Date	Service	AU 58	MS 60	MS 62	MS 63	MS 64	MS 65	MS 66	MS 67	MS 68	MS 69
1946	NGC	9	2	27	93	738	1022	428	70	2	0
1946	PCGS	20	2	23	241	1264	1294	390	45	1	0
1946	Combined	29	4	50	334	2002	2316	818	115	3	0

Date	Service	AU 58	MS 60	MS 62	MS 63	MS 64	MS 65	MS 66	MS 67	MS 68	MS 69
1946 D	NGC	3	0	7	59	426	604	256	61	5	0
1946 D	PCGS	0	1	11	111	713	787	245	33	0	0
1946 D	Combined	3	1	18	170	1139	1391	501	94	5	0

Date	Service	AU 58	MS 60	MS 62	MS 63	MS 64	MS 65	MS 66	MS 67	MS 68	MS 69
1946 S	NGC	6	0	18	72	524	843	408	100	7	0
1946 S	PCGS	5	0	21	178	1108	1211	373	56	0	0
1946 S	Combined	11	0	39	250	1632	2054	781	156	7	0

Date	Service	AU 58	MS 60	MS 62	MS 63	MS 64	MS 65	MS 66	MS 67	MS 68	MS 69
1947	NGC	1	0	1	8	194	389	128	7	0	0
1947	PCGS	0	0	1	27	411	605	152	4	0	0
1947	Combined	1	0	2	35	605	994	280	11	0	0

Date	Service	AU 58	MS 60	MS 62	MS 63	MS 64	MS 65	MS 66	MS 67	MS 68	MS 69
1947 D	NGC	0	0	2	12	125	305	128	7	0	0
1947 D	PCGS	0	0	1	28	276	385	111	2	0	0
1947 D	Combined	0	0	3	40	401	690	239	9	0	0

Date	Service	AU 58	MS 60	MS 62	MS 63	MS 64	MS 65	MS 66	MS 67	MS 68	MS 69
1947 S	NGC	1	0	3	7	121	325	204	22	0	0
1947 S	PCGS	2	0	2	32	262	542	225	6	0	0
1947 S	Combined	3	0	5	39	383	867	429	28	0	0

Date	Service	AU 58	MS 60	MS 62	MS 63	MS 64	MS 65	MS 66	MS 67	MS 68	MS 69
1948	NGC	0	0	0	2	108	393	200	11	0	0
1948	PCGS	0	0	0	10	320	659	186	2	0	0
1948	Combined	0	0	0	12	428	1054	386	13	0	0

Date	Service	AU 58	MS 60	MS 62	MS 63	MS 64	MS 65	MS 66	MS 67	MS 68	MS 69
1948 D	NGC	0	0	0	4	94	378	218	26	0	0
1948 D	PCGS	0	0	0	21	349	622	217	9	0	0
1948 D	Combined	0	0	0	25	443	1000	435	35	0	0

Date	Service	AU 58	MS 60	MS 62	MS 63	MS 64	MS 65	MS 66	MS 67	MS 68	MS 69
1948 S	NGC	0	0	4	11	86	377	299	63	1	0
1948 S	PCGS	0	0	1	19	261	645	245	6	0	0
1948 S	Combined	0	0	5	30	347	1022	544	69	1	0

Date	Service	AU 58	MS 60	MS 62	MS 63	MS 64	MS 65	MS 66	MS 67	MS 68	MS 69
1949	NGC	0	0	0	4	118	329	252	18	0	0
1949	PCGS	0	0	0	26	334	650	237	7	0	0
1949	Combined	0	0	0	30	452	979	489	25	0	0

Date	Service	AU 58	MS 60	MS 62	MS 63	MS 64	MS 65	MS 66	MS 67	MS 68	MS 69
1949 D	NGC	0	0	1	9	122	322	206	21	0	0
1949 D	PCGS	0	0	2	31	361	599	237	15	0	0
1949 D	Combined	0	0	3	40	483	921	443	36	0	0

Date	Service	AU 58	MS 60	MS 62	MS 63	MS 64	MS 65	MS 66	MS 67	MS 68	MS 69
1949 S	NGC	0	0	0	4	80	280	341	53	0	0
1949 S	PCGS	0	0	1	21	206	707	376	19	0	0
1949 S	Combined	0	0	1	25	286	987	717	72	0	0

Date	Service	AU 58	MS 60	MS 62	MS 63	MS 64	MS 65	MS 66	MS 67	MS 68	MS 69
1950	NGC	0	0	0	6	95	270	150	13	0	0
1950	PCGS	0	0	2	14	241	468	164	2	0	0
1950	Combined	0	0	2	20	336	738	314	15	0	0

Date	Service	AU 58	MS 60	MS 62	MS 63	MS 64	MS 65	MS 66	MS 67	MS 68	MS 69
1950 D	NGC	0	0	0	3	112	273	120	14	0	0
1950 D	PCGS	0	0	0	21	274	460	167	3	0	0
1950 D	Combined	0	0	0	24	386	733	287	17	0	0

Date	Service	AU 58	MS 60	MS 62	MS 63	MS 64	MS 65	MS 66	MS 67	MS 68	MS 69
1950 S	NGC	1	0	5	20	175	446	350	60	0	0
1950 S	PCGS	2	0	9	48	410	882	412	19	0	0
1950 S	Combined	3	0	14	68	585	1328	762	79	0	0

Date	Service	AU 58	MS 60	MS 62	MS 63	MS 64	MS 65	MS 66	MS 67	MS 68	MS 69
1951	NGC	2	0	9	33	384	556	103	10	1	0
1951	PCGS	1	0	3	85	693	634	156	5	0	0
1951	Combined	3	0	12	118	1077	1190	259	15	1	0

Date	Service	AU 58	MS 60	MS 62	MS 63	MS 64	MS 65	MS 66	MS 67	MS 68	MS 69
1951 D	NGC	0	0	0	6	97	285	177	34	0	0
1951 D	PCGS	0	1	1	18	237	471	206	9	0	0
1951 D	Combined	0	1	1	24	334	756	383	43	0	0

Date	Service	AU 58	MS 60	MS 62	MS 63	MS 64	MS 65	MS 66	MS 67	MS 68	MS 69
1951 S	NGC	0	0	1	4	47	262	275	60	0	0
1951 S	PCGS	0	0	0	9	131	537	361	28	0	0
1951 S	Combined	0	0	1	13	178	799	636	88	0	0

Up to grade MS-65 these coins should be acquired only for the joy of collecting. Interest in the series is lacking: were this to change, prices would rise.

Most people who own B.T.W. MS-64 coinage usually observe enough surface negatives to not even consider slabbing, given the cost of doing so, and the low prices for B.T.W.s. The census would be much higher if such collectors submitted. Should you desire MS-64 coinage, the sleeper is the 1951-S issue. Then consider the 1949-S, and 1950-P strikings. There is average potential in these coins.

At current levels and based on current demand, all sets are fairly priced, but if the series is promoted when the market heat arrives, prices will rise.

The 1947-D, 1950-P, and 1950-D are the lowest populations within the MS-65 rating. The 1946-P and S strikings are the most abundant and easiest to obtain.

Unless you desire the complete set in MS-65 condition, I would recommend only the 1947-D, 1950-D, and 1950-P for type acquisition, and only if the pieces are attractive. Except for the most common issues, which possess little potential, the less abundant dates such as the 1947-D, 1950-P, and 1951-D offer reasonable future potential. I would reduce population figures for each date between 10% and 20%.

As you may have gathered, the real value is for the rarer individual type coins, and some sets are unjustly held down by the more abundant MS-64 and MS-65 1946–1951 B.T.W. coinage within the series. Population figures in total certainly reflect large availability, should a type coin be needed. What should matter is attractiveness: too many coins that I have encountered didn't give a flicker, even though they were graded MS-65. Unless all you want is a representative example, do not buy a common variety.

I would rate the 1947-D and 1951-P the rarest issue in MS-66 condition, along with the 1950-P and 1950-D. One's chance of finding an MS-66 B.T.W. type coin or set lies in the 1946-S, 1946-P, and 1950-S productions. Most collectors would find a complete eye-appealing B.T.W. MS-66 set desirable.

In MS-67 condition, the 1946-S issues make up most of the population, followed by the 1946-P, 1951-S, 1946-D, and 1951-S productions. Observe those low population issues such as the 1947-D, 1947-P, 1948-P, 1950-P, 1950-D and 1951-P: these would be a delight to add to your collection. One beautiful slabbed NGC rainbow-toned 1947-D specimen sold for $25,300; the bid price for the set was $2,000. What this bid means is that there is excellent future potential for this lofty grade. Two 1946-P pieces sold for $3,105 and $3,335. An MS-68 1946-D example brought $3,795. As an indication of the importance of a coin's makeup, note that five 1946-D MS-67 NGC encapsulations ranged from $775 to $2,530, and three sold in the $775 to $805 range. Some person believed the $2,530 coin would upgrade to an MS-68, but it did not. Values will vary widely for the entire issue.

Numismatic Guaranty Corporation (NGC) Proof-like Booker T. Washington Census

Date	Service	PL 58	PL 60	PL 62	PL 63	PL 64	PL 65	PL 66	PL 67	PL 68	PL 69
1946	NGC	0	0	0	0	0	0	0	0	0	0
1946 D	NGC	0	0	0	0	0	0	0	0	0	0
1946 S	NGC	0	0	0	1	7	4	1	0	0	0
1947	NGC	0	0	0	0	0	0	0	0	0	0
1947 D	NGC	0	0	0	0	0	0	0	0	0	0
1947 S	NGC	0	0	0	4	23	49	18	5	0	0
1948	NGC	0	0	0	0	0	2	0	0	0	0
1948 D	NGC	0	0	0	0	0	0	0	0	0	0
1948 S	NGC	0	0	0	0	0	12	11	1	2	0
1949	NGC	0	0	0	0	2	6	0	0	0	0
1949 D	NGC	0	0	0	0	0	0	0	0	0	0
1949 S	NGC	0	0	0	0	0	1	0	0	0	0
1950	NGC	0	0	0	0	0	0	0	0	0	0
1950 D	NGC	0	0	0	0	0	0	0	0	0	0
1950 S	NGC	0	0	0	0	8	23	14	0	0	0
1951	NGC	0	0	0	0	0	1	0	0	0	0
1951 D	NGC	0	0	0	0	0	1	0	0	0	0
1951 S	NGC	0	0	0	0	2	12	18	4	0	0

Should one possess a proof-like MS-63 piece, it will pay to submit it if it is not cleaned or whizzed. Such a coin will certainly bring much more money than if kept unslabbed (a PL surface must be present on both sides of the coin). These coins were produced from re-polished dies, and are not abundant. I know of collectors who will pay many times over bid for the issue. Early strikes resemble near brilliant proofs on both sides. There is excellent future potential for these in all grades. Note that the PL designation of later strikings can be debatable, if the proof-like look is limited or borderline.

To determine if your coin is proof-like, you should be able to read the reflected small print (10-point: approximately one-eighth of an inch high) on a standard business card held from two to approximately four inches away from the coin. How strong is the coin you are examining? At what distance does the print begin to blur on both sides? Is it 2.5 inches or 3.8 inches? (For more information, see the section "PRICING PROOF-LIKE COMMEMORATIVE COINAGE" in Topic 2, "Commemorative Proof-like Coinage.")

Collectors should watch out for raw or unslabbed PL specimens unscrupulously offered for sale. Many that were evaluated in coin collections or have crossed my path at coin shows had been polished or, on a few occasions, dipped in liquid mercury, to dupe the uninformed. Other legitimate pieces were whizzed on Washington's portrait to improve the coin's appearance and grade, or they were cleaned, and are not eligible to be encapsulated; others were PL on one side only.

These general rules concerning B.T.W. proof-like pieces can be applied to all proof-like designated commemoratives: for example, the Isabella quarter dollar; half dollars like the Washington–Carvers, Boone, Cincinnati, Columbians, Delaware, Lincoln, Maine, New Rochelle, Rhode Island, Roanoke, San Diego, and Texas; or gold dollars like Jefferson–McKinley, Lewis and Clark, and the 1916 and 1917 McKinley dollars. Many dealers consider NGC's PL designation as borderline.

George Washington Carver–Booker T. Washington

Reason for Issue:	To commemorate the lives of Booker T. Washington and George Washington Carver.
Authorization:	Act of September 21, 1951: Supplementary Act allowing the un-issued Booker T. Washington authorization to be used for the Carver–Washingtons. Therefore, authorization was 3,415,631, consisting of 1,834,000 un-coined and 1,581,631 melted B.T.W.s.
Issued by:	Carver–Washington Coin Commission
Official Sale Price:	$10 per set of 3 coins. (However, many 1952 Philadelphia coins were sold at or near face value by banks, as were the 1953-S and, to a lesser degree, the 1954-S issue.)

Production Figures

Date	Business Strikes	Assay Coins	Proofs	Melted	Net Mintage
1951	110,000	118	0	70,000*	40,000*
1951 D	10,000	4	0	0	10,000
1951 S	10,000	4	0	0	10,000
1952	2,006,000	292	0	883,000	1,123,000*
1952 D	8,000	6	0	0	8,000
1952 S	8,000	6	0	0	8,000
1953	8,000	3	0	0	8,000
1953 D	8,000	3	0	0	8,000

Date	Business Strikes	Assay Coins	Proofs	Melted	Net Mintage
1953 S	108,000	20	0	60,000*	48,000*
1954	12,000	6	0	40,000	8,000
1954 D	12,006	6	0	4,000	8,000
1954 S	122,000	24	0	80,198*	41,802*

* Estimate

Current Market Values

Date	MS-60	MS-63	MS-64	MS-65	MS-66	MS-67	MS-68
Type Specimen	$21	$23	$45	$95	$315	$500+	$3,500+
1951 PDS set	$110	$185	$210	$525	$3,400	$9,000	$40,000+
1952 PDS set	$110	$230	$195	$400	$1,650	$9,000+	$40,000+
1953 PDS set	$110	$200	$210	$550	$1,700	$8,500+	$40,000+
1954 PDS set	$110	$180	$190	$400	$1,700	$10,000+	$45,000+

DESIGNS BY ISAAC SCOTT HATHAWAY

Obverse

The accolated busts of the botanist and scientist George Washington Carver (c.1864–1943) and the educator Booker Taliaferro Washington (1856–1915), facing right. "UNITED STATES OF AMERICA", "IN GOD WE TRUST", and "E PLU-RIBUS UNUM" form an outer border with three decorative stars. An inner border is formed by the names and the denomination. The date of issue is at the nape of Carver's neck.

Reverse

A map of the United States superimposed with the initials "U.S.A." The inscription "FREEDOM AND OPPORTUNITY FOR ALL" and the word "AMERICANISM" separated by two decorative stars on each side run around the outer border. The Mint mark, when present, is located above the letters "IC" of "AMERICANISM".

Origins of the Carver–Washington

Dr. Sidney J. Phillips, President of the Booker T. Washington Birthplace Memorial of Rocky Mount, Virginia, had to sell the balance of the original Booker T. Washington authorization by the August 7, 1951 deadline, but this was impossible. In order to raise more funds, he helped engineer the passage of a bill that became the supplementary Act of September 21, 1951. A clause was inserted stating that profits would be used "to oppose the spread of Communism among Negroes, in the interest of the national defense." Remember that this was taking place during the McCarthy anti-communist hysteria years. The magic words were successful, as the bill was passed and quickly signed by President Truman. To Dr. Phillips, this victory meant being able to use the remaining 1,834,000 B.T.W. authorization, plus the melting and reincarnating into new coinage of the balance held by his Birthplace Memorial Commission and the Treasury Department. Now 3,415,631 Carver–Washingtons would become a reality.

The original anti-communist designs created by Hathaway were rejected by Dean Acheson, Secretary of State. Virtually all of the accepted composition had to be altered by Chief Mint Engraver Gilroy Roberts. This was especially true of the reverse: the map of America was higher than the border of its design, with the result that the coin would not stack. In addition, the lettering was poor. A coin with this design would be impossible to strike, because of metal flow problems. Also, careful examination of the map reveals that Delaware and part of Maryland are omitted.

In December 1951, the Philadelphia Mint struck 110,000 Carver–Washingtons; the branch Mints each produced 10,000. Official distributors were Bebee's, Stack's, and R. Green of Chicago. Sets were sold at $10 each; individual coins were offered at $5.50. During March 1952, the Philadelphia Mint struck 2,006,000 coins. These numbers were justified by the hope that various banks could distribute quantities of individual pieces at premium prices. The concept was a failure, however, as large numbers were sold at or close to face value. Both Denver and San Francisco produced 8,000 pieces. They were distributed by the same firms, at the same set price.

In January 1953, Philadelphia and Denver each struck 8,000 Carver–Washingtons, and the San Francisco facility produced 108,000 pieces. Stack's did not care to offer its services. Distributorships were now opened to almost any firm. The sets were sold at $10 each. During January 1954, the Mints each produced 6,000 half dollars, and they did in February. Between August 1 and August 6, the San Francisco Mint struck 110,000 additional halves. After this date, no more commemorative coinage would be minted until July 1, 1982. The three-piece set sold for $10. By the end of the year sales had come to a standstill. Few cared about the issue. The writing was on the wall, and some 1,091,198 Carver–Washingtons were returned for melting.

The Carver–Washington Today

As with the B.T.W. issue, the larger 1952-P, 1953-S, 1954-P, and 1954-S issues can be located with no trouble in grades EF-AU through MS-64. The value spread is almost nonexistent, so collectors should aim for MS-64. When promoted, the sets rise in worth to some degree; however, when the promotion is over, prices return to past levels. The best bets are singles within the series. They are the 1953-D and 1951-S. Acquire these for the joy of collecting. The future lies in the MS-65 category. The best MS-65 singles within the series are the 1951-P, 1952-D.

Rarity order for sets in MS-65 condition: 1953, 1954, 1951, and 1954; rated MS-66: 1954, 1953, 1951, and 1952.

Luster will range from strong semi-proof-like, to very brilliant satiny, to satiny, to dull satiny. I have seen some semi-proof-like 1952 Philadelphia pieces. Strike will cause a grade-value lowering. Weakness will be observed on the heads of the two portraits, as well as on the superimposed letters ("U.S.A.") – especially the period after the "S" – and on the map. What really downgrades this coin are numismatic negatives such as bag marks, lack of metal fill marks, slide marks, hairline scratches, and abrasions on the primary focal portraits and the reverse map, and then on the surrounding fields. Attempt to locate eye-appealing Carver–Washingtons that are virtually free of detracting marks and are well struck. I have seen pieces rated MS-66 with too many obvious surface negatives on the obverse portraits, which should downgrade these coins to MS-64+. Collectors should be aware that some dealers exclaim, 'That's why the MS-66 census or populations have risen from limited numbers to much higher figures!' If acquiring just for the joy of collecting, look for a coin or set that is fully original and is attractive. It should not display ugly deep bag marks or cuts or deep scratches, which really take away from the coin's beauty. Some pieces display clash marks within the outer border inscriptions. These coins may prove more valuable in the future. However, value should be based on the coin's condition. Many collectors assemble the three-piece or complete 12-piece set via individual purchases over a period of time. Of all the commemorative coinage produced from 1892 through 1954, this design has been voted the least popular, followed by the Rhode Island obverse.

The only error coinage I have encountered for this issue was a "railroad wheel": a partial collar-struck coin. It was created by a striking press malfunction that caused the collar to be in an incorrect coining position. Although not classified as error material, die clash marks are created when the obverse and reverse dies come together without a planchet or coin blank located in the press collar. The result is that part of the obverse design will appear on the reverse die or vice-versa. Should the clash marks not be removed and die polished, they will be observed on coins produced thereafter. Clash marks can be observed on the 1951 and 1952 Philadelphia coins on their obverse and reverse – within the lettering adjacent to the rim.

There are no known counterfeits for this, the last commemorative to be struck for the classic issues of 1892–1954.

Is Your Carver–Washington Circulated or Mint State?

Obverse

A metal loss will first be noticed on the cheekbone of Carver. Look for a difference in texture and fine crisscross scratches in this area, which usually reveals a poor strike and lack of fill marks, resembling small cuts and scratches. This area is a prime target for the coin doctors.

Reverse

Examine the letters "U.S.A." for first loss of metal. The period after the "S" of "U.S.A." is usually seen weakly struck or not as pronounced as the other periods. At times, it is almost nonexistent.

Related Material

This issue was distributed in a cellophane coin envelope, which was placed in a paper envelope. The larger mintage issues were sent out on approval by the Booker T. Washington Birthplace Memorial Foundation in a small envelope, housing one coin. If you liked the souvenir after inspection, you were to send $2 to the Peoples National Bank of Rocky Mount, Virginia. It was also noted in 15 lines of dark red imprint that $1.50 is deductible for tax purposes and a supply of these coins could be obtained from your Federal Reserve Bank. Small quantities were also mailed out in two types of Christmas cards with a cutout for one coin. The envelopes can be valued from $25 to $50; the Christmas cards, between $350 and $500.

Future Potential of the George Washington Carver–Booker T. Washington Half Dollar

Population Figures

Date	Service	AU 58	MS 60	MS 62	MS 63	MS 64	MS 65	MS 66	MS 67	MS 68	MS 69
1951	NGC	1	0	13	75	419	204	27	2	0	0
1951	PCGS	4	1	20	125	514	179	38	0	0	0
1951	Combined	4	1	33	200	933	383	65	2	0	0

Date	Service	AU 58	MS 60	MS 62	MS 63	MS 64	MS 65	MS 66	MS 67	MS 68	MS 69
1951 D	NGC	0	0	3	24	222	272	45	0	1	0
1951 D	PCGS	1	0	2	66	457	363	74	0	0	0
1951 D	Combined	1	0	5	90	679	635	119	0	1	0

Date	Service	AU 58	MS 60	MS 62	MS 63	MS 64	MS 65	MS 66	MS 67	MS 68	MS 69
1951 S	NGC	0	0	0	10	137	407	171	18	0	0
1951 S	PCGS	0	0	1	19	312	727	124	1	0	0
1951 S	Combined	0	0	1	29	449	1134	295	19	0	0

Date	Service	AU 58	MS 60	MS 62	MS 63	MS 64	MS 65	MS 66	MS 67	MS 68	MS 69
1952	NGC	24	2	46	235	1441	1187	282	21	1	0
1952	PCGS	22	4	38	410	1874	1067	220	7	0	0
1952	Combined	46	6	84	645	3315	2254	502	28	1	0

Date	Service	AU 58	MS 60	MS 62	MS 63	MS 64	MS 65	MS 66	MS 67	MS 68	MS 69
1952 D	NGC	0	0	1	25	210	208	10	1	0	0
1952 D	PCGS	0	0	3	56	459	255	30	0	0	0
1952 D	Combined	0	0	4	81	669	463	40	1	0	0

Date	Service	AU 58	MS 60	MS 62	MS 63	MS 64	MS 65	MS 66	MS 67	MS 68	MS 69
1952 S	NGC	0	0	1	8	123	328	132	8	0	0
1952 S	PCGS	0	0	1	17	418	542	106	5	0	0
1952 S	Combined	0	0	2	25	541	870	238	13	0	0

Date	Service	AU 58	MS 60	MS 62	MS 63	MS 64	MS 65	MS 66	MS 67	MS 68	MS 69
1953	NGC	0	0	1	27	186	218	65	3	0	0
1953	PCGS	0	0	6	95	474	281	57	1	0	0
1953	Combined	0	0	7	122	660	499	122	4	0	0

Date	Service	AU 58	MS 60	MS 62	MS 63	MS 64	MS 65	MS 66	MS 67	MS 68	MS 69
1953 D	NGC	0	0	1	16	227	149	11	1	0	0
1953 D	PCGS	0	0	2	74	493	218	38	0	0	0
1953 D	Combined	0	0	3	90	720	367	49	1	0	0

Date	Service	AU 58	MS 60	MS 62	MS 63	MS 64	MS 65	MS 66	MS 67	MS 68	MS 69
1953 S	NGC	1	0	5	20	325	602	124	14	0	0
1953 S	PCGS	1	0	3	72	665	650	95	5	0	0
1953 S	Combined	2	0	8	92	990	1252	219	19	0	0

Date	Service	AU 58	MS 60	MS 62	MS 63	MS 64	MS 65	MS 66	MS 67	MS 68	MS 69
1954	NGC	0	0	0	20	334	289	58	3	0	0
1954	PCGS	0	0	2	88	598	382	65	1	0	0
1954	Combined	0	0	2	108	932	671	123	4	0	0

Date	Service	AU 58	MS 60	MS 62	MS 63	MS 64	MS 65	MS 66	MS 67	MS 68	MS 69
1954 D	NGC	0	0	2	27	335	240	24	1	0	0
1954 D	PCGS	0	1	3	102	589	270	28	0	0	0
1954 D	Combined	0	1	5	129	924	510	52	1	0	0

Date	Service	AU 58	MS 60	MS 62	MS 63	MS 64	MS 65	MS 66	MS 67	MS 68	MS 69
1954 S	NGC	1	0	4	36	441	447	102	5	0	0
1954 S	PCGS	3	0	9	149	718	573	69	2	0	0
1954 S	Combined	4	0	13	185	1159	1020	171	7	0	0

Date	Service	PL 58	PL 60	PL 62	PL 63	PL 64	PL 65	PL 66	PL 67	PL 68	PL 69
1951	NGC	0	0	0	2	0	0	0	0	0	0
1951 D	NGC	0	0	0	0	0	0	0	0	0	0
1951 S	NGC	0	0	0	0	0	0	0	0	0	0
1952	NGC	0	0	0	0	0	0	0	0	0	0
1952 D	NGC	0	0	0	1	5	2	0	0	0	0
1952 S	NGC	0	0	0	0	1	1	0	0	0	0
1953	NGC	0	0	0	0	0	0	0	0	0	0
1953 D	NGC	0	0	0	0	1	0	0	0	0	0
1953 S	NGC	0	0	0	0	0	0	0	0	0	0
1954	NGC	0	0	0	0	0	0	0	0	0	0
1954 D	NGC	0	0	0	2	1	2	0	0	0	0
1954 S	NGC	0	0	0	0	0	0	0	0	0	0

As noted previously, buy this issue only for the joy of collecting in all grades up to MS-65. The only dates that I like – if strictly graded – are as follows: 1951-P and 1952-D. I would like to reinforce the rarity of individual dates especially in grades MS-66. They are the 1953-D, 1952-D, 1954-D, and 1951-P. Check out their census: there is excellent future potential for these coins. The remaining MS-66 issues have a very good future potential; the 1952-P is the highest population issue. The MS-67 combined encapsulation figures are limited, except for the 1952-P, 1951-S, and 1953-S. There is almost no population in MS-67 for the series which makes pricing difficult. To date a 1951-D and 1952-P encapsulated by NGC are rated MS-68. There is not much out there. There is excellent future potential in loftier grades. At present many MS-67 Carver–Washingtons are rare pieces. Values will vary between $2,000 and $4,000 to $2,000 and $16,000. Coins with excellent makeup and rarity will find buyers at the high range of prices.

1982 250TH ANNIVERSARY OF GEORGE WASHINGTON'S BIRTH

Reason for Issue:	To commemorate the 250th anniversary of George Washington's birth.
Authorization:	Act of December 23, 1981.

Facts and Figures

Denomination	Date/Mint	Pre-issue Price	Regular Price	Maximum Authorized	Net Mintage	Market Value
Silver Half Dollar	1982 D UNC	$8.50	$10	10,000,000	2,210,458*	$14
	1982 S Proof	$10.50	$12		4,894,044*	$14

*Alone among the post-1982 commemoratives, coins were struck in anticipation of sales. When sales did not meet production, coins were returned to the Mint and melted. The Mint struck 2,689,204 uncirculated coins, with 478,716 melted; 5,762,370 Proofs were struck, with 868,326 melted. In later programs, coins were struck to order, with no official melting.

Designs

Obverse by Elizabeth Jones

George Washington on horseback, shown at about 50 years of age. "George Washington" and "250TH Anniversary of Birth 1982" appear in the upper and lower fields, respectively. The word "Liberty" is in the central left field; the designer's initials (EJ) are adjacent to the lower forearm. The Mint mark, either D or S, is to the left of the horse's lower mane.

Reverse by Elizabeth Jones and Matthew Peloso

The eastern facade of Mount Vernon, Washington's home on the banks of the Potomac. "UNITED STATES OF AMERICA" arcs above; "HALF DOLLAR" below. "IN GOD WE TRUST" is in smaller letters in the upper field. Below the building rests the heraldic eagle, bearing the banner "E PLURIBUS UNUM". The designer's initials (EJ) appear below the columns in the right field and Matthew Peloso's initials are cleverly placed and hardly noticeable in the first section of foliage opposite the left rim.

Origins of the Washington Half Dollar

It has been many years since the first 1982 George Washington half dollar made its debut, so this might be a good time to pause and take a look at how U.S. commemoratives came to be reborn.

The 1920's and 1930's were the golden age of U.S. commemorative coinage—or, more precisely, the silver age. That was when the preponderance of U.S. commemoratives was struck.

The 1960's and 1970's were, by sharp contrast, the dark ages. The series ended in 1954, when the U.S. Mint completed production of the Washington–Carver half dollar—and, for nearly 30 years thereafter, commemorative coins were a dead issue at the Treasury.

There seemed to be no reason to look for new life in the series as the 1980's got under way. It is true that Ronald Reagan's victory in the 1980 presidential election did serve notice that changes would be made in the nation's capital, but only cockeyed optimists held any serious hope that the changes would trickle down to commemorative coins.

Most observers of the numismatic scene took only casual note in the early days of the 97th Congress in 1981 when the Georgia congressman Douglas Barnard, Jr., announced his intention to introduce a new coinage bill to authorize production of a commemorative half dollar honoring George Washington on the 250th anniversary of his birth. Nor was there any perceptible gasp of excitement on March 16th of that year, when Barnard actually did introduce the legislation.

The bill picked up important support when Rep. Frank Annunzio of Illinois, Chairman of the House Subcommittee on Consumer Affairs and Coinage, joined Barnard in co-sponsoring it. Still, even then, few gave it very much chance of success. Numerous other bills proposing special coins had come up for discussion through the years, but—with the exception of the Bicentennial coinage legislation—anything that sounded remotely like a new commemorative coin faced Treasury opposition.

This time, however, something totally unexpected took place. Instead of opposing the bill, the new Treasury leadership, made up of Reagan appointees, went along with it.

U.S. Treasurer Angela M. Buchanan disclosed this astounding new attitude on May 7, 1981, when she testified before Annunzio's panel:

While the Department of the Treasury has a history of objecting to the issuance of commemorative coins for the benefit of private sponsors and organizations, it has not objected to special coinage authorized by Congress for the government's own account (such as the proposal we are discussing today).

The Treasury Department, thus, did not object to the Eisenhower 40-percent silver dollar program, enacted in 1970, or the American Revolution Bicentennial 40-percent silver set program, enacted in 1973.

The Treasury Department believes that the 250th anniversary of the "Father of Our Country" is an occasion which justifies the issuance of a special non-circulating commemorative coin.

It was my privilege and pleasure to be in attendance at that hearing—for I, too, had been invited by Chairman Annunzio to present my views on the bill as an expert witness. I was, of course, delighted by the Treasurer's remarks—and it's interesting to note that in my prepared testimony, I had called upon the Treasury and the Mint for just such a change of heart, for what I described as "a simple softening of their stance."

"Let us put an end to this continuous neglect of inadequately honoring those exceptionally important events in our nation's great history," I declared. "Remember the U.S. moon landing? On whose coinage is it commemorated? Isn't it time that we begin remembering our heroes? Let us revive the custom of striking commemoratives—the most colorful coinage of the United States of America."

Annunzio's subcommittee gave the bill its immediate and unanimous approval. Less than two weeks later, on May 19, 1981, the full House did likewise in a voice vote.

Progress was slower in the Senate. Sen. James McClure of Idaho introduced a companion bill on May 18, the day before the final House approval, but the Senate didn't act for more than six months. Finally, on December 9, the Senate passed the bill and sent it to President Reagan, who signed it into law on December 23.

Clearly, the Treasury's willingness to accept the Washington coin was a key to its eventual approval. And, by taking the position it did, the department not only cleared the way of this specific coin, but also reopened the books on commemorative coinage as a whole.

Treasurer Buchanan insisted, however, that there really hadn't been a fundamental change in department policy:

We appreciate the reasons why past administrations have opposed commemorative coins and believe there was a lot of solid reasoning involved. But we also feel that each proposal deserves to be reviewed on its own merits, rather than being rejected with a flat, across-the-board statement.

Whatever the official thinking may have been, hobbyists naturally hailed what was taking place as a welcome sign of new cooperation and new consideration by the Treasury.

I think it is especially fitting that this first new commemorative honored George Washington, a man who was himself a first in many important respects. "First in war, first in peace, first in the hearts of his countrymen" is an epigram often used to describe the nation's first president.

The legislation authorizing the Washington half dollar specified that the coin be composed of 90 percent silver, as had all previous U.S. commemorative halves. Up to 10 million examples could be struck, with production continuing through 1983 if necessary, even though all the coins would be dated 1982. The coins would be sold for a premium, reflecting the actual costs of production and distribution, plus a surcharge of not more than 20 percent.

An unusual amendment inserted by Annunzio specified that all profits from sale of the Washington coin would be used to help reduce the national debt. "When George Washington was president," the congressman pointed out, "our country had almost no debts."

By an interesting coincidence, the Washington half dollar gained final approval in Congress only a few weeks after the swearing-in of Elizabeth Jones as new Chief Sculptor/Engraver of the Mint. Thus, it was only natural that Jones, the first woman ever to hold that post, should get the pleasant assignment of being the coin's designer.

Jones set out at once to give the coin a distinctive appearance: instead of simply using a traditional bust of George Washington, she got the idea of showing him on horseback.

> I knew right away that I wanted to put Washington on a horse. He was so famous as a horseman and a general, and there are so many equestrian statues and paintings of him, that I thought it would be appropriate to show him in that part of his life, rather than just in his older years when he was president.
>
> I wanted to make a break with tradition. I have seen so many collections of medals and coins of Washington where everything is either a head or a profile view. They're all variations on the same basic theme. But this is something different, something we haven't seen much in the U.S. coinage tradition.

Equestrian designs hadn't been totally foreign to U.S. coinage. One earlier commemorative coin, the 1925 Stone Mountain half dollar, shows two Confederate generals—Robert E. Lee and Thomas "Stonewall" Jackson—on horseback. Another, the 1900 Lafayette dollar, depicts an equestrian statue of the Marquis de Lafayette. Still, as Jones noted, U.S. coinage had tended to be conservative and repetitive, especially in its treatment of Washington. Thus, her design was an interesting departure from the norm. In creating the design, she had drawn on an 1824 Rembrandt Peale portrait that hangs in the portrait gallery of Philadelphia's Second Bank of the United States.

The Washington quarter dollar is the only regular-issue U.S. coin ever produced in Washington's honor– and, of course, it shows him in a standard profile portrait. Two earlier commemorative coins had carried his likeness; but, there, too, the portraits were standard. The most recent coin to depict George Washington, a 1999 $5 half eagle commemorating the 200th anniversary of his death in 1799, also uses a standard profile.

Curiously, two of the previous commemoratives had depicted Washington along with somebody else. He appeared with Lafayette on the 1900 dollar and with Calvin Coolidge on the 1926 half dollar marking the sesquicentennial of U.S. independence.

In authorizing the 1982 commemorative, Congress stipulated that both sides of the coin should bear designs "emblematic" of the Washington anniversary. At first, Jones intended to show the house where Washington was born—a little-known dwelling in Wakefield, Virginia—on the reverse. She later reconsidered, though, and showed his famous homestead at Mount Vernon. The reason, she explained to me, was that after completing her original design, she learned that the present-day "Washington birthplace" at Wakefield is a total reconstruction.

Jones got a helping hand in fashioning the reverse. Using her artwork, Matthew Peloso, an assistant staff engraver at the Mint, prepared the plaster model. Numismatic sleuths will find Peloso's initials hidden in the shrubbery to the left of Mount Vernon. It was Jones's suggestion that he include his initials. Peloso, feeling honored, decided to conceal them, for whatever reason, in the shrubbery design. Mint Director Donna Pope became aware of the hidden initials only during the ceremony when the coin galvanos were displayed and interpreted. Pope privately told Jones that she must be informed about such occurrences in the future. Business-strike Washington half dollars were produced at the Denver Mint and Proof specimens were struck at San Francisco. July 1, 1982, marked the start of production, and special ceremonies took place on that day at both locations.

It was, of course, a truly historic occasion: the dawn of a new age in U.S. commemorative coinage. For that reason, I consider myself extremely fortunate to have been a participant in the program—even though I had to do some fancy cross-country flying to be on hand for both sets of ceremonies.

At Denver, I was privileged to strike the fifth ceremonial piece, after the first four had been struck by Donna Pope, Denver Mint Superintendent Nora W. Hussey, Denver Mayor William H. McNichols, Jr., and American Numismatic Association President Adna G. Wilde, Jr. The first ceremonial coin was struck at 9:16 a.m. Mountain Time. Silver used to make this coin came from the 14.3 million ounces stored up for the Eisenhower dollar program.

The whole thing seemed like a dream. I was almost walking on air as I stepped up and selected one of the 16 remaining silver planchets. Then I placed it on the press, and within a few seconds a coin emerged. I examined it at once, and found to my delight that its fields were semi-proof-like.

Following the program in Denver, I left at once and headed for the airport, along with some of the others, for a quick flight to San Francisco, where similar ceremonies were scheduled just a few hours later. I found the second part of the day's double-header an equally exhilarating experience.

Initially, I suspect, there were doubters—at the Treasury and also in the hobby—who didn't expect the Washington coin to make very much of a splash. Even those who liked it, including me, had no real way of gauging its sales potential, since three decades had passed since the last new commemorative, and the market had changed dramatically.

As things turned out, there was no cause for concern. Orders poured in, and the Mint had to work full blast to keep up with demand. There were 3,084 dies produced by the Philadelphia Mint for this issue during the fiscal year of 1983. By the time production ended, on December 31, 1983, some 8 million pieces—all bearing the original 1982 date—had been struck. The overwhelming majority of these were sold. By December 31, 1985, when sales officially ended, the Mint had sold a total of nearly 4.9 million Proof San Francisco examples and more than 2.2 million Denver Uncirculated pieces—not meant for circulation—at issue prices of $10.50 and $8.50, respectively. This is a grand total of more than 7.1 million coins. That made this the most successful commemorative coin, from the standpoint of sales, in U.S. history. A profit of more than $36 million was made, which was deposited in the Treasury's General Fund to help reduce the national debt. It is interesting to note that Proof coins outsold business strikes by a 2-to-1 margin. This was a numismatic first: never before had this happened with any U.S. coin that was offered for public sale in both versions.

The Washington half dollar has proven to be popular not only with the public but also with coinage critics. In 1984 Krause Publications chose it as the winner of the first annual "Coin of the Year" contest, in head-to-head competition with new coin issues from all over the world. The entries were judged on the basis of their beauty and historical significance.

I, too, give the Washington coin high marks, especially from the standpoint of historical significance. After a full generation with no new commemorative coins, the Washington half dollar got the United States back on the track.

I strongly suspect that hobbyists of the future will view two dates as particularly special in the history of U.S. commemorative coinage: 1892, when the series was born, and 1982, when it was born again.

The Washington Half Dollar Today

One of my favorite late-date designs happens to be the Washington half dollar. However, it is also the most abundant and easily located of all the post-1982 commemorative coins. Based on their mintage, the method of handling and pre-packaging of the uncirculated version, and the high level of care in handling the proof coinage make them not really worth much more than current value levels. Values will rise and fall based on the bullion value of silver. Early 1982 Denver Mint Uncirculated coins often had a small field scratch or two, or a nick, which naturally lowered their grade. The Mint received complaints. I was told that planchets that were delivered from the San Francisco Mint were lacking in quality. Officials at the San Francisco Mint responded by saying the

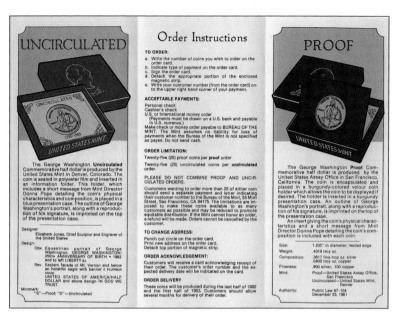

George Washington promotional flyer—inside.

planchets were not properly handled by the Denver Mint after they were delivered. Whatever the cause, this situation was remedied with later productions receiving better care, and, therefore, higher grades. Many of the high mintage Proof pieces (4,894,044) will grade between Proof 65 and Proof 69, while a large percentage of the Uncirculated specimens (2,210,458) will grade between MS-64 and MS-68.

Several errors are known. There are two very rare Proof Washington half dollars that were struck ten percent off center. One sold for $5,000. Also, when examining the date 1982, one may notice its digit "8" will resemble the open letter "S" (the date looks like "19S2"). This common polishing variety was created when the die surface was cut below the level of part of the digit, eliminating sections of the "8."

This issue's proof coin is encapsulated in a plastic coin holder, housed within a burgundy cardboard box. The encapsulation is located in an opening of a velour-lined coin holder with a rear picture-frame stand allowing the coin to be displayed. A descriptive insert is contained. The top of the box cover is imprinted with a silver outline of Washington's bust and a reproduction of his autograph. The inner top lid is covered with silver paper.

The Uncirculated version is sealed in Mylar or polyester film wrap, housed within a descriptive insert with an opening to view the coin, and placed within a bluish green box. This container is exactly the same as the burgundy box, except the inner bottom is elevated by a piece of cardboard covered by a bluish-green paper.

Ceremonial press kits containing galvano photos and information about the issue are rare, as are the official Mint invitations to the ceremony. These were produced in very limited numbers. Two were sold in 1999 for $275 and recently for $700. Probably 99.9 percent of these coins will not be removed from their Mint encapsulations. Thus they vary little in grade and have not received the abuse of earlier commemorative issues (1892–1954). Grading information of modern commemorative coinage is irrelevant when compared to classic commemorative coins, which were treated far more roughly in the minting process than their modern counterparts. Modern commemoratives are individually produced and given careful handling from the moment they are removed from the press to their encapsulation and packaging. The older issues were created in the way regular circulating coinage is struck, with no special care given after striking. They were bagged, counted, shipped, delivered, and further abused.

However, any coin can bring a smile to a child or adult's face when given as a gift. This can act as a catalyst and create a new coin collector, now or 10 years from now, as it did with me. I received a 1952 Proof set when I was 10½ years old as a Christmas present.

The future potential of this coin is highly dependent on the grade. To date, no MS-70 pieces have been encapsulated. I recommend that collectors acquire this coin only for the pure joy of collecting, not for investment. That is unless an MS-69 coin is desired. The Mint State census is low for the MS-69. One PCGS MS-69 encapsulation sold for $400 almost three years ago but its population figure was much lower than it is now. I have seen MS-69s going for $150 to $210 recently. PCGS has encapsulated 14,737 Proof Deep Cameos (PFDC) in PF-69, including 4,005slabs with Donna Pope's signature, while only 261 (92 with Pope signatures) were rated PF-70.

Your odds of getting the perfect grade rated MS-70 are very slim, though your coin could be submitted and you might very well be blessed. To date, neither NGC nor PCGS has assigned the MS-70 rating to a specimen. Just remember that there are huge numbers of this issue that can be submitted for slabbing in the future. NGC labels the equivalent of PCGS's "Proof Deep Cameo" (PFDC) as "Ultra Cameo" (UC) and they tend to sell at auction in the $25 to $30 range for the PF-69 ultra cameo grade.

1982-D 50¢

Grading Service	MS 68	MS 69	MS 70
NGC	838	72	0
PCGS	1601	474	0
Combined	2439	546	0

1982-S 50¢

Grading Service	PF 68	PF 69	PF 70
NGC	225	4801	263
PCGS	438	9412	261
Combined	515	13,558	524

1983–1984 Los Angeles Olympics

Reason for Issue:	To commemorate and support the 1984 Los Angeles Olympic Games.
Authorization:	Act of July 22, 1982: silver dollars (combined 1983 and 1984 authorization); gold ten dollar coins.

Facts and Figures

Denomination	Date/Mint	Pre-issue Price	Regular Price	Maximum Authorized	Net Mint-age	Market Value
Silver Dollar	1983 P UNC	-	$28	50,000,000	294,543	$40
	1983 D UNC	-			174,014	$40
	1983 S UNC	-			174,014	$40
	1983 S Proof	$24.95	$29/$32		1,577,025	$40
	1984 P UNC	-	$28		217,954	$40
	1984 D UNC	-			116,675	$40
	1984 S UNC	-			116,675	$40
	1984 S Proof	$32	$35		1,801,210	$40
Gold $10	1984 P Proof	-	$352	2,000,000	33,309	$840
	1984 D Proof	-	$352		34,533	$840
	1984 S Proof	-	$352		48,551	$840
	1984 W UNC	-	$352		75,886	$840
	1984 W Proof	-	$352		381,085	$840

Silver dollar PDS Uncirculated set, $89; later $100. Denver and San Francisco Uncirculated specimens sold in sets only. All three coins were included in other Mint packaging options. Maximum authorization is by denomination. Proof and Uncirculated coins combined make up the maximum. Net mintage figures shown represent the net quantity distributed by the Mint. According to the 1985 annual report of the director of the Mint, the actual number of 1983 and 1984 dollars melted was not declared. It is estimated that 1,170,511 pieces were destroyed.

1983 Dollar Designs

Obverse by Elizabeth Jones

A figure of the Discus Thrower inspired by the ancient work of the Greek sculptor Myron. Around the border of the coin is the inscription "Los Angeles XXIII Olympiad" and the word "Liberty". The date 1983 appears beneath the Thrower's thighs; the designer's initials (EJ) are below his foot. In the right field is the motto "In God We Trust" and the Olympic Star in Motion symbol. The horizontal bars express the speed of the competitors while the repeated star shape represents the spirit of competition between equally outstanding physical forms. Below is the Olympic rings logo.

Reverse by Elizabeth Jones and John Mercanti

The head and shoulders of an American eagle. In the outer border are "United States of America" and "One Dollar" separated by olive branches. In the left central field is the motto "E Pluribus Unum". The designers' initials (EJ–JM) are behind the eagle's neck.

1984 DOLLAR DESIGNS BY ROBERT GRAHAM

Obverse

The artist's Olympic Gateway sculpture of two headless figures separated by an Olympic flame on a lintel, supported by two columns. In the background is an outline of the Los Angeles Memorial Coliseum (where Robert Graham's actual bronze sculptures were placed). The word "LIBERTY" and the inscription "LOS ANGELES 1984 XXIII OLYMPIAD" are in the outer border. The motto "IN GOD WE TRUST" is in the central field. The Mint mark is above the second "E" of "ANGELES".

Reverse

The full figure of a perched American eagle looking right, holding an olive branch. Beneath the eagle is the motto "E PLURIBUS UNUM". In the field under the olive branch are the designer's initials (RG). In the upper field is "UNITED STATES OF AMERICA" and "ONE DOLLAR".

1984 GOLD $10 DESIGNS

Obverse by John Mercanti, from a sketch by James M. Peed

Two Olympic torch runners. To the left of the runners (as you view the coin) are the words "LOS ANGELES"; below are the Olympic rings. To the right is the motto "IN GOD WE TRUST". Directly below is the date and Mint mark. In the upper field arcs "LIBERTY" and in the lower field (the exergue) is "OLYMPIAD XXIII". The engraver's initials (JM) and designer's initials (JP) appear below the actual right foot of the male torch runner.

Reverse by John Mercanti

The Great Seal of the United States, which is slightly modified. In the outer border is "UNITED STATES OF AMERICA". The lower part of the border displays the coin's denomination, "TEN DOLLARS". Below the eagle's tail feathers are the designer's initials (JM).

Origins of the Los Angeles Olympics Coins

Rich in history and controversial from the day they were first proposed is how one might describe these Olympic commemorative silver dollars and gold eagles.

For a full understanding of the turmoil that surrounded the birth of the United States Olympic coin program, some historical context is necessary. In 1981, the United States had been without commemorative coin production for almost three decades. The commemorative coin program had ceased to be an active part of the Mint's yearly activities because of a checkered past that included programs with too many coins, some programs in which the private marketing of the coins was suspect, and others where even the reason for the commemorative was suspect. While many of the coins may have been beautiful and exciting, the programs that had given rise to them were often marginal—if not simply embarrassing. Under this cloud, the commemorative program had been stopped.

In 1981, there was reason to believe that there was a thaw in the frosty attitude of Congress toward commemorative programs. A proposal for a George Washington commemorative half dollar, which was viewed as a non-controversial way of making a modest venture into a potentially new era of commemoratives, had received strong support in the House of Representatives. It must be remembered that there were many at the time who did not trust the notion of commemorative coins because of the past problems.

Into this atmosphere, where even talk of a single commemorative coin was enough to send sparks of excitement through collector ranks, came a bolt of lightning. A peculiar threesome stunned everyone by calling for an Olympic commemorative coin program involving 26 basic coin designs and denominations to be produced in gold, silver, and copper-nickel in both Proof and Uncirculated versions, for a total of 53 coins for a complete set. The threesome was Occidental Petroleum and its colorful chairman, Dr. Armand Hammer, the banking house Lazard Frères, and the Franklin Mint.

The basic outline for the huge program appeared in legislation introduced on May 20, 1981, by Senator Alan Cranston of California. The Cranston bill (S. 1230) called for four different $100 gold pieces, four different $50 gold pieces, 16 different $10 silver pieces, and five different copper-nickel dollars. The silver and gold coins were to be produced in both Proof and Uncirculated versions, with the dollars produced only as business strikes, for a total of 53 different coins.

Sen. Cranston was hardly alone in supporting a large Olympic commemorative program. In the House of Representatives, a similar bill (H.R. 3958) was introduced by Representative Jerry M. Patterson of California on June 17, 1981. The proposals had the backing of groups such as the United States Olympic Committee (USOC), which stood to gain from the sale of the coins. USOC supplied noted athletes to testify in support of the proposals. Amended in committee, a 25-coin proposal passed the Senate. The bill among other things called for the private marketing of the Olympic coins, with some of the profits going to the three firms doing the marketing.

When the Cranston bill moved over to the House of Representatives, it ran into a hailstorm of opposition headed by the powerful chairman of the House Subcommittee on Consumer Affairs and Coinage, Representative Frank Annunzio of Illinois, and a wide range of hobby leaders. As the proposed legislation would have to pass the subcommittee that Annunzio chaired, its fate was sealed early. Annunzio would have no part of 53 coins or private marketing.

Understanding the problems, Rep. Patterson introduced a new measure (H.R. 5933) that called for 17 coins, including four gold coins, 12 silver coins, and one copper-nickel coin. The Senate passed this measure, but Annunzio again stood firm in his opposition.

Sensing the time had come for a final struggle, the proponents rallied behind H.R. 6058, a 17-coin proposal introduced by House Banking Committee Chairman Fernand St. Germain and supported by Deputy Secretary of the Treasury Tim McNamar, a host of lobbyists, President Reagan, the Los Angeles Olympic Organizing Committee, and USOC.

The 17-design or 33-coin (with Proof and Uncirculated versions of all but the one copper-nickel coin) proposal had carried the day in committee by a 32-to-7 margin. Still carrying the private-marketing provision and complete with a $30 million guarantee to the Los Angeles Olympic Organizing Committee, the 33-coin proposal was all but signed, according to most.

For his part, Annunzio stuck by his principles. He countered the proposal with a three-coin bill (H.R. 6158) that followed other unsuccessful efforts to gain approval for a limited coin bill. The three-coin proposal called for 1983 and 1984 silver dollars with an authorization limit of 50 million coins. It also called for a 1984 $10 gold eagle with an authorization of 2 million pieces. The coins were to be sold in the United States by the Treasury and overseas by a private corporation. Prices were to be sufficient to cover production costs plus a surcharge of at least $10 on the silver dollars and at least $50 on the gold coin. The money collected through the surcharges was to be split evenly between the Los Angeles Olympic Organizing Committee and USOC.

The final showdown took place on May 20, 1982, on the floor of the House of Representatives. Debate was over the 33-coin proposal, and it lasted for hours. When it came time for a vote, all were stunned when by a margin of 302–84 the House of Representatives voted "No" on 33 coins and approved instead the Annunzio plan for three Olympic coins.

Faced with three coins or none, the Senate agreed to go along with the House on July 1, 1982. On July 22, 1982, President Reagan signed Public Law 97-220, making the three-coin (six if you count separate Proof and Uncirculated versions) bill into law.

The troubles with the Olympic coins did not end with the final House showdown. In fact, the ink had barely dried on the bill before the next round of difficulties surfaced. The next problem was over the designs. Working under severe time constraints Treasury Department officials unveiled preliminary sketches for the three coins. The response was well short of enthusiastic. In fact, there were howls of protest.

Although probably the least criticized of the Olympic coin designs, the 1983 dollar obverse was considered by many to be too similar to a Soviet platinum 150-ruble coin. It was the first U.S. commemorative coin to bear the P Mint mark.

The 1984 Olympic silver dollar was the work of Robert Graham, an American sculptor. The Coliseum design, in particular, drew reviews that were well short of raves, and was likened to an automobile hood ornament by at least one critic. Others were critical of the headless athletes that were a part of Graham's sculpture.

Although the two dollar coins were not exactly popular, it was the $10 gold eagle, the first commemorative coin of that denomination and the first U.S.

gold coin since 1933, that particularly upset the critics. With an obverse of two runners, one male and one female, bearing an Olympic torch and a reverse modeled after the Great Seal of the United States, the $10 gold designs were greeted with outrage. The most quoted comment came from none other than Annunzio, who suggested that the two figures on the obverse looked like "Dick and Jane." Even the person responsible for the design was in dispute: the sketches were prepared by James Peed, an exceptional graphic artist with the U.S. Mint, while the later modifications necessary to turn the two-dimensional concept into a three-dimensional coin design fell to John Mercanti.

The whole design controversy ultimately found its way to the House Subcommittee on Consumer Affairs and Coinage where Chairman Annunzio and others vented their anger, while Treasurer Angela "Bay" Buchanan and few others supported the designs. Finally, with some modifications, the designs were used.

The Treasury Department began taking orders for the Olympic coins on October 14, 1982. At the time, Proof dollars were offered from San Francisco along with a Proof $10 gold coin that was produced at West Point, New York, and carries the first W Mint mark in the history of American coins. Had the eventual coins produced been limited to those three, it is likely that there would have never been a strong possibility for buyers to profit from the Olympic commemorative coins.

However, Treasury officials decided there were ways to create more coins, thus increasing sales and revenue. Ultimately, Proof $10 gold coins were struck at West Point, Denver, San Francisco, and Philadelphia. An Uncirculated version was also produced at West Point. The silver dollars were struck in Uncirculated condition at the Philadelphia, Denver, and San Francisco Mints; Proofs were produced at San Francisco only. In total, 13 different coins were struck and sold to collectors, well beyond anything that had been imagined when Annunzio won his victory in the House of Representatives.

As might be expected, all the different coins and the cost of the gold coins prevented most collectors from obtaining complete sets. The large majority of the silver dollar orders were for the San Francisco Proofs of 1983 and 1984. The Proof 1983 dollar finished with total sales of 1,577,025. For the Proof 1984 dollar, total sales were 1,801,210. The Uncirculated dollars are a completely different story, with 294,543 Philadelphia uncirculated 1983 dollars sold and 174,014 uncirculated 1983 dollars sold each from both Denver and San Francisco. In 1984, Uncirculated Philadelphia dollar sales were 217,954 while sales at Denver and San Francisco were 116,675. Clearly the Olympic silver dollars are not equal in rarity.

The official ceremonial striking for the 1984 $10 Proof issue occurred at the West Point Bullion Depository on September 13, 1983. Present were Cliff Barber, its superintendent; Donald T. Regan, Secretary of the Treasury; Donna Pope, Director of the U.S. Mint; Colonel F. Don Miller, executive director of USOC; and Edwin W. Steidle, senior vice president of the Los Angeles Olympic Organizing Committee. Olympic medalists present were Floyd Patterson,

Donna de Varona, and Melissa Belote(-Hamlin). I personally enjoyed the music of the U.S. Military Academy Band.

The W Mint mark was the eighth used on U.S. coinage. (Let us not forget that there was a Branch Mint in Manila, the Philippines, under U.S. sovereignty in 1920 and after. The M Mint mark was used.) No special law was passed for the new Mint mark. Mint Director Pope made the decision, according to an interim memo she signed in January 1983.

Sales of the $10 gold coin were much lower than those of the silver dollars (Proof, 381,085 and Uncirculated, 75,886), and they soon came to a standstill. A South Korean entrepreneurial group was happy, since it previously purchased a very large number of Uncirculated specimens. Its primary objective was to sell this modern low-mintage striking at much higher prices to collectors in the very near future, when Seoul would hold the Olympic Games.

However, in an effort to revive sales, Mint officials decided that Proof $10 coinage would be produced at Philadelphia, Denver, and San Francisco, bearing their respective Mint marks. The act called for one design—but it did not specify that only one facility would be permitted to produce the issue. Not only were the South Koreans angry, collectors were also angry! They would have preferred to choose the lowest mintage issue and/or the Mint of their choice. Also, if they wanted all five coins the total cost would be $1,747.

This was the first gold commemorative struck since the 1926 Sesquicentennial quarter eagle. It was the only U.S. commemorative design to be struck by four different Mints, and it was the first Proof-only issue of any denomination to be created by the Denver facility. It was the first gold coin to be produced by the Denver Mint since the rare 1931-D Saint-Gaudens $20 double eagle. The 1984-P gold coin was Philadelphia's first gold coin since the rare 1933 Indian Head $10 eagle and the 1933 Saint-Gaudens double (which federal officials claim is illegal to own). The 1984-S eagle was the first gold coin struck at the San Francisco Mint since the rare 1930-S Indian Head eagle and 1930-S Saint-Gaudens double eagle.

Because of the sale of 4.7 million 1983 and 1984 silver and gold Olympic coins, the Treasury received $307 million. Approximately $67.7 million was collected to help support the Olympic program through the surcharges. However, an audit by the Government Accounting Office showed plainly that only $6.4 million of the $49.2 million given to the United States Olympic Organizing Committee was used to train athletes. The balance was placed in interest-bearing investments. Unquestionably, this was not the intent of the original legislation.

While the Olympic coin program had more than its share of troubles, it was still a program of major importance. It gave birth to the first U.S. commemorative silver dollars since the Lafayette dollar in 1900. It provided the first U.S. gold commemorative coin since 1926, and the first U.S. gold $10 commemorative coin. In addition, it provided collectors with the first W Mint mark and the first gold U.S. coin since 1933. That is an impressive list of achievements for any program. Considering the troubles, the Los Angeles Olympic Games was a remarkable commemorative program.

Figure 1—photo courtesy of NGC.

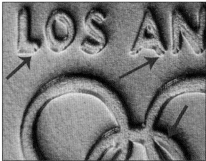

Figure 2—photo courtesy of NGC.

Figure 3—photo courtesy of NGC.

Figure 4—photo courtesy of NGC.

Figure 5—photo courtesy of NGC.

Error Coinage

In 2006 NGC identified and attributed a 1984-W $10 Double Die Obverse almost 18 years after the coin was issued. The doubling is well pronounced throughout the obverse of the coin and the greatest spread is visible on the designer's initials (see the photo below). To date only four specimens have been identified but there are surely more lurking among the unslabbed population of more than 74,000. Be vigiliant.

The key identification points for the Double Die Obverse are shown above:

The 1983 Los Angeles Olympics Dollar Today

Since virtually all the coinage produced for this program in 1983 received the best of care and Mint encapsulation, I suggest acquiring these only for the pure joy of collecting, not for investment purposes. Raw, MS-69, PF-69, and lower graded silver and gold issues are now selling slightly above bullion levels.

By the way, there were 12 ceremonial 1983-S Olympic dollars produced on Press 19 at the San Francisco Assay Office on February 10, 1983. I had the honor of striking the last Proof coin. Unfortunately, even with three blows from the press, a section of the eagle's feathers and neck area did not strike up well. All were destroyed. Design modifications were made. It was believed these pieces could be very valuable if they escaped the Mint, but none did.

According to a personal friend working at the San Francisco Mint, a small number of Proof 1983-S dollars were accidentally produced with a 180-degree reverse die misalignment. This means the obverse discus thrower and reverse eagle will both be in an upright position as you rotate the coin. The belief is that "all were destroyed, but it's possible some may have escaped." Therefore, it is suggested collectors examine their Proof 1983-S Olympic dollars to see if such a rare error coin reposes in their collections. It would be very valuable.

The three P, D, and S Uncirculated dollars were offered as a set and housed in a blue box. Offered individually, the uncirculated 1983-P dollar was housed in a blue box; the Proof version in a burgundy velvet case. The burgundy case was also included with the standard 1983 Proof coinage (one cent through half dollar), creating the very first Prestige Proof set. The issue price in 1983 was $59. All other such sets produced from 1984 through the 1991 Mount Rushmore set have decreased in value. From the 1992 Olympics set through the 2001 Buffalo set values have shown moderate to excellent increases.

The 1984 Los Angeles Olympics Dollar Today

Out of the four coins struck for this issue, the only 1984 dollar possessing a possible numismatic future is the 1984-D coin (116,675). One might say the Uncirculated San Francisco dollar has the same mintage, making it somewhat underrated. However, those looking for a representative 1984-S dollar can also choose the more impressive looking Proof coin (1,801,210). The same cannot be said for the Denver Mint dollar, which is well distributed and undervalued. To acquire the uncirculated 1984-D dollar—which was not sold individually by the Mint—one had to purchase the three-piece uncirculated set. At auction, REGISTRY SET buyers have paid head scratching prices for extremely low population MS-70 encapsulations. As populations increase values will decrease, and beware of price manipulations on e-bay.

Specimens displaying obverse machine doubling are rather common and offer no extra value, unlike the unrelated and more desirable doubled die. Machine doubling is created by the die bouncing on the coin after it was struck. Many collect doubled die coins, such as the famous 1955 double die obverse Lincoln cent, but few collect machine doubled coins.

The Uncirculated 1984 Philadelphia and San Francisco dollars may exhibit near and far rims (small or large inside diameter) depending on the hub that was used to produce the die. All Denver dollars should have far rims (large inside diameter).

The Uncirculated 1984-P dollars and Proof 1984-S dollars should be acquired only for the joy of collecting, not for investment. As with the 1983 dollars, many of these pieces will grade MS-69/PF-69 and in some cases MS-70/PF-70. Collectors should not be too impressed with these loftier grades, since they exist in large numbers because of the high level of care the coins received.

Offered individually, the uncirculated 1984-P dollar was housed in a blue box; the proof dollar was presented in a burgundy velvet case. The proof dollar was also included with the standard 1984 Proof coinage (one cent through half dollar) in a Prestige Proof set. All three uncirculated P, D, and S dollars were sold as a set and housed in a blue box.

The Los Angeles Olympics $10 Today

At present, the West Point Proof (75,886) and Uncirculated (381,085) coins, as well as the San Francisco gold coins are selling at moderate premiums. Any future for the coin is in the Philadelphia version (33,309) and the Denver coin (34,533). However, the coins can be difficult to locate in quantity. There are some small hoards of these well-distributed low-mintage eagles. Since these pieces can be removed from their coin capsules, a small percentage have been abused. Pass on those that display fingerprints or hairline scratches. Full frosted pieces are desirable. The Philadelphia and Denver mint strikings graded PF-70 or better with low populations are recommended.

All proof $10 coinage was offered individually in dark blue velvet cases; the uncirculated version was housed in a blue box. The proof $10 coinage was also distributed in a dark blue cardboard numbered holder, measuring 2 × 3½ inches. The cardboard holder was housed in the dark blue velvet case. The number on the holder has no relationship to the coin's striking order at the mint facility where it was manufactured. The three-piece uncirculated set included the 1984-W $10 coin, plus the 1983 and 1984 silver dollars, housed in a burgundy velvet case (there were 29,975 sets sold at $395 each). A three-piece Proof set, offered before the creation of the Proof 1984-S $10 coin was envisioned, comprises the 1983-S and 1984-S dollars, plus the Proof 1984-W eagle. At $352, there were 260,083 sets sold.

When the San Francisco eagle was struck, another three-piece set was conceived. It comprises the 1983-S and 1984-S dollars, plus the Proof 1984-S eagle. There were 4,000 of the latter sold, first at $352, then at $416. All of these coins were housed in a burgundy velvet case. Descriptive literature was included, and each coin was encapsulated.

A six-piece set contained in a cherry wood box consisted of the following coins: Uncirculated 1983 and 1984 Philadelphia and San Francisco dollars, the low-mintage Proof 1984-P $10 coin, and the Uncirculated 1984-W $10 eagle at $850 per set. There were 8,926 of these sets sold. I have examined some of the sets where the rarer $10 1984-P eagle was replaced with the common Proof 1984-W $10 coin and the descriptive literature was missing. Be alert.

The future potential for this issue is limited. The census figures are high for all issues rated MS-69 or PF-69, especially the proof and uncirculated 1984-W $10. The future can be bright for the 1983 and 1984 dollar low-population specimens that are encapsulated in MS-70, as long as the census numbers remain on the low side.

1983-P $1.00

Grading Service	MS 60	MS 62	MS 63	MS 64	MS 65	MS 66	MS 67	MS 68	MS 69	MS 70
NGC	0	0	0	0	0	1	4	17	1193	21
PCGS	0	0	0	1	1	2	22	129	1815	14
Combined	0	0	0	1	1	3	26	146	3008	36

1983-D $1.00

Grading Service	MS 60	MS 62	MS 63	MS 64	MS 65	MS 66	MS 67	MS 68	MS 69	MS 70
NGC	0	0	0	0	0	4	7	34	867	3
PCGS	0	0	0	0	0	13	68	153	1210	5
Combined	0	0	0	0	0	17	75	187	2077	8

1983-S $1.00

Grading Service	MS 60	MS 62	MS 63	MS 64	MS 65	MS 66	MS 67	MS 68	MS 69	MS 70
NGC	0	0	0	3	0	0	3	26	966	6
PCGS	0	0	0	3	0	3	36	110	1221	5
Combined	0	0	0	6	0	3	39	136	2187	11

Grading Service	PF 60	PF 62	PF 63	PF 64	PF 65	PF 66	PF 67	PF 68	PF 69	PF 70
NGC	0	0	0	0	2	4	31	101	3080	21
PCGS	0	1	1	3	17	21	85	229	2455	9
Combined	0	1	1	3	19	25	116	330	5535	30

1984-P $1.00

Grading Service	MS 60	MS 62	MS 63	MS 64	MS 65	MS 66	MS 67	MS 68	MS 69	MS 70
NGC	0	0	0	1	1	0	5	28	984	30
PCGS	0	0	0	4	4	21	58	136	1590	28
Combined	0	0	0	5	5	21	63	164	2574	58

1984-D $1.00

Grading Service	MS 60	MS 62	MS 63	MS 64	MS 65	MS 66	MS 67	MS 68	MS 69	MS 70
NGC	0	0	0	0	0	1	8	52	751	5
PCGS	0	0	0	0	0	11	63	147	1210	5
Combined	0	0	0	0	0	12	71	199	1961	10

1984-S $1.00

Grading Service	MS 60	MS 62	MS 63	MS 64	MS 65	MS 66	MS 67	MS 68	MS 69	MS 70
NGC	0	0	0	0	0	1	13	63	736	2
PCGS	0	0	1	1	2	6	55	145	1030	5
Combined	0	0	1	1	2	7	68	208	1766	7

Grading Service	PF 60	PF 62	PF 63	PF 64	PF 65	PF 66	PF 67	PF 68	PF 69	PF 70
NGC	0	0	0	1	1	9	36	126	2749	79
PCGS	0	0	1	4	2	10	31	106	2103	117
Combined	0	0	1	5	3	19	67	232	4852	196

1984-P $10.00

Grading Service	PF 60	PF 62	PF 63	PF 64	PF 65	PF 66	PF 67	PF 68	PF 69	PF 70
NGC	0	1	0	0	0	0	9	32	1594	107
PCGS	0	0	3	6	26	27	43	112	2217	38
Combined	0	1	3	6	26	27	52	144	3811	145

1984-D $10.00

Grading Service	PF 60	PF 62	PF 63	PF 64	PF 65	PF 66	PF 67	PF 68	PF 69	PF 70
NGC	0	0	1	0	0	1	44	16	1605	172
PCGS	0	0	1	2	6	9	38	109	2159	39
Combined	0	0	2	2	6	10	82	125	3764	211

1984-S $10.00

Grading Service	PF 60	PF 62	PF 63	PF 64	PF 65	PF 66	PF 67	PF 68	PF 69	PF 70
NGC	0	0	0	0	3	0	4	11	1419	370
PCGS	0	0	1	2	2	10	31	106	2013	117
Combined	0	0	1	2	5	10	35	117	3432	487

1984-W $10.00

Grading Service	MS 60	MS 62	MS 63	MS 64	MS 65	MS 66	MS 67	MS 68	MS 69	MS 70
NGC	0	0	0	0	0	0	0	6	1070	431
NGC (DDO)	0	0	0	0	0	0	0	1	3	1
PCGS	0	0	0	2	0	2	13	90	2436	117
Combined	0	0	0	2	0	2	13	97	3509	549

1984-W $10.00

Grading Service	PF 60	PF 62	PF 63	PF 64	PF 65	PF 66	PF 67	PF 68	PF 69	PF 70
NGC	0	3	1	0	2	8	19	85	4431	847
PCGS	0	3	6	4	20	33	100	224	7276	207
Combined	0	6	7	4	22	41	119	309	11707	1054

1986 Statue of Liberty–Ellis Island Centennial

Reason for Issue:	To commemorate the centennial of the Statue of Liberty.
Authorization:	Act of July 9, 1985.

Facts and figures

Denomination	Date/Mint	Pre-issue Price	Regular Price	Maximum Authorized	Net Mintage	Market Value
Copper-Nickel Clad Half Dollar	1986 D UNC	$5	$6	25,000,000	928,008	$4
	1986 S Proof	$6	$7		6,925,627	$4
Silver Dollar	1986 P UNC	$20.50	$22	10,000,000	723,635	$40
	1986 S Proof	$22.50	$24		6,414,638	$40
Gold $5	1986 W UNC	$160	$165	500,000	95,248*	$425
	1986 W Proof	$170	$175		404,013*	$425

*The complete authorization was struck. Total net mintage or distribution reflects 499,261 pieces. The missing 739 pieces were presumably used to replace damaged or lost shipments. Maximum authorization is by denomination. Proof and Uncirculated specimens combined make up the maximum. Net mintage figures shown represent the net quantity distributed by the Mint.

HALF DOLLAR DESIGNS

Obverse by Edgar Z. Steever IV

The growing New York City skyline, circa 1913, with the statue's uplifted hand, welcoming an inbound liner seen against the sun rising in the east, conveying the start of a new or different life in the New World. The word "LIBERTY" and the motto "IN GOD WE TRUST" are in the outer field, with the date in the lower field. The Mint mark appears to the left of the second "T" of "TRUST".

Reverse by Sherl Joseph Winter

An immigrant family of four people with luggage behind them, standing on a pier or wharf at Ellis Island, observing the New York City skyline and New York harbor. "UNITED STATES OF AMERICA" is in the upper border; below this are the words "A NATION OF IMMIGRANTS". In the lower field is the denomination; above it, the motto "E PLURIBUS UNUM".

DOLLAR DESIGNS

Obverse by John Mercanti

The Statue of Liberty with the main building at Ellis Island seen in the background. Above the building are the words "ELLIS ISLAND"; in smaller letters underneath is "GATEWAY TO AMERICA". To the right of the famous statue (officially known as Liberty Enlightening the World) is the motto "IN GOD WE TRUST". Underneath the first "T" of "TRUST" are the designer's initials (JM); below the letter "U" is the Mint mark. Above the statue is the word "LIBERTY".

Reverse by John Mercanti, assisted by Matthew Peloso

Liberty's hand, holding her torch, which emits flaming light. Below are four lines taken from Emma Lazarus's poem, "The New Colossus" (November 2, 1883): "GIVE ME YOUR POOR, YOUR HUDDLED MASSES YEARNING TO BREATHE FREE" (part of lines 10 and 11); underneath is "E PLURIBUS UNUM" and the denomination. To the right of the denomination are the designers' initials (MP and JM). In the upper border is "UNITED STATES OF AMERICA".

GOLD $5 DESIGNS

Obverse by Elizabeth Jones

The bold head of the Statue of Liberty as seen from below, as she gazes toward the future of freedom and opportunity. In the upper right field is the date 1986. Along the right outer border is the word "LIBERTY", with its letters "E" and "Y" incused within two of the statue's rays in order to keep the lettering below the coin's rim (the other letters are positioned between three of the five rays depicted. The Mint mark is located in lower right field beneath Liberty's hair. The designer's initials (EJ) are above the fourth window of the crown, in the field.

Reverse by Elizabeth Jones and Philip Fowler

This design pays homage to gold coinage of the 19th century by combining the traditional layout and lettering with a contemporary treatment of the usual eagle symbol. "UNITED STATES OF AMERICA" appears in the outer field; beneath, separated by the eagle, are "E PLURIBUS UNUM" and "IN GOD WE TRUST". In the lower field is the denomination. To the left of the word "FIVE" are six five-pointed stars; to the right of the word "DOLLARS" are seven stars. Fowler, the engraver, executed only a part of the initial modeling; thus no designer's or engraver's initials appear on the design.

Origins of the Statue of Liberty Coins

The 100th anniversary of the Statue of Liberty and its need for restoration were widely discussed before there was even a suggestion of a commemorative coin program.

The hints of a possible Statue of Liberty coin stretched back to the Republican national convention in 1984, when, in her keynote address, Treasurer of the United States Katherine Dávalos Ortega stated, "My fellow Americans, on the minted dollar of the United States is the face of Liberty, the profile of the woman of that great statue whose centennial we celebrate in 1986, the midterm year of the second Reagan administration."

Ortega continued, "There is on the face of Liberty on that coin ... the words 'In God We Trust' and the words 'E Pluribus Unum'—'Out of many, one.'" Ortega was hardly alone, or even the first in suggesting that something might be done in conjunction with the anniversary of the Statue of Liberty. Thelma Marcus Beckerman, an artist from Brooklyn, New York, had written to the Statue of Liberty–Ellis Island Centennial Foundation in 1983 about a coin. In fact, Beckerman had prepared a design titled "Miss Liberty" that had been part of an exhibit organized by the American Medallic Sculpture Association in late 1983.

A final public force for a Statue of Liberty commemorative coin program was Chrysler Chairman Lee Iacocca. Iacocca was also chairman of the Centennial Foundation, and he took this position very seriously. Iacocca wanted a commemorative coin program, and he was willing to use his considerable influence to get one.

There was really very little question that a Statue of Liberty commemorative proposal would have its day in the 99th Congress. The only real question was the type of program to be proposed. That question was answered on January 3, 1985, when Frank Annunzio, still chairman of the House Subcommittee on Consumer Affairs and Coinage, introduced legislation for Statue of Liberty commemorative coins.

The Annunzio legislation (H.R. 47) was matched in the Senate by a bill introduced by Sen. Al D'Amato of New York. Both bills showed that lessons from previous programs had been learned: no-one wanted the Statue of Liberty commemorative program to endure the sort of legislative fighting that had accompanied the effort for Olympic commemoratives.

The Statue of Liberty proposals called for a $5 gold coin weighing 8.359 grams and composed of .900 fine gold, identical specifications to the traditional half eagle. The legislation also called for a .900 fine silver dollar weighing 26.73 grams, also the traditional specifications. The final coin authorized in the legislation was a copper-nickel half dollar, the first commemorative coin of this composition.

As with the Olympic program, surcharges were authorized, but they were reduced to $35 for the gold coin, $7 for the silver dollar, and $2 for the half dollar.

The legislation allowed for both Uncirculated and Proof versions of the coins, but it also stipulated that all coins of a denomination and condition had to be struck at the same facility, thus eliminating the possibility of what happened in the Olympic commemorative program where Mint mark varieties were created by having coins struck at various facilities.

The coins were to be marketed and distributed by the Mint with maximum mintage figures set at 500,000 for the gold coin, 10 million for the silver dollar, and 25 million for the half dollars, all more realistic than the enormous allocations authorized for the Olympic commemoratives.

The legislation also had features that were clearly a consequence of the Olympic coins program and the problems experienced in its designing process. As many, including Annunzio, had been very unhappy with the initial designs for the Olympic coins, some guidance for the Statue of Liberty designs was incorporated into the legislation. The gold coin was to symbolize the Statue of Liberty. The silver dollar was supposed to depict Ellis Island as the major entry point for new immigrants. The half dollar was to depict the contributions of immigrants to the nation.

In addition, the legislation required that the Treasury Secretary consult with the chairman of the U.S. Commission of Fine Arts as well as with the chairman of the Centennial Foundation, which was in charge of the restoration project. Clearly Annunzio wanted no repetition of the Olympic coin problems.

Annunzio had sought in the legislation to avoid other potential problems. The bill contained a provision exempting the program from federal procurement procedures, thus avoiding a time-consuming competitive bidding process. Another provision was that the silver dollars could be struck from any federally owned stock of silver, a clause designed to gain support of senators from silver-producing states.

To the surprise of no one, the Statue of Liberty coinage bill virtually sailed through the House of Representatives. On March 5, 1985, the bill was passed by the House on a voice vote and sent to the Senate, where backers hoped that a quick passage would follow.

In the Senate, however, the Statue of Liberty coinage proposal sat, and sat some more. The problem was really that the proposal was too popular. It had become an inviting vehicle for those with less popular ideas. Attached to the Statue of Liberty bill, a more marginal proposal might get the added votes it needed. As the days turned into months, leaders became concerned. Finally steps were taken to break the logjam. Senate leaders helped to strip away some of the various riders, and on June 21, 1985, the Senate passed its version of the Statue of Liberty coinage program. The version still had one rider attached, an authorization for a silver bullion coin (which became the American Eagle).

Senate and House versions were not identical, and the measure returned to the House where Annunzio once again took over. There he faced a last stand by those who wanted not just a silver bullion coin, but also gold bullion coins. Representative Jerry Lewis of California was the prime force behind a gold bullion provision, and before dropping his objection to passing the bill without such a provision, Lewis was given assurances from Annunzio that the gold bullion coin would receive his attention once the Statue of Liberty legislation had passed. With this assurance, Lewis went along; the legislation was adopted and sent to the White House for the president's signature.

Designing the Statue of Liberty coins was necessarily a rapid project. All of the engraving staff submitted design proposals. Chief Engraver Elizabeth Jones designed the five dollar gold coin. The silver dollar, with the statue and Ellis Island on the obverse and torch on the reverse, was the work of John Mercanti, assisted by Matthew Peloso. The half dollar featured the statue and New York skyline behind an inbound liner on the obverse and the reverse depicted immigrants on Ellis Island. It was the work of Edgar Z. Steever IV and Sherl J. Winter. The designs were actually not released until the coins were ready to be struck. By that time the designs had been approved by J. Carter Brown, Chairman of the Commission of Fine Arts.

While the designs were moving along on one front, the Mint was engaged in a range of activities, including designing friction-fitted plastic capsules for the coins and developing a marketing plan that held forth the potential for sales in excess of anything enjoyed before in other commemorative programs.

A marketing program was not needed in the case of the five dollar gold coin. With a 500,000 mintage limit, many suspected it might well sell out—and those suspicions were correct. Orders placed before January 1, 1986 received discounts, and collectors used that opportunity wisely. By the time the pre-issue discount period had ended, enough orders were on hand to enable officials to announce a couple of weeks later that the gold coin was sold out.

With the sellout, the only question remaining on the gold coins was how high their prices would rise. With four out of every five orders for gold coins being for Proofs, it was the uncirculated version that would experience the greatest price increase. Before the peak was reached, a three-coin uncirculated set had climbed from a $165 issue price to around $750 retail. A three-coin Proof set rose from $175 to about $550 retail.

In the months following the gold coin sellout, the government continued with its marketing plans and educational programs designed to help interest Americans in the dollar and half dollar. By the time the program ended December 31, 1986, the sales of the six Statue of Liberty coins had reached record levels. Surcharges alone reached more than $78 million while gross sales stood at $292.8 million. Clearly the program had been a success beyond anyone's expectations.

The revenue raised by the Statue of Liberty coin sales played an important role in the restoration effort and the celebration of the statue's centennial. Similarly, collectors had benefited with the investment success of the gold coin. All had benefited through the educational programs launched in the nation's schools, as a whole new generation was being exposed to coins. Coupled with extensive television advertising, it is safe to suggest that the Statue of Liberty commemorative program helped increase public awareness of coins and thus probably planted many new seeds that will later develop into the hobby needs of new collectors.

The Statue of Liberty commemorative program was a success in every way. It showed the true potential for moderately priced commemoratives both in terms of popularity and in terms of the revenue their sale might raise for worthy projects, and appeared to be an excellent springboard for future programs.

The Statue of Liberty $5 eagle striking ceremony took place at the West Point Mint on October 18, 1985. Secretary of the Treasury James A. Baker III struck the first two Proof gold coins, the first at 12:47 p.m., the second at 12:49 p.m. Others to strike this popular issue were Iacocca, Annunzio, Donna Pope, Ortega, and Florence Schook, the American Numismatic Association president. After having the honor of striking one of these ceremonial pieces, I examined the coin closely and said to both the Mint Director and the Treasurer: "This coin will sell out in three months": It ended up taking just two and a half months. In fact, it was the only issue struck from 1982 through 1991 that sold out the maximum authorization. The first coin struck by Baker will not be seen until October 28, 2086. This half eagle was placed in a time capsule at the Statue of Liberty Museum in New York, where it is scheduled to rest for 100 years.

A special striking ceremony was held for the dollar the same day at the San Francisco Mint. The first piece was struck by Deputy Mint Director Eugene Essner upon authorization (via telephone) from Baker, at 12:20 p.m., from West Point.

After the ceremonial Statue of Liberty dollars were struck by telephone order from Baker, it was time for the striking of the first clad Proof coinage. The first piece was struck by Thomas H. Miller, officer in charge of the San Francisco Assay Office. (The San Francisco facility regained its Mint status on March 31, 1988.) Nora Hussey, superintendent of the Denver Mint, struck the first commemorative clad half dollar on December 9, 1986 at the Denver facility during a small ceremony.

The Statue of Liberty Half Dollar Today

This issue was the first copper-nickel clad U.S. commemorative coinage. Its two outer layers consist of a copper-nickel alloy (.750 copper and .250 nickel) bonded to an inner core of pure copper.

Combined, it also has the highest production or distribution figure of all commemorative coinage produced from 1892 through 2005—928,008 Denver Uncirculated coins and 6,936,627 San Francisco Proof coins.

With sales figures like these, this issue should be purchased only for the pure joy of collecting, not for investment. However, check out the MS-70 low population figures at NGC and PCGS. Only procure these serivces. Have one? Place it at auction!

The coin was sold individually in blue felt-lined boxes and offered for sale with the other denominations within the issue. Its Proof version (along with the dollar) was included with the regular Proof coinage for the year and offered as the Prestige Proof set.

The Statue of Liberty Dollar Today

With a huge 6,414,638 Proof mintage, plus an uncirculated total of 723,635 existing dollars, I strongly suggest, again, acquisition only for the pure joy of collecting, not for investment. Check out the low population MS-70 dollars.

The Proof San Francisco dollar was distributed in a blue velvet case, and the Philadelphia uncirculated version was sold in a blue cardboard box. The Proof dollar was sold along with the Proof Statue of Liberty half dollar in a two-coin set. The Uncirculated dollar and uncirculated half dollar were also combined to create two-coin sets. All coinage was encapsulated. Most coins will grade between MS-68 and MS-69 or PF-68 and PF-69 respectively. The Proof dollar and half dollar were combined with the regular Proof coinage for the year (one cent through half dollar) and offered as the Prestige Proof set.

The Statue of Liberty Gold $5 Today

Both versions were well distributed. The Proof coin (sales of 404,013) is more impressive looking. The underrated coin is the uncirculated version graded PF-70 by PCGS. However, one should remember that there are many raw specimens in the hands of collectors that could be submitted for encapsulation in the future, permitting an increase in population figures.

Proof half eagles were offered individually or along with the Proof half dollar and dollar in a three-coin set. They were housed in a blue velvet box, accompanied by a descriptive insert. The Uncirculated coinage was sold the same way, but placed in a blue box. Each coin was encapsulated. A six-coin set was offered in a cherry wood box containing all versions of the coins, accompanied by a descriptive insert. Advance sale price was $375, later increased to $439.50. There were 39,102 sets sold.

Buy this issue for the joy of ownership. The exception, at present, appears to be the MS-70 half dollars and the MS-70 1986-P dollar, as long as population figures do not increase drastically.

1986-D 50¢

Grading Service	MS 69	MS 70
NGC	1419	28
PCGS	2146	15
Combined	3565	43

1986-S 50¢

Grading Service	PF 69	PF 70
NGC	7754	369
PCGS	4957	49
Combined	12,711	418

1986-P $1.00

Grading Service	MS 69	MS 70
NGC	3019	174
PCGS	3046	99
Combined	6065	273

1986-S $1.00

Grading Service	PF 69	PF 70
NGC	7754	369
PCGS	6191	159
Combined	13,945	528

1986-W $5.00

Grading Service	MS 69	MS 70
NGC	1639	1973
PCGS	3777	292
Combined	5416	2265

Grading Service	PF 69	PF 70
NGC	6407	3399
PCGS	10,756	603
Combined	17,163	3902

Reason for Issue:	To commemorate the 200th anniversary of the United States Constitution.
Authorization:	Act of October 29, 1986.

Facts and Figures

Denomination	Date/Mint	Pre-issue Price	Regular Price	Maximum Authorized	Net Mintage	Market Value
Silver Dollar	1987 P UNC	$22.50	$26	10,000,000	451,629	$40
	1987 S Proof	$24	$28		2,747,116	$40
Gold $5	1987 W UNC	$195	$215	1,000,000	212,225	$425
	1987 W Proof	$200	$225		651,659	$425

Maximum authorization is by denomination. Proof and Uncirculated coins combined make up the maximum. Net mintage figures shown represent the net quantity distributed by the Mint.

DOLLAR DESIGNS BY PATRICIA LEWIS VERANI

Obverse

A quill pen lying across a sheaf of parchments and the inscription "WE THE PEOPLE". Originally, these first three words of the Constitution were part of the reverse design, but they were moved to the obverse by the Treasury. To the right of the second "E" of "PEOPLE" in the field is the Mint mark. The anniversary inscription "THE U.S. CONSTITUTION 200TH ANNIVERSARY" occupies the outer border. At the bottom border is "1787 LIBERTY 1987". Above the parchments is the motto "IN GOD WE TRUST"; below it are 13 five-pointed stars.

Reverse

Thirteen human figures in diverse dress, representing the wide cultural and social spectrum of the United States across more than 200 years. Below the group is the word "DOLLAR". Directly above the second "S" of "STATES" is the digit "1," thus the denomination appears as "DOLLAR 1". "UNITED STATES OF AMERICA" and "E PLURIBUS UNUM", separated by three circular links, appear around the outer border. The designer's initials (PV) are in the field below the back right figure.

GOLD $5 DESIGNS BY MARCEL JOVINE

Obverse

A highly stylized flying eagle with a quill pen in its talons. The word "LIBERTY" appears in the left border. The motto "IN GOD WE TRUST" is below the upper wing; the date is in the lower field. The designer's logo is on the second lower feather to the right of the date digit "7."

Reverse

A quill pen in a vertical position. "WE THE PEOPLE" appears calligraphically across the pen's lower section; the denomination is below. To the left of the pen is the date "SEPT 17, 1787"; to the right is "E PLURIBUS UNUM". The upper border consists of "UNITED STATES OF AMERICA" with an arc of 13 stars split by the top of the quill. The bottom border is "BICENTENNIAL OF THE CONSTITUTION". The West Point Mint mark is opposite the letter "U" of the word "CONSTITU-TION".

Origins of the Constitution Coins

The first-strike ceremony for the dollar took place at the Philadelphia Mint on July 1, 1987. It officially began at 11:15 a.m. with a welcome by Anthony

H. Murray, Jr., superintendent of the facility. After Treasury Secretary James A. Baker III struck and displayed the first Uncirculated Constitution dollar, he then pressed a palm button (located alongside the stage area) marked "West Point." An electronic impulse was transmitted over telephone lines through modems to West Point. The signal activated the press, and the first Constitution gold specimen was created within a fraction of a second. His nine-year-old daughter, Mary Bonner Baker, struck the second dollar and $5 gold piece. Members of the Society for U.S. Commemorative Coins, including Helen Carmody and me, had the honor of striking one of those ceremonial dollars. This coinage is highly desired by collectors.

The Constitution Dollar Today

With sales of 451,629 uncirculated coins and 2,747,116 Proof coins, I suggest this issue be acquired only for the pure joy of collecting, not as an investment. Because of the high level of care given to these coins, many will grade between Mint State and Proof 68 through 69. The dollars were sold individually, in navy blue velvet cases, and in two-coin Uncirculated and Proof sets, each accompanied by the respective $5 gold piece (also placed in navy blue velvet cases). The Proof dollar was included along with the standard 1987 Proof coinage (one cent to half dollar), and offered as the Prestige Proof set.

The Constitution Gold $5 Today

With 214,225 Uncirculated and 651,659 Proof half eagles sold, I recommend collectors acquire these coins only for the pure joy of collecting, not for investment. Both coins have recently sold just above melt or bullion value. The half eagle was sold individually, housed in a blue velvet case that was placed in a blue cardboard box. Each version was also sold along with the respective Proof or Uncirculated dollar coin. These two-piece sets, accompanied by a descriptive insert, were packaged similarly to the individual offerings. All four coins were presented in a mahogany case that included a certificate of authenticity. This set was originally offered at $465, then $525; in total 89,258 sets were sold. Every coin was encapsulated by the Mint.

The future potential for this issue will be based on the rise and fall of silver bullion. Collectors should buy only for the thrill of ownership. At present, the 1987-S proof dollar population is low in the PF-70 census. This can easily change in the future should the low census become more obvious. This could lead to large numbers being submitted in the hope of obtaining a PF-70 rating—ultimately causing a price fall. MS-70 encapsulations should be sold at major auction houses. Be somewhat skeptical of values attained elsewhere.

1987-P $1.00

Grading Service	MS 69	MS 70
NGC	2526	395
PCGS	2980	185
Combined	5506	580

1987-S $1.00

Grading Service	PF 69	PF 70
NGC	3805	133
PCGS	4077	153
Combined	7882	286

1987-W $5.00

Grading Service	MS 69	MS 70
NGC	2405	4878
PCGS	2100	231
Combined	4505	5109

Grading Service	PF 69	PF 70
NGC	7716	7984
PCGS	14,441	1829
Combined	22,157	9813

1988 Games of the XXIV Olympiad

Reason for Issue:	To support training of American athletes for the 1988 Olympic Games.
Authorization:	Act of October 28, 1987.

Facts and Figures

Denomination	Date/Mint	Pre-issue Price	Regular Price	Maximum Authorized	Net Mintage	Market Value
Silver Dollar	1988 D UNC	$22	$27	10,000,000	191,368	$40
	1988 S Proof	$23	$29		1,359,366	$40
Gold $5	1988 W UNC	$200	$225	1,000,000	62,913	$425
	1988 W Proof	$205	$235		281,465	$425

Maximum authorization is by denomination. Proof and Uncirculated coins combined make up the maximum. Net mintage figures shown represent the net quantity distributed by the Mint.

Dollar Designs

Obverse by Patricia Lewis Verani

Two hands, one holding the Statue of Liberty's torch and the other an Olympic torch; the separate flames merge into a single symbolic flame. Olive branches, symbolic of peace, encircle the torches. The upper and lower fields show the words "Olympiad" (the original design read "Olympiad XXIV") and "Liberty", respectively, in large letters. The motto "In God We Trust" is in the center left field; the date and Mint mark are in the center right field. Patricia Verani's initials (PV) are positioned between the hand and lower section of Olympic torch.

Reverse by Sherl Joseph Winter

The five interlocking rings logo of the U.S. Olympic Committee (USOC), framed by a pair of olive branches. Above this symbol and the letters "USA" is the digit "1", the word "Dollar" below it in smaller letters. In the lower field is the motto "E Pluribus Unum"; "United States of America" encircles most of the outer border. We thus have the statutory inscription as well as the letters "USA" on the reverse. Between the "C" and "A" of "America", and adjacent to the branch stem, are the designer's initials (SJW).

Gold $5 Designs

Obverse by Elizabeth Jones

Nike, goddess of victory, wearing a crown of olive leaves. The word "Liberty" in large letters is placed partially in field and across her neck; "In God We Trust" is in the ribbon of the wreath. The date 1988 is in the left center field; the designer's initials (EJ) are incused in the lower neck, below the letter "E" of "Liberty".

Reverse by Marcel Jovine

A stylized Olympic flame evoking the spectacle of the Games and the renewal of its spirit every four years. Situated above is the Olympic logo. Beneath are the motto "E Pluribus Unum", the denomination, and "United States of America". The W Mint mark is to the left of letter "E" of "America". To the left of the W Mint mark, within the lowest flame, is the designer's monogram.

Initially, there were those collectors and admirers of the Jones design in the numismatic community who believed that the classical obverse and modernistic reverse designs should not be combined. The creators felt likewise.

Origins of the 1988 Olympic Coins

It didn't matter that the Games of the XXIV Olympiad were not to take place in the United States. The primary objective of the decision to produce commemorative coinage was to raise funds for the American athletes participating in the 1988 Olympic Games, in Calgary, Alberta, and Seoul, South Korea. During the creation of the dollar design, USOC stated that it would not authorize use of its logo unless the letters "USA" were situated above the rings in a specific manner. The Mint at first objected to the addition of these letters, because the inscription "UNITED STATES OF AMERICA" was already incorporated within the design. However, allowances were made and the United States is acknowledged twice.

A first-strike ceremony took place at the Denver Mint on May 2, 1988. Secretary of the Treasury James A. Baker III struck the first two silver dollars.

When Baker struck the first 1988 Olympic dollar at the Denver Mint ceremony, he gave the OK—through audio hook-ups—for 1984 Olympic gold-medal swimmer Theresa Andrews to proceed with the initial coining of the Olympic $5 gold piece at the West Point Mint. This marked the first time that a Secretary of the Treasury, Mint Director, or Mint Superintendent did not strike the very first ceremonial coin of a particular series.

The 1988 Olympic Dollar Today

With 191,368 Uncirculated and 1,359,366 Proof pieces sold for this attractive issue, I strongly suggest that they be acquired only for the joy of collecting, not for investment. Both versions were sold individually in burgundy velvet cases. The Proof coin was included in the Prestige Proof set, which comprises the commemoratives and the standard 1988 Proof coinage. The uncirculated dollar rated MS-69 is a better proposition than its proof brethren.

The 1988 Olympic Gold $5 Today

Most collectors believe Elizabeth Jones's obverse design makes this coin popular. This is especially true of the 281,465 Proof mintage issue. It should be acquired for the pure joy of collecting. If there is to be a future for this coin, it is with the 62,913 uncirculated coins. They were sold individually in a burgundy velvet case, or offered in two-coin, Uncirculated or Proof sets (each containing the dollar and half eagle), housed in a similar case. A four-coin set was sold in a mahogany box at $550, later reduced to $510; 13,313 four-coin sets were sold. All coins were encapsulated. Because of the care given to these coins, many grade Mint State and Proof 69 for both the dollar and the five dollar issues. A collector's best choice when selecting the five dollar issue has to be the uncirculated version.

As for future potential, the census numbers looks quite low and inviting for the dollar issues rated MS-70 and PF-70, but buy the very popular gold issues only for the joy of ownership. Sell the MS-70 issue at auction or through a trusted dealer. Value will be based mainly on demand.

1988-D $1.00

Grading Service	MS 69	MS 70
NGC	1565	41
PCGS	1535	24
Combined	3100	65

1988-S $1.00

Grading Service	PF 69	PF 70
NGC	3433	65
PCGS	2138	105
Combined	5671	170

1988-W $5.00

Grading Service	MS 69	MS 70
NGC	1082	1149
PCGS	2698	234
Combined	3780	1383

Grading Service	PF 69	PF 70
NGC	5663	3417
PCGS	8394	437
Combined	14,057	3854

1989 Congress Bicentennial

Reason for Issue:	To commemorate the Bicentennial of the United States Congress.
Authorization:	Act of November 17, 1988.

Facts and Figures

Denomination	Date/Mint	Pre-issue Price	Regular Price	Maximum Authorized	Net Mintage	Market Value
Copper-Nickel Clad Half Dollar	1989 D UNC	$5	$6	4,000,000	163,753	$8.50
	1989 S Proof	$7	$8		767,897	$8
Silver Dollar	1989 D UNC	$23	$26	3,000,000	135,203	$40
	1989 D UNC Rotated Reverse				Estimated at about 40-50 specimens of the 135,203	$1,900+
	1989 S Proof	$25	$29		762,198	$40
Gold $5	1989 W UNC	$185	$200	1,000,000	46,899	$425
	1989 W Proof	$195	$225		164,690	$425

Maximum authorization is by denomination. Proof and Uncirculated coins combined make up the maximum. Net mintage figures shown represent the net quantity distributed by the Mint.

Half Dollar Designs

Obverse by Patricia Lewis Verani

The bust of Thomas Crawford's Statue of Freedom atop the U.S. Capitol dome. In the outer border is "Bicentennial of Congress" and the word "Liberty" in large letters. Above the latter, is the motto "In God We Trust"; in the central left field is the date 1789; diagonally below its digit "9" are the designer's initials (PV). In the central right field is the date 1989; the Mint mark is below.

Reverse by William Woodward, modeled by Edgar Z. Steever IV

A full view of the Capitol surrounded by a wreath of 13 stars. In the upper border is "United States of America"; below the Capitol is the motto "E Pluribus Unum". Directly above the motto's "E" are the designer's initials (WW); above the "M" of "Unum" are the modeler's initials (EZS). The denomination "Half Dollar" is in the lower field.

Dollar Designs

Obverse by William Woodward, modeled by Chester Young Martin

The bronze Statue of Freedom, which stands atop the dome of the U.S. Capitol. In the background, the sun's rays emanate from clouds. "Liberty" appears in large letters in the coin's upper border; the motto "In God We Trust" is located in the lower border. On each side of Freedom are the anniversary dates, 1789 and 1989, with the Mint mark below the latter.

Reverse by William Woodward, modeled by Chester Young Martin

The mace of the House of Representatives, topped by an eagle astride a world globe. "UNITED STATES OF AMERICA" and "ONE DOLLAR" encircle the outer border. To the left of the mace is the motto "E PLURIBUS UNUM", and to the right the words "BICENTENNIAL OF THE CONGRESS". The designers' initials (WW and CYM) appear at either side of the bottom of the mace.

GOLD $5 DESIGNS

Obverse by John Mercanti

A rendition of the Capitol dome. Above in large letters is the word "LIBERTY". According to Mint officials, the letter "Y" in "LIBERTY" appears odd or backward because the engraver used artistic license. However, what actually occurred is that the shading was done on the wrong side of the "Y". Somewhere along the transfer process, the side to be shaded was transposed. Below are the anniversary dates 1789–1989; at the dome's right base is the Mint mark. The motto "IN GOD WE TRUST" is in the central left field.

Reverse by John Mercanti

A majestic American eagle overlooking the canopy of the Old Senate Chamber. Above is "BICENTENNIAL OF THE CONGRESS". Beneath the eagle is the motto "E PLURIBUS UNUM"; "UNITED STATES OF AMERICA" is separated by the eagle. At the canopy's right base are the designer's initials (JM); in the lower field is "FIVE DOLLARS".

Origins of the Congress Bicentennial Coins

The original legislation provided that the half dollar and dollar coins could be struck in Uncirculated and Proof versions, but not more than one Mint would be permitted to produce any combination of denomination or quality. It also required that the $5 gold coin be struck at the West Point Mint. The coins were minted in 1989 and 1990 (all were dated 1989).

The U.S. Capitol Bicentennial program was historic in that for the first time since 1792, official U.S. coins were struck outside a Mint facility. Four coin presses painted light blue were set up for the first-strike ceremony, which took place on the Capitol grounds. At 11:11 a.m. on June 14, 1989, Secretary of the Treasury Nicholas F. Brady struck the first ceremonial Proof 1989-W $5 gold half eagle, which bore the West Point W Mint mark despite being struck in Washington, D.C. It received two blows from the press. After displaying the coin to the media and onlookers, Brady went to the opposite end of the podium to strike the first ceremonial dollar coin. Would you believe the press jammed? Using the backup press that was also set up with San Francisco Proof dollar dies, the coin was struck using three blows from the press. Several members of the House of Representatives then struck the dollar commemorative, which depicts the House mace. A number of senators did likewise with the Proof $5 gold coin, which portrays the eagle design adapted from one appearing in the Old Senate Chamber. Mint Director Donna Pope coined the last ceremonial half eagle. Shortly thereafter, she asked the Associate Director of the Mint to telephone the West Point and San Francisco facilities to tell them to begin production. At this point, Deputy Mint Director Eugene Essner then requested the invited guests to strike additional ceremonial coins.

The Congress Bicentennial Half Dollar Today

Sales figures for the Uncirculated (163,753) and Proof (767,897) copper-nickel clad half dollars are rather large. I suggest collectors acquire them only for the pure joy of collecting, not for investment. The half dollar was individually offered for sale in a brown velvet-lined box (Uncirculated) and in a brown velvet case. The silver and gold issues are bullion value coins.

The Congress Bicentennial Dollar Today

With large Uncirculated (135,203) and Proof (762,198) sales figures, I suggest that these coins also be acquired only for the joy of collecting, not for investment. The good news for some fortunate owners of the Uncirculated Denver Mint dollar is that approximately 40 to 50 extremely rare pieces accidentally escaped detection by the U.S. Mint and were already shipped to collectors with "medal" alignment instead of the normal coin alignment. In other words, when the coin is flipped left to right (not top to bottom), medal orientation will show an upright reverse design. The proper coin obverse–reverse relationship will, upon rotation, show the reverse motif upside down. The belief that one coin press struck the Congress uncirculated dollar with normal alignment and another produced the issue with the medal alignment is totally erroneous. I strongly recommend collectors examine their 1989-D coins. The rotated dies error is a major rarity that has sold in the past for between $1,200 and $4,500. I highly recommend its acquisition.

Both versions of the dollar were sold individually, housed in a dark brown box (Uncirculated) and brown velvet case (Proof), and as a two-piece Uncirculated set (in a dark brown box) and a two-piece Proof set (in a brown velvet case), accompanied by the respective half dollar. The latter two commemorative coins were combined with regular 1989 Proof coinage and sold as the Prestige Proof set.

The Congress Bicentennial Gold $5 Today

While uncirculated (46,899) and Proof (164,690) sales figures for the $5 gold piece were rather low at the time, it appears that those who wanted the issue made their purchases. Currently, there is little demand for the issue: its future, if any, appears to be only in the uncirculated state. Acquire the Proof Gold $5 coin for the joy of ownership, not for investment.

Both the dollar and five dollar coins were sold individually; in three-piece Uncirculated or Proof sets (half dollar, dollar, and five-dollar); and in cherry wood boxes housing all six Congress Bicentennials. Every specimen was encapsulated. There were 24,967 of the six-coin sets sold at $435, then at $480.

The best future potential lies with the medallic alignment 1989-D dollar: it is a wonderful issue to possess, a rare item with a great future. The proof and uncirculated half dollar and dollar coins rated 70 could turn out to be sleeper issues. Procure everything else for the joy of collecting.

1989-D 50¢

Grading Service	MS 69	MS 70
NGC	879	6
PCGS	1273	3
Combined	2152	9

1989-S 50¢

Grading Service	PF 69	PF 70
NGC	1747	58
PCGS	1724	8
Combined	3471	66

1989-D $1.00

Grading Service	MS 69	MS 70
NGC	1951	23
PCGS	1450	3
Combined	3401	26

1989-S $1.00

Grading Service	PF 69	PF 70
NGC	2361	23
PCGS	1929	39
Combined	4290	62

1989-W $5.00

Grading Service	MS 69	MS 70
NGC	1073	1070
PCGS	2100	231
Combined	3173	1301

Grading Service	PF 69	PF 70
NGC	2947	2202
PCGS	4692	501
Combined	7639	2703

1990 EISENHOWER CENTENNIAL

Reason for Issue:	To commemorate the 100th anniversary of the birth of Dwight D. Eisenhower.
Authorization:	Act of October 3, 1988.

Facts and Figures

Denomination	Date/Mint	Pre-issue Price	Regular Price	Maximum Authorized	Net Mintage	Market Value
Silver Dollar	1990 W UNC	$23	$26	4,000,000	241,669	$40
	1990 P Proof	$25	$29		1,144,461	$40

Maximum authorization is by denomination. Proof and Uncirculated coins combined make up the maximum. Net mintage figures shown represent the net quantity distributed by the Mint.

DESIGNS

Obverse by John Mercanti

A right-facing profile of Dwight D. Eisenhower, the 34th President of the United States, superimposed on a left-facing profile of General Eisenhower, wearing five stars. The two portraits symbolize Eisenhower's peacetime leadership and military service. The words "EISENHOWER CENTENNIAL" appear in the coin's outer border; the anniversary dates 1890–1990 are beneath the presidential bust. The word "LIBERTY" is in the lower left field, with the Mint mark underneath; the motto "IN GOD WE TRUST" is in the right field. The designer's initials (JM) are adjacent to the bottom bar of the letter "Y" of "LIBERTY", on President Eisenhower's jacket.

Reverse by Marcel Jovine, modeled by Chester Young Martin
The retirement home of Dwight and Mamie Eisenhower at the Gettysburg National Historical Site, and not Eisenhower's birthplace, which was Dennison, Texas. Below the left section of the building are the words "EISENHOWER HOME". Above the first "E" of his name, in the shrubbery, is the designer's logo. In the lower right field is the motto "E PLURIBUS UNUM" and in the center the denomination; "UNITED STATES OF AMERICA" arcs over the home.

Origins of the Eisenhower Centennial Dollar
On January 16, 1990, a special ceremony was held in Gettysburg, Pennsylvania: the Proof Eisenhower dollar was displayed by Mint Director Donna Pope for all invited guests to view. It had been previously struck without any formal ceremony (no coins were struck at the Gettysburg event). Two additional pieces were presented to U.S. Treasurer Catalina Villalpando and Pennsylvania Representative Bill Gooding, sponsor of the legislation authorizing the issue. The Philadelphia Mint struck the Proof issue; the Mint is in the state to which Eisenhower retired. The West Point Mint produced the uncirculated version: Eisenhower graduated from the U.S. Military Academy at West Point on June 12, 1915. This dollar marked the first time the W Mint mark was placed on a silver dollar coin. Less than three months after production began, more than 1 million coins were sold. However, sales began to slow down soon afterward.

The Eisenhower Centennial Dollar Today
The Eisenhower is the only U.S. commemorative coin that portrays more than one portrait of the same person on the same side. It should be acquired for the pure joy of collecting, especially in proof condition. Any future potential lies with the uncirculated version. Both versions of the coin were offered individually, encapsulated in dark green velvet presentation cases. The Proof coin was also included with the standard 1991 yearly Proof coinage, to create the Prestige Proof set.

The MS-70 coinage looks inviting at present, as long as populations remain low; otherwise buy for the joy of ownership.

1990-W $1.00

Grading Service	MS 69	MS 70
NGC	1610	136
PCGS	1838	87
Combined	3448	223

1990-P $1.00

Grading Service	PF 69	PF 70
NGC	2658	60
PCGS	4879	108
Combined	7537	168

Reason for Issue:	To commemorate the 38th anniversary of the ending of the Korean War and in honor of those who served. The funds raised were applied to the Korean War Veterans Memorial in West Potomac Park, Washington, D.C.
Authorization:	Public Law 101-495, October 31, 1990.

Facts and Figures

Denomination	Date/Mint	Pre-issue Price	Regular Price	Maximum Authorized	Net Mintage	Market Value
Silver Dollar	1991 D UNC	$23	$26	1,000,000	213,049	$40
	1991 P Proof	$28	$31		618,488	$40

Maximum authorization is by denomination. Proof and Uncirculated coins combined make up the maximum. Net mintage figures shown represent the net quantity distributed by the Mint.

DESIGNS

Obverse by John Mercanti

A military figure charging up a hill. Naval ships are in the foreground, F-86 Sabre jets fly overhead, and eight decorative stars are in the upper border. The anniversary inscription "THIRTY EIGHTH ANNIVERSARY COMMEMORATIVE KOREA" is in four lines in the left field; below is the motto "IN GOD WE TRUST". The anniversary dates 1953–1991 are on the hill. In the lower border is the word "LIBERTY"; the designer's initials (JM) are in front of the foremost ship's bow.

Reverse by T. James Ferrell

A map of Korea with the yin and yang symbol located below the 38th degree North parallel, in South Korea. To its right is the earnest-looking head of an American bald eagle; below its neck is the Mint mark. The denomination and "UNITED STATES OF AMERICA" are in the upper and lower borders, with the motto "E PLURIBUS UNUM" in the left central field. The designer's initials (TJF) are above the second "S" of "STATES". The words "38TH PARALLEL" and the United Nations seal, on the original sketch, were excluded.

Origins of the Korean War Memorial Dollar

On May 6, 1991, a first-strike ceremony was held at the Philadelphia Mint. U.S. Treasurer Catalina Villalpando, Mint Director Donna Pope, General Richard G. Stilwell, the Counsel General of the Embassy of the Republic of Korea, national commanders of 16 leading veterans organizations, Myongbai Kim, Chairman of the Korean War Veterans Memorial Advisory Board, American Numismatic Association President Kenneth Hallenbeck, and other invited guests were present and struck examples of the Proof dollar.

While the coin was issued on the 38th anniversary of the ending of combat, that unusual anniversary date has nothing to do with the 38th Parallel, the line on a map separating North Korea and South Korea. Instead, the date was a coincidence, since the primary goal of the legislation was to raise funds for the Korean War Veterans Memorial and not to commemorate a special date.

The Korean War Memorial Dollar Today

These dollars should be acquired only for pride of ownership. Any possible future potential lies with the uncirculated version. Yet with 213,049 uncirculated specimens minted, this will never be a scarce issue.

Both coins were sold individually in a turquoise velvet-lined case. A total of $5.8 million in surcharges was raised toward the construction of the first national memorial honoring all who served in Korea, from 1950 to 1953. Small quantities of the proof coinage show a 90-degree reverse rotation. The Philadelphia Mint thought all such coins were destroyed, but this was not the case, and these coins can be valuable pieces.

Regarding future potential at this time, I especially like the proof and uncirculated versions rated 70. Anything graded 69 or below should be considered only for the joy of ownership.

1991-D $1.00

Grading Service	MS 69	MS 70
NGC	1657	225
PCGS	2020	138
Combined	3677	363

1991-P $1.00

Grading Service	PF 69	PF 70
NGC	2043	23
PCGS	1799	23
Combined	3842	46

1991 Mount Rushmore Golden Anniversary

Reason for Issue:	To commemorate the 50th anniversary of the Mount Rushmore National Memorial.
Authorization:	Public Law 101-332, July 6, 1990.

488

Facts and Figures

Denomination	Date/Mint	Pre-issue Price	Regular Price	Maximum Authorized	Net Mintage	Market Value
Copper-Nickel Clad Half Dollar	1991 D UNC	$6	$7	2,500,000	172,754	$23
	1991 S Proof	$8.50	$9.50		753,257	$23
Silver Dollar	1991 P UNC	$23	$26	2,500,000	133,139	$48
	1991 S Proof	$28	$31		738,419	$46
Gold $5	1991 W UNC	$185	$210	500,000	31,959	$425
	1991 W Proof	$195	$225		111,991	$425

Maximum authorization is by denomination. Proof and Uncirculated coins combined make up the maximum. Net mintage figures shown represent the net quantity distributed by the Mint.

HALF DOLLAR DESIGNS

Obverse by Marcel Jovine
The world's largest carved stone sculpture, the Mount Rushmore Memorial in South Dakota, created by Gutzon Borglum, and a sunburst. Above is the word "LIBERTY" in large letters; in the lower field is the memorial's name. Below the sculpture are the motto "IN GOD WE TRUST" and the date 1991; diagonally below Lincoln's beard is the designer's monogram, resembling hieroglyphs.

Reverse by T. James Ferrell
The classic design of the great North Western American bison, native to the Black Hills of South Dakota. (The buffalo is native to Europe, Eurasia, and Africa. Because the bison is similar, it is commonly referred to as the buffalo.) Above the bison are the words "GOLDEN ANNIVERSARY" (which replaced the original inscription, "50th Year Anniversary"). Beneath, by the animal's left front hoof are the designer's initials (TJF); behind the bison is the Mint mark. "UNITED STATES OF AMERICA" and "HALF DOLLAR" encircle the design, and a circle of stars surrounds all.

DOLLAR DESIGNS

Obverse by Marika H. Somogyi, modeled by Chester Young Martin
The famous mountainside carving portraying the busts of George Washington, Thomas Jefferson, Theodore Roosevelt, and Abraham Lincoln. Below in small letters are the inscriptions "GOLDEN ANNIVERSARY" and "MOUNT RUSHMORE NATIONAL MEMORIAL". At the lower border are two crossed laurel wreaths, with

the motto "IN GOD WE TRUST" incused in the ribbon. Underneath the right evergreen stem are the designers' initials (MHS and CYM).

Reverse by Frank Gasparro

The well-known eagle crest from the Great Seal of the United States, with a background sunburst and a depiction of most of North America (the portion south of the U.S. is omitted and most of the northern portion is obscured by the Great Seal). A five-point star on the map marks the location of Mount Rushmore. Beneath is the inscription "SHRINE OF DEMOCRACY"; "UNITED STATES OF AMERICA" arcs above; "E PLURIBUS UNUM" and "ONE DOLLAR" appear below. In the left field are the designer's initials (FG); the Mint mark is in the field off the Virginia coast. The designer, Frank Gasparro, was formerly Chief Engraver of the U.S. Mint.

GOLD $5 DESIGNS

Obverse by John Mercanti

An American eagle in flight over Mount Rushmore. The eagle holds sculpting tools, a chisel and mallet, in its claws; the ribbon in its beak displays the incused motto "IN GOD WE TRUST". The inscription "LIBERTY" and large date 1991 are in the central field, opposite six decorative stars. The famous carving is situated mostly in the lower-right quarter of the coin. The designer's initials appear within the left mountain base, diagonally below the mallet.

Reverse by Robert Lamb, modeled by William C. Cousins

The calligraphic inscription "MOUNT RUSHMORE NATIONAL MEMORIAL". Encircling the outer border is "UNITED STATES OF AMERICA", "FIVE DOLLARS", and the motto "E PLURIBUS UNUM". Beneath the word "MEMORIAL" are the designers' initials (RL and WC) and the Mint mark.

Origins of the Mount Rushmore Coins

On February 15, 1991, U.S. Treasurer Catalina Villalpando announced the official launch of Mount Rushmore commemorative coinage. The primary objective was to raise funds to preserve and restore the South Dakota landmark and its surrounding National Park, which receives more than two million visitors each year. All three coins—which were struck without any first-strike ceremony—were unveiled at a ceremony held in Ford's Theatre in Washington, D.C. The event was officiated by John Robson, Deputy Secretary of the Treasury. Present were the Treasurer, Mint Director Donna Pope, South Dakota Representative Tom Johnson (prime sponsor of the legislation), members of the Mount Rushmore National Committee, Mary Ellis Borglum Powers (Gutzon Borglum's daughter), and invited guests. The same coins were later displayed at the U.S. Mint's booth during the 1991 American Numismatic Association's Mid-Winter Convention in Dallas. Coins were first offered to collectors in spring 1991.

I personally believe a commemorative design similar to the reverse of the $5 gold coin, if submitted between 1892 and 1954 to the U.S. Commission of Fine Arts, might have been rejected. It seems more appropriate for a medal reverse than a coin's reverse. To me, it lacks a decorative composition; there are no figures or symbols in the design, which is solely comprised of lettering. This is a first in U.S. commemorative history.

Sales for this program totaled 35 percent of the authorized maximums. Surcharges raised $12 million, half of which was paid to the Mount Rushmore National Memorial Society to enlarge and renovate the memorial. The other half of the surcharges were placed in the Treasury General Fund to reduce the national debt.

The Mount Rushmore Half Dollar Today

The beautiful proof issue should be acquired only for the pure joy of collecting. The uncirculated version, with the much lower mintage of 172,754, offers the best future potential for the clad half dollar denomination. The uncirculated coin was sealed in a Mylar envelope; the Proof coin was encapsulated in plastic. Both were housed in a gray cardboard box. This coin's Proof (753,257) half dollar was included (along with the Proof dollar) in the Prestige Proof set, accompanied by the standard Proof coinage of 1991.

The Mount Rushmore Dollar Today

For future potential, collectors should concentrate on the lower mintage uncirculated issue instead of the Proof version, which are equally valued at present. Both pieces were sold individually, or in two-piece Proof or Uncirculated sets, housed in gray cardboard boxes. The Mount Rushmore half dollar and dollar were added to the standard 1991 coinage for that year's Prestige Proof set.

The Mount Rushmore Gold $5 Today

Acquire the half eagles only for the pure joy of ownership, not for investment. Both pieces were offered individually or in three-piece Uncirculated or Proof sets, accompanied by the clad half dollar and silver dollar. They were housed in a gray cardboard box.

Any future potential is to be found with the 1991-D half dollar, rated MS-70 and PF-70 and while populations remain small. Check current population figures for increased activity. Procure this issue only because you like the design.

1991-D 50¢

Grading Service	MS 69	MS 70
NGC	865	47
PCGS	1449	22
Combined	2314	69

1991-S 50¢

Grading Service	PF 69	PF 70
NGC	1876	180
PCGS	2426	49
Combined	4302	229

1991-P $1.00

Grading Service	MS 69	MS 70
NGC	1010	454
PCGS	1635	247
Combined	2645	701

1991-S $1.00

Grading Service	PF 69	PF 70
NGC	2685	93
PCGS	2551	107
Combined	5236	200

1991-W $5.00

Grading Service	MS 69	MS 70
NGC	558	993
PCGS	1768	307
Combined	2326	1300

Grading Service	PF 69	PF 70
NGC	2183	1613
PCGS	4079	351
Combined	6262	1964

1991 USO 50th Anniversary

Reason for Issue:	To commemorate the 50th anniversary of the United Service Organization (USO), founded at the beginning of World War II in 1941.
Authorization:	Public Law 101-404, October 2, 1990.

Facts and Figures

Denomination	Date/Mint	Pre-issue Price	Regular Price	Maximum Authorized	Net Mintage	Market Value
Silver Dollar	1991 D UNC	$23	$26	1,000,000	124,958	$40
	1991 S Proof	$28	$31		321,275	$40

Maximum authorization is by denomination. Proof and Uncirculated coins combined make up the maximum. Net mintage figures shown represent the net quantity distributed by the Mint.

DESIGNS

Obverse by Robert Lamb, modeled by William C. Cousins

A pennant based directly on the design of the USO flag. Above is the calligraphic inscription "50TH ANNIVERSARY" and the motto "IN GOD WE TRUST". The designers' initials (AL and WC) appear above the letter "L" of "LIBERTY", which is located in the lower field, adjacent to the coin's date, 1991. Cousins executed the modeling for this design (as well as for the 1991 Mount Rushmore Golden Anniversary $5 gold commemorative issue) because Lamb was extremely busy with other planned undertakings.

Reverse by John Mercanti

An American bald eagle perching on top of a globe, holding in its beak a ribbon, incused with the letters "USO"; "United States of America" arcs above. The USO's anniversary theme is split into the left and right fields. At the left appears "Fifty Years Service"; underneath the letters "SE" of "Service" are the designer's initials (JM). In the right field is the remainder of the theme, "To Service People"; under the second "E" of "People" is the Mint mark. The motto "E Pluribus Unum" is seen across the Southern Hemisphere; below the globe is an arc of 11 decorative stars and the denomination.

Origins of the USO Dollar

There was no official first-strike coin ceremony for this issue. It made its formal entrance into the numismatic world on June 8, 1991, as part of a Desert Storm Victory Parade. Onlookers were treated to a 10-foot reproduction of the obverse, part of a float that presented a lifelike representation of a classic USO performance.

A $7 surcharge imposed on each coin raised $3.1 million dollars, half of which was paid to the USO to fund its programs. The other half of the funds went toward reducing the national debt.

The USO Dollar Today

During late 1992 and early 1993 subscribers to the numismatic newsletter the *Swiatek Report* were advised that because of renewed promotional efforts, USO commemorative dollars retailing in the $35 to $37 range were about to rise to the $75 to $80 retail range. When both the Proof (321,275) and Uncirculated (124,958) versions had reached the $60 wholesale level, readers were advised to sell. One month later, prices for both versions dropped before stabilizing at the $18.00 and $21.50 levels. Mintage figures mattered not, as the primary objective of the promoters was to sell, sell, sell—while there were buyers. Were the market to get hot in the future and this issue was promoted again, this coin could be a moneymaker for its owners. The issue was offered individually in Uncirculated and Proof versions, housed in a blue velvet case. It was not included in the 1991 Prestige Proof set.

Consider issues rated MS-69 and PF-69 solely for the pride of possession. The 70-rated offerings look good at present, especially in the in the proof condition. Collectors should confirm that there has been no rapid increase of populations before procuring and beware price manipulation on the internet.

1991-S $1.00

Grading Service	MS-69	MS-70
NGC	1557	235
PCGS	1956	177
Combined	3413	412

Grading Service	PF-69	PF-70
NGC	1691	38
PCGS	1358	36
Combined	3049	74

1992 COLUMBUS QUINCENTENNIAL

Reason for Issue:	To commemorate the 500th anniversary of the first voyage by Christopher Columbus to the New World.
Authorization:	Public Law 102-281, May 13, 1992.

Facts and Figures

Denomination	Date/Mint	Pre-issue Price	Regular Price	Maximum Authorized	Net Mintage	Market Value
Copper-Nickel Clad Half Dollar	1992 D UNC	$6.50	$7.50	6,000,000	135,702	$15
	1992 S Proof	$8.50	$9.50		390,154	$12.50
Silver Dollar	1992 D UNC	$23	$28	4,000,000	106,949	$47
	1992 P Proof	$27	$31		385,241	$47
Gold $5	1992 W UNC	$180	$210	500,000	24,329	$425
	1992 W Proof	$190	$225		79,730	$425

Maximum authorization is by denomination. Proof and Uncirculated coins combined make up the maximum. Net mintage figures shown represent the net quantity distributed by the Mint.

HALF DOLLAR DESIGNS

Obverse by T. James Ferrell

A full-length portrait of Christopher Columbus at landfall, with his arms out-stretched. Behind is his disembarking crew with their small boat, as well as the *Santa Maria*. "LIBERTY" partially encircles the explorer; the anniversary dates 1492 and 1992 are in the lower foreground; to the right is the motto "IN GOD WE TRUST". The designer's initials (TJF) are at the right rim, just below the tufts of beach grass. The Mint mark is placed below the "Y" of "LIBERTY".

Reverse by T. James Ferrell

Columbus's three ships under sail, within an inner circle. The inscription "500TH ANNIVERSARY OF COLUMBUS DISCOVERY" circles above; "E PLURIBUS UNUM" floats on the waves below. "UNITED STATES OF AMERICA" arcs around the upper border; "HALF DOLLAR" appears below.

DOLLAR DESIGNS

Obverse by John Mercanti

A full-length portrait of Christopher Columbus holding a banner in his right hand and scroll in his left, standing next to a globe atop a pedestal. Below the pedestal are the designer's initials (JM). To the right of the globe is the motto "IN GOD WE TRUST", with the date 1992 below; the Mint mark is below the date. Around the bottom border is the inscription "COLUMBUS QUINCENTE-NARY"; the word "LIBERTY" appears at Columbus's elbow. At the top, in the background, are three vessels at sea.

Reverse by Thomas D. Rogers, Sr.

A split image of the *Santa Maria* and the space shuttle *Discovery* with the Earth and a star or sun to the shuttle's upper right. The designer's initials (TDR) appear below the wing, to the right of the engines. "UNITED STATES OF AMERICA" arcs above; "ONE DOLLAR" appears in the right field, "E PLURIBUS UNUM" just below it. The anniversary dates 1492–1992 are at the bottom border.

GOLD $5 DESIGNS

Obverse by T. James Ferrell

A profile of Christopher Columbus looking left at a map of the New World. His name is at the bottom center within a circular border. Near his shoulder are the designer's initials (TJF). "LIBERTY" appears at the upper border; "IN GOD WE TRUST" at the lower. The anniversary dates 1492 and 1992 are at the nine o'clock and three o'clock positions, respectively.

Reverse by Thomas D. Rogers, Sr.

The crest of Columbus, given the rank of Admiral of the Ocean Sea by Ferdinand and Isabella. The crest overlaps a map of the western Old World with the date 1492. "E PLURIBUS UNUM" is above the crest and map. "UNITED STATES OF AMERICA" arcs above, "FIVE DOLLARS" below. The Mint mark is near the last "A" of "AMERICA". In the lower left field are the designer's initials (TDR).

Origins of the Columbus Quincentennial Coins

Public Law 102-281 authorized the Mint to produce a gold half eagle, silver dollar, and clad half dollar to mark the 500th anniversary of Columbus's first voyage of discovery. Surcharges of $35, $7, and $1 respectively were imposed to raise funds to establish and endow the Christopher Columbus Fellowship Fund.

The Columbus Quincentennial Coins Today

By all rights, this commemorative program should have been a monster. Not only was the 500th anniversary of the major turning point in the second millennium to be noted, but the coin also brought the U.S. commemorative program full circle—it had been one hundred years since the first commemorative, which marked the World's Columbian Exposition in 1892. But the program seems to have been widely ignored by the general populace. A dilution of the commemorative market by too many coins authorized by Congress may have had some effect. (In 1992 alone, there were three coins for the Columbus anniversary, three more for the Olympics, and the White House dollar.)

Also, Columbus suffered from a wave of politically motivated thinking. Demoted from hero to villainous conqueror by some, at many of the tie-in events around the country Columbus became a victim to demonstrations for one special interest cause or another. Then, too, the United States failed to participate in the worldwide Age of Discovery coin marketing program that experienced phenomenal success in Europe and elsewhere.

In any case, at this point I recommend purchase of these coins only for enjoyment of ownership. One may ponder why the half eagle piece is not worth much more than the higher proof production. Our answer lies in the greater availability of the proof issue. It is easier for a dealer to locate the latter through other dealers, who usually have only the proof coins in stock or want more money for the uncirculated piece than the dealer wants to pay. Greater sales for the proofs cause the bid values to increase for the coin. Lower sales for the rarer uncirculated coin cause values to rise more slowly, unless there is demand pressure.

The popular copper-nickel clad half dollar produced in the uncirculated version has been promoted from time to time. When it is promoted, expect values to rise, as the issue is rather well distributed, like most other modern commemorative coins.

Future potential seems to be in the clad 1992-S proof half dollar and proof dollar. Populations are low for the proof dollar but look at those production figures. Otherwise collectors should procure these only for the pride of ownership.

1992-D 50¢

Grading Service	MS 69	MS 70
NGC	667	142
PCGS	1228	86
Combined	1895	228

1992-S $1.00

Grading Service	PF 69	PF 70
NGC	2008	31
PCGS	1984	34
Combined	3992	65

1992-S 50¢

Grading Service	PF 69	PF 70
NGC	1799	295
PCGS	1974	72
Combined	3763	367

1992-W $5.00

Grading Service	MS 69	MS 70
NGC	452	818
PCGS	1514	281
Combined	1966	1099

1992-D $1.00

Grading Service	MS 69	MS 70
NGC	1159	257
PCGS	1513	101
Combined	1672	358

Grading Service	PF 69	PF 70
NGC	1359	1323
PCGS	2976	350
Combined	4335	1673

Reason for Issue:	To support the training of American athletes participating in the 1992 Olympic Games.
Authorization:	Act of October 3, 1990.

Facts and Figures

Denomination	Date/Mint	Pre-issue Price	Regular Price	Maximum Authorized	Net Mintage	Market Value
Copper-Nickel Clad Half Dollar	1992 D UNC	$6.00	$7.50	6,000,000	161,607	$12
	1992 S Proof	$8.50	$9.50		519,645	$11

Denomination	Date/Mint	Pre-issue Price	Regular Price	Maximum Authorized	Net Mintage	Market Value
Silver Dollar	1992 D UNC	$24	$29	4,000,000	187,552	$46
	1992 S Proof	$28	$32		504,505	$46
Gold $5	1991 W UNC	$185	$215	500,000	27,732	$425
	1991 W Proof	$195	$230		77,313	$425

Maximum authorization is by denomination. Proof and Uncirculated coins combined make up the maximum. Net mintage figures shown represent the net quantity distributed by the Mint.

HALF DOLLAR DESIGNS

Obverse by William C. Cousins

A female gymnast in motion, against a background of a partial American flag. In the upper bar of the flag is "IN GOD WE TRUST". The date 1992, the inscription "USA", and the interlocking Olympic rings are under the gymnast's outstretched leg. Below that in large letters is the word "LIBERTY".

Reverse by Steven Bieda

The Olympic torch crossed by an olive branch, along with the inscribed Olympic motto "CITIUS ALTIUS FORTIUS" (meaning "faster, higher, stronger"). "UNITED STATES OF AMERICA" arcs above, "HALF DOLLAR" below. The motto "E PLURIBUS UNUM" is in the right field.

DOLLAR DESIGNS

The Uncirculated 1992 Olympic dollar has a combination reeded and lettered edge design. In addition to the reeding, which is about 50 percent finer than normal, appear the words "XXV Olympiad" four times, two of which are inverted. This was a first for commemorative coinage.

Obverse by John R. Deecken, modeled by Chester Y. Martin

A baseball player, firing the ball to home plate. Many coin and baseball card collectors claim it resembles Texas Rangers star pitcher Nolan Ryan as depicted on the 1991 Fleer baseball card Number 302. Mint officials discount this and judge the resemblance purely coincidental. "LIBERTY" is widely spaced around the upper border. "USA" and the Olympic rings are in the left field; "IN GOD WE TRUST" appears to the right. The designers' initials (JRD and CYM) are below and to the left of the pitcher's mound.

Reverse by Marcel Jovine

The Union shield with Olympic logo above and one vertical olive branch on each side of the shield. "United States of America" and the denomination form the outer border. The motto "E Pluribus Unum" is incused on the banner below the shield.

Gold $5 Designs

Obverse by Jim Sharpe

A male sprinter, reminiscent of the Olympic track legend Jesse Owens, in a burst of speed with the American flag (resembling a track) in the background. "Liberty" appears at the top border; "USA" and the Olympic rings are to the left, the date and "In God We Trust" to the right.

Reverse by James M. Peed

A modernistic American eagle with Olympic logo above. "United States of America" arcs above, "Five Dollars" below. The Mint mark is in the center right field; the designer's initials (JP) are above the "V" in "Five".

Origins of the 1992 Olympic Coins

The coins were offered individually, or in two-piece (half dollar and dollar) Uncirculated and Proof sets and in three-piece Uncirculated and Proof sets, all housed in burgundy cases or in the six-piece complete set housed in a cherry wood box.

This issue's half dollar and dollar were also combined with the standard 1992 five-coin (1 cent through half dollar) Proof set to form the Prestige Proof set.

The 1992 Olympic Coins Today

I suggest acquiring the coins just for the pride of ownership. The low-mintage uncirculated version is priced the same as the Proof striking. When interest in the series seriously develops, expect the Uncirculated value to rise, since the issue was well distributed and is not as readily available.

Any future potential can be found in the 1992-S $1 issue rated PF-70. The other issues should at present be collected simply for the joy of ownership.

1992-P 50¢

Grading Service	MS 69	MS 70
NGC	550	288
PCGS	1036	116
Combined	1586	404

1992-S 50¢

Grading Service	PF 69	PF 70
NGC	1661	341
PCGS	1660	83
Combined	3321	424

1992-D $1.00

Grading Service	MS 69	MS 70
NGC	2833	127
PCGS	2035	84
Combined	4868	211

1992-S $1.00

Grading Service	PF 69	PF 70
NGC	2072	21
PCGS	1801	44
Combined	3873	65

1992-W $5.00

Grading Service	MS 69	MS 70
NGC	526	991
PCGS	1722	342
Combined	2248	1333

Grading Service	PF 69	PF 70
NGC	1509	1508
PCGS	2864	276
Combined	4373	1784

Reason for Issue:	To commemorate the 200th anniversary of the laying of the cornerstone of the White House on October 13, 1792. Construction was supervised by the Irish architect James Hoban.
Authorization:	Public Law 102-281, May 13, 1992.

Facts and Figures

Denomination	Date/Mint	Pre-issue Price	Regular Price	Maximum Authorized	Net Mintage	Market Value
Silver Dollar	1992 D UNC	$23	$28	500,000	123,803	$44
	1992 W Proof	$28	$32		375,849	$44

Maximum authorization is by denomination. Proof and Uncirculated coins combined make up the maximum. Net mintage figures shown represent the net quantity distributed by the Mint.

Designs

Obverse by Edgar Z. Steever IV

The north portico of the White House with the dates 1792 and 1992 inscribed above and "In God We Trust" below. "The White House" arcs around the top border, "Liberty" around the lower. The designer's initials (EZS) appear in the field below the left corner of the building as you view the coin.

Originally, John Mercanti worked on this issue's design. On Mercanti's coin, behind and above the White House, was the prayer recited by John Adams, the first president to live in the White House: "May none but honest and wise men ever rule under this roof…" The design was deleted, according to some, by an influential woman government employee who found the male reference offensive.

Reverse by Chester Y. Martin

The bust of James Hoban, the original architect of the White House, and the main entrance he designed. "James Hoban" is inscribed beneath the bust, with "United States of America" along the top border and "One Dollar" at the bottom center. "E Pluribus Unum" is at the right; the designer's initials (CYM) are on Hoban's sleeve.

Origins of the White House Bicentennial Dollar

Public Law 102-281, which was signed by the first President Bush May 13, 1992, authorized this commemorative dollar. Included in the price of each coin was a $10 surcharge, paid to the White House Endowment Fund. The fund serves as a permanent source of support for the White House collection of fine art and historic furnishings, as well as for the maintenance of the historic public rooms.

This famous building became the official presidential residence November 1, 1800. Although the building was unfinished, John Adams, the second president, moved in. At the time, it was called the President's House, and later was known as the Executive Mansion. It was not until 1901 that the name "White House" appeared on presidential stationery (Theodore Roosevelt's). Thomas Jefferson opened it to the public in 1801. When it was burned almost to the ground by the British in 1814, all that remained was the scorched sandstone walls. It was rebuilt from 1815 to 1817, using part of the original walls. Today, the brass plate detailing the laying of the cornerstone remains buried within its stone walls. In 1902, the West Wing offices were constructed. They were enlarged in 1909, when the first Oval Office was built for William Howard Taft. Since the original interior walls and wooden beams revealed significant deterioration, in 1948 Harry Truman ordered a complete renovation and construction of the building's interior (which was gutted). This effort continued into 1952. Today, the rooms reflect the cultural heritage of the United States.

The White House Bicentennial Dollar Today

The 500,000 maximum authorized is normal for a modern commemorative silver issue offering comprised of just one design and denomination. The White House was a popular theme; otherwise the proposed maximum sales of 500,000 might have been too ambitious. Sales are dependent on various circumstances, such as popularity of the issue, level of demand, marketing, timing, and the number of other issues being produced. The White House dollar sold out before the order cutoff date. Sales figures reveal that about three-fourths of the mintage is the Proof version, while the remainder is the uncirculated variety.

The Proof dollar, housed in a blue presentation case, rose to approximately four times the pre-issue price. The Uncirculated dollar, housed in a blue gift box, also rose to four times its pre-issue price in 1992. Besides collectors, a large number of dealers and speculators had purchased the coins. Several European dealers ordered 1,750 pieces for their clients, but were having some difficulty filling their orders. Thus, prices were forced upwards—to $85 for either coin. In addition to dealer hype of the issue's "rarity," a large percentage of dealers who have the coins in their possession are selling only limited numbers, reinforcing the hype. As values fall, watch the supply become more available. Although less than one-third the proof mintage, this version sells for less than the proof issue—because it is easier to locate and more readily saleable.

For future potential the PF-70 coin looks good; otherwise procure only for the pride of ownership in the PF-69 and MS-69 ratings.

1992-W $1.00

Grading Service	MS 69	MS 70
NGC	1449	335
PCGS	1229	160
Combined	2678	495

1992-W $1.00

Grading Service	PF 69	PF 70
NGC	2243	44
PCGS	1950	64
Combined	4193	108

1993 (1991–1995) World War II 50th Anniversary

Reason for Issue:	To commemorate the 50th anniversary of the involvement of the United States in World War II.
Authorization:	Public Law 102-414, October 14, 1992.

Facts and Figures

Denomination	Date/Mint	Pre-issue Price	Regular Price	Maximum Authorized	Net Mintage	Market Value
Copper-Nickel Clad Half Dollar	1991-95 (1993) P UNC	$8	$9	2,000,000	197,072	$22
	1991-95 (1993) P Proof	$9	$10		317,396	$22

Denomination	Date/Mint	Pre-issue Price	Regular Price	Maximum Authorized	Net Mintage	Market Value
Silver Dollar	1991-95 (1993) D UNC	$23	$28	1,000,000	107,240	$42
	1991-95 (1993) W Proof	$27	$31		342,041	$41
Gold $5	1991-95 (1993) W UNC	$170	$200	300,000	26,342	$425
	1991-95 (1993) W Proof	$185	$220		67,026	$425

Maximum authorization is by denomination. Proof and Uncirculated coins combined make up the maximum. Net mintage figures shown represent the net quantity distributed by the Mint. The utter disregard for any type of dating convention throws this issue into classification limbo. Bearing the dual anniversary dates of 1991 and 1995, the actual date of issue is 1993, and so can arguably be classified as undated.

HALF DOLLAR DESIGNS

Obverse by George Klauba

Three service personnel: an Army infantryman in helmet, a sailor with hat and broad collar, and a woman military nurse. In the computer-enhanced drawings included with the press kit, the three soldiers share similar facial characteristics, but in the struck coin they are more distinctive. The three are superimposed over a large letter "V" for Victory at the center. At the top are five five-pointed stars and a World War II-era bomber, perhaps a Boeing B-29 Superfortress. "LIBERTY" traces the rim at lower left; the dual dates 1991–1995 are at the lower right rim. "IN GOD WE TRUST" appears above the soldier's helmet. The dates 1991 and 1995 represent 50 years from the beginning and the end of U.S. involvement in World War II. Nowhere on this copper-nickel clad half dollar or any other in the series is the actual date of issue, 1993, shown.

Reverse by Bill Leftwich

An American soldier with a M1 Carbine belly-crawling up a South Pacific beach while landing craft, a naval ship, and a fighter plane approach in the background. "UNITED STATES OF AMERICA" traces the top border; "E PLURIBUS UNUM" and "HALF DOLLAR" are stacked at the bottom. The Mint mark appears at about the four o'clock position, beneath the palm frond lying on the ground. Interestingly, changes were also made to Bill Leftwich's reverse design. In the drawings included with the press kit, the beach is relatively smooth. On the struck coin, however, there are footprints in the sand, the soldier's position has changed somewhat, and there is an overall more chaotic appearance to the scene.

Dollar Designs by Thomas D. Rogers, Sr.

Obverse

A soldier running onto the beach from the surf, while other soldiers can be seen approaching the beach and in landing craft in the background. The authorizing legislation for this issue specified that the dollar coin be emblematic of the Battle of Normandy, when some 176,000 Allied soldiers stormed the beaches of northern France and arguably turned the tide of the war. At the top of the coin is the inscription "D-Day June 6, 1944". At the right center are the anniversary dates 1991 and 1995 in two lines divided by a short line. "Liberty" is at the bottom right; "In God We Trust", in four lines, is at the left behind the soldier. Rogers's initials are below the soldier's foot.

Reverse by Thomas D. Rogers Sr.

The shoulder-sleeve insignia of the Supreme Headquarters Allied Expeditionary Force, a long inscription: "I have full confidence in your courage, devotion to duty and skill in battle. We will accept nothing less than full victory!", and an attribution of the speaker, Dwight D. Eisenhower on June 6th, 1944. "United States of America" appears in large letters along the upper rim; "E Pluribus Unum" is in smaller letters just below it. At the bottom rim is "One Dollar". The Mint mark is in exergue below Eisenhower's name. Overall, this is a text-heavy design.

Gold $5 Designs

Obverse by Charles J. Madsen

A soldier with a M1 Garand rifle and clenched fist; mouth agape in an apparent "Hurrah!" By law, the gold coin was to be emblematic of the Allied victory. "Liberty" appears in large letters at the upper rim; "In God We Trust" is in small letters just below. The dual dates are in two lines in the right field.

Reverse by Edward Southworth Fisher

A large, three-dimensional letter "V" with the Morse code for the letter, "dot-dot-dot-dash," superimposed. The "V" is framed by laurel branches to the right and left. At the top is "United States of America" in three lines; "5 Dollars" appears in two lines below, with the Mint mark between that and the bottom rim. "E Pluribus Unum" is superimposed over the striated "V".

Origins of the World War II 50th Anniversary Coins

The 50th anniversary of World War II was almost too large to be captured in a single coin program, but Congress gave it a gallant effort. Specifying in legislation that the silver dollar was to be emblematic of D-Day, and the gold coin emblematic of Victory, the directive was both specific and vague.

While the American Battle Monuments Commission received top billing in the press releases as recipients of surcharges, in fact the first $3 million was earmarked for the Battle of Normandy Foundation. The foundation was to use funds to create, endow, and dedicate on the 50th anniversary of D-Day—June 6, 1994—the Battle of Normandy Memorial in Normandy, France. This proved to be not without controversy, as allegations of financial mismanagement—including claims that up to 90 percent of the funds were used for "administration"—and outright fraud clouded the nominal good works. Ultimately it was Steven Spielberg's film *Saving Private Ryan* that fixed the Normandy invasion in the minds of 1990's Americans, but when the tourists arrived in France in homage to Spielberg's film, at least they found a nice Memorial Garden, funded in part by American coin collectors.

The World War II 50th Anniversary Coins Today

In addition to the usual packaging combinations, and in an apparent move to capitalize on the popularity of the Bill of Rights–Madison options, an Uncirculated half dollar was issued in a Young Collector's Edition, and in a Coin and Victory Medal set featuring a reproduction of the World War II Victory Medal awarded to military personnel who served in the war. Each set had a limited production of 50,000. Both sets sold out during the pre-issue period at $35.

A two-coin set with a silver dollar and a French D-Day/6 Juin 1944 silver franc was offered for sale by the Battle of Normandy Foundation; it cannot be considered an official Mint issue. (Priced $50.)

World War II Commemorative Coin and Medal Set—outside.

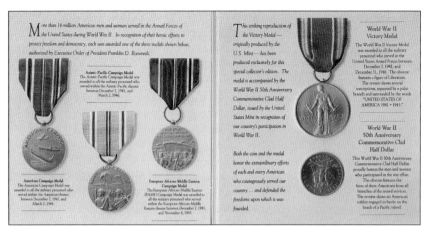

World War II Commemorative Coin and Medal Set—inside.

I recommend that collectors procure the 50th anniversary coinage for the pure joy of ownership, aiming for the lower mintage Uncirculated coins. Remember that any of these issues can be promoted. Such promotion causes a temporary value increase lasting until the promotion ceases. Prices can the drift back to the pre-promotional level or stabilize at new higher levels.

At present the half dollar and dollar designs rated PF-70 offer future potential. Buy the other coins in this issue because you like them.

1991-1995 (1993)-P 50¢

Grading Service	MS 69	MS 70
NGC	736	56
PCGS	1197	54
Combined	1933	110

Grading Service	PF 69	PF 70
NGC	1562	47
PCGS	1736	11
Combined	3298	58

1991-1995 (1993)-D $1.00

Grading Service	MS 69	MS 70
NGC	991	65
PCGS	1822	143
Combined	2813	208

1991-1995 (1993)-W $1.00

Grading Service	PF 69	PF 70
NGC	2587	55
PCGS	2054	54
Combined	4641	109

1991-1995 (1993)-W $5.00

Grading Service	MS 69	MS 70
NGC	574	476
PCGS	1055	141
Combined	1629	617

Grading Service	PF 69	PF 70
NGC	1740	640
PCGS	3856	171
Combined	5596	811

Reason for Issue:	To commemorate the Bill of Rights and the role James Madison played in its adoption.
Authorization:	Public Law 102-281. May 13, 1992.

Facts and Figures

Denomination	Date/Mint	Pre-issue Price	Regular Price	Maximum Authorized	Net Mintage	Market Value
Silver Clad Half Dollar	1993 W UNC‡	$9.75	$11.50	1,000,000	193,346	$22
	1993 W UNC Special Serial Number Pieces	Not Applicable	15		9,656	$40 to $700 depending on very low serial number
	1993 S Proof	$12.50	$13.50		586,315	$19
Silver Dollar	1993 D UNC	$22	$27	900,000	98,383	$44
	1993 S Proof	$25	$29		534,001	$44
Gold $5	1993 W UNC	$175	$205	300,000	23,266	$425
	1993 W Proof	$185	$220		78,651	$425

Maximum authorization is by denomination. Proof and Uncirculated coins combined make up the maximum. Net mintage shown represents net quantity distributed by Mint. The Uncirculated silver half dollar was available individually from the Mint in the Young Collector's Edition.

HALF DOLLAR DESIGNS

Obverse by T. James Ferrell

James Madison penning the Bill of Rights. Montpelier, the Virginia home of James and Dolley Madison is in the right center field, with the inscription "JAMES MADISON FATHER OF THE BILL OF RIGHTS" above and "IN GOD WE TRUST" below. The Mint mark appears in the lower right field. The word "LIBERTY" is in the upper border; the issue date 1993 at the bottom. Below Madison's elbow are the designer's initials (TJF).

Reverse by Dean E. McMullen

A hand holding the torch of freedom; on the wrist are the designer's initials (DEM). "THE BILL OF RIGHTS" is inscribed in the left field, "OUR BASIC FREEDOMS" in the right. "UNITED STATES OF AMERICA" and "E PLURIBUS UNUM" arc above, "HALF DOLLAR" below.

DOLLAR DESIGNS

Obverse by William J. Krawczewicz, modeled by Thomas D. Rogers, Sr.

James Madison facing three-quarters right. In the otherwise stark field are the words "LIBERTY" and "JAMES MADISON" and the Mint mark. At the bottom border is "IN GOD WE TRUST" with the date 1993. The designers' initials (WJK and TDR) appear on Madison's collar.

Reverse by Dean E. McMullen, modeled by Thomas D. Rogers, Sr.

Montpelier, home of the Madisons. Above is the motto "E PLURIBUS UNUM"; below is "MONTPELIER". "UNITED STATES OF AMERICA" arcs above, "ONE DOLLAR" below. McMullen's initials (DEM) are under the left wing of Montpelier, Rogers's initials (TDR) under the right.

GOLD $5 DESIGNS

Obverse by Scott R. Blazek, modeled by William C. Cousins

Madison studying the Bill of Rights; his name and the date 1993 are inscribed below. "IN GOD WE TRUST" appears at the lower left border; "LIBERTY" seems to emanate from Madison's forehead. The border at the right is formed by 13 five-pointed stars; the Mint mark is near the last star, at about the four o'clock position. The designers' initials are on Madison's sleeve.

Reverse by Joseph D. Pena, modeled by Edgar Z. Steever IV

An eagle holding a parchment in its talons is at the top; below is the title "BILL OF RIGHTS", followed by the inscription "EQUAL LAWS PROTECTING EQUAL RIGHTS ARE ... THE BEST GUARANTEE OF LOYALTY AND LOVE OF COUNTRY": the words are Madison's. At the left border is a torch; at the right, a laurel branch. The designers' initials appear on either side of the laurel stem. "UNITED STATES OF AMERICA" arcs above, "E PLURIBUS UNUM" and "FIVE DOLLARS" below.

Origins of the Bill of Rights–Madison Coins

The designs for these coins were chosen from 815 entries received by the Mint in an open competition. Public Law 102-281 provides for a surcharge of $30 on each gold coin, $6 for each dollar, and $3 on each half dollar. According to a Treasury Department press release, all surcharges received from the sale of the coins were paid to the James Madison Memorial Fellowship Trust Fund to encourage teaching and graduate study of the Constitution of the United States.

For the Madison program, the Mint experimented with some unusual packaging options. The most popular was the Young Collector's Edition, which quickly sold out its 50,000 allotment. Another popular option was the Madison Coin and Medal set, which included an Uncirculated silver half dollar accom-

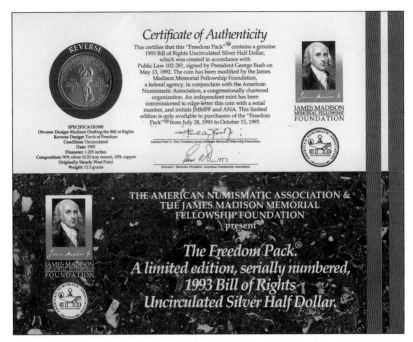

1993 Madison Young Collector's Edition—outside.

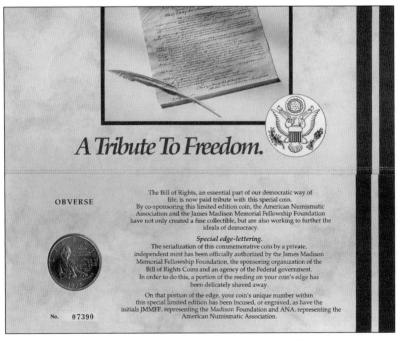

1993 Madison Young Collector's Edition—inside.

panied by a bronze James Madison presidential medal (a replica of the original issued during his administration) and a 25-cent stamp. The Coin and Medal sets were also limited to 50,000, and also quickly sold out. The pre-issue price was $13.50; it was later raised to $14.50. At this writing it is $50.

The Uncirculated half dollar was not available by itself from the Mint. Other than the sets, it could be purchased in bulk lots of $5,000 or more.

Proof coins were issued individually in blue presentation cases. The Uncirculated coins were packaged in blue gift boxes as two-coin (half dollar, dollar) or three-coin (half dollar, dollar, and five dollar) sets. The issue was also offered as a six-piece set (three Proof and three uncirculated coins) in a wooden box for $445, with the price later raised to $495.

The Bill of Rights–Madison Coins Today

The Madison silver half dollar, at the time of issue, had the lowest Mintage authorized for its denomination since 1940. It broke the string of copper-nickel clad commemorative half dollars issued since the 1986 Statue of Liberty program. It was also the first half dollar to bear the W Mint mark of the West Point Mint. It was offered with the Madison dollar in the 1993 Prestige Proof set, making this Prestige Proof set the first to offer two silver commemoratives in addition to the usual Proof coinage.

The Madison Foundation and the American Numismatic Association offered 9,656 Uncirculated pieces, the edges of which were privately marked with a serial number (0001 through 9656), as well as the initials of the Madison Foundation and the ANA. These special pieces were altered privately by Silver-Towne L.P. (www.silvertowne.com), a numismatic firm in Winchester, Indiana, and not by the United States Mint. Each piece is nicely packaged and well distributed. The early numbers (0001–0100) are in demand; some collectors have paid amounts as high as $175 to $500 for them. Number 0001 resides at American Numismatic Association headquarters in Colorado Springs. The numbers 0002 through 0099 are the most desired, when available. Later pieces have sold for between $40 and $60. With a production figure of 193,346, any investment potential for the issue lies in the altered-edge coins (0001 - 0100) and not the unaltered specimens.

The silver dollar and gold $5 authorizations are also not that low by today's standards. At this point I would recommend acquiring these coins for the joy of collecting, not for investment. Later lower mintage strikings of other issues that are equally (or almost equally) valued—at this time—can prove to be better acquisitions, should you like those coinage designs. Examples include the 1997 uncirculated Jackie Robinson gold $5 and the 1996 Olympic uncirculated silver dollars (Tennis, Paralympics, Rowing and High Jump).

The possible sleeper of this issue is the 1993-S proof half dollar and dollar, but collectors are advised to watch the population numbers for any marked increases before buying.

1993-W 50¢

Grading Service	MS 69	MS 70
NGC	788	163
PCGS	1229	90
Combined	2017	253

1993-S 50¢

Grading Service	PF 69	PF 70
NGC	1768	28
PCGS	1229	90
Combined	2997	118

1993-D $1.00

Grading Service	MS 69	MS 70
NGC	981	151
PCGS	1501	79
Combined	2482	230

1993-S $1.00

Grading Service	PF 69	PF 70
NGC	1567	30
PCGS	1837	26
Combined	3404	56

1993-W $5.00

Grading Service	MS 69	MS 70
NGC	487	813
PCGS	1737	252
Combined	2224	1065

Grading Service	PF 69	PF 70
NGC	1955	1200
PCGS	3520	241
Combined	5475	1441

Reason for Issue:	To commemorate the 250th anniversary of the birth of Thomas Jefferson, third President of the United States.
Authorization:	Public Law 103-186, December 14, 1993.

Facts and Figures

Denomination	Date/Mint	Pre-issue Price	Regular Price	Maximum Authorized	Net Mintage	Market Value
Silver Dollar	1993 P UNC	$27	$32	600,000	266,927	$40
	1993 S Proof	$31	$35		332,891	$40

Maximum authorization is by denomination. Proof and Uncirculated coins combined make up the maximum. Net mintage figures shown represent the net quantity distributed by the Mint. Although it bears the dual date 1743–1993, and will often be classified as a 1993 issue, this coin was actually produced and sold in 1994.

Designs by T. James Ferrell

Obverse

The head of Jefferson in classical style, facing left; it was modeled after a portrait medallion by Gilbert Stuart. The original medallion is in Harvard University's Fogg Art Museum. "Thomas Jefferson Architect of Democracy" circles above; "Liberty" is in large letters below. "In God We Trust" is in two lines at the nape of Jefferson's neck, and the anniversary dates 1743 and 1993 appear at the left and right.

Reverse

A realistic and attractive view of Monticello, Jefferson's famed Virginia estate. Both obverse and reverse designs are a far cry from the highly stylized Jefferson and Monticello on the currently circulating 5-cent coin (excluding the 2005 to present obverses). "UNITED STATES OF AMERICA" circles at top, offset clockwise so that "AMERICA" is fully engulfed in tree foliage. "MONTICELLO" appears above the mansion; with the motto "E PLURIBUS UNUM" below. The Mint mark is just to the right of the motto; the denomination "ONE DOLLAR" is at the bottom.

Origins of the Jefferson Dollar

The Jefferson coins were produced and sold in 1994, but effectively backdated to the anniversary date 1993. As with the George Washington silver half dollar of 1982, the issue that led the rebirth of commemorative coins in the United States, there is no shortage of questions as to why, of all the commemorative-worthy subjects, a president fully honored by his appearance on a circulating coin needs a commemorative. The pairing again of Monticello on the reverse side might indicate to future generations that Renaissance-man Jefferson's chief contribution to American culture is the house he lived in.

The design elements were no accident, as the authorizing legislation specifically required them. In a hilarious example of "cut-and-paste" bill writing, the text of the law states: "... shall be emblematic of a profile of Thomas Jefferson and a frontal view of his home Monticello." Emblematic of "Liberty"—yes—of World War II—sure—but emblematic of a profile and a frontal view? There's not much left to interpret artistically.

The coin program was introduced at the request of and to benefit the Jefferson Endowment Fund, which received surcharges from the first 500,000 coins sold as an endowment for the support of Monticello and its furnishings, and for educational programs. The balance of the surcharge revenue was paid to the Corporation for Jefferson's Poplar Forest, to be used for the restoration and maintenance of Jefferson's Blue Ridge Mountain retreat near Lynchburg, Virginia.

The Jefferson Dollar Today

A packaging inspiration touched off a short-lived speculative firestorm around the Jefferson issue. A set consisting of the uncirculated 1993-P Jefferson silver dollar, a Crisp Uncirculated 1976 Bicentennial $2 bill (presumably from the Federal Reserve's vast stockpile), and a 1994-P Jefferson 5-cent coin aroused the interest of many coin collectors. The 5-cent coin, it was later determined, had been double struck from sandblasted dies. While no official designation as such was given by the Mint, the nickels are essentially matte proof (although *Coin World* describes the coin as having a Matte Finish in its Trends and annual Price Guide). To enhance their desirability even more, the specially prepared 5-cent coin was sold only with the set, and a final net mintage of 167,703 ensued. (The

Jefferson Coin and Currency Set—outside front.

Jefferson Coin and Currency Set—outside back.

Jefferson Coin and Currency Set—inside.

Mint had intended to sell no more than 50,000 such sets, but forgot to mention that limitation in its sales literature; it thus produced the sets to order.)

It has been speculated but by no means numismatically proven that the sandblast dies, after a relatively few strikes, were reassigned to the circulation presses. Many collectors at the time of issue and a few even now insist that many 1994-P Jefferson 5-cent coins exhibit a richer-than-usual surface texture: maybe so—maybe it is just wishful thinking.

Once the secret was out, these sets ballooned in value, and eventually dealers began breaking up the sets to assemble "rolls" of matte proof 5-cent coins. The Uncirculated Jefferson dollar enjoyed a brief run-up in value to about double its issue price, before settling back down to today's levels. The item is well distributed, with good future potential because of the Matte Finish 5-cent coin.

Collectors should beware of individual Philadelphia Mint, single-struck 5-cent coins that were doctored or lightly sandblasted outside the Mint, or are Brilliant Proof pieces produced by the San Francisco Mint—the wrong facility—and lightly sandblasted. Procure the original set or coins that have been encapsulated by a respected grading service.These are undervalued at the current price of $60 per set.

The issue as a whole was relatively popular, effectively selling out its 600,000 maximum authorization; it can easily be promoted to higher levels for the uncirculated and proof versions.

The sleeper of this issue is the 1993-S proof dollar rated PF-70. The MS-69 and PF-69 ratings should be considered only for the joy of ownership, not for investment.

1993-P $1.00

Grading Service	MS 69	MS 70
NGC	1481	473
PCGS	3177	252
Combined	4658	725

1993-S $1.00

Grading Service	PF 69	PF 70
NGC	1817	23
PCGS	1429	48
Combined	3246	71

1994 World Cup USA

Reason for Issue:	To commemorate the first World Cup soccer games held in the United States.
Authorization:	Public Law 102-281, May 13, 1992.

Facts and Figures

Denomination	Date/Mint	Pre-issue Price	Regular Price	Maximum Authorized	Net Mintage	Market Value
Copper-Nickel Clad Half Dollar	1994-D UNC	$8.75	$9.50	5,000,000	168,208	$11
	1994-P Proof	$9.75	$10.50		609,354	$10
Silver Dollar	1994-D UNC	$23	$28	5,000,000	81,524	$40
	1994-S Proof	$27	$31		577,090	$40
Gold $5	1994-W UNC	$170	$205	750,000	22,447	$425
	1994-W Proof	$185	$220		89,614	$425

Maximum authorization is by denomination. Proof and Uncirculated coins combined make up the maximum. Net mintage figures shown represent the net quantity distributed by the Mint.

HALF DOLLAR DESIGNS

Obverse by Richard T. LaRoche, modeled by John Mercanti

A single player dribbling a soccer ball toward the right and in front of a large "1994". "LIBERTY" appears in the left field, "IN GOD WE TRUST" in the lower right. The initials of the two artists are below the player's left foot. Richard LaRoche's design was selected from an open competition.

Reverse by Dean E. McMullen

The official World Cup USA 1994 logo flanked by laurel branches; the reverse is common to all three denominations. "UNITED STATES OF AMERICA" circumscribes the rim from nine o'clock to three o'clock; the denomination "HALF DOLLAR" is at the bottom. "E PLURIBUS UNUM" is tucked into the exergue; the Mint mark is at the four o'clock position. McMullen's initials are near the stem of the left laurel branch.

DOLLAR DESIGNS

Obverse by Dean E. McMullen, modeled by T. James Ferrell

Two players contend for the ball. "LIBERTY" appears in large letters at the top, the letters interspersed with five-pointed stars; "IN GOD WE TRUST" is at the bottom rim and the date 1994 is in the left field. The artists' initials are at either end of "IN GOD WE TRUST".

Reverse by Dean E. McMullen

The reverse is common to all three denominations.

GOLD $5 DESIGNS

Obverse by William J. Krawczewicz, modeled by Edgar Z. Steever IV

The World Cup trophy. "LIBERTY" is modestly arranged to the left; "IN GOD WE TRUST" appears in two lines at right. The date 1994 is between the bottom of the trophy and the rim. William J. Krawczewicz, the creator of this stark and elegant obverse, was a Mint visual information specialist. The designers' initials are at the four o'clock position along the rim.

Reverse by Dean E. McMullen

The reverse is common to all three denominations.

Origins of the World Cup USA Coins

The World Cup, which has long been arguably the greatest sports spectacle in the world outside the United States, finally came to American shores for the first time in 1994. To commemorate, or at least capitalize on, that event, this series of coins was conceived.

World Cup USA 1994 logo.World Cup USA 1994 logo. There must have been no shortage of optimists in the crowd because the maximum authorized mintage of 5 million silver dollars was the highest authorization for that denomination since the 1988 Olympics coins. And the World Cup program matched the dismal performance of those previous Games, selling barely 13 percent of its authorized maximum (the 1988 Games did a bit better, selling 15 percent of its

Young Collector's Half Dollar packaging.

World Cup USA 1994 logo

authorized 10 million coins). While the World Cup event itself did manage to garner moderate support from Americans, the coin program was received about as warmly as a nil–nil tie.

Nevertheless, there was enough money generated in the program to raise suspicions of wrongdoing, as the World Cup USA 1994 organizing committee awarded its director a rather large bonus, a good chunk of which was formerly in coin collectors' bank accounts.

The World Cup USA Coins Today

Uncirculated and PF-70 half and dollar coins offer future potential. The coins were sold in all the usual combinations, including the now-requisite Young Collector's Edition, which sold out during the pre-issue period. However, even packaging rarities couldn't save this program, and in a strange turn of terminology, the net fell well short of the goal.

Acquire graded MS-69 pieces for the joy of collecting. William J. Krawcze-wicz's stylish gold $5 obverse would make a beautiful, motivating charm for the aspiring soccer professional. Best bets at present are the 1994 half dollar rated MS-70 or PF-70; other issues should be considered pride of ownership coinage.

The Young Collector's Set contains the uncirculated half dollar; the Special Edition Set houses the proof clad half dollar and silver dollar coins. The sets sell at a moderate premium to collectors of modern commemoratives because of their limited-quantity packaging. Registry set buyers will pay for these sets!

1994-D 50¢

Grading Service	MS 69	MS 70
NGC	697	56
PCGS	1907	1
Combined	2604	57

1994-P 50¢

Grading Service	PF 69	PF 70
NGC	1445	28
PCGS	1907	1
Combined	3352	29

1994-D $1.00

Grading Service	MS 69	MS 70
NGC	991	65
PCGS	1154	38
Combined	2145	103

1994-S $1.00

Grading Service	PF 69	PF 70
NGC	1688	69
PCGS	2182	74
Combined	3870	143

1994-W $5.00

Grading Service	MS 69	MS 70
NGC	547	476
PCGS	1534	77
Combined	2081	553

Grading Service	PF 69	PF 70
NGC	1404	635
PCGS	3465	106
Combined	4869	741

1994 Vietnam Veterans Memorial

Reason for Issue:	To commemorate the 10th anniversary of the Vietnam Veterans Memorial.
Authorization:	Public Law 103-186, December 14, 1993.

Facts and Figures

Denomination	Date/Mint	Pre-issue Price	Regular Price	Maximum Authorized	Net Mintage	Market Value
Silver Dollar	1994-W UNC	$27	$32	500,000	52,290	$78
	1994-P Proof	$31	$35		332,891	$40

Maximum authorization is by denomination. Proof and Uncirculated coins combined make up the maximum. Net mintage figures shown represent the net quantity distributed by the Mint.

DESIGNS

Obverse by John Mercanti

A hand reaching out toward the engraved names on the memorial Wall, with the Washington Monument in the background at right. "LIBERTY" and the date 1994 appear at the top; "IN GOD WE TRUST" is at the left of the Washington Monument and "VIETNAM VETERAN'S MEMORIAL" is in two lines at the bottom. Mercanti's initials (JM) are at the right rim. Several of the names on the wall are quite legible, and can be identified as appearing in Panel 03E, casualties incurred on or around November 17, 1965: on the Memorial names are arranged chronologically by date of casualty rather than alphabetically.

Reverse by Thomas D. Rogers, Sr.

Three medals issued during the war. "UNITED STATES OF AMERICA" circles above; "E PLURIBUS UNUM" appears in three lines above the central medal, and "ONE DOLLAR" is in two lines below. The Mint mark is at the lower right rim; the designer's initials (TDR) are at the lower left.

Origins of the Vietnam Veterans Memorial Dollar

This dollar may be the only commemorative coin to date that marks the anniversary of a memorial: 10 years of the Vietnam Veterans Memorial (even though by the time the coins were issued, it had been 12 years). The coin was also designed to raise surcharge funds for the continued upkeep and updating of the memorial.

The Vietnam Veterans Memorial wall is arguably the most emotionally involving of the monuments and memorials in Washington, D.C. Unlike the abstract Washington Monument that stands in contrast on the coin's obverse, or the gigantic scale of the Lincoln Memorial in whose shadow the Wall literally rests, the Vietnam Veterans Memorial displays the actual names of the young men and women killed in that long conflict. This memorial is both human, in its tactile design and appalling, in its vast expanse.

The Vietnam Veterans Memorial Dollar Today

Somewhat more than half the allotted 500,000 coins were sold. The emotional context they carry is immense. It may be that an aftermarket will appear where part of the design is ground off and the name and service particulars of individuals are engraved onto the coins as personal mementos. How wonderful and sobering that would be for numismatists generations hence. This coin was well distributed.

The sleeper coin of this issue could very well be the 1994-P proof dollar rated PF-70, if population numbers remain low. All other members of this issue should be acquired only for the pride of ownership.

1994-W $1.00		
Grading Service	**MS 69**	**MS 70**
NGC	1047	457
PCGS	1456	232
Combined	2863	689

1994-P $1.00		
Grading Service	**PF 69**	**PF 70**
NGC	2217	10
PCGS	1580	26
Combined	3797	36

1994 Prisoners of War Museum

Reason for Issue:	To commemorate Americans who have been prisoners of war.
Authorization:	Public Law 103-186, December 14, 1993.

Facts and Figures

Denomination	Date/Mint	Pre-issue Price	Regular Price	Maximum Authorized	Net Mintage	Market Value
Silver Dollar	1994 W UNC	$27	$32	500,000	54,893	$90
	1994 P Proof	$31	$35		224,449	$45

Maximum authorization is by denomination. Proof and Uncirculated coins combined make up the maximum. Net mintage figures shown represent the net quantity distributed by the Mint.

Designs

Obverse by Tom Nielsen, modeled by Alfred Maletsky

An eagle in flight, escaping from a ring of barbed wire. Around the eagle's left talon is a broken chain, still manacled. "Liberty" appears above, between the eagle's upswept wings, and "Freedom" is at the right, in the foreground. "In God We Trust" is below the eagle's head in two lines, and the date appears below, inside the barbed wire ring. The designers' initials (TMN and AM) appear at lower left and lower right, between the barbed wire and the rim. Tom Nielsen was an employee of the Department of Veterans Affairs; his design was rendered into plasticine by Alfred Maletsky of the Mint engraving staff.

Reverse by Edgar Z. Steever IV

A straight-on depiction of the National Prisoner of War Museum in Andersonville, Georgia, site of the most infamous of the Civil War prison stockades. Uniformly sized lettering at the top spells out "E PLURIBUS UNUM", "UNITED STATES OF AMERICA", and "ONE DOLLAR". In smaller letters in exergue is "NATIONAL PRISONER OF WAR MUSEUM" in three lines. The Mint mark is at the lower right. The designer's initials are at left, just below the building.

Origins of the Prisoners of War Museum Dollar

The National Prisoner of War Museum opened to the public in April 1998 at Andersonville, in southern Georgia. The museum does not focus entirely on Andersonville, but communicates the prisoner of war experience regardless of when or where prisoners served or how they were captured. Sadly, the coin's designs fail to express even a small hint of that experience.

Throughout the museum grounds are brick walls depicting prisoners in agonizing poses seemingly encased in the brick relief. It is a haunting view even in photographs, and must be a chilling experience first-hand, especially for former POWs visiting the site.

According to information at the museum, more than half the funds to build the museum came from donations, the majority of which was the result of the sale of the commemorative coins. This commemorative program must be judged a success, if purely on these terms.

The Prisoners of War Museum Dollar Today

Just more than half the allotted maximum was sold, so the money raised was earmarked for construction. A maintenance endowment for the museum and for national Veterans Administration cemeteries missed the cut. A rather sizeable and varied subset of modern U.S. commemorative coins could be assembled around war themes. The POW Museum coins would certainly complete that collection.

There are an estimated 56,000 former POWs living in the United States; fewer than 55,000 uncirculated silver dollars were sold. If each former POW decides he needs a coin, tremendous demand would develop as redistribution occurs. This would have an effect on the higher-mintage Proof version. No such demand has materialized as of yet.

The low population numbers in the PF-70 can increase. The mintage is extremely high. Any future potential is based on bullion value. Should you possrssa PF-70 sell into auction for best return.

1994-W $1.00		
Grading Service	MS 69	MS 70
NGC	1021	544
PCGS	1299	309
Combined	2320	853

1994-P $1.00		
Grading Service	PF 69	PF 70
NGC	1638	13
PCGS	1669	13
Combined	3307	26

1994 WOMEN IN MILITARY SERVICE MEMORIAL

Reason for Issue:	To commemorate all women, past and present, who served in the U.S. Armed Forces.
Authorization:	Public Law 103-186, December 14, 1993.

Facts and Figures

Denomination	Date/Mint	Pre-issue Price	Regular Price	Maximum Authorized	Net Mintage	Market Value
Silver Dollar	1994 W UNC	$27.00	$32.00	500,000	69,860	$42
	1994 P Proof	$31.00	$35.00		249,278	$42

Maximum authorization is by denomination. Proof and Uncirculated coins combined make up the maximum. Net mintage figures shown represent the net quantity distributed by the Mint.

DESIGNS

Obverse by T. James Ferrell

Left-facing profiles of servicewomen representing the five branches of the U.S. military. The wording "ARMY MARINES NAVY AIR FORCE COAST GUARD", separated by five-pointed stars, almost completely encircles the obverse design. "LIBERTY" in large letters, "IN GOD WE TRUST" in smaller letters, and the date 1994 fill the lower central area. Ferrell's initials (TJF) are at the lower left rim, between the legend and the date.

Reverse by Thomas D. Rogers, Sr.

The approved design for the Women in Military Service Memorial. "UNITED STATES OF AMERICA" circles the upper left rim, and "ONE DOLLAR" appears horizontally in two lines at the three o'clock position. "WOMEN IN MILITARY SERVICE MEMORIAL" is located centrally above the structure; "E PLURIBUS UNUM" is in the foreground at the bottom. The Mint mark is at the eight o'clock position near the rim.

Origins of the Women in Military Service Memorial Dollar

From legislation through marketing, the Women in Military Service Memorial coins have been categorized with the Vietnam Veterans Memorial and Prisoners of War Museum coins. Technically, though, they are separate issues, and benefit different organizations, albeit similarly themed ones.

The memorial was authorized by Congress in 1986, although without federal funding. It is located in Arlington National Cemetery, and incorporates and repurposes part of that historical landmark's structures. The memorial was dedicated on October 18, 1997.

The Women in Military Service Memorial Dollar Today

Sale of these three veterans commemorative dollars was scheduled to cease on April 30, 1995, but the U.S. Mint granted the issues a three-month extension. Towards the year's end, a sales agreement was made between the U.S. Mint and the Women in Military Service for America Memorial Foundation, Inc. (www. womensmemorial.org). This was a first for the modern commemorative coin program. The foundation was able to purchase at an undisclosed bulk discount 16,828 uncirculated and 21,469 proof 1994 Women in Military Service Memorial dollars that were unsold and stored at the Philadelphia Mint. Production figures presented at the time represented only the purchased coinage. Three-coin sets housing the U.S. Veterans pieces were sold in the uncirculated and proof versions

Special financing was arranged because the foundation's assets were being used for the memorial construction. The first payment was made in January 1996; the debt was paid off in December 1998.

With the bulk sale of the uncirculated and proof dollars listed above, the best bet for collectors is the 1994-P proof issue rated PF-70. Carefully review the PF-70 populations before your procurement for any large increases, and purchase accordingly. Obtain any other member of this coinage issue for the sheer joy of collecting.

1994-W $1.00

Grading Service	MS 69	MS 70
NGC	2183	821
PCGS	1977	246
Combined	4160	1067

1994-P $1.00

Grading Service	PF 69	PF 70
NGC	1097	16
PCGS	1036	4
Combined	2133	20

1994 United States Capitol Bicentennial

Reason for Issue:	To commemorate the 200th anniversary of the United States Capitol.
Authorization:	Public Law 103-186, December 14, 1993.

Facts and Figures

Denomination	Date/Mint	Pre-issue Price	Regular Price	Maximum Authorized	Net Mintage	Market Value
Silver Dollar	1994 D UNC	$32	$37	500,000	68,332	$40
	1994 S Proof	$36	$40		279,579	$40

Maximum authorization is by denomination. Proof and Uncirculated coins combined make up the maximum. Net mintage figures shown represent the net quantity distributed by the Mint.

Designs

Obverse by William C. Cousins

A view of the Capitol dome. A ring of 13 stars circles the Statue of Freedom; "Liberty" and the date 1994 are in large letters at top; "In God We Trust" is in smaller letters below "Liberty". "Bicentennial of United States Capitol" appears in three lines in the left field.

Reverse by John Mercanti

An eagle, shield, and flags as portrayed in a stained glass window in the Capitol. Uniform lettering "United States of America" and "One Dollar" encircle the central device. Mercanti's initials (JM) appear near the bottom of the flag

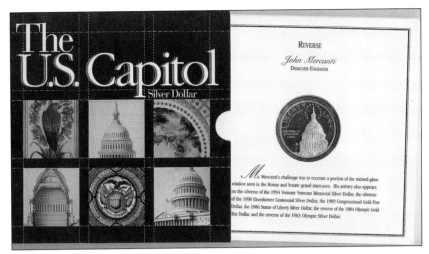

1994 U.S. Capitol proof coin in special collector sleeve packaging.

at left, and the Mint mark is in the lower right field. "E PLURIBUS UNUM" is incorporated into a ribbon being held by the eagle.

Origins of the United States Capitol Bicentennial Dollar

A steep $15 per coin surcharge raised funds to construct a Visitor Center under the Capitol's East Plaza. In 1793 George Washington laid the cornerstone to the Capitol, and the building has been undergoing construction, renovation, or addition pretty much ever since. The famed dome is by now familiar to coin collectors, having already appeared on the half dollar and half eagle in the 1989 Bicentennial of Congress program.

The United States Capitol Bicentennial Dollar Today

Sales were mediocre—low enough to indicate soft demand, too high to create any real rarities, and today's market value bears that out. If you collect architecture on coins, or Washingtonia (material relating to the District of Columbia, that is), then this piece is a must. The best bet is the 1994-S proof dollar rated PF-70. All others I recommend purchasing only for the joy of collecting.

<table>
<tr><td colspan="3">1994-D $1.00</td></tr>
<tr><th>Grading Service</th><th>MS 69</th><th>MS 70</th></tr>
<tr><td>NGC</td><td>857</td><td>496</td></tr>
<tr><td>PCGS</td><td>1484</td><td>279</td></tr>
<tr><td>Combined</td><td>2341</td><td>775</td></tr>
</table>

<table>
<tr><td colspan="3">1994-S $1.00</td></tr>
<tr><th>Grading Service</th><th>PF 69</th><th>PF 70</th></tr>
<tr><td>NGC</td><td>1401</td><td>40</td></tr>
<tr><td>PCGS</td><td>1369</td><td>58</td></tr>
<tr><td>Combined</td><td>2770</td><td>98</td></tr>
</table>

1995 ATLANTA CENTENNIAL OLYMPIC GAMES

Reason for Issue:	To commemorate the Games of the XXVI Olympiad in Atlanta.
Authorization:	Public Law 102-390, October 6, 1992.

Facts and Figures

Denomination	Date/Mint	Pre-issue Price	Regular Price	Maximum Authorized	Net Mintage	Market Value
Copper-Nickel Clad Half Dollar Basketball	1995 S UNC	$10.50	$11.50	2,000,000	171,001	$23
	1995 S Proof	$11.50	$12.50		169,655	$24
Copper-Nickel Clad Half Dollar Baseball	1995 S UNC	$10.50	$11.50	2,000,000	164,605	$25
	1995 S Proof	$11.50	$12.50		118,087	$23
Silver Dollar Gymnastics	1995 D UNC	$27.95	$31.95	750,000	42,497	$68
	1995 P Proof	$30.95	$34.95		182,676	$45
Silver Dollar Cycling	1995-D UNC	$27.95	$31.95	750,000	19,662	$145
	1995-P Proof	$30.95	$34.95		118,795	$49
Silver Dollar Track & Field	1995 D UNC	$27.95	$31.95	750,000	24,976	$100
	1995 P Proof	$30.95	$34.95		136,935	$45
Silver Dollar Paralympics, Blind Runner	1995 D UNC	$27.95	$31.95	750,000	28,649	$75
	1995 P Proof	$30.95	$34.95		138,337	$49
Gold $5 Torch Runner	1995 W UNC	$229	$249	175,000	14,645	$850
	1995-W Proof	$239	$259		57,442	$450

The U.S. Olympic Coins of the Atlanta Centennial Olympic Games

Release 1 - January 1995

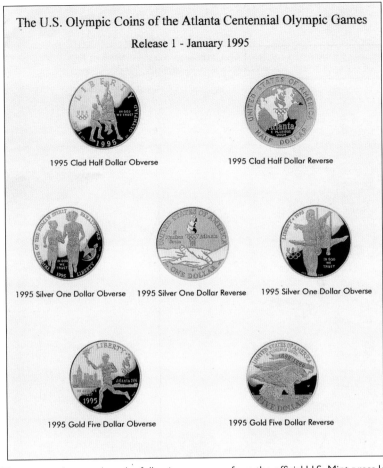

1995 Clad Half Dollar Obverse   1995 Clad Half Dollar Reverse

1995 Silver One Dollar Obverse   1995 Silver One Dollar Reverse   1995 Silver One Dollar Obverse

1995 Gold Five Dollar Obverse   1995 Gold Five Dollar Reverse

The images above and on the following pages are from the official U.S. Mint press kit for this issue. The 1996 $5 Olympic Cauldron and 1996 $5 Flag Bearer coins had their release dates switched because of "production issues" at the Mint.

Denomination	Date/Mint	Pre-issue Price	Regular Price	Maximum Authorized	Net Mintage	Market Value
Gold $5 Atlanta Stadium	1995-W UNC	$229	$249	175,000	10,579	$2,350
	1995 W Proof	$239	$259		43,124	$450
Copper-Nickel Clad Half Dollar Swimming	1996 S UNC	$10.50	$11.50	3,000,000	49,533	$150
	1996 S Proof	$11.50	$12.50		114,315	$38

The U.S. Olympic Coins of the Atlanta Centennial Olympic Games

Release 2 - July 1995

1995 Clad Half Dollar Obverse

1995 Clad Half Dollar Reverse

1995 Silver One Dollar Obverse

1995 Silver One Dollar Reverse

1995 Silver One Dollar Obverse

1995 Gold Five Dollar Obverse

1995 Gold Five Dollar Reverse

Denomination	Date/Mint	Pre-issue Price	Regular Price	Maximum Authorized	Net Mintage	Market Value
Copper-Nickel Clad Half Dollar Soccer	1996 S UNC	$10.50	$11.50	3,000,000	52,836	$140
	1996 S Proof	$11.50	$12.50		112,412	$105
Silver Dollar Tennis	1996 D UNC	$27.95	$31.95	1,000,000	15,983	$265
	1996 P Proof	$30.95	$34.95		92,016	$95

The U.S. Olympic Coins of the Atlanta Centennial Olympic Games

Release 3 - January 1996

1996 Clad Half Dollar Obverse

1996 Clad Half Dollar Reverse

1996 Silver One Dollar Obverse

1996 Silver One Dollar Reverse

1996 Silver One Dollar Obverse

1996 Gold Five Dollar Obverse

1996 Gold Five Dollar Reverse

*Change - To be released
Spring 1996

Denomination	Date/Mint	Pre-issue Price	Regular Price	Maximum Authorized	Net Mintage	Market Value
Silver Dollar Rowing	1996 D UNC	$27.95	$31.95	1,000,000	16,258	$300
	1996 P Proof	$30.95	$34.95		151,890	$78
Silver Dollar High Jump	1996 D UNC	$27.95	$31.95	1,000,000	15,697	$325
	1996 P Proof	$30.95	$34.95		124,502	$48

The U.S. Olympic Coins of the Atlanta Centennial Olympic Games

Release 4 - Spring 1996

1996 Clad Half Dollar Obverse

1996 Clad Half Dollar Reverse

1996 Silver One Dollar Obverse

1996 Silver One Dollar Reverse

1996 Silver One Dollar Obverse

1996 Gold Five Dollar Obverse

1996 Gold Five Dollar Reverse

*Change - To be released
January 1996

Denomination	Date/Mint	Pre-issue Price	Regular Price	Maximum Authorized	Net Mintage	Market Value
Silver Dollar Paralympics, Wheel Chair Athlete	1996 D UNC	$27.95	$31.95	1,000,000	14,497	$300
	1996 P Proof	$30.95	$34.95		84,280	$95
Gold $5 Olympic Cauldron	1996 W UNC	$229	$249	300,000	9,210	$2,550
	1996 W Proof	$239	$259		38,555	$450

Denomination	Date/Mint	Pre-issue Price	Regular Price	Maximum Authorized	Net Mintage	Market Value
Gold $5 Flag Bearer	1996 W UNC	$229	$249	300,000	9,174	$2,550
	1996 W Proof	$239	$259		32,886	$450

Maximum authorization is by denomination. Proof and Uncirculated coins combined make up the maximum. Net mintage figures shown represent the net quantity distributed by the Mint.

Half Dollar Designs

1995 Basketball Obverse by Clint Hansen, modeled by Alfred Maletsky

Three basketball players in action. According to the U.S. Mint, the sports depicted on the clad half dollars were chosen for their special appeal to young people, so we have basketball and baseball in 1995 and swimming and soccer in 1996. "Liberty" in large letters arcs above and the date 1995 is below. To the left is "USA" and the five rings logo, and to the right "In God We Trust". At the lower left and lower right rim, separated by quite some distance, is "XXVI Olympiad". Hansen's initials are (CPH) at the lower left, Maletsky's (AM) at the lower right.

1995 Baseball Obverse by Edgar Steever

A batter awaits an oncoming pitch, the catcher is poised behind him, and in what may be the only appearance of an official rather than a competitor on an Olympic commemorative, the umpire crouches to make the call. "Liberty" is in large letters at the upper left rim; "USA" and the five rings logo appear just above the umpire's head. "In God We Trust" is in three lines just to the right of the batter's knee. The date 1995 appears at the bottom. Steever's initials (EZS) are at the rim below the umpire's feet. Baseball was a newcomer to the Olympic Games in Atlanta, and this choice of design clearly states "These are the Olympic Games today."

1995 Common Reverse by T. James Ferrell

The half dollars of this date share a common reverse, as do the half dollars of 1996, the silver dollars of each date, and the gold half eagles of each date. Ferrell's 1995 half dollar reverse shows a hemispheric globe centered on the Atlantic Ocean. The ice cream cone-like logo of the Centennial Games is formed from the number 100 with the five rings stacked above the number, and a stylized flame and three stars rise from it. The torch elements fill most of the Atlantic above the equator. Below the equator is "Atlanta" and "E Pluribus

Unum", the latter appearing in two lines. "United States of America" and "Half Dollar" circle the entire design in a double-rim configuration. Ferrell's initials (TJF) are located, approximately, in South America (Argentina) and the Mint mark is positioned in West Africa (Angola).

1996 Swimming Obverse by William Krawczewicz, modeled by E. Z. Steever IV

A goggled swimmer moving right, probably in the butterfly stroke, water splashing around. "USA" and the five rings logo are located on the swimmer's cap; above and centered are "Liberty", in large letters, and "In God We Trust", in two lines and smaller letters. The date 1996 is centered below. At the left and right, respectively, of the pool's lane marker are Krawczewicz's initials (WJK) and Steever's (EZS).

1996 Soccer Obverse by Clint Hansen, modeled by William C. Cousins

Two pony-tailed young women compete to control a soccer ball. "Liberty" in large letters arcs above; "USA" and the five rings logo are at the left, "In God We Trust" to the right. Around the lower rim is "Atlanta 1996 XXVI Olympiad". Hansen's initials (CPH) are behind the heel of the left player; Cousins's monogram is near the leg of the right player.

1996 Common Reverse by Thomas D. Rogers, Sr., modeled by Malcolm Farley

Malcolm Farley's common reverse for the 1996 half dollars is practically a cleaner version of the 1995 reverse, without the map. Inside a double-rim, "United States of America" and "E Pluribus Unum" circle the outside, punctuated by five-pointed stars. In smaller letters, "Atlanta 1996" is at the bottom. The Centennial Games flame and stars logo is the main central device, splitting the words "Half Dollar". Farley's initials are at the lower-left inner rim, Rogers's at the lower right. The Mint mark floats in the right field.

Dollar Designs

1995 Paralympics Obverse by Jim Sharpe, modeled by Thomas D. Rogers, Sr.

According to the program's design guidelines, the silver dollars portray individual sports and highlight human achievement. In addition, one of the four designs for each year features a Paralympics design, a separate set of events tailored to physically challenged athletes. Jim Sharpe's obverse portrays a blind runner and her sighted companion runner. The two hold a kerchief to keep in touch during the race. Around the rim are the inscriptions: "Triumph of the Human Spirit", "Paralympics 1995", and "Liberty". "In God We Trust" is in three lines between the runners. The Paralympics logo is positioned at the right, and the artists' initials are between that and the right rim; above the Paralympics logo is the Braille phrase "SPIRIT".

1995 Gymnastics Obverse by Jim Sharpe, modeled by Thomas D. Rogers, Sr.

A young female gymnast standing large, arms outstretched in the background, while in the right foreground a male gymnast performs a split press maneuver on the rings. "LIBERTY" and "1995" are at the upper left rim and "IN GOD WE TRUST" appears in three lines in the lower right field. "USA" and the five rings logo are in the left field. The artists' initials are at either side of the female gymnast's knees at the lower rim.

1995 Cycling Obverse by John Mercanti

Three cyclists pedal toward the viewer. At the right are "USA" and the five rings logo; to the left, "XXVI OLYMPIAD" appears in two lines, with "LIBERTY" below. Centered at the bottom in small letters are "IN GOD WE TRUST" and, in larger numerals, 1995. Mercanti's initials are at the lower left, at the conjunction of the roadway with the rim.

1995 Track and Field Obverse by John Mercanti

In a highly geometric design, running lanes are clearly marked and labeled 2, 3, 4, and 5 down the right side. Lunging toward the finish line are two runners. Above are "USA" and the five rings logo; behind the runners are "LIBERTY" and "XXVI OLYMPIAD". At the bottom are "IN GOD WE TRUST" and the date 1995. Mercanti's initials are at the left, near the trailing runner's trailing foot.

1995 Common Reverse by William Krawczewicz, modeled by T. James Ferrell

Clasped hands in heavy outline, with the Centennial Olympics logo above. "UNITED STATES OF AMERICA" arcs above in this token-like design, and "ONE DOLLAR" appears at the bottom. "E PLURIBUS UNUM" is in the upper left field and "ATLANTA" to the upper right. Krawczewicz's initials are at the lower left, Ferrell's to the lower right. The Mint mark is centrally located above "ONE DOLLAR".

1996 Paralympic Obverse by Jim Sharpe, modeled by Alfred Maletsky

An athlete in a wheelchair, arms outstretched, approaches the viewer. Above in two lines is "TRIUMPH OF THE HUMAN SPIRIT"; at the rim below are "PARALYMPICS", "LIBERTY", and the date 1996. "IN GOD WE TRUST" is in three lines in the left field below the athlete's arm; the Paralympics logo is to the right. Above, near the athlete's mouth, is the Braille phrase "SPIRIT." The artists' initials are at the lower right and lower left.

1996 Tennis Obverse by Jim Sharpe, modeled by T. James Ferrell

A female tennis player makes a forehand strike at a ball, seemingly about to knock it through the "USA" inscription and the five rings logo in the left field. At the left rim are "LIBERTY", "1996", and "ATLANTA", punctuated by five-pointed stars. "IN GOD WE TRUST" is at the lower right rim; the artists' initials are stacked behind the tennis player's knee.

1996 Rowing Obverse by Bart Forbes, modeled by T. James Ferrell

A four-man crew rows its craft. "XXVI OLYMPIAD" is above left; "USA" and the five rings logo are centered above the rowers. "IN GOD WE TRUST" appears in two lines of small lettering below the waterline; "LIBERTY" and the date 1996 are at the lower rim. Forbes's and Ferrell's initials are left and right below the waterline.

1996 High Jump Obverse by Calvin Massey, modeled by John Mercanti

A high jumper clears the bar in the backward-over-the-bar "Fosbury Flop," first introduced to the Olympics in 1968 by American gold medalist Dick Fosbury. "LIBERTY" in large letters follows the jumper's arc above; below the jumper are "IN GOD WE TRUST" in two lines, "USA", the five rings logo, and the date 1996. The artists' initials are at the lower right rim.

1996 Common Reverse by Thomas D. Rogers, Sr.

The Centennial Olympics logo is at the left, with "E PLURIBUS UNUM" and "ATLANTA 1996 CENTENNIAL OLYMPIC GAMES" at the right. "UNITED STATES OF AMERICA" arcs above, with "ONE DOLLAR" below. The Mint mark is above the "E" of "ONE". The artist's initials are between the "U" of "UNITED" and the "O" of "ONE".

GOLD $5 DESIGNS

1995 Torch Runner Obverse by Frank Gasparro, modeled by Thomas D. Rogers, Sr.

A runner bearing a torch carrying the Olympic flame held high in his right hand; a city skyline is in the background. While here and in legend the torch-bearer's task is portrayed as a lonely vigil, in fact the torch-bearing ceremony is an almost endless months-long public relations photo opportunity involving tens of thousands of participants. "LIBERTY" is positioned above, with the Centennial Olympics logo and "ATLANTA 1996" behind the runner. "IN GOD WE TRUST" and the date 1995 appear to the left, below the cityscape. The artists' initials are at the lower right on either side of the runner's trailing foot.

1995 Stadium Obverse by Marcel Jovine

The Centennial Olympics logo is prominent over Atlanta Stadium; trailing from the top of the flame, the logo's stars begin to warp into the word "LIBERTY" and another distorted five-pointed star, evoking a trail of smoke from the torch. "THE CENTENNIAL GAMES" is located in the upper field; "IN GOD WE TRUST" is at the left. "ATLANTA" is nested under the lower left of the stadium and the date 1995 is centered at the bottom. Barely visible in the relief of the stadium's lower left pavement is Jovine's monogram; this renowned Italian–American sculptor brought a touch of playfulness to the design.

1995 Common Reverse by Frank Gasparro, modeled by John Mercanti

There is no obvious reference to the Olympics at all, save for the 1896–1996 centennial years inscribed on the banner being carried in the beak of a Union-style striding eagle. "UNITED STATES OF AMERICA" arcs above; "E PLURIBUS UNUM" is just below. "FIVE DOLLARS" is incused at the lower rim; Gasparro's familiar initials are at the left, Mercanti's at the right. The Mint mark floats in the right field, where the eagle seems to be watching it suspiciously. The bold, patriotic theme of the 1995 common reverse is pure Gasparro. The longtime chief engraver of the United States Mint is perhaps best known to coin collectors as the designer of the Susan B. Anthony and Eisenhower dollar coins, the Lincoln Memorial reverse on the cent, and the Kennedy half dollar reverse.

1996 Olympic Cauldron Obverse by Frank Gasparro, modeled by T. James Ferrell

Gasparro's stylized, almost Art Deco scene of a torchbearer lighting the Olympic cauldron seems somehow cold and impersonal compared to the image of a shaky but still defiant Muhammad Ali mustering every last bit of strength and dignity at the actual Atlanta flame-lighting ceremony. "LIBERTY" appears in large letters at the left rim; "USA", the five rings logo, and "IN GOD WE TRUST" are positioned in the right field. The date 1996 is inscribed onto the base of the cauldron pedestal, and the artists' initials are at either end of a line defining the lower field.

1996 Flag Bearer Obverse by Patricia Lewis Verani

A flag bearer, carrying America's Old Glory, leads a trail of other athletes, coaches, and officials, waving at the crowd. The composition—a central foreground figure with a trail of followers in perspective—is quite reminiscent of Verani's reverse on the 1987 Constitution Bicentennial dollar. "LIBERTY" is at the upper left rim; "IN GOD WE TRUST" is at the lower left; "USA" and the five rings logo are in the upper right field, and the date is prominent in the lower field. Verani's initials are hidden in the folds of the clothing on the parade participant behind the flag bearer. In contrast to the near parity of events for men and women in the modern Olympics, Patricia Lewis Verani was the only woman to design any of the Olympic coins. Her obverse depicts a scene described by many Olympic participants as among their most memorable and treasured: the parade of participants that opens and closes the Games.

1996 Common Reverse by William Krawczewicz, modeled by Thomas D. Rogers, Sr.

The Centennial Olympics logo at the center, with "ATLANTA", "E PLURIBUS UNUM", and the Mint mark (W) below it. On either side is a sprig of laurel, the traditional victor's wreath. "UNITED STATES OF AMERICA" arcs above; "FIVE DOLLARS" is at the bottom. The artists' initials are located at the bottom of each laurel sprig.

Origins of the Atlanta Olympic Coins

Numismatists who have followed the rise and fall and rebirth of commemorative coins in the United States may remember the heated controversy surrounding a proposed 53-coin program to raise funds for the 1984 Olympic Games in Los Angeles. That proposal was eventually rejected as unwieldy and unfair to coin collectors, and was replaced by a more modest 13-coin program. Apparently, the authors of the Atlanta Games coin program selectively forgot this recent history.

The Games themselves became an icon for merchandising excess, and it is perhaps appropriate that the coin program was such a bloated and labyrinthine one. The coins were sold by subscription, with four release periods beginning in January 1995 and continuing through the Games in the summer of 1996. Subscriptions for 32 and 16 coins were offered. Worldwide subscriptions were limited to 10,000 of the 32-coin sets and 20,000 of the 16-coin sets. The 16-coin set consisted of all the Uncirculated 1995 and 1996 Olympic coinage or, if preferred, all the Proof strikings of the same productions. The 32-piece set contained all of the 1995 and 1996 Olympic coins struck in Proof and Uncirculated condition. While the Mint claimed "overwhelming interest" from the international market, clearly not all interested parties signed up. The subscription offered a discount in addition to the pre-issue discount of individual coins, and the Mint even offered installment payment plans. Good thing, because the 32-coin subscription cost $2,261 and the 16-coin subscription, $1,162.

Sales were so poor that in an effort to salvage any profits, the coins were still for sale late into 1997, a full year after the Games had taken place. The program was so ambitious that, even in failure, surcharges of $50 per gold coin, $10 per silver coin, and $3 per clad half dollar raised more than $25 million for the Games.

It is important to understand that the Olympic Committee, or any similar organization, envisions the creation of a commemorative coin as a dual-purpose venture. It will not only honor their cause or event, but will help generate a tremendous amount of income for it. The belief, which seems logical, is that the greater the number authorized for production by Congress, the greater the amount of money to be derived through the sale of these coins—to collectors.

What really matters, of course, is the number of collectors and buyers who want to buy this coin (which determines the final mintage or, in this case, the production figure) and the overall market mood for the modern commemorative series. By 1994, collectors and dealers for the most part became disenchanted with the 1982–1994 U.S. modern commemorative issues. Too many of them had declined 50 percent or more in value. Compare the issue price for these productions with current values and see for yourself. The feeling that developed certainly influenced the buying demand for the 1995 Olympic coinage— and particularly the 1996 coins. Just compare the authorized amounts with the actual production numbers: you can bet generated funds from the issue were far less than expected.

When the 1996 Olympic Uncirculated and Proof coins were offered, there was very little interest. This didn't change when the low, but not final, production figures were released. Nor did it matter that the issue was widely distributed and no hoards were available. The *Swiatek Report* highly recommended this acquisition in 1997 and in 1998. Eventually, eyes opened, as values increased as much as five times; these low-mintage half dollars and dollars have proven to be winners.

The Atlanta Olympic Coins Today

Press materials touted the staggering numbers surrounding the Olympic Games—twice as large as the 1984 Los Angeles Games, more than $400 million in construction projects, 3,000 hours of television coverage, and more than 10,000 athletes.

1995 Young Collectors Set—front.

1995 Young Collectors Set—back.

The coinage numbers are not quite so staggering as previous issues. In fact, this program presents some low productions for the modern commemorative series. Fewer than 10,000 each of the 1996 Uncirculated gold half eagles were sold, presenting a pretty small bottleneck for future completionists. The Uncirculated silver dollars of 1996 all hover in the 14,000 to 16,000 range. The low-mintage Uncirculated dollar issues are the 1996-D Wheelchair Athlete (14,497), 1996-D High Jump (15,697), 1996-D Rowing (16,258), 1995-D Cycling (19,662), and 1995-D Track and Field (24,796).

The Young Collector's Set houses either an uncirculated 1995-S Basketball, with a value of $25; a 1996-S Soccer, valued at $120; or a 1996-S Swimming clad half dollar.

The key to the entire issue is its extreme popularity with the collector base. The real sleeper coinage at present is the PF-70 1996 dollar creations, as well as the 1995-P PF-70 productions. Your 1996 MS-70 dollars offergood future potential. Suggest purchase the proof before the 1995 MS-70 encapsulations. Also the PF-70 1995 and 1996 half dollars. Populations are presently low. Also with good future potential are the uncirculated 1996-W Olympic Flame and 1996-W Flag bearer $5 half eagles. Keep checking for increased activity for all of these. Procure what you like rated MS-69 just because you want it.

1995-S 50¢ Basketball

Grading Service	MS 69	MS 70
NGC	828	401
PCGS	1485	112
Combined	2313	513

Grading Service	PF 69	PF 70
NGC	1433	201
PCGS	1300	13
Combined	2733	214

1995-S 50¢ Baseball

Grading Service	MS 69	MS 70
NGC	721	229
PCGS	1767	77
Combined	2488	306

Grading Service	PF 69	PF 70
NGC	1187	166
PCGS	957	16
Combined	2144	182

1995-D $1.00 Gymnastics

Grading Service	MS 69	MS 70
NGC	1080	254
PCGS	1660	196
Combined	2740	450

1995-P $1.00 Gymnastics

Grading Service	PF 69	PF 70
NGC	1832	58
PCGS	1597	24
Combined	3429	82

1995-D $1.00 Cycling

Grading Service	MS 69	MS 70
NGC	536	213
PCGS	948	99
Combined	1484	312

1995-P $1.00 Cycling

Grading Service	PF 69	PF 70
NGC	1142	22
PCGS	1073	27
Combined	2215	49

1995-D $1.00 Track & Field

Grading Service	MS 69	MS 70
NGC	475	213
PCGS	817	98
Combined	1292	311

1995-P $1.00 Track & Field

Grading Service	PF 69	PF 70
NGC	1161	38
PCGS	1509	22
Combined	2670	60

1995-D $1.00 Blind Runner

Grading Service	MS 69	MS 70
NGC	796	302
PCGS	1216	185
Combined	2012	487

1995-P $1.00 Blind Runner

Grading Service	PF 69	PF 70
NGC	1274	39
PCGS	1591	56
Combined	2865	95

1995-W $5.00 Torch Runner

Grading Service	MS 69	MS 70
NGC	264	645
PCGS	1354	182
Combined	1618	827

Grading Service	PF 69	PF 70
NGC	1158	583
PCGS	2357	151
Combined	3515	734

1995-W $5.00 Atlanta Stadium

Grading Service	MS 69	MS 70
NGC	360	488
PCGS	1581	159
Combined	1941	647

Grading Service	PF 69	PF 70
NGC	1098	650
PCGS	1924	154
Combined	3022	804

1996-S 50¢ Swimming

Grading Service	MS 69	MS 70
NGC	418	98
PCGS	683	40
Combined	1101	138

Grading Service	PF 69	PF 70
NGC	751	68
PCGS	934	18
Combined	1685	86

1996-S 50¢ Soccer

Grading Service	MS 69	MS 70
NGC	340	175
PCGS	641	86
Combined	981	261

Grading Service	PF 69	PF 70
NGC	725	55
PCGS	899	21
Combined	1624	76

1996-D $1.00 Tennis

Grading Service	MS 69	MS 70
NGC	525	67
PCGS	907	115
Combined	1432	182

1996-P $1.00 Tennis

Grading Service	PF 69	PF 70
NGC	1003	8
PCGS	947	6
Combined	1950	14

1996-D $1.00 Rowing

Grading Service	MS 69	MS 70
NGC	484	106
PCGS	755	106
Combined	1239	212

1996-P $1.00 Rowing

Grading Service	PF 69	PF 70
NGC	1015	5
PCGS	962	9
Combined	1977	14

1996-D $1.00 High Jump

Grading Service	MS 69	MS 70
NGC	462	77
PCGS	912	75
Combined	1374	152

1996-P $1.00 High Jump

Grading Service	PF 69	PF 70
NGC	1062	4
PCGS	983	1
Combined	2045	5

1996-D $1.00 Wheel Chair

Grading Service	MS 69	MS 70
NGC	570	134
PCGS	906	101
Combined	1476	235

1996-P $1.00 Wheel Chair

Grading Service	PF 69	PF 70
NGC	1096	6
PCGS	1145	9
Combined	2241	15

1996-W $5.00 Cauldron

Grading Service	MS 69	MS 70
NGC	411	284
PCGS	1393	56
Combined	1804	340

Grading Service	PF 69	PF 70
NGC	1536	609
PCGS	1735	112
Combined	2271	721

1996-W $5.00 Flag Bearer

Grading Service	MS 69	MS 70
NGC	291	317
PCGS	1342	102
Combined	1633	419

Grading Service	PF 69	PF 70
NGC	868	365
PCGS	1534	122
Combined	2402	487

Reason for Issue:	To commemorate the 100th anniversary of the beginning of the protection of Civil War battlefields.
Authorization:	Public Law 102-379, October 5, 1992.

Facts and Figures

Denomination	Date/Mint	Pre-issue Price	Regular Price	Maximum Authorized	Net Mintage	Market Value
Copper-Nickel Clad Half Dollar	1995 S UNC	$9.50	$10.25	2,000,000	113,045	$47
	1995 S Proof	$10.75	$11.75		326,801	$45
Silver Dollar	1995 P UNC	$27	$29	1,000,000	51,612	$75
	1995 S Proof	$30	$34		327,686	$65
Gold $5	1995 W UNC	$180	$190	300,000	12,623	$850
	1995 W Proof	$195	$225		54,915	$425

Maximum authorization is by denomination. Proof and Uncirculated coins combined make up the maximum. Net mintage figures shown represent the net quantity distributed by the Mint.

Half Dollar Designs

Obverse by Donald Troiani, modeled by T. James Ferrell

A simple standing portrait of a drummer, a broken fence in the background. "Liberty" appears above, "In God We Trust" below, and the date 1995 in the upper right field. Troiani's and Ferrell's initials (DT and TJF) initials are at the left, below the fence; the Mint mark is at the right. The Connecticut artist Donald Troiani created all three obverse designs for this issue.

Reverse by T. James Ferrell

A cannon in the foreground is aimed ominously toward a farmhouse in the far distance, in a scene reminiscent of Gettysburg. "United States of America" circles above; "E Pluribus Unum" appears nested below it. Across the central field is the inscription "Enriching our future by preserving the past", in three lines; "Half Dollar" appears below. Ferrell's initials are at the right, below the cannon's caisson.

Dollar Designs

Obverse by Donald Troiani, modeled by Edgar Z. Steever IV

One soldier helps a wounded comrade drink from a canteen. Troiani continues in his cleanly elegant, vignette style scene here, and it is this touching scene, more than any other, that underscores the great personal losses and individual heroism in war. "Liberty" appears in large letters at the upper left rim, "In God We Trust" is in two lines in the lower left, and the date 1995 is centered at the bottom. The two sets of initials (DT and EZS) appear at the lower left. Alone in the right field is the Mint mark, in a brilliantly asymmetrical arrangement.

Reverse by John Mercanti

At the top "UNITED STATES OF AMERICA" and "E PLURIBUS UNUM" are separated by a scroll device. An inscription dominates the design: "IN GREAT DEEDS SOMETHING ABIDES. ON GREAT FIELDS SOMETHING STAYS, FORMS CHANGE AND PASS, BODIES DISAPPEAR: BUT SPIRITS LINGER TO CONSECRATE GROUND FOR THE VISIONPLACE OF SOULS. — JOSHUA CHAMBERLAIN". Chamberlain was a college professor from Maine, a hero at Gettysburg, and winner of the Medal of Honor for his defense of Little Round Top in that battle. Almost secondary to the design is a long-range view of a tower perched on a hilltop. "ONE DOLLAR" is superimposed over the frothing sea, and Mercanti's initials (JM) are notched into the right at the rim. As if in counterpoint to Troiani's simple yet eloquent obverse, Mercanti's reverse reads like the opening pages of a history book.

GOLD $5 DESIGNS

Obverse by Donald Troiani, modeled by Thomas D. Rogers, Sr.

A bugler on horseback. "LIBERTY" is above, the date 1995 is at the bottom, and "IN GOD WE TRUST" appears in two lines at the right. The designers' initials (DT and TDR) appear below the horse's rear hooves; the Mint mark is just below "IN GOD WE TRUST".

Reverse by Alfred Maletsky

A period depiction of an eagle, holding in its beak a ribbon inscribed "LET US PROTECT AND PRESERVE". Maletsky's initials appear below and to the right. "UNITED STATES OF AMERICA" is at the top, with "E PLURIBUS UNUM" and "FIVE DOLLARS" appearing below the eagle.

Origins of the Civil War Battlefields Coins

It may seem odd to commemorate the battlefields of the Civil War, sites of so much personal tragedy. But the battlefields remain as tangible reminders of this period, and raising money to preserve those reminders is a worthy aim.

The barest historical connection is claimed for this issue, marking the 100th anniversary of the establishment of the Gettysburg National Military Park in 1895.

The Civil War Battlefields Coins Today

Among other sales options, two are particularly appropriate to the subject matter. Two-coin and three-coin "Civil War Photo Case Editions" comprised Proof sets packaged in reproductions of Civil War-era photo cases. The original photo cases were made of a composite of shellac and wood—an early form of plas-

1995 Civil War Young Collector's packaging.

tic—colored and molded to hold heirloom early photos. Their emotional context, bearing images of far-away loved ones during a time of grave danger, coupled with the then-miraculous daguerreotype images, have endured as a symbol of family separation during the Civil War.

At present, potential value lies in the half dollar and dollar designs encapsulated PF-70, because of low populations, but collectors should be aware that these low numbers can change upwards—sometimes drastically—within a span of months if a large number of half dollar and dollar designs are submitted for grading. Acquire the other issues for the joy of collecting.

The Young Collector's Set contains an Uncirculated Half Dollar and currently commands a modest premium because of the limited edition packaging; but it offers no real potential in the long run.

1995-S 50¢

Grading Service	MS 69	MS 70
NGC	1022	312
PCGS	552	84
Combined	1574	396

1995-S 50¢

Grading Service	PF 69	PF 70
NGC	1309	68
PCGS	1767	16
Combined	3076	84

1995-P $1.00

Grading Service	MS 69	MS 70
NGC	934	111
PCGS	1346	109
Combined	2310	220

1995-S $1.00

Grading Service	PF 69	PF 70
NGC	2387	43
PCGS	2166	77
Combined	4453	120

1995-W $5.00

Grading Service	MS 69	MS 70
NGC	226	503
PCGS	1028	132
Combined	1254	635

Grading Service	PF 69	PF 70
NGC	1215	529
PCGS	3255	133
Combined	4470	662

1995 Special Olympics World Games

Reason for Issue:	To recognize the achievements of developmentally challenged persons.
Authorization:	Public Law 103-328, September 29, 1994.

Facts and Figures

Denomination	Date/Mint	Pre-issue Price	Regular Price	Maximum Authorized	Net Mintage	Market Value
Silver Dollar	1995 W UNC	$29	$31	800,000	89,301	$40
	1995 P Proof	$31	$35		352,449	$40

Maximum authorization is by denomination. Proof and Uncirculated coins combined make up the maximum. Net mintage figures shown represent the net quantity distributed by the Mint.

Designs

Obverse by Jamie Wyeth, modeled by T. James Ferrell

A portrait of Eunice Kennedy Shriver was offered by the artist Jamie Wyeth to be used as a design for this commemorative. The artistic merit of Wyeth's profile was quickly overwhelmed, however, by a tide of controversy. First, the originator of the Special Olympics, Anne Burke of Chicago, was entirely forgotten in favor of Shriver, whose interest, money, and influence took the concept nationwide. Numismatically, a larger controversy loomed as both the Citizens Commemorative Coin Advisory Committee and the U.S. Commission of Fine

Arts opposed the portrait of a living person on a commemorative issue (Eunice Kennedy Shriver died in 2009). But the Kennedy influence (in the person of Senator Ted Kennedy) dominated in this instance. Circling above is the legend "SPECIAL OLYMPICS WORLD GAMES". "LIBERTY" appears below Shriver's chin; "IN GOD WE TRUST" is in two lines below her hair and the date 1995 is at the bottom. Wyeth's initials are on Shriver's neck, Ferrell's are below, at the nape. The Mint mark is below "IN GOD WE TRUST"

Reverse by Thomas D. Rogers, Sr.

A rose (the first depiction of this flower seen on any U.S. commemorative struck from 1892 to 1995), a Special Olympics medal, and the inscription: "AS WE HOPE FOR THE BEST IN THEM, HOPE IS REBORN IN US, EUNICE KENNEDY SHRIVER, FOUNDER". In letters of equal size, "UNITED STATES OF AMERICA", "E PLURIBUS UNUM", and "ONE DOLLAR" completely circle the rim. Rogers's initials (TDR) appear just above the "O" in "ONE".

Origins of the Special Olympics World Games Dollar

Despite the undisputed good works attributed to the Special Olympics, and the noble aim of raising money through a commemorative coin program, hardly anything kind can be said about this issue. Wyeth's portrait of Shriver was described as unflattering, in a flurry of derogatory and colorful criticism. The status of Shriver as "founder" of the Special Olympics is a matter of some debate by various unhappy individuals.

The Special Olympics World Games Dollar Today

Collectors greeted the Special Olympics coins unkindly, as sales languished badly throughout most of the offering. But seemingly a white knight on a stallion rode to the rescue at the 11th hour, when a bulk purchase of some quarter million coins became publicly known. The buyer was at the time anonymous, but it is now known that the "hero" was the Phoenix Home Life Mutual Insurance Company of Hartford, Connecticut.

Phoenix Home Life's last-gasp arrangement mere days before the end of the sales period more than doubled the final net mintage figures, boosting sales of the Proof coins by 200,000 and of the uncirculated coins by 50,000 pieces. The coins were to be used for an incentive program and given to Special Olympics athletes.

At a $10 per coin surcharge, the purchase added an additional $2.5 million to the Special Olympics coffers and, according to sources, the 1995 games finished in the black.

Collectors may not be so fortunate; however, as the quarter million coins were acquired by those with little interest in the coins as numismatic collectibles. It remains to be seen how many of the Phoenix Home Life's trove ultimately find their way back into numismatic collections. Too many pieces can be encapsulated because of the large hoard of both issues. I suggest collectors purchase them only for the joy of ownership, not for investment. Should you have the coins, especially the low population proof, your best return will be by placing them in auction or selling to a reputable dealer. Remember, it must be encapsulated by NGC or PCGS to attain the highest return.

1995-W $1.00

Grading Service	MS 69	MS 70
NGC	609	186
PCGS	877	65
Combined	1486	251

1994-P $1.00

Grading Service	PF 69	PF 70
NGC	1099	36
PCGS	1066	38
Combined	2165	74

1996 NATIONAL COMMUNITY SERVICE

Reason for Issue:	To commemorate the millions of Americans who contribute to community service projects.
Authorization:	Public Law 103-328, September 29, 1994.

Facts and Figures

Denomination	Date/Mint	Pre-issue Price	Regular Price	Maximum Authorized	Net Mintage	Market Value
Silver Dollar	1996-S UNC	$30	$32	500,000	23,500	$190
	1996-S Proof	$33	$37		101,543	$65

Maximum authorization is by denomination. Proof and Uncirculated coins combined make up the maximum. Net mintage figures shown represent the net quantity distributed by the Mint.

DESIGNS

Obverse by Thomas D. Rogers, Sr.

A female Liberty inspired by an Augustus Saint-Gaudens medal design for the Women's Auxiliary of the Massachusetts Civil Service Reform Association. Rogers replaces Saint-Gaudens's staff with a lamp emanating rays of light, in a stylistic nod to John Mercanti's 1986 Statue of Liberty silver dollar reverse. "LIBERTY" appears at the top, among the rays; "NATIONAL COMMUNITY SERVICE" is positioned in the lower left field, with the date 1996 below. "IN GOD WE TRUST" is in the right field. Rogers's initials are at the bottom, near Liberty's feet, and the Mint mark is at right, near the shield.

Reverse by William C. Cousins

The inscription "Service for America" encircled by a laurel wreath with "E Pluribus Unum" in small letters below inside the wreath. "United States of America" arcs above, with "One Dollar" below. Cousins's initials are at the lower left, just inside the wreath.

Origins of the National Community Service Dollar

The justification for this issue was so vague (the authorizing legislation is called the "Riegle–Neal Interstate Banking and Branching Efficiency Act of 1994") that the Mint really had little else to hang the marketing on but the tenuous connection to Saint-Gaudens. The obverse design, "inspired" by a medal designed by Saint-Gaudens, seems like a remote connection, but in a desperate-seeming grasp, a Saint-Gaudens coin and stamp set was offered, comprising a Proof dollar and a 3-cent postage stamp featuring Saint-Gaudens.

A $10 per coin surcharge generated $1.24 million to be paid to the National Community Service Trust to fund innovative community service programs at American universities.

A promotional brochure distributed by the Mint stresses the importance of community service to our country:

> It's the very foundation of America's greatness. From the Minutemen who won our country's freedom to the retired executive who helps build homes for the underprivileged; from Clara Barton caring for wounded soldiers to a student volunteer teaching someone how to read. Our nation's soul has been shaped by the spirit of community service. Now, the United States officially recognizes these selfless acts of generosity. Authorized by Congress, the National Community Service commemorative Silver Dollar honors the contributions, past and present, of those who have defined the character of our nation.

The National Community Service Dollar Today

The Uncirculated coin is beautifully designed and has a low mintage that was well distributed: it sells at a premium against its original regular issue price. In the past dealer stock of the uncirculated version was quite limited. Because of this, collectors who must have the issue and can't wait to procure the uncirculated issue choose the higher production proof strikings as a substitute, thus driving the prices on the proof issue.

This popular issue has good potential in both versions rated MS-70.

1996-S $1.00

Grading Service	MS 69	MS 70
NGC	598	205
PCGS	980	86
Combined	1578	291

Grading Service	PF 69	PF 70
NGC	1277	81
PCGS	1154	125
Combined	2431	206

National Community Service Commemorative Coin and Stamp Set— outside front.

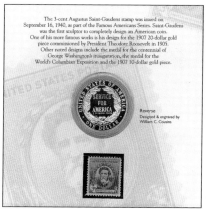

National Community Service Commemorative Coin and Stamp Set— inside back.

Reason for Issue:	To commemorate the sesquicentennial of the founding of the Smithsonian Institution.
Authorization:	Public Law 104-96, January 10, 1996.

Facts and Figures

Denomination	Date/Mint	Pre-issue Price	Regular Price	Maximum Authorized	Net Mintage	Market Value
Silver Dollar	1996 D UNC	$30	$32	650,000	31,320	$145
	1996 P Proof	$33	$37		129,152	$65

Denomination	Date/Mint	Pre-issue Price	Regular Price	Maximum Authorized	Net Mintage	Market Value
Gold $5	1996 W UNC	$180	$205	100,000	9,068	$825
	1996 W Proof	$195	$225		21,772	$425

Maximum authorization is by denomination. Proof and Uncirculated coins combined make up the maximum. Net mintage figures shown represent the net quantity distributed by the Mint.

Dollar Designs

Obverse by Thomas D. Rogers, Sr.

A rendering of the "Castle," the original Smithsonian building on the Mall in Washington, D.C. Flanking the Castle are sprigs of congratulatory laurel. Arcing above are "Liberty" in large letters and "In God We Trust" in smaller letters. Below the Castle are "Smithsonian" and the anniversary dates 1846–1996.

Reverse by John Mercanti

A hooded female figure sitting on top of the world; in her left hand she holds a torch, and in her lap a scroll is inscribed—upside-down to her—"Art History Science". In the right field, she is facing the inscription "For the Increase and Diffusion of Knowledge". Arcing above is "United States of America"; "E Pluribus Unum" and "One Dollar" appear below.

Gold $5 Designs

Obverse by Alfred Maletsky

A left-facing bust of benefactor James Smithson; his name is inscribed below. Arcing above is the legend "For the Increase and Diffusion of Knowledge"; "Liberty" in large letters arcs at the bottom. The anniversary dates 1846–1996 are below Smithson's chin to the left; "In God We Trust" is behind his head to the right. Maletsky's initials (AM) are rather prominently tattooed on Smithson's shoulder.

Reverse by T. James Ferrell

The Smithsonian's sunburst logo, with "Smithsonian" spelled out below, all within an inner rim and a matte field. Within the double rim, "United States of America" arcs above; "E Pluribus Unum" and "Five Dollars" appear below.

Origins of the Smithsonian Coins

The Smithsonian Institution, the national repository of art, science, history, and popular culture, contains within its Museum of American History arguably the most important collection of American numismatic items in the world. A quick perusal of the *Comprehensive Catalog and Encyclopedia of United States Coins*, especially in the sections on patterns and pioneer gold, reveals numerous citations of "unique, Smithsonian." While the Smithsonian's Josiah K. Lilly Collection of gold coins garners all the glory, unfortunately the collection is no longer on prominent display. The *History of Money and Medals* exhibition closed in August 2004, but the Lilly Collection's true treasure is in the rows and rows of storage vaults containing rare and unique glimpses into the history of American and world numismatics.

The numismatic press had long called for a commemorative coin program with surcharges to benefit the Smithsonian's National Numismatic Collection. It is perhaps unfortunate that when this call was finally heeded, it came in the wake of the vast, exhausting, lumbering behemoth that was the 1996 Atlanta Olympic Games program, and the Smithsonian coins became an also-ran in 1996.

Surcharges of $10 per silver dollar and $35 per gold half eagle raised something over $2.6 million, 85 percent of which went to the Smithsonian proper, with 15 percent, or less than $400,000, earmarked specifically for the National Numismatic Collection. While that sum may keep the lights on for a few more years, the National Numismatic Collection contains numerous individual pieces with market values far exceeding $400,000.

In 1764, Elizabeth Keate Macie bore an illegitimate son of the Duke of Northumberland. The child, James Smithson, who could never attain the ducal title because of the status of his birth, nevertheless became a brilliant scholar and mineralogist of some note. Smithson had no children. He willed the bulk of his estate to his nephew, and should his nephew have children, then to them. However, Smithson's nephew, Henry James Hungerford, also died without heirs. A provision in Smithson's will bequeathed the entire estate, more than $500,000 in British gold sovereigns (a fortune inherited from his mother), to the United States to create in Washington, D.C., an institution to be named for him "for the increase and diffusion of knowledge among men."

Strangely, Smithson had never visited the United States, but his remains were brought to Washington in 1904 and interred in a room near the north entrance of the Smithsonian Castle. Located by the vessel that contains his remains is a sculptured bust of Smithson. The portrait rendered by Maletsky on the gold coin bears a strong resemblance in proportion and style to this bust.

In September 1996, a pair of two-coin Proof sets was carried into orbit around the Earth by the space shuttle *Atlantis*. The high-altitude coins now reside in the Smithsonian's Air and Space Museum collection in Washington.

The Smithsonian Coins Today

With barely 9,000 uncirculated gold coins sold and just about 30,000 Uncirculated and Proof (21,772) half eagles combined, future completionists may have a hard time finding one of these coins. While initial collector demand was almost nonexistent, these coins must be considered fully distributed. The proof versions can easily be promoted. This is a very popular issue. Your best bet at present is the $1 proof versions rated 70, as long as the populations do not rise significantly from their present levels. The other issues look good as well. Just keep an eye out for population increases.

1996-D $1.00

Grading Service	MS 69	MS 70
NGC	505	374
PCGS	831	71
Combined	1336	445

1996-P $1.00

Grading Service	PF 69	PF 70
NGC	1409	31
PCGS	1254	37
Combined	2663	68

1996-W $5.00

Grading Service	MS 69	MS 70
NGC	429	333
PCGS	831	71
Combined	1260	404

Grading Service	PF 69	PF 70
NGC	883	302
PCGS	1748	65
Combined	2631	367

Reason for Issue:	To commemorate the opening of the Franklin Delano Roosevelt Memorial in Washington, D.C.
Authorization:	Public Law 104-329, October 20, 1996.

Facts And Figures

Denomination	Date/Mint	Pre-issue Price	Regular Price	Maximum Authorized	Net Mintage	Market Value
Gold $5	1997-W UNC	$180	$205	100,000	11,805	$1430
	1997-W Proof	$195	$225		29,233	$425

Maximum authorization is by denomination. Proof and Uncirculated coins combined make up the maximum. Net mintage figures shown represent the net quantity distributed by the Mint.

Designs

Obverse by T. James Ferrell

Roosevelt from about midsection up. The image is based on one of Roosevelt's favorite photographs of himself, in which he is shown windblown on the bridge of the Northampton-class heavy cruiser *USS Houston* (CA-30, sunk March 1, 1942 in the Battle of Sunda Strait), wearing a wool cloak that flaps in the breeze, his right arm casually cocked over the rail, a look of utter delight on his face. Arcing above is the inscription "Franklin Delano Roosevelt". Before him, in the right field, are the date 1997 and "In God We Trust"; "Liberty" is in a straight line below. Ferrell's initials are at the left below the portrait. Although this issue is perhaps not at the best scale for a $5 gold coin (which is slightly larger than the circulating Roosevelt dime), Ferrell's obverse design exhibits as much personality as has ever been attributed to a president on a coin, commemorative or otherwise. It provides a happy contrast to the dour "death-mask-like" left-cheek profile on the circulating Roosevelt dime.

Reverse by James Peed, modeled by Thomas D. Rogers, Sr.

The presidential seal from Roosevelt's 1933 inaugural. An eagle looks left with wings outstretched, superimposed over a round shield adorned with stars. Thomas Harding's rendering of this eagle appears in the Franklin Delano Roosevelt Memorial. Arcing above the eagle are the legends "UNITED STATES OF AMERICA" in large letters and "E PLURIBUS UNUM" in smaller letters; "FIVE DOLLARS" arcs below. Peed's initials are above the "V" in "FIVE" and Rogers's initials can be found above the "A" in "Dollars". The Mint mark is in the right field. Barely visible until pointed out, the eagle carries in its talons a plaque bearing the date 1933, the year of Roosevelt's first inaugural.

Origins of the Roosevelt Gold $5

The Roosevelt commemorative, at the time, was the only "gold coin only" program since the rebirth of American commemorative coins in 1982. For this reason, some have accused Congress of elitism in making the coins too expensive for many collectors to own.

Both Proof and Uncirculated versions were struck at the West Point Mint. This is especially fitting for this issue as, among FDR's many acts during his four terms, he signed the law creating the West Point Silver Bullion Depository, now functioning as the West Point Mint.

Some collectors were critical of this issue for another reason. Many members of the numismatic community found it quite ironic that Roosevelt, whose executive order (below) limited Americans' rights to own gold coins, was himself depicted on a gold coin.

> "By virtue of the authority vested in me by Section 5(B) of The Act of October 6th, 1917, as amended by section 2 of the Act of March 9th, 1933, in which Congress declared that a serious emergency exists, I as President, do declare that the national emergency still exists; That the continued private hoarding of gold and silver by subjects of the United States poses a grave threat to the peace, equal justice, and well-being of the United States; and that appropriate measures must be taken immediately to protect the interests of our people.
>
> Therefore, pursuant to the above authority, I herby proclaim that such gold and silver holdings are prohibited, and that all such coin, bullion or other possessions of gold and silver be tendered within fourteen days to agents of the Government of the United States for compensation at the official price, in the legal tender of the Government. All safe deposit boxes in banks or financial institutions have been sealed, pending action in the due course of the law. All sales or purchases or

movements of such gold and silver within the borders of the United States and its territories, and all foreign exchange transactions or movements of such metals across the border are hereby prohibited.

Your possession of these proscribed metals and/or your maintenance of a safe-deposit box to store them is known to the Government from bank and insurance records. Therefore, be advised that your vault box must remain sealed, and may only be opened in the presence of an agent of The Internal Revenue Service.

By lawful Order given this day, the President of the United States."

Senator Carter Glass of Virginia, who when Chairman of the Senate Finance Committee had sponsored the legislation that created the Federal Reserve System in 1913 and the Glass–Steagall Act of 1933, which established the Federal Deposit Insurance Corporation (FDIC) and included various banking reforms, and who later served as Secretary of the Treasury, denounced FDR's gold seizure and subsequent dollar devaluation:

It's dishonor, sir. This great government, strong in gold, is breaking its promises to pay gold to widows and orphans to whom it has sold government bonds with a pledge to pay gold coin of the present standard of value. It's dishonor, sir.

Senator Thomas Pryor Gore of Oklahoma was more succinct: "Why, that's just plain stealing, isn't it, Mr. President?" It should be noted that in the 1936 elections FDR personally financed Gore's Democratic primary rival and succeeded in unseating the Senator as retribution.

THE ROOSEVELT GOLD $5 TODAY

In the past this issue was well distributed with dealers processing limited stock of both issues. Populations are somewhat large, and the collector should obtain this issue simply for the sheer joy of collecting. Excellent promotional issue.

1997-W $5.00

Grading Service	MS 69	MS 70
NGC	349	414
PCGS	1482	207
Combined	1831	621

Grading Service	PF 69	PF 70
NGC	1145	459
PCGS	2196	159
Combined	3341	618

Reason for Issue:	To commemorate the accomplishments of baseball legend and civil rights icon Jackie Robinson on the 50th anniversary of his breaking the color barrier in baseball's National League.
Authorization:	Public Law 104-329, October 20, 1996.

Facts and Figures

Denomination	Date/Mint	Pre-issue Price	Regular Price	Maximum Authorized	Net Mintage	Market Value
Silver Dollar	1997 S UNC	$30	$32	200,000	30,180	$90
	1997 S Proof	$33	$37		110,002	$105

Denomination	Date/Mint	Pre-issue Price	Regular Price	Maximum Authorized	Net Mintage	Market Value
Gold $5	1997 W UNC	$180	$205	100,000	5,174	$3,200
	1997 W Proof	$195	$225		24,072	$575

Maximum authorization is by denomination. Proof and Uncirculated coins combined make up the maximum. Net mintage figures shown represent the net quantity distributed by the Mint.

Dollar Designs

Obverse by Alfred Maletsky

A sliding Robinson stealing home and kicking up a cloud of dust. "Liberty" in large letters arcs above to the left; "In God We Trust" is at the right, with the Mint mark just below it; the date 1997 is at the bottom.

Reverse by T. James Ferrell

The logo of the Jackie Robinson Foundation is at the center; the Foundation was ostensibly the beneficiary of the surcharges from this issue. Surrounding in large letters are "United States of America" and "One Dollar". In smaller letters circling the logo and separated by stars are "Rookie of the Year 1947", "Hall of Fame 1962", and "E Pluribus Unum".

Gold $5 Designs

Obverse by Alfred Maletsky

A portrait of Robinson. "Jackie Robinson" circles above, with "Liberty" below. The date 1997 and the Mint mark are to the left; "In God We Trust" is to the right.

Reverse by James Peed

A baseball forms a central circle, inscribed with "1919–1972" (the years of Robinson's birth and death) and "Legacy of Courage". Surrounding the baseball are the legends "United States of America", "Five Dollars", and "E Pluribus Unum".

Origins of the Jackie Robinson Coins

In 1947, if you played baseball in the Major Leagues, you were white. Despite the demonstrated excellence of play in the Negro Leagues, and despite surreptitious attempts to break it, the color barrier survived until after World War II.

It might be thought that Robinson's breakthrough would have been heralded at the time, but in fact the opposite was true. He faced frequent threats against his person, even his life, both on and off the field. Yet he persevered and excelled (winning Rookie of the Year in 1947, in a vote by the Baseball Writers Association of America) and paved the way for the true integration of the races in baseball and, in fact, in all professional sports.

The Jackie Robinson Foundation was founded in 1973 by friends and family of Robinson. The foundation grants scholarships to students of demonstrated ability, character, and need. Until the commemorative coin program, the foundation had never sought government funding, and surcharges from the sale of the coins were to be paid to the foundation to continue its work and make more scholarships available to economically disadvantaged youth.

Except—that provision appears in paragraph (ii). Paragraph (i) of the legislation states that surcharges from the sale of the first 100,000 silver dollars were to be paid to the National Fund for the United States Botanic Garden.

That's right. Despite the fact that the Botanic Garden commemorative program had already trumped the Smithsonian program, the first 100,000 silver dollars sold in the Jackie Robinson program—that's 100,000 of 135,000 net—didn't even benefit the Jackie Robinson Foundation, but the Botanic Garden instead!

A limited edition of 50,000 of the Jackie Robinson Legacy Sets, featuring a Proof Gold $5 Coin and a specially authorized reproduction of the 1952 Topps Jackie Robinson baseball card. Also featured is a full-color limited edition lapel pin made exclusively for the Mint, which duplicates the 50th Anniversary uniform patch being worn by all Major League baseball players for the 1997 season. As a free bonus to purchasers of the Legacy Set the U.S. Mint also provided the actual patch being worn by Major League players for the 1997 season. It was priced at $311 (Jackie Robinson's lifetime batting average was .311) for the

pre-issue discount period from July 3 through August 15, 1997. After the pre-issue discount period, the Legacy Set sold for $325. There were 10,271 sets sold. All remaining baseball cards were destroyed as required by the U.S. Mint.

THE JACKIE ROBINSON COINS TODAY

The Jackie Robinson Uncirculated $5 gold coin is a true rarity—a net of just more than 5,000 pieces sold. That number defines the maximum number of complete commemorative sets that may be assembled from the post-1982 era. A PCGS MS-67 sells for $4500. If the official number stands at 5,174, then it slips under the Cincinnati Music Center half dollars of 1936, and you need to go back to the later years of the Texas, Arkansas Centennial, and Boone Bicentennial issues of the Depression-ridden 1930s to find a lower mintage. Mintage-wise, for gold commemoratives, the Jackie Robinson rivals in rarity the 1922 Star/No Star gold dollar varieties of the Grant Memorial issue. It is rarer even, in terms of number of coins released by the Mint, than all but a handful of dates of circulating half eagles, which became "extinct" in 1929. However, we must be aware that the Jackie Robinson issue was struck, handled, and packaged with extreme care, as is all modern commemorative coinage since 1982. Commemorative coins produced between 1892 and 1954 were struck, handled, counted, and bagged in much the same way as coinage produced for circulation purposes.

Fifteen years ago, I exclaimed that this $195 uncirculated low-mintage $5 issue would sell retail for $5,000. It did, but unfortunately it now retails for approximately $3,200 rated MS-69. I strongly advise that buyers research the market trends before procuring the uncirculated $5 piece for their collections. There can be little doubt that this will be a very desirable coin now and in the future: it is an issue that is well distributed and easy to promote.

Those who cannot afford the uncirculated issue at the present time should acquire the proof version of the $5 coin. Procure the silver dollar issues rated 69 only for the joy of ownership. At present the dollar coins look good.

1997-S $1.00

Grading Service	MS 69	MS 70
NGC	755	97
PCGS	1235	49
Combined	2090	146

Grading Service	PF 69	PF 70
NGC	1344	38
PCGS	1223	68
Combined	2567	106

1997-W $5.00

Grading Service	MS 69	MS 70
NGC	446	213
PCGS	849	44
Combined	1295	257

Grading Service	PF 69	PF 70
NGC	837	393
PCGS	1600	127
Combined	2437	520

Reason for Issue:	To commemorate the sacrifice of law enforcement ZZ
Authorization:	Public Law 104-329, section 101.6, October 20, 1996.

Facts and Figures

Denomination	Date/Mint	Pre-issue Price	Regular Price	Maximum Authorized	Net Mintage	Market Value
Silver Dollar	1997 P UNC	$30	$32	500,000	28,575	$175
	1997 P Proof	$32	$37		110,428	$105

Maximum authorization is by denomination. Proof and Uncirculated coins combined make up the maximum. Net mintage figures shown represent the net quantity distributed by the Mint.

DESIGNS BY ALFRED MALETSKY

Obverse

United States Park Police officers Robert Chelsey and Kelcy Stefansson touching a fellow officer's name on the Memorial wall. The image was inspired by a photograph taken at the Memorial by Larry Ruggeri, and largely because the design is emblematic rather than a precise depiction of the actual people shown, this issue was not surrounded by the controversy of whether living people should appear on coins. Circling is the legend "NATIONAL LAW ENFORCEMENT OFFICER'S MEMORIAL", with "LIBERTY 1997" at the bottom. "IN GOD WE TRUST" is in small letters above the central device; Maletsky's initials appear just below the Memorial.

Reverse

An unadorned law enforcement shield draped with a single long-stemmed rose, with the legend "To Serve and Protect" below. "E Pluribus Unum" is in smaller letters below, and the Mint mark is centered below that. Arcing above is "United States of America"; below arcs "One Dollar".

Origins of the National Law Enforcement Officers Memorial Dollar

Surcharges on the coins were to support the long-term maintenance of the National Law Enforcement Officers Memorial, located at Judiciary Square in Washington, D.C. The memorial opened and was dedicated in 1991.

One of the sales options offered by the Mint was the Insignia set, which included the Proof dollar, a cloisonné enamel emblem pin, and an embroidered emblem.

Production and sales for this lovely coin were halted on December 15, 1998. The National Law Enforcement Officers Memorial Fund received approximately $1.4 million from the silver dollar sales. A $10 surcharge, included in the sale price of each coin, was set aside for the memorial's maintenance fund.

The National Law Enforcement Officers Memorial Dollar Today

Both issues were well distributed and offer the collector good future potential, especially the harder to locate uncirculated striking. This striking has become quite popular.

This issue has been sought out by non-collector Law Enforcement Officers (LEOs) as retirement ceremony mementos, thus elevating prices. The proof coin has been the more popular for this use. Such non-collector demand is similar to what has been occurring to the 2001 Buffalo commemorative coin. Why the proof over the uncirculated? Non-collectors like the bright shiny mirrored surfaces. Currently the prices now reflect the scarcity of the uncirculated coin.

Procure this issue only for pride of ownership, since non-collector LEO demand cannot be depended upon to continue, and in turbulent financial times, retirees and estates will quickly dump these coins back onto the market. Additionally, the mintages and slabbed populations are too high for any real potential to emerge. At present, MS-70 and PF-70 LEOs are low, but watch for population increases which can cause value declines.

1997-P $1.00

Grading Service	MS 69	MS 70
NGC	406	182
PCGS	801	105
Combined	1207	287

Grading Service	PF 69	PF 70
NGC	1215	63
PCGS	1044	88
Combined	2259	151

1997 U.S. Botanic Garden

Reason for Issue:	To commemorate the 175th anniversary of the founding of the U.S. Botanic Garden in Washington, D.C.
Authorization:	Public Law 103-328, September 29, 1994.

Facts and Figures

Denomination	Date/Mint	Pre-issue Price	Regular Price	Maximum Authorized	Net Mintage	Market Value
Silver Dollar	1997 P UNC	$30	$32	500,000	57,272	$49
	1997 P Proof	$33	$37		264,528	$49

Maximum authorization is by denomination. Proof and Uncirculated coins combined make up the maximum. Net mintage figures shown represent the net quantity distributed by the Mint.

Designs

Obverse by Edgar Z. Steever IV

A straight-on view of the façade of the U.S. Botanic Garden building, adding another edifice to the list of Washington structures depicted on commemorative coins. "Liberty" in large letters arcs above; below the building, at the extreme right, are the artist's initials. "One Dollar" and the date of issue 1997 are centrally located, with the Mint mark below the date. Arcing below are "In God We Trust" and "United States of America" at the rim.

Reverse by William C. Cousins

A rose in the center, with a rose garland arcing above. It is perhaps known by few that the rose is America's national flower—little known because it wasn't so declared until a 1986 Act of Congress. As an interesting sidelight, when the proposal to make the rose the national floral emblem was introduced in Congress in 1985, there was actually competition. In a battle somewhat less dramatic than Benjamin Franklin's legendary proposal to make the American Turkey rather than the Bald Eagle the national mascot, Representative Robert Michel of Illinois offered a proposal to make the American marigold the national floral emblem. Representative Michel's offering died in committee and the rose was named in 1986 (Public Law 99-449). This issue is also the second U.S. commemorative to depict a rose. The first is the 1995 Special Olympics dollar (reverse). Below the rose in straight lines is the inscription "UNITED STATES BOTANIC GARDEN 1820–1995". "E PLURIBUS UNUM" arcs at the bottom rim. Cousins's distinctive monogram is located at the right rim, between the garland and the rim.

Origins of the U.S. Botanic Garden Dollar

Why does a commemorative coin marking an anniversary two years past, and for an institution barely known to the American public, sell at twice the rate of a commemorative marking the 150th anniversary of the Smithsonian, arguably this country's most treasured asset? One word: packaging.

In 1997, with the marketing of the Botanic Garden coins, the Mint announced the end of the Prestige Proof set. Since 1983, with the exception of 1985, a set of coins incorporating the regular five-coin circulating coin Proofs with select commemorative Proofs in special packaging was sold. The Prestige Proof sets quickly peaked in popularity with the 1986 set, which included the Immigrant half dollar and the Ellis Island silver dollar from the Statue of Liberty program. But by 1996, the Prestige Proof program had languished to just under 60,000 sets sold, incorporating coins from the abusive Atlanta Olympics commemorative travesty. Thus did the death knell sound.

With the 1997 Prestige set, a limit of 80,000 sets was established, and the authorization relatively quickly sold out. The 80,000 silver dollars included in these sets boosted the Proof sales to more than double the Smithsonian silver dollar net. The rest of the program benefited from this air of rarity.

Another factor, albeit a smaller one, was the attempt to recreate the excitement around the 1994 Jefferson "Matte Finish" 5-cent coin set. The Mint created a tenuous connection between the Botanic Garden and Thomas Jefferson (the garden was created by legislation signed by James Monroe in 1820, long after Jefferson's presidency) and created the U.S. Botanic Garden Coinage and Currency set. Limited to 25,000, the set included the Uncirculated Botanic Garden silver dollar, an Uncirculated Series 1995 $1 Virginia Federal Reserve note featuring the bank seal with the letter E, and a matte finish 1997 Jefferson 5-cent coin. (See the "1993 Thomas Jefferson's 250th Anniversary of Birth" entry for additional information concerning this special nickel.)

These two special sets account for almost half the net sales. One can only speculate how many Coinage and Currency sets were snapped up by collectors hoping to cash in on another unofficial Matte Finish 5-cent coin.

THE U.S. BOTANIC GARDEN DOLLAR TODAY

Packaging rarities notwithstanding, this is an attractive design. Buy any grade less than the "70" for the pride of ownership, but do not expect any significant future potential. Consider the low population "70" encapsulations. Just keep vigil for population increases.

1997-P $1.00

Grading Service	MS 69	MS 70
NGC	890	155
PCGS	1424	90
Combined	2314	245

Grading Service	PF 69	PF 70
NGC	1165	43
PCGS	1118	39
Combined	2283	82

Reason for Issue:	To commemorate contributions of black Americans during the Revolutionary War, and the 275th anniversary of the birth of Crispus Attucks.
Authorization:	Public Law 104-329, section 101.3, October 20, 1996.

Facts and Figures

Denomination	Date/Mint	Pre-issue Price	Regular Price	Maximum Authorized	Net Mintage	Market Value
Silver Dollar	1998-S UNC	$30	$32	500,000	37,210	$170
	1998-S Proof	$33	$37		75,070	$120

Maximum authorization is by denomination. Proof and Uncirculated coins combined make up the maximum. Net mintage figures shown represent the net quantity distributed by the Mint.

DESIGNS

Obverse by John Mercanti

A facing representation of Crispus Attucks, the first colonist killed by British troops during the Boston Massacre. "LIBERTY" in large letters arcs above; "IN GOD WE TRUST" appears at the left. "CRISPUS ATTUCKS 1723–1770" (the years of his birth and death) appears to the right. The date is below, with Mercanti's initials engraved into Attucks's shoulder.

Reverse by Ed Dwight, modeled by Thomas D. Rogers, Sr.

A Revolutionary Era black family, honoring not only the men who fought but the families who supported them. The group is a representation of a portion of the Black Revolutionary War Patriots Memorial sculpture in Washington, D.C. "UNITED STATES OF AMERICA" and "E PLURIBUS UNUM" arc above, "ONE DOLLAR" below.

Origins of the Black Revolutionary War Patriots Dollar

The $1 million raised in surcharges from the sale of these coins was earmarked to help build the Black Revolutionary War Patriots Memorial on the Mall in Washington; General Motors also contributed $1.5 million.

In the late Boston winter of 1770, tensions between the emboldened American colonists and the increasingly threatened British loyalists reached fever pitch. A lone shot rang out, leaving the agitated crowd shocked that a free, 54-year-old black man, Crispus Attucks, lay dead from British gunfire. What would come to be known as the Boston Massacre ignited the flames of independence that led to the Revolutionary War and, ultimately, to the formation of the United States.

Offered as part of this issue were 20,000 Black Patriots Coin-and-Stamp sets. The sets included a Proof dollar and four postage stamps in a leather case for $79. The stamps feature Frederick Douglass, Harriet Tubman, Benjamin Banneker, and Salem Poor. Alone among this quartet, Salem Poor was a Revolutionary War soldier: he fought at Bunker Hill. Douglass and Tubman were heroes of the Civil War era, and Banneker was an inventor and scientist, most famed for recreating from memory the plans for Washington, D.C., after Pierre L'Enfant took the working plans with him when he was dismissed as architect and planner of the city.

The Black Revolutionary War Patriots Memorial is still under development in Washington at Constitution Gardens, Constitution Avenue and 17th Street NW. Development of the Memorial is now in the hands of the Liberty Fund D.C. The Black Revolutionary War Patriots Foundation disbanded in 2005, when its fourth extension from Congress expired. Money raised by the Foundation to build the Memorial seems to have disappeared, including more than $1 million raised from the sale of the Crispus Attucks commemorative coin. To date, investigation has revealed no wrong doing.

THE BLACK REVOLUTIONARY WAR PATRIOTS DOLLAR TODAY

This issue was purchased by many non-collectors—those individuals who do not normally buy coins from the U.S. Mint; this indicates the issue was well distributed. I would recommend the uncirculated version over the proof, especially since the dealers' holdings are limited at present. There is good future potential for the uncirculated coin, and very good possibilities for the PF 70 version and the Young Collector's set. Keep vigil on those population numbers!

Benjamin Banneker 15-cent stamp; Scott#1804

Harriet Tubman 13-cent stamp; Scott#1744

Frederick Douglass 25-cent stamp; Scott#1290

Salem Poor 10-cent stamp; Scott#1560

The Black Revolutionary War Patriots set containing a proof silver dollar and four U.S. Postal Service stamps Honoring Benjamin Banneker (15 cents, Scott catalogue of postage stamps reference #1804), Harriet Tubman (13 cents, Scott #1744), Frederick Douglass (25 cents, Scott #1290), and Salem Poor (10 cents, Scott #1560) is valued at a marginal premium.

Populations for this issue have risen to new all-time highs, and at present it could be in for a price correction. Still, if you desire the issue buy it—but be sure to evaluate the market trends right before you do so.

Black Revolutionary War Patriots Commemorative
Coin and Stamp Set.

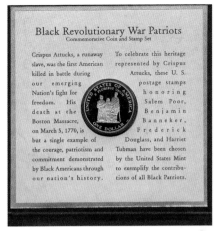

Black Revolutionary War Patriots
Commemorative Coin and Stamp Set.

1998-S $1.00

Grading Service	MS 69	MS 70
NGC	753	244
PCGS	1030	141
Combined	1783	385

Grading Service	PF 69	PF 70
NGC	1081	49
PCGS	1032	51
Combined	2113	100

Reason for Issue:	To commemorate Robert F. Kennedy thirty years after his assassination.
Authorization:	Public Law 104-328, September 29, 1994.

Facts And Figures

Denomination	Date/Mint	Pre-issue Price	Regular Price	Maximum Authorized	Net Mintage	Market Value
Silver Dollar	1998 S UNC	$30	$32	500,000	106,422	$45
	1998 S Proof	$33	$37		99,020	$45

Maximum authorization is by denomination. Proof and Uncirculated coins combined make up the maximum. Net mintage figures shown represent the net quantity distributed by the Mint.

DESIGNS

Obverse by Thomas D. Rogers, Sr.

A facing portrait of Robert Kennedy, his familiar shirt and tie somewhat askew. According to the Mint, Kennedy's widow personally supervised the sculpture of the model. "ROBERT F. KENNEDY" arcs above in large letters. "IN GOD WE TRUST" is at the left, with the date 1998 and "LIBERTY" at the right. Rogers's initials are below Kennedy's right shoulder (to the viewer's left).

Reverse by James Peed, modeled by Thomas D. Rogers, Sr.

The defiant eagle of the Department of Justice is the large central device; "JUS-TICE" arcs above. Superimposed is the smaller emblem of the U.S. Senate. The designer's initials are just below the Justice emblem, and the Mint mark to the right of the Senate emblem. The legends "UNITED STATES OF AMERICA" and "ONE DOLLAR" completely circle the design. Kennedy served in two national posts: as Attorney General in the Department of Justice, and as Senator from New York; both roles are represented on the reverse.

Origins of the Robert F. Kennedy Dollar

Of all the key chains, money clips, baseball cards, Young Collector's sets, embroidery, cloisonné, doodads and what-nots cobbled up by Mint marketers to manufacture buyer interest in commemorative coin programs over the years, one set in this program stands far above all else in terms of historical significance and emotional impact. The Kennedy Collector's set combines in simple, under-stated packaging an Uncirculated Robert F. Kennedy silver dollar and a specially prepared John F. Kennedy silver half dollar. The half dollar was made with the sandblast matte finish process, on a 90 percent silver planchet reserved for silver Proof set pieces. The set bears the San Francisco (S) Mint mark, and sells in the $170–$185 range at present.

The set had no upper sales limit, other than those imposed by the Robert F. Kennedy program as a whole. However, sales were limited to just six weeks. Collectors responded, ordering some 64,000 of the sets during the limited sales window. As a result, the Robert F. Kennedy Uncirculated mintage exceeds the Proof mintage, a rarity for modern commemorative coin programs.

This issue marks a first in U.S. history, in that at no other time have broth-ers appeared on American coins. That both were assassinated—publicly and indelibly in the American consciousness—makes this set a double "what might have been." After John Kennedy's assassination in his first term as President, his Vice President, Lyndon B. Johnson, took office. Johnson was elected in his own right to the presidency in 1964. Robert Kennedy resigned his office of Attorney General and was elected Senator from New York.

Funds from surcharges are to support the Robert F. Kennedy Memorial, which is not a monument-type memorial at all, but a working foundation for education and civil rights.

THE ROBERT F. KENNEDY DOLLAR TODAY

With higher numbers than recent programs in the uncirculated version, one might wonder about this coin's market power in the future. However, the Ken-nedy mystique, the unique brothers-on-coins aspect, and the Matte Finish silver half dollar in the set, may keep this issue high in collectors' interests for some time to come. However, I would procure only for the pure joy of collecting. The three-piece set, which is quite popular among collectors, shows some good but limited future potential. PF-70 populations are low at this time. The problem is that a large hoard can be graded and the PF-70 census can suddenly increase. Be alert should you procure one of these encapsulations.

1998-S $1.00

Grading Service	MS 69	MS 70
NGC	1726	520
PCGS	2076	194
Combined	3802	714

Grading Service	PF 69	PF 70
NGC	1155	57
PCGS	982	32
Combined	2137	89

1999 Dolley Madison

Reason for Issue:	To commemorate the 150th anniversary of the death of Dolley Madison, wife of the fourth President.
Authorization:	Public Law 104-329, section 101.1, on October 20, 1996.

Facts and Figures

Denomination	Date/Mint	Pre-issue Price	Regular Price	Maximum Authorized	Net Mintage	Market Value
Silver Dollar	1999 P UNC	$30	$32	500,000	89,104	$42
	1999 P Proof	$33	$37		224,403	$42

Maximum authorization is by denomination. Proof and Uncirculated coins combined make up the maximum. Net mintage figures shown represent the net quantity distributed by the Mint.

Designs

Obverse by Tiffany & Company, modeled by T. James Ferrell

Portrait of Dolley Madison: a luminescent, low-cut design evocative of the French designs of Louis Oscar Roty (1846–1911) a century ago. She is surrounded by her favorite flower, the Cape Jasmine gardenia. In the background right is the domed portico over the icehouse at the Madison estate, Montpelier, near Charlottesville, Virginia. Take away the inscription "Dolley Madison" crowding the center below the icehouse and this design would be among the finest in American portraiture on coins. The date 1999 is tucked in near the flowers; "Liberty" in large, widely spaced letters arcs above; "In God We

Trust" is attached to Dolley's temple. The historic "t&co" hallmark of Tiffany & Company appears at the lower right; Ferrell's initials are at the lower left. The renowned jeweler and silversmith Tiffany & Company, perhaps more famous for its stained glass lamps, is the credited designer of this coin. One look at it, and it is apparent that the Dolley Madison really stands out artistically from the recent crowd.

Reverse by Tiffany & Company, modeled by Thomas D. Rogers, Sr.

The columned front portico of Montpelier, bounded by foliage and willows. "United States of America" and "One Dollar" completely circle the design, although the Tiffany artists allowed the circle to be partially open, and closed by the viewer's own eye. "E Pluribus Unum" appears above the the building's pediment, with "Montpelier" below. The "t&co." hallmark and Mint mark are at either end of the porch steps. Rogers's initials are in the lawn under the willows at right. This design is artistically coherent but not as commanding as the stronger obverse.

Origins of the Dolley Madison Dollar

The Tiffany connection threatens to overwhelm all other factors surrounding this issue. Still, Dolley Madison is notable in her own right. She virtually invented the Washington political-social circle—for good or bad—that still exists today.

Her most famous act took place during the War of 1812, when the British soldiers were attempting to burn Washington to the ground. Despite being begged to flee for her life, she stayed behind at the White House and began removing items she judged of national importance. Among them was the Gilbert Stuart portrait of George Washington. Tiffany & Company became involved with this program through its association with the National Trust for Historic Preservation. Seeking funds to preserve and maintain Montpelier, the trust commissioned Tiffany, who donated the design.

I was personally invited to attend a White House ceremony on January 11, 1999, to help launch the issue. Michael J. Kowalski, Tiffany's president, was also present. This the third issue to display private advertising on coinage. The first was the 1926 Sesquicentennial half dollar, and the second was the Liberty Bell design (with the inscription naming Pass and Stow as makers of the bell) on the Franklin half dollars of 1948–63.

Somewhat surprisingly, the coins were issued either individually or as two-coin sets, but without the typical "collector's sets" and associated money clips, key chains, and other items so prevalent in recent programs.

THE DOLLEY MADISON DOLLAR TODAY

The artistic beauty of this design and the historic first of a Tiffany-designed coin may entice some collectors, but, unfortunately, mintage figures are too high. This issue is a buy purely for the joy of collecting; there is very little future potential here.

1999-P $1.00

Grading Service	MS 69	MS 70
NGC	1053	830
PCGS	2038	321
Combined	3091	1151

Grading Service	PF 69	PF 70
NGC	1821	401
PCGS	2254	210
Combined	4075	611

Reason for Issue:	To commemorate the 200th anniversary of the death of George Washington.
Authorization:	Public Law 104-329 section 101.2, October 20, 1996.

Facts and Figures

Denomination	Date/Mint	Pre-issue Price	Regular Price	Maximum Authorized	Net Mintage	Market Value
Gold $5	1999 W UNC	$180	$205	100,000	22,511	$420
	1999 W Proof	$195	$225		41,693	$420

Maximum authorization is by denomination. Proof and Uncirculated coins combined make up the maximum. Net mintage figures shown represent the net quantity distributed by the Mint.

DESIGNS

Obverse by Laura Gardin Fraser

A bust of George Washington, facing right. In 1931, a design competition was held to create a design for a quarter dollar commemorating the 200th anniversary in 1932 of the birth of George Washington. The competition's rules dictated that the likeness of Washington be based on the life mask bust of Washington sculpted by Jean-Antoine Houdon. Laura Gardin Fraser, wife of James Earle Fraser—the designer of the Indian Head 5-cent coin (the "Buffalo nickel")—and designer of commemorative coins in her own right in the 1920s, won the competition. But in a pique of unknown motivation, Treasury Secretary William Woodin declared instead that John Flanagan's designs would be used. The circulating commemorative quarter dollar was struck in 1932, and that was that.

The bicentennial commemorative design was used on the circulating quarter dollars of 1934 (none was struck in 1933, in the depths of the Great Depression), and production of the Flanagan designs continued until 1999, when a slightly modified and reduced bust was introduced for the 50 State Quarters program.

But, in that same year of 1999, the Laura Gardin Fraser design resurfaced, this time on the elite if not widely held denomination of the $5 gold half eagle. Using Fraser's original plasters as a guide, the bold portrait of Washington was repurposed for the 250th anniversary of his death.

The chief difference between Fraser's and Flanagan's Washington likeness is that Flanagan's faces left while Fraser's faces right. In fact, for a commemorative, the Fraser coin is remarkably banal in design. "LIBERTY" appears above and is partially obscured by Washington's head. "IN GOD WE TRUST" is to the left, behind his queue, or ponytail. The date 1999 and the Mint mark (W) are located below his chin. Fraser's queue is tightly bound, whereas Flanagan's is tied with a bow. Fraser's hair appears less "coiffed," but most importantly Fraser finally gets full credit, as her initials (LFG) appear on the truncation of the bust.

Reverse by Laura Gardin Fraser

An eagle with wings spread faces right and clutches a sheath of arrows in its talons. "UNITED STATES OF AMERICA" and a field of 13 stars appear above; "E PLURIBUS UNUM" and "FIVE DOLLARS" are below. This is Fraser's original reverse, also snubbed by Treasury Secretary William Woodin.

Origins of the George Washington Gold $5

One begins to wonder how many ways and for how many anniversaries we will be able to honor the Father of Our Country. The first American coin to honor Washington was, of course, not the quarter dollar but Charles Barber's Lafayette Monument dollar of 1900 (this portrait was also based on Houdin's bust). In 1926, John Ray Sinnock offered his take on this bust, pairing Washington with Calvin Coolidge on the obverse of the Sesquicentennial of American Independence half dollar. As mentioned, the 1932 circulating quarter dollar was issued to commemorate the 200th anniversary of Washington's birth. Then, in 1982, chief engraver Elizabeth Jones created the obverse of the silver half dollar that signaled the rebirth of commemorative coins in America, but she departed from the Houdon portrait by showing Washington on horseback.

This is the first U.S. gold coin to depict Washington.

Surcharges of $35 per coin were paid to the Mount Vernon Ladies' Association for the preservation of Washington's historic estate, and for educational purposes. The program launch ceremony was held at Mount Vernon, in Virginia, just outside of Washington, D.C.

THE GEORGE WASHINGTON GOLD $5 TODAY

This coin has an attractive design. Buy it only if you like it or must have a specimen for your complete commemorative set. The high mintage figures and corresponding elevated population figures mean that the future potential of this issue is doubtful. As the value of gold fluctuates, so shall the value of this issue.

1999-W $5.00

Grading Service	MS 69	MS 70
NGC	637	727
PCGS	1933	133
Combined	2570	860

Grading Service	PF 69	PF 70
NGC	1121	762
PCGS	2879	154
Combined	4000	916

Reason for Issue:	To commemorate the 125th anniversary of the establishment of Yellowstone National Park as the first National Park in the United States, and the birth of the National Park idea.
Authorization:	Public Law 104-329, section 101.5, October 20, 1996.

Facts and Figures

Denomination	Date/Mint	Pre-issue Price	Regular Price	Maximum Authorized	Net Mintage	Market Value
Silver Dollar	1999 P UNC	$30	$32	500,000	82,563	$46
	1999 P Proof	$33	$37		187,595	$40

Maximum authorization is by denomination. Proofs and Uncirculated coins combined make up the maximum. Net mintage figures represent the net quantity distributed by the Mint.

DESIGNS

Obverse by Edgar Z. Steever IV

An erupting geyser and a fountain of steam and hot water rising before a forested hillside. When you mention the word "Yellowstone" to almost any American, two images come to mind: the Old Faithful geyser and the bison. Both of these symbols are prominently displayed on the Yellowstone silver dollar. Although the central obverse image is not specifically identified as Old Faithful, the park's star attraction, noted for its legendary (and somewhat exaggerated) regularity, most people will make that association. "YELLOWSTONE" arcs above; "IN GOD

WE TRUST" is in small letters in the left field, and the designer's initials are at the lower left. "LIBERTY" and the date 1999 are in two lines in exergue; the Mint mark is at the lower right.

Reverse by William C. Cousins

A classic American bison, or buffalo, faces left, while the sun sets majestically with rays filling the sky above distant mountains. Within a double circle, "United States of America" arcs above, and "One Dollar" below. "E Pluribus Unum" is in smaller letters between the inner circle and the bison's hooves.

Origins of the Yellowstone National Park Dollar

On the theory that "late is better than never," the issue marking the 125th anniversary of America's first National Park appeared two years after that anniversary year. In 1872 an Act of Congress signed into law by President Ulysses S. Grant established the National Park System and created Yellowstone as the first National Park in the world. The unique landscape of the world's largest conglomeration of geysers and other thermal features was set aside for the enjoyment of the public, and to preserve and protect its delicate nature. Today, Yellowstone receives more than three million visitors per year, almost all of them in the months from June through September.

In 1997, Yellowstone celebrated its 125th anniversary. A variety of commemorative items was available for sale at the park and through other channels—T-shirts, posters, mugs, key chains, stuffed animals—but no coins. Given the scope of the anniversary marketing efforts in 1997 and the vast numbers of visitors to the park, one can only wonder whether the entire 500,000 maximum mintage might not have been sold over the counter had they been available to the park's several souvenir shops in that year. Of the $10 surcharge added to the price of each coin sold by the Mint, half was earmarked for Yellowstone and half for the National Park Foundation.

THE YELLOWSTONE NATIONAL PARK DOLLAR TODAY

The issue is popular but it is hampered by the high production numbers, which became the final mintage figures. Currently the lower uncirculated version is the best bet: I would procure for the joy of ownership at present.

The issue was also sold in a two-piece set containing a proof and uncirculated coin. The current value of the set is determined by adding the values of the two coins; there no discernible premium for the set at this time and collectors should buy it only for the sheer joy of collecting.

1999-P

Grading Service	MS 69	MS 70
NGC	1004	394
PCGS	1711	202
Combined	2715	596

Grading Service	PF 69	PF 70
NGC	1721	90
PCGS	1478	47
Combined	3199	137

Reason for Issue:	To commemorate the Bicentennial of the Library of Congress.
Authorization:	Public Law 105-268, October 19, 1998.

Facts and Figures

Denomination	Date/Mint	Pre-issue Price	Regular Price	Maximum Authorized	Net Mintage	Market Value
Silver Dollar	2000 P UNC	$25	$27	500,000	53,400	$42
	2000 P Proof	$28	$32		196,900	$42
Gold-Platinum Bimetallic $10	2000 P UNC	$380	$405	200,000	6,683	$4700
	2000 P Proof	$395	$425		27,167	$1250

Maximum authorization is by denomination. Proofs and Uncirculated coins combined make up the maximum. Net mintage figures shown represent the net quantity distributed by the Mint.

Silver Dollar Designs

Obverse by Thomas D. Rogers, Sr.

An open book superimposed over the torch from the Library's dome. "Library of Congress" and the bicentennial dates 1800 and 2000 arc above. "In God We Trust" and "Liberty" are below in exergue.

Reverse by John Mercanti

A flying saucer-like depiction of the Library's dome, "United States of America" and "E Pluribus Unum" are in two lines arcing above. Below is "One Dollar".

Gold-Platinum Ringed Bimetallic $10 Designs

Obverse by John Mercanti

The hand of Minerva, the Greek goddess of wisdom, raising the torch of learning above the dome of the Thomas Jefferson Building of the Library of Congress. "Liberty" and the date 2000 are above, split by the torch's flame. "Library of Congress" arcs below in the gold ring. In the platinum central portion, "In God we Trust" is at the left.

The designer's initials are below and to the left. The hand and torch are in the platinum portion (inner core) of the coin; the flame is the gold portion (the outer ring).

Reverse by Thomas D. Rogers, Sr.

The Library of Congress seal, surrounded by laurel leaves. "E Pluribus Unum" is in small letters inside the platinum slug (the inner core). "United States of America" and "Ten Dollars" surround the design in the gold ring.

Origins of the Library of Congress Bicentennial Coins

The authorizing legislation for the Library of Congress coins specifies a silver dollar and a $5 gold coin, but with a provision allowing the Mint to substitute for the gold coin a $10 coin made of gold and platinum. Despite the production challenges, the Mint went with the ringed bimetallic coin—so called because a central slug is surrounded by a ring of a different metallic composition.

The Library of Congress $10 coin is the first ringed bimetallic coin struck by the U.S. Mint, although ringed bimetallic coins have been popular in other countries for some time.

The surcharge on the silver dollar was reduced from that of recent issues—$10 per coin—to $5 per coin. This resulted in lower prices for the collector. The ringed bimetallic $10 coin, however, came with a hefty $50 per coin surcharge.

The authorizing legislation specified a maximum of 100,000 gold $5 coins, but up to 200,000 bimetallic $10 coins, so that the Library of Congress Trust

Fund Board, recipients of the surcharge windfall, would not be adversely affected by the halving of the silver dollar surcharge.

The Library of Congress Bicentennial Coins Today

Based on the sales figures for all issues, except the $10 bimetallic issue, I suggest acquisition only for the joy of ownership at present.

Production of the $10 Proof version experienced a staggering 40 percent rejection rate for technological reasons. One might ponder whether this is a good reason to acquire the first U.S. bimetallic coin ever produced. That said, a good promotion can drive prices higher—at some point. The bimetallic coin's sales figure appears too high for any serious long-term value increase.

Concentrate on the $10 uncirculated striking and the associated 6,683 mintage—these have good future potential. I like the low-mintage uncirculated $10 piece, but procure these coins only because you want one

2000-P $1.00

Grading Service	MS 69	MS 70
NGC	795	644
PCGS	1385	182
Combined	2180	826

Grading Service	PF 69	PF 70
NGC	1598	43
PCGS	1310	56
Combined	2908	99

2000-W $10.00

Grading Service	MS 69	MS 70
NGC	418	804
PCGS	1377	368
Combined	1795	1172

Grading Service	PF 69	PF 70
NGC	1796	386
PCGS	3756	437
Combined	5552	823

Reason for Issue:	To commemorate the 1,000 years of history since Leif Ericson landed in and established settlements in the New World.
Authorization:	Public Law 106-126, sections 101-107, December 6, 1999.

Facts and Figures

Denomination	Date/Mint	Pre-issue Price	Regular Price	Maximum Authorized	Net Mintage	Market Value
U.S. Silver Dollar	2000 P UNC	$30	$32	500,000	28,150	$75
	2000 P Proof	$33	$37		58,612‡	$65
Icelandic 1000 Kronur	2000 Proof	$33	$37	150,000	15,947‡	$25

Denomination	Date/Mint	Pre-issue Price	Regular Price	Maximum Authorized	Net Mintage	Market Value
Two-piece Proof Set	2000 P Proof 2000 Proof	$63	$68	Unknown	86,136	$88

Maximum authorization is by denomination. Proofs and Uncirculated coins combined make up the maximum. Net mintage figures shown represent the net quantity distributed by the Mint.

The Proof single sales figure must be combined with the two-piece Proof set sales figures to arrive at the correct mintage figure.

1000 Kronur Designs

The Iceland commemoratives, like the modern U.S. silver dollar commemoratives, were struck from 26.73 grams of 90 percent silver. Proof production took place at the Philadelphia Mint "on behalf" of the Republic of Iceland—but the coins bear no P Mint mark.

The 1000 Kronur proof-only issue was offered individually and as part of the first ever jointly released United States Mint two-coin set, accompanied by the United States Proof Leif Ericson dollar.

Obverse by Throstur Magnusson, modeled by T. James Ferrell

An image of Stirling Calder's sculpture of Leif Ericson, which was presented to Iceland by the United States in 1930.

Reverse by Throstur Magnusson, modeled by John Mercanti

The eagle, the dragon, the bull, and the giant from the Icelandic coat of arms. This same design can be found on several other Iceland coinage issues—both commemorative and circulating.

Silver Dollar Designs

Obverse by John Mercanti

A bearded, flowing-haired Leif Ericson facing right, wearing an iron-banded helmet. A chain circles 90 percent around, the date 2000 at the bottom. "Leif Ericson" arcs above, inside the chain, split by the peak of the helmet. "In God We Trust" is in three lines at the left. "Liberty" and the Mint mark are below Ericson's chin. The designer's initials are at the nape of the neck.

Reverse by T. James Ferrell

A tall-prowed Viking ship under square sail heads toward the New World, as Ericson stands dramatically in the bow. The presumptuous title "Founder of the New World" arcs above; "One Dollar" in two lines is to the windward of the sail; "E Pluribus Unum" in three lines precedes the bow of the ship; "United States of America" is in three lines below the ship.

Origins of the Leif Ericson Millennium Coins

Leif Ericson, or Leifur Eiriksson, depending on which side of the Big Pond you are from, was an Icelandic venture seaman who some ten centuries ago set sail westward and wound up bouncing along the North American coastline. Recent archaeological and anthropological studies have given additional credit to Scandinavia's claim, once thought more legend than fact, to be the discoverers and settlers of the New World centuries before Mediterranean Europeans launched the Age of Discovery and the conquest of the Americas. (It should be noted that Asians seem to have found their way to North America some 15,000 years ago via the Bering land bridge connecting Siberia and Alaska.)

Proceeds from the $10 surcharge on each silver dollar were paid to the Leifur Eiriksson Foundation for the purpose of funding student exchanges between the United States and Iceland. The surcharges will also fund a Fulbright scholarship at the University of Virginia to promote student exchanges between the two countries.

The U.S. Mint symbolically turned over a check to Steingrimer Hermansson, Chairman of the Board of Trustees of the Leifur Eiriksson Foundation, and John Casteen III, President of the University of Virginia, on November 15, 2005. The $1,728,980 in surcharge proceeds had actually been transferred to the Leifur Eiriksson Foundation in May 2005. The delay of the formal ceremonial payment was because the sponsors of the legislation, Representative James A. Leach and Senator Tom Harkin, both of Iowa, were not available for the ceremony until November 2005.

The Leif Ericson Millennium Coins Today

The sales figures displayed in the above tables total 34.5% of the authorized U.S. coinage to be sold in this commemorative issue. Coins of this set should be procured only for the joy of ownership and collecting at present. Buy the 1,000 Kronur issue for the pure joy of collecting. It is overvalued in many price guides at $28—it is a $10 retail coin.

At this time the PF-70 issue could be a sleeper with its currently low population, but this could change in the future. Buy the other coins in this issue for the joy of collecting only.

2000-P $1.00

Grading Service	MS 69	MS 70
NGC	682	418
PCGS	1367	122
Combined	2049	540

Grading Service	PF 69	PF 70
NGC	1512	17
PCGS	1336	30
Combined	2848	47

Reason for Issue:	The coin was authorized to mark the opening of the National Museum of the American Indian, part of the Smithsonian Institution in Washington, D.C., and to supplement the museum's ongoing endowment and educational funds.
Authorization:	Public Law 103-375, October 27, 2000.

Facts and Figures

Denomination	Date/Mint	Pre-issue Price (May 4, 2001 - June 21, 2001)	Regular Price	Maximum Authorized	Net Mint-age	Market Value
Silver Dollar	2001-D UNC.	$30	$32	500,000	227,131	$175
	2001-P Proof	$33	$37		272,869	$180
	2-coin Proof and Uncirculated Set	$59.95	$64.95			$355
	Coin & Currency set	$54.95	$59.95			$320

Maximum authorized mintage was 500,000 for both uncirculated and proof issues combined. This also included the two-coin proof and uncirculated set ($59.95) and the Coin & Currency set ($54.95) of which 50,000 were issued.

DESIGNS

Obverse

A rendition of the obverse by James Earle Fraser (1876–1953) originally used for the Buffalo Nickel and struck from 1913 through mid-1938. It portrays an American Indian thought by many to represent Big Tree, a Kiowa; or Chief Iron Tail, an Oglala Lakota; or Two Moons, a Cheyenne. While Fraser's memory was failing him in later years he is quoted as saying: "In making that portrait the face of the magnificent old Indian, Chief Iron Tail, was uppermost in my mind." Fraser was also known for his famous western sculpture, *The End of the Trail*. Additionally, Fraser designed the Buffalo Pan-American Exposition Medal; the Victory Army and Navy medal; the Navy Cross Medal; and the Norse American Centennial medal.

"Liberty" crescents in front of the American Indian's eyes along the rim; the date 2001 and Fraser's initial (F) are at the seven o'clock position at the base of the neck.

Reverse

The profile of Black Diamond, a bison Fraser had observed at New York City's Central Park Zoo. This reverse design is like that of the original Buffalo Nickel. Fraser stated that in his search for American symbols, "I found no motif within the boundaries of the United States as distinctive as the American buffalo."

The coin also features an incuse Mint mark, the first such type of Mint mark to appear on an American commemorative. "United States of America" and "In God We Trust" arc above the bison's back and "E Pluribus Unum" appears below his beard; "One Dollar" is on the mound supporting the animal.

Packaging: $5 Currency Replica

A $5 currency replica was officially produced exclusively for these sets in an extremely limited edition of just 50,000 by the United States Bureau of Engraving and Printing. The printing plate was prepared from an original master die of the bill. This is the only issue of United States paper money for which an American Indian was chosen as the central motif. The likeness shown on this bill is that of Ta-to-ka-in-yan-ka also known as Running Antelope of the Hunkpapa Lakota Tribe based on an 1872 photograph by Alexander Gardner in the Smithsonian Institution. The original plate was crafted by the world-renowned U.S. Treasury Engraver, George F.C. Smillie (1854–1924).

Origins of the American Buffalo Dollar

This coin was issued to mark the opening of the Smithsonian National Museum of the American Indian. A portion of the proceeds from the sale of each coin is authorized to support the museum and to supplement its endowment and educational outreach funds.

The National Museum of the American Indian is in a 260,000-square-foot building on the National Mall that faces the Capitol and is adjacent to the Air and Space Museum. The museum also has a fine permanent exhibition facility in New York City and a state-of-the-art collections research and study center in Suitland, Maryland. The new building has a collection of 800,000 Native objects spanning 10,000 years, unquestionably the largest and most comprehensive collection ever assembled. Since Native Americans themselves pre-

$5 currency replica: front.

$5 currency replica: back.

dominantly planned this new museum, it enables the world to explore the past, present, and future through the eyes of Native people of the United States.

THE AMERICAN BUFFALO DOLLAR TODAY

This coin became a big seller from the minute sales were opened to the public. Some of the demand was fueled by buzz in various online forums, such as the Internet newsgroup "rec.collecting.coins": its long interactive threads gave many dealers the incentive to speculate correctly that demand would be high and the newsgroup's own speculation caused the demand to go even higher. Within two weeks of release the issue was sold out. It may have sold out even more quickly had not the overloaded U.S. Mint website and telephone ordering systems failed several times under the crush of collectors and non-collectors trying to order this much sought-after coin.

With approximately 50,000 more proofs one wonders why the uncirculated piece fails command the higher price. This has been attributed to the large number of non-collectors interested in the piece and enticed by the shiny proof surfaces. A similar but more subtle effect of this phenomenon can be seen with the 1997 Law Enforcement proof that is very popular with non-collectors of the Law Enforcement community as presentation pieces for retirement ceremonies, etc.

While the proof coin is enjoying a premium over its scarcer uncirculated brethren, one must remember that both coins are above the 225,000+ mark in population, thus both issues have a high population for coins in the commemorative series. Non-collectors generally have little price tolerance: if prices climb too high these will quickly drop out of the market, causing prices to fall. A sufficient rise in silver bullion prices may also drive a lot of these pieces onto the market. Non-collectors will not be reluctant to "dump and run" with their windfall profits. Remember when the then-billionaire Hunt brothers had driven silver to its highs in late 1979 and early 1980? Many coins found their way on to the marketplace after unknowledgeable individuals retrieved coins from their sock drawers, etc., where they had resided for many years. A spike in silver bullion could send a lot of Buffalos stampeding to the marketplace. As noted, this issue is extremely popular with collectors and non-collectors; this is the reason for its current value—despite the high production figures.

At this time joy of ownership should be the decisive factor. Acquire this beautiful coin only if you feel you must have it.

2001-D $1.00

Grading Service	MS 69	MS 70
NGC	10,315	1505
PCGS	10,377	541
Combined	20,692	2046

2001-P $1.00

Grading Service	PF 69	PF 70
NGC	10,645	1418
PCGS	11,829	504
Combined	22,474	1922

Reason for Issue:	To celebrate the first meeting of the Congress in the new U.S. Capitol in 1800, and to help fund the Visitor Center Building.
Authorization:	Public Law 106-126, sections 201-208, December 6, 1999.

Facts and Figures

Denomination	Date and Mint	Pre-issue Price	Regular Price	Maximum Authorized	Net Mint-age	Market Value
Clad Half Dollar	2001 P UNC	See pricing section below		750,000	99,157	$17
	2001 P Proof				77,962	$19
Silver Dollar	2001 P UNC			500,000	35,380	$40
	2001 P Proof				143,793	$40
Gold $5	2001 W UNC			100,000	6,761	$2,950
	2001 W Proof				27,652	$430

PRICING OPTIONS

Pre-issue Sales Price (February 28, 2001–April 20, 2001)

- Three-coin set in presentation case, $225
- Gold Five Dollar proof in presentation case, $200
- Gold Five Dollar proof in mailer, $195
- Gold Five Dollar proof $177
- Gold Five Dollar uncirculated in presentation case, $180
- Gold Five Dollar uncirculated in mailer, $175
- Silver Dollar proof in presentation case, $33
- Silver Dollar proof in mailer, $29
- Silver Dollar proof uncirculated in gift box, $30
- Silver Dollar proof uncirculated in mailer, $27
- Clad Half Dollar proof in tray and sleeve, $11.25
- Clad Half Dollar proof in mailer, $10.75
- Clad Half Dollar uncirculated in Mylar and envelope, $7.75
- Clad Half Dollar uncirculated in mailer, $8.75
- Clad Half Dollar uncirculated collector set, $16.50

Regular Sales Price (after April 20, 2001)

- Three-coin set in presentation case, $250
- Gold Five Dollar proof in presentation case, $225
- Gold Five Dollar proof in mailer, $207
- Gold Five Dollar proof uncirculated in presentation case, $205
- Gold Five Dollar proof uncirculated in mailer, $200
- Silver Dollar proof in presentation case, $37
- Silver Dollar proof in mailer, $33
- Silver Dollar uncirculated in gift box, $32
- Silver Dollar uncirculated in mailer, $29
- Clad Half Dollar proof in tray and sleeve, $12
- Clad Half Dollar proof in mailer, $11.50
- Clad Half Dollar uncirculated in Mylar and envelope, $8.50

- Clad Half Dollar uncirculated in mailer, $9.75
- Clad Half Dollar uncirculated collector set, $17.50

CLAD HALF DOLLAR DESIGNS

Obverse by Dean McMullen

The original U.S. Capitol building, with an outline of the Capitol dome from the post-1864 renovation. The image is encircled with stars; a horse and buggy, with a driver and passenger, trot past the building. The designer's initials are in front of the horse; "LIBERTY" dominates the top of the austere field; "IN GOD WE TRUST" hangs inside the ring of stars. "U.S. CAPITOL" and the date 1800 in two lines provide something for the horse and buggy to plod across. The date 2001 is at the bottom.

Reverse by Marcel Jovine and Alex Shagin

Sixteen stars and the inscriptions: "6TH CONGRESS", "SENATE" and "HOUSE"; "32 SENATORS"; "106 MEMBERS". The stars represent the number of states and the inscriptions reflect the number of members in the 6th Congress—the first to meet in the new Capitol in 1800. "E PLURIBUS UNUM" is at the bottom of the inner ring of stars; "HALF DOLLAR" and "UNITED STATES OF AMERICA" are in the outer portion of the design. The Philadelphia Mint mark can be found next to the final "A" in "AMERICA".

The designer Alex Shagin was born in Russia in 1947 and has created works for the U.S. Mint, the Singapore Mint, the Israel Government Mint, the American Numismatic Association, the Leningrad Mint, and The White House (Ronald Reagan's Medal of Liberty). Marcel Jovine designed the official medal for the 1980 Winter Olympics in Lake Placid, New York, and the 125th Anniversary Medal for the American Numismatic Society (ANS). For the U.S. Mint, he designed the Mount Rushmore Clad Half Dollar obverse and the Bicentennial of the Constitution Gold Five Dollar obverse and reverse.

SILVER DOLLAR DESIGNS

Obverse by Marika H. Somogyi

The original U.S. Capitol superimposed on the image of today's Capitol building. The contrasting images illustrate the growth of the nation. "LIBERTY" arcs across the top of the design. The date 2001 is in the upper left field, and the date 1800 is in the lower right. "IN GOD WE TRUST" and "U.S. CAPITOL" are at the bottom.

Marika Somogyi trained at the Beaux Arts College in Budapest. Her work has been seen in art museums around the world, including the permanent collections of the Smithsonian Institution and the British Museum. She designed the U.S. Mint's Mount Rushmore Commemorative Silver Dollar obverse.

Reverse by John Mercanti

A bald eagle cloaked in a banner inscribed "U.S. Capitol Visitor Center." "United States of America" and "E Pluribus Unum" dominate the upper portion of the design. The Mint mark (P) is directly below the word "Capitol" in the banner. "One Dollar" is at the lower rim.

Gold $5 Designs by Elizabeth Jones

Elizabeth Jones was the first woman to hold the position of U.S. Mint Chief Sculptor/Engraver.

Obverse

An intricate carving of a single Corinthian column, the type found on the Capitol building. "Liberty" is in the upper rim; the date 1800 and "First Convening of Congress in Washington" are in six stacked lines next to the column. The date 2001 at the lower rim forms the base of this linguistic column, a companion to the architectural one. "In God We Trust" snakes along the right hand rim, almost as an afterthought.

Reverse

An image of the original Capitol structure, beautifully portraying the edifice where the first congressional session was held. "United States of America" and "E Pluribus Unum" arc over the building. The West Point Mint mark (W) sits above "Five Dollars", below the Capitol.

Origins of the Capitol Visitor Center Coins

This issue was a controversial program from its inception and resulted in a political tempest. The non-inspiring designs on most of the coins in the series ultimately led to lackluster sales and massive collector apathy. Critics argued that the viability of the entire commemorative coin program was threatened. The issue was strenuously opposed both by the Chairman of the House Banking Subcommittee on Domestic and International Monetary Policy and the Chairman of the Citizens Commemorative Coin Advisory Committee.

The coin's issuance raised strong objections and complaints for several reasons:

- The proposed program violated the requirements of the 1996 Commemorative Coin Reform Act, stating that no more than two commemorative programs per year be authorized by Congress.
- It also violated the 1996 Reform Act by authorizing mintages far in excess of limits of 500,000 set by the Act.
- The proposed program imposed excessive surcharges on the sale prices of the coins. How excessive? As much as two-and-one-half times the standard surcharge levels usually associated with commemoratives. Some collectors considered the surcharges to be a

2001 Capitol Visitor Center 607

tax on their hobby instead of a levy to help a worthy cause.
- The Capitol had been the subject of two prior commemorative coin programs in recent years that already had raised funds for the construction of a visitor center. Moreover, two other authorized coin programs have benefited institutions associated with the Congress: the U.S. Botanic Garden and the Library of Congress.
- Congressional passage of the Capitol Visitor Center Commemorative Coin Act violated House committee rules designed to ensure restraint and deliberation in considering commemorative programs. It also circumvented the congressionally-mandated role of the Citizens Commemorative Coin Advisory Committee in weighing the merits of proposed coin programs.

The methods used by some special interests to push through this coin program revealed Washington politics at its starkest.

The exceptions to the 1996 Commemorative Coin Reform Act prompted the Citizens Commemorative Coin Advisory Committee to make the following recommendations to Congress: "We strongly urge against extension of sales periods for any commemorative coin programs. This is critical to repairing relationships between Congress and the coin collecting community who purchase ninety percent of all commemorative coins authorized by Congress."

The Visitor Center

The main reason for this coin program was to fund the U.S. Capitol Visitor Center. The center was to provide visitors with a secure and accessible environment from which to visit the seat of the U.S. government. The architecturally and historically significant United States Capitol is the center of American democracy. In addition to its active use by Congress, it serves the American people as a museum of American art and history and is home to scores of priceless paintings and sculptures portraying significant people and events that helped shape U.S. history.

Surcharges from the proceeds from the sale of each coin are authorized to be paid to the Capitol Preservation Fund for the purpose of aiding the construction, maintenance, and preservation of the new Capitol Visitor Center. The surcharges for each coin were $35 for gold, $10 for silver, and $3 for clad.

Packaging Options

This issue was unique in that it was the first and to date the only issue to allow the purchaser to choose among various packaging options at different prices. Each option included its own official Certificate of Authenticity. The numerous choices of packaging and pricing only added confusion to prospective buyers. The fact that many buyers were trying to make the purchase selection decision online (often their first such purchase) led most to choose the mail order option, or not to order the coin at all. Even with the U.S. Mint dropping the delivery charge for orders taken online, sales were disappointing.

The ordering options were:

- U.S. Capitol Visitor Center Proof Silver Dollar in Presentation Case
- U.S. Capitol Visitor Center Proof Silver Dollar, Encapsulated in Mailer
- U.S. Capitol Visitor Center Uncirculated Silver Dollar in Gift Box
- U.S. Capitol Visitor Center Uncirculated Silver Dollar, Encapsulated in Mailer
- U.S. Capitol Visitor Center Proof Clad Half Dollar, Encapsulated in Tray and Sleeve
- U.S. Capitol Visitor Center Proof Clad Half Dollar, Encapsulated in Mailer
- U.S. Capitol Visitor Center Uncirculated Clad Half Dollar in Mylar and Envelope
- U.S. Capitol Visitor Center Uncirculated Clad Half Dollar, Encapsulated in Mailer
- U.S. Capitol Visitor Center Uncirculated Clad Half Dollar Collector Set
- U.S. Capitol Visitor Center Proof Gold Five Dollar, Encapsulated in Mailer
- U.S. Capitol Visitor Center Uncirculated Gold Five Dollar in Presentation Case
- U.S. Capitol Visitor Center Uncirculated Gold Five Dollar, Encapsulated in Mailer
- U.S. Capitol Visitor Center Three-Coin Proof Set in Presentation Case (Silver, Gold, and Clad)

The Capitol Visitor Center Coins Today

Like the 2001 American Buffalo commemorative, this coin was conceived as a way to fund a building project within the confines of Washington, D.C. Unlike its American Buffalo cousin, the Capitol Visitor Center project did not seem to have a grassroots supporting constituency. Lack of an interested non-collector subscriber base seemed quite evident as sales were sluggish at best. An example of the poor sales and limited interest by both collectors and non-collectors could be seen during 2001, when one internet bullion vendor (www.tulving.com) was selling PCGS encapsulated MS-69 specimens at only $10 above the pre-issue price and at one point dropped the price to equal to the issue price.

The U.S. Mint caught many collectors off-guard by announcing an abrupt cessation of production of the coins in December 2001. Thus many last-minute buyers of the issue using the "wait and see" tactic were frozen out of obtaining a low-mintage uncirculated $5 gold piece, and a spike in prices resulted almost immediately.

The clad half dollar specimens in MS-69 and PF-69 in both uncirculated and proof should be procured only for the joy of ownership. Unlike its siblings,

U.S. Capitol Visitor Center Uncirculated Clad Half Dollar Collector Set.

it contains no valuable metal content, was distributed in vast numbers, and its uninspiring design does not excite many collectors. Only those few collecting every commemorative specimen available will seek out this coin. The PCGS MS-70 and PF-70 look good at this time.

The silver dollar proof version has a 143,793 mintage, while the uncirculated version of the dollar has a lower mintage of 35,380 pieces. Both coins, again, are recommended only for the joy of ownership. In the future, the uncirculated striking should do better than the proof simply because of its lower mintage numbers. Both coins are not scarce enough to command any appreciable premium. The exceptions are those graded "70" by PCGS.

The gold piece, unlike the clad half or the silver dollar, could show some real potential for appreciation, but only in the uncirculated version: the proof $5 coin has 27,652 pieces minted, the uncirculated version only 6,761 pieces. This was caused by the early cessation of sales declared by the Mint. The latter has appreciated over its issue price, and the uncirculated $5 coin is now undoubtedly one of the "semi-keys" of the modern commemorative issues, joining the ranks of the 1997-W Jackie Robinson $5 uncirculated coin, the 1996 uncirculated Olympic gold coins, and the 1996 uncirculated Smithsonian gold coin. The proof gold coin is recommended only for the joy of ownership. Only dealer promotion may create any price increases in the near future. Collectors should note that some dealers procured moderate numbers of the coins prior to the abrupt cessation of the program, and promotion by one or two of these dealers could make the price rise. If you were lucky enough to obtain one of the uncirculated gold coins directly from the Mint—hold onto it.

Population figures have been rising for the UNC gold issue. This increase might be caused by many in the hobby finally realizing this unappreciated coin is one of the modern commemorative semi-key coins that serious collectors will demand in the future. Study the market before you acquire the uncirculated gold coin. Only time will tell what the true trend is.

At present, the proof half dollar looks like a sleeper, if graded PF-70. PCGS has not graded a PF-70 half of this issue. Should you get lucky, auction same or sell to your trusted dealer. Procure all Capitol Visitor Center issues because you want them or need a complete modern commemorative set.

2001-P 50¢

Grading Service	MS 69	MS 70
NGC	1652	1711
PCGS	1247	57
Combined	2899	1768

Grading Service	PF 69	PF 70
NGC	1739	121
PCGS	1640	54
Combined	3379	175

Grading Service	PF 69	PF 70
NGC	1165	13
PCGS	981	0
Combined	2146	13

2001-W $5.00

Grading Service	MS 69	MS 70
NGC	846	1074
PCGS	2608	216
Combined	3484	1290

2001-P $1.00

Grading Service	MS 69	MS 70
NGC	1152	473
PCGS	1386	78
Combined	2538	551

Grading Service	PF 69	PF 70
NGC	1128	654
PCGS	1964	146
Combined	3092	800

Reason for Issue:	To support the Olympic Winter Games at Salt Lake City, Utah.
Authorization:	Public Law 106-435, November 13, 2000.

Facts and Figures

Denomination	Date/Mint	Pre-issue Price	Regular Price after 25 February 2002	Maximum Authorized	Net Mintage	Market Value
Silver Dollar	2002 P UNC	$30	$32	400,000	40,257	$40
	2002 P Proof	$33	$37		166,864	$40

Denomination	Date/Mint	Pre-issue Price	Regular Price after 25 February 2002	Maximum Authorized	Net Mintage	Market Value
Gold $5	2002 W UNC	$195	$225	80,000	10,585	$425
	2002 W Proof	$210	$235		32,877	$425

SILVER DOLLAR DESIGNS

Obverse by John Mercanti

The Crystal Emblem of the 2002 Olympic Winter Games, the Olympic rings, and the Games' secondary identity mark, the jagged line known as "Rhythm of the Land." "LIBERTY" arcs around the top; "XIX OLYMPIC WINTER GAMES" is in three lines in the field near the nine o'clock position. "SALT LAKE 2002" is above the interlocking Olympic rings, "IN GOD WE TRUST" below. Mercanti's initials are near the rim at the eight o'clock position.

Reverse by Donna Weaver

The Salt Lake City skyline with the Rocky Mountains in the background. The stylized "fire and ice" design dominates the top of the motif with "XIX OLYMPIC WINTER GAMES" just below it. Below the skyline are "E PLURIBUS UNUM", "ONE DOLLAR", and the Mint mark. Tracing the lower rim is the inscription "UNITED STATES OF AMERICA". The initials of Donna Weaver, the U.S. Mint Sculptor/Engraver, are directly up from "NIT" in "UNITED" at the bottom of the skyline.

GOLD $5 DESIGNS

Obverse by Donna Weaver

A modernistic crystalline snowflake dominates. "LIBERTY" arcs along the rim at the upper left; "IN GOD WE TRUST" competes for space at the nine o'clock position; a bold lettered "SALT LAKE" is superimposed over the snowflake. The date 2002 almost gets lost near the lower rim of the design; Weaver's initials are near the rim at the four o'clock position.

Reverse by Donna Weaver, modeled by Norman E. Nemeth

The Olympic flame in relief atop a cauldron. "UNITED STATES OF AMERICA" arcs across the top of the flames; the inscription "FIVE DOLLARS" arcs upwards beneath the cauldron. "E PLURIBUS UNUM" is prominent to the left of the flames; the stylized "fire and ice" design finishes off the lower portion. The West Point Mint mark (W) is directly to the right of the cauldron. The designers' initials are in the "fire and ice" device, near the rim: Donna Weaver's at the eight o'clock position, Norman E. Nemeth's at the four o'clock position.

Origins of the Winter Olympics Coins

Like its cousins the 1984 and 1996 Olympic issues, these coins were meant to generate funds to support U.S. Olympic athletes. A portion of the proceeds from the sale of each coin—$35 for gold and $10 for silver—was authorized to help fund the 2002 Salt Lake Olympic Winter Games.

Many foreign governments large and small often issue Olympic coins to support their athletes or just to make money from collectors. As with the previous Olympic issues, this commemorative coinage had to compete in a marketplace saturated with foreign Olympic productions. Additionally, the designs on the U.S. coins were considered by many collectors to be too avant-garde for their tastes.

The two previous Olympic strikings together raised more $130 million. That revenue figure from the surcharges may seem high, but consider the number of coins issued 1995–96 alone. As of January 2003, the two coins in the 2002 issue had generated only enough income for the U.S. Mint to forward $3.6 million to the Salt Lake and U.S. Olympic committees. Unfortunately, unlike its cousins in 1984 and 1995–96, these pieces did not generate much excitement or funds for the athletes.

The Winter Olympics Coins Today

Sales of these coins were not spectacular. The motif, though original, did not inspire collectors to run out and obtain a specimen or two. The gold and the silver coins did not even reach the halfway point for their respective maximum mintages. Maybe the Mint will eventually learn that the Olympics are not a good subject for commemorative coins. They could produce low number production runs for collectors that would be sure sellouts. This would create a wonderful secondary market for such issues, but would not help the Olympic revenues. In fact the Olympics have become such a popular subject with mints around the world that one could (and should) write a book devoted to this niche subject, though sales of the book might mimic those of Olympic coins. The Olympic theme seems to have been overdone.

A note to collectors: this issue, along with the 2002 West Point Bicentennial commemorative coin, were part of the U.S. Mint's bulk sales discount program. This program allows pre-certified dealers to buy large pre-set amounts (500- to 1,000-piece lots, or more) of a coin from the U.S. Mint at a discounted price. This discounted price is lower than the pre-issue and the issue prices. How much lower? It depends on the deal the dealer and the U.S. Mint arrive at in negotiations. Industry sources tell me that the discount amount, depending on the issue and time of purchase, can be as high as 20% to 30% off the issue price. These figures cannot be fully verified since the U.S. Mint requires a confidentiality agreement with the dealers in the program. Coin dealers bought large numbers of these coins and some may still have sizable amounts in their inventories, thus depressing prices until these coins become fully dispersed into the collecting community.

Procure this coin only for the thrill of collecting or if you feel you must have one specimen of every issue. Future profits from this issue will depend on the rise or fall of bullion value.

2002-P $1.00

Grading Service	MS 69	MS 70
NGC	695	654
PCGS	1878	281
Combined	2573	935

Grading Service	PF 69	PF 70
NGC	1657	183
PCGS	1416	53
Combined	3073	236

2002-W $5.00

Grading Service	MS 69	MS 70
NGC	538	616
PCGS	1591	214
Combined	2129	830

Grading Service	PF 69	PF 70
NGC	592	578
PCGS	1579	214
Combined	2171	792

2002 United States Military Academy
(West Point Bicentennial)

Reason for Issue:	To commemorate the bicentennial of the founding of the United States Military Academy in West Point, New York.
Authorization:	Public Law 103-328, section 207, September 29, 1994.

Facts and Figures

Denomination	Date/Mint	Pre-issue Price	Regular Price	Maximum Authorized	Net Mintage	Market Value
Silver Dollar	2002 W UNC	$30	$32	500,000	103,201	$40
	2002 W Proof	$33	$37		288,293	$40

Designs

Obverse by T. James Ferrell

A cadet color guard in parade with the Military Academy's Washington Hall and Cadet Chapel in the background. The inscription "Liberty", separating the bicentennial dates, arcs across the top rim; "In God We Trust" is in three lines just below the date 2002. The engraver's initials (JF) are on the left in the parade ground field, just below one of the cadet dormitories.

Reverse by John Mercanti

The West Point Bicentennial logo. The inscriptions "West Point " and "Bicentennial", with the dates, compose the outer rim of the design. "United States of America" arcs over the plume of the classical battle helmet; the W Mint mark and "E Pluribus Unum" appear near the faceguard. "One Dollar" forms a display pedestal for the helmet; Mercanti's initials are near the end of the scabbard.

Origins of the United States Military Academy Dollar

On March 16, 1802, President Thomas Jefferson signed into law a bill passed by Congress authorizing the establishment of "a military academy to be located at West Point in the State of New York." During 2002, the bicentennial of the founding of the United States Military Academy was observed at West Point and at other designated places throughout the world.

The purpose of the coin program is to commemorate the founding of the academy and its contributions to the nation and to the allies of the U.S., who have sent their own students to be trained at this historic institution.

The West Point Bullion Depository and the West Point Mint

Built in 1937, the West Point Bullion Depository was originally designed to store silver bullion and was nicknamed the "Fort Knox of Silver." From 1973 to 1986, West Point produced 1-cent coins (though none of those coins bore a distinguishing Mint mark) and in 1980 began striking gold medallions, commonly referred to as "Postal Medallions", since they were available for ordering only through the U.S. Post Office. Approximately $20 billion worth of gold was also stored in its vaults, making it the second-largest repository of gold after the Fort Knox Bullion Depository. The West Point Mint is also one of the major producers of collectible and bullion gold coins for the U.S. government.

The West Point facility officially became a U.S. Mint on March 31, 1988. The West Point Bullion Depository is still a storage facility, but the minting division also manufactures and packages gold and silver commemorative coins, and American Eagle Bullion coins in proof and uncirculated condition. In 2000 it struck the first ever gold and platinum bimetallic coin by a U.S. Mint, the Library of Congress ringed $10 design. With this 2002 issue, the West Point Mint is also the only Mint to issue a legal tender coin commemorating itself.

THE UNITED STATES MILITARY ACADEMY DOLLAR TODAY

Predictions were that this coin would have wide appeal, since West Point alumni and their families, most not regular collectors, were expected to join the regular collector base in procuring this commemorative issue. Unlike the 2001 American Buffalo commemorative dollar, this issue generated no stampede of buyers when sales opened, but sales did proceed at a steady pace. Some collectors complained that the obverse was too busy and the reverse too stark in comparison. Such contrasts in styles were jokingly referred to as giving the coin a "Dr. Jekyll and Mr. Hyde" aesthetic personality.

This coin seems to be well dispersed among collectors and non-collectors, with some dealers also possessing some bulk quantities. Time will tell if the coins that fell into non-collector hands will ever re-enter the marketplace. This issue and the 2002 Winter Olympics coins were the first commemoratives to be included in the U.S. Mint's bulk sales discount program (described in the 2002 Olympic Winter Games entry). Known dealer quantities could make the West Point a target for a promotion, but little upside should be expected.

Procure either the popular proof or the uncirculated coin only for the joy of ownership. I recommend the lower-mintage uncirculated piece if you feel you must obtain this issue. Graded populations are too high to expect any real future potential. Value will rise and fall with the price of bullion.

2002-W $1.00

Grading Service	MS 69	MS 70
NGC	1892	2295
PCGS	3841	858
Combined	5733	3153

Grading Service	PF 69	PF 70
NGC	3453	1636
PCGS	2769	174
Combined	6222	1810

Reason for Issue:	To commemorate the Wright Brothers and the centennial of the first manned flight, made at Kitty Hawk, North Carolina, on December 17, 1903.
Authorization:	Public Law 105-124, December 1, 1997.

Facts and Figures

Denomination	Date/Mint	Pre-issue Price	Regular Price	Maximum Authorized	Net Mint-age	Market Value
Clad Half Dollar	2003 P UNC	$9.75	$10.75	750,000	57,122	$18
	2003 P Proof	$12.50	$13.50		109,710	$19
Silver Dollar	2003 P UNC	$31	$33	500,000	53,533	$40
	2003 P Proof	$33	$37		190,240	$40
Gold $10	2003 W UNC	$340	$375	100,000	10,009	$995
	2003 W Proof	$350	$365		21,676	$875

CLAD HALF DOLLAR DESIGNS

Obverse by John Mercanti

An upward-looking perspective of the Wright Monument, sitting atop its star-shaped base on Big Kill Devil Hill, North Carolina. "LIBERTY" circles above the monument, with "IN GOD WE TRUST" in the left field. The words "WRIGHT MONUMENT" are below, with the date 2003 at the bottom along the rim. Mercanti's initials (JM) can be found in the rear base of the monument on the right.

Reverse by Donna Weaver and Al Maletsky

The 1903 *Wright Flyer* as it soared after take-off near the dunes of Kitty Hawk. "UNITED STATES OF AMERICA" arcs across the top; "E PLURIBUS UNUM" is centered directly below it. The Mint mark (P) can be found just below the running figure of Wilbur Wright; "HALF DOLLAR" dominates the lower portion. The designers' initials are opposite the Mint mark, below the horizon of the design.

SILVER DOLLAR DESIGNS

Obverse by T. James Ferrell

A portrait of Orville and Wilbur Wright, based on the classic design by George T. Morgan that was used on the Wright Brothers Congressional Medal in 1909. The centennial dates 1903 and 2003 bracket the brothers' profiles. "LIBERTY" and "IN GOD WE TRUST", arc across the top. The words "ORVILLE & WILBUR WRIGHT" fill the lower portion of the design.

Reverse by Norman E. Nemeth

The 1903 *Wright Flyer* soars near Kitty Hawk. "ONE DOLLAR" dominates the upper portion; the Mint mark (P) and "E PLURIBUS UNUM" are at the three o'clock position, and "UNITED STATES OF AMERICA" is incused into the sand dune that the *Wright Flyer* is flying over. Nemeth's initials (NEM) are at the five o'clock position near the rim.

Gold $10 Designs

Obverse by Donna Weaver

A frontal portrait of the brothers, with the inscription "Orville & Wilbur Wright"; "First Flight Centennial" appears below the portrait. "In God We Trust" and the centennial dates flank the two brothers with "Liberty" filling the obverse at the top. Donna Weaver's initials are on Wilbur's shoulder directly below the "20" in "2003".

Reverse by Donna Weaver

The 1903 *Wright Flyer*, with an American bald eagle soaring above it. "United States of America" fills the upper rim. The inscription "E Pluribus Unum" appears in front of the eagle; Donna Weaver's initials are on the left of the horizon near the rim and the Mint mark (W) is on the opposite side. "Ten Dollars" spans the lower rim.

Origins of the First Flight Coins

On December 17, 1903, the Wright brothers inaugurated the modern age of aeronautics with their successful first flight of a heavier-than-air craft at Kitty Hawk, North Carolina. The airplane, known as the *Wright Flyer* and sometimes referred to as the *Kitty Hawk Flyer*, was the culmination of a four-year endeavor of research and development conducted by the Wrights beginning in 1899.

The First Flight Coins Today

Unfortunately, this coin did not "fly" off the U.S. Mint's warehouse shelves, but the sales were respectable. As happens with every coin issued by the Mint, some collectors and critics voiced an opinion that the coins were not unique—in this case suggesting they were just "big North Carolina state quarters," since the design was so similar to that coin, issued in 2001.

Indeed the Mint missed an opportunity to honor Wilbur and Orville's sister who enabled their bicycle business in Dayton, Ohio to operate while the two brothers experimented in the sands of North Carolina's Outer Banks. Katherine Wright is thought to have chosen the fabric, the "Pride of the West" muslin, that covered the delicate skeleton of the flyer and enabled the craft to achieve self-powered flight. Katherine Wright's contribution was so integral to the success of her brothers that it is a shame the Mint officials did not seize the opportunity to grant her any recognition. Including Katherine in the homage may have also prevented the gold ten dollar's obverse designed by Donna Weaver from acquiring the derogative nickname the "Smothers Brothers" Eagle from some overly critical collectors.

This issue also has been included in the U.S. Mint's bulk sales program, and some dealers may have sizable quantities of the coins in their inventory, reducing secondary market prices until those supplies are exhausted.

Buy this issue only if you like it. The populations are too high for any appreciable profit potential in the future.

2003-P 50¢

Grading Service	MS 69	MS 70
NGC	969	1066
PCGS	1325	176
Combined	2294	1242

Grading Service	PF 69	PF 70
NGC	1618	155
PCGS	1058	50
Combined	2676	205

Grading Service	PF 69	PF 70
NGC	2539	196
PCGS	1586	47
Combined	4125	243

2003-W $10.00

Grading Service	MS 69	MS 70
NGC	447	1361
PCGS	1486	440
Combined	1933	1801

2003-P $1.00

Grading Service	MS 69	MS 70
NGC	1915	1051
PCGS	1595	201
Combined	3510	1252

Grading Service	PF 69	PF 70
NGC	958	499
PCGS	1467	93
Combined	2425	592

Reason for Issue:	Commemorating the bicentennial of the Lewis and Clark Expedition of 1804–06.
Authorization:	Public Law 106-126, December 6, 1999.

Facts and Figures

Denomination	Date/Mint	Pre-issue Price	Regular Price	Maximum Authorized	Net Mint-age	Market Value
Silver Dollar	2004 P UNC	$33	$35	500,000	142,015	$40
	2004 P Proof	$35	$39		351,989	$40
	Coinage and Currency Set	$90	$90		49,943	$55
	Coin and Pouch Set	$120	$120		49,441‡	$60

Mintage figures do not take into account refunds by the United States Mint for certain 2004 Lewis and Clark Coin and Pouch Sets by the Shawnee Nation United Remnant Band of Ohio.

DESIGNS BY DONNA WEAVER

Obverse

Meriwether Lewis and William Clark on a stream bank planning their travel and exploration. Lewis is holding his expedition journal; the dates 1804 and 1806 mark the start and completion of their historic journey. "LIBERTY" and "IN GOD WE TRUST" arc above Lewis and Clark. The date 2004 is at the men's feet, with the words "LEWIS & CLARK BICENTENNIAL" tracing the bottom rim. Donna Weaver's initials are directly above the "L" in "BICENTENNIAL" in the water of the stream.

Reverse

Two feathers representing the Native American cultures touched by the Corps of Discovery Expedition. The reverse also features a peace medal, inscribed with "PEACE AND FRIENDSHIP", that was presented to leaders of the Native American Nations during the expedition on behalf of President Jefferson. Seventeen stars represent the number of states in the Union as of 1804. The Mint mark (P) can be found under the stem of the right feather. The words "ONE DOLLAR" separate the two feathers below the peace medal. "E PLURIBUS UNUM" follows the rim along the top; "UNITED STATES OF AMERICA" curves at the bottom.

Packaging

This coin was offered in two distinct premium packaging options, the Lewis and Clark Coinage and Currency Set and the Lewis and Clark Coin and Pouch Set.

The Lewis and Clark Coinage and Currency Set, which is a limited edition of only 50,000 sets, inclusive of the 500,000 maximum mintage, was priced at $90 each. The set features an uncirculated Lewis and Clark Bicentennial Silver Dollar, a silver-plated bronze duplicate of the Jefferson Peace Medal, a specimen of the two uncirculated 2004-dated nickels in the Westward Journey Nickel Series, and a 2004-dated uncirculated Golden Dollar depicting Sacagawea. Also included in the package are two insightful booklets written by archivists from the National Archives and Records Administration about the expedition and the Louisiana Purchase. Additionally, the set includes three Lewis and Clark expedition stamps from the United States Postal Service and a replica Series 1901 Ten Dollar Bison United States note from the Bureau of Engraving and Printing, which bears the likenesses of Lewis and Clark on either side of a majestic bison. Trivia fans will recognize the Ten Dollar Bison United States note as the central subject in the O. Henry short story "Tale of the Tainted 'Tenner.'"

The Lewis and Clark Coin and Pouch Set also had a limited edition of up to 50,000 sets priced at $120 each. Each set contains a proof Lewis and Clark Bicentennial Silver Dollar and a handmade American Indian pouch with its own Certificate of Authenticity. Each uniquely hand-crafted pouch was individually signed by the American Indian artisan who made it. This product option was delayed until September 7, 2004, because of the time required to hand-craft each pouch. It is an item I would buy for the joy of collecting, but collectors should be aware that the pouch can be duplicated.

Origins of the Lewis and Clark Bicentennial Dollar

The design for this commemorative coin was officially unveiled at a ceremony held in Monticello, Virginia, on January 18, 2003. It is meant to commemorate the bicentennial of the historical exploration and charting of the Louisiana Purchase territory and the important discoveries that were made during the expedition. The price of each coin includes a $10 surcharge, with two-thirds of the surcharges authorized to be paid to the National Lewis and Clark Bicentennial Council and one-third to the National Park Service.

THE LEWIS AND CLARK BICENTENNIAL DOLLAR TODAY

The Lewis and Clark Coinage and Currency Set sold out almost immediately after being offered for sale to the general public. One must remember that collector interest is in the packaging option and not in the coin itself. Coincidentally, in 2007, the U.S. Mint reluctantly, at first, offered refunds of up to $130 to anyone who owned a 2004 Lewis and Clark Coin and Pouch Set if the pouch was from the Shawnee Nation United Remnant Band of Ohio. The refund was offered because neither the State of Ohio nor the Federal authorities recognized the group as an official American Indian tribe. At the time of publication there were no accurate figures of how many refunds were made by the U.S. Mint and what was done with the returned coins.

I highly recommend procuring this coin for the joy of ownership only. The sales and graded populations are too high for any appreciable future profit potential.

2004-P $1.00

Grading Service	MS 69	MS 70
NGC	2437	1426
PCGS	2902	546
Combined	5339	1972

Grading Service	PF 69	PF 70
NGC	4389	692
PCGS	3671	717
Combined	8060	1409

Reason for Issue:	To mark the 125th anniversary of Thomas Alva Edison's invention of the light bulb in 1879.
Authorization:	Public Law 105-331, October 31, 1998.

Facts and Figures

Denomination	Date/Mint	Pre-Issue Price	Regular Price	Maximum Authorized	Net Mint-age	Market Value
Silver Dollar	2004-P UNC	$31	$33	500,000	92,132	$40
	2004-P Proof	$33	$37		211,184	$40

DESIGNS

Obverse by Donna Weaver

A portrait of the Edison holding an early experimental light bulb at his work bench. "LIBERTY" spans across the top of the design; "THOMAS ALVA EDISON" and the date 2004 are in the right field, "IN GOD WE TRUST" in the left. Donna Weaver's initials are by Edison's right elbow directly below "IN GOD WE TRUST".

Reverse by John Mercanti

A rendering of Edison's first light bulb. The image is encircled above by the legend "125TH ANNIVERSARY OF THE LIGHT BULB" and below by the dates 1879 and 2004, and the inscriptions "UNITED STATES OF AMERICA", "ONE DOLLAR", and "E PLURIBUS UNUM". John Mercanti's initials are above the "20" in "2004" and just below the fourth (from the center) stylized light ray.

Origins of the Thomas Alva Edison Dollar

Public Law 105-331, which authorized the mintage, declared that the designs of the coins "shall be emblematic of the light bulb and the many inventions made by Thomas A. Edison throughout his prolific life."

Proceeds from the sale of these coins is authorized to be paid to the Port Huron, Michigan, Museum of Arts and History; the Edison Birthplace Association; the National Park Service; the Edison Plaza Museum; the Edison Winter Home and Museum; the Edison Institute; the Edison Memorial Tower; and the Hall of Electrical History, for purposes of repairing, refurbishing, and maintaining the various facilities.

The Thomas Alva Edison Dollar Today

While sales of this issue were not as electrifying as Mint officials hoped, the sales figures and graded populations are high enough to make this issue a candidate for procuring only for the joy of ownership: buy only if the design and the topic appeal to you. Low population PCGS "70" coinage looks good. Just monitor any real population increase.

2004-P $1.00

Grading Service	MS 69	MS 70
NGC	1700	776
PCGS	1930	555
Combined	3630	1331

Grading Service	PF 69	PF 70
NGC	2681	331
PCGS	1634	77
Combined	4315	408

Reason for Issue:	To commemorate the 250th anniversary of the birth of Chief Justice John Marshall.
Authorization:	Public Law 108-290, August 6, 2004, stating that the coins may be minted and issued only between January 1 and December 31, 2005.

Facts and Figures

Denomination	Date/Mint	Pre-issue Price until June 27, 2005	Regular Price	Maximum Authorized	Net Mintage	Market Value
Silver Dollar	2005 P UNC	$33	$35	400,000	67,096	$40
	2005 P Proof	$35	$39		196,753	$40

Designs

Obverse by John Mercanti

A portrait of John Marshall based on one by the French painter Charles-Balthazar-Julien Fevret de Saint-Mémin (March 1808). The words "Chief Justice United States Supreme Court 1801–1835" skirt the rim at the top. "In God We Trust" and the Mint mark (P) are near Marshall's hair ribbon. Mercanti's initials (JM) are at the end of Marshall's tied-back hair. In the left field are the words "John Marshall" and "Liberty"; the date 2005 is at the eight o'clock position against the rim.

Reverse by Donna Weaver

A view of the Old Supreme Court Chamber, located inside the Capitol building, on the side that now houses the United States Senate. The words "E PLURIBUS UNUM", "ONE DOLLAR", and "UNITED STATES OF AMERICA" cascade toward the rim. Weaver's initials (DW) are at the base of the court clerk's partition near the rim.

Origins of the Chief Justice John Marshall Dollar

On February 4, 1801, John Marshall was sworn in as Chief Justice of the United States. He was the fourth man to serve in that capacity after the Court was created in 1789, and served for 34 years.

Under Marshall's leadership, the English practice of each Justice writing his own opinion was replaced with the Court's speaking with one majority voice, a practice that remains to the present day. Marshall wrote the Court's opinion in 519 of the 1,106 cases decided during his tenure—almost half. He championed the primacy of the Court through his power of persuasion, congenial manner, and shrewd sense of policy.

In 1803, only two years after Marshall became Chief Justice, the Court announced its opinion in *Marbury versus Madison*, asserting that the judicial branch has the authority to judge the validity of an Act of Congress, and to overturn the Act if it is not in conformity with the United States Constitution. This doctrine of judicial review has become a cardinal principle of U.S. constitutional law. Marshall also wrote many landmark opinions establishing the supremacy of national law and the authority of the Constitution.

The surcharge proceeds from the sales of the coin were earmarked to go to the Supreme Court Historical Society to support historical research and educational programs about the Court, the Constitution, and related topics.

THE CHIEF JUSTICE JOHN MARSHALL DOLLAR TODAY

Sales of this issue were lackluster, yet they were sufficient take this issue out of the scarce category. Collector interest was ambivalent at best with many of the sales to Registry Set collectors or to others keeping up with the latest Mint issue. So-so mintage numbers and questionable dispersion among the high graded populations mean that collectors should buy this issue only for the joy of ownership.

2005-P $1.00

Grading Service	MS 69	MS 70
NGC	865	1202
PCGS	1258	328
Combined	2123	1530

Grading Service	PF 69	PF 70
NGC	2014	857
PCGS	1300	170
Combined	3314	1027

Reason for Issue:	To mark the 230th anniversary of the United States Marine Corps.
Authorization:	Public Law 108-291, August 6, 2004, authorizing the minting of 500,000 coins for a one-year period beginning January 1, 2005.

Facts and Figures

Denomination	Date/Mint	Pre-issue Price until June 27, 2005	Regular Price	Maximum Authorized	Net Mintage	Market Value
Silver Dollar	2005-P UNC	$33	$35	500,000 (initial maximum) 600,000*	49,671	$47
	2005-P Proof	$35	$39		548,810	$50

* A "floating sell out" was declared by the U.S. Mint in mid-September 2005. Metal composition of the coin is 90% silver and 10% copper. The coin's diameter is 1.5 inches and it weighs 26.73 grams.

Designs

Obverse by Norman E. Nemeth

A rendition of Associated Press photographer Joe Rosenthal's photograph, taken on February 23, 1945, depicting the raising of an American flag by Marines at Iwo Jima. Many believe this to be the most reproduced image in the history of photography. The word "Liberty" crescents across the top; "In God We Trust" hovers above the five Marines; the inscription "Marines" and the commemorated dates 1775 and 2005 are in the field to the left of the group. Nemeth's initials (NEN) are incused just below the right foot of the first Marine raising the flag.

Reverse by Charles L. Vickers

An engraving of the Eagle, Globe and Anchor, which make up the official emblem of the Marine Corps. This emblem has remained virtually unchanged since 1868, when the Secretary of the Navy, Gideon Welles, approved the design as recommended by Brigadier General Commandant Jacob Zeilin. Vickers's initials (CLV) are below the tip of South America on the emblem. "UNITED STATES OF AMERICA" arcs across the top along the rim; the inscription "E PLURIBUS UNUM" is just below it. Below the emblem is the Latin motto of the Corps: "SEMPER FIDELIS" meaning "Always Faithful". Below this motto is the Philadelphia Mint mark (P); the words "ONE DOLLAR" are at the bottom of the design.

Origins of the Marine Corps Dollar

Two hundred and thirty years ago, following skirmishes in and around Lexington and Concord, Massachusetts, delegates to the Second Continental Congress assembled in Philadelphia. On November 10, 1775, they authorized the formation of two United States Marine battalions to serve as a landing force for the fledgling colonial Navy. It was the first deployment of U.S. Marines in what became a distinguished line of heroic service that parallels the length of United States history.

THE MARINE CORPS DOLLAR TODAY

This coin sold out according to its initial mintage limit of 500,000 and there was no attempt by Treasury Secretary John W. Snow to invoke the additional 100,000 under Title 31 of the U.S. Code, Section 5112(m)(2)(B). This stated that "the Secretary of the Treasury can waive the mintage level for commemorative coins if independent, market-based research conducted by a designated recipient organization indicates the mintage level will not meet public demand."

Various items in the retail marketplace with the USMC logo enjoy brisk sales with many current and former members of the Marines, proud of their identification with this branch of the service. Thus this issue will be a ripe candidate for promotion at some time in the future. The demand in the future for this issue could increase premiums, but at present you should procure only for the joy of collecting, since the census populations are too high. Yet keep a watchful eye out for promotional activities by dealers, especially with the 49,671 Mint State variety.

Additionally, this coin could also be incorporated into many Marine Corps ceremonies by service men and women. This would increase demand, most likely for the uncirculated version of the coin, thereby degrading the Mint State supply of this issue by non-numismatic handling (unintentional abuse). Do you remember the end of the 1982 movie *An Officer and a Gentleman?* The graduating naval officer cadets symbolically pay their Marine drill instructor with an "actual" silver dollar and the Sergeant salutes each newly commissioned officer for the first time. I can envision a grateful cadet passing his former drill instructor a USMC commemorative coin in deep gratitude.

At this time, however, this special issue should be acquired for the joy of ownership only. Census figures are too lofty.

2004-P $1.00

Grading Service	MS 69	MS 70
NGC	4919	6278
PCGS	3740	553
Combined	8659	6831

Grading Service	PF 69	PF 70
NGC	10,288	2912
PCGS	4261	715
Combined	14,549	3627

Founding Father

Scientist

Reason for Issue:	To commemorate the 300th anniversary of Benjamin Franklin's birth.
Authorization:	Public Law 108-464, December 21, 2004.

Facts and Figures

Denomination	Date/Mint	Pre Issue Price until March 14th, 2006	Regular Price	Maximum Authorized	Net Mint-age‡	Market Value
Founding Father Silver Dollar	2006-P UNC	$33	$35	250,000 (across all product options)	58000	$44
	2006-P Proof	$35	$39		142,000	$44

Denomination	Date/Mint	Pre Issue Price until March 14th, 2006	Regular Price	Maximum Authorized	Net Mint-age‡	Market Value
Scientist Silver Dollar	2006-P UNC	$33	$35	250,000 (across all product options)	58000	$50
	2006-P Proof	$35	$39		142,000	$46

‡Market value is for raw or unencapsulated Mint State 69 or Proof 69 examples. The cost of encapsulation, or slabbing, by a grading service is not included in the given values.

DESIGNS (SCIENTIST)

Obverse by Norman E. Nemeth

An image of Franklin in his younger years, flying a kite. The motif recalls the groundbreaking success of Franklin's experiments into the nature of electricity in June 1752. The words "LIBERTY", "IN GOD WE TRUST", and "BENJAMIN FRANKLIN SCIENTIST" and the tercentenary dates 1706 and 2006 are featured within the design. The Mint Mark (P) appears below "IN GOD WE TRUST".

Reverse by Charles L. Vickers

A reproduction of Franklin's famous political cartoon published in the *Pennsylvania Gazette* on May 9, 1754. The severed snake conveyed Franklin's belief that colonial unity was truly a matter of life and death, hence "Join, or Die." The inscriptions "UNITED STATES OF AMERICA" and "E PLURIBUS UNUM" are above the cartoon; "ONE DOLLAR" dominates the lower portion of the design. The designer's initials (CLV) are just outside the lower right-hand corner of the frame.

DESIGNS (FOUNDING FATHER)

Obverse by Don Everhart

A more familiar image, capturing Franklin in the autumn of his years, as a Founding Father. The inscriptions "BENJAMIN FRANKLIN TERCENTENARY" and "LIBERTY" bisected with a star form a semi-crescent around the rim of the coin. The tercentenary dates, "IN GOD WE TRUST", and the Mint Mark (P) fill in the field near Franklin's cheek. Franklin's signature inside an oval field dominates the lower portion of the coin. This is also the first commemorative coin to feature a specific person's signature.

Reverse by Donna Weaver

A faithful homage to the 1776 Continental Currency dollar designed by Franklin, and highlighting his contributions as statesman, businessman, and scientist. The inscriptions "UNITED STATES OF AMERICA", "E PLURIBUS UNUM", and

"ONE DOLLAR" separated by five-pointed stars encircle the reproduced image of the 1776 Continental Currency dollar design. The design elements of the 1776 Continental Currency dollar coin had been sketched by Franklin and had been incorporated on a few Continental currency notes attributed to Elisha Gallaudet.

Patterns using Franklin's designs were struck in pewter, brass, and silver, and many tin specimens circulated for a time in the colonies. While the Continental Congress waited for a loan of silver from their allies in France to use in minting coins for the colonies, several unknown intermediaries arranged for the New Jersey engraver Elisha Gallaudet to make the actual dies for the Continental Currency dollar. Gallaudet employed the popular renderings—attributed to both Gallaudet and Franklin—of the sundial and chain, with each state engraved one to a link.

Origins of the Benjamin Franklin Dollar

Born in 1706, Franklin pursued a variety of interests. He is credited with bringing new ideas to science and journalism while serving as one of the primary leaders of the American Revolution. For nearly six decades, Franklin conducted experiments and published wisdom that still holds true today.

Most school children are familiar with his experimenting with electricity, inventing bifocals, and writing *Poor Richard's Almanack*, the pamphlet with aphorisms such as "Early to bed, and early to rise, makes a man healthy, wealthy and wise." But most people are unaware that Franklin invented the flexible catheter, swim fins, and the lightning rod. He also founded the first hospital and the first volunteer fire-fighting company in America. Franklin's interests in atmospheric phenomena led him to establish the field of meteorology, when he realized that some storms travel.

Franklin also became the only person, at the age of 81, to sign all four of the cornerstone documents instrumental to the founding of the United States—the Declaration of Independence, the United States Constitution, the Treaty of Paris, and the Treaty of Alliance, Amity and Commerce, in which France recognized and supported the United States.

Some 48,452 sets of the 2006 United States Mint American Legacy Collection™, priced at $135 were produced. The set contained a proof Founding Father Benjamin Franklin Commemorative Silver Dollar and a proof San Francisco Old Mint Silver Dollar, as well as proof versions of all 2006-dated circulating coins.

The coins were also featured in a Benjamin Franklin Coin & Chronicles Set that was priced at $65. This set contained a Scientist uncirculated silver dollar and a collection of four stamps honoring Franklin from the United States Postal Service. The set also featured a reproduction by the Government Printing Office of *Poor Richard's Almanack*. The reproduction was modeled after an original edition provided by The Library Company of Philadelphia. An intaglio print was also included in the set, printed by the Bureau of Engraving and Printing, honoring Franklin's contribution to the drafting of the Declaration of

Independence. The Benjamin Franklin Coin & Chronicles Set's shipping was delayed until April 2006 to coincide with the official release of the U.S. postage stamps that were included in the set.

Surcharges from the sales of the coin are earmarked to be paid to the Secretary to the Franklin Institute for the purposes of the Benjamin Franklin Tercentenary Commission.

THE BENJAMIN FRANKLIN DOLLAR TODAY

I suggest that collectors procure only for the joy of ownership. The population census is already too high for this issue to realize any value potential in the future.

2006-P $1.00 (Founding Father)

Grading Service	MS 69	MS 70
NGC	1385	6510
PCGS	2156	567
Combined	3541	7077

Grading Service	PF 69	PF 70
NGC	2457	7219
PCGS	1957	536
Combined	4414	7755

2006-P $1.00 (Scientist)

Grading Service	MS 69	MS 70
NGC	2094	5329
PCGS	2188	368
Combined	4282	5697

Grading Service	PF 69	PF 70
NGC	5395	4041
PCGS	2133	200
Combined	7528	4241

Reason for Issue:	To commemorate San Francisco's Old Mint Building, its importance to California, and its role in maintaining the spirit of San Francisco after the 1906 earthquake and fire.
Authorization:	Public Law 109-230, June 15, 2006.

Facts and Figures

Denomina-tion	Date/Mint	Pre-issue Price be-tween August 15 and October 17, 2006	Regular Price	Maximum Authorized	Net Mintage	Market Value
Silver Dollar	2006-S UNC	$33	$35	500,000 (across all product options)	67,100	$42
	2006-S Proof	$35	$39		160,870	$40

Denomina-tion	Date/Mint	Pre-issue Price be-tween August 15 and October 17, 2006	Regular Price	Maximum Authorized	Net Mintage	Market Value
Gold $5	2006-S UNC	$220	$245	100,000 (across all product options)	17,500	$480
	2006-S Proof	$230	$255		44,174	$425

SILVER DOLLAR DESIGNS

Obverse

An image of the San Francisco Old Mint, based on the obverse design of the San Francisco Mint medal by Sherl J. Winter. Winter's initials can be found below the right of the mint edifice above the "Y" of "RECOVERY". The building is identified by its nickname, "THE GRANITE LADY", given beneath "OLD MINT". "LIBERTY" arcs above, "INSTRUMENTAL IN SAN FRANCISCO'S RECOVERY" below. "E PLURIBUS UNUM" is in the left field, the centennial dates in the right.

Reverse

A reproduction of the 1904 Morgan Silver Dollar eagle reverse originally designed by George T. Morgan. "UNITED STATES OF AMERICA" and "ONE DOLLAR" circle above and below; "IN GOD WE TRUST" is between the eagle's wings. The Mint mark (S) is above the "DO" of "DOLLAR".

Surcharges from the sale of these coins are authorized to be paid to the San Francisco Museum and Historical Society for the purpose of rehabilitating the Historic Old Mint in San Francisco as a city museum and an American coin and Gold Rush museum.

GOLD $5 DESIGNS

Obverse

The San Francisco Old Mint, modeled after the original 1869 construction drawings created by the supervising architect, A.B. Mullett. "LIBERTY" arcs above, "SAN FRANCISCO EARTHQUAKE AND FIRE CENTENNIAL" below. "E PLURIBUS UNUM" is beneath the building's entrance portico; the centennial dates 1906 and 2006 are above the Old Mint's left and right wings.

Reverse

A reproduction of the 1906 Half-Eagle Coronet Liberty eagle reverse, originally designed by Christian Gobrecht. "UNITED STATES OF AMERICA" and "FIVE D." circle the coin. "IN GOD WE TRUST" is in a banner above the eagle. The S Mint mark of the U.S. Mint at San Francisco is below the eagle's talons.

Origins of the San Francisco Mint Coins

Nancy Pelosi of California, at the time House Minority Leader, and Representative Mike Castle of Delaware sponsored the commemorative coin legislation in the House of Representatives. Senators Dianne Feinstein and Barbara Boxer of California and John Ensign of Nevada sponsored the bill in the Senate. Pelosi lobbied vigorously with Feinstein and members of the San Francisco Museum and Historical Society to promote the passage of the San Francisco Old Mint Commemorative Coin Act.

Originally established in 1852, The San Francisco Mint was built in response to the need to convert California Gold Rush discoveries into coinage. The first mint facility was quickly outgrown, giving rise to the building depicted in the 2006 San Francisco Mint Commemorative coins. The "Granite Lady", as the second San Francisco Mint came to be known, struck its first coins in 1874.

Because of her superior structural design, the Granite Lady remained standing following the 1906 earthquake. The Mint was the only financial institution capable of functioning immediately after the disaster, and served as a clearing house for relief funds, helping the city to get on its feet much more quickly.

Some 48,452 sets of the 2006 United States Mint American Legacy Collection™, priced at $135 were produced. The set contained a proof Founding Father Benjamin Franklin Commemorative Silver Dollar and a proof San Francisco Old Mint Silver Dollar, as well as proof versions of all 2006-dated circulating coins.

THE SAN FRANCISCO MINT COINS TODAY

While some collectors hoped that the retro reverses would spur a demand similar to that for the 2001 American Buffalo dollar, this did not happen. Collectors should buy this issue purely for the joy of ownership: with fairly sizable mintages, this coin continues to languish in the secondary market. Only the uncirculated $5 coin, with a sales figure of 17,500 (compared to the proof at 44,174), may produce any noticeable premium in the future, if it is properly promoted.

2006-P $1.00

Grading Service	MS 69	MS 70
NGC	1644	2675
PCGS	2654	501
Combined	4298	3176

Grading Service	PF 69	PF 70
NGC	6159	1789
PCGS	3501	279
Combined	9660	2068

2006-W $5.00

Grading Service	MS 69	MS 70
NGC	897	1826
PCGS	2013	331
Combined	2910	2157

Grading Service	PF 69	PF 70
NGC	1773	2017
PCGS	2644	439
Combined	4417	2456

Reason for Issue:	To commemorate the 400th anniversary of the founding of the English settlement at Jamestown, Virginia, in 1607.
Authorization:	Public Law 108-289, August 6, 2004.

Facts and Figures

Denomination	Date/Mint	Pre-issue Price until February 12, 2007	Regular Price	Maximum Authorized	Net Mintage	Market Value
Silver Dollar	2007-P UNC	$33	$35	500,000 (across all product options)	75,645	$40
	2007-P Proof	$35	$39		212,103	$40
Gold $5	2007-W UNC	$220	$245	100,000 (across all product options)	16,969	$425
	2007-W Proof	$230	$255		43,399	$425

Market value is for raw or unencapsulated Mint State 69 or Proof 69 examples. The cost of encapsulation, or slabbing, by a grading service is not included in the given values.

Silver Dollar Designs

Obverse by Donna Weaver (design) and Don Everhart (sculptor/engraver)

Three faces of diversity—Native American, White European, Black African—representing the cultures that lived and worked together to ensure the success of the colony at Jamestown, which is represented by a stockade and buildings in the background. "Liberty" and, in smaller letters, "In God We Trust" are at the upper left. "Founding Jamestown" is ranged across the three figures, with the commemorative dates 1607 and 2007 circling below. Donna Weaver's initials (DW) can be found in the woman's clothing near the rim at approximately the seven o'clock position; Don Everhart's initials (DE) are in the chief's robe near the rim at approximately the four o'clock position.

Reverse by Susan Gamble (design) and Charles Vickers (sculptor/engraver)

The *Susan Constant*, the *Godspeed*, and the *Discovery*, the three ships that carried the English settlers to the Virginia shoreline are sailing toward the viewer. "United States of America" arcs above, "One Dollar" below. "E Pluribus Unum" is in a smooth field in front of the ships, with the Mint mark (P) to the right. Susan Gamble's intitials (SG) can be found in the water near the rim between the seven and eight o'clock positions; Charles Vickers's initials (CLV) can be found in the water, just above the "BU" in "Pluribus".

Gold $5 Design

Obverse by John Mercanti

Captain John Smith in conversation with an American Indian, who is holding a bag of maize (corn); a ship is in the background. The outer rim inscriptions are "Liberty" above, with the commemorative dates to either side, and "Founding of Jamestown" below. "In God We Trust" is between Smith and the Indian. John Mercanti's initials are along the rim of the internal design, just above the "AM" in "Jamestown".

Reverse by Susan Gamble and Norman E. Nemeth

The remains of the Jamestown Memorial Church. "United States of America" arcs above, "Jamestown Memorial Church" below. "$5" is at the left of the structure and "E Pluribus Unum" is beneath it. The Mint mark (S) is above the final "H" in "Church". The designers' initials are just below the fence, Susan Gamble's (SG) on the left, Norman E. Nemeth's (NEN) on the right.

Origins of the Jamestown Coins

In the spring of 1607, three ships carried to the New World more than 100 settlers sponsored by the Virginia Company of London. The settlers made landfall

April 1607 at a place they named Cape Henry, and set up a cross and gave thanks for their safe landing. They then set about exploring what is now Hampton Roads and a Chesapeake Bay outlet they christened the James River in honor of their king, James I of England and VI of Scotland.

Jamestown had followed no fewer than 18 previous failed attempts at European colonization of North America, including the famous Lost Colony at Roanoke Island in what is now Dare County, North Carolina. The Jamestown settlement was located some 15 miles from the ill-fated Spanish Ajacan Mission, established 36 years earlier by Jesuit priests. The Virginia Company was charged with establishing a settlement in North America; its employees were the first permanent English settlers in what would eventually become the United States. The continued viability of the settlement at Jamestown marked a major milestone in the exploration of North America.

THE JAMESTOWN COINS TODAY

Like many of its numismatic brethren, the 2007 Jamestown issue continues to languish in the secondary market. Mintages are too high for serious collectors and many enthusiasts find the designs uninspiring. While the coin is somewhat dispersed, this has not helped prices in the secondary market, where bids approximate, at best, the issue price when the rise in bullion metals is factored in. Collectors should buy this issue purely for the joy of ownership.

2007-P $1.00

Grading Service	MS 69	MS 70
NGC	2722	4684
PCGS	2032	907
Combined	4754	5591

Grading Service	PF 69	PF 70
NGC	4942	5457
PCGS	3171	693
Combined	8113	6150

2007-W $5.00

Grading Service	MS 69	MS 70
NGC	758	2400
PCGS	1037	704
Combined	1795	3104

Grading Service	PF 69	PF 70
NGC	1489	2524
PCGS	2116	515
Combined	3605	3039

2007 Little Rock Central High School Desegregation

Reason for Issue:	To recognize and pay tribute to the strength, courage, and determination displayed by the African American high school students who enrolled in the all-white Central High School in the fall of 1957.
Authorization:	Public Law 109-146, December 22, 2005.

Facts and Figures

Denomination	Date/Mint	Pre-issue Price until June 13, 2007	Regular Price	Maximum Authorized	Net Mintage	Market Value
Silver Dollar	2007-P Proof	$35	$39	500,000 (across all product options)	90,196‡	$38
	2007-P Uncirculated	$33	$35		61,920†	$42

†23,777 were included in the Little Rock Coin & Medal set, cost $40

‡24,389 were packaged in the American Legacy Set. Total set cost: $139

Designs

Obverse by Richard Masters and Charles L. Vickers

The walking feet of students accompanied by an armed National Guardsmen, on the way to school. The design also includes nine stars, symbolic of the first nine students who faced the threats of violence in a segregated society unable to accept that "all men are created equal." "LIBERTY" spans across the top of the rim. "DESEGREGATION IN EDUCATION" supports the vignette of walking feet in two lines with the date 2007 underneath it. "IN GOD WE TRUST" follows the lower rim. The initials of the designer Richard Masters (RM) are directly left of the "D" in "DESEGREGATION"; the initials of the engraver Charles L. Vickers (CLV) are on the left of the "N" of the word "IN".

Reverse by Don Everhart

The Little Rock Central High School circa 1957. Designated a National Historic Site in 1998, the structure still operates as an educational institution. "ONE DOLLAR" and "E PLURIBUS UNUM" arc over the school building. "LITTLE ROCK CENTRAL HIGH SCHOOL", the Mint mark (P), and "UNITED STATES OF AMERICA" occupy the foreground at the bottom. Don Everhart's initials are in the grass of the school lawn directly above the final "A" in "AMERICA".

Origins of the Little Rock Dollar

In the landmark 1954 decision of *Brown versus the Board of Education* of Topeka, Kansas, the United States Supreme Court declared racial segregation in the public schools unconstitutional. The events in Little Rock, Arkansas in 1957 were an important attempt to bring racial equality to the public education systems of the United States. The American Civil Rights movement viewed the successful integration of Little Rock Central High School as a milestone, and Dr. Martin Luther King, Jr., personally attended the 1958 commencement for the school's first African American graduate.

Surcharges collected through the sale of the coins are to be used for the protection and preservation of the Little Rock Central High School National Historic Site and to assist in the preservation and restoration of the historic Park Street and Daisy L. Gatson Bates Drive corridors adjacent to the site.

This coin was also a component of the 2007 American Legacy Set that featured proof versions of the Jamestown 400th Anniversary Silver Dollar and the Little Rock Central High School Desegregation Silver Dollar along with proof versions of all 14 circulating coins for 2007, including the five quarters from the 50 State Quarters Program (Montana, Washington, Idaho, Wyoming, and Utah) and the four $1 coins from the first year of the Presidential $1 Coin Program (Washington, Adams, Jefferson, and Madison). The set is presented in unique packaging with a strictly limited issuance of 50,000 sets.

Another option for the Little Rock Central High School Desegregation commemorative is a set that included the uncirculated dollar and a Little Rock Nine bronze medal, designed by Marjorie Williams-Smith, measuring 1½ inches. The bronze medal was created to honor the selfless heroism of the first nine students during 1957. The obverse of the medal features the students being escorted up the steps of the school by National Guardsmen. The names of each of the Little Rock Nine appear on the reverse, as well as the words "COURAGE BRAVERY JUSTICE OPPORTUNITY".

Little Rock Nine bronze medal.

The Little Rock Dollar Today

Serious numismatic interest in this commemorative issue is limited. The almost voyeuristic obverse featuring walking feet punctuated by the butt of a National Guard M1 Garand rifle leaves the viewer with little inspiration. The reverse featuring the Little Rock Central High School building fares not much better. One sarcastic coin dealer was heard to exclaim: "I've seen better renditions [of a building] on my real estate agent's Multiple Listing Service!" To be fair, the designer is given photos of a building and told to select and create. He or she can't make it resemble the White House or Buckingham Palace.

Equally uninspiring are the 2007 Little Rock sales figures on the secondary market, with bids for certified examples barely reaching the issue price of the original coin. Though this piece was fairly well distributed, there were several organizations that bought (perhaps "propped up" sales for) this piece for numerous political reasons or to garner political favors.

To make this issue's history even more interesting, Representative Melvin Watt of North Carolina introduced legislation, the Civil Rights Quarter Dollar Coin Act of 2008 (H.R. 6701), to establish a circulating quarter program with the reverse designs emblematic of 40 prominent civil rights leaders and events. One of the designs seriously talked about by the sponsors of this bill was—you guessed it—the Little Rock commemorative obverse. Why? I am not sure. Considering the lackluster interest in this issue by both collectors and the general public, the whole idea of a civil rights series of quarters does not seem to be a viable program.

This bill was referred to the House Committee on Financial Services in 2008 but it was not reintroduced in the 111th Congress by Mr. Watt. Yet, if this bill ever does become law, and the Little Rock obverse is featured as a reverse on a circulating quarter, it would be the first design to span two denominations since

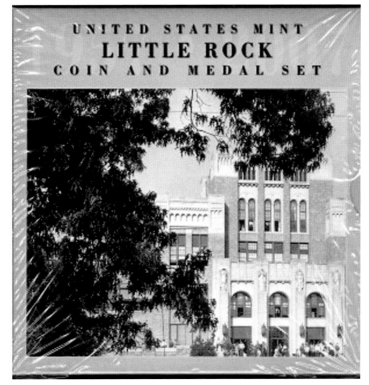

U.S. Mint Little Rock Coin and Medal Set.

the Barber series, and the first ever to be both an obverse and a reverse design element. This would make the environment quite ripe for promotion, pushing up prices. But for the here and now, mintage figures are too high for there to be any real future potential for the Little Rock. Procure for the joy of ownership. It appears that the value of the issue will increase only if silver bullion prices rise or the issue is promoted.

2007-P $1.00

Grading Service	MS-69	MS-70
NGC	745	1698
PCGS	1094	314
Combined	1839	2012

Grading Service	PF-69	PF-70
NGC	1345	1487
PCGS	1182	289
Combined	2527	1776

2008 Bald Eagle

Reason for Issue:	To celebrate the comeback from the brink of extinction of the American national symbol, the 35th anniversary of the Endangered Species Act of 1973, and the removal of the Bald Eagle from the Endangered Species List.
Authorization:	Public Law 108-486, December 23, 2004.

Facts and Figures

Denomina-tion	Date/Mint	Pre-issue Price until February 14, 2008	Regular Price	Maximum Authorized	Net Mintage	Market Value
Clad Half Dollar	2008-S UNC	$7.95	$8.95	750,000 (across all product options)	120,887 *	$15
	2008-S Proof	$9.95	$10.95		221,293	$16
Silver Dollar	2008-P UNC	$35.95	$37.95	500,000 (across all product options)	120,237	$40
	2008-P Proof	$39.95	$43.95		296,942 †	$40
Gold $5	2008-W UNC	$284.95	$309.95	100,000 (across all product options)	15,133	$490
	2008-W Proof	$294.95	$319.95		60,022	$425

* 22,814 were packaged in Young Collector's set option priced at $14.95.

27,505 were packaged in the Coin and Medal set option priced at $44.95.

† 21,821 were packaged in the American Legacy Collection priced at $100.00

Market value is for raw or unencapsulated Mint State 69 or Proof 69 examples. The cost of encapsulation, or slabbing, by a grading service is not included in the given values.

CLAD HALF DOLLAR DESIGNS

Obverse by Susan Gamble (designer) and Joseph Menna (sculptor)

Baby eaglets in a nest with an unhatched egg. "Liberty" arcs at the upper left, separated from the date 2008 by a star. "In God We Trust" is in two lines above the head of the left-hand eaglet. Joseph Menna's initials (JFM) are between the four and five o'clock position superimposed on the leaf bordering the eagle's nest. Susan Gamble's initials (SG) are at the seven o'clock position near the rim, superimposed on the branch.

Reverse by Donna Weaver (designer) and Charles L. Vickers (sculptor)

The legendary Bald Eagle "Challenger," with the American flag in the background. The inscriptions "E PLURIBUS UNUM", "CHALLENGER", and "HALF DOL-LAR" circle around the rim. "UNITED STATES OF AMERICA" is beneath the flag, and the Mint mark (S) between this inscription and "HALF DOLLAR". Donna Weaver's initials (DW) are at the eight o'clock position on the eagle's folded wing near the rim; Charles Vickers's initials (CLV) are at the seven o'clock position near the rim on the eagle's breast feathers.

Silver Dollar Designs

Obverse by Joel Iskowitz (designer) and Don Everhart (sculptor)

A mature eagle soars majestically through the sky, flying over a lake with a mountain and a forested shoreline in the background. "Liberty" circles between the eagle' wings; "In God We Trust" is between the foremost wing and the mountain. The date 2008 is at the lower rim. Joel Iskowitz's initials (JI) are just below the neck by the lake's horizon; Don Everhart's initials (DE) are at the four o'clock position between the eagle's tail feathers and the shoreline.

Reverse by Jim Licaretz

A design based on a replica of the first Great Seal of the United States, used between 1782 and 1841. In the outer rim, "United States of America" arcs above, "One Dollar" below. Jim Licaretz's initials (JL) are below the eagle's left claw, with the Mint mark (P) above it.

Gold $5 Designs

Obverse by Susan Gamble (design) and Phebe Hemphill (sculptor)

Young eaglets perched on a branch in their natural habitat. "Liberty" circles above; the date circles below. "In God We Trust" is in three lines in the upper central field. Phebe Hemphill's initials (PH) are at the five o'clock position below the leaf near the rim, and Susan Gamble's (SG) are at the seven o'clock position near the rim below the branches and leaves.

Reverse by Don Everhart

The current Great Seal of the United States as engraved in 1903. "United States of America" and "Five Dollars" circle the coin, separated by stars. The Mint mark (W) is between the "E" of "Five" and the "D" of "Dollars"; Don Everhart's initials (DE) are to the right of the eagle's tail feathers.

Origins of the Bald Eagle Coins

The Second Continental Congress in 1782 officially selected the Bald Eagle (*Haliaeetus leucocephalus*) as the national emblem. The Congress also designated the eagle as the centerpiece of the Great Seal of the United States. For more than two centuries, the majestic Bald Eagle became known internationally as a symbol of America's freedom, strength, and democracy.

Once abundant throughout the nation, Bald Eagles were unfortunately victims of poaching, loss of habitat, and unintended pesticide contamination. These stresses reduced the population from the estimated 100,000 nesting pairs in the late 1700s to just over 400 nesting pairs in the early 1960s.

The efforts of both government and private organizations determined to save the eagle prompted bans on the use of certain pesticides such as DDT in 1972.

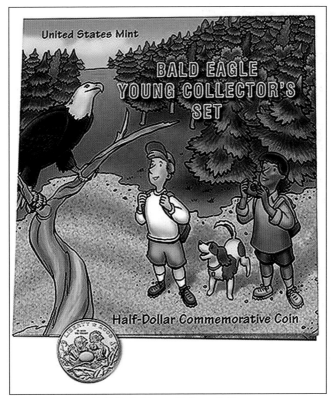

Bald Eagle Young Collector's Set.

Bald Eagle Coin and Medal Set.

The protections provided under the Endangered Species Act of 1973, and captive breeding and nest-watch programs, gave Bald Eagles the respite they needed in order to survive. The success of the Bald Eagle's recovery culminated in its official removal from the Endangered Species List in 2007. Currently, about 10,000 nesting pairs can be found throughout the continental United States.

Surcharges collected from this commemorative program are authorized to be paid to the American Eagle Foundation of Tennessee for the purposes of continuing its work to save and protect Bald Eagles nationally.

The clad half dollar was also available in a Young Collector's Set. While there was no limit except for the clad half's 750,000 production limit, the number of sets created was based on orders received between January 15 and April 15, 2008.

The Bald Eagle Coin and Medal Set option was limited to 50,000 units and features a Bald Eagle uncirculated silver dollar and a bronze Bald Eagle medal from the National Wildlife Refuge System's Centennial Medal Series. The obverse of the bronze medal honors President Theodore Roosevelt and the reverse design depicts a Bald Eagle in flight with a treetop background, and the inscription "BALD EAGLE" at the top right.

THE BALD EAGLE COINS TODAY

Collectors should buy for the sheer joy of ownership. Any potential value appreciation might occur with the rise of bullion prices as well as promotion of the UNC $5 gold piece.

2004-S Half Dollar

Grading Service	MS-69	MS-70
NGC	1189	5471
PCGS	1440	734
Combined	2629	6205

Grading Service	PF-69	PF-70
NGC	9108	3806
PCGS	3589	261
Combined	12,697	4067

Grading Service	PF-69	PF-70
NGC	2856	5681
PCGS	2371	360
Combined	5227	6041

2004-W $5.00

Grading Service	MS-69	MS-70
NGC	116	880
PCGS	513	462
Combined	629	1342

2004-P $1.00

Grading Service	MS-69	MS-70
NGC	2331	635
PCGS	2083	720
Combined	4414	1355

Grading Service	PF-69	PF-70
NGC	350	1311
PCGS	1458	422
Combined	1808	1733

Reason for Issue:	To celebrate the life and presidency of one of America's great leaders.
Authorization:	Public Law 109-285, September 27, 2006.

Facts and Figures

Denomina-tion	Date/Mint	Pre-issue Price (February 12, 2009 to March 12, 2009)	Regular Price	Maximum Authorized	Net Mint-age	Market Value
Silver Dollar	2009-P UNC	$31.95	$33.95	500,000	125,000‡	$55
	2009-P Proof	$37.95	$41.95		375,000‡	$65

‡ Preliminary sales figures (actual sales figures have not been released by the U.S. Mint at the time of publication).

Designs

Obverse by Justin Kunz (designer) and Don Everhart (sculptor)

A bust of Lincoln inspired by Daniel Chester French's famous sculpture in the Lincoln Memorial in Washington, D.C. The inscriptions "Liberty" and "In God We Trust" circle the rim. The date 2009 is between Lincoln's chin and the "R" and "T" of "Liberty"; the Philadelphia Mint mark (P) is below the date.

Reverse by Phebe Hemphill

A centered inscription, consisting of the last 43 words of the Gettysburg Address:

> we here highly resolve that these dead shall not have died in vain—
> that this Nation, under God, shall have a new birth of freedom—and

that government of the people, by the people, for the people, shall not perish from the earth.

The inscription is flanked on both sides by a laurel wreath. Above the wreath is the inscription "UNITED STATES OF AMERICA" and below it, on a curling banner, is Lincoln's signature between the inscriptions "ONE DOLLAR" and "E PLURIBUS UNUM".

Origins of the Abraham Lincoln Dollar

Abraham Lincoln was born in present-day LaRue County, Kentucky, on February 12, 1809. Lincoln's legacy in attaining the presidency through a combination of honesty, integrity, and intelligence is celebrated here. Most Americans have learned of Lincoln's firm belief that all men are created equal and of his of efforts to end the institution of slavery in the United States while guiding the country through a tumultuous Civil War. But very few people understand that he was also one of the most excoriated presidents—attacked both by his opponents and by members of his own political party.

Lincoln's popularity rose and waned with the fortunes and misfortunes of the war. Ultimately, he became the symbolic last casualty of the Civil War, dying from an assassin's bullet on April 15, 1865, just days after Confederate General Robert E. Lee signed the treaty ending the war at Appomattox Court House, Virginia.

During the dedication of the Gettysburg National Cemetery on November 19, 1863, at the site of one of the fiercest and costliest battles of the war, Lincoln reminded the country why the war was being waged, and spoke the words that are inscribed on this coin.

Today, the Gettysburg Address is recognized as one of the most important statements in American history.

THE ABRAHAM LINCOLN DOLLAR TODAY

After a month of sales by the U.S. Mint the Lincoln coins sold out all of the 450,000 allotted coins for the individual options. Later in the year the Mint offered the Lincoln Coin and Chronicles Set, which included the proof version of the 2009 Lincoln silver dollar. This specially issued set was limited to 50,000, and sold out within days.

Currently the 2009 Lincoln silver dollar enjoys brisk sales on the secondary market; the proof has a $10 premium at $65 over the uncirculated version at $55. Sales figures for this coin are still in the preliminary stage: the Mint has yet to release final mintage figures at the time of writing. The price imbalance for the more available proof coin, at approximately 375,000 issued, is the result of buying by non-astute collectors seeking the shiny flash of the proof specimen over the dull finish of the uncirculated business strike coin. At approximately 125,000 uncirculated coins released to collectors, this variant probably has too high a population to enjoy any appreciable future gains, though it can easily be promoted by dealers because of its almost eternal subject matter. For any real appreciation in price, look to the scarcer lower-mintage uncirculated coin. Because of the astronomical populations, collectors should buy either specimen only for the joy of ownership.

2009-P $1.00

Grading Service	MS-69	MS-70
NGC	1496	7928
PCGS	2435	2972
Combined	3931	10,900

Grading Service	PF-69	PF-70
NGC	10,275	6689
PCGS	5973	2303
Combined	16,248	8992

Reason for Issue:t	To celebrate the bicentennial of Louis Braille's birth and his invention of the Braille method of reading and writing. Braille's invention has allowed countless millions of sight-impaired people to become literate and less dependent upon the sighted world.
Authorization:	Public Law 109-247, July 27, 2006.

Facts and Figures

Denom-ination	Date/Mint	Pre-issue Price (March 26, 2009 to April 27, 2009)	Regular Price	Maximum Authorized	Net Mintage	Market Value
Silver Dollar	2009-P UNC	$31.95	$33.95	400,000	48,863	$40
	2009-P UNC Easy-Open Capsule	$31.95	$33.95		23,078	$40
	2009-P UNC Braille Educa-tion Set (limit 25,000)	N/A	$44.95		10,698	$40
	2009-P Proof	$37.95	$41.95		135,235	$40

Designs

Obverse by Joel Iskowitz (designer) and Phebe Hemphill (engraver)

A bust view of Louis Braille with "Liberty" tracing the rim of the design from the eight o'clock to the four o'clock positions. "Louis Braille" is prominent along the bottom rim under the portrait. The dates 1809 and 2009 are on either side of the bust; the Philadelphia Mint mark (P) is below the latter date.

"In God We Trust" is nestled between the portrait and the "T" and "Y" of "Liberty".

Reverse by Susan Gamble (designer) and Joseph Menna (engraver)

A child holding a cane with his bent arm and reading a book in Braille. The word "Braille" in Braille code is depicted in a tactile representation. "United States of America" arcs along the upper rim, "One Dollar" along the lower. "E Pluribus Unum" is behind the blind child. The word "Independence" is written into the top fascia board of the bookshelf. The titles of the books in the bookshelf have been "Greeked out" making them illegible. The U.S. Mint missed a great opportunity for a bit of whimsy: imagine a bookshelf filled with some of the great tomes from the American Numismatic Association.

This issue is not the first U.S. coin to feature Braille. Alabama's 2003 State Quarter, honoring Helen Keller, includes her name spelled in English and Braille. The 1995 and 1996 Paralympic silver dollars, minted to commemorate the 1996 Atlanta Olympics, also featured Braille. It should be noted that the Braille on those coins was too small to be read by the visually impaired.

Origins of the Louis Braille Dollar

Louis Braille was born on January 4, 1809 in Coupvray, France. At the age of three he was blinded in one eye accidently with one of the awls from his father's leather-making shop. He later lost sight in the other eye because of complications caused by sympathetic ophthalmia, an inflammation of both eyes following trauma to one eye.

Braille's intelligence and creativity allowed him to attend the local school with other children of his age, an unusual practice for the time. At the age of ten Braille was given a scholarship by an impressed local nobleman that allowed him to continue his studies at the Royal Institute for Blind Children in Paris, becoming the school's youngest pupil.

In 1821, Charles Barbier de la Sierra, a captain in the French Army, visited the school. Barbier shared his invention called "ecriture nocturne" (night writing), a code of twelve raised dots and a number of dashes that let soldiers share top-secret information on the battlefield without having to speak. The code was too difficult for Braille to understand and he later adapted the system to consist of a series of patterns of six raised dots to form what we today call Braille.

Ironically, the Braille system was not even taught at the Royal Institute until after Braille's death on January 6, 1852. Even then, the Braille system was not promoted until several patrons of the British Royal National Institute for the Blind began publicizing the method and advocating its teaching.

Braille's genius also touched the world of print. He developed the concept of the raphigraph (needle writer), which allowed the sight-impaired to write regular print on a machine now regarded as the world's first dot-matrix printer. The first Braille writing machines appeared in 1892.

A $10 surcharge is included in the price of the coin, and the proceeds are earmarked to go to the National Federation of the Blind to promote Braille literacy. This issue will also be eligible for discounted bulk sales by the U.S. Mint.

This issue also broke new ground with a unique mint packaging option, an Easy-Open Capsule (for those who wish to feel the tactile features of the coin), which was available only for the Uncirculated silver dollar.

THE LOUIS BRAILLE DOLLAR TODAY

During the distribution period, two Louis Braille commemorative silver dollars were sent into space on the space shuttle *Atlantis*. The hope was that some 50,000 coins would be sold during the 11-day flight. The "coins in space" event was coordinated with the National Federation of the Blind in order to raise awareness that only 10 percent of blind children are learning Braille today.

With approximately 54% of the maximum mintage dispersed during the sales period collectors didn't exactly embrace this issue. The proof version of this coin, as expected, sold better than the uncirculated version, even though the uncirculated coin was offered in three packaging options aimed at boosting sales.

Although estimates vary, the American Foundation for the Blind states that there are approximately 10 million blind and visually impaired people in the United States. This issue had the potential to be popular—but it wasn't.

Some collectors are hoping that the uncirculated Easy-Open option will be a popular issue with the visually impaired. If it is, one must surmise that the physical handling of the Easy-Open option coins will decrease the population of high grade uncirculated specimens. Only time will tell. This may be an interesting commemorative issue to watch in the future, but, even with lackluster sales, appreciable gains are not predicted. Procure only for the joy of ownership, since population figures are already too high for serious commemorative collectors.

2009-P $1.00

Grading Service	MS-69	MS-70
NGC	1764	1473
PCGS	1075	375
Combined	2839	1848

Grading Service	PF-69	PF-70
NGC	3574	553
PCGS	1343	105
Combined	4917	658

2010 2010 Boy Scouts of America Centennial.

2010 American Disabled for Life Silver Dollar.

At the time of printing of this book the 2010 American Veterans Disabled for Life Silver Dollar and the 2010 Boy Scouts of America Centennial Silver Dollar had just finished distribution with the Veterans commemorative selling over 250,000 of the allotted 350,000 mintage while the Boy Scout issue sold out completely. Due to rising price of precious metals many non-collectors also participated in sales of the issue. The NGC MS-70 census already reports over 5,400 for the Boy Scout Issue and the MS-70 figures for the Veterans issue is already over 3,000. NGC's census also reports that both issues in PFUC-70 have exceeded 3,000. These are both beautiful coins but populations are already too high and that these issues should only be procured for the joy of collecting.

Additionally, 2011 Medal of Honor Commemorative Coin and 2011 Medal of Honor Commemorative Coin Programs look to have high sales figures even with the US Mint temporarily halting sales and hiking prices on the gold commemorative coins significantly thus making these issues too candidates for the joy of collecting.

1995 AND 1996 CANCELLED
OLYMPIC COMMEMORATIVE COIN DIES

1996 Reverse Proof die.
Photo courtesy of CoinWorld, Amos Press Publishing, Inc.

1995 Gymnast Proof die.
Photo courtesy of Fred Weinberg.

1996 Tennis Proof die.
Photo courtesy of Fred Weinberg.

Reason for Issue:	To raise additional funds for the 1996 U.S. Olympic Committee.
Authorization:	None required.

Facts and Figures

The "X" canceled 1995 and 1996 Atlanta Centennial Olympic coin dies were sold by the U.S. Mint in 1997 for $49.95 each. The dies were featured in the Mint's 1997 Holiday catalog and sales began on August 29, 1997. Sales of the dies were discontinued less than two weeks later when Mint officials reported that the supplies of available dies for sale were exhausted from inventory.

The U.S. Mint marketed a reported total of 2,833 Proof, as well as uncirculated obverse and reverse dies used to strike the Olympic $5 gold half eagles and Olympic silver dollar coins. From each of these dies, numbers from only a handful to as many as several thousand coins were created before the dies were removed from production. Each die was later cancelled and sold.

Collectors were able to place orders for as many of the Olympic dies as they wanted, without being able to specify a particular die. During a phone conversation with the error specialist Fred Weinberg, I was informed that Fred had ordered 500 dies ($24,750), using three different credit cards. How many did he receive? The Mint ultimately restricted the dies to one per order, selling out its entire complement within two weeks of open sales. Fred received only one Olympic die per order. Each was selected at random by Mint staff and shipped to the customers.

The Olympic dies were defaced by cutting an "X" across the die face to prevent reuse. The "X" defacing design was cut into the face of the die using a saw and each part of the "X" required several passes of the saw since the kerf (the width of a groove or notch made by a cutting tool, such as a saw or an ax) of the saw blade was not wide enough to insure that the defacing "X" could not be filled back in by nefarious characters. Generally, most dies received two cutting passes of the saw. Some "X" cuts exhibit a small ridge line in the cancelling "X" while others do not. This is normal, since the saw blade settings may have moved slightly during the cutting process. Spotting and rusting of the dies are most often first observed in and around the cancelling "X" grooves, and these areas should be one of the first areas examined by collectors.

THE OLYMPIC COIN DIES TODAY

In 2002 the coin dies were selling on the secondary market for up to $1,000, depending on the die and its condition. Because of their limited numbers, plus the fact that they have been distributed into the strong hands of serious numismatic collectors, this already scarce item has become even scarcer in the secondary market. Generally there tends to be no clear difference between the prices of rarer dies, such as the 1995-W $5 Torch Runner die with 19 pieces known to be distributed by the Mint, and more common dies, such as the 1996-P $1 Proof reverse die with 632 pieces shipped. While the pricing table above does list a price differential between the dies, this is postulated from the most recent die sales information. Other factors also need to be considered. Some dies with aesthetically pleasing defects, such as starring, spalling or cracking, that add to the eye appeal of the specimen and set it apart from its brethren, often command higher bids.

Because these dies are often thinly traded and prices can be gauged only by known public transactions, true valuation can be quite difficult to determine at this time. Additionally, serious modern commemorative collectors are too preoccupied with the ongoing process of finding and obtaining the best numismatic specimens for their registry collections to devote much time to these ancillary collectibles that in the future may make their collections stand out.

While more astute collectors would be willing to offer higher premiums for the 1995-W $5 Torch Runner die because of its scarce numbers, collectors should understand that the total number of dies reported may not be as accurate and well documented as one would like to believe. While researching this very subject I turned up a 1996-P uncirculated or business strike silver reverse die that was not included in Mint reports or previous *Numismatic News* and *Coin World* articles. The generally accepted number of 2,833 dies may need to be increased or the 632 figure for the proof 1996-P reverse dies may need to be sub-divided to account for some uncirculated dies that were counted as proof dies. My belief is that the 1996-P silver reverse proof die figure of 632 may actually be the combination of the proof and uncirculated figures combined acciden-tally when they were reported by the U.S. Mint. Even though the reverse die populations are higher, the price differential is the same for the lower popula-tion obverse dies. This increased price is caused by demand from collectors who already have the obverse die and wish to obtain the reverse die in order to create a "complete die set."

Discrepancies aside, these coin dies were probably also the last defaced coin dies to leave the U.S. Mint with much of their original designs intact. Under a new policy, all retired dies are now either "puddled," the design being melted off with a very high temperature torch, or ground off with a grinding wheel leaving a totally defaced die face. Dies have also been observed having the design lathed off, leaving a raised dimple in the center surrounded by concentric rings as the only recognizable patterns of the die face. This new policy removes any possibil-ity that these dies could be used for any nefarious purposes.

One rumored reason for the "puddling" edict from the U.S. Mint was tied to the distribution of the Olympic dies. The rumor states that some unscrupulous individuals were trying to manufacture fake 10 to 20 percent off-center double strike versions of the silver Olympic dollars with the un-defaced portions of the dies. No reliable documentary reports have surfaced to verify this. The change of procedure by the Mint regarding the handling of worn-out dies may have evolved naturally from similar counterfeiting activity reported by mints in Asia in late 1996 with old or stolen dies. The quick sell-out of these dies seems to give credence to the many collectors who believed that the dies were quickly pulled from the market by the U.S. Mint, thus perpetuating the counterfeiting myth.

The fact the U.S. Mint has stated is that it will continue to only sell "pud-dled" dies in the future has enhanced the numismatic premium of these items as the last modern numisteria to leave the Mint is such a condition. The continued expectation that these dies will become sought after in the future as adjuncts to any registry set collection would not be unreasonable. If a savvy marketing person at one of the first-tier certification services were to start certifying and grading these dies, then you should expect a whole new ball game in terms of pricing and collector demand for them.

Since many of the dies are made of steel and may not be stored properly, rust and oxidation can quickly develop, causing serious damage. A thin coat of premium grade machinery oil will offer them protection. I recommend using Break Free CLP, www.break-free.com (MIL-L-63460, NATO Code S-758 9150-01-079-6124) from Armor Holdings Corporation. I do not have any financial or other interest in Armor Holdings, or its products, but have had great success in treating minor rust and spotting on dies with this product. It can be found at most firearms dealers, auto parts suppliers, or on the Internet.

Collectors should be aware that the non-die-face engraved portions of the die often do exhibit rusting, scratch marks and even anaerobic metal glue residue (similar to Loctite®) on the die stems and body. Glue residue, most commonly looking like some sort of red or blue paint, was used to insure that the die would stay secure in worn minting press die holders during production. As long as the rusting does not adversely affect the die face or the structural integrity of the die as a whole, you should be fine. Do expect to see unwarranted premiums paid by some collectors for pristine, residue- and totally rust-free examples since that is generally the nature of numismatic collectors. The collector needs to remember that these dies are in reality used machine tool parts and needs to judge their cosmetic condition accordingly.

The collector should also expect to see some pin-point rust specs on the dies, most notably along the defacing cuts. These dies were all used at one time in the production process; they later faced the defacing process. Both exposed them to moisture. It would probably be safe to speculate that a limited number of the 2,833 dies sold probably have succumbed to some sort of advanced, irreversible oxidation. Their unknowledgeable owners have unknowingly stored the dies in unstable environments. Bank safe deposit boxes must be included in this category: the humidity of a depository's air is increased in order to prevent important paper documents from becoming brittle. Remember that moisture is the foe of our metallic coinage, as well as of stamps. It serves as a catalytic agent for chemical reactions. Should you possess a problem die, I highly recommend your marketing it. That is unless you desire it for the joy of collecting.

Negligent storage of dies will make the surviving pristine specimens even rarer. If you are lucky enough to posses one of these dies, hold onto it! Demand will surely build and the numismatic premiums will continue to rise at a steady progression over time. Such pieces will certainly be sought out by collectors in the future.

50 State Quarters

Origins of the 50 State Quarters Coins

Make no mistake—this was a valid commemorative coin program. Just because the coins were available via normal circulation, and through banks for face value, without surcharges, and not produced in pricey precious metals, don't think for a moment that the regularly updated quarters you see in your pocket change are not "real" commemoratives. In fact, the original 10-year (now 11-year) series is the purest form of commemorative: specific event, limited issue, and no ulterior fund-raising motives (although a little seigniorage and profits from Proof and Uncirculated sets won't hurt the national debt).

When Public Law 105-124 was signed December 1, 1997, an unprecedented era of fresh circulating coin designs was born. Beginning in 1999, and five times a year through 2008, until all 50 states had their turn, the reverse design of the workhorse of United States coinage changed (quarters for the District of Columbia and five U.S. territories were added in 2009). At the first strike ceremonies of the program, held at the Philadelphia Mint on December 7, 1998, U.S. Treasurer Mary Ellen Withrow struck the first ceremonial Delaware commemorative quarter, on a special medal press, at 11:54:08 A.M. At 12:19:38 P.M., she activated two presses simultaneously, which began production for circulation purposes. My wife Gloria and I also struck early ceremonial coinage.

The 50 designs are easily recognizable with even the most casual glance. No microscopic varieties here: anyone can see the difference between a Georgia peach and the Connecticut Charter Oak. Whether the program ultimately results in creating more coin collectors remains to be seen, but one thing is certain—our pocket change is a lot more interesting!

Each design is emblematic of the state it honors. Mint design standards prohibit head and shoulders portraits of favorite sons or living persons. The sequence of issue is based on the order in which the states joined the Union. Thus, the 1999 State Quarters issued were Delaware, Pennsylvania, New Jersey, Georgia, and Connecticut—the first five states of the original thirteen.

Each state was required to submit three to five possible designs. Some states held competitions open to the general public. A template was provided, outlining the area reserved for the inscription. The governor of each state sent his or her choices to Washington, D.C., for the final design selection by the Secretary of the Treasury. Upon approval, Mint staff engravers or others rendered the design concepts into three-dimensional designs. Since the U.S. Mint Sculptor/Engravers created, from a concept, a viable or workable coin design, they are recognized as the coin's designer. Thus, their initials appear on the quarters they composed.

This led to some interesting, even heated, interstate competitions as the program unfolded; for example, both North Carolina and Ohio claimed bragging rights to the Wright Brothers and the first powered flight.

The mintage of the coins was large, but limited. Each design was produced for only ten weeks. Because of circulation demands, roughly one half billion to a billion coins of each design, more or less evenly split between the Philadelphia and Denver Mints, were produced. Any 40-piece roll issue can be promoted at any time. Illinois, Tennessee, Connecticut and California are such candidates, as well as the U.S. Territories issues with their lesser mintages.

Are these quarters likely to be worth considerably more than face value? Probably not. The real money is to be made in the error coinage of these creations. This is discussed in the State Quarters Errors section on page 694.

Common George Washington obverse, redesigned by William C. Cousins

The head of George Washington facing left as it has appeared since 1932, but slightly reduced to make room for statutory inscriptions. Compared to the pre-50 State Quarters obverse, "LIBERTY" is reduced in size and moved to the lower left under Washington's chin, displacing "IN GOD WE TRUST", which has been moved, in three lines, to the right—behind Washington's head. The Mint mark is in about the same place, now beneath "IN GOD WE TRUST", but is slightly reduced in size. To make room for commemorative inscriptions, those previously on the reverse have been moved to the obverse. "UNITED STATES OF AMERICA" arcs above, with "QUARTER DOLLAR" below, where the date (now moved to the reverse) had previously appeared.

The high point, the first to show wear, is George Washington's eyebrow.

The George Washington quarter was initially issued in 1932. It was designed by John Flanagan. His initials appear next to those of William Cousins at the base of Washington's neck (JF WC).

Reverse Designs

There is design consistency on all of the 50 State Quarters reverses. At the top is the state name, with the statehood year just below it. At the bottom are the issue date and the motto "E PLURIBUS UNUM".

1999 DELAWARE

| MINTAGE: | PHILADELPHIA: 373,400,000 |
| | DENVER: 401,424,000 |

Delaware was admitted into the Union on December 7, 1787, becoming the 1st state. Design: Caesar Rodney on horseback. The words "CAESAR RODNEY" are at the left below the horse's head; "THE FIRST STATE" appears at the right. Caesar Rodney was a delegate to the Continental Congress, but was by some accounts quite ill and at home in Delaware while the Declaration of Independence was being drafted in Philadelphia. The other two Delaware delegates disagreed on whether to support the Declaration, so Rodney, according to legend, rode 80 miles to cast the tie-breaking vote, thus starting the Revolutionary ball rolling. He served as governor of Delaware, but there is no known portrait of him: this portrayal is an idealization.

William Cousins's initials (WC) are near the horse's front-most hoof, near the rim.

Look for wear to occur first on Caesar Rodney's leg.

1999 Pennsylvania

MINTAGE: PHILADELPHIA: 349,000,000
DENVER: 358,332,000

Pennsylvania was admitted into the Union on December 12, 1787, becoming the 2nd state. Design: the main element is an outline of the state. A keystone (Pennsylvania's nickname and symbol), appears in the upper-left part of the state outline. At the center is Commonwealth, the statue that stands atop the Pennsylvania Capitol dome. Some think she appears ready to slam-dunk a basketball. The motto "Virtue, Liberty, Independence" is at the right.

John Mercanti's initials (JM) are above Commonwealth's right ankle as you look at the coin.

Wear will first appear at Commonwealth's left knee (to the right, as the coin is viewed).

1999 New Jersey

MINTAGE: PHILADELPHIA: 363,200,000
DENVER 299,028,000

New Jersey was admitted into the Union on December 18, 1787, becoming the 3rd state. Design: George Washington and crew crossing the Delaware River from Pennsylvania into New Jersey to attack the Hessian encampment at Trenton. The image is taken from Emanuel Leutze's 1851 painting, now hanging in the Metropolitan Museum of Art in New York. The inscription "Crossroads of the Revolution" is below.

Alfred Maletsky's initials (AM) are near the coin's rim at the three o'clock position.

The high point of the design and location of first wear is the hand of the third oarsman from the left, which grasps the oar.

1999 GEORGIA

MINTAGE: PHILADELPHIA: 451,188,000
DENVER: 488,744,000

Georgia was admitted into the Union on January 2, 1788, becoming the 4th state. Design: an outline of Georgia, flanked by live oak sprigs. The state motto "WISDOM, JUSTICE, MODERATION" is on a three-part banner. Central to the design is a peach. Some casual collectors reported "upside-down" peach varieties of the coin, but these later proved to be misunderstandings. Interestingly, "Peach State" is not Georgia's official nickname: this is "Empire State of the South."

T. James Ferrell's initials (TJF) are next to the right oak sprig's stem. The point of first wear on the design is found at the top of the "A" in "MODERATION".

The Georgia issue marks a sudden inflation in the mintage for circulation, nearing 1 billion coins in just 10 weeks. This is indicative of the strong public demand for State Quarters. A $10 face value roll of 40 pieces currently sells for double that amount. Howbeit, look at those mintage figures!

1999 CONNECTICUT

MINTAGE: PHILADELPHIA: 688,744,000
DENVER: 657,880,000

Connecticut was admitted into the Union on January 9, 1788, becoming the 5th state. Design: a new depiction of the Charter Oak (Connecticut Governor John Rowland held a design competition, and the state's Commission of Fine Arts fairly quickly landed on the predictable). The Connecticut Charter Oak also appeared on the 1935 Connecticut Tercentenary half dollar, designed by Henry Kreiss.

The story of the Charter Oak relates that in 1687 King James II issued an order to revoke Connecticut's royal charter. At the high point of the negotiation someone blew out the candles and a rapscallion absconded with the Charter, hiding it in an oak tree. Of course, without the parchment, the king's henchmen were unable to revoke the Charter.

T. James Ferrell's initials (TJF) are next to the rim at the five o'clock position.

The trunk of the tree, the high point of the design, will be the first to show wear. An uncirculated roll of 40 pieces currently sells for close to double the ten dollar face value.

2000 Massachusetts

MINTAGE: PHILADELPHIA: 628,600,000
            DENVER: 535,184,000

Massachusetts was admitted into the Union on February 6, 1788, becoming the 6th state. Design: a map of the state onto which is superimposed Daniel Chester French's Minute Man statue. The statue is also on the 1925 Lexington–Concord Sesquicentennial commemorative half dollar. The nickname "The Bay State" is on the right.

Massachusetts had a wealth of patriotic images from which to choose; the city of Boston is arguably the most historic Revolutionary-period city, with the possible exception of Philadelphia. The design competition was open to schoolchildren only, in a strict interpretation of the authorizing legislation's nod to education.

Thomas D. Rogers's initials (TDR) are in the field below the western tip of the state's outline.

The high point of the design and the first to show wear is the Minute Man's cap, where the cap meets the hair just above the ear.

2000 Maryland

MINTAGE: PHILADELPHIA: 678,200,000
            DENVER: 556,532,000

Maryland was admitted into the Union on April 28, 1788, becoming the 7th state. Design: the dome of the Maryland State House, where the Treaty of Paris was ratified, officially ending the Revolutionary War. The inscription is the state nickname, "The Old Line State", which is attributed to George Washington. According to some sources, the Maryland State House is the oldest state capitol still in legislative use; it was built in 1772. Flanking the dome are branches of white oak, the state tree.

Thomas D. Rogers's initials (TDR) are near the base of the right white oak branch.

First wear will appear on the right white oak branch, on the stem at the second set of leaves from the bottom.

2000 South Carolina

MINTAGE: PHILADELPHIA: 742,576,000
            DENVER: 566,208,000

South Carolina was admitted into the Union on May 23, 1788, becoming the 8th state. Design: the state outline and familiar state symbols: the Carolina wren, yellow jessamine (the state flower), and a palmetto tree. "THE PALMETTO STATE" and a star representing the state capital, Columbia, complete the design.

Thomas D. Rogers's initials (TDR) are to the right of the base of the palmetto tree.

The first design element to show wear will be the center of the wing of the wren.

2000 NEW HAMPSHIRE

MINTAGE: PHILADELPHIA: 673,040,000
                    DENVER: 495,976,000

New Hampshire was admitted into the Union on June 21, 1788, becoming the 9th state. Design: a face in the rock reminiscent of those of Mount Rushmore. The inscription "THE OLD MAN OF THE MOUNTAIN" refers to a natural formation in Franconia Notch State Park that, from a certain angle, appeared to be a human face (in early accounts it was known as the Great Stone Face). The Old Man was not so natural before his demise on May 3, 2003. The formation had been heavily trussed with cable and pitons over a period of several years, but this could not prevent the inevitable collapse of the formation. It is thus perhaps ironic that the Revolutionary era motto "LIVE FREE OR DIE" appears in the left field. At the left rim, in a rare nod to symbolism over literalism in this modern era, nine stars are symbolic of New Hampshire being the ninth state to join the Union. The design of this quarter borrows heavily from the United States Postal Service's 3-cent stamp.

William Cousins's initials (WC) are in the field above the "M" of "Unum".

The Old Man's jowl, just below and to the left of the "M" in "Mountain" will show the first wear.

Old Man of the Mountain Sesquicentennial Stamp, June 21, 1955:
125,944,400 issued; Scott #1068.

2000 Virginia

MINTAGE: PHILADELPHIA: 943,000,000
             DENVER: 651,616,000

Virginia was admitted into the Union on June 25, 1788, becoming the 10th state. Design: three sailing ships, representing the quadricentennial (if a bit early) of the Jamestown landing in 1607. The ships' names are the *Godspeed*, the *Discovery*, and the *Susan Constant*: these ships ferried Captain John Smith's contingent up the James River. Virginia had a long Colonial and early state history from which to select; it is perhaps surprising and certainly delightful that these ships were selected.

Edgar Z. Steever's initials (EZS) are part of the crestless waves in the lowest-right section of the ocean.

The bowsprit of the foremost ship, where the forward foresail crosses, will be the first area to show wear.

Soon after the launch of the State Quarters program the U.S. Mint refrained from designating any one person as the designer, sculptor and/or engraver of a specific state coin reverse, and the Virginia was the last State Quarter to include a designer's initials. This was partly in response to some individuals the U.S. Mint felt were trying to commercialize and promote their involvement with the program. The concept of the program was for the citizens of the honored states to participate by selecting and formally recommending a design concept to the Mint. Additionally the Mint believed that the design and production of the State Quarters represented a group effort and that many people, not one individual, provided the input and ideas that shaped the quarters in the program. Unfortunately, the group input idea did not always have a positive influence, as highlighted by the Louisiana and Missouri design mistakes, or—more politically correct—"discrepancies."

2001 New York

MINTAGE: PHILADELPHIA: 655,400,000
             DENVER: 619,640,000

New York was admitted into the Union on July 26, 1788, becoming the 11th state. Design: the Statue of Liberty superimposed over an outline of the state along with the inscription "Gateway to Freedom". Also incorporated into the state features is a line highlighting the path of the Hudson River and the route of the Erie Canal.

This New York design celebrates the "Empire State" as a point of entry for millions of immigrants seeking political freedom and democracy. President Grover Cleveland accepted the Statue of Liberty as a gift from the people of France on behalf of the United States on October 28, 1886. "Liberty Lighting the Way" was designated a National Monument on October 15, 1924 and underwent an extensive restoration for her centennial on July 4, 1986. New York Governor George E. Pataki asked the U.S. Mint to add the line tracing the Hudson River and the route of the Erie Canal because of the developmental role of the waterways in the state's history. Additionally, the waterway element prevented upstate pundits from arguing that the Liberty design favored the downstate regions of New York. This design captured 76 percent of the votes of New Yorkers who voiced their opinion on the various proposals.

Alfred Maletsky's initials (AM) appear along the southern border of New York State.

The left breast of Miss Liberty will show the first signs of wear.

2001 NORTH CAROLINA

MINTAGE: PHILADELPHIA: 627,600,000
               DENVER: 427,876,000

North Carolina was admitted into the Union on November 21, 1789, becoming the 12th state. Design: an image based on the famous 1903 photograph "The First Flight at Kitty Hawk." On December 17, 1903 Orville Wright piloted the first successful flight of a heavier-than-air, self-propelled flying machine. The craft, the 1903 *Wright Flyer*, traveled a distance of approximately 37 meters (120 feet) on this flight and ushered in the modern aviation age.

Collectors' interest was piqued by detail differences in the design on the quarter and that of the well-known photograph that usually accompanied the quarter in newspaper and magazine articles. Some hopeful collectors thought that they had discovered an error, thinking "FIRST FLIGHT" should have said "First in Flight" after the popular state license plate series that preceded the quarter.

John Mercanti's initials (JM) are on the horizon near the rim at approximately the four o'clock position.

The middle of the beach in front of Wilbur Wright will be the first place on this coin to exhibit wear.

2001 RHODE ISLAND

MINTAGE: PHILADELPHIA: 423,000,000
               DENVER: 447,100,000

Rhode Island was admitted into the Union on May 29, 1790, becoming the 13th state. Design: a vintage sailboat sailing through Rhode Island's famous Narragansett Bay, with an image of the Pell Bridge in the background, and the nickname "THE OCEAN STATE" near the sail. With more than 400 miles of coast-line, Rhode Island, physically the smallest state in the Union, has more than 100 fresh water and salt water beaches within its boundaries. Known as the "sailing capital of the world," Rhode Island was home to the America's Cup for more than 50 years.

U.S. Mint engraver Thomas D. Rogers's initials are conspicuously absent from the design. This omission was caused by the Mint's dispute with Daniel Carr, a designer from Colorado who had been one of seven finalists for the reverse of the Sacagawea dollar and initial designer of the Rhode Island quarter.

From "50-State Quarters: Credit where credit is due, state quarter artists speaks out about contest rules" by Leon Worden, *COINage* magazine, December 2005:

> Carr got the nod for the New York and Rhode Island quarters. On instructions from the Mint, he modified his initial designs to appease state officials. Gov. George Pataki wanted a line to run across the map of New York to signify the Erie Canal; Carr added the line. Gov. Lincoln Almond wanted a historic ship from Rhode Island instead of Carr's initial generic sailboat; Carr changed the boat.
>
> Carr's exact designs were sculpted and minted. The Mint paid him $2,500 for each. He got the cash, but only the Mint sculptors got the credit.
>
> "The only proof I have that I designed the quarters is a letter from the Mint asking me to redo the Rhode Island quarter with a specific ship on it," Carr said.

The middle section of the left back smaller sail will be the first area to show metal loss on this coin.

2001 VERMONT

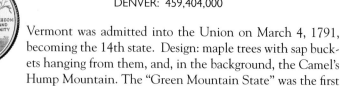

MINTAGE: PHILADELPHIA: 423,400,000
            DENVER: 459,404,000

Vermont was admitted into the Union on March 4, 1791, becoming the 14th state. Design: maple trees with sap buckets hanging from them, and, in the background, the Camel's Hump Mountain. The "Green Mountain State" was the first state admitted into the Union after the original 13 colonies. Vermont is most famous for its skiing and the production of maple sugar and syrup. Until the 19th century, when cane sugar was introduced, Americans relied on Vermont's maple sugar for much of their sugar supply. Also featured on the quarter is the one of the state's most prominent landmarks, Camel's Hump Mountain in the northern half of the Green Mountains. Camel's Hump is recognizable from its unique double-humped profile and is one of the highest peaks in the state.

T. James Ferrell's initials (TJF) are on the horizon near the rim at approximately the four o'clock position.

The left-most hanging bucket will show the first signs of wear on this design.

2001 KENTUCKY

MINTAGE: PHILADELPHIA: 353,000,000
DENVER: 370,564,000

Kentucky was admitted into the Union on June 1, 1792, becoming the 15th state. Design: the stately mansion Federal Hill, with the inscription "MY OLD KENTUCKY HOME"; a thoroughbred race horse is shown behind a fence in the foreground. Kentucky was the first state on the then "western frontier" to join the Union. It is one of the four states in the union to call itself a "commonwealth." Kentucky is also home to the longest-running annual horse race in the country, the Kentucky Derby, and to the famous Kentucky bluegrass country, known for producing some of the world's finest racehorses. Federal Hill in Bardstown is where Stephen Foster wrote the state song, "My Old Kentucky Home."

Collectors should examine their Kentucky quarters where the fence meets the rim of the coin for what appears to be an extra blob of metal in the design. Some coinage dies started to fail at this point of the design and broke away, leaving a pattern that error coin collectors refer to as a "cud." If this "cud" is present, the coin is rare, and can easily be worth $25 instead of 25 cents.

T. James Ferrell's initials (TJF) are near the first fence post at approximately the four o'clock position.

The vertical railing under the horse's head will exhibit the first signs of wear on this coin.

2002 TENNESSEE

MINTAGE: PHILADELPHIA: 361,600,000
DENVER: 286,468,000

Tennessee was admitted into the Union on June 1, 1796, becoming the 16th state. Design: a celebration of the state's contributions to the nation's musical heritage; it incorporates several musical instruments and a score with the inscription "MUSICAL HERITAGE" on a banner. Three stars represent Tennessee's three regions, and the instruments symbolize each region's distinct musical style. The fiddle represents the Appalachian music of eastern Tennessee, the trumpet stands for the blues of western Tennessee and Memphis, and the guitar is for central Tennessee, home to Nashville, the capital of country music.

Astute collectors immediately realized that the guitar on the quarter has six tuning pegs—but only five strings. Additionally, the trumpet's mouthpiece on the coin is on the wrong side, although there are a few left-handed trumpets made that way. U.S. Mint spokesman Matt Kilbourne was quoted as saying "the federal engraver who worked out the details on the design, suggested by the state, took some liberties to try to make the guitar and trumpet images more realistic for the naked eye ... You've heard of artistic license. Art a lot of the time is about compromise, especially when we're working on images this small. The goal of our artists is to convey an image that is both visually appealing and physically accurate. It's a balancing act."

As defensive as the U.S. Mint may have been about the strings on the guitar and the trumpet's mouthpiece, the whole episode made the collecting experience a little more interesting. As Stephen Bobbitt, a past spokesman for the American Numismatic Association, stated: "This gives collectors something more to look for... This makes collecting more interesting for them ... providing things that they will note in their collection—the little glitches."

Donna Weaver's initials (DW) are nestled between the book and the banner.

Either side of the bottom of the banner, where the lettering either begins or ends, will be the first place to exhibit metal loss. The area where the strings of the fiddle meet will also be one of the first places for wear to show on this design. The Denver Mint coinage sells for $31 per roll, while the "P" Mint is offered at $20. It is a popular and very promotable issue.

2002 OHIO

MINTAGE: PHILADELPHIA: 217,200,000
             DENVER: 414,832,000

Ohio was admitted into the Union on March 1, 1803, becoming the 17th state. Design: an early aircraft and an astronaut, superimposed as a group on the outline of the state, honor Ohio's contribution to the history of aviation. The design also includes the inscription "BIRTHPLACE OF AVIATION PIONEERS".

Ohio was the birthplace of the history-making astronauts Neil Armstrong and John Glenn, as well as Orville Wright, co-inventor of the airplane. Orville and his brother, Wilbur Wright, also built and tested one of their later aircraft, the 1905 *Flyer III*, in Ohio.

Donna Weaver's initials (DW) are just below the south west corner of the state outline.

The right side of the astronaut around the hip area (the astronaut's left hip) will be the first place on this design to show signs of wear.

2002 LOUISIANA

MINTAGE: PHILADELPHIA: 362,000,000
                DENVER: 402,204,000

Louisiana was admitted into the Union on April 30, 1812, becoming the 18th state. Design: images of Louisiana's state bird, the pelican, a trumpet with musical notes, and the outline of the Louisiana Purchase territory, along with the inscription "LOUISIANA PURCHASE".

Thomas Jefferson bought the Louisiana Territory from Napoleon Bonaparte in 1803 for $15 million. Dubbed the "greatest real estate deal in history," the Louisiana Purchase eventually added 13 new states to the Union, nearly doubling its size and making the United States, in area, one of the largest countries in the world.

The trumpet on the coin is a tribute to the state's heritage of jazz music heard and played by millions of enthusiasts around the globe. Jazz reputedly was born in New Orleans more than a hundred years ago with its roots drawing upon a combination of elements from blues, ragtime, and marching band music. A multitude of musicians propelled jazz from New Orleans' French Quarter onto the world stage, making the style a dominant force in 20th-century music and continuing its influence into the 21st century.

John Mercanti's initials (JM) are just off shore of the Florida panhandle.

Below the pelican's eye is the first place to look for signs of wear on this design.

2002 INDIANA

MINTAGE: PHILADELPHIA: 362,600,000
                DENVER: 327,200,000

Indiana was admitted into the Union on December 11, 1816, becoming the 19th state. Design: the image of a racecar superimposed on an outline of the state with the inscription "CROSSROADS OF AMERICA"; this displays state pride in the famous Indianapolis 500 race. The 19 stars signify Indiana as the 19th state.

The Indianapolis Motor Speedway is a 2.5-mile track built in 1909 for automotive research and testing. The track has been, and still is, used for research, but is best known for hosting the famous Indy 500, the oldest continuously held auto race in the world. It has been run every year, except during the two World Wars, since 1911. The winner of the first Indy 500 was Ray Harroun, whose car, the *Marmon Wasp*, is thought to have been the first to have a single seat and

Model of the Marmon Wasp.

to use a rear-view mirror. Since Harroun's victory, the Indy 500 has become an international event, synonymous with auto racing around the world.

Donna Weaver's initials (DW) are just below the southeast corner of the state outline.

Examine the hood of the race car for the first indications of wear on this design.

2002 MISSISSIPPI

MINTAGE: PHILADELPHIA: 290,000,000
DENVER: 289,600,000

Mississippi was admitted into the Union on December 10, 1817, becoming the 20th state. Design: the state flower, in all its beauty and elegance, combining the blossoms and leaves of two magnolias with the inscription "THE MAGNO-LIA STATE". This *Magnolia grandiflora*, named after the French botanist Pierre Magnol, is strongly associated with the South and the state of Mississippi, where the flower thrives. It became enormously popular after it was introduced from Asia into local gardens and landscapes. Mississippi adopted the magnolia as the state flower in 1952.

Donna Weaver's initials (DW) hide in the details of the leaf near the rim at the four o'clock position.

Examine the two leaves directly below the "M" of "MAGNOLIA": this is where the first signs of wear will be apparent on this design.

2003 ILLINOIS

MINTAGE: PHILADELPHIA: 225,800,000
                  DENVER: 237,400,000

Illinois was admitted into the Union on December 3, 1818, becoming the 21st state. Design: a young Abraham Lincoln within the outline of the state. A farm scene and the Chicago skyline appear to the left and to the right of the state's outline. Twenty-one stars border the coin, representing Illinois as the 21st state.

The inscription "LAND OF LINCOLN" pays tribute to the nation's 16th president. Young Mr. Lincoln lived and practiced law in Springfield before becoming one of America's greatest leaders and the subject of many other commemorative issues.

Donna Weaver's initials (DW) are just below the southeast corner of the state outline.

Metal loss will first occur at the edge of the book held by Lincoln.

At present an uncirculated roll of this issue sells for $40. It's a wonderful promotional creation.

2003 ALABAMA

MINTAGE: PHILADELPHIA: 225,000,000
                  DENVER: 232,400,000

Alabama was admitted into the Union on December 14, 1819, becoming the 22nd state. Design: an image of Helen Keller with her name in English, and in a reduced-size version of Braille. It should be noted that the Alabama quarter is the first U.S. circulating coin to feature Braille. An Alabama long leaf pine branch and magnolias grace the sides of the design, and a banner inscribed "SPIRIT OF COURAGE" underlines the central image.

Helen Adams Keller was born at Ivy Green in Tuscumbia, Alabama, in 1880. When she was a small child, illness, most likely scarlet fever or meningitis, destroyed her senses of sight and hearing, and deprived her of the means by which we normally learn to speak. Despite her disabilities, Helen Keller learned to speak and read using the raised and manual alphabets, and Braille. Miss Keller graduated with honors and received her Bachelor of Arts degree from Radcliffe College in 1904. She went on to publish numerous books, articles, and essays. Helen Keller lived out her life writing and addressing social issues for disabled persons and for women.

Norman E. Nemeth's initials (NEN) are below the word "SPIRIT" in the banner.

Wear will be first noticed at the top of Helen Keller's head.

2003 MAINE

| MINTAGE: | PHILADELPHIA: 217,400,000 |
| | DENVER: 231,400,000 |

Maine was admitted into the Union, as part of the Missouri Compromise, on March 15, 1820, becoming the 23rd state. Design: the Pemaquid Point Light atop a granite coast, with a schooner at sea in the distance.

Pemaquid Point Light is located in New Harbor, marking the entrance to Muscongus Bay and John Bay. Since the beginning of shipping activity in this area, a shoal or shallow place presented a navigation hazard, and caused many shipwrecks. As maritime trade and traffic increased so did the need for a permanent lighthouse, and in 1826 Congress appropriated funds to build one at Pemaquid Point. The original structure was replaced in 1835. Its light still provides a navigation beacon for ships and remains one of Maine's most popular tourist attractions. The schooner resembles *Victory Chimes*, the last three-masted schooner of the Windjammer Fleet. *Victory Chimes*, a Chesapeake Bay Ram built in Bethel, Delaware in 1900, is synonymous with Maine windjamming. In 1997 *Victory Chimes* became one of only 127 vessels designated as an American National Historic Landmark.

Donna Weaver's initials (DW) are hidden in the rocks along the shoreline at approximately the eight o'clock position near the rim.

Wear will first occur below the house on the cliff's edge.

2003 MISSOURI

| MINTAGE: | PHILADELPHIA: 225,000,000 |
| | DENVER: 228,200,000 |

Missouri was admitted into the Union, as part of the Missouri Compromise, on August 10, 1821, becoming the 24th state. Design: Lewis and Clark's historic return to St. Louis down the Missouri River, with the Jefferson National Expansion Memorial (Gateway Arch) in the background and the inscription "CORPS OF DISCOVERY 1804-2004".

Much of Missouri's history is tied to the rivers that flow through the "Show Me State." The state got its nickname because of the devotion of its people to simple common sense. In 1899, Representative Willard D. Vandiver said, "Frothy eloquence neither convinces nor satisfies me. I'm from Missouri. You've got to show me." Missouri was the launching point for Lewis and Clark on their adventurous trek into the uncharted Louisiana Purchase territory. The expedition's 8,000-mile journey westward and back, which some proponents claim was the greatest U.S. military expedition ever mounted, began in St. Charles,

Missouri, just 20 miles west of the present-day city of St. Louis in 1804 and ended when Lewis and Clark returned to St. Louis in 1806.

This quarter stirred up a lot of controversy after the U.S. Mint changed many of the coin's design features. The controversy forced the Mint to amend its procedures for dealing with situations when a design submitted from a state requires changes.

Alfred Maletsky's initials (AM) are near the riverbank between the three and four o'clock positions.

A difference in metal texture or wear will first be noticed on the elbow of the first rower at the front of the boat.

2003 ARKANSAS

MINTAGE: PHILADELPHIA: 228,000,000
             DENVER: 229,800,000

Arkansas was admitted into the Union on June 15, 1836, becoming the 25th state. It was acquired through the Louisiana Purchase and later became the Arkansas Territory before gaining statehood. Design: images of rice stalks, a diamond, and a mallard gracefully flying above a lake, all symbolic of the state's natural resources.

The "Natural State" is Arkansas's official nickname. The state has more than 600,000 acres of natural lakes and is known for its outdoor sports. Mallard hunting is a main attraction for hunters across the nation, hence the portrayal of the flying mallard. Visitors to Arkansas can search the Crater of Diamonds State Park for precious gems, including diamonds. The mine at this park is reportedly the oldest diamond mine in North America, and the only one in the United States open to the public where visitors get to keep what they find. The rice stalks allude to plentiful harvests of rice produced by the state's many farms; Arkansas is one of the prime producers of rice in the U.S.

John Mercanti's initials (JM) are in the marsh lands directly below the mallard duck at approximately the four o'clock position.

Metal loss will first be noticed on the mallard's breast.

2004 MICHIGAN

MINTAGE: PHILADELPHIA: 233,800,000
             DENVER: 225,800,000

Michigan was admitted into the Union on January 26, 1837, becoming the 26th state. Design: an outline of the state and the Great Lakes that surround it. The quarter bears the inscription "GREAT LAKES STATE".

As suggested by the state's nickname, much of Michigan's history is tied to the Great Lakes: Superior, Michigan, Huron, Erie, and Ontario. These are five of the world's largest lakes, which together cover more than 38,000 square miles and form the largest system of fresh water bodies in the world. Michigan borders four of the five Great Lakes, more than any other state; standing anywhere within the state you are within 85 miles of one of the lakes. The Great Lakes also were responsible for assisting in development of the Michigan's well-known automobile industry, since iron ore, coke, coal, and other products were all shipped on the lakes.

Donna Weaver's initials (DW) can be found along the southern shore of Lake Erie.

The upper peninsula of the state, approximately where Sault Ste. Marie is located (upper left-hand side as you look at the coin), is where the design will show the first signs of metal loss and wear.

2004 FLORIDA

MINTAGE: PHILADELPHIA: 240,200,000
            DENVER: 241,600,000

Florida was admitted into the Union on March 3, 1845, becoming the 27th state. Design: the legend "GATEWAY TO DISCOVERY", a Spanish galleon, palm trees, and a space shuttle.

The design was an interesting composite of ideas. The Spanish galleon represents Florida's original Spanish heritage, when the territory belonged to Spain. The palm tree represents the ubiquitous image of Florida to the state's millions of domestic and international visitors. The space shuttle, interestingly enough never identified as *Discovery*, represents the state's notable contributions to the U.S. space program, and to space exploration. Florida is also the launching point of many U.S. and foreign-owned space satellites and probes.

T. James Ferrell's initials (TJF) are just under the first palm tree near the rim at approximately the four o'clock position.

The central section of the space shuttle will be the first area to show metal loss.

2004 TEXAS

MINTAGE: PHILADELPHIA: 278,800,000
            DENVER: 263,000,000

Texas was admitted into the Union on December 29, 1845, becoming the 28th state. Design: the Star, "deep in the heart of Texas," is almost obligatory as a representation of the state, since it has been ingrained in the public psyche through books, song, stage, film, television, and comics. The legend "The Lone Star State" pays homage to Texas' brief life as the Republic of Texas. The simple but elegant rope borders evoke memories of Western films set in the state's vast wide-open spaces.

Norman E. Nemeth's initials (NEN) are just above the "M" of "*UNUM*" and near the southern tip of the state outline.

Wear will first be noticed on the center of the right arm of the star pointing almost to the three o'clock position.

2004 Iowa

MINTAGE: PHILADELPHIA: 213,800,000
           DENVER: 251,800,000

Iowa was admitted into the Union on December 28, 1846, becoming the 29th state. Design: a focus on education, inspired by a painting by an Iowa native, Grant Wood. Wood's painting, *Arbor Day*, features a one-room schoolhouse on the prairie with children and adults planting trees. The legend "Foundation in Education" is to the left of the schoolhouse; the name of the artist appears just below the tree-planting scene.

The state of Iowa was originally a territory of Wisconsin west of the Mississippi River, and it derived its name from the Iowa River, itself named after the Iowa Indians who lived in the territory. The tribal name "Ayuxwa" was spelled by the French as "Ayoua" and by the English as "Ioway." "Ayuxwa" means "one who puts to sleep."

The popular nickname for the state, the "Hawkeye State," is said to have come from the scout, Hawkeye, in James Fenimore Cooper's *The Last of the Mohicans*, published in 1826. According to the Iowa State website, "Two Iowa promoters from Burlington are believed to have popularized the name." The nickname was given approval by "territorial officials" in 1838, twelve years after the book was published and eight years before Iowa became a state. The nickname did not make it onto the coin, even though similar tags are almost standard in the State Quarters series.

John Mercanti's initials (JM) are near the rim at approximately the eight o'clock position.

Wear will first occur at the top of the schoolhouse's steeple.

2004 Wisconsin

MINTAGE: PHILADELPHIA: 226,400,000
           DENVER: 226,800,000

Wisconsin was admitted into the Union on May 29, 1848, becoming the 30th state. Design: the head of a black and white Holstein cow, a partial wheel of cheese, and an ear of corn represent the state's abundant agricultural production. The motto "FOR-WARD" was introduced in the 1851 revision of the state seal and coat of arms. Wisconsin's first governor, Nelson Dewey, asked the University of Wisconsin Chancellor John H. Lathrop to design a new seal. The motto was apparently selected during a chance meeting between Dewey and Edward Ryan, who would later become Chief Justice of the Wisconsin Supreme Court, when the governor went to New York City, carrying the Lathrop design to the engraver. Ryan objected to the Latin motto, "Excelsior," which Lathrop had proposed. According to tradition, Dewey and Ryan sat down on the steps of a Wall Street bank, designed a new seal, and chose "Forward" on the spot.

Alfred Maletsky's initials (AM) are just below the banner, near the "*D*" in "*FORWARD*".

Metal loss will first occur at the cow's right nostril (viewer's left), above the "*OR*" in "*FORWARD*".

2004 WISCONSIN VARIETIES

Some 2004-D Wisconsin quarter dollars feature an interesting die variety that some hobbyists are describing as "extra leaves." Generally described as an "Extra Leaf Up" or an "Extra Leaf Down," the unusual coins have die gouges or what could be described as raised lines along the left side of the ear of corn on the reverse that some say resemble extra "leaves" on the ear of corn. The cause of these extra "leaves" is uncertain. Mint officials who have examined photographs of the two "varieties" claim they are nothing more than random damage (or gouges) to the two dies responsible for the struck coins. Some dealers and collectors theorize that the dies may have been altered by a U.S. Mint employee, but at present no concrete evidence has been put forward to support such a claim. I personally believe this is the explanation.

Only coins struck by the Denver Mint are known to feature this unusual characteristic. They can be identified by the D Mint mark on the obverse of the

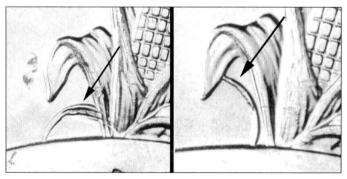

Lower leaf die gouge.   Upper leaf die gouge.

Normal ear of corn on reverse.

coin, to the right of the back of George Washington's neck and below the motto "IN GOD WE TRUST".

2005 CALIFORNIA

MINTAGE: PHILADELPHIA: 257,200,000
               DENVER: 263,200,000

California was admitted into the Union on September 9, 1850, becoming the 31st state. Design: the naturalist and conservationist John Muir, walking stick in hand, admiring Yosemite Valley's monolithic granite edifice known as Half Dome. This design also incorporates a soaring California condor.

Muir had made his home in the Yosemite Valley, describing the Sierra Nevada Mountains as "the Range of Light… the most divinely beautiful of all the mountain chains I have seen." He devoted his life to the conservation of such natural beauties, publishing more than 300 articles and some 10 books that espoused his philosophy. In 1890 Congress established Yosemite National Park, and in 1892 Muir helped to found the Sierra Club to protect Yosemite. He served as the President of the Sierra Club until his death in 1914.

The California condor, with a wingspan as wide as nine feet, is also featured on the coin as a tribute to the successful repopulation and reintegration of the once nearly extinct bird. The concept designer of this coin, Garret Burke, is a personal friend.

Don Everhart's initials (DE) can be found hidden in the rocks near the three o'clock position by the rim.

Metal loss will first be noticed on the middle of the rock in front of Muir.

2005 Minnesota

MINTAGE: PHILADELPHIA: 239,600,000
              DENVER: 248,400,000

Minnesota was admitted into the Union on May 11, 1858, becoming the 32nd state. Design: a tree-lined lake with two people fishing, a loon on the water, and a textured outline of the state surrounding its nickname, "Land of 10,000 Lakes". The state actually possesses more than 15,000 such bodies of water, with a total shoreline exceeding 90,000 miles—more than the shorelines of California, Hawaii, and Florida combined.

Lined with Norway Pines, many of the states lakes offer residents much in the way of outdoor recreation. The graceful loon featured in the design is Minnesota's official state bird.

Charles Vickers's initials (CLV) are hidden in the reeds near the four o'clock position.

Wear will first occur on the body of the loon, right above the date 2005.

2005 Oregon

MINTAGE: PHILADELPHIA: 316,200,000
              DENVER: 404,000,000

Oregon was admitted into the Union on February 14, 1859, becoming the 33rd state. Design: a portion of Crater Lake, viewed from the south-southwest rim. At 1,943 feet, it is the deepest lake in the United States and the seventh deepest in the world. Also featured in the design are Wizard Island, as well as Watchman and Hillman Peaks on the lake's rim, plus conifer trees. The coin bears the inscription "Crater Lake".

Congress and President Theodore Roosevelt established Crater Lake National Park in 1902, with the lake itself featured as the park's crown jewel. It is the sixth oldest National Park in the country.

Donna Weaver's initials (DW) can be found next to the trunk of the tallest pine tree.

Metal loss will first be observed on the top of the pine tree on the coin's right side.

2005 Kansas

MINTAGE: PHILADELPHIA: 263,400,000
              DENVER: 300,000,000

Kansas was admitted into the Union on January 29, 1861, becoming the 34th state. Design: two of the state's most recognized symbols, the state animal and flower, respectively the bison and the sunflower (*Helianthus annuus*: Kansas is the "Sunflower State"). These two design elements provide a visual reminder of America's heartland, and both feature prominently in the history of the territory and state of Kansas. Both were found in abundance throughout the region in the mid-19th century, when Kansas became a state.

Norman E. Nemeth's initials (NEN) are hidden in the grass near the four o'clock position.

A difference in metal texture, or wear, will be seen in the center of the bison's actual right leg (viewer's left).

2005 WEST VIRGINIA

MINTAGE: PHILADELPHIA: 365,400,000
            DENVER: 356,200,000

West Virginia was admitted into the Union on June 20, 1863, becoming the 35th state. Design: symbols that combine the natural physical beauty of the state with the triumph of human engineering, portrayed by the New River Gorge Bridge. At 3,030 feet long and 69 feet wide, the bridge is the world's largest steel span bridge and the second highest bridge in the United States, rising 876 feet above the New River Gorge in southern West Virginia. In 1978, 53 miles of the New River was added to the National Park System as the New River Gorge National River.

Prior to gaining statehood, the area that is now West Virginia formed the western part of the state of Virginia. Many settlers in this western section favored joining the federal Union when Virginia announced its secession in 1861, during the Civil War. In the western part of the state, the Restored Government of Virginia in Wheeling drafted a state constitution in 1862. The new state, now called West Virginia, petitioned Congress for admission into the Union. Congress approved the request with one condition, that the new state abolish slavery. The citizens of West Virginia complied with the congressional request, and President Lincoln signed the West Virginia statehood bill. West Virginia is only new state to be comprised of territory derived from another state already part of the United States.

John Mercanti's initials (JM) are in the water near the riverbank at approximately the four o'clock position.

Look for wear to occur first at the top of the mountain at the right side of the bridge where the arch descends to the mountainside.

2006 Nevada

MINTAGE: PHILADELPHIA: 312,800,000
             DENVER: 277,000,000

Nevada was admitted into the Union on October 31, 1864, becoming the 36th state. Design: three wild mustangs and a sunrise behind snow-capped mountains. Sagebrush fronds bracket the scene and a banner reads "The Silver State".

Nevada became a territory in 1861, several years after a Mormon Battalion in the Mexican War discovered gold and silver in the area of Virginia City—the famous Comstock Lode. Nevada is home to more than 50 percent of the wild horse population of the United States.

Don Everhart's initials (DE) are nestled in the banner and the sagebrush fronds near the four o'clock position.

Look for wear to occur first at the top of the lead horse's shoulder.

2006 Nebraska

MINTAGE: PHILADELPHIA: 276,400,000
             DENVER: 318,000,000

Nebraska was admitted into the Union on March 1, 1867, becoming the 37th state. Design: an ox-drawn covered wagon carrying pioneers, with Chimney Rock in the background. The natural formation of Chimney Rock rises from the valley of the North Platte River and is 445 feet high. Chimney Rock was designated a National Historic Site on August 9, 1956; the Nebraska State Historical Society is responsible for its custodianship.

The covered wagon is a symbol that reminds travelers that anywhere they may go in Nebraska they will encounter evidence of America's westward expansion. The state is crisscrossed by the Oregon and Mormon Trails, the Pony Express route, the Lewis and Clark Trail, the Texas–Ogallala Trail, and the Sidney–Deadwood Trail.

Charles Vickers's initials (CLV) can be found directly below the "K" in "Rock".

Look for wear to occur first at the head of the ox closest to the rim (viewer's left) and then at the top of Chimney Rock.

2006 Colorado

MINTAGE: PHILADELPHIA: 294,200,000
             DENVER: 274,800,000

Colorado was admitted into the Union on August 1, 1876, becoming the 38th state. Design: a sweeping panorama of the state's majestic Rocky Mountains, framed with evergreen trees and a banner carrying the inscription "COLORFUL COLORADO". Colorado's statehood was gained less than one month after the 100th anniversary of the signing of the Declaration of Independence, giving it the nickname "Centennial State."

Colorado's Rocky Mountains are home to some of the nation's most awe-inspiring natural wonders. Among these, rising approximately 10,000 feet from the valley floor in Northwest Colorado, Grand Mesa is the largest flat-top mountain in the world, and is home to more than 200 lakes and many miles of scenic hiking trails.

Norman E. Nemeth's initials (NEN) are hidden in the pine tree near the rim at approximately the four o'clock position.

Look for wear to occur first at the top of the trees on the left and on the mountain ridges.

2006 NORTH DAKOTA

MINTAGE: PHILADELPHIA: 359,000,000
DENVER: 305,800,000

North Dakota was admitted into the Union on November 2, 1889, becoming the 39th state. Design: two grazing American bison in the foreground and, in the background, a sunset view of the buttes and canyons found in the state's Badlands region.

President Theodore Roosevelt signed Congress' Antiquities Act in 1906, designating the North Dakota Badlands for preservation and protection. The area is now known as Theodore Roosevelt National Park, and is home to herd of more than 400 wild bison, an animal once on the brink of extinction.

Donna Weaver's initials (DW) can be found hidden in the grass just below the hind foot of the foreground bison at approximately the four o'clock position.

Look for wear to occur first at the top of the horn and shoulder of the foreground bison and at the ridge of the butte.

2006 SOUTH DAKOTA

MINTAGE: PHILADELPHIA: 265,800,000
DENVER: 245,000,000

South Dakota was admitted into the Union on November 2, 1889, becoming the 40th state. Design: an image of the state bird, a Chinese ring-necked pheasant, in flight above a depiction of the Mount Rushmore National Monument. The design is flanked by shafts of wheat.

Sculptor Gutzon Borglum began drilling into the 5,725-foot Mount Rushmore, in the Harney National Forest, in 1927. His creation of the "Shrine of Democracy" took 14 years and cost approximately $1 million.

John Mercanti's initials (JM) can be found chiseled in the rocks just below Lincoln's beard.

Look for wear to occur first on Jefferson's nose and cheek, and on the pheasant's back and left wing.

2007 MONTANA

MINTAGE: PHILADELPHIA: 256,240,000
                DENVER: 257,000,000

Montana was admitted into the Union on November 8, 1889, becoming the 41st state. Design: a bison skull depicted above the Montana landscape, with the inscription "BIG SKY COUNTRY".

This nickname reminds residents of Montana's open lands and pioneering values. Additionally, the bison skull is a powerful and sacred symbol to many of Montana's Indian tribes. This symbol is seen throughout the state on the logos of schools, businesses, and government offices. It evokes memories of the native traditions of Montana, which was once home to the Crow, the Cheyenne, and other tribes. After exploration by Lewis and Clark, Montana initially became a prime destination for fur trappers. The region attracted gold prospectors in the 1860s, and eventually cattle ranchers also made their way west to Montana.

Don Everhart's initials (DE) can be found in the lowlands near the four o'clock position.

Look for wear to occur first at the top of the skull's snout.

2007 WASHINGTON

MINTAGE: PHILADELPHIA: 280,000,000
                DENVER: 265,000,000

Washington was admitted into the Union on November 11, 1889, becoming the 42nd state. Design: a king salmon jumping out of the water, with Mount Rainier in the background, and the inscription "THE EVERGREEN STATE" below it. Newsman and pioneer real estate tycoon C.T. Conover is credited with coming up with Washington's nickname, honoring the state's many lush forests.

Most non-residents of Washington State are unaware that Mount Rainier is an active volcano. It is also the symbolic bridge between the eastern and western parts of the state. The salmon is a traditional symbol of the indigenous Pacific Northwest culture, and was revered as an essential food source for the native populations.

Charles Vickers's initials (CLV) can be found near the rim at the three o'clock position.

Look for wear to occur first at the top of Mount Rainier and on the lower jaw of the salmon.

2007 IDAHO

MINTAGE: PHILADELPHIA: 286,800,000
DENVER: 294,600,000

Idaho was admitted into the Union on July 3, 1890, becoming the 43rd state. Design: a peregrine falcon above an outline of the state, with the state capital, Boise, indicated by a star. The inscription "ESTO PERPETUA" is the state motto and means "May it be forever."

The peregrine falcon is one of the fastest birds in the world. Once an endangered species, it can now be found throughout Idaho and elsewhere, because of many conservation efforts both inside and outside the state.

Don Everhart's initials (DE) can be found in the falcon's wing feathers directly above the "E" in "E PLURIBUS UNUM".

Look for wear to occur first at the top of the "eyebrow" of the falcon and the shoulder of the wing.

2007 WYOMING

MINTAGE: PHILADELPHIA: 320,800,000
DENVER: 243,600,000

Wyoming was admitted into the Union on July 10, 1890, becoming the 44th state. Design: the well-known image of a bucking horse and rider silhouette that first appeared in 1936 on Wyoming passenger vehicle license plates. The horse and rider symbolize the state's Wild West heritage. The design also bears the inscription "THE EQUALITY STATE".

Wyoming's nickname refers to the state's historical role in establishing equal voting rights for women. Wyoming was the first territory to grant female suffrage and became the first state to allow women to vote, serve on juries, and hold public office. In 1924 Nellie Tayloe Ross became the first woman elected Governor of Wyoming, and in 1933 she became the first woman appointed Director of the United States Mint.

Norman E. Nemeth's initials (NEN) seem almost lost in the plain field directly above the "M" in "E PLURIBUS UNUM".

Look for wear to occur first at the periphery of the rider and horse's silhouette.

2007 Utah

MINTAGE: PHILADELPHIA: 253,200,000
            DENVER: 255,000,000

Utah was admitted into the Union on January 4, 1896, becoming the 45th state. Design: two locomotives flanking the golden spike that joined the Central Pacific and Union Pacific railroads. The historic connection on May 10, 1869 at Promontory, Utah linked the East coast to the West and transformed both the Utah Territory and the United States. The inscription is "Crossroads of the West".

Joseph Menna's initials (JFM) are just below the last railroad tie near the rim at the three o'clock position.

Look for wear to occur first at the top of the spike.

2008 Oklahoma

MINTAGE: PHILADELPHIA: 194,600,000
            DENVER: 222,000,000

Oklahoma was admitted into the Union on November 16, 1907, becoming the 46th state. Design: an image of the state bird, the scissortail flycatcher, soaring over the state wildflower, the Indian blanket, along with a field of various wildflowers.

Indian blanket (*Gaillardia pulchella*) symbolizes Oklahoma's rich Native American heritage and the tallgrass prairies that are abundant in wildlife. Oklahoma was formed by the combination of the Oklahoma Territory and the Indian Territory of the Five Civilized Tribes: Choctaw, Creek, Seminole, Chickasaw, and Cherokee. The state's name is derived from the Choctaw words "okla" and "homma," meaning "red" and "people."

Phebe Hemphill's initials (PH) are just below the wildflower near the rim at the four o'clock position.

Look for wear to occur first at the top of the bird's right wing and the crest of the bird's head.

2008 New Mexico

MINTAGE: PHILADELPHIA: 244,200,000
            DENVER: 244,400,000

New Mexico was admitted into the Union on January 6, 1912, becoming the 47th state. Design: the Zia Sun symbol over a topographical outline of the state. The design also features the inscription "Land of Enchantment".

The influence of Native American cultures can be found throughout New Mexico. The Zia tribe believed that the sun symbol represented the giver of all good, who gave gifts in groups of four. From the circle representing life and love without beginning or end, emanate four groups of four rays representing the four directions, the four seasons, the four phases of a day (sunrise, noon, evening, and night), and the four divisions of life (childhood, youth, middle years, and old age).

Don Everhart's initials (DE) are inside the New Mexico state map near the location of the city of Carlsbad in the southeast corner of the state.

Look for wear to occur first on the rays of the Zia Sun symbol.

2008 ARIZONA

MINTAGE: PHILADELPHIA: 244,600,000
DENVER: 265,000,000

Arizona was admitted into the Union on February 14, 1912, becoming the 48th state, and the last territory to become a state within the confines of the continental United States. Design: an image of the Grand Canyon with a Saguaro cactus in the foreground. A ribbon banner reading "GRAND CANYON STATE" bisects the landscape.

Joseph Menna's initials (JFM) can be found at the base of the Saguaro cactus.

Look for wear to occur first on the upper arms of the Saguaro cactus and canyon ridges on the left.

2008 ALASKA

MINTAGE: PHILADELPHIA: 251,800,000
DENVER: 254,000,000

Alaska was admitted into the Union on January 3, 1959, becoming the 49th state. Design: a grizzly bear (*Ursus arctos horribilis*) clutching a salmon in its jaw. The design also includes the North Star and the inscription "THE GREAT LAND".

The grizzly bear and salmon symbolize Alaska's natural beauty and abundant wildlife. The widespread grizzly population in Alaska can be observed in places such as Denali and Katmai National Parks, Kodiak Island, and Admiralty Island; more than 98 percent of the country's grizzly population is found in Alaska.

The name Alaska comes from the Aleutian word "Alyeska," meaning "the Great Land." The state was for centuries populated by Indians, Eskimos, and Aleuts. Alaska was first explored by Europeans in 1741, when Russia established a colony to protect its lucrative fur-trading interests. On March 30, 1867 Russia sold Alaska to the United States for $7.2 million, or two cents per acre, when it could no longer afford to maintain the colony. The transaction was called "Seward's Folly", "Seward's Icebox," and Andrew Johnson's "polar bear garden" by short-sighted critics. The state of Alaska celebrates the purchase on Seward's Day, the last Monday of March.

The 11-member Alaska Commemorative Coin Commission, appointed by former Governor Frank Murkowski, invited Alaskans to submit design ideas for the quarter. From the 850-plus submissions, four concepts were forwarded to the U.S. Mint for consideration. These concepts were developed into design candidates by the Mint's Sculptor/Engravers and artists in its Artistic Infusion Program. On April 26, 2007, Governor Sarah Palin announced her selection of the grizzly bear and salmon design following a statewide comment period.

Charles Vickers's initials (CLV) can be found near the rim at the four o'clock position.

Look for wear to occur first at the top of the bear's snout near the nose.

2008 HAWAII

MINTAGE: PHILADELPHIA: 254,000,000
            DENVER: 263,600,000

Hawaii was admitted into the Union on August 21, 1959, becoming the 50th state. Design: the Hawaiian monarch King Kamehameha I, a revered figure in Hawaiian history, stretching his hand over the eight major islands of the 137 islands and atolls that comprise the Hawaiian Islands. The main inscription is the state motto "UA MAU KE EA O KA 'AINA I KA PONO" ("The life of the land is perpetuated in righteousness").

Hawaii, spelled "Hawai'i" in the Hawaiian language, is nicknamed the "Aloha State". In the Hawaiian language, "Aloha" can mean "hello" or "good-bye," but it also means love and affection. The word "Aloha" itself is used in a combination with other words, such as "aloha kakahiaka," which means "good morning"; "aloha auinala," used as a greeting, means "good afternoon"; and "aloha ahiahi" means "good evening."

Don Everhart's initials (DE) can be found near the rim, by King Kamehameha's heel.

Look for wear to occur first at the top of the king's left hand holding the spear and the spear shaft over his left knee.

DISTRICT OF COLUMBIA AND THE UNITED STATES TERRITORIES ISSUES

2009 DISTRICT OF COLUMBIA

MINTAGE: PHILADELPHIA: 83,600,000
             DENVER: 88,800,000

The District of Columbia was created in 1790 and officially became the nation's capital on December 1, 1800. Design: a portrait of the composer and musician, and D.C. native son, Duke Ellington, seated at a grand piano. The inscription "DISTRICT OF COLUMBIA" arcs across the top along the rim; "DUKE ELLINGTON" is inscribed on the piano's fall (key cover) and "JUSTICE FOR ALL", the District of Columbia's motto, is just above "E PLURIBUS UNUM" and the date 2009, which rock along the lower rim.

This was the first of the 2009 commemorative quarters released in the District of Columbia and U.S. Territories Quarters Program. The coin celebrates the area chosen personally by President George Washington to fulfill the need for a new Federal district, created in order that no state could boast that it hosted the seat of the federal government. The 10-square-mile site was ceded from Maryland and Virginia.

The engraver Don Everhart's initials (DE) are on the piano leg just above the date.

Look for wear to appear first on Ellington's right hand, holding the sheet music.

2009 THE COMMONWEALTH OF PUERTO RICO

MINTAGE: PHILADELPHIA: 53,000,000
             DENVER: 86,000,000

Design: a view of the Caribbean Sea from the sentry box in the Old San Juan fort; clouds float above and at the right is a hibiscus. The inscription "PUERTO RICO" arcs across the top along the rim. "ISLA DEL ENCANTO" ("Isle of Enchantment" in Spanish) is between the hibiscus and the word "RICO". "E PLURIBUS UNUM" and the date 2009 rock across the bottom along the rim.

Puerto Rico means "rich port" in Spanish. Christopher Columbus arrived in 1493, and the island soon became a colony and important military outpost for the Spanish. Over the succeeding years there were numerous attempts by the French, the Dutch, and the English to conquer Puerto Rico, but it remained a significant part of the overseas provinces of Spain until the Spanish–American War. Under the Treaty of Paris of 1898, Puerto Rico was ceded to the United States, and civilian government was established in 1900 by the Foraker Act. Puerto Rican residents became American citizens when the Jones–Shafroth Act was signed into law by Woodrow Wilson on March 2, 1917. It wasn't until July 3, 1950 that Congress passed a law (P.L. 81-600) authorizing Puerto Rico to draft its own constitution. The territory became a United States commonwealth on July 25, 1952.

The designer Joseph Menna's initials (JFM) are directly below the bottom hibiscus leaf.

Look for wear to occur first along the upper and lower radii of the sentry box.

2009 Guam

MINTAGE: PHILADELPHIA: 45,000,000
           DENVER: 42,600,000

Design: a topographical outline of the island of Guam flanked by symbols associated with it. At approximately ten o'clock is a sailing vessel known as a "flying proa". At approximately four o'clock is a latte, a stone pillar used in ancient houses. The inscription "Guam" is along the rim at the top. "Guahan I Tanó Man-Chamorro" ("Guam—Land of the Chamorro" in the native language, Chamorro) is at approximately three o'clock. "E Pluribus Unum" and the date 2009 rock across the lower rim.

Guam (Guåhån in Chamorro) is an organized, unincorporated island territory of the United States in the western Pacific Ocean; it is the largest and southernmost of the Mariana Island chain. The island's capital is Hagåtña (formerly Agana). It is believed that Guam was first discovered by people from southeastern Indonesia around 2000 BC.

The United States took control of Guam in the 1898 after the Spanish–American War, as part of the Treaty of Paris. The Guam Organic Act of 1950 established Guam as an unincorporated territory of the U.S., created the framework of the island's civilian government, and granted the people U.S. citizenship.

The engraver Jim Licaretz's initials (JL) are to the right of the base of the latte.

Look for wear to occur first on the mountainous features of the topographical outline.

2009 American Samoa

MINTAGE: PHILADELPHIA: 42,600,000
           DENVER: 39,600,000

Design: items used in special Samoan ceremonies, set against the background of the Samoan coastline and a palm tree. The items include an ava bowl, which is used to make ceremonial drinks, and a whisk and staff, which represent the rank of Samoan orator. The inscription "AMERICAN SAMOA" arcs across the top along the rim. "SAMOA MUAMUA LE ATUA" ("Samoa, God is First" in the native language) is above the ava bowl; "E PLURIBUS UNUM" and the date 2009 rock across the lower rim.

The sculptor Charles Vickers's initials (CLV) are at the base of the whisk, directly above the date.

Look for wear to occur first in the leaves of the palm tree and on the rim of the ava bowl.

2009 U.S. VIRGIN ISLANDS

MINTAGE: PHILADELPHIA: 41,000,000
DENVER: 41,000,000

Design: a bird known as the banana quit is pictured next to three yellow cedar flowers. Behind the bird is a tyre palm, which, unlike most species of palms, is native to the Virgin Islands. The background includes an outline of the three main islands. The inscription "U.S. VIRGIN ISLANDS" arcs across the top rim; "UNITED IN PRIDE AND HOPE" is stacked in three lines just below the outline of the three islands. "E PLURIBUS UNUM" and the date 2009 rock along the lower rim.

The sculptor Joseph Menna's initials (JFM) are directly above the 2 in 2009.

Look for wear to occur first on the edge of the wing of the bird, the petals of the lowest flower, and the top of the palm tree.

2009 NORTHERN MARIANA ISLANDS

MINTAGE: PHILADELPHIA: 35,200,000
DENVER: 37,600,000

Design: symbols of the islands' culture and wildlife. These include a latte, a native two-piece carved stone pillar, which also appears on the Guam quarter; coconut trees, wild plants, flying native birds, and a sailing canoe are also featured. A garland of teibwo, also known as Pacific basil, frames the design. The inscription "NORTHERN MARIANA ISLANDS" arcs along the top rim of the coin; "E PLURIBUS UNUM" and the date 2009 rock along the lower rim.

The sculptor Phebe Hemphill's initials (PH) are at the end of the teibwo garland near the rim at about the four o'clock position.

Look for wear to occur first on the latte and at the various high points of the teibwo garland and the lower bird.

Important note about the state quarter series

The end has arrived for this series. Remember that the mintage figures are very high for these creations but all coinage has not been fully released by the Treasury Department. Don't expect these quarters to be worth considerably more than face value. These Territorial issues are great promotional candidates. Should your state quarter submissions to PCGS or NCG be graded MS-69, I suggest selling at auction or to your trusted dealer. Populations are zero to a few pieces. The exceptions at this time are the Tennessee (54), Louisiana (43), and Ohio (54) coins. NGC has rated only (1) California and (3) Minnesota coins MS-70. PCGS has rated none MS-70 to date. Remember that these coins were struck as regular coinage for commerce. The proof issues received specil care.

State Quarters Errors

The state quarter error coins are the real profit makers of the series. With U.S. Mint production in the hundreds of millions, there will be no rarities in the State Quarters series. Collectors desiring uniqueness will turn to the striking— in both senses of the word—error coins being discovered.

Even though production numbers are astronomical, each quarter design is produced for just a few weeks, as five different designs must pass through the presses in a given year.

Rotated die errors have already been discovered on several of the issues. Rotated dies occur when one of the dies in the press is improperly set, resulting in the obverse and reverse design not matching up as intended. The Mint allows 5 degrees rotation as normal tolerance, so any rotation larger than 5 degrees may be considered a collectible error. (Consider a clock face: the rotation from 12 to 1 is 30 degrees "clockwise"; from 12 to 9, 90 degrees "counterclockwise"; from 12 to 6, 180 degrees.)

Some reports sensationalized some early rotated die discoveries on the Pennsylvania issues, and reported values of up to $500. That figure is generally unrealistic, however. If not discovered soon after setting, a rotated die pair may produce tens of thousands of error coins, at a rate of several hundred per minute. If one does not check specifically for rotation, these coins otherwise look normal, and will pass normally through the error checking and counting mechanisms at the Mint, to escape easily into circulation. Dealer price lists place the value at more like $50 for pronounced rotation.

The value of error coins is related to how spectacular the error, the "freak quotient." Error coins that are misshapen have a much harder time escaping the Mint undetected, so are much rarer in collector hands. Occasionally, genuine spectacular striking errors do escape, and collecting examples of these is a legitimate branch of numismatics.

Consider so-called off-center strikes. These are coins that have been struck when the planchet, or blank coin, has not been properly placed between the dies. These strikes are generally classified by percentage off center, the higher

1999 Delaware State Quarter double-struck 30 percent off-center.

the percentage of error, the more valuable the coin. Of course, enough of the design must be visible to identify the coin, but the design regularities of the State Quarters make that relatively easy, even for the most pronounced off-center errors. Witness the Delaware quarter struck (just barely) some 90 percent or more off center, as reported in *Coin World* by a Maryland collector. There is just a shred of "LAW" from "DELAWARE", but it is enough to identify the piece.

Multiple strikes are another type of error that has been reported in the State Quarter series. These occur when a coin fails to be fully ejected after striking, and it receives another blow. Generally the secondary hit is somewhat off-center, and the degree to which both strikes can be discerned is the key to value.

Coins can get stuck in the press and get hit several times. At least one 1999-P Georgia quarter is known with four distinct strikings, a rare quadruple strike. Such an error could be worth upward of $4,000.

Sometimes multiple strikes occur and additional blanks continue to feed into the press. This can cause what is known as a brockage, where the design of a struck coin acts as a die, impressing the unstruck face of a new planchet. Several have been reported.

All kinds of bad planchets may be struck, resulting in collectible errors. One class of these are incomplete planchet errors or "clips," where the planchet was mis-punched, resulting in either a curved or straight bite out of the circle. Clips can be smooth or irregular. Some coins may exhibit planchets clipped on two sides. Again, value depends upon the ability to identify the intended piece and the extent of the error.

Sometimes the planchet metal, which is a sandwich of copper-nickel over a copper core, can break apart into layers. When this happens after striking, you may end up with what looks like half a coin—one side correctly struck, with only a faint image, if any, on the other side. If it happens before striking, the design may be all there, but in a bright coppery color on one side, if the grayish copper-nickel covering is gone. Many such pieces (struck after splitting) have been reported, and their value depends on how coppery and fully detailed the design. Note that some unscrupulous coin chemists may try to fake such errors by plating or by acid-dissolving the thin copper-nickel outer surface. Such pieces must be authenticated by honest and knowledgeable experts.

1999 Georgia State Quarter with a obverse brockage.

A Delaware quarter struck on a fragment of aluminum has been verified. No U.S. coins are currently made of aluminum. The aluminum fragment is a part of the press equipment known as the feeder finger. In any case, this rare gem of a mutant may be worth $8,000 to $12,000.

Another very desirable type of State Quarter error is the capped die error. These sensational rarities, like brockage errors, are created when a coin planchet sticks to a die (errors produced by die caps cease to be brockages when the original design is obliterated from the die). A planchet is repeatedly struck by the hammer, or upper die, creating a capped die strike (a form of struck-through error). The reverse design will be sharply struck, while the obverse image can range from almost nonexistent to attractive, but distorted. The capped die strike also can be reversed depending on how it forms in the minting press: the obverse design will be sharply struck, while the reverse image can range from almost nonexistent to attractive, but distorted Depending on how spectacular they are, capped die errors have sold for between $4,000 and $5,000. There is great future potential for these pieces.

Coins struck on blanks intended for other denominations also occur, as un-struck planchets sometimes stick to the insides of tote bins and come loose at fortuitous times. A State Quarter struck on a dime planchet has a value of $8,000 to $10,000.

The rapid turnover of designs in the State Quarters program invites some interesting error possibilities. We have even had overstrikes of one state onto another. These errors—especially the major creations—are excellent numismatic items to put away for the grandchildren. Just be certain they are encapsulated by NGC or PCGS.

GLOSSARY OF COIN TERMS

accolated Portraits on a coin, medal, or escutcheon that are overlapping and facing in the same direction.

acid-treated / acid-dipped Coins that have been dipped in a mild acid solution to remove dirt, patina, or tarnish.

ask price Price quoted by a dealer to buy a coin for a certain year, Mint, and condition.

assay coin Coin specifically struck as a quality control sample to be tested to ascertain if it contains the correct amount of precious metal or metals. These coins normally are, or should be, destroyed after testing.

AU About Uncirculated: a shorthand notation for a coin grading between AU-50 and AU-59 on the Sheldon scale. Can also mean Almost Uncirculated.

bag marks Nicks, wear, scuffs, and scratches found on a coin's surface from contact with other coins, from the practice of storing coins in bags. When the bags are handled the coins rub and grind against each other.

Barber coinage The Liberty Head dimes, quarters, and half dollars struck from 1892 until 1916 (1915 for the half dollar); designed by Charles E. Barber.

Bebee's The late Aubrey Bebee's coin business. Bebee began assembling his world-class collection of U.S. paper money in 1941. The collection eventually grew to include many spectacular rarities, including a Series of 1934 $10,000 Federal Reserve notes. Bebee and his wife (and collecting partner), Adeline, donated the Bebee collection to the American Numismatic Association in 1988.

bezel A jewelry item used to hold a coin for the purposes of adornment.

bid (bid level, bid price, bid value) Price quoted by a dealer to sell a coin for a certain year, Mint, and condition.

blast An attribute of intense mint luster of a newly struck coin.

bondoed *See* **puttied**.

brockage A minting error occurring when a mirror image of a coin is struck on both sides of the planchet. This error typically occurs when a coin remains stuck on either die after striking, and the next coin fed into the coining chamber receives the image from the die, though its blank other side also receives the image of the previously struck coin: the result is an incuse mirror image. Most brockages are partial; a full brockage is rare and potentially valuable.

BU Brilliant Uncirculated: a shorthand notation for a coin corresponding to a grade between MS-60 and MS-70 on the Sheldon scale.

buffed A cleaned, polished coin that has a grainless finish of high luster.

business strikes Coins intended for use in circulation.

cameo effect An unintentional matte finish created on coins from new dies that have not been fully polished.

cameo frost A matte finish on part of a coin device or lettering that is created by treating the relevant part of the die with an acidic solution. The frosted area contrasts with the surrounding field(s).

cartwheel Slang for a silver dollar coin.

clad A coin with two or more types of metal sandwiched or layered together to form a composite planchet for the coining process. The most common clad coins have layers of copper and nickel.

clash marks Marks that appear on a coin when a blank fails to feed into the press and the dies hit each other without the blank between to absorb the blow. This imprints images from the obverse on the reverse and vice versa.

collar The part of the minting press that keeps the blank planchet centered between the two dies, and restrains the metal as it expands during striking. The collar also embosses the reeded edge on most coins.

copper spot On gold coins, an area of copper concentration that has oxidized and caused a spot, stain, or discoloration. Copper spots or stains can range from tiny dots to large blotches. Some issues and years are known to suffer from copper spotting, and the grading of these coins takes this abnormality into account.

counter-stamping The secondary post-stamping of a coin by either a government or organization. Historically, counter-stamping was done by many countries to certify that foreign coinage was acceptable for domestic usage. Several groups have counter-stamped U.S. commemorative coins to create a sub-type of a particular commemorative: an example is the 1936 Cleveland, counter-stamped by the Western Reserve Numismatic Club.

crack out Slang for removing a certified coin from its encapsulation holder, usually for resubmitting the coin to a grading agency in hope of receiving a higher grade.

date-and-mint set A set of a particular coin that includes one example from every different Mint for every year of issue.

denticle A small tooth-like element in a coin's design, usually seen around the rim.

die A steel rod that is engraved, punched, etc., with a coin's design (inscriptions, dates, devices, and emblems).

die abrasions Abrasions, scratches, and general wear on the die caused by misfed planchets coming into the stamping chamber or by coins leaving the stamping chamber of the mint press.

die clash A minting error occurring when the obverse and reverse dies strike each other with no planchet in between them, resulting in damage to the coin dies. This usually imparts part of the obverse image to the reverse die and vice versa.

die marriage The documentation of the pairing of two specific sets of dies to create a coin variety.

eagles

   double eagle A $20 gold piece.

   eagle A $10 gold piece.

   half eagle A $5 gold piece.

   quarter eagle A $2.50 gold piece.

early-struck One of the first coins struck from a new pair of dies. Also known as "early die state" (EDS), to error collectors and die marriage collectors.

EF Extremely Fine: a shorthand notation for a coin showing little, but noticeable, wear. Most of the major features of the coin are clearly defined and a fair amount of mint luster is still visible.

encapsulated A coin that has been placed in a special container to preserve it, generally a grading service slab.

exergue The space below the device on a coin or medal, sometimes separated from the field by a horizontal line or bar.

flash An attribute of the mint luster of a newly struck coin.

fractional currency Notes issued by the U.S. government in denominations of 3, 5, 10, 15, 25, and 50 cents, necessitated by the hoarding of metal coins during and after the Civil War. The notes were used until 1876, and were redeemable by the U.S. Post Office at face value in postage stamps.

frost A crystalline or matte effect.

galvano An epoxy-coated plaster relief model of a coin, used to produce master hubs, which in turn produce the coin dies.

gem Description of coins graded MS-65 to MS-70.

grading services Companies that evaluate coins submitted for their review and certify them as being in designated grades. Two of these services enjoy far greater market acceptance than the others: the Professional Coin Grading Service (PCGS), founded in 1985, and the Numismatic Guaranty Corporation (NGC), founded in 1987.

hairlines Fine lines visible when a coin is viewed at an angle.

hub A steel apparatus used to produce a die. It bears the exact design (a positive image) that will appear on the coin. The die that is created will be a negative (mirror) image of the coin.

incuse design (incused) A recessed design hammered or stamped into the metal of a coin. Examples are the star on the 1922 Grant Memorial and the 2X2 on the 1921 Alabama.

Janvier reducing lathe A machine that transfers designs from the galvano to the master die. The lathe turns clockwise very slowly, taking days to cut a master die.

kerf The measurement of the width of a saw blade cut.

lack of metal fill marks / metal flow marks When a coin is pressed between two dies the metal on the surface instantaneously melts and fills all the cracks and crevices of the dies. When a planchet is not formed correctly there is insufficient metal fully to occupy all the details of the die, thus creating a coin design that shows lack of metal fill and/or apparent metal flow marks where there was insufficient material.

luster A blending of sheen, brilliance, contrast, and the effect observed on a coin when rotated in a proper light source, such as incandescent or halogen light.

matte proof A double-struck coin dipped in nitric acid (at the Philadelphia Mint) to create a matte or dull and flat finish.

Merrick press The first powered coining press to be used at the U.S. Mint in Philadelphia. This steam-powered press is often thought to have been imported by Merrick, Agnew & Tyler in 1836, but this is not the case. The firm built the press in 1836, using drawings and plans designed in Paris by Pierre-Antoine Thonnelier in 1833.

metal flow marks *See* **lack of metal fill marks**.

milling The process of removing metal by machining.

milling mark A blemish that can result when the reeded edge of a coin strikes the surface of another coin. This may produce one mark only or a series of marks. Also known as a reeded mark.

mint bloom Slang term for the metallic luster of a newly minted coin.

Mint State Uncirculated; as a coin grade, abbreviated MS.

mirrored Reflective surface of a coin created from a highly polished die; normally seen in proof coins.

monogram An emblematic or decorative letter or letters; often the applied initial of a coin designer or coin sculptor that is included among a coin's devices as a "signature."

Morgan silver dollar The Liberty Head silver dollar struck from 1878 until 1904 and again in 1921; designed by George T. Morgan.

non-upset Planchets that have not had a primary or rudimentary rim milled onto them in preparation for minting.

originality The attributes of a coin when it leaves the Mint; used in comparison with the coin's current state, perhaps after dipping or cleaning.

over-dipped Slang for a coin that has been over chemically treated to clean or enhance its appearance, often resulting in the coin's becoming dull.

pallet A shaping tool used by potters and sculptors, consisting of a flat blade or plate with a handle at one end.

pattern An experimental coin design or full-scale mock-up that is minted to verify metal flow, design wear, and mintage press pressures, and to test how many die blows are required and how much die wear and fatigue is caused by each impression. Patterns may be made in metals other than the one proposed for the coin, and are not intended for commerce.

planchet A coin blank; the blank disk of metal before it is struck and transformed into a coin.

powdery Having a blanched appearance: used of a frosted device or detail on a coin.

primary focal area The location of a coin's design to which the eye is quickly or instinctively drawn.

promotion (promotable) A dedicated marketing effort by one or more coin dealers to generate interest and demand among collectors to buy a specific type and/or year of a coin.

proof A specimen coin minted on a high-quality planchet that is struck several times with highly polished dies to give the coin a jewel-like appearance.

proof-like / semi-proof-like Description of a business strike coin with exceptional detail, luster, or mirrored surfaces, making it look as if it could be a proof coin. Such coins are usually created inadvertently from a combination of above-average planchets and brand new, or newly polished, coinage dies.

proof sets
> **Standard** Set that includes the one cent through the one dollar coins, minted in a particular year.
>
> **Prestige** Set that includes the coins in the Standard proof set, plus any commemorative coins minted in a particular year. It is usually packaged by the Mint in a premium package.

puttied Slang for a coin that has been doctored with some type of filler to hide scratches, abrasions, or other type of abuse.

rare A term indicating that a coin is very difficult to find in a certain grade or condition, either because of low survival rates or low market availability. Even coins with high initial mintages can be rare. Many coins were minted in San Francisco in the 1850's, but because of the Mint's geographical isolation, almost all San Francisco coins were used extensively. Thus very few San Francisco 1850-era Mint State examples survive, making those grades "rare" despite the mintages. "Rare" does not correspond with "value". For example, early United States Philippine issues are rare in most Mint State grades, but because few collectors are in the market for these coins their values are correspondingly low. The reader may encounter references to a Rarity Scale in other numismatic sources: the scale is an estimate of what is believed to exist. I do not use the scale in this book, as it does not generally apply to commemoratives, but readers should be aware of it.

(R) Rarity Scale:

R-1 Common
R-2 Not So Common
R-3 Scarce
R-4 Very Scarce (population estimated between 76 and 200)
R-5 Rare (31–75)

R-6 Very Rare (13–30)
R-7 Extremely Rare (4–12)
R-8 Unique or Nearly So (1, 2 or 3)

raw Slang for a coin that has not been encapsulated by a grading service.

red book Slang for *A Guide Book of United States Coins*, currently edited by Kenneth Bressett. This book has been the standard value guide for coin collectors and dealers since 1947, and lists the retail prices for U.S. coins, Colonial coins, Error coins, Mint and Proof sets, Commemoratives, and gold coins.

reeded Having grooves embossed onto the edge of a coin to prevent the filing off of small amounts of precious metal and thus debasing the coin.

reeded mark See **milling mark**.

reflectivity The amount of light reflected back to the observer's eye. As a coin tarnishes the reflectivity decreases.

registry set A set of coins that is registered with a major third party organization that verifies the quality and ownership of the coins in that set. NGC and PCGS track the completion and quality of specific graded coin series collections. Registry sets are divided into two parts, All-Time Finest (ATF) and Current Finest (CF). The ATF registry is the most highly graded collection of coins for that series or collection at any given time since registry sets have been tracked.

satiny Luster that possesses a semi-glossy, sleek, and smooth appearance.

seigniorage The amount of money derived from the difference between the face value of a coin and the cost of producing, distributing, and circulating it. More generally, the profit generated from the printing or coining of currency.

semi-key A specific year and mintage of a type of coin that is in the top three to five lowest mintages for that series.

Sheldon scale A 70-point scale for grading coins. It was developed by Dr. William Sheldon in 1949 for grading copper coins. A slightly modified form of the Sheldon scale has become the *de facto* standard for grading all U.S. coins today.

slab Slang for a coin grading service capsule or holder.

slabbed Slang for a coin that has been submitted to a grading service for authentication, grading, and encapsulation.

slider Slang for an About Uncirculated (AU) coin that can be passed off as an uncirculated (UNC) coin to inexperienced coin collectors.

spit spot A blemish commonly caused inadvertently by saliva ejected from the mouth that lands on a coin and oxidizes its surface. Brown or black spots occur from basic or alkaline saliva; green spots are commonly formed from acidic saliva. Food particles have been also known to accompany spit spots on coins.

spot A discolored area on a coin, which can affect the coin's grade, depending on severity and location.

statutory inscriptions Wording that by law that must appear on a coin. These inscriptions are "UNITED STATES OF AMERICA", "E PLURIBUS UNUM", "IN GOD WE TRUST", "LIBERTY", and the date and denomination of the coin.

strike The degree to which a coin's intended design has been completely transferred to the coin in the minting process.

toned Coin with tarnish or patina on its surface.

tote bins Large bins used for the temporary storage and transport of coins within a minting facility.

Trend values (Trends) Slang for Coin World's CoinValues, originally Coin World Trends, a pricing periodical that provides retail values for more than 65,000 specific types, years, and mintages of U.S. coins.

type set A collection of one representative piece for each denomination. If there has been more than one design for a denomination then these are also included.

UNC Uncirculated: a shorthand notation for a coin that corresponds to a grading between MS-60 and MS-70 on the Sheldon scale.

variety A specific sub-type of a coin by year and mintage. Varieties are generally defined as distinctive die types or variations and different die marriages.

whizzed Slang for a coin that has been treated with a fine wire brush to enhance its appearance.

wire edge A thin, knife-like coin rim caused by metal flowing between the collar and the dies during the minting process.

Further Reading

Alexander, David T. (editor), *Coin World Comprehensive Catalog and Encyclopedia of United States Coins*, 2nd edition, Sidney, Ohio: Amos Press, 1998 (ISBN 0944945244)

Bowers, Q. David, *A Guide Book of United States Type Coins: A Complete History and Price Guide for the Collector and Investor*, Atlanta: Whitman, 2008 (ISBN 0794822835)

Bressett, Kenneth and Abe Kosoff (editors), *The Official American Numismatic Association Grading Standards for United States Coins*, 6th edition, Atlanta: Whitman, 2005 (ISBN 0794819931)

Fivaz, Bill and J.T. Stanton, *Cherrypickers' Guide to Rare Die Varieties of United States Coins*, 5th edition, 2 vols, Atlanta: Whitman, 2009 (ISBN 0794820530)

Swiatek, Anthony, *Commemorative Coins of the United States: Identification and Price Guide*, New York: Avon, 1993; 2nd edition, Sidney, Ohio: Amos Press, 2001 (ISBN 0944945376)

Travers, Scott A., *The Coin Collector's Survival Manual*, 6th edition, New York: House of Collectibles, 2006 (ISBN 0375723056)

Wood, Howland, *The Commemorative Coinage of the United States (Numismatic Notes and Monographs 16)*, New York: American Numismatic Society, 1922

Yeoman, R.S., *A Guide Book of United States Coins (2010 Official Red Book)*, edited by Kenneth Bressett, 63rd edition, Atlanta: Whitman, 2009 (ISBN: 0794827667)

Coin World's CoinValues (periodical, originally *Coin World Trends*), 2003–

Anthony Swiatek, known as "Mr. Commem," is a past President (1997–99) of the American Numismatic Association (ANA), the world's largest organization for collectors of coins, tokens, medals, and paper money. He is highly respected by collectors, dealers, and colleagues in the numismatic world, and is a recognized contemporary authority on silver and gold commemoratives. In 2002, the ANA awarded him numismatics' highest honor, the Farran Zerbe award.

Swiatek's Commemorative Coins of the United States (1993, 2nd edition 2001), covering coinage from 1892, won the Numismatic Literary Guild (NLG)'s award for Best Investment Book. He is co-author of the *Encyclopedia of United States Silver and Gold Commemorative Coins* (1981), of which this is the third edition; the second edition (1990) received the NLG's Book of the Year Award. His *The Walking Liberty Half Dollar* (1983, updated 1984) received the NLG's Best Book on U.S. Coins award. In 2008, Swiatek received the NLG's highest honor, the Clemy award.

A full-time professional numismatist since 1979, and now one of numismatics' most influential coin dealers, he is publisher and editor of the popular *Swiatek Report*, which has frequently been voted the Best Numismatic Investment Newsletter of the Year. Swiatek has a guest column in *Coin World*, and has written for numerous journals, manuals, and guidebooks.

As a commemorative specialist, Swiatek has been invited to participate in several ceremonial strikings, including the 1982 Denver George Washington half dollar, the 1983 San Francisco proof Olympic dollar, the uncirculated 1984 West Point Olympic gold eagle, and the 1986 Statue of Liberty gold $5 uncirculated coin. In 1984 he and his wife Gloria were invited to the Reagan White House for the gold Olympic coin ceremonies. In 1999, the Swiateks were twice invited to the White House by Hillary Clinton to help launch the Sacagawea dollar program. He has held several offices with the Society for U.S. Commemorative Coins, including President (1983–84, 2001) and was editor of the Society's newsletter, *Commemorative Trail*.

An educator, Swiatek is on the Board of Governors and lectures at the Institute of Numismatic Studies at Adelphi University, New York. He has sponsored and written home study courses for the ANA and lectured at educational forums and coin shows throughout the United States. His goal is to help educate as many "young and senior" collectors and investors as possible, teaching them about the pros and cons of coin collecting and coin investing. In addition to his writings and lectures, he has spread the numismatic news on radio, television, and video tapes. Swiatek received his Bachelor's and Master's degrees from the City College of New York, and taught Science for ten years in the New York City school system.

Swiatek is also a consumer advocate. He has testified before the House Subcommittee on Consumer Affairs and Coinage regarding U.S. commemorative coinage, and his opinions and work are cited in the Library of Congress study

"Issuing Commemorative Coins: A Historical Overview." Before the same Subcommittee, Swiatek testified in support of its Chairman, Frank Annunzio, in his quest to attain better Olympic coinage designs for the collector and hobbyist. Swiatek is noted for his exceptional fairness in dealing with collectors, dealers, and investors, and in 2000 received an NLG award for promoting consumer protection and awareness. He is a consultant to the coin grading services ANACS, Numismatic Guaranty Corporation, and Professional Coin Grading Service. Additionally, Swiatek is the Numismatic Expert for the Eastern Division of the U.S. Attorney's Office and has counseled the U.S. Postal Police and the U.S. Secret Service in the areas of numismatic fraud.

Anthony Swiatek has received numerous awards, offices, and citations for his work in numismatics, and belongs to numerous clubs and organizations, national and local, throughout the United States. His most recent award is the 2009 Presidential Award from Florida United Numismatists.

For more information, visit: www.anthonyjswiatek.com
Contact email: uscoinguru@aol.com

INDEX